**Customer review for *The Elvis Films* on the Elvis Inform:**

"Let me say that I am a fan of the author's earlier works...

I knew Jon Abbott would infuse his coverage of the eclectic Elvis film canon with a pop culture sensibility and an appreciation beyond the narrow minded perspective of many film critics. The author provides a general overview of the narrative of each film and demonstrates a perceptive understanding of how elements play off each other (and) infuses his discussion with a heady mix of behind the scenes anecdotes offering a rich source of tantalising nuggets of information. He also comments perceptively on Elvis' seminal role in the growth of teen culture.

While I may not agree with everything he has written, I appreciate and respect his consideration and interpretation of Elvis' body of film work and its wider implications and influences. In discussing each film Abbott also goes off in juicy tangential diversions to enlighten the reader about the non-Elvis film careers of many of his co-stars, film producers and directors. Pop culture addicts (like me) will particularly welcome these explorations.

His is a "fan" perspective with a healthy dose of pop culture treats and cogent analysis... an abundance of facts, opinion and anecdote to enjoy and reflect on. Abbott's off-center 'pop culture' perspective gives *The Elvis Films* a different feel to most other books on Elvis' celluloid career and for this reason it is a fresh and invigorating read. However, the author and I will have to agree to disagree about the value of Elvis' late 60s films"

(see the full review on elvisinfonet.com)

**Customer reviews on Amazon U.S. for Jon Abbott's *Cool TV of the 1960s***

"Jon Abbott's earlier works on Irwin Allen and Stephen J. Cannell occupy pride of place on my bookshelf. Here he tackles a trio of American 1960s television shows which became pop culture phenomena--*The Man from UNCLE, Batman* and *The Monkees* ...intelligent and thought-provoking. His section on *UNCLE* is worth the cost of the book alone..."

"Great new take on three classic shows! ...intelligent and insightful. It is clear the author very much loves these shows... a fresh perspective on their importance relative to their place in pop culture. The book features an episode guide with thoughtful commentary and analysis for all three shows... well worth the price"

"Very detailed about three great shows. Hope there is a sequel with more shows and how they influenced television and the 1960s"

"Each part has a full season by season episode guide with summaries and cast... Must read if you love these shows!"

"A complete, extremely well researched guide to three of the most popular shows of the 1960s: *The Man from UNCLE*, *Batman*, and *The Monkees*. As a kid, I watched only *UNCLE* every week, *Batman* in its beginnings, and *The Monkees* almost never, but I found what he had to say interesting and perceptive. I didn't always agree with his views (he found one of my favorite *UNCLE* guest actresses "annoying") but his points are clear and he often offers comparisons to other shows of the genres and information that I had not known before reading this. The detail and research that went into the formation of 'cast and crew' information is indeed remarkable and the book is worth its price for that information alone. Highly recommended if you have any interest in even one of these shows".

**Customer reviews on Amazon U.K. for Jon Abbott's *Cool TV of the 1960s***

"A good read in relation to the culture of the times... very well written and brings back many good memories".

"Really interesting book, enjoyed it"

**Customer reviews on Amazon U.S. for Jon Abbott's *Strange New World: Sex Films of the 1970s***

"Mr. Abbott tackles the herculean task of reviewing somewhere (around 500) films, most of which are some variety of crap, and manages to write something interesting about each one... There are a plethora of witty remarks on hand, and Mr. Abbott is especially adept at insulting English sexploitation films from the decade in question... As an overview of an immense body of work spanning more than a decade, this is an excellent primer. Perhaps he strives a little too hard to have a fun quip about every bad film he sees, but it does keep the tone light and enjoyable. There are many illustrations and the chapters are organised in a relatively intelligent way. Very impressive overall, just not perfect, like the movies that are detailed within."

After expressing his reservations, this reviewer writes:

"Still, this is *great* idea for a book and Abbott genuinely does an admirable job (he even has a whole chapter on Gloria Guida and Italian sex comedies!). If I sound a little critical, it's only because this would be a truly wonderful book if the author ... would bite-back his harsh personal opinions just a little bit."

"I received my voluminous tome (some 700 pages) about a week ago and haven't been able to put it down since. Jon Abbott obviously has a real passion for the same movie genre that I am also obsessed with and he writes of the films in a very informative, knowledgeable and easy read way. Any criticism of him being opinionated is unjustified and other reviewers appear to not have read his Preface which gives great explanation of his writing/reviewing style."

"Jon Abbott, known for his books and articles about vintage television, began writing this chunky tome for a publisher who wanted a serious scholarly book on the topic of seventies sex films. He found he couldn't keep to a serious tone when writing about sex movies so ended up self-publishing. The fact that he makes no attempt to restrain his personality is a large part of what makes the book such an entertaining read. His cornball humor, cranky rants and special pleading on behalf of terrible movies which just happen to feature his own personal lust objects... make for a rollicking fun time. His writing can be insightful, especially when writing about classic films like *Klute, Don't Look Now* or *The Beguiled*. And he gives a good run-down of particular sexploitation genres, such as nurse movies and women-in-prison films. He does well with his coverage of Russ Meyer and Roger Corman's New World Pictures, but I would have liked to see him delve as far into the absolute rubbish that was coming out of the U.S. as he did into the absolute rubbish coming out of Europe and the U.K. What I look for from this kind of book is that it inform me about movies I've never heard of, inspire me to revisits those I've seen, maybe make me laugh and challenge me with opinions which clash with my own. This book did all of that. While all the coverage of interchangeable Jess Franco and Jean Rollin films might drag a little, mostly it's a romp through the sublime, the hilariously godawful and the sizzlingly sexy. You are bound to read about many titles with which you were unfamiliar."

### Customer reviews on Amazon U.S. for Jon Abbott's *The Elvis Films*

"I was keen to learn more about the oft-derided Elvis films and this book doesn't disappoint. Jon is clearly a fan and the book takes an overall sympathetic look at the Elvis films whilst happily thrashing a few that deserve it. If I had to criticise something I would say that in my opinion there is an excess of detail on the supporting cast members but maybe they deserve more than a footnote in the Elvis story. Though I totally disagree with some of the opinions in Jon's book it was a good read and very enjoyable. Well done Jon".

"I like this book. For one thing, the author points out that though these movies were not respected by the film community, or, even by Elvis himself, they *were* what people were wanting to see, stood in line, and paid to see. They were the blockbuster movies of their time. If he was unhappy making them, he really was a great actor because in each film he is so absorbed in each scene, beautiful himself, of course, and always seemed to be having a great time.

The aim of the author is to put the reader in the place of the then viewer, and then explain why it would be so appealing to the ticket buyer as well as a new viewer. And he does an excellent job".

**Customer reviews on Amazon U.K. for Jon Abbott's *The Elvis Films***

"Jon Abbott has written a well researched book on the Elvis Presley films and he has his prejudices and likes as we all do. I found my eyes glazing over when the TV credits of every starlet who ever appeared with Elvis were listed and so I think the book could have omitted large chunks of this information and been all the better for it... Instead, I would have liked more information on the songwriters... Not a bad book to pick up and refer to from time to time".

"Well worth a read for any Elvis fan. Takes a different slant than most books covering this part of Elvis' career... It's written by someone who actually likes Elvis' movies and is very well versed in them. A lot of information many fans won't have come across before".

"A good read, some unusual facts"

**Customer reviews on Amazon for *Irwin Allen Television Productions, 1964-1970: A Critical History* (hardback and softback, U.S. and U.K. sites)**

"Jon Abbott has done an amazing job compiling four of Irwin Allen's classic 1960s sci-fi TV shows into one great book... informative background history... synopsis of every episode with a detailed review, complete with guest cast, it also includes who wrote and directed each episode. This is a perfect example of how a book like this should be done. In other words this is the only book you need on these four shows because it's all there—the plots, writers, directors, guest stars and the author's review of each episode filled with trivia and fun facts... this book is the best episode guide out there. I look at it like a more detailed version of the excellent 1977 book *Fantastic Television*...".

"...an excellent critical appraisal of these particular shows. It's clear from the outset that the author has a deep affection for Allen's output and he's not shy to admit it, but neither is he afraid to highlight the many inconsistencies and absurdities... substantial information... there's so much to get your teeth into here that you'll find yourself revisiting this book many times over... a very worthy and compelling read. His style is open and accessible, yet knowledgeable and authoritative. I like that, and having read the book, I certainly feel more empowered to discuss each show's respective merits with confidence and clarity..."

"If you enjoy Irwin Allen's work, this is a must-purchase. You may not agree with some of the episode assessments but it's an enjoyable and sometimes thought provoking book. And there isn't really anything else quite like it on the subject..."

"What makes this book different from most others is the author's viewpoint and 'critical history' of the shows themselves; not everybody may be in agreement, good or bad, with his statements, but it is very interesting".

"Jon Abbott's book should not be looked on as just another TV series episode guide. There are already many of those available and that's not what Mr. Abbott's book is about. Instead, the author guides us episode by episode through the four science fiction series that Irwin Allen produced back in the '60s, giving his critical evaluations of each hour-long show. Since we're dealing with opinions here, one might find them at variance with the author. I personally find that refreshing..."

"I always thought *Lost in Space* got too silly by the third season, but this book made me go back and re-watch the episodes again. That's a good book".

"I absolutely loved this book. I read it a couple years ago and enjoyed every moment of it. If you enjoyed sitting in front of that tv watching any or all of Irwin's series, you will love it too".

Thank you to all those reviewers! (See the full reviews, and others, on those sites)

*This book is dedicated to the memory of Robert Culp, perhaps the finest television actor the medium ever saw; to the underrated Roy Thinnes; to the classy and intelligent Anne Francis; to Gary Conway for staring down John Cassavetes; to Gene Barry for being Gene Barry; and to the efforts of Dick Powell, Sheldon Leonard, Robert Culp, Joseph Stefano, and Leslie Stevens for raising the standards of the medium.*

# Cool TV 2: More Cult TV from the 1960s

**The Outer Limits, Burke's Law,**

**Jonny Quest, Honey West,**

**Amos Burke—Secret Agent,**

**The Green Hornet, The Invaders**

**Jon Abbott**

ISBN -13: 978-1977980359

ISBN-10: 197798035X

Text © Jon Abbott, 2017

# Cool TV 2: More Cult TV from the 1960s

**Jon Abbott**

**Also by Jon Abbott**

*Irwin Allen Television Productions, 1964 – 1970:*
*A Critical History of Voyage to the Bottom of the Sea, Lost in Space,*
*The Time Tunnel, and Land of the Giants*
McFarland, 2006

*Stephen J. Cannell Television Productions: A History of All Series and Pilots*
McFarland, 2009

*The Elvis Films*
Createspace Independent Publ., 2014

*Cool TV of the 1960s: Three Shows That Changed the World*
*The Man from UNCLE, Batman, and The Monkees*
Createspace Independent Publ., 2015

*Strange New World: Sex Films of the 1970s*
Createspace Independent Publ., 2015

*One Hundred of the Best, Most Violent Films Ever*
Createspace Independent Publ., 2016

*The Great Desilu Series of the 1960s*
*The Untouchables, The Lucy Show, Star Trek, and Mission: Impossible*
Createspace Independent Publ., 2016

*for further details search Jon Abbott on Amazon and/or see the back pages*

# contents

### Spoiler statement

There are 'spoilers'—that is to say giveaway plot points—throughout this book; if there weren't, there would be no book. In order to properly discuss the content of the episodes, I may, in some cases, reveal the endings and other relevant plot points. There's no other way to seriously consider these films in the context of an informative reference work; I must assume comparable knowledge, or the desire for same. I can't believe there's anyone left in the world who doesn't know how, say, *Planet of the Apes* or *The Wicker Man* turn out, and I would expect this book to be read mostly by those who have seen most of the episodes herein, but as I always work on the assumption that someone, somewhere, is going to be seeing these films for the first time, consider yourselves warned.

Also, I thought it might be fun (sorry if it isn't) to examine exactly what David Vincent actually achieved in his one-man fight against the aliens in *The Invaders,* so there's an "end result" section in each *Invaders* review. The best way to approach all the episode guide comments is to think of them as after-episode discussions if you've forgotten or not seen them. If you have, and you know the events and outcome as well as I do, then hopefully it will provoke an overwhelming desire to revisit the shows. Let's face it, it's gotta be better than watching whatever dismal 'reality' show or talent-free 'talent' show is on 21st century television tonight…!

## introduction

Hi, and welcome to *Cool TV 2*, the follow-up book to *Cool TV of the 1960s: Three Shows That Changed the World*. I can't promise you shows that changed the world this time, but then there's not too many of those about (that was kind of the point of the first one). What I *can* promise you is twice as much bang for your buck in the number of shows covered... three more really brilliant shows that, even if they didn't change the world, were just as good as those in the first book — *The Outer Limits*, *Burke's Law*, and *The Invaders* — and four really interesting single season obscurities — *Honey West* and *Amos Burke — Secret Agent* (two spin-offs from *Burke's Law*), *Jonny Quest*, the first ever animated adventure show, and still unsurpassed today, and *The Green Hornet*, from the producers of the legendary *Batman* TV series — that are well worth looking up. You may, of course, be reading this book because you already know and love these shows, grew up with them perhaps, as I did, or you may be smart enough to just be curious about film and TV made before you were even born. Either way, I trust you'll find these trips back through time as informative and provocative as my previous books. As usual, there'll be facts and there'll be opinions, and it should be easy to spot which is which.

I love these old shows (I'm not blind to their occasional failings, as you'll see), and my intention, as ever, is to spread the word and document them properly, accurately, and fairly for future generations. Whether they'll be of any interest to those future generations who follow us is something I cannot know, but I'm inspired and encouraged by a quote from the extraordinary, madly eccentric, and super-intelligent media sage Marshall McLuhan (the man who, around the time these shows were made, coined the term 'global village' for the media world we live in now in the 21st century). It opens one of my other books on 1960s TV produced in this style, *The Great Desilu Series of the 1960s*. He predicted, in 1952 (that's at the very dawn of television, before *anything* of merit had been produced):

*"The next medium, whatever it is — it may be the extension of consciousness — will include television as its content, not as its environment, and will transform television into an art form. A computer as a research and communication instrument could enhance retrieval, obsolesce mass library organisation, retrieve the individual's encyclopaedic function and flip into a private line to speedily tailored data of a saleable kind"*

Wow. He didn't know about the forthcoming saturation take up of home video recorders, about time-shifting, camcorders, computer games, cable TV, satellite TV, Blockbuster, DVDs, digital technology, home computers, the internet, Amazon, e-bay, the IMDB, You Tube, Facebook, Createspace, Twitter, Wikipedia, i-pods, i-pads, i-phones, selfies, Netflix, Amazon Prime, or anything else, and sadly passed away on December 31st, 1980 at the age of 69, literally as everything he had predicted was starting to happen, and before he could know for sure just how right he was. After all, classic television is everywhere now, more accessible now than it was at the time. How unfair that he couldn't hang on for another three decades, and see it all occur before his eyes. But he knew, thirty years earlier, that somehow, from somewhere, great things were coming, and that they would be stored and remembered, both by humanity and technology. The least I can do is try and study, interpret, understand, and document, some of that "saleable product" that I do believe is also Great Art.

*Cool TV 2* was ready a lot quicker than I thought it would be, simply because a lot of the work was already done. *The Green Hornet* had been prepared for the first *Cool TV* book, but had to come out for space reasons, and I'd already written a ton of stuff about *The Outer Limits* and *The Invaders,* both for my magazine work in the 1980s and '90s and for my personal pleasure. I'm a compulsive writer, finding it impossible to watch or read something and *not* review it, and now I'm self-publishing I don't have to spend months looking for publishers or writing back and forth to editors (even though I've always been lucky enough to have good ones). The bulk of the work to do was on *Burke's Law,* which was no hardship, as it's a show I personally love and has a strong nostalgia element for me. It was a pleasure to go back and re-watch the series through yet again. What a strange world we live in, where a murder mystery show can be warm and fuzzy 'comfort TV'. Unfortunately, on many episodes, I'm now starting to remember whodunnit!

*Amos Burke — Secret Agent* was a show I hadn't seen for literally forty years, since it first aired and vanished, seemingly forever. Then, just a few years ago, it suddenly turned up in Blighty on an obscure arts channel, of all places, a cash-starved service looking to fill ungodly hours as cheaply as possible, with shows nobody else wanted. But we TV buffs *did* want! While most would agree that the original *Burke's Law* format was vastly superior to what was, at the time, a disastrous reboot, to unearth seventeen hours of lost spy-fi featuring all the usual suspects from the '60s... well, let's just say I suddenly knew how those archaeologists must feel when they stumble unexpectedly onto a Roman village or Pharaoh's tomb. And it's always fun to revisit *Honey West.*

*Jonny Quest* was a late addition, and replaced the series I was originally going to cover, the wonderful *I Spy.* As this book nears completion, the Bill Cosby story has yet to play out. This is probably for the best, as I have little to say but this. Initially I felt that this book was reviewing the series, not the man, and so I would proceed, but I've found that in the current climate I'm too angry and depressed by what we already know to be true and has not been denied, that consequently I simply could not watch and enjoy the three seasons of the series, as much as I tried to separate the art from the artist. It's not fair to the late, great Robert Culp, one of my TV heroes whom I respect enormously, it's not fair to Sheldon Leonard, who — with Culp's blessing and co-operation — gave an entire ethnic group a chance by giving one man a chance, it's not fair to the other actors, or the writers, directors, and craftsmen who made it one of the coolest and most significant shows of the '60s, but it's how I feel at the moment. Yes, I know a lot of frauds and fantasists will be coming out of the woodwork to get a piece of celebrity, but I also know what he's already admitted to. This was a man with more charm, money, prestige, respect, and opportunity than the gods give anybody. Where is the motive, the rationale? Whichever way things go, it remains a tragedy for all concerned, a terrible way to end an extraordinary legacy. *

* If you feel particularly aggrieved about my dropping *I Spy* this go-round, I'm happy to point you towards an excellent research source and good read, 2007's pre-scandal *I Spy: a History and Episode Guide,* by fellow TV historian Marc Cushman for the publishers McFarland, also publishers of some of my own work. Marc is best known for his self-published in-depth study of *Star Trek,* the three volumes of *These Are the Voyages,* as well as three equally intriguing volumes on *Lost in Space.*

Finally, although I've been luckier than I dared hope, I must apologise for the quality of the photo reproduction in certain sections of this book. This is not the fault either of myself, the producers of the series concerned, the present owners and distributors, or the publishers Createspace. It has been extraordinarily difficult finding pictures for some of the shows that are of the quality I would prefer, particularly for *Burke's Law, Amos Burke – Secret Agent,* and *Honey West.* While it is ultimately the words that count, I am not naive enough to believe that the pictorial content doesn't matter. So—I beg your indulgence as I document sixty year old TV shows, some of them orphaned and without anyone to care for them, and I thank my good friend and contact Mark Phillips, a fellow writer in Canada who covers this wonderful period of pop culture on the same beat, for helping out where possible. We've never met, but we've corresponded regularly by e-mail for the past few years exchanging news, thoughts, information… and publicity stills. Thanks again, Mark.

If you like my work, please take a few minutes to leave me a good review. When you see a good review for one of my books, you know it's for real, because I don't go out asking all my friends for five star favors. And it's really obvious, and quite embarrassing, when writers write their own reviews, as some clearly do. You'll know from some of the stranger ones on my various Amazon sites that I don't! If you don't like my work, be polite and tell me exactly what you didn't care for, and I'll try and respond in the comments section. Some people think it's bad form to reply to reviews, and in the bad old days it probably was, but the internet is a new medium that has moved the goalposts. Reviews are at point of sale now, not in obscure journals seen by only a few, and they directly prompt or discourage sales; I'm grateful for good ones and disappointed by bad ones, so let me fix it or explain myself. Everything about the internet everywhere you look is first and foremost about communication and contribution, and while I don't at present have enough time in the day for Facebook, Twitter, and blogs any more than I used to have the time or inclination to keep a diary or write long letters, I do believe in correspondence when it has purpose and a point. Misunderstandings only happen when people don't talk. So don't be backward about coming forward. After all, Marshall McLuhan might be out there somewhere, floating on some astral plane, waiting to see what we do next…!

On the other hand, he's probably already figured it out…!

Jon Abbott, 2017

For one thing, we can have no notion of what the new civilisation will be... For another thing, the people who live in that civilisation will, by the fact of belonging to it, be different from ourselves...

Every change we make is tending to bring about a new civilisation of the nature of which we are ignorant, and in which we should all of us be unhappy. A new civilisation is, in fact, coming into being all the time. The civilisation of the present day would seem very new indeed to any civilised man of the eighteenth century, and I cannot imagine the most ardent or radical reformer of that age taking much pleasure in the civilisation that would meet his eye now...

We have to admit, in comparing one civilisation with another, that no one age realises all the values of civilisation... What is certain is that in realising some we lose the appreciation of others.

Culture may even be described simply as that which makes life worth living.

—*T.S. Eliot, Notes Toward the Definition of Culture, 1945*

## The Outer Limits

**September 16th, 1963 — January 16th, 1965**

*"Instead of tending towards a vast Alexandrian library the world has become a computer, an electronic brain, exactly as an infantile piece of science fiction. And as our senses have gone outside us, Big Brother goes inside. So, unless aware of this dynamic, we shall at once move into a phase of panic terrors, exactly befitting a small world of tribal drums, total interdependence, and superimposed co-existence... Terror is the normal state of any oral society, for in it everything affects everything all the time... In our long striving to recover for the Western world a unity of sensibility and of thought and feeling we have no more been prepared to accept the tribal consequences of such unity than we were ready for the fragmentation of the human psyche by print culture"*

— Marshall McLuhan, *The Gutenberg Galaxy*, 1962 (sourced from Wikipedia)

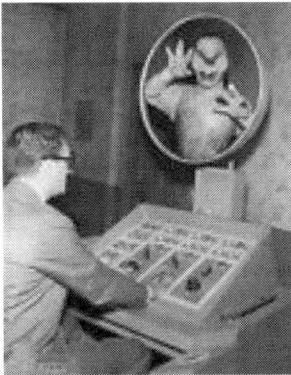

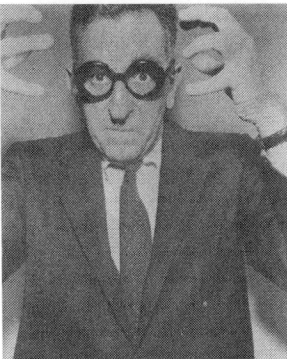

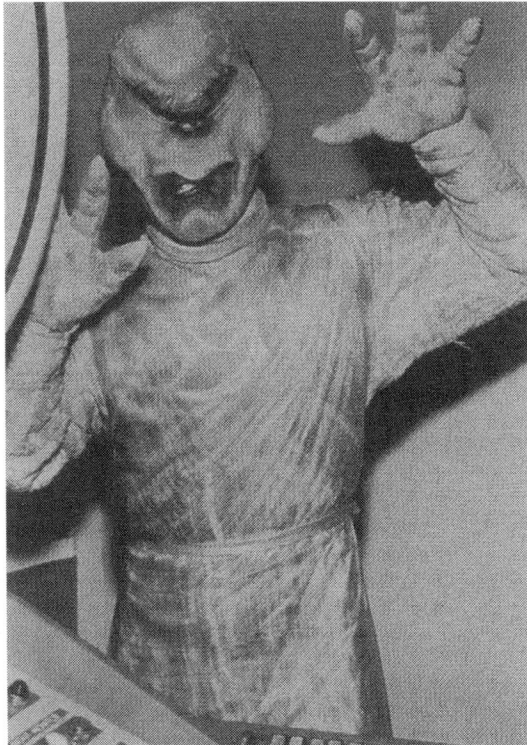

*"Most good science-fiction starts with the premise What If...? So - what if... you thought you had tracked down and seen every good, bad, and mediocre sci-fi creature feature from the '50s and '60s ever made? What if... you thought that every golden oldie worth seeing had already been released on video? What if... you thought that the truly superior TV SF of the past consisted of* **Star Trek, The Twilight Zone,** *and the first few episodes of most other shows?*

*But what if... there were 49 individual TV episodes of a gothic horror/sci-fi anthology show that were the equivalent of fifty minute 1950s monster movies? What if... a lot of them were light years better than many sci-fi adventures of the period made for the big screen? What if... they hadn't been broadcast in Britain since 1979-'80 in the middle of the night, shortly before video recorders became part of the household furniture? What if... despite being critically acclaimed TV classics, they'd only been broadcast twice in the U.K.... one of those times being when they were first made, back in the early '60s?*

*If you're familiar with* The Outer Limits, *or you vaguely remember those 49 episodes from ten, or even thirty years ago, then you'll be as thrilled as I was to learn that the series is at last about to be released on video. If it's all news to you and you've never heard of the show, then I envy you... because you are about to participate in a great adventure... you are about to experience the awe and mystery which reaches from the inner mind... to the Outer Limits...!"*

So went my first draft for an article in a 1990 issue of the long-gone *Video Buyer* magazine. A few months later, the episodes started airing on U.K. TV again, via the 'squarials' of the short-lived BSB satellite network. Sky TV inherited them, and when they were done, the Sci-Fi Channel snatched them up. Happily, they were available fairly consistently throughout the 1990s, and, like many golden oldies in the sci-fi genre, they've been more readily accessible and frequently aired than when they were first made (in Britain, ITV aired episodes around the regions when the series was first produced, both in primetime and in afternoon slots). The 1979-'80 run was offered by BBC2, and attracted attention and considerable coverage in such trend-setting publications as *Time Out, City Limits,* and *The Face* (see left). A few episodes were aired at the fashionable London cinema The Scala at around the same time by a group calling itself Wider Television Access. That power to the people finally arrived in the years to follow, via the video recorder and satellite television, then DVDs and the internet. Nearly 2000 people have looked at my DISCOVER list of the best episodes since I put it on the IMDB in 2013, fifty years after they were made.

First aired in September 1963, *The Outer Limits* was on the cusp of 1950s and 1960s attitudes towards the science and technology of the space race, bridging the fear, apprehension, and paranoia of the 1950s view of the Atomic Age with the excitement, thrill, and adventurousness of the 1960s Space Age. Most episodes of this extraordinary anthology series — despite their mere fifty minute length — stand on their own as individual productions boasting all the quality, care, thoughtfulness and significance of the very best classic science-fiction and horror films made for the cinema. The best are almost too good to be 'just TV' and stand effortlessly alongside most of the acknowledged film classics of the 1950s. The weaker, 'ordinary' episodes (mostly from the more conventional, cheaper-looking second season) are as good as any of the other SF films of the period. Long before the arrival of video recorders, subscription movie channels, and the internet, *The Outer Limits* was blurring the boundaries between TV and cinema.

The exploration of the universe's secrets was just beginning when *The Outer Limits* was conceived in 1963, and we're not much wiser today. *The Outer Limits* preoccupied itself with dire warnings, as did many of the SF films of the time, but it substituted hope and optimism for fear and despair, even as it presented us with the casualties of those first stumbling confrontations. In *The Outer Limits*, humankind's first encounters with alien life are constantly presented as clumsy betrayals or misunderstandings fostered by either greed, ignorance, or selfishness, or else insidious, callous plots hatched by fearsome and demonic monsters (courtesy of Wah Chang's formidable gallery of brilliantly horrific bug-eyed creatures). Yet through all this fatalism and lack of communication, hope continually shines through the madness. In many tales, one side or the other will redeem itself, often in an act of supreme self-sacrifice ("The Galaxy Being", "The Man With the Power", "The Man Who Was Never Born", "A Feasibility Study", "The Bellero Shield", etc. etc.), as if to

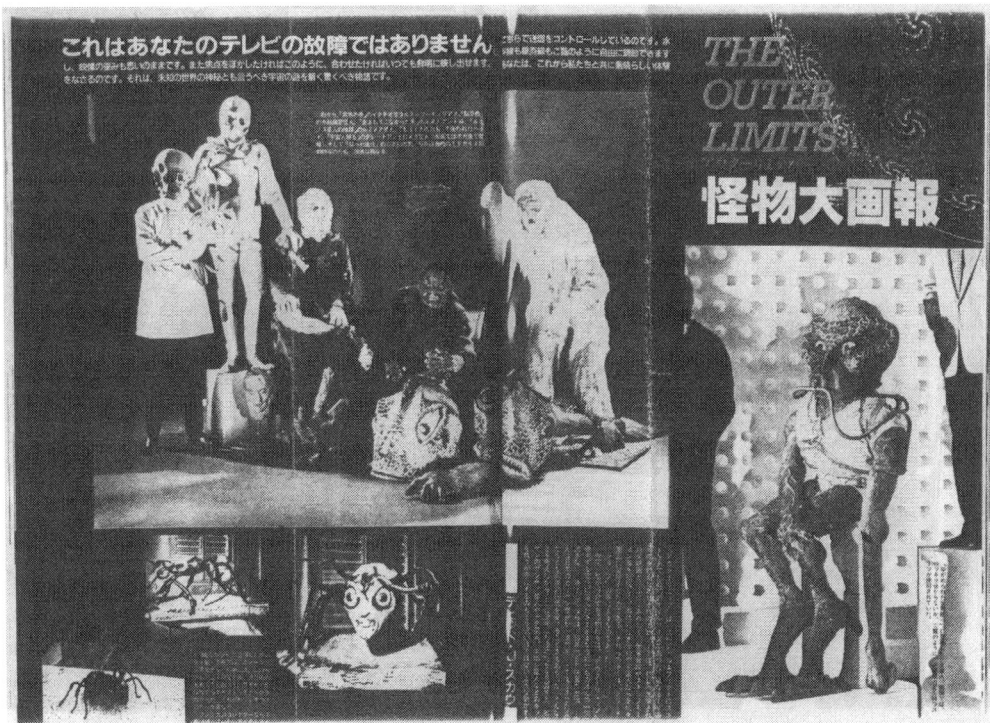

say—next time we'll know better. The familiar SF image of man as child in the universe is constantly emphasised.

Despite the episodes showing their age today (like most filmed SF, the series belongs firmly to its period), *The Outer Limits* was and still is literate, intelligent, enthralling and beautifully crafted, relying on characterisation, ideas, and clever camera tricks and make-up to get its ideas across. Whatever direction Leslie Stevens, Joe Stefano and the staff of production company Daystar took, they had promised the ABC network one thing—a monster every week—and it is these creations that *The Outer Limits* is best remembered for. These bizarre exhibits, defiantly and boldly thrown in the faces of those who insist that less is more, were provided by a legion of Hollywood's finest make-up men and effects people; huge claws, teeth, mandibles and glaring eyes adorn almost all of *The Outer Limits'* wide range of alien creatures— those that weren't hard-faced horrors were blobby, tendril-covered indeterminate lumps of nastiness! The absence of any other elaborate special effects was more than compensated for by the work of the creative talents on the series—brilliant writers and inspired directors, and Stefano's insistence on a stylish, almost European photography and camerawork virtually alien to TV. The series' lack of color was made a virtue rather than a handicap, particularly by the gothic look filmed by Gerd Oswald, who never bettered his work here. Many of the stories, themes, and ideas are on a par with much of the abundance of SF today released to cinemas, video, TV or cable, and this is no great coincidence. Many of the plots may now be suspiciously familiar simply because many later film-makers were reared on episodes of *The Outer Limits* and *The Twilight Zone* throughout their formative years. For example, Guillermo del Toro freely references it as a childhood inspiration (along with Rod Serling's *Night Gallery*), and his films *Chronos, Mimic, Pan's Labyrinth* (particularly) and *The Devil's Backbone* could not be better examples of what *The Outer Limits* would be doing today if it had been truly revived in spirit rather than name only. Rarely does a month go by without some new film or series offering a theme previously explored on *The Twilight Zone* or *The Outer Limits*.

*The Outer Limits* was the product of two distinctly different and ambitious creative talents, the first of whom was playwright and producer Leslie Stevens. By all accounts, Stevens was a dynamic and optimistic individual, who—having conquered Broadway and written plays for television in New York—had moved west to break into Hollywood, where he formed his own production company, Daystar. Having provided the ABC network with the rodeo-based modern western *Stoney Burke*, starring Jack Lord, Warren Oates, Bruce Dern, and Robert Dowdell, Stevens was commissioned by the network to produce a science-fiction anthology for them. He had an entirely free hand, but for two things—they wanted monsters, and they wanted a 'name' associated with it to give it gravitas and respectability.

That name would be Joseph Stefano, an old songwriting buddy from Stevens' lean years in Greenwich Village, who had since become a successful screenwriter for films and TV, and whose greatest claim to fame was as the author of Hitchcock's film adaptation of Robert Bloch's *Psycho*. Intending to begin with TV work, Stefano's first submission to the 1950s anthology dramas had instead become the feature film *The Black Orchid*, with Sophia Loren. Subsequently mixing film with TV, Stefano worked for 20th Century Fox on features and on such long-forgotten TV series as *Saints and Sinners, Mr. Novak,* and *The Detectives,* as well as numerous one-off dramas.

Stevens' pilot for the series, which he wrote and directed himself, was "The Galaxy Being", starring Cliff Robertson, who became the first of many soon-to-be-known performers to make journeys to *The Outer Limits* in the early stages (or in a few cases, final stages) of their careers. "The Galaxy Being" details the first tentative, clumsy steps toward intergalactic communication with alien life, made between two rebel radio hams experimenting against the wishes of their respective authorities, each grasping at grainy, blurred cosmic straws to exchange ideas and information. Their first stumbling steps of discovery costs one of the communicators his life... sort of.

Playing the part of the Galaxy Being was mime William Douglas Jnr., who was clad in a dark rubber suit coated in reflective oils and then photographed in negative. Sound effects were a combination of vacuum cleaner

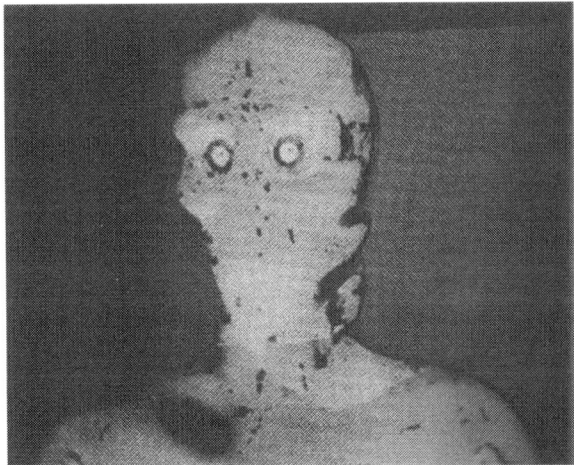

*The Galaxy Being. Left, Allyson Ames, with monsters from "The Man Who Was Never Born", "Don't Open Till Doomsday", "Tourist Attraction", "Nightmare", "The Bellero Shield".*

noises and distorted wildlife sounds originally recorded for the Morlocks in the film *The Time Machine*. When the alien turns sideways, you'll see he has a pot belly like Snoopy or E.T. This was because the face mask covered his head completely, and the stomach conceals an oxygen tank feeding a hidden tube to Douglas' mouth.

"We didn't want some lumbering stunt-man in a suit" Stevens told David Schow and Jeffrey Frentzen, authors of the indispensable reference work *The Outer Limits Companion*. "Douglas added a touch of weirdness to the way he walked by using a preying mantis as his model. You can see how he looks and turns with his whole body. The creature perceives a world that, to him, is made of glass. He can't keep his balance, as though he's about to fall off this transparent place".

Douglas went on to portray a number of other aliens in the series. Sometimes the actors themselves suited up (and those who did included Martin Landau, David McCallum, Robert Duvall, Simon Oakland, John Hoyt, and John Anderson), while other non-human roles were taken by stunt-men, and in a few cases veteran monster maker Janos Prohaska, whose unusual creations adorned episodes of such shows as *Lost in Space, Bewitched, Voyage to the Bottom of the Sea* and *Star Trek*. Contrary to some accounts, Stevens and Stefano had no qualms about ABC's insistence on a 'monster of the week'. While Stevens and Stefano had the same dispiriting experience with SF writers that *Star Trek's* Gene Roddenberry would have a couple of years later (none of these writers with such a disparaging view of the medium could begin to understand the mechanisms for writing for it), they decided, unlike Roddenberry, to embrace the request for monsters. Stefano called it "the bear", after the old vaudeville practice of bringing on a man in a bear suit—or even a live bear—when the audience started to shift in their seats. It was a requisite Prohaska would have been able to deal with quite literally—during the late '60s and early '70s he was the infamous Cookie Bear on *The Andy Williams Show!*

*Sometimes they did get a lumbering stunt-man in a suit, but at least here it's Janos Prohaska as the iconic Thetan from "The Architects of Fear".*

For all their integrity, ambition and intellect, Stevens and Stefano were pragmatic professionals who understood the needs of the marketplace. These bizarre creatures and their weapons and vehicles were the product of a legion of Hollywood's best and most creative make-up men and effects people, including Wah Chang, Byron Haskin, John Chambers, Fred Phillips, Gene Warren and stop motion expert Jim Danforth. Anybody who was anyone in special effects worked in some capacity on *The Outer Limits*. Wah Chang made most of the hideous alien heads that appeared in the show, and gave them the piercing, ferocious mad-eyed look of a marriage between 1950s bug-eyed monsters of the Paul Blaisdell variety and Oriental mythology and art. John Chambers was a master of extending the physical appearance of actors, and went on to create the masks for the *Planet of the Apes* films with Dan Striepke. He also provided disguises for *Mission: Impossible* and *The Wild, Wild West,* transformed Robert Culp into an Oriental warlord for *I Spy*

("The Warlord", written by Culp), created an army of Doctor Smiths for *Lost in Space* ("The Space Destructors"), produced some of Spock's ears for *Star Trek*, gave us a dissolving alien in *The Invaders* ("The Enemy"), and also worked on *Voyage to the Bottom of the Sea* and *Night Gallery*. His main claim to fame on *The Outer Limits* was transforming David McCallum into a man of the future for the episode "The Sixth Finger". Also brought in to assist with the special effects, but ending up mostly directing, was legendary old curmudgeon Byron Haskin, who had directed such big screen predecessors as *War of the Worlds, Conquest of Space, From the Earth to the Moon*, and—after *The Outer Limits*—*Robinson Crusoe on Mars, Captain Sindbad*, and *The Power*.

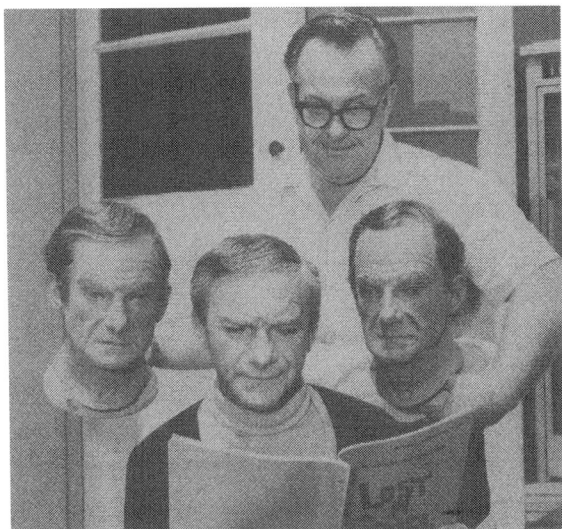

*Jonathan Harris of Lost in Space hamming it up for a publicity picture with make-up magician John Chambers, whose other work includes the masks shown, for an episode titled "The Space Destructors".*

Haskin also worked without credit on the *Star Trek* pilot "The Cage" (although he and Roddenberry eventually fell out), and in fact many of the behind-the-scenes personnel on *The Outer Limits*, including assistant director Robert Justman, went straight from *The Outer Limits* to *Star Trek*.

Like most of those concerned with the series, Byron Haskin was responsible for some outstanding episodes, and a couple of turkeys. Jerry Sohl's "The Invisible Enemy", almost a trial run for his film *Robinson Crusoe on Mars* the following year, complete with Adam (*Batman*) West and Martian setting, is a splendid idea pre-dating both *Jaws* and *Alien*, both of which it resembles, but Haskin was also responsible for directing the abysmal "Behold Eck", which old-time Marvel or *Mad* readers might have been more inclined to refer to as "Behold Echh"! Here, a friendly, but clumsy two-dimensional alien can only see and be seen with the aid of special glasses constructed by the optometrist he befriends. A nice idea putting across the notion that an extraterrestrial might be encountered in the most unlikely of places was completely fudged. Yet Haskin promptly followed this with the remarkable "Demon with a Glass Hand", one of the best episodes ever produced.

*Robert Culp, made up by Chambers for his role in "The Warlord", for I Spy.*

Similarly, "A Feasibility Study" is a moving, almost flawless masterpiece from the first season, moody, atmospheric, and powerfully effective, both in moments of sudden, shocking horror (such as the pre-credits jump to the ceiling where a businessman, lost in an inexplicable and deepening fog, abandons his car and then runs to the camera from pursuing monsters only to have a hideous claw suddenly jump up between him and the camera). Of several marvellous sequences, there are particularly the closing moments, strongly reminiscent of the quiet moments in the church in Haskin's immortal *War of the Worlds*. Haskin was also responsible for directing the brilliant and astonishing "The Architects of Fear" (an intriguing variation on the premise of *The Day the Earth Stood Still*), which followed on from the fascinating, over-the-top paranoid fantasy "One Hundred Days of the Dragon", a Red-bashing Cold War fantasy from the typewriter of future *Mission: Impossible* story editors and scriptwriters William Read Woodfield and Allan Balter, with special effects sequences that range from really good to rotten and a magnificent central performance from Sidney Blackmer. Consistency was not one of Haskin's strong points; he contributed to some of the best and some more variable episodes, but to his credit, in subsequent interviews he recognised which were which, even if he wouldn't take the blame. Given material he liked, Haskin's work was masterful, but given an assignment he didn't care for, he seemed to fall asleep at the wheel with indifference. In "The Invisible Enemy" for example, we're treated to the ludicrous sight of a crewman who spots a botanical specimen to take back to Earth as an example of rare alien plant life, and then picks it from the stem! Was this really the work of the same director who aimed for such credibility and accuracy in *Conquest of Space*? When convinced he'd been handed a lemon to squeeze, Haskin seemed to go out of his way to make sure he was proven right...

"A Feasibility Study"

Although Stevens had turned the reins over to Joseph Stefano once *The Outer Limits* was in production, he contributed three other first season episodes, sadly three of the weaker ones. Ordinarily, when a series' creator scripts a story it can be relied upon to be one of the better ones, but Stevens' contributions were merely stop-gap measures when time or money ran short and a cheap and easy episode had to be rustled up on the spot. Stevens' "The Borderland", with the series' favorite theme of science abused by selfish or over-ambitious individuals (less successfully employed here than in the superior "OBIT", "The Bellero Shield", "The Architects of Fear",

"The Sixth Finger", "The Man Who Was Never Born", or "It Crawled Out of the Woodwork"), failed to sustain its sense of wonder and dramatic tension, becoming instead a tedious and empty exercise in style and visual effects (with some early occasionally unintentionally funny techno-babble). A similar fate befell "Production and Decay of Strange Particles", also written and directed by Stevens, although both are certainly moody and unusual pieces of television. The light-hearted and budget-conscious "Controlled Experiment", thrown together in four days as opposed to the usual seven or eight, told the tale of two humanoid 'martians' replaying a human murder with a time-shifting device (amusingly pre-dating the abilities of contemporary VCRs) at different speeds in order to fully understand this exclusively human behavior. Instead of employing the usual 'cheater' technique of stitching together clips from previous episodes with a new framing sequence (which would not have worked for a unique and diverse anthology series, a point adequately proven by the 1990s version of the show), Stevens was able to employ the same murder footage repeatedly. Unconvincing and obvious in its premise, it was nevertheless an entertaining diversion thanks primarily to the enjoyable performances of Carroll O'Connor and Barry Morse as the aliens and Star Trek's Grace Lee Whitney as the murderess.

*Above: "Nightmare". Right: If the episode was weak, you could still admire the alien – "Fun and Games"*

Stefano, on the other hand, was responsible for nine of the series' strongest and most eloquent scripts out of twelve he contributed. As Gene Roddenberry later found out with *Star Trek*, hiring science fiction writers didn't necessarily result in ready-for-film TV scripts, although many of those who contributed to *The Outer Limits* had SF credits, including Meyer (Mike) Dolinsky, David Duncan, Harlan Ellison, and Jerry Sohl, and many of them (and other *Outer Limits* writers) went on to contribute to other TV SF productions, notably *The Invaders* and *Voyage to the Bottom of the Sea*. However it was Stefano's episodes that read like a checklist of the finest first season episodes, and include "Nightmare", "It Crawled Out of the Woodwork", "The Zanti Misfits", "The Mice", "Don't Open Till Doomsday", "The Invisibles", "The Bellero Shield", "A Feasibility Study", and "The Form of Things Unknown", one of the most bizarre pieces of film ever produced for television. For the record, the other three Stefano scripts were the marginally weaker "Fun and Games" (which at least had a great Wah Chang alien) and "The Chameleon" (ditto), both co-written, and "The Special One". Of these twelve scripts, eight were directed by Gerd Oswald, the series' best and most distinguished director. This was not a coincidence; as producer's perks, Stefano took the liberty of ensuring that his episodes were almost always directed by Oswald.

Gerd Oswald was a refugee with his family from Hitler's Germany, and travelled through Austria, France, and England before settling in America. He worked in theatre, and then became an assistant director on B-pictures from Monogram and Republic. Later, he worked for Paramount and Fox, becoming a production manager. Enlisted for *The Outer Limits* by Leslie Stevens, the series was already well underway when Oswald came aboard, pitching in to helm the hokey "Specimen: Unknown", a corny tale of killer plant life that had little to recommend it but for a clever punchline—**spoiler coming**—the plant seeds contaminate Earth, but are *destroyed* by rainfall, rather than nourished.

Oswald's first notable episode was Meyer Dolinsky's "OBIT", a grim Big Brother parable starring Peter Breck, (later of the popular western series *The Big Valley*, story edited by Lou Morheim), actor, teacher, and director Jeff Corey, a survivor of Hollywood's McCarthy era, and Harry Townes, known to SF buffs for his appearances in *The Twilight Zone, The Invaders, Star Trek,* and an exceptional performance in the superior *Incredible Hulk* two-parter "The First", itself unusually reminiscent of *The Outer Limits* for monster sequences shot in sun-speckled woodland, an *Outer Limits* trademark. Oswald's next was "Corpus Earthling", the least well-known of the three episodes to feature Robert Culp, this time cast as a desperate man who overhears alien beings planning a takeover of the Earth, but it was with Stefano's second script, "It Crawled Out of the Woodwork", that he made his first big splash. In the familiar *Outer Limits* setting of a scientific research establishment, a life-form is created spontaneously out of the energy growing out of

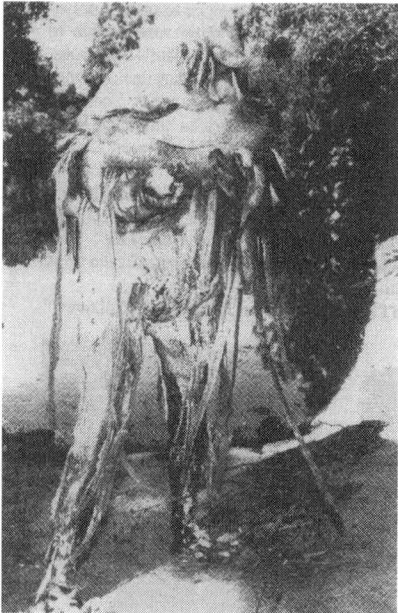

"The Mice"

the dust in a cleaner's vacuum cleaner, and eventually taking up residence at the end of a 'last mile'-style corridor. Again, exploitation of alien forces comes into play, when a scientist realises that he can kill off intruders and colleagues alike and then bring them back to life with a pacemaker-like device under his control. One by one, people take the long, fearful, hypnotic walk down the corridor...

The chilling and visually haunting "The Mice" followed, and then the nightmarish "Don't Open Till Doomsday", an extraordinary episode in which Miriam Hopkins, an old-time movie actress, plays a jilted and now aged and demented bride whose husband-to-be, still young, is imprisoned in a black box by a very Freudian dimension-traversing alien blob who wants to get out and invade the Earth. Hopkins' Mrs. Kry comes across as equal parts Gloria Swanson in *Sunset Boulevarde* and June Foray's Witch Hazel in Chuck Jones' *Bugs Bunny* cartoons as she prowls her Bates Motel-style residence attempting to lure two underage eloping lovers into her spider's web to take their places. John Hoyt, a supporting player in numerous sci-fi films and TV series, turns up in several *Outer Limits* episodes (as the alien in "The Bellero Shield" and later in "I, Robot"), and here plays the sour but loving father of the bride.

Of the remaining first season episodes directed by Oswald, particular mention might be made of "The Invisibles", a combination of the later series *The Invaders*, the classic *Invasion of the Body Snatchers*, and the old William Castle shocker *The Tingler*, all by way of Heinlein's novel "The Puppet Masters". Here, Don Gordon is a grim government agent infiltrating a subversive organisation of two-bit fascists, only to discover that its operatives are slaves of grotesque parasitic slugs surgically implanted in their gullible hosts. The operation to insert the parasite is shown to be a particularly slow and painful surgical affair, as opposed to the usual SF cliche of having the host simply go glassy-eyed or develop monotone speech patterns. Oswald's sweeping, tilted cameras and the masterful, leering performance of screen villain George MacReady (an actor used to less effect in "Production and Decay of Strange Particles") make the episode a horrific delight. The supporting cast are superb, from Walter Burke's deformed implant-that-went-wrong Igor-type, to Dee Hartford's Jackie Kennedy-ish politician's wife, and Richard Dawson's smarmy, fey recruiter to Neil Hamilton's delightfully deranged invisible-controlled authority figure.

Of Oswald's other contributions, "Fun and Games" was the only episode to feature a cackling comic-book cliche of an evil alien, which made the episode a novelty in that respect at least, even if the extraterrestrial's dialogue was pure Irwin Allen. The alliance between Oswald and Stefano ended in a blaze of glory with the captivating backdoor pilot "The Form of Things Unknown", with Vera Miles, queen of the TV movies, and, left, Barbara Rush (of *It Came from Outer Space*) accompanying future UNCLE agent David McCallum in a curious gothic oddity of murder, malice, and guilt.

Director of photography on the series was Conrad Hall, whose mentor, Ted McCord, had worked on numerous Joan Crawford and Bette Davis movies, as well as classics such as *Treasure of the Sierra Madre* and *East of Eden*. When McCord fell ill and was forced to retire during the making of *Stoney Burke*, Daystar's first and only other TV series commission, Hall took over, and his inventiveness and innovation proved an immeasurable asset to the unique visual style of *The Outer Limits*, which was quite unlike anything else on TV at the time or since. "I had the chance to experiment a lot", Hall told Schow and Frentzen for *The Outer Limits Companion*. "Anything I ever heard about, dreamt about, or thought up—I tried everything in the book. *The Outer Limits* became a school for the development of my craft". "He could get so much out of so little" Stevens confirmed. "Once he was shooting someone on a balcony, through the branches of a willow tree. He tied a rope to the branches from below and had someone pull it very gently, giving the branches this wonderful subtle motion. It cost fifteen cents more and made all the difference in the world. Another time, he lit an actress from the centre of her forehead with a tiny light used for close-ups. Every time she blinked, these tiny shadow-lines of eyelash were thrown all the way down her face. Now when you think of what you're getting for those extra two minutes (to set it up), that's incredible" (Oswald also used the eyelash trick on actress Susan Flannery in "Hail to the Chief", an episode of *Voyage to the Bottom of the Sea*). The talent that worked alongside Hall was equally impressive, and all went on to bigger things in Hollywood.

The music for the series was provided by Dominic Frontiere, an old friend of Stevens who later went on to score *The Invaders* (the theme for that series, and much of the incidental music, had been made for Stefano's unsold pilot *The Unknown,* and you can still hear it in "The Form of Things Unknown", the series episode that pilot became). In those days, before the musician's union stepped in, studios accumulated music libraries of the scores composed for other films and series and re-used them on later shows when applicable, and variations of Frontiere's themes for *The Outer Limits* were not only occasionally employed on *The Invaders,* but could also frequently be heard on such other non-SF shows as *Branded* and *The Fugitive.* For the second season, a new score was provided by Harry Lubin, a hauntingly moving and melodic piece (as opposed to Frontiere's fearful and ominous chords), which bore a striking resemblance to his theme for the earlier supernatural anthology show *One Step Beyond.*

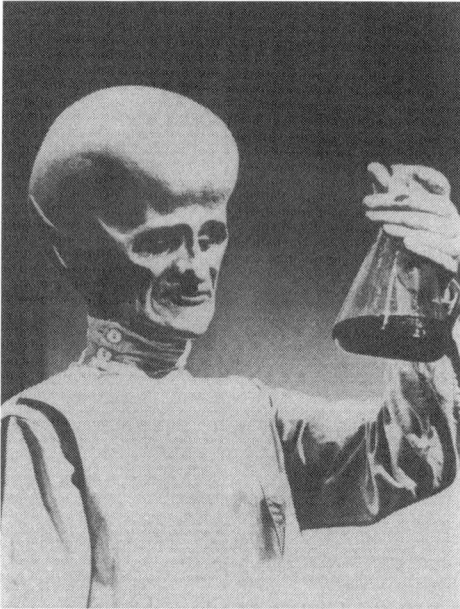

*David McCallum as the Future Man in "The Sixth Finger"*

Two other key contributors were voice artists. The legendary Control Voice which narrated the series was provided by busy bit player and voice artist Vic Perrin, whose numerous on-screen bit parts included aliens in "People Are Alike All Over" for *The Twilight Zone,* "Summit Meeting" for *The Invaders,* "Mirror Mirror" for *Star Trek,* "Judgement from Outer Space" for *Wonder Woman,* and "The Guardians" for *Buck Rogers in the 25th Century,* the irate pedestrian bumped into by a giant-sized Kurt Kasznar in "Genius at Work" for *Land of the Giants,* and numerous cartoon voices including Cyclops, the Silver Surfer, Hawkman, *Birdman's* Vulturo and *Space Ghost's* Creature King in the '60s, Thor, Sub-Mariner, and *Super-Friends'* Sinestro in the '80s, and the villainous Doctor Zin in episodes of *Jonny Quest,* TV's first adventure cartoon. Most of the other alien voices for *The Outer Limits* were provided by Bob Johnson, a singer and announcer from Seattle who was Daystar's accountant! Whenever an ominous alien vocal was needed, Johnson would sprint upstairs from his desk and take the microphone! But he went on to occupy an even more prestigious place in TV history a few years later, as the man who delivered each and every tape-recorded assignment on the self-destructing messages for *Mission: Impossible.*

Inevitably, *The Outer Limits* attracted the services of a number of fine young actors (and a couple of distinguished veterans), some of them already established masters of their craft, others going on to become well-known in films or TV in the years to follow. These included David McCallum, Martin Landau, Robert Culp, Donald Pleasance, Bruce Dern, Ed Asner, Sally Kellerman, Martin Sheen, Warren Oates, Robert Duvall, Gloria Grahame, Miriam Hopkins, Sir Cedric Hardwicke, Vera Miles, Barbara Rush, Adam West, William Shatner, Leonard Nimoy, and James Doohan.

David McCallum, later to achieve world-wide fame just a few months later in *The Man from UNCLE* appeared as he is usually seen in "The Form of Things Unknown", but underwent an extraordinary and remarkably designed transformation as a super-evolved man in "The Sixth Finger", a brilliant early episode written by Ellis St. Joseph and directed by James Goldstone. McCallum plays a miner who is exploited by a scientist (Edward Mulhare of *The Ghost and Mrs. Muir* and *Knight Rider*) who puts him through a process to speed up his evolution and transform him into a man of the future. Inevitably, the already bitter and surly young fellow becomes an arrogant menace with a dangerous superiority complex as his intellect and appearance advances. John Chambers' make-up work is exemplary on this, one of the few episodes to require a noticeably human visage on the alien, rather than the totally different look most often achieved on the series with a complete headpiece. Chambers manages not only to make the future man still clearly resemble McCallum, but also to make him appear smug, intelligent, and threatening at the same time. The finished effect is quite extraordinary.

Robert Culp also undergoes a tragic metamorphosis in "The Architects of Fear", as the unfortunate scientist who draws the short straw to be transformed into a highly unusual alien menace to blackmail the world into peace *Day the Earth Stood Still*-style into behaving itself, only to have the alien emotions transformation process understandably drive him insane. In "Corpus Earthling", Culp found himself the increasingly paranoid intended victim of rock specimens which he could hear plotting against him and humanity in general!

"The Man Who Was Never Born" also breathes life into that oldest of SF cliches, the traveller in time who prevents his own birth and 'cancels himself out' by changing the future. Here though, the action is deliberate, the man not without valid

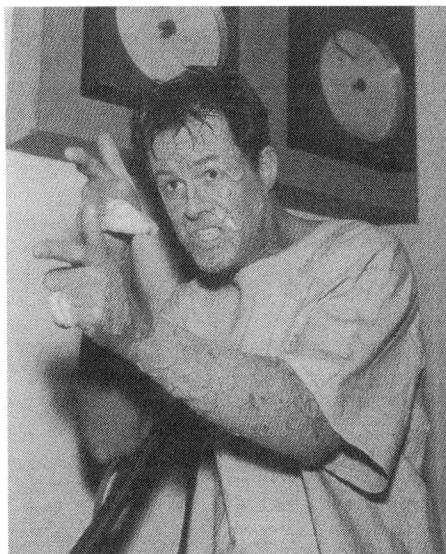

*Robert Culp in "The Architects of Fear"*

reason and just cause. He is a horribly deformed mutant (although he has the hypnotic ability to transform himself into a more average, acceptable appearance) who returns to an idyllic past on Earth completely at odds with his harsh, barren future world, to prevent the holocaust that a young woman's unborn, not-yet-conceived son will one day cause. In a sequence reminiscent of James Whale's *Frankenstein,* the hideous mutant has just arrived in his past (our present), and approaches a young girl playing by a stream (this time, a teenage woman). He follows her back to her lodgings, but when she spins around, taken by surprise, the moment of expected horror is instantly defused as a natural-looking man (Martin Landau) stands before her... still somehow strangely... not right. The rest of the episode shows equal visual ingenuity, particularly in the closing sequence. The final shot, as mutant Andros quietly fades away, is poignantly and masterfully executed as their spaceship dissolves to leave only the woman he has seduced alone, seated on a single chair in the darkness as the camera pulls away.

An equally chilling ending graced the extraordinary "The Bellero Shield", also starring Landau, this time as a weak scientist dominated by his power-hungry status-seeking wife (Sally Kellerman of the second *Star Trek* pilot) and self-serving father (the wonderful Neil Hamilton) who makes contact with alien life by chance. They destroy themselves personally and the alien literally. In "The Guests", an episode that is pure Stefano, but in fact written by *Twilight Zone* writer Charles Beaumont and *Boris Karloff's Thriller* regular Donald Sanford, a drifter stumbles onto a house full of hateful individuals frozen in time and all going slightly mad. No wonder—a grotesque glob of an alien parasite is unfeelingly stripping their souls bare to analyse their emotions while searching for the missing factor none of them possess... until the young man finds elusive—obsessive?—love at first sight.

Undoubtedly though, the most memorable episode for many people remains the extraordinary "The Zanti Misfits", with its wild-eyed and insanely malevolent grinning human-faced ants! The alien ants (the Zanti misfits of the title) are both horribly nightmarish and ludicrous at the same time (as indeed are 'real' nightmares), and the episode even has the structure of a bad dream—a slow, lonely build-up with a man in flight, leading to a crowded and claustrophobic frantic conclusion of mounting hysteria. Not only are the ants typically 1950s B-movie-ish, but so is the acting, consisting of mostly unknowns, with Michael Tolan as the traditional tweedy young scientist, Robert F. Simon in the 'Morris Ankrum' role of army general, and the then-unknown Bruce Dern as a fleeing criminal, all of it occurring in vintage SF's favorite setting, the desert (Vasquez Rocks, no less)... The episode cleverly but casually avoids the usual SF simplification that a race of alien beings must be 'all-good' or 'all-bad'. The Zanti are callous, indifferent, and pragmatic. However, there is a superb twist at the end.

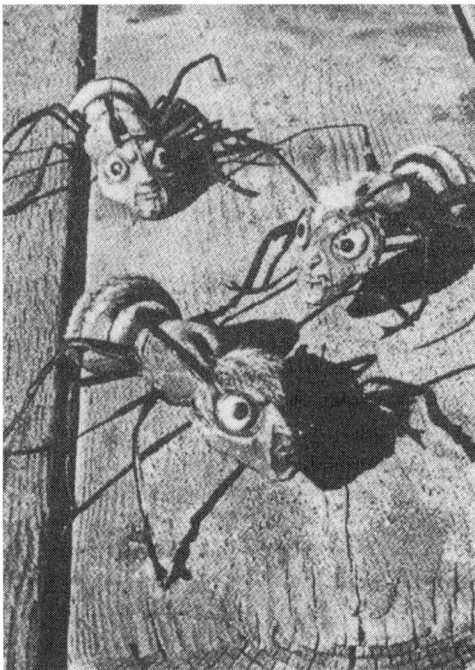

"The Zanti Misfits"

ABC had found themselves with an inexplicable and unexpected hit on their hands, albeit a modest one, and their inevitable interference with a winning formula that they could not understand but insisted on controlling resulted in the series being shifted from its successful Monday evening slot to a Saturday night position opposite a particularly popular mainstream lowbrow comedy show. Stevens and Stefano protested the move bitterly, and for Stefano, it was the last straw in a continuous battle with the network that had culminated in their refusal to let him direct. Angrily, he left the series, and feeling and support was so strong (a strike, threatening to stop production unless Stefano directed *The Unknown* had already been squashed by lawyers) that many production staff left too. Others found themselves pushed or pressured out by the new producer's people.

Undeterred by Stefano's decision to go, ABC brought in one of their own executives, professional line producer Ben Brady, to take charge of the second season, in order that he might work out his final year under contract to them. As far as they were concerned, they still had *The Outer Limits* because they had a program called *The Outer Limits*. The new story editor was Seeleg Lester, and Stevens credits the continuing quality of many of the scripts to Lester's work (years later, when developing the David McCallum series *The Invisible Man*, Stevens hired Lester as story editor on that show). Stevens and Stefano had guessed correctly that the change of time and day would kill the series in the ratings, and the even more traditional and familiar approach to creature features proffered by Brady failed to attract viewers from the more typical mainstream Saturday night fare. Stevens and Stefano had known that *The Outer Limits* in any form would prove more than a little inaccessible to the traditional Saturday night stay-at-homes, losing its strong teenage following in a weekend time-slot when last season's core audience were out on the town. With the show's audience, and its unique flavor severely depleted, the show was cancelled mid-season. Fortunately for posterity, a TV season in the 1960s was considerably longer then than today (from 26 to 30 episodes a year, as opposed to 18 to 22 today), and so we have 32 Stefano-supervised stories to enjoy, followed by 17 from Brady's botched and budget-conscious half-season.

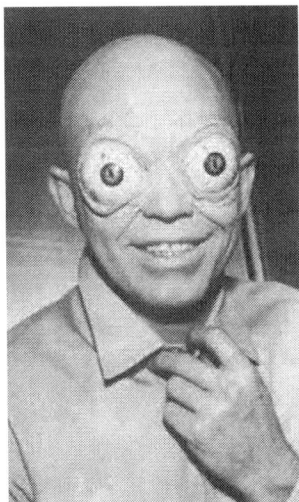

*"Tourist Attraction" and "The Mutant" – not so bad?*

As Stevens' and Stefano's work was so creative, outrageous, and unusual, and Brady's so workmanlike and pedestrian, it's common to read that the first season was uniformly wonderful and the second season complete rubbish. Objectively though, the second season had its moments and the first season certainly had its fair share of stinkers, which even Stefano, Stevens, and their colleagues acknowledge. "Moonstone", "Second Chance", and "Specimen: Unknown" were openly accepted to be failures, even at the time. Others, such as "Tourist Attraction" and "The Mutant" (left), are not as bad as some have suggested.

### The Second Season

While most of the criticisms levelled at the second season of *The Outer Limits* are justified, TV SF buffs spoiled by the superior first season produced by different hands, and appalled by the heavy handed network interference that cut those hands off at the wrists, are inclined to dismiss too quickly the remaining episodes of *The Outer Limits* that were produced without creators Stefano and Stevens. Admittedly hindered by low budgets and more conventional in their approach to the medium, the second season had much that would have been acclaimed had it belonged to another, earlier series separated from the Stefano season—the fine performances in "Cold Hands, Warm Heart" and "I, Robot", the cleverness of "Demon with a Glass Hand" and "Soldier", the humanity of "The Inheritors", the mounting hysteria of "Cry of Silence", the thoughtfulness and suspense of the *Twilight Zone*-ish "The Premonition" and "The Probe", even the malevolent alien creatures of "Keeper of the Purple Twilight".

*Robert Webber poses with the aliens from "Keeper of the Purple Twilight"*

Ben Brady was a conventional and competent line producer whose previous TV work had been in the popular courtroom drama *Perry Mason*, but he was quite capable of dealing with the day-to-day realities of making a TV show. He had no personal vision like Stevens or Stefano, but hired the right people to do the right jobs with what he had. Like Stefano and story editor Lou Morheim before him, Brady discovered very early on that most science-fiction novelists were quite incapable of writing material for television. Harlan Ellison was a rare exception who wrote regularly for television until the late '70s (*Burke's Law, Cimarron City, The Flying Nun, Voyage to the Bottom of the Sea, Star Trek, The Man from UNCLE, The Young Lawyers, The Starlost, Logan's Run*), but had a volatile personality and was always taking his name off finished scripts due to network foolishness or rewrites. For those SF writers who did dare to dabble in television, even for exemplary, prestigious series, the disappointment was often a two-way street. SF writer Jerry Sohl was also destined to be mostly let down by his experiences with both *The Outer Limits* and *Star Trek*.

No article on *The Outer Limits* seems to pass without mention of the two episodes penned by Ellison, who revolutionised the SF medium of the written word, not just with his own stories, but with his mid-'60s anthology *Dangerous Visions*, in which he collected together all the unpublished and rejected works of established SF authors which for one reason or another had been turned down by editors or publishers for being too controversial or different. Needless to say, some were turkeys and others quite magnificent, but the collection redefined what you 'could' and 'couldn't' do in SF. He also produced two collections of fraught, highly partial and laughably side-taking TV criticism reproduced from a regular column he wrote for *The Village Voice* in the late '60s and early '70s, *The Glass Teat* and *The Other Glass Teat*. Ellison was no less a maverick in television, although he lost more battles than he won when fighting for his scripts. A script conference for an episode of *Voyage to the Bottom of the Sea* apparently ended with Ellison hurtling down a lengthy polished boardroom table to punch out the lights of a TV executive he was having a dispute with! A regular writer for TV in the '60s, such as *The Man from UNCLE* and *Burke's Law*, and part-author of his acclaimed "The City on the Edge of Forever", one of the finest ever *Star Trek* episodes, Ellison had been a natural for the unrestrained creativity of *The Outer Limits*, contributing two above average episodes — "Soldier" and "Demon with a Glass Hand" — to the persistently mundane but occasionally inspired second season. Ellison is one of the few — if not only — to hold the opposing view to most commentators that the second season was better than the first.

"Demon with a Glass Hand", which offers no demon, was a typical Ellison mystery populated with characters with odd yet typically un-SF names (Arch, Battle, Budge, and Breech — a dictionary is a wonderful tool for writers). Despite the absence of Stefano and Hall, the episode was strong on atmosphere, a dark and brooding thriller with an eerie otherworldly mood to it, timeless, and despite its abandoned office block setting, quite unearthly and cold. Carrying the glass hand of the title was Robert Culp as the unfortunate Trent, an excellent and way above average TV performer later to take the lead in the groundbreaking mid-'60s spy series *I Spy* (1965-'68) and who had already turned in inspired performances in two first season episodes, the magnificent "The Architects of Fear" and the slower but competent and effective chiller "Corpus Earthling". In all three episodes, he was playing the troubled and haunted victim of the creeping out-of-control excesses of the unknown. Ellison's "Soldier", more conventional second season fare, was a powerful militaristic piece exposing the futility off the military mindset, with Michael Ansara in the first of three 1960s roles as an alien warrior (the others were in *Lost in Space* and *Star Trek*), here stranded on Earth during a battle.

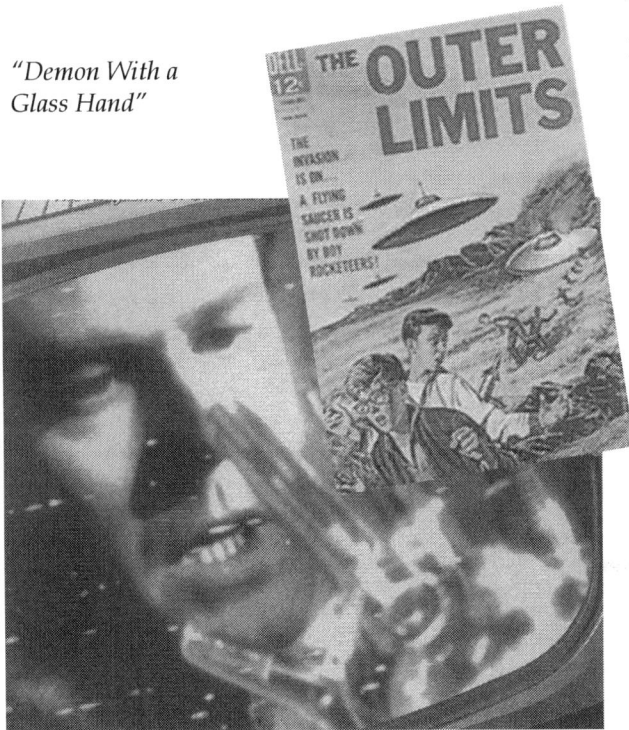

*"Demon With a Glass Hand"*

"Cold Hands, Warm Heart" is also well known, with *Star Trek's* William Shatner as a pre-Kirk astronaut who witnesses an alien life form (similar to Spielberg's *Close Encounters* Roswellian alien) outside his capsule and returns to Earth shivering and unable to get warm. Shatner gives his usual pre-'70s outstanding performance and there are a few nice lines in the dialogue department. "Cry of Silence" has Eddie Albert and June Havoc as Mr. and Mrs. Average American menaced in a desert cabin by sentient tumbleweeds, and despite the absurdity of the idea (no doubt springing from exposure to numerous sagebrush westerns), the finished piece manages some

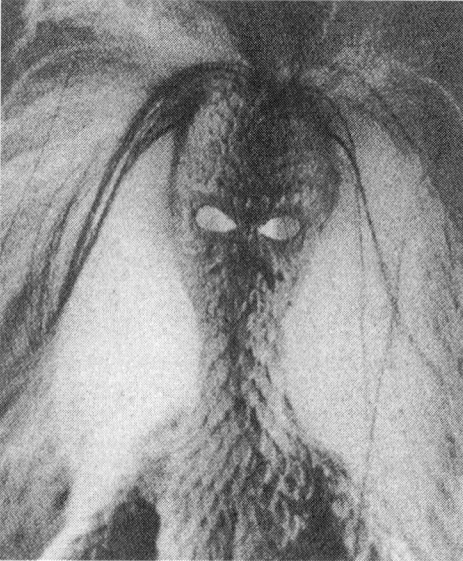

*"Cold Hands, Warm Heart"*

nicely spooky and atmospheric moments. "I, Robot" is an adaptation of Asimov's law that no robot may harm his human masters. Leonard Nimoy and Howard Da Silva give particularly strong performances of a straightforward but literate script. A courtroom story, even with a robot on trial, was probably almost inevitable given Brady's lengthy stint on *Perry Mason*. "Counterweight" and "The Probe" are both barren episodes pitting groups of panicky or resolute people against the unknown, but certainly to less effect than first season episodes such as "A Feasibility Study" or "The Mutant", while "The Premonition" is a pleasing *Twilight Zone*-ish tale of two people who find that time is mysteriously suspended long enough to avert a personal tragedy, if only they can figure out how to act before time resumes. Dewey Martin, the cowardly and selfish astronaut in the *Twilight Zone* episode "I Shot an Arrow..." has the lead in this tale uncharacteristically directed by Gerd Oswald in daylight and wide open spaces.

The only two-parter produced for *The Outer Limits* was "The Inheritors", helmed by James Goldstone. The resolution, typical of *The Outer Limits,* was a grand reversal of audience expectations from what initially appears to be a standard B-movie bodysnatching saga. Starring a then-unknown Robert Duvall (who had already appeared as a bogus alien in the earlier "The Chameleon") as a government agent hunting down a number of missing soldiers taken over by an invading alien intelligence, the episode has the structure, appearance, and dialogue of a traditional hokey '50s pulp yarn but is redeemed by its unusual climax and some brief flashes of *Outer Limits* brilliance shining through. At one point, one of the possessed Earthmen chosen for their 'special skills' (Ivan Dixon, later a TV director) is seen in a church, poignantly praying for "just a sign of some kind" to indicate that by obeying the alien commands and not resisting, he's "doing the right thing". Whatever views on religion the viewer might hold, churches and faith make for great drama and emotion, and it's a moving scene despite its brevity within the main body of the story, a flat, grey, cop show style hunt for the aliens' pawns.

"The Inheritors" and the Ellison episodes were not the only second season offerings to retain some of the first season magic. Although the aliens in "Keeper of the Purple Twilight" are in the more traditional SF role of brutal menace (and very effectively so — like many of the show's aliens, they look as though they just stepped out of one of Stan Lee's pre-Marvel Super Hero fantasy yarns), the drama and the horror is alleviated by some appropriately contrasting scenes of quiet discomfort, as a rebel, Ikar (with the later familiar face of regular 1970s TV guest star Robert Webber alternating with the hideous headpiece) attempts to learn the ways of humans. The scientist hero (Warren Stevens, Irwin Allen regular and co-star in *Forbidden Planet*) drives home one night, idly talking aloud to himself and contemplating suicide. Silently, the peaceful alien of the motley crew, makes an appearance in the back seat, materialising silently in ghostly fashion to quietly admonish him. Stevens is half-way through an absently-given reply before he freezes! There's a brilliantly primed pause for realisation before the alien vanishes as silently as he came, and Stevens glances up to his mirror to find himself alone in his car.... It makes a superbly chilling scene, and a familiar one — we've all had that feeling at some time.

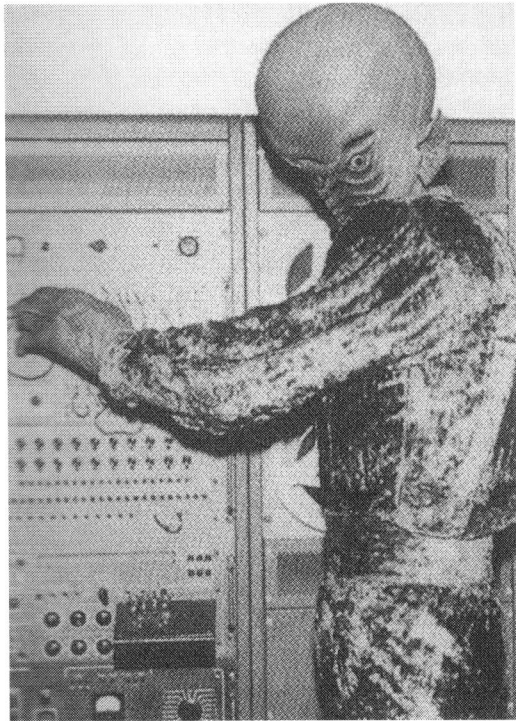

Despite the deliberate emphasis on fear, *The Outer Limits* was not a negative series. Quite the reverse. It did not reinforce the Cold War paranoia of so many of the 1950s feature films dealing with alien visitors from outer space. Neither did it indulge in the naive, starry-eyed and simplistic approach of *Close Encounters of the Third Kind* and its ilk. The approach of *The Outer Limits* was logic and intelligence tempered with caution and reason, and epitomised by the closing narration of the pilot episode:

*"We must see the stranger in a new light — the light of understanding"*

Common sense, caring, and an attempt to comprehend the incomprehensible were the attitudes advocated by the series, even in the lamer episodes. The aliens were a fair mix of good guys and bad guys, as were the humans who came into contact with them, but even then things were not always clear cut. The series dealt not only with real people and their faults and flaws, but alien creatures who were often as confused, uncertain, or helpless. Not only did the series deal with humankind's confrontations with alien life, but also the alien visitors' confrontations with us. Often, the audience was invited to identify as much with the alien as those who encountered it, and these were not surprisingly the better episodes.

The risk in relating story outlines of the often complex and always compelling plots of *The Outer Limits* in cold print is that it almost does an injustice to a series dominated so strongly by powerful visuals and creative camerawork. *The Outer Limits* was quite literally a show that has to be seen to be believed. All these years on, there has been nothing to compare with it (the successful 1990s series exploiting the name has had its ups and downs, but looks and feels no different than any of the other numerous anthology series from the 1970s to the present), although much contemporary SF, particularly from the 1980s on, when the series' young audience was making films itself, owes a huge debt. It is no exaggeration to say that virtually every SF or fantasy film from the start of the 1980s on that was not directly influenced by Spielberg and Lucas owes some sort of debt to *The Twilight Zone* and *The Outer Limits,* and deliberately or by chance most of them can be traced back to the episode listings and story synopses in this book.

**The Outer Limits**

**episode guide**

**First Season**

**(1963-'64)**

**The Galaxy Being**

wr. and dir. Leslie Stevens

An inspired but introvert radio ham makes contact with an alien being of solidified sound, but when he is forced to leave his discovery temporarily, a substitute disc jockey inadvertently draws the alien to Earth, where the incredulous creature causes havoc

*with Cliff Robertson (Allan Maxwell), Jacqueline Scott (Carol Maxwell), Lee Phillips (Gene 'Buddy' Maxwell), William O. Douglas Jnr./ Charles McQuarry (Andromedan), Burt Metcalfe (relief d.j.), Allyson Ames (Buddy's date), Joseph Perry (police chief), Don Harvey (military officer), Roy Sickner (caretaker)*

Wonderful effects, and Robertson's delivery of some inspired lines makes this meeting of minds a worthy opening to *The Outer Limits*. He plays a radio ham tinkering with sound waves at the expense of his local radio station who suddenly makes contact with an extraterrestrial being. He alienates his family and friends, who are concerned with more earthly matters, such as whether he will deign to turn up at a dinner in his name, or lose their sponsors and livelihood for the sake of his experiments. Distant, obsessed, and cold, he mirrors his environment and the likeminded intelligence he contacts, two life forms defying their colleagues, to reach across the stars and make contact. His wife, furious he's not ready for their engagement, and in no mood to listen to stories about his discovery, forces him to leave the creature unattended for an hour by threatening to bring the party to him if he doesn't show. The relief d.j., also ignoring instructions, takes the opportunity to boost the station's radio signal so that he'll be heard further afield, and inadvertently transports the alien creature to our own, incompatible dimension.

*Cliff Robertson and Jacqueline Scott in a publicity pose for "Galaxy Being"*

37

The Outer Limits sets out its stall to perfection in this opening effort. This is a show where the lead's first action on seeing an alien being is not to pull a gun, but to ask simple, obvious, intelligent questions. On 1960s television, that immediately made The Outer Limits quite unique. ABC was known as the junior network, downmarket for dummies, populist to a fault even above CBS and NBC, but The Outer Limits put the lie to that. What is particularly notable is that this is science fiction with real people, who behave just like real people.

This was to be Cliff Robertson's only notable work in fantasy TV, although he did do an okay but routine Twilight Zone; he had previously had the lead role in the 1950s series Rod Brown of the Rocket Rangers, and would later appear as the demented cowboy Shame in the Batman series. More recently he has portrayed Uncle Ben in the 2002 Spider-Man film and its sequels.

Jacqueline Scott took another trip to The Outer Limits during the second season, but it was quite a comedown — she was in the diabolically bad "Counterweight". William O. Douglas Jnr. would play further alien creatures during the run of The Outer Limits, returning as the creature in "The Human Factor", "OBIT", and "The Children of Spider County". He can be seen in human form as Agent Spain's ill-fated contact in "The Invisibles". The alien effect here is cheap, simple, and incredibly effective, a bodysuit coated in oil and filmed in negative. The alien's pot belly is the actor's oxygen tank. He looks fantastic, especially when he breaks loose and slithers through into our world. All the rest is sound effects and a wind machine as the alien inadvertently causes chaos. See also the main feature.

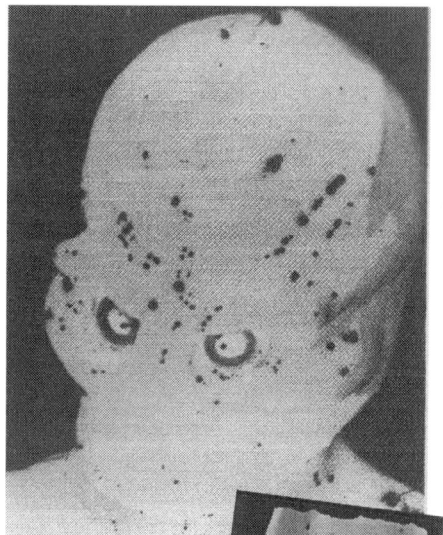

Cliff Robertson contacts alien life in "The Galaxy Being"

The Galaxy Being and gum card version

THE TELEVISION TERROR

38

Lee Phillips, who plays best buddy Buddy was originally up for the lead until Robertson agreed to do it. Allyson Ames was a bit player who became the girlfriend and later wife (for a year) of Leslie Stevens; she appears again in Stevens' "Production and Decay of Strange Particles" and episodes of *Burke's Law* and *Honey West*.

### The Borderland

wr. and dir. Leslie Stevens

An industrialist has the finance and facilities to hire a group of scientists to try to contact his prematurely deceased son in limbo...

*with Peter Mark Richman (Ian Frazer), Nina Foch (Eva Frazer), Gladys Cooper (Mrs. Palmer), Alfred Ryder (Edgar Price), Philip Abbott (Lincoln Russell), Barry Jones (Dwight Hartley), Gene Raymond (Benson Sawyer), Noel De Souza (Dr. Sung)*

On several occasions, and in the main feature, I have remarked that almost every sci-fi or fantasy film since the beginning of the '80s is an extrapolation of an idea or storyline from either *The Twilight Zone* or *The Outer Limits*. I feel this is a point that can not be made too often. However, even these two venerable and innovative series inevitably drew from previous creations. "The Borderland" has a similar theme to the 1941 Boris Karloff feature *The Devil Commands*, in which a mad scientist attempts to contact his dead son from a privately owned power station.

For the first episode of the series to be produced following the pilot, Stevens creates a cast of old-dark-house characters and then does nothing with them. He gives us a scheming aide in the corporation, who slimes around the scientists plotting, but is ultimately full of hot air and does nothing; he gives us a lovelorn assistant to the scientist, who covets his wife, but again nothing happens; and he gives us two charlatan mediums, who skulk around and pointlessly sabotage the

*Peter Mark Richman and Nina Foch pose for "The Borderland"*

scientific experiment. In short, we either get characters with motivation who do nothing, or characters who act, but without motivation. Having set the stage, Stevens simply gave us three acts of what we today call 'techno-babble'.

When the episode ends, the story just stops, with some rather pathetic platitudes about love—not a very scientific resolution for a story focussed entirely on the (excellent) special effects at the expense of story. Despite the quality of the visuals, and a lot of sound and fury signifying nothing, the mounting hysteria of the experiments goes on for so long that it actually tries the patience, and gives the impression that the show is being awkwardly, obviously, and desperately padded out—yet the Schow and Frentzen book on the series, *The Outer Limits Companion*, an excellent source book, reproduces dialogue—good dialogue—that was cut from the script. Stevens quite clearly cared more about the science than the characters (so much so, that the corporate plotter presumably comes out the winner at the end of the story, as Stevens doesn't even bother to have him exposed) which is a shame, because he had a strong cast. To add insult to injury, ABC's insistence on a clip from the episode as a teaser at this time blatantly gives away the climax of the episode (a problem that also plagued *The Untouchables* during this period, when key plot points were thoughtlessly revealed). The DVDs also include these giveaway trailers, so be sure to skip them.

Mark Richman (sometimes billed as Peter Mark Richman) returned to *The Outer Limits* in "The Probe", the final episode in the series. He made numerous appearances in SF TV of the '60s, also guesting twice in *The Invaders*, and twice in *Voyage to the Bottom of the Sea*. He was also in *The Man from UNCLE*, *Land of the Giants*, and *Star Trek: the Next Generation*. He's well cast as the obsessed scientist, although we never find out what drives him. Stage and film actress Gladys Cooper, by now elderly, also guested in *The Twilight Zone* at this time, in the episodes "Nothing in the Dark", "Passage on the Lady Anne", and "Night Call". She's fine as the phoney medium. Alfred Ryder, overacting as the medium's stooge, also appeared in *The Invaders* and *Voyage to the Bottom of the Sea*, three

times each. He is best remembered as Professor Crater in "The Man Trap" for *Star Trek*. Philip Abbott, later a regular on *The FBI*, is the scientist in "Zzzzz"; he appeared twice in *The Twilight Zone*, and appeared in several 1970s sci-fi shows, such as *The Six Million Dollar Man*, *The Bionic Woman*, and *The Incredible Hulk*. During the 1990s, he voiced the animated Nick Fury. Indian-born bit player Noel De Souza also appears in "Tourist Attraction", and was still working in the 1990s, when he portrayed Mahatma Gandhi in an episode of *Star Trek—Voyager*.


### The Human Factor

wr. David Duncan, dir. Abner Biberman

When a delicate and pioneering experiment is interrupted by an earthquake, a scientist inadvertently exchanges brains with his psychopathic patient—whose paranoia and guilt over a wrong decision being uncovered has provoked him to try and destroy the Arctic military base they are stationed at.

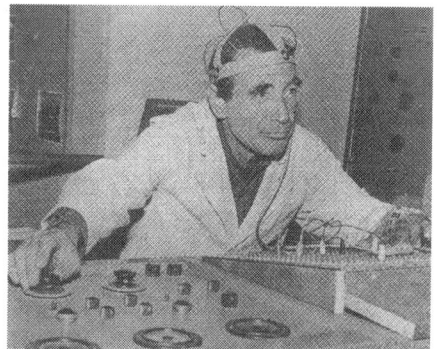

*with Gary Merrill (Dr. Hamilton), Harry Guardino (Major Brothers), Sally Kellerman (Ingrid), Joe De Santis*

(Colonel Campbell), Ivan Dixon (Major Giles), Shirley O'Hara (Dr. Soldini), James B. Sikking (orderly), John Newton (Peterson), Art Alisi (Sergeant), Jane Langley (Nurse), William O. Douglas Jnr. (ghost)

The setting is an Arctic base, the premise the old switcheroo—an experimental machine examining brainwaves overloads and switches the minds of patient and doctor. The doctor ends up strapped to a table and sedated while claiming who he really is, while the patient, now in the doctor's body, goes about his intended plan to destroy the base and thus, he hopes, the ghost of the man he didn't bother to rescue (the episode's creature, a figment of his imagination). As with *The Invaders* (which re-used much of Dominic Frontiere's haunting score here), this episode's suspense comes from the clever dilemma of the only man who knows the truth; his story of switching bodies is plainly preposterous—but the viewer knows it just happens to be true. The scene where the psychopath, in the body of the doctor, calls in the guards to take away his hopelessly incurable 'patient', is superbly chilling, as the raving man obviously appears to be pulling an idiotic stunt that only a madman would try. The more the doctor rants about who he really is, the more he appears to be the crazy man the 'doctor' claims. But the scenes in which the agitated lunatic comes unglued because he must listen to his commanding officer discuss his own madness puts the psychopath through equal emotional turmoil!

The performances in this one are fine, but the series was still warming up, if you'll pardon the pun. It's a perfectly watchable episode, but its ordinariness will make newcomers to the show wonder what the fuss is about if they see it first. Seen in sequence, one can see the series gradually picking up the pace, becoming more confident and experimental. Watching the episodes in the order ABC broadcast them, and as subsequently ordered on the DVD, the show inevitably begins with more of a bang, as the stronger ones were naturally brought forward. I've opted to review them in the order they were produced to study the development of the show. Either way, you're in for a treat, whichever sequence you watch the episodes in.

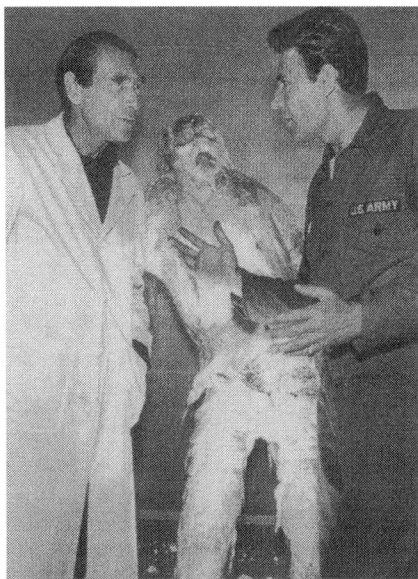

The publicity pictures for this one are a bit bizarre, for two reasons. Firstly, in the episode, only Guardino's character can see the ice ghost, which is his hallucination. Secondly, the creature originally designed for the episode was for some reason not used, and re-designed for broadcast in more human-like form. Inside the costume is the stoic William Douglas, who portrayed "The Galaxy Being" in the pilot.

Gary Merrill was later the cost-cutting Senator LeRoy Clark in the pilot for *The Time Tunnel*, and stood in for Richard Basehart in "The Menfish", an episode of *Voyage to the Bottom of the Sea*. He also starred in the SF B-movie *Destination: Inner Space*. Sally Kellerman, then doing mostly minor roles in TV and film, took a second role in *The Outer Limits*, appearing in the superior episode "The Bellero Shield". She was also in the second *Star Trek* pilot, "Where No Man Has Gone Before", and an interesting episode of *The Invaders*, "Labyrinth".

*Harry Guardino poses with his demon in "The Human Factor".*

Although she did much TV in the '60s, and worked in film and TV constantly thereon (she was the original 'Hot Lips' in the feature film *MASH*), these three are probably her best roles. Harry Guardino is probably best recognised for playing the politically compromised boss of *Dirty Harry*, perhaps also his best role. He did a lot of TV, but not much sci-fi, usually being cast in urban cop dramas.

Ivan Dixon, later a busy director with assignments including fantasy series *Wonder Woman* and *Greatest American Hero*, was best known in the '60s for his role in the slapstick sit-com *Hogan's Heroes*. Also appearing in *The Twilight Zone* at around this time, his two episodes of *The Outer Limits* (he's back as one of the possessed soldiers in "The Inheritors") gave him a rare chance to demonstrate his talents properly; Stevens used him again to excellent effect in his superior late-'60s drama *The Name of the Game*. And despite appearing in over 200 guest roles and bit parts on TV, James B. Sikking will be forever known as Howard Hunter on *Hill Street Blues*; he played numerous minor roles in '60s TV, turning up again during the second season of *The Outer Limits*, in "Cold Hands, Warm Heart", and as an army man getting zapped by *The Invaders* in "The Watchers".

An actor turned director, and more often working on cop shows or westerns, this was Abner Biberman's only *Outer Limits*, although he did direct four *Twilight Zones*. Author David Duncan broke into sci-fi screenwriting by scripting the U.S. version of Toho's *Rodan*, a wonderful and often moving Japanese rip-off of *Them* with giant birds instead of ants. He then turned out the scripts, stories, or both for routine 1950s creature features *The Monster That Challenged the World*, *The Black Scorpion*, *Monster on the Campus*, and *The Leech Woman*, also contributing to the TV series *Men in Space*. His most significant works were the screenplays for *The Time Machine* and *Fantastic Voyage*. He did not confine himself to pulp sci-fi, and ended his screenwriting career working regularly on the series *Daniel Boone*.

### Tourist Attraction

wr. Dean Reisner, dir. Laslo Benedek

When an aggressive adventurer discovers giant sea creatures in a river running through a banana republic, the local despot sees his chance at aggrandisement in the eyes of his people and the world.

*with Ralph Meeker (John Dexter), Henry Silva (General Mercurio), Janet Blair (Lynn Arthur), Jerry Douglas (Tom Evans), Jay Novello (Professor Arrivelo), Willard Sage, Edward Colmans (reporters), Jon Silo (Oswaldo), Francis Ravel (Captain Fortunato), Stuart Lancaster (Skipper), Martin Garrelega (Paco), Henry Delgado (Mario), Marco Antonio (manservant)*

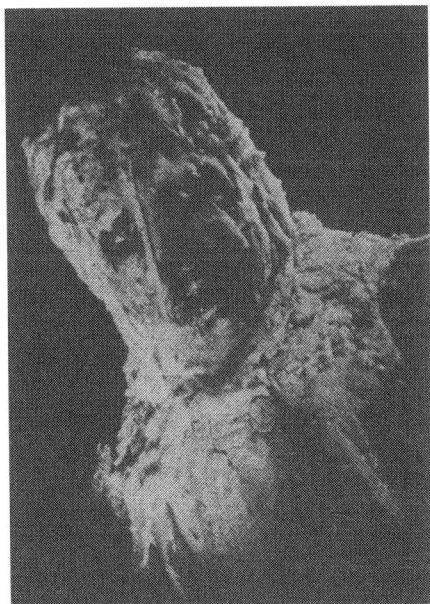

*William O. Douglas in the more realistic creature suit that was ultimately used for the ghost of the frozen-to-death soldier in "The Human Factor".*

Shamelessly inspired by *The Creature from the Black Lagoon*, but veering off in an entirely different direction, this episode isn't nearly as bad as some would have you believe (including my younger self; I've been a little hard on this one in the past). Maybe I've softened up over the years, but looking at it today there's some nice character stuff (the anthology format allows *all* the lead characters to be deeply unpleasant),

*The earthborn prehistoric creatures from "Tourist Attraction"*

the fish monsters (filming supervised by *Voyage to the Bottom of the Sea's* Paul Stader) aren't so bad, there's a fair comment to be made on the nature of power, publicity, and peoples' perception of it, and as I've always said, the show is more than redeemed by Henry Silva's powerful presence as Mercurio, who holds the episode together. Equally intriguing is Janet Blair's sell-out journalist, slowly but surely getting her comeuppance.

The underlying theme of two strong egotistical men on individual power trips of differing natures (Silva and *Kiss Me Deadly's* Ralph Meeker) is well-realised and the creatures are ultimately made to work. Like the monster in "The Architects of Fear", another show on which there were difficulties realising the creature, this is achieved through clever editing. Also, having the creatures of earth origin rather than extraterrestrial made a nice switch.

this foreign country, and the manner in which the creature is released could have happened anywhere; had it taken place in New York, no doubt a *Playboy*-reading joik from Brooklyn would have fallen asleep at the switch, in California it would have been the fault of a couple of airheads or teenagers sneaking around looking for a quiet place to have sex. It's the scene that's stereotypical, not the blue-collar bunglers, and it's written and performed in sledgehammer style.

*Jay Novello, Jerry Douglas, Ralph Meeker, and Henry Silva examine the creature, sans stuntman.*

Nevertheless, the show went wildly over-budget, the monsters created numerous problems and a couple of injuries, and writer Dean Reisner (best known for his work on the *Dirty Harry* films) was no great lover of science-fiction, reluctantly contributing to the show as a favor, all of which tainted the show for the production team. Some have commented that at one point the monster is released by stupid 'ethnic stereotypes'—but the story is set in

However, it's very difficult *not* to do a story set in South America and avoid falling into stereotypes, as what isn't genuinely a part of their culture is defiantly manufactured for visitors, including those who are patronisingly politically correct, and then go home and complain about cliches. If it's all been seen and done before, it's hardly the fault of the country, or the production. It's just the way it is.

But Laslo Benedek's direction—or perhaps his editor—is careless; even though there's a perfectly good shot of the creature hiding, there's a full reveal much too soon in the proceedings. And the production's lack of confidence in the material causes the insertion of quite extraneous and unnecessary narration, always a sign of an episode perceived to be in trouble. But the second time I saw it, I liked it.

Henry Silva would be back as the convict in "The Mice".


### The Architects of Fear

wr. Meyer Dolinsky, dir. Byron Haskin

A well-meaning but misguided scientific cabal attempt to terrify the world into peace by turning one of their number into an unearthly alien menace...

*with Robert Culp (Allen Leighton), Geraldine Brooks (Yvette Leighton), Leonard Stone (Dr. Gainer), Martin Wolfson (Dr. Herschel), Douglas Henderson (Dr. Fredericks), Janos Prohaska (Leighton as Thetan), Hal Bokar (duck hunter)*

With "The Architects of Fear", *The Outer Limits* came into its own, with its first truly notable episode since the pilot. A series of nuclear close calls during a Cold War situation drive a cabal of worried scientists to a desperate measure. To unite the nations of the world, the educated inhabitants of a smoky room at the Advanced Biological Studies Group have concocted a dreadful plan with fellow brains involved in the space race—to fuse a tiny alien creature from the planet Theta (we assume—it's never made clear) with a human volunteer from their number and create a terrifying being that will pretend to menace the Earth and draw the people of the world together in fear, so concentrating the minds of those who would otherwise be pursuing the petty personal agendas that lead to war. The man whose name is pulled out of the hat to be transformed into a believable otherworldly menace that will fool their colleagues in the scientific world is doctor of physics Allen Leighton. To achieve total credibility, nervous, guilt-ridden Doctor Philip Gainer will transform every organ in the stoic and determined idealist's body. And Allen Leighton must die.. in a 'plane crash over the Andes...

"The Architects of Fear" is *The Day the Earth Stood Still* in reverse—a group of well-meaning fools try to force the world into an uneasy peace through fear of an alien scarecrow. Unlike the usual Bondish world rulers of other sci-fi (including Culp's own Captain Shark in an early *Man from UNCLE*), with whom they share only arrogance, genius, and the ability to over-extend themselves, they mean well (although how long they could have resisted becoming benevolent dictators is questionable; see also *Our Man Flint* and UNCLE film *How to Steal the World*). The result is a debacle, months of planning undone in minutes—their phoney spaceship crashes, the 'alien' is disgorged into the middle of duck hunting country instead of the city, and a good man's life is ended miserably in truly stupid and tragic circumstances.

What makes the episode work is the sheer foolishness of the scientists' intentions and the grim consequences and waste of a man's future that is the result of it, enhanced by Robert Culp's ability to convey charm, passion and pain with equal skill. These are some of the greatest intellects in the world, brilliant men capable of making Culp's terrible transformation a reality, and yet it takes his wife, a simple woman with no greater ambition than to 'catch' a man and have babies, to see instantly the idiocy and insanity of the plan.

*Unable to cope with being physiologically transformed into an alien being, Robert Culp goes nuts in "The Architects of Fear"*

Although the deceit is intended on a grand scale, the entire scenario ends up as a group of conspiratorial men trying to put one over on a woman, Leighton's oddly psychic wife. With the marriage, romance, and pregnancy to the fore, and Culp blandly, treacherously reassuring in his betrayal of her trust, love, and faith in him, the personal drama has the air of a simple extra-marital affair conducted behind her blissfully ignorant back.

Behind the drama and poignancy of what was then an extremely powerful extra-terrestrial horror film were some wild and wacky anecdotes. Brusque, big-mouthed Byron Haskin, the colorful director of the episode (he had directed George Pal's wonderful Americanised update of *War of the Worlds* ten years earlier, and would later fall out with Gene Roddenberry while acting as an advisor on *Star Trek* pilot "The Cage") took exception to the over-enthusiasm of Robert Culp, an actor who never gave less that 101 percent to even the shabbiest project; legendary monster man Janos Prohaska, a regular resource of *The Outer Limits,* found himself staggering around on the stilts inside the Thetan costume because of fumes from the glue that hadn't yet dried, resulting in very little usable footage; and some local U.S. TV station executives in the boonies panicked when they saw what there was of the monster and blacked it out for being too horrific to show (naturally, huge photos of the too-scary monster then appeared in all the papers in the morning).

*Boo!!*

Infuriating as it was for the unhappy audience (who made their opinions known in papers across the country the next day), the publicity for the show was invaluable.

On a more sober note, the Thetan ray gun disintegrates things in much the same way as the 'real' alien weapons in *Earth vs. the Flying Saucers* and *The Invaders*. As ever, the only weak point was the traditionally pathetic *Outer Limits* spaceship. My god, they are so bad. The 'panic in the streets' footage that opens the episode was lifted from the 1955 feature *It Came from Beneath the Sea*.

*The Outer Limits* provided early work for many fine, powerful actors who would later go on to make their names in movies, including Martin Sheen, Robert Duvall, and Warren Oates. Robert Culp, although he made a number of interesting feature films as a supporting player, never quite escaped the confines of the small screen, but that has undoubtedly been to television's eternal advantage. Charismatic and intelligent, Culp had a huge body of TV work of which he could be proud, including starring in the series *Trackdown*, appearing in two other memorable episodes of *The Outer Limits*, "Corpus Earthling" and "Demon with a Glass Hand",

three superb episodes of *Columbo* (two written by future TV legends Stephen Cannell and Steven Bochco, one directed by Spielberg), a number of top notch TV movies, a starring role as super-cool spy Kelly Robinson in the classy and underrated *I Spy*, and a co-starring role as uptight FBI agent Bill Maxwell in Cannell's superior super-hero send-up *Greatest American Hero*. Culp did his fair share of junk to pay the bills, particularly in later years as his hair greyed, and invariably brought something—even if it was only a snapping pencil in *Combat Academy* —to the roles he took on. The tough-to-impress Harlan Ellison was in awe of him; he wrote and directed episodes of *I Spy* on merit, not because producers were throwing him bones; the fool and hypocrite Bill Cosby owed his career to his generosity. As a frustrated villain, Culp's famous slow burn is legend, and his ability to exploit a cliche, simultaneously sending it up while indulging in it, was matched only by his skill in never giving the same performance twice while remaining indefinably the Robert Culp viewers wanted and expected.

There is a strong argument to be made that "The Architects of Fear" could only have been carried off by Culp. He plays several roles here—madman, tense idealist, fool, charmer, and glib deceiver. All three of his performances in *The Outer Limits* were completely different, despite the similarity in the roles; his 'golf ball' scene in *Columbo*, looking very much from series star Peter Falk's reaction like an ad-lib, instantly defined the premise of the entire series (right under Columbo's nose, Culp's villain plucks his ball out of the rough and flicks it onto the green, leering that he can throw the ball back and get away with it, "...and nobody will ever know!"). He could play flawed hero and admirable bastard effortlessly, and never the same way twice. In *I Spy*, as a hero, he could do both fun-loving hedonist and tortured patriot without seeming remotely inconsistent. Discussing his work in *The Outer Limits* for *Filmfax* magazine, Mark Burbey wrote: "Culp's idiosyncratic style is a joy to watch; he turns something as simple as putting on a jacket into a flourish of bridled conflict". From icy, remorseless loner (*Hannie Caulder*) to perky, gullible sucker (*Sunday in New York*), from sad, silly, jealous swinger (*Bob and Carol and Ted and Alice*) to phoney, gladhanding politician (*Turk 138*), Culp delivered the goods.

*Janos Prohaska models the Thetan monster suit on the backlot; you barely get to see it in the episode, but still some of the local yokels in the ABC affiliates panicked, and incredibly blacked out screens.*

Geraldine Brooks took another 'faithful wife' role, this time married to William Shatner, in the second season's "Cold Hands, Warm Heart". Leonard Stone was the showman Farnum, the one good thing in two poor episodes of *Lost in Space*, "A Day at the Zoo" and "Space Beauty". He also appeared in *I Spy*, *The Invaders*, and several episodes of *Mission: Impossible* and *Land of the Giants*. Martin Wolfson, the other prominent member of the scientific cabal, had a strong role in a superior episode of *The Invaders*, "Task Force". Douglas Henderson appeared in the films *King Dinosaur* and *Invasion of the Saucermen* and several episodes of *The Invaders* and *The Wild Wild West*. He had supporting roles in two further *Outer Limits* episodes, "The Chameleon" and "Behold, Eck". Hal Bokar was the cop in *Star Trek's* "City on the Edge of Forever".

Director Byron Haskin had been in the film industry since the 1920s and achieved the rare feat of becoming known for a large body of sci-fi and fantasy work while maintaining a presence in other genres as well. His other fantasy films besides *War of the Worlds* included *Conquest of Space*, *Captain Sindbad*, and *Robinson Crusoe on Mars*. He worked on the special effects for the 1935 film of *A Midsummer Night's Dream* and uncredited as a designer and advisor on *The Outer Limits*, directing "The One Hundred Days of the Dragon", "A Feasibility Study", "The Invisible Enemy", "Behold Eck", and "Demon with a Glass Hand" (also with Culp). Writer Meyer Dolinsky contributed two more *Outer Limits* scripts that became classics—"OBIT" and "Zzzzz", as well as the less impressive "Plato's Stepchildren" for *Star Trek*.

And the Thetan—too horrible to be seen on television—adorned the cover of *Famous Monsters of Filmland*, ads in *TV Guide*, and several bubble gum trading cards.

In many ways, *The Outer Limits* was over-extending itself in ambition in much the same way as the scientists in this episode. After the fiasco of filming "Tourist Attraction", which went way over budget due to unforeseen difficulties filming the monsters, exactly the same thing had happened with this episode, except that this time the producers barely got any footage of their creature in the can. Considering the elaborate nature of the suit, particularly the brilliantly clever design of the stilt legs, which are ultimately never shown onscreen, we barely get to see the creature at all, with or without the help of the censors, and what we do see is pathetically lame. As with the original ice monster for "The Human Factor", the Thetan has played a far greater and more effective role in the publicity and iconography of the series than it ever got the chance to on screen.

**Controlled Experiment**

wr. and dir. Leslie Stevens

A 220-year-old Martian caretaker masquerading as a pawn shop owner prepares to welcome his superior, an inspector who has come to Earth to witness a murder, a peculiar phenomenon exclusive to the Earth which they fear may be a contagious threat to the galaxy

*with Carroll O'Connor (the Caretaker), Barry Morse (the Inspector), Grace Lee Whitney (Carla Duveen), Robert Fortier (Bert Hamil), Linda Hutchins (Arlene Schnabel), Bob Kelljan (shifty customer)*

By the producers' own admission, this was a contrivance dashed off to produce an episode as quickly and as cheaply as could be done. Deliberately devised to use the same footage as often as possible, it was saved by Stevens' amusing script, both witty (O'Connor's explanations for Earth behavior) and childish (both Martians are amazingly, coincidentally named after Earth's names for Mars' moons), and most of all by the busy, lively performances of leads Carroll O'Connor and Barry Morse.

Entrusted to lesser mortals, this cheapo quickie would have looked like exactly what it was. As it is, the episode is more like a *Twilight Zone* than an *Outer Limits*, with its frivolous approach, imaginatively corny unearthliness, and hammy, knowing performances... and as with many episodes of that illustrious series, time has not been kind to it—the novelty of seeing film run backwards and forwards, speeded up and slowed down, and printed in negative is no longer the spectacle that it must have been in 1964, when in today's age of video trickery, everyone with a VCR, DVD, or home computer can conduct a 'controlled experiment' with any film they please. Stevens' cute Earthlings-through-alien-eyes routine is also pure Serling, and is again a little old to all but newcomers to the genre. Bizarrely, and decidedly anti-Serling, the curiously dismissive ending has

*Grace Lee Whitney, trapped in a murderous time-loop in "Controlled Experiment"*

Earth apparently doomed to a holocaust if the two sentimental Martians let the womaniser live— which they do, in a pre-*Star Trek* switch-around of the theme of "The City on the Edge of Forever", in which saving a life will also doom a world. It wouldn't have taken much effort to tidy up and make the victim's survival a necessity rather than a threat, although at least this careless peculiarity makes "Controlled Experiment" original!

From today's perspective, the most appealing concept is not that of the murder being replayed back and forth and every which way, but the charming notion of bureaucratic authoritarian aliens in our midst in human form.

Carroll O'Connor was being considered for the role of Doctor Smith in *Lost in Space* at around the time this episode was made; he's superb in a dual role in an episode of *The Time Tunnel*, "The Last Patrol", and also turned up around this time in episodes of *Voyage to the Bottom of the Sea*, *The Man from UNCLE*, *The Wild Wild West*, and *Mission: Impossible*, none of which really exploited his considerable

talents. Barry Morse would later co-star in the first run of the 1970s series *Space: 1999*, but is best known for the role of Lt. Gerard in Quinn Martin's *The Fugitive*. That series lead to Martin being assigned production of the similarly themed *The Invaders*, another man-on-the-run show, for which Morse guested in "The Life Seekers".

Grace Lee Whitney later starred as Yeoman Rand in the first few episodes of *Star Trek*; among her numerous other TV roles were appearances in episodes of *The Untouchables, Bewitched* and *Batman*. Robert Fortier, who has the toughest role of all in this episode, quite literally standing still for all manner of treatment, guested in two other episodes of *The Outer Limits,* Stevens' own "Production and Decay of Strange Particles", also written and directed solo by Stevens, and the superb second season masterpiece "Demon with a Glass Hand". He also appears in the *Star Trek* episode "By Any Other Name", memorably intoxicated with James Doohan's Scotty. Leslie Stevens himself provided the Martian voice.

**The Hundred Days of the Dragon**

wr. Allan Balter, Robert Mintz, dir. Byron Haskin

From behind the 'Bamboo Curtain' comes a sinister scheme to replace the President of the United States with an impostor, a scheme made possible by a ghastly form of plastic surgery executed with a metal faceplate and a serum that makes the subject's face malleable!

*with Sidney Blackmer (William Lyons Selby), Phil Pine (Theodore Pearson), Nancy Rennick (Carol Selby Conner), Joan Camden (Ann Pearson), Richard Loo (Li Chin-Sung), Mark Roberts (Dr. Conner), Aki Aleong (Dr. Su-Lin), Clarence Lung (Major Ho Chi-Wong), James Hong (Wen Lee), James Yagi (Li Kwan), Bert Remsen (Frank Summers), Dennis McCarthy (Carter), Richard Gittings (Briggs), Robert Brubaker (Bryan)*

A sci-fi version of *The Manchurian Candidate*, this episode is a grim monster-free espionage yarn reeking of political hysteria; Sidney Blackmer is superb as the tragic newly-elected President and his sinister replacement. Most of the hostility toward this episode comes once again from reviewers who are unable to get beyond the supposed 'stereotypes' on offer. It is true that this episode is laced with the political paranoia of the period. However, it is the evocation of this fear (at the time, a genuine one) that gives the episode its atmosphere and power, and it needs to be understood and appreciated from that perspective.

Asian actors certainly benefitted from the 'Bamboo Curtain' era of U.S. TV, and contrary to assumptions, they didn't always play similar stereotypical roles. Parts ranged from dictators to shopkeepers to scientists to servants to spies. What they never were, were leads — but then white guys didn't take the lead in asian films.

Aki Aleong is back in a second season episode, "The Expanding Human", and has a quite extraordinary role in that. He had a regular role in *V – the series*, and also later appeared in episodes of *Airwolf, Streethawk, SeaQuest 2032,* and *Babylon 5.* Richard Loo also appears in episodes of *Voyage to the Bottom of the Sea, The Man from UNCLE, Amos Burke – Secret Agent, Honey West, I Spy, The Wild Wild West, Bewitched, I Dream of Jeannie,* and *The Incredible Hulk.* Similar parts adorn the credits of Lung and Yagi. As for the ubiquitous James Hong, working solidly from 1954 to time of writing in 2017, it would be quicker to list the series he *hasn't* been in at one time or another; a mere smattering of titles would include *The Man from UNCLE, I Dream of Jeannie, The Bionic Woman, Wonder Woman,* numerous 1980s adventure series, *The X-Files, Seinfeld, Friends, The Big Bang Theory,* and *Agents of SHIELD.*

### The Man with the Power

wr. Jerome Ross, dir. Laslo Benedek

Meek schoolteacher Harold Finley is thrilled to be of service to his heroes in the space program with his extraordinary telekinetic abilities, but his rages of frustration at the mundane lack of vision of those around him cause his power to take a deadly dangerous form that he cannot control.

*with Donald Pleasance (Harold Finley), Priscilla Morill (Vera Finley), Edward Platt (Dean Radcliffe), Fred Beir (Steve Crandon), Frank Maxwell* *(Dr. Keenan), John Marley (Dr. Hindemann), Paul Lambert (Dr. Henschell), James McCallion (Dr. Tremaine), Paul Kent (police detective), Ann Loos (Emily Radcliffe), Harry Ellerbee (Finley's doctor), Diane Stromm (Radcliffe's secretary), Pat O'Hara (surgeon), Jane Barclay (nurse), Saul Gross, Fred Crane (workmen in truck)*

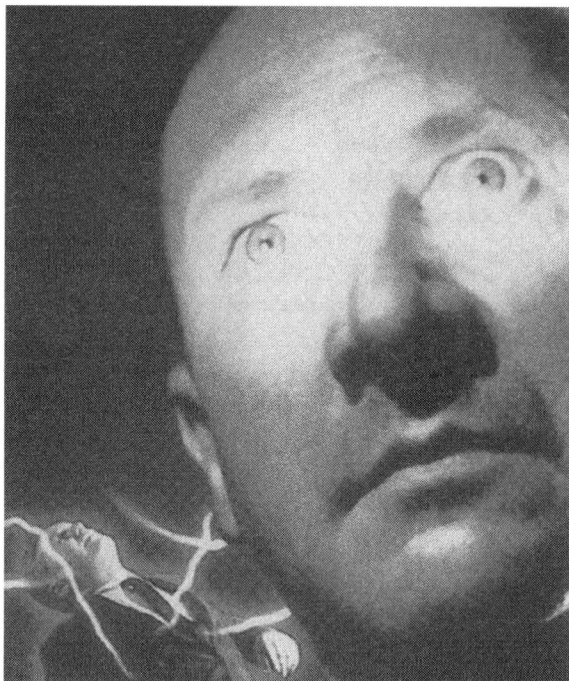

*Donald Pleasance as "The Man With the Power"*

A superb mix of horror and science-fiction. Donald Pleasance excels as a hen-pecked nobody who volunteers for a scientific experiment that finds him unleashing a powerful electrical cloud that selectively seeks out and assaults those who offend him. A nice subversive touch from the norm is that it is the man with vision surrounded by the small minded who is the menace rather than the local yokels, who on this occasion haven't done anything but be themselves... and, occasionally, victims.

Harold Finley is a good but insignificant man, fully aware of his insignificance, who has been cajoled into submitting himself to an unorthodox scientific procedure to boost his self-image. He has a petty, spiteful, small-minded wife, a dull, intransigent, blinkered employer, and is in envious, almost schoolboy-ish awe of a young astronaut working in the same science project.

*Donald Pleasance in his iconic role as Ernst Blofeld in the Bond film You Only Live Twice.*

Finley's embarrassment and shame when his cruel wife humiliates him in front of the astronaut he idolises is painfully real. "Some women like to take their husbands by the hand, and say—together we'll reach the stars... but not you... never you"

fumes the embittered man to his shrewish wife, a superb performance by Priscilla Morrill, particularly when he unleashes his power and she begs for her life pathetically as Finley recoils jointly from both the ugly horror and insincerity of her behavior and what he is able to do. But what finally sinks Finley's shot at nobility is not his harridan of a wife, but his own initial ambivalence to the carnage he causes in life and property with the force, which he closes his mind to because the force is all he has to improve his standing with the scientific community he worships. Here is a man who could never have been more than he was. He didn't have the substance of a hero. Instead, he finds redemption through suicide when he finally realises what he has done.

Credibility is briefly hurt by highly visible wires on the large 'rock' that Finley moves across the room with his mind (although watching in widescreen mostly removes these), but a bravura performance from Pleasance and an intelligent, macabre and suspenseful script more than compensate. In many of today's SF productions, poor special effects sink the entire project, because it is often nothing without them; with *The Outer Limits,* such failings were a mere irritation, a minor distraction from the excellent writing... and the other effects are excellent, particularly when the force obliterates people at the episode's close. Leslie Stevens devised the opticals, electrical sparks superimposed on ink in water. Also very effective is (presumably) director Laslo Benedek's idea of shining a light into Pleasance's expressive eyes every time the force is about to break loose.

Donald Pleasance did not stay within the confines of television for very long, although he flitted between the U.S. and the U.K. throughout his career doing both film and TV. He had worked in theatre and television in Britain throughout the '50s (including half-a-dozen episodes of syndicated series *The Adventures of Robin Hood* as King John), and went on to make his name with roles in such 1960s film classics as *The Great Escape, You Only Live Twice,* and *Fantastic Voyage*. His first role in the U.S. was for *The Twilight Zone*, in a similar part but in a (slightly) more uplifting story, "The Changing of the Guard". He invariably played weak men, cruel men, or weirdoes, finding frequent but not exclusive employment in horror films.

This was Priscilla Morrill's first filmed TV role; she went on to guest parts and recurring roles in many series throughout the rest of her career. Ed Platt, best known in the '60s for his comic turn as 'the Chief' in spy send-up *Get Smart*, appeared three times in *The Outer Limits*; he returns in "The Special One" and "Keeper of the Purple Twilight" in similar authoritarian roles. Fred Beir, a fine actor when given the opportunity to shine, had memorable roles in *The Twilight Zone* in "Death Ship" and *Kolchak: the Night Stalker* in "Firefall". Frank Maxwell worked regularly throughout the '50s to the mid-'80s, invariably cast as cops or military men.

## A Feasibility Study

wr. Joseph Stefano, dir. Byron Haskin

An entire town is transported to an alien world for study.

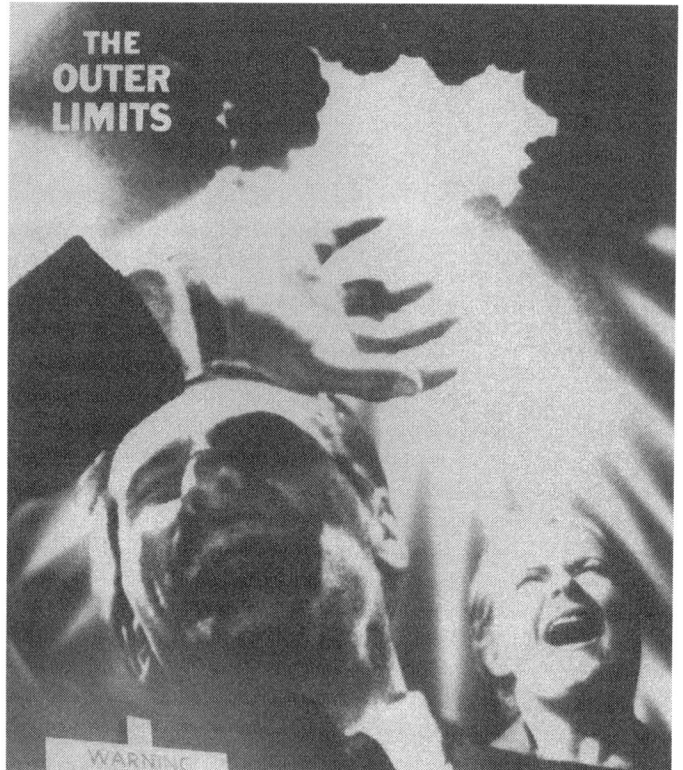

*Sam Wanamaker and Joyce Van Patten are part of "A Feasibility Study" in this art from my TV Zone feature.*

*with Sam Wanamaker (Dr. Simon Holm), Phyllis Love (Andrea Holm), David Opatoshu (Ralph Cashman), Joyce Van Patten (Rhea Cashman), Frank Puglia (Father Fontana), Ben Wright/Robert Justman (Luminoid Leader), Glenn Cannon (Luminoid teenager)*

54

The residents of Midgard Drive and five surrounding blocks awake to find the day dry, hot and humid. A strange mist pervades everything. Harassed husband Ralph Cashman prepares to flee on a Sunday morning to avoid his needy, whiny wife Rhea, while next door, bored dissatisfied Andrea Holm prepares to leave her arch-conservative doctor husband Simon after a year of having her ambitions stifled... unaware that there is nowhere to leave to. During the night, their entire neighborhood has been spirited away to the alien world of Luminos, where the inhabitants intend to test a small sampling of Earth people for their suitability as slaves.

When Doctor Holm's car won't start, neighbor Ralph Cashman offers him a lift. After they leave, Cashman's wife spots the problem—no engine. As she gapes in amazement, it reappears. In Ralph's car, Cashman remarks that they've been neighbors for a year now, without ever really knowing each other. When Holm's impending separation is revealed, they commiserate. Driving on alone through the mist, Cashman finds he can't pick up any stations on his radio. It becomes increasingly difficult to see, and even breathe. A strange inhuman hand slumps down onto the windscreen. Stumbling from his car, Cashman finds himself crawling across rocky alien terrain. Three strange, scruffy rock creatures shamble toward him, but when he turns to flee, another alien blocks his way. Back at the Holm house, Andrea is still there when Simon returns. She can't use the 'phone to call her taxi, she

explains. Once again, they argue—she can't adapt to the life of a housewife, he can't bend in his expectations of her to conform. With him back, she'll borrow their car. Suddenly, it works.

As they argue, Cashman staggers into view, dishevelled and covered in some form of contagion. "We're not on Earth" he tells his wife and neighbors... and disappears in a beam of light that teleports him away.

The abducting aliens, the Luminoids, we are told, atrophy with age, eventually becoming immobile in maturity. With this lack of mobility comes pure intellect—but no way to act on their ideas. For this, they need strong, healthy slaves to make their dreams a reality... humans resistant to the contagion that afflicts them. The Earth people will submit to slavery, they assume, under threat of contamination.

Holm discovers that they are safe if they stay clear of the infected and keep to the six blocks of Earth terrain... but they can never be safe from Luminoid slavery. And soon, they will be in slave camps with the rest of Earth's population. For now, they still possess free choice—the choice to stop the Luminoids here.

Each holds hands, passing the infection through them. They have defiantly demonstrated to the Luminoids that Earth people make poor slaves. Meanwhile, on Earth there is a huge crater where Midgard Drive and its neighboring streets used to stand, and a world unaware of the immense sacrifice and poignant martyrdom that has taken place to save it from being sold into slavery for the Luminoids' dreams.

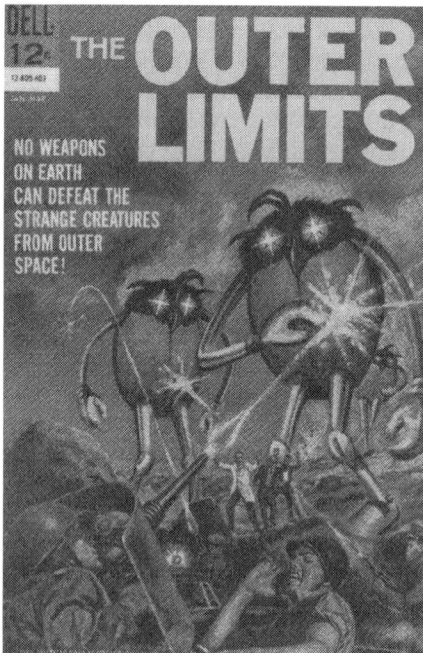

*Dell Publishing produced a series of Outer Limits comic-books which didn't scrimp on the extraterrestrials, but Marvel's pre-super-hero monster comics of the 1950s were closer in tone.*

"A Feasibility Study" opens with an alien abduction with a difference— an entire block of suburbia has been spirited away into the night. It was one of the earliest scripts for the original early 1960s version of *The Outer Limits*, and it was written (as were thirteen other marvellous episodes of the series) by Joseph Stefano, who had planned on contributing a considerably smaller number of scripts but had just discovered what Gene Roddenberry would later realise, when making *Star Trek*—that the vast majority of SF novelists can't or won't write for TV. Their snobbery and/or incompetence was our gain, and Stefano's minuscule SF output after *The Outer Limits* our loss. He was a perfectionist, bullied into leaving *The Outer Limits* after the first season, and his refusal to compromise where his work was concerned resulted in him refusing many later offers. In many ways, his attitude to the television industry was reflected by the congregation in "A Feasibility Study"—to go quietly into the night rather than acquiesce.

However, television being the beast it is, there were adjustments to be made to "A Feasibility Study", some reasonable, some less so. Stefano was obliged to focus the story on the Holm and Cashman households rather than include incidents with other people on the block... and he was also required to take all the children out of the picture, infanticide being a definite network no-no (although director Haskin manages to sneak in a babe-in-arms).

Completed a week before the series first went on the air, the contentious themes of slavery and suicide made the network nervous, and caused the episode to air close toward the end of the first phenomenal season, some nine months after it had been filmed. Although we are spared any heavy-handed analogies with American history, the Luminoid youth's parroted propaganda on the subject of slavery leaves us in no doubt that, as Rod Serling once confirmed in older brother *The Twilight Zone,* people are indeed alike all over. Andrea Holm also likens her marriage vows to slavery, and Simon Holm finally sees her point of view after his excursion into the Luminoid world.

Despite the minor production difficulties along the way, director Byron Haskin—whose 1950s classic *War of the Worlds* also featured powerful scenes in a church, to which this episode's scenes bear a strong resemblance—creates some stylish jolts throughout, primarily in the mist sequences. Particularly striking was the scene used as the pre-credits teaser—David Opatoshu running from a trio of shadowy rock-men toward the camera, only to be dramatically halted by an upraised hand that darts jumpily into view to block his way to a crescendo of grandly hysterical music from what was quite literally the biggest orchestra in television.

There are a few misfires—the silly alien spaceship spitting fire like a *Flash Gordon* leftover (as mentioned earlier, and proven on numerous occasions, spacecraft were not *The Outer Limits'* strong point), the ludicrous, almost *Simpson*-esque and unintentionally hilarious "have you seen this city block?" notice at the end, agonisingly read aloud to compound the absurdity, the crappy contagion make-up (the teenage Luminoid looks like he had a tough time shaving) and the disappearing and reappearing car engine sequence which is both silly and illogical. A sum total of about two

minutes in an otherwise superior forty-nine. Lost in the text are blink-and-you-miss-'em references to the Luminoid young opposing the 'morality adjustment' of their elders and the interesting notion that being inanimate gives a being more time to think, and thus greater intellect, a

wonderful defence next time you're accused of being a couch potato. Midgard, rather cornily, is of course the Norse gods' name for Earth—what a cool City Hall.

Once again, a valiant effort went into effects that didn't work. When Ben Wright, the voice artist hired to play the alien, was unable to fit into the creature's headpiece, it became a task that subsequently fell to Bob Justman, right-hand man on *The Outer Limits* production staff, and later *Star Trek*. While Wright, while still providing the smug and superior dialogue of the Luminoid leader as only a British old timer can, read his lines from the side of the stage, Justman, under the mask, mouthed them—but you can barely see the mouthpiece moving anyway, even on the DVDs, let alone vintage TV sets; a false perspective planet set was built, with dozens of Luminoid cut-outs being subtly moved to suggest numerous aliens milling around in the background—but again, even with modern technology you can barely see them against the rocks. Both these must have been barely visible on 1960s TV screens. Exteriors were filmed on the MGM backlot suburbia employed in numerous other films and series, but all attempts to create the alien planet's misty environment with fog machines were blown to the winds, as the natural outdoor wind gusted away the Luminoid smoke, which later had to be added optically.

"A Feasibility Study" became the second of the original *Outer Limits* episodes to be remade for the 1990s incarnation of the series (the first was "I, Robot", stunt-casting Leonard Nimoy, who appeared in both). The remake features David McCallum, who appeared twice in the original series prior to his fame in *The Man from UNCLE*, although not in this episode. Curiously, the one niggling flaw in the original, rather than being corrected, is even more pronounced in the remake. While the ultimate sacrifice of everyone is indeed profoundly noble and uplifting, everybody takes the leading man's quite fanciful story with an astonishing amount of faith considering they are being asked to succumb to a horrible death. I think most of us would have been inclined to investigate all the other options,

and indeed validate his story, before we took part in any Jonestown line-dancing. For all they knew, they were being suckered into another Halle-Bopp debacle. Besides, this is the movies—isn't the cavalry coming over the hill? Aren't a team of dedicated saviours going to arrive with Captain Kirk-like efficiency and aplomb with a miracle cure or super weapon?

The answer of course, is no. "A Feasibility Study", in both its forms, is about courage and noble sacrifice. It is a 'message' picture painting a portrait of victory, selflessness and defiance. Yet at the same time, that message is still one of defeat, suicide and despair—the Luminoids' guinea-pigs make their last stand before they've made a first. At no time does anybody take up arms or employ intellect toward debate or escape, or even enter into discussion with the aliens. The most drastic decision is taken first. The remake should surely have been a two-parter, as should the original, showing a couple of failed escape attempts. At that point, the congregation's act becomes defiant rather than defeatist.

One superb image compensates for all these minor flaws though. Thirty years of advances in special effects finally allowed Stefano to visualise what had previously only been in his mind and in the original could only be done with the cheesiest of animated sequences. In the 1990s version of "A Feasibility Study" we finally see the awesome image we were denied thirty years earlier. The sight of the suburban block being carved out of the ground and lifted into the sky is magnificent. This is how and why remakes should be made; the only justification is to do it better, not worse. Sadly, the premise, while faithfully adhered to, was not revised upwards. As so often oddly happens with remakes, the mistakes were also remade.

## Specimen Unknown

wr. Stephen Lord, Joseph Stefano, dir. Gerd Oswald

When a spacecraft becomes infected with deadly plant spores of alien origin, the military must decide whether to risk allowing the capsule to return to Earth...

*with Stephen McNally (Colonel MacWilliams), Richard Jaeckel (Captain Doweling), Russell Johnson (Major Benedict), Arthur Batanides (Lt. Gavin), Peter Baldwin (Lt. Halper), Dabney Coleman (Lt. Howard), Gail Kobe (Janet Doweling), John Kellogg (Major Jennings), Walt Davis (Sergeant)*

From the sublime to the ridiculous. Director Gerd Oswald would helm many of the best episodes of *The Outer Limits*, but his debut on the show was an inauspicious one to say the least. "Specimen: Unknown" was a major embarrassment to the series, at the time, and today, and another early episode plagued with problems, not the least of which was running short. An entire lengthy sequence had to be added to the front of the episode to bring it up to time, with then bit player Dabney Coleman (later to play other minor roles in "The Mice" and "Wolf 359") acting out a scene that had previously only been referred to in the script as having already occurred. Although this padding, directed belatedly by Robert Justman with the one actor, revealed the spores sooner than

originally intended, it actually helped make the slow and stodgy episode more suspenseful with the audience already 'in on it'. The male leads were wooden and uninspired, and the female lead another of the series' fragile hysterical women (of whom there were far too many on this show), a simpering wife who looks and behaves more like her supposed husband's mother.

The storyline is standard Z-movie stuff, and one absurdity follows another. Realising the plants are the cause of their contamination, the Captain bravely and quite correctly suggests they self-destruct the ship before it returns to Earth with a potential global catastrophe on board. Everyone is already infected with this unknown and rapidly fatal condition, and the plants are multiplying. What a poignant episode this would then be. No-one ever confronts the issue that the Captain was completely right to not want to bring the ship down, and the Colonel an absolute fool to bring it back from space; he's literally risked the safety of every man, woman and child on Earth for four lives already half-gone. All of this is spelled out at great length *by the Colonel himself*, who then places the lives of these four half-dead contaminated astronauts over the safety of thousands, maybe millions of civilians, but we're supposed to be cheering him on, and rooting for the plucky members of the space shot. To add insult to idiocy, when the ship lands (crash-lands, mind you, with one of the four already dead), *even knowing what's on board,* no-one is wearing any kind of protective gear whatsoever. Not that this would have helped, as the plants are already outside the broken ship and seeding, the Captain's wife is sitting in her car surrounded by the alien plants with the windows open, and the military rescue back-up from the base haven't even turned up as requested ("Where are all the flame throwers?" bleats the Colonel, surrounded by the killer daffodils he brought to Earth; thirty or forty minutes away apparently, and that's ten minutes *after* the ship came down).

Then the ship hatch is opened up (prised open by a guy dressed like a janitor) and the contaminated astronauts are physically hauled out by hand to be taken to a nearby hospital! You'll fall off the sofa ROFL when having loaded the four astronauts into the ambulance, everyone in their day clothes, doors and windows wide open, the distraught wife is told she can't ride along "because they don't know what the contamination potential is". Luckily, she gave him a great big hug anyway, when they pulled him from the ship.

"What about Lt. Halper's body?" she asks / "We'll have to leave it for the decontamination squad" is the severe reply.

*Now* they're thinking about decontamination... except there were four bodies in the ambulance, so who was the fifth? Meanwhile, the plants appear to be watching the proceedings with the same stunned disbelief as the audience, occasionally spitting out a few spores just to remind everyone they're still around.

"Heaven help us" says the Major. "They said there's a ninety percent probability of rain. How much faster will these things spread if it rains?". Uh, well, yeah... Good question, dummy. All the false jeopardy is caused by sheer stupidity, and you would think the blithering Janet is the only person on the planet who mattered. That the Earth survives this infestation is *literally* sheer dumb luck. Can't I say *anything* nice? Gerd Oswald pulls off some nice picture compositions in the final act from assorted imaginative angles, and the resolution is a clever twist. But to what avail? Nothing can overcome this plot or dialogue.

So much of the visual style of filmed sci-fi between the early '50s and the mid-'60s was defined by the constant recycling of props, costumes, stock footage, and sound-effects. The space station here was a prop from '50s series *Men into Space,* while the rocket ship exterior was later re-used in *Twilight Zone's* "Probe Seven, Over and Out". Bizarrely, this unmitigated turkey, a bit of a steal from *Day of the Triffids,* a schlocky British sci-fi novel that had only just been filmed (badly), was the show's highest rating episode, but, as Stevens pointed out to Schow and Frentzen, a good episode will pull in extra viewers on word of mouth the next week, while a turkey will diminish the *following* week's figures. At least, that was the rationale that helped him deal with it.

The spore-spraying plants from space would prove a popular plot device in 1960s sci-fi, reappearing in *Lost in Space* ("Attack of the Monster Plants"), *Star Trek* ("This Side of Paradise"), *Voyage to the Bottom of the Sea* ("Night of Terror" and again in plain old all-around non-specific generic "Terror"), and *Land of the Giants* ("The Unsuspected"). This is easily the dumbest of them all.

### The Sixth Finger

wr. Ellis St. Joseph, dir. James Goldstone

A reclusive scientist studying evolution is persuaded to use an ambitious young villager in his experiments, and creates a super-being from the future whose anger turns to arrogance when combined with intellect.

*with David McCallum (Gwyllm), Edward Mulhare (Professor Mathers), Jill Haworth (Cathy Evans), Constance Cavendish (Gert Evans), Robert Doyle (Wilt Morgan), Nora Marlowe (Mrs. Ives), Janos Prohaska (Darwin/ monkey), George Pelling (motorcycle cop)*

Quite what Welsh playwright Emlyn Williams thought, had he chanced upon this sci-fi yarn quite plainly built on the premise of his most famous work, the semi-autobiographical play *The Corn is Green,* is not known, but it suffered far worse indignities, including the success of the rip-off *How Green Was My Valley* the following year (from the film of which this episode nicks its stock footage), followed later by an American adaptation re-set in the South being booed off the stage after one performance, and a drubbing from the *Monty Python* team, both in the early '70s, so this perhaps was the least of it. Whatever the case, "The Sixth Finger" is one of the finest episodes of *The Outer Limits,* one of the greatest hours of SF TV ever accomplished, and also one of the most memorable pieces of television ever made. With all the hyperbole out of the way, let's have a proper look at it.

*Jill Haworth and David McCallum in "The Sixth Finger".*

Dominating a perfectly written, performed, and directed episode throughout is the flawless performance of a very young David McCallum in one of his earliest roles. Just months away from international fame in the worldwide hit series *The Man from UNCLE,* he doesn't put a foot wrong while playing several very different incarnations of the same person.

Note the changes in his manner, voice, and particularly his walk as Gwyllm goes through his various phases of evolution — the madness of his middle phase, the calmness of his final phase, the brittle anger and inferiority of his frustrated young man, too good for the mines, not good enough for anything else, a boy doomed by his stifling environment, an all too familiar dilemma for young men. It's not just about what McCallum does, it's about what he doesn't do; all his acting choices are not only correct, they're occasionally inspired. He is undoubtedly aided by the superb make-up job devised by the brilliant John Chambers and executed by *Star Trek's* Fred Phillips, which in other less thoughtful hands could have so easily been a deal-breaking, performance-crushing disaster. Instead, McCallum's transformation goes beyond simple horror to become more awesome and unnerving with every phase, from hideous and deformed to almost serene and noble.

At no point is McCallum embarrassed or overwhelmed by his make-up, nor should he be. So often, even in the best sci-fi yarns about transformations, the actor disappears, like Bottom under his donkey-head; here, like Karloff's Frankenstein, McCallum is always visible, ever-present, still *acting*. It's a wonderful performance, perhaps the best in the series — and in a series boasting Oates, Duvall, and three turns by Robert Culp, that is surely the highest compliment.

Although troubled by ABC censors pandering to the Bible Belt on the subject of evolution, still a contentious subject in religious corners of America even today, the episode slipped through onto 1964 airwaves relatively safely, with only a couple of irritating dialogue changes comfortably obscured by Stefano's trademark flowery poetic prose. Although we learn from Schow and Frentzen that Stefano whittled down the characters and the carnage, in the first case this was probably right for timing, and in the second helped to make the episode special. Just as McCallum's evolved

MAN FROM TOMORROW

*A series of thoroughly silly and enjoyable garish and gaudy trading cards came out in the 1960s, splattered with vivid color. The card for this episode is relatively subdued in comparison with some of the others!*

being is about to go on the expected vengeful rampage in the village, he evolves into his next phase and loses the negative emotions of spite, anger, revenge, and power-seeking. Now even more curious and scholarly, no longer callous but still disdainful and superior, and finally benevolent, he naively trusts Cathy to send him into a further advanced state... and she, of course, takes the opportunity to return him to the form of human she loved, his normal, natural self. Outwitted by

emotion. What remains of the supporting roles are very well played by Doyle, Cavendish, and Marlowe.

Flaws? Well, there are a couple of very incongruous American-style motor-cycle cops policing this tiny Welsh village with Constable Wilks (there would have instead been one pointy-hat on a bicycle in the U.K. at this time), but at least this scene gives us the classic line "Your ignorance makes me ill and angry!", so it can be forgiven. This was the sequence that was originally to lead to the aborted attack on the village, which would have begun at the mine, and while it would have been enjoyable on a visceral level to see the super-brain run amok, the episode is better served without it.

Also, an embarrassing and silly potentially disastrous and laugh-inducing ending with the evolution machine was also narrowly avoided. At one point, McCallum almost came back as a monkey, but for once the network's idiot fear of creationists worked in the episode's favor.

Ellis St. Joseph is a writer whose contributions to sci-fi TV were so excellent that some people can't even believe they were his! He was ludicrously and erroneously outed by British magazine *Cult Times* as a pen-name for Harlan Ellison (he plainly wasn't, and besides which, a little less random speculation and a spot of research, even pre-IMDB, would have unearthed *Starlog* interviews by my colleague Mark Phillips), and he has fellow TV writer John Kneubuhl (*Wild Wild West, The Invaders*) listed as a pseudonym on his IMDB page at time of writing. But Ellis St. Joseph was Ellis St. Joseph, a busy TV jobsworth throughout the 1950s and early '60s, who did indeed produce some other extraordinary and legendary SF TV moments besides "The Sixth Finger" for posterity, all of which were his own. Although his Sandman episode of *Batman* with Michael Rennie was botched by the producers it was still a reasonable entry in the series, and St. Joseph authored "The Day the Sky Fell In", the landmark Pearl Harbor episode widely and rightly regarded as the finest hour of *The Time Tunnel*, as well as the classic *Land of the Giants*, "The Weird World", originally intended as the follow-up episode to the pilot and featuring the infamous 'spider in the air vent' scene.

James Goldstone was a jobbing TV director who also had some superior SF credits to his name, including the second season's two-parter "The Inheritors", four first season *Voyage to the Bottom of the Sea,* and memorable episodes of *Amos Burke – Secret Agent* and *Star Trek* (the second pilot, "Where No Man Has Gone Before", and "What Are Little Girls Made Of?"). Thus, two of television's greatest monsters, McCallum's future-man (and he was most certainly a monster for a while), and Ted Cassidy's Ruk, were memorably filmed to advantage by James Goldstone.

The supporting cast is uniformly excellent. Edward Mulhare, Henry Higgins on Broadway in *My Fair Lady,* and the ghostly sea captain in the romantic TV series *The Ghost and Mrs. Muir,* both roles previously essayed by Rex Harrison, probably remains best known as Devon Miles on the early '80s hit *Knight Rider.* As well as being Harrison's understudy and successor on *My Fair Lady,* he worked alongside his son Noel Harrison on an episode of *The Girl from UNCLE.* British-born Jill Haworth also made it to Broadway, but ended up in obscure TV guest roles and seedy horror films. This was easily her finest moment in either TV or horror.

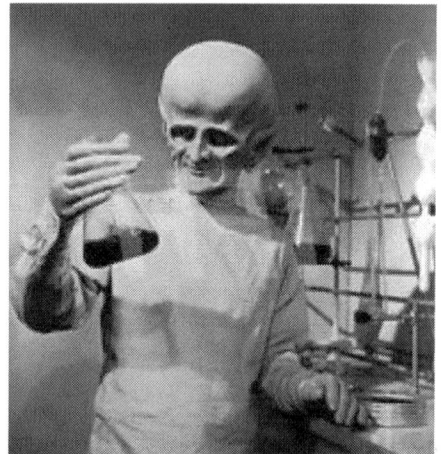

It should be noted that all the supporting players hold their own against the overwhelming and bravura central performance of McCallum, grabbing their various moments and making the most of them. Robert Doyle was the go-to guy in the '60s whenever directors needed a young man who was slightly, or seriously, unhinged; he goes nuts in episodes of both *UNCLE* series, and one of his larger roles was as the vengeful son of a disgraced navy man in "And Five Of Us Are Left" during the second season of *Voyage to the Bottom of the Sea.* He returns in the second season's "The Expanding Human".

Kept busy in numerous minor roles and bit parts for three decades, Nora Marlowe closed her career with a recurring role in *The Waltons*. Monster man Janos Prohaska ("The Architects of Fear", "The Probe") took out this particular monkey suit for numerous 1960s television appearances, including episodes of *Bewitched*, *Lost in Space*, and *The Lucy Show*. McCallum is so good and central to the episode that Prohaska's clever and perfectly judged performance as the educated simian is always overlooked.

### The Man Who Was Never Born

wr. Anthony Lawrence, dir. Leonard Horn

An astronaut time-travels into the ruined future of a biologically destroyed future Earth, giving a mutated survivor the chance to prevent the tragedy by returning to the undamaged past to kill the man responsible before he can act. Instead, he finds he has travelled back to the courtship of the man's young parents, putting before him an appalling moral dilemma worsened by his growing passion for the mother-to-be...

*with Martin Landau (Andro), Shirley Knight (Noelle), Karl Held (Captain Reardon), John Considine (Bertram Cabot), Maxine Stuart (Mrs. McCluskey), Marlowe Jensen (Minister)*

Martin Landau is probably best known, by my generation at least, for his three seasons on *Mission: Impossible*, a series he ill-advisedly departed for greener pastures that were fifteen years coming, yet another TV star who thought he was bigger than his show. However, his two finest pieces of work might well be his two episodes of *The Outer Limits*. He was lucky enough, alongside David McCallum and Robert Culp, to star in no less than *two* classic episodes — in his case, "The Man Who Was Never Born" and "The Bellero Shield".

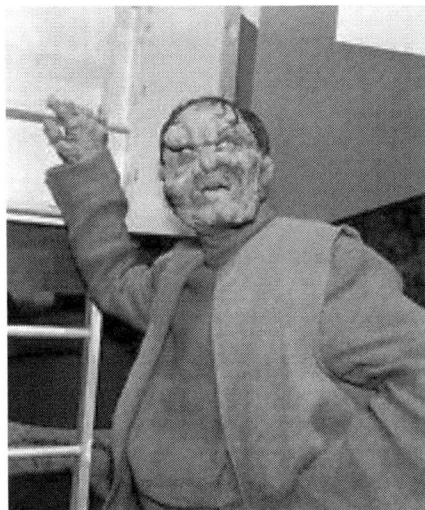

Director Leonard Horn was himself behind the camera for two other classic episodes, the notorious "The Zanti Misfits" and the lyrical "The Children of Spider County", two stories resembling 1950s Marvel monster comics bought to life. He was also responsible for several first season *Voyage to the Bottom of the Sea* episodes and a superior *Lost in*

*Space*, "Invaders from the Fifth Dimension". He was, without a doubt, the most inventive and creative director of television sci-fi of all time (even above Sutton Roley, whose flourishes were sometimes indulgent and unsuccessful, slipping him down to second place), and this episode is equally without a doubt, his masterpiece, a perfect piece of television from start to finish.

"The Man Who Was Never Born" is one of the oldest sci-fi plots of all time, married to the fairy-tale *The Frog Prince* (when Andro first spies Noelle, she is even tenderly studying a frog she's netted from the river), and is a joy from start to finish, both as art and entertainment, one of those hours of television that gives you tingling hope for the entire medium.

This, then, is the terrible truth about the anthology show; while a *Star Trek*, or a *Lost in Space*, or a *Voyage to the Bottom of the Sea* will always be an episode of that series, varying only slightly in quality from week to week, *The Outer Limits* could veer wildly from a "Controlled Experiment" to a "Sixth Finger", or have a "Man Who Was Never Born" in production at the same time as a "Specimen: Unknown" or "Moonstone". Was *The Outer Limits* a mediocre series that suddenly spun gold every so often, or a wonderful series that occasionally dropped a turd? While it all depended which week you were watching, happily the gems far outnumbered the lemons,

particularly in the first season, where—in my opinion—only two episodes seriously embarrass the show, :Specimen: Unknown" and "Second Chance", while "Controlled Experiment", "The Special One", and the dated but adequate "Moonstone" merely disappoint.

Deceptively, the story begins with another man's tale, the astronaut Reardon, but he turns out to be just a plot device cruelly dispatched so that we can follow the mutant Andro to Earth, where he intends to change the past to avoid his catastrophic dead world future

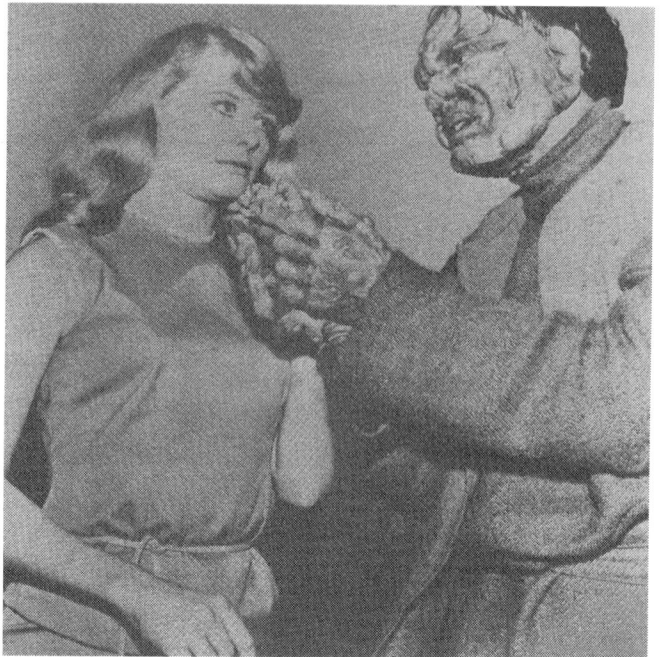

(interestingly, this episode inadvertently illustrates just how shallow the bland never-mind-the-future platitudes of "Controlled Experiment" were). Andro wants to murder the selfish and careless power-monger Bertram Cabot Jnr., who inadvertently wiped out humanity while experimenting with extraterrestrial microbes. He travels back in time with Reardon, who disappears, unable to return through the time warp that brought him into the future. Reardon vanishes into limbo exhorting him to "kill Cabot, kill Cabot", but although Andro shows up in exactly the right place (it's never shown how he does this), he has miscalculated the *time,* and arrives before Cabot is conceived.

He encounters and falls in love with the man's mother, plotting instead to prevent the marriage that will father Earth's bacteriological mass murderer, but when he attempts to take her back (or perhaps I should say forward) to a new future, it is he who can't return this time, and he dissolves into nothing, leaving the poor girl in limbo (filmed, but excised for time, was a scene showing Noelle arriving in a safe and clean future world, but alone).

Horn's · directorial flourishes, too numerous to list, are constant— the sudden introductory lurch of the mutant over the rock as Reardon explores the ruined future Earth, the transformations, back and forth, between mutant and man, as Landau and his double effortlessly switch places between Horn's fluid camera moves, the hideous creature following the chatty, carefree landlady up the stairs, the invisible money Andro counts out, staring with dishonest eyes as he pays his rent with thin air, a glint of sunlight on Andro's teeth, and a particularly brilliant sequence when Andro transforms into his human self without even a cutaway, just Landau, back to camera, adjusting his gait, and the by now familiar ripple of transformation music suggesting it.

There are oddities. Reardon prowls around on the ruined Earth of the future with a handgun drawn like a TV cop or a cowboy, all-American astronaut that he is, a curious lapse for a thoughtful and intelligent series like this, and counter to the series' in-built intelligent philosophy. Two times, without any attempt at explanation, the protagonists land exactly where they need to be, in front of the individual they need to meet, in order to advance the story. Reardon may be on automatic pilot, but he certainly didn't leave from a woodland grove. And he announces to Andro that he has come to 2148 from the year 1963, yet this is the year the episode was filmed, and audiences knew perfectly well that space travel was not that advanced. Why not make it 1973, 1983, or 1993, or 2023? It

would also explain why Reardon couldn't return; perhaps his future birth or timeline had been made void by Andro's butterfly effect alterations in '63. Perhaps he too had never been born, or taken a different path.

And Noelle doesn't seem as creeped out as she should be by all Andro's ramblings about her unborn son. She should be running from this bug-eyed weirdo like her summer dress is on fire. The last two acts seem absurdly condensed. And yet, despite all this, the episode is absolutely captivating.

Landau's monster make-up is superb. As with David McCallum in "The Sixth Finger", it is clearly apparent that it is Landau under the mask, which melds to Landau's features perfectly and once again is the work of John Chambers and Fred Phillips, fixing a botched job by the credited company. His performance is equally well-judged, the appliance, like McCallum's, allowing him to express himself, with none of the over-acting that occasionally found its way into his *Mission: Impossible* episodes.

*Andro in human form, looking remarkably like Martin Landau from Paramount's Mission: Impossible.*

The remaining players, Shirley Knight as the fluttery, soppy Noelle, John Considine as the stiff, jilted military man, and Maxine Stuart as the likeable landlady, all fulfil their roles with precision.

**Moonstone**

wr. William Bast, dir. Robert Florey

A lunar expedition stumbles onto a tiny spherical spaceship containing fugitive aliens

*with Ruth Roman (Professor Brice), Alex Nichol (General Stocker), Tim O'Connor (Major Anderson), Curt Conway (Dr. Mendl), Hari Rhodes (Lt. Travers), Ben Wright (alien voice), Leslie Stevens (scanner outpost voice)*

This is the later and better known "Zanti Misfits" in reverse. Whereas in that one, hypocritical aliens sent their criminal rebels to Earth to be destroyed by this planet's predictable but quite understandable response to them, in "Moonstone", an Earth outpost on the moon has to protect fugitive life forms seeking asylum from their murderous and ideologically unsound aggressors.

The astronauts have found a spherical globe that houses a selection of very-unlike-us alien life forms, cleverly realised plant-like eyes languidly floating in liquid. Circumstances are complicated by all-too-human romantic, idealistic, and ethical conflicts dating back some years between the two military protagonists (the future is close enough for the men to have been involved in the Korean war) that mirror their current predicament. Cloaked in the style and cliches of the era's sci-fi presumptions and limitations (flimsy spacesuits and spherical helmets, crisp, clear lunar landscapes, humming computer banks, techno-babble, English-speaking aliens, Washington v. Moscow), it is both less successful and less ambitious than "Zanti Misfits" (or many other episodes), but interesting in an anachronistic early '50s way (once again, *Men into Space* hand-me-downs provide costumes). It's not quite the dud its reputation has it, but you wouldn't want it to be the first episode you saw, or the one your friends stumbled on after you'd talked the series up as a television masterpiece.

*Oh no! Quicksand! On the moon!*

As in "Specimen: Unknown", no precautions or protection are evident when the scientists examine their alien find; they guard their eyes from their own laser beams, but handle the moonstone with bare hands and without any form of shield or protective apparel. There is traditional jeopardy (quicksand, would you believe), and the actors have to plod around mimicking slow motion, rather than being more convincingly filmed slowly from inside the camera. There is cornball romantic dialogue and traditional well-written early '60s TV-style human conflict, with veteran TV guest star Tim O'Connor easily walking away with the acting accolades.

O'Connor, who went on to play Dr. Huer in Universal's *Star Wars*-influenced *Buck Rogers* revival just under twenty years later, plays an antagonistic trouble-maker whose constant picking at old wounds has finally provoked his higher-ranked rival, wooden plank Alex Nichol, to send him back to Earth. The quality of O'Connor's acting and dialogue here next to his bland second banana scripts for *Buck Rogers* (a project Leslie Stevens was also briefly involved with) serves only to painfully illustrate how superior even a routine episode of a 1960s sci-fi show was to the TV SF product of the 1970s, which was without exception kiddie show b-a-a-d, and —to compound its sins—boring, which you could rarely say about 1960s kid-vid.

Ultimately though, what separates "Moonstone" from so many of the rank and file and gives it that *Outer Limits* stamp of approval is that it steers away from the frequent assumption that all members of alien races feel exactly the same way about everything. So often, alien races are presented as 'friendly' or 'hostile', as if an entire planet's population have reached a massive consensus representative of a sole political faction or ideology. Life on other worlds, should it be out there, is surely no less complex or fractious than our own, but even on *Star Trek* we are told that a whole 'world' is this or that, never just a region or country. But if the moonstone-encased rebels hold an opposing view to the rest of their species (five minds possessing advanced knowledge), how is it that

"there is no leader" and "their minds are linked", yet ideologically opposed to the "tyranny" of their pursuers? And if they failed to reach the Earth for lack of power, how did they revive and restore to life with magic beams the drunken Anderson after his electrocution? These guys hold the "secrets of the universe", and have studied us to the point of speaking our language in the voice of an elderly Englishman from a London members only club, but have only just now found out that the planet they tried to get to for refuge was a complete non-starter, incompatible with their basic needs. They also haven't figured out that the rescue signal beam they send to their allies will also be picked up by the bad guys—which, of course, it is.

And as for the Korean sub-plot, if Stocker had "hundreds of men", it should have been worth a try at defending the village and honoring his promise. Anderson, even though portrayed as a bitter jerk, appears to be right in my view, but suddenly everyone appears to be sympathetic to Stocker. Stefano and Bast appear to be trying to make some sort of comparative point between the situation in Korea with the villagers and on the moon with the aliens, but I'm afraid it's lost on me; they seem to be trying to justify a typical example of the worst excesses of American military meddling in foreign affairs—go in, fuck up, and get out. By all means intervene for humanitarian or even ideological reasons, if justified... but finish what you started and honor your promises, surely? The aliens blow themselves up rather than let the enemy acquire their knowledge, taking the same way out as the humans in "A Feasibility Study", but if they'd waited until they were aboard the enemy ship to self-destruct, they could have taken the tyrants with them. I see no parallels between the aliens' actions and Stocker's inexcusable decision in Korea to leave the villagers to their fate, but suddenly everybody "understands".

Tim O'Connor would be back for the second season's "Soldier". And dear Ben Wright, hopelessly British, provides the unintentionally hilarious alien voice.


## OBIT

wr. Meyer Dolinsky, dir. Gerd Oswald

Big Brother manifests itself in the form of a grotesque alien interloper when government investigators study a surveillance system that has been appropriated by alien invaders exploiting corporate and government paranoia

*with Jeff Corey (Byron Lomax), Peter Breck (Senator Orville), Alan Baxter (Colonel Grover), Harry Townes (Dr. Scott), Joanne Gilbert (Mrs. Scott), Sam Reese (Clyde Wyatt), Konstantin Shane (Dr. Fletcher), Jason Wingreen (OBIT Operator), Robert Beneveds (Captain Harrison), Lindsay Workman (Dr. Anderson), Chuck Hamilton (Armand Younger), William O. Douglas Jnr. (creature)*

Every so often *The Twilight Zone* and *The Outer Limits* would do a dark and sober episode about the dangers of fascism, and the bleak and sterile environment such a political philosophy produces. They were worthy, oppressive, and valuable pieces of work, if not always one's first choice from the shelf. One approves and admires, but there is a strong sense that such

sombre intellectual fare merely preaches to the converted. Whether episodes like this and the following "Nightmare" appealed to the audience for the *Destination Moon/ Conquest of Space*-style adventures of the likes of "Specimen: Unknown", "Moonstone", and the forthcoming "Second Chance" is highly debatable. "OBIT", with a great opening, descends into a single set courtroom enquiry pretty fast, but is one of the more entertaining ones, a collection of individual sequences of strength and poignancy rather than a satisfying whole. Author Meyer Dolinksy wrote the similarly dark "Plato's Stepchildren" for *Star Trek*.

Director Gerd Oswald's debut with "Specimen: Unknown" had been awkward, but he was quickly able to prove himself here, employing stylish visual tricks to subtly heighten the mood of suspicion, fear, and paranoia, and Oswald's efforts made him Stefano's golden boy and the third name in the *Outer Limits* troika after Stevens and Stefano, most closely associated with making the series the triumph it was. Unlike many *1984* clones, the people here actually realise their terrible mistake, and fear what they have done, which makes the revelations all the more chilling. The monster, a good one, while not exactly necessary to the plot, is a worthwhile addition to the mix, unobtrusive but giving substance to the hour in the opening and closing scenes. A few years later he would turn up in "If a Martian Answers, Hang Up", an episode of *The Munsters,* as a punch-line to a gag.

The storyline here is reminiscent of one of my favorite science-fiction short stories, by Isaac Asimov. In it, the government has access to technology that provides a visual window to the past, not unlike the satellite technology that can zero in on any part of the world today, but much more specific and spanning all of history. Naturally there is much humanity wants to learn, but the government controls access benevolently but firmly.

A professor with an interest in Byzantine pottery has been trying to take his turn for years, but his modest interests are always superseded by others with more important concerns, and he and his priorities remain at the bottom of the list. To cut a short story shorter, he allies himself with a group of anarchists, and ultimately they obtain and publish the blueprints to the technology, and make it available to the whole world; no longer will the authorities decide who can, and who can't, explore visual history. But the authorities belatedly but patiently explain their rationale to him at story's end.

Yes, everyone now has access to the great moments of Earth's history… but this is not how the vast majority of the public will use this newfound science. A small number will study the past in a scholarly manner, as intended… but most people, it is pointed out, will use their machines to spy on wives, husbands, children, lovers, business rivals, neighbors, and for general intrusions of privacy. The anarchists have changed the whole of society irrevocably, in a way they hadn't intended, and Asimov, in many ways, had predicted the consequences of the internet. In "OBIT", which seems in no way to be inspired by this story incidentally, it is that same good old-fashioned human nature that alerts the authorities to the insidious OBIT machines. While spying on their

own staff for corporate reasons, they have uncovered the sexual affairs of the controller's wife.

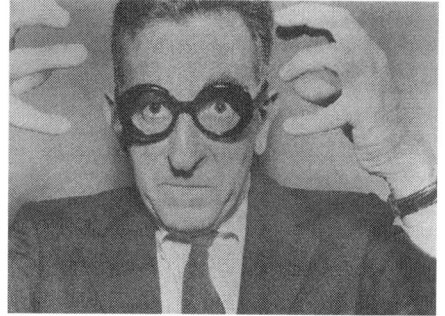

Jeff Corey appeared in "OBIT" shortly after being blacklisted for ten years by the McCarthy hearings, so the theme of the episode undoubtedly resonated with him.

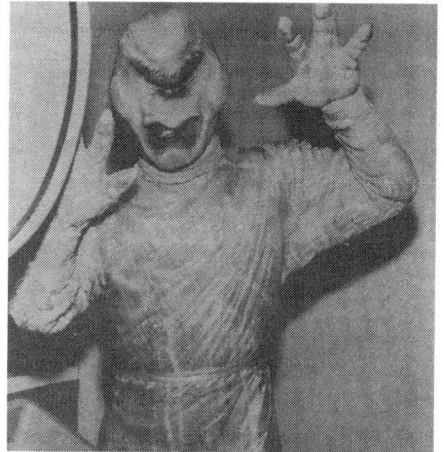

His SF roles include *Superman and the Mole People*, *Star Trek's* "The Cloud Minders" and *The Wild Wild West*. Peter Breck was a former Warners contract player who starred in two western series, *Black Saddle* and *The Big Valley*. Harry Townes' numerous guest appearances included memorable roles in *Star Trek* ("Return of the Archons") and *The Incredible Hulk* ("The First"). Sam Reese returns in "Behold Eck", Konstantine Shayne returns in "The Duplicate Man".

Bit player Jason Wingreen was rarely off the screen for half a decade, and appears three times in *The Outer Limits*. Wingreen comes to a sticky end in the opening teaser of "The Special One". He was an everyman bit-player whose greatest claim to fame is probably for providing the voice of *Star Wars* character Boba Fett (I've been aware of Jason Wingreen for over forty years, but I only found that out last year!).

### Nightmare

wr. Joseph Stefano, dir. John Erman

Military men involved in Earth's first war with extraterrestrials are subjected to brutal physical and psychological interrogation

*with Ed Nelson (Colonel Stone), James Shigeta (Major Jong), Martin Sheen (Private Dix), Bill Gunn (Lt. Willowmore), David Frankham (Captain Brookman), Sasha Harden (Lt. Krug), John Anderson (Ebonite interrogator), Ben Wright (British officer), Bernard Kates (psychiatrist), Whit Bissell, Willard Sage (project controllers), Lillian Adams (Dix's mother), Lisa Mann (Krug's Governess), Paul Stader (Ebonite guard)*

Please note the warning at the beginning of the book about spoilers, as it is particularly relevant here!

Luke Stone and his men, a pre-*Star Trek* multi-cultural force — American, Chinese, African, English, and German — are the latest combatants on their way to the planet Ebon to be taken prisoner by the Ebonites, who are found to be brittle, glassy-eyed, remorseless extraterrestrial interrogators with evil alien torture devices. Cold, ruthless, and unforgiving, the Ebonites swiftly deprive a screaming youngster of his voice (this is a very young Martin Sheen, father of Charlie Sheen and Emilio Estevez) and another (Bill Gunn) of his sight. They then play cruel psychological games with them, including the use of hallucinations to trick them into revealing information, and later, inevitably, more direct, brutal methods.

The false reassuring appearance of people from the subjects' pasts is reminiscent both of the 1970s mini-series made of Bradbury's *Martian Chronicles* and *Twilight Zone's* underrated "Death Ship". The Ebonites, genuine aliens who, far from being invaders, became implicated after they inadvertently assaulted Earth in a tragic misunderstanding, are reluctant participants in what the military have decided is a perfect opportunity to test the will and resolve of their men in the event of a genuine attack from space. It's all a brutal sham (soldiers have, in reality, been subjected to psychological experiments by the military, such as debilitating survival courses and faked impending air crashes, for example). As Schow and Frentzen perceptively point out in their *Outer Limits Companion*, to the soldiers, aliens, and generals here, war is a game, described and perceived as such throughout, in all their dialogue exchanges. The generals are testing the soldiers, the soldiers are testing themselves.

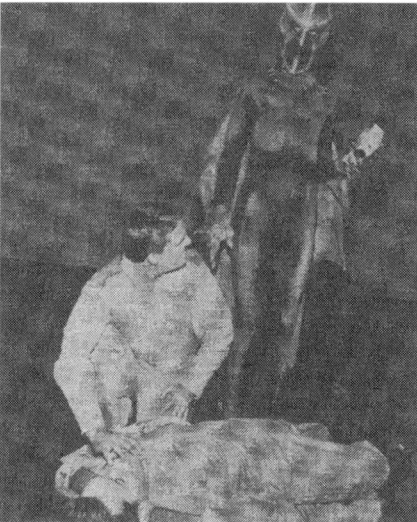

"Nightmare" is bleak, but beautifully lit, photographed, and directed (although apparently tinkered with in the editing suite by Stefano, dissatisfied), with a persistent, nagging score different from the usual tracked pieces associated with the series. The performances (other than the usual flat, uninspired blandness of Whit Bissell, as ever cast as a general) are superb, and dominate. Stefano's dialogue is beautiful (this is probably the best script in the series, and there was a hell of a lot of competition), with James Shigeta

getting to make a particularly incisive speech when accused of betrayal:

*"Now — let us consider Private Dix. They had demonstrated that they could return his power of speech if he talked. An uneducated man rarely refuses the opportunity to speak. And Lt. Willowmore. He had his sight to gain, a very precious thing, especially to a man who's had to endure the blindness of other people's minds. And Colonel Stone, who thought he slept, but might have been in a hypnotic trance. A man who chooses men-in-arms over the arms of a beautiful woman is not a particularly natural man. Perhaps he loves his fellow man so fervently because he cannot face his hatred of them. That's Sunday supplement psychology Colonel. But what spiteful, damaging things might such a man say under hypnosis?".*

Ed Nelson was best known as housewives heart-throb Doctor Rossi in the 1960s soap *Peyton Place*, but he could act when given the opportunity. Martin Sheen spent the 1960s in television before breaking into movies with the excellent *Badlands* in the early '70s. He is best known for his role in *Apocalypse Now*, and the TV series *The West Wing*, one of many politically-themed roles over the years. James Shigeta's sci-fi roles were not necessarily the best in his extensive credits, but included another *Outer Limits*, the Gene Roddenberry pilot *The Questor Tapes*, and guest spots in *Greatest American Hero*, *Airwolf*, *seaQuest 2032*, and *Babylon 5*. In between the inevitable typecasting as foreign despots and sinister spies, he managed to acquire more diverse roles in films ranging from *Paradise, Hawaiian Style*, in which he played a buddy of Elvis running a sightseeing helicopter business, and *Die Hard*, as a witty and pragmatic but ill-fated head of a corporation.

Neither Bill Gunn or David Frankham did as much as they should have or deserved to, although Frankham appeared in *Boris Karloff's Thriller* four times and returns to *The Outer Limits*. Kates did much theatre, but his TV work was thin; he appeared as Sigmund Freud on *Star Trek – the Next Generation*. This is the first of three small roles in the series for bit player Willard Sage, who also appeared in Erman's "The Empath" for *Star Trek*, a third-rate retread of this episode's themes.

BRING IN THE EARTHMEN

Shigeta, alongside Sheen (in his Hollywood debut), Frankham, and Wright have probably never been better, and they are always good. Bill Gunn is solid, and Anderson spot-on as the alien. The IMDB tells us that the title "Nightmare" has been used for over sixty different TV shows alone, including fellow '60s sci-fi series *The Invaders, Voyage to the Bottom of the Sea,* and *Land of the Giants,* as well as the usually insipid

1990s *Outer Limits* revival-in-name-only, but this must surely rival the *Invaders* entry as the most genuinely nightmarish of all.

PLOTTING DESTRUCTION

### Corpus Earthling

wr. Louis Charbonneau, Orin Borsten, dir. Gerd Oswald

When the husband of a lab assistant meets his wife from work, a metal plate in his head inadvertently allows him to overhear telepathic alien voices emanating from rock specimens preparing to take over humankind. He then hears the creatures' telepathic voices plotting his imminent death. Fleeing to Mexico with his worried wife more out of fear than conviction, he is pursued by the aliens' zombie slave.

*with Robert Culp (Paul Cameron), Salome Jens (Laurie Cameron), Barry Atwater (Dr. Temple), David Garner (physician), Ken Renard (caretaker), Bob Johnson (rock voices)*

75

Another exercise in paranoia exploiting the same dilemma as that faced by the heroes of "The Human Factor" and the TV series *The Invaders*—the absurd is true. The clever twist here is that Culp's Paul Cameron, a man who literally has rocks in his head, is the cast member who denies the possibility of his fears being real, while it is his concerned wife and her colleague who are prepared to admit his bizarre claims might be true. And happily, the episode doesn't bog itself down by spending the hour showing Culp vainly trying to persuade his friends and colleagues of the truth of his story, but swiftly moves on into true horror.

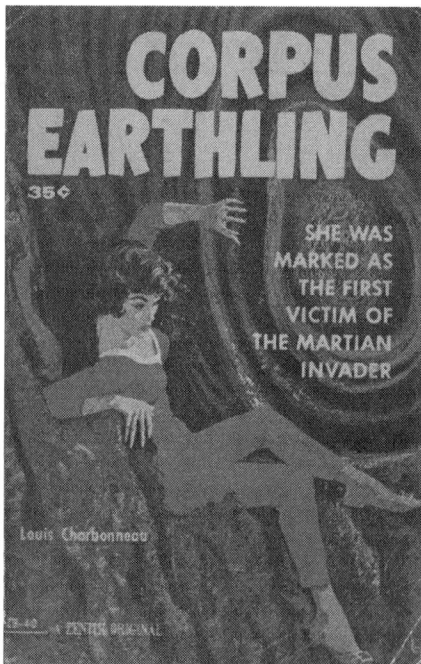

The problem with this episode is the rocks as a menace. It's not the concept, but the execution. Visually, the rocks would actually be far more menacing if the camera just held on them, inanimate; the production's efforts to make them look more sinister and otherworldly by moving as if breathing simply looks silly and B-movie-ish. They're also as dumb as rocks. Had they not spoken aloud in Culp's presence a second time, they would not have had to make, or attempt to carry out, their empty dime-store novel threats to kill him; he had just been swayed into believing that the voices were figments of his imagination, brought on by his concussion, when they they start blabbing all over again. Similarly, the globs the rocks morph into, although well done, are cliched and unnecessary; *Star Trek's* "The Naked Time" later showed the way to go with its simple droplet effect.

More effective are the zombies the rocks create, amalgams of the creatures in *Night of the Living Dead* and *The Omega Man,* both features some years in the future at this time. Culp's performance, as ever, is brilliant, and with the aid of Orin Borsten's brilliant script, loosely adapted from the book by Louis Charbonneau and worthy of Stefano himself, is totally convincing. Whereas in "The Architects of Fear" Culp was actually going mad, in "Corpus Earthling" he only thinks he is. Although this is the least respected of Culp's three episodes, it may be his best of his three performances.

*Salome Jens in 1958's Terror from the Year 5,000*

Salome Jens had previously appeared as an alien in the time travel film *Terror From the Year 5000*; more recently she was Martha Kent in the *Superboy* TV series, and back to playing aliens again in *Star Trek — the Next Generation*, *Star Trek: Deep Space Nine*, and the 2011 *Green Lantern* film. Barry Atwater, the poor chap turned into a zombie but barely mourned, played another nightmarish creature some years later in the TV movie *The Night Stalker*, progenitor of the *Kolchak* series.

## The Zanti Misfits

wr. Joseph Stefano, dir. Leonard Horn

*with Michael Tolan (Professor Grave), Robert F. Simon (General Hart), Claude Woolman (Major Hill), Bruce Dern (Ben Garth), Olive Deering (Lisa Lawrence), Lex Johnson, Joey Tata, George Sims, Mike Mikler (military personnel), Bill Hart (sentry)*

The Zantis dispose of their rubbish by dumping it on backward planets. In the deserted ghost town of Morgue, California, military man Major Hill and historian and scholar Professor Grave await the arrival of the Zanti ship, which turns out to be a small unassuming capsule. As Hill speculates on whether the Zanti are "super-human or sub-human", Graves idly flicks a bug from a post, thinking nothing of the tiny life he has snuffed out. "Or non-human" he responds prophetically.

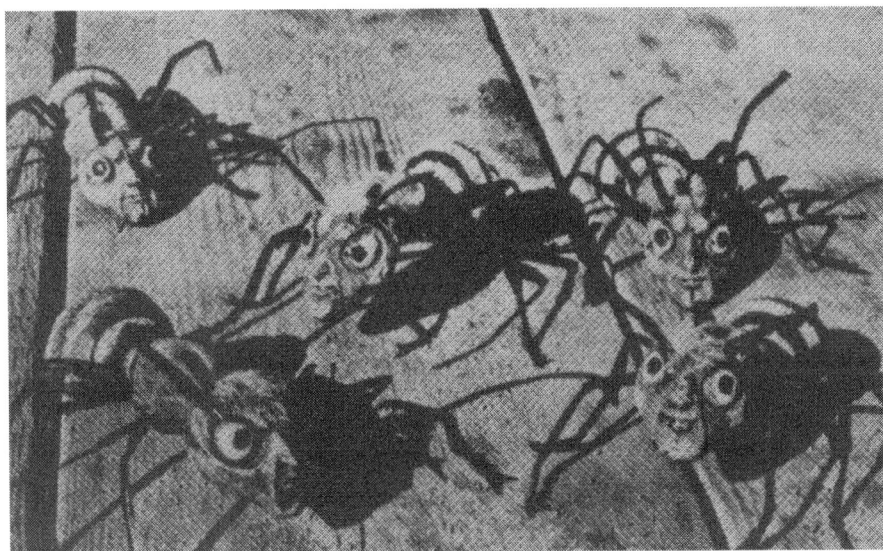

Nervous military men helplessly await the secret arrival of a party of evil aliens sent to Earth by their race as a punishment... but a psychotic bank robber has broken through into the restricted area for the landing of their spacecraft

Director Leonard Horn has done some classy TV SF in his time, but if "The Man Who Was Never Born" is undoubtedly his finest hour, this is the most well-remembered and famous episode of *The Outer Limits*. No corny and naive Close Encounter this, but a dark, despairing dirty deal with the military establishment, a horrific tale eagerly exploiting humankind's fear of that which is not human, with a secretive military keeping very quiet about the fact that the Zanti have announced the arrival of a prison-ship on Earth, and there's nothing anyone in authority can do except welcome it. No monstrous saucers blocking the sunlight one morning, no robots landing in Washington or New York, no covert bodysnatchers posing as the next door neighbors, just a quiet, compliant, devious little arrangement through the back door that, if it doesn't exactly backfire tragically for the Earth, is a sordid little first contact for the history books.

*Bruce Dern and Olive Deering pose somewhat unconvincingly with the Zanti and their spaceship.*

The Zanti, good and bad, turn out to be hideous little bug-eyed rat-sized ants with evil goblin-like faces. If good, friendly Zanti had arrived on Earth, we might well have put our boots on and started stamping. The military may have been crazy for doing the deal, or they may have been acting pragmatically and making the best of a bad lot. We know Bruce Dern is crazy from the moment he opens his mouth—"I would never kill a reasonable man. That guard was not a reasonable man!"—and he's been playing nutters ever since. Although he's very quickly finished off here, he makes the most of the screen-time he has, and the scene where he skulks around the spaceship is one of the scariest moments in the show. As with many future film actors who took early TV roles (Warren Oates, Robert Duvall, Jack Nicholson, Sissy Spacek, Gene Hackman, Martin Sheen), you can see that something extra that has them destined for the big screen; watch the thought and intensity that goes into Dern's discovery of the spaceship, and the way he goes to touch the wing of the craft and then decides against it. These are the almost imperceptible touches that separate an actor from someone who's just going through the motions.

Dern's speciality is portraying loonies who are one straw away from going completely over the edge. To see him at his best in non-SF roles, catch him as the beauty contest organiser in the wicked *Smile*, or as the demented cop in the extraordinary *The Driver*. He's also done lots of stuff for Roger Corman, including the superb gangster film *Bloody Mama*.

Olive Deering is cast well for her role, and goes beyond the standard screamer cliches; she's also saddled with the only misjudged scene in the show, when—having just been saved from the poison of the Zanti Regent—she suddenly launches into a mercifully brief but poetic resume of her rotten life... rather than fleeing an area about to be obliterated by army missiles. This is hardly what would have been coming out of her mouth at the time, and is pretty clumsy stuff; her character has already been superbly sketched by Stefano in previous scenes, and this is all extraneous. Women pausing to talk about their feelings just when every second counts (while male and female audience members alike shout "Shut up and move!" at the screen) is one of the oldest Hollywood cliches in film history, and still prevalent today (it turns up more than once in the 1990s *Outer Limits*). However, the scene in which she's trapped in her car by the Zanti, and then foolishly dares leave, is masterfully horrible.

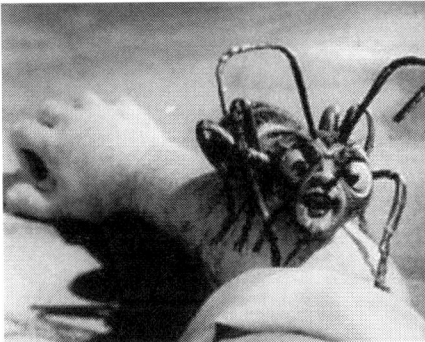

Michael Tolan is the typically wooden heroic scholar of a thousand bug-eyed monster movies, and Robert F. Simon the archetypical General (although in a nice twist, we discover that he's not the usual gung-ho warmonger of a billion B-movies that call in the army, when he talks of fearing war with the Zanti, and "broken lives and broken hearts"). Simon played military men for over two decades; he was also Darrin's father in some episodes of *Bewitched*, and J. Jonah Jameson in the short-lived *Spider-Man* series of the 1970s. Special mention should go to the character and performance of Claude Woolman as the voice-of-

doom Major Hill, who makes some cogent comments before completely cracking up; Woolman has a couple of *UNCLE* episodes to his credit and a couple of nondescript *Mission: Impossible*. The Zanti voices, and a typically early '60s d.j. gabbing about the latest 'saucer scare' over the radio, were provided by the series' regular voice artistes Vic Perrin (the show's narrator) and Bob Johnson (also the guy on the self-destructing tape in *Mission: Impossible*).

The battle scene is spectacular and horrific, and quite unique for television, with only the shots of the Zanti being killed by point-blank gunfire looking like modelwork (today they'd have exploded filled with goo!). In the giant ant film *Them*, the ants kill their victims with formic acid; we never do find out exactly how the Zanti ants dispose of the big hulking soldiers, an accomplishment left chillingly to the imagination. A shot of the ants coming down the wall outside the building, and then on the outside through the window, is especially striking, as is a scene of a soldier tumbling down some stairs covered in the ants. In another scene, one is seen crawling up a soldier's trouser-leg, to do what harm we dare not think about! Throughout the episode, Horn goes for the sudden jolt, the instant shock effect. For all its pretensions to thoughtful philosophical discourses on the nature of humankind, at the end of the day this is a good old BOO! film... and well done *The Outer Limits* for providing both simultaneously. Fun SF and thinking SF don't have to be mutually exclusive.

"The Zanti Misfits" is the perfect example of what we have both lost and gained from the arrival of CGI. Yes, the wires are visible when the ants troop down the outside of the windows. Yes, no matter how tight the editing, we can see a couple of shots that clearly don't work when the soldiers are shooting the ants. Yes, we can "see how it's done". And yes, today it could all be done super-smoothly and on a grand scale with computer technology. But much of the fun—for my generation at least—is the level of creativity involved in accomplishing what *has* been achieved. Just as theatre and the limitations of the stage, a medium with its own virtues and values, can be enjoyed and appreciated on a different level than the spectacle of big screen cinema, so can the organic, primitive, ingenious

effects of yesterday's SF provide a contrast to the easy and unlimited spectacle of modern film and TV.

The special effects team were Projects Unlimited, who had previously worked in films before receiving regular work on *The Outer Limits*. Their movies include George Pal's *tom thumb, Atlantis – the Lost Continent, The Time Machine,* and *The Wonderful World of the Brothers Grimm,* as well as *Dinosaurus, Master of the World,* the delightful *Jack the Giant Killer,* and *Flesh Gordon.* Some of their effects work was undeniably ropey, even for the time, and occasionally had to be re-done completely, but with "The Zanti Misfits" they excelled themselves. Horn wisely uses the ants sparingly until this final climatic battle; the desert ghost town in which the confrontation occurs is instantly recognisable from innumerable westerns. Observant TV SF fans will have no trouble spotting the unmistakeable terrain of dear old Vasquez Rocks near L.A., where many SF films and series episodes have been filmed around its dry brush and distinctive rock formations, most notably and famously "Arena" for *Star Trek.* As the tension mounts in the last ten minutes, regular *Outer Limits* viewers will recognise the stomping menacing theme from "The Architects of Fear".

## It Crawled Out of the Woodwork

wr. Joseph Stefano, dir. Gerd Oswald

When a rigid scientist arrives in town with his insecure hanger-on brother to take a position at a research establishment, he stumbles into a nightmarish scenario where he and his fellow scientists are enslaved by an energy monster that controls them from 'the pit' with pacemaker devices.

*with Scott Marlowe (Joey Peters), Michael Forest (Stuart Peters), Ed Asner (Detective Siroleo), Barbara Luna (Gaby Christian), Kent Smith (Dr. Bloch), Joan Camden (Professor Linden), Gene Darfler (first security guard), Ted De Corsia (second security guard), Lea Marmer (cleaning lady), Tom Palmer (coroner)*

Fear of the atomic age meets the old dark house in this twisting and turning story that constantly defies traditional formulaic expectations, bumping off the affable scientist hero we've assumed is the lead, exposing the easy-going happy-go-lucky brother as inept, psychologically damaged, and strung-out, and introducing a hard-nosed cop midway through the story to tie things up. Stefano used the same trick writing Hitchcock's *Psycho,* killing off the character we'd become involved with and going off in a different direction, and he employs it again here. The menace is a crackling, malevolent energy creature very similar—identical, in fact—to the one in "The Man With the Power", lurking at the end of a corridor in a room melodramatically termed "the pit" and turning all the humans it comes into contact with into tormented living-dead slaves. The over-the-top 'pit', mad scientist, and murder victims re-animated and controlled by pacemaker boxes strapped around them, create a blackly comedic aura of gruesome death and destruction that present a done deal before the story even begins; there's no-one to be saved, just something to be stopped. All the characters begging for life are already dead.

Gerd Oswald directs dark and shadowy; Stefano gives great Spillane-ish dialogue to Asner's cop, almost the only normal human being in the episode, although Barbara Luna's suddenly committed girlfriend warrants developing, but

81

is abandoned as the story careens off into, well, the outer limits. Oddly, perhaps for timing reasons, this episode starts with an opening scene before the credits, leading into the episode, instead of the usual giveaway teaser clip. Although it opens the story, it also acts perfectly as a teaser, but it's confusing. So with this episode, don't avoid the teaser, start at the beginning. (Incidentally, although the teaser implies the cleaning lady is the creature's first victim, she must have lived, as the staff know how the energy monster first appeared; the only way they could know this is if she lived to tell the tale… or lived on in death, like the others). And as horrific as this episode is in parts — there are some terrifying and cruel deaths (and re-deaths) — it is a mere foretaste of what is to come in the less morbid, but darker still "The Invisibles".

Scott Marlowe appeared in "The Death Trap", the Abraham Lincoln episode of The Time Tunnel; he would return in "The Form of Things Unknown". Michael Forest was Atlas for Roger Corman and Star Trek's Apollo in "Who Mourns for Adonais?". Joan Camden was an actress throughout the '50s who retired after this appearance; she previously had a minor role in "One Hundred Days of the Dragon".

While everyone else tensely plays one level below hysteria, Siroleo the cop saunters in to sort it out; "Stuart Peters had scar tissue as fresh as tomorrow's milk" he says at one point. "If he'd been in any better health, they'd have given him a morning show on television". These are the sort of lines that need an Ed Asner to drawl them… and happily, they've got him. But the weary seen-it-all stance soon evaporates, and he

gets the chance to join in the panic, which he does with conviction…

Asner, best known for his long-running role as Lou Grant in The Mary Tyler Moore Show and Lou Grant in the 1970s, played cops or heavies throughout the '60s. His SF roles included appearances in Voyage to the Bottom of the Sea, Amos Burke – Secret Agent, The Man from UNCLE, The Girl from UNCLE, The Wild Wild West, and The Invaders.

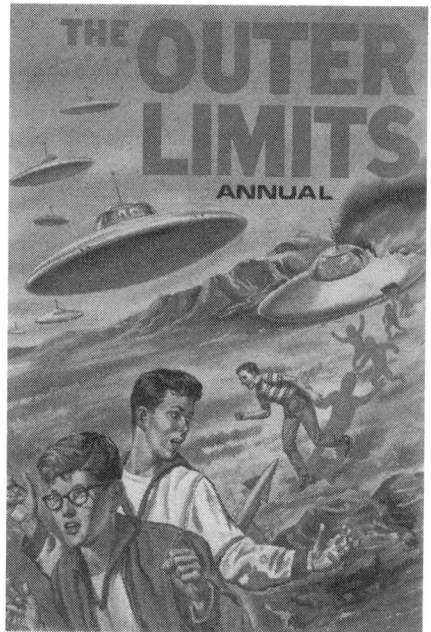

Kent Smith returned to The Outer Limits for "The Children of Spider County", and later took a co-starring role in The Invaders during the series' second season. His character here is confusing. In his early scenes, his dialogue implies he is keen to have Forest's scientist release him from the creature's servitude, dropping lots of nudging hints for help, but in the final scenes, he suddenly becomes a comic-bookish villain, lord of the creature. Barbara Luna, left to do little but be supportive, is best known to sci-fi buffs for Star

*Trek's* "Mirror Mirror". She also appeared in episodes of *Amos Burke – Secret Agent, The Man from UNCLE, The Wild Wild West, The Invaders, The Six Million Dollar Man, Project UFO, The Amazing Spider-Man,* and *Buck Rogers in the 25th Century.*

*Diana Sands, menaced by the Chromite in "The Mice".*

### The Mice

wr. Bill Ballinger, Joe Stefano, dir. Alan Crosland Jnr

A convict who has volunteered as a 'guinea-pig' for a military experiment in collaboration with supposedly amiable aliens uncovers treachery

*with Henry Silva (Chino Rivera), Diana Sands (Dr. Harrison), Michael Higgins (Dr. Kellander), Ronald Foster (Dr. Richardson), Dabney Coleman (Dr. Williams), Don Ross (Haddon, convict), Gene Tyburn (Goldsmith, convict), Francis De Sales (prison warden), Hugh Langtry (creature)*

Another first contact story. The monster suit is excellent, but there are a few instances where it's far too clear there's a man inside, and these might have been excluded with careful, tighter editing and more cautious camerawork; the top half is a complex affair, gelatinous and ugly, like a giant lump of snot with an eating ability built in, but the lower half consists solely of trouser legs. Any scene which shows the lower half of the costume, with the towering stunt-man Hugh Langtry (also an imposing alien menace in "Keeper of the Purple Twilight") running or walking, betrays the illusion.

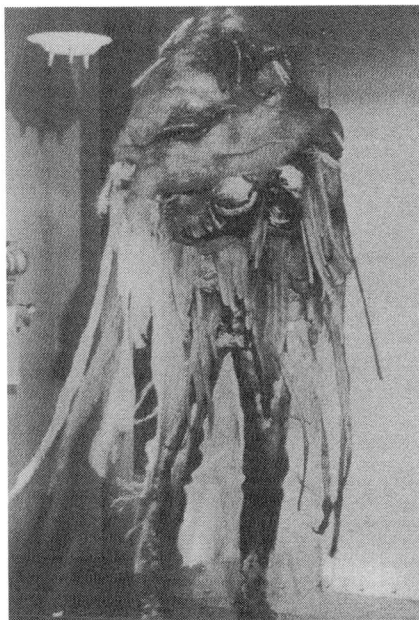

But the disgusting-looking slimy alien is the high point of the story, which also offers Henry Silva, the saving grace of "Tourist Attraction", as the focal point for the human element, otherwise poorly served by a cluster of cardboard lab-coat types. He plays a sly, energetic convict, a street thug imprisoned for a sympathetic crime of passion, who volunteers to be a guinea-pig—or "mouse"—for the experiments of a bunch of dull, detached, and naive scientists collaborating with deceitful cynical aliens. The episode belongs to him.

Diana Sands, a stage actress in a rare television appearance, is excellent in a role that could very easily have been one of *The Outer Limits'* usual hysterical female routines, but which she invests with sympathy and compassion. Added to the mix are a bunch of Keystone Kops who provide the establishment's pitiful security. The scenes with the visiting creature (the aliens' 'mouse') given free rein outside the complex (shot on MGM's outdoor backlot and the familiar tree-lined straight-line lane of "The Sixth Finger", "The Children of Spider County", and many *Twilight Zones* and *UNCLE* adventures) offer a lyrical beauty in sharp contrast to the oppressive shadows of many of the previous episodes ("OBIT", "Nightmare", "It Crawled Out of the Woodwork", and the forthcoming "The Invisibles"). The final line—an angry and despairing "You only had to *ask!!*"—deserves to be up there with *Twilight Zone's* "It's a cookbook!"

and *Star Trek's* "Let me help" speech. Just for once, Earth's scientists and authorities are not inept bunglers, gun-waving aggressors, or self-interested bullies.

### The Invisibles

wr. Joe Stefano, dir. Gerd Oswald

Bodysnatching alien parasites recruit disaffected loners and outcasts as foot soldiers to enable them to infiltrate the highest echelons of society

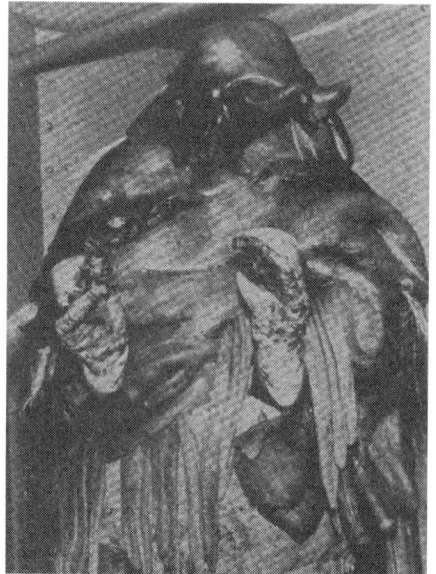

*with Don Gordon (Luis Spain), Tony Mordente (Genero Planetta), George MacReady (Governor Hillmond), Neil Hamilton (General Clarke), Dee Hartford (Mrs. Clarke), Richard Dawson (Oliver Fair), Walter Burke (Hillmond's aide), Chris Warfield (Castle), John Graham (doctor), William O. Douglas Jnr. (Johnny/Spain's contact), Len Lesser (security guard)*

A shadowy figure discreetly watches three new recruits—hard

man Spain, shy neurotic Planetta and dimbulb Castle—arrive at the wet, shabby and spartan hideaway of the Society of Invisibles. A white-haired figure enters a room full of boxes holding evil-sounding growling, panting alien insects, large thick-shelled creatures with scuttling legs. We see that he is clearly, agonisingly, in thrall to them. Later, calm and collected, he addresses the new volunteers to join his 'subversive, illegal, powerful and large' secret organisation. Each of the new recruits—bitter, disenfranchised losers and social misfits—will be inoculated against infection by the aliens and despatched around the United States to secure specific hosts in high places for these parasitic 'Invisibles'. Spain recognises the white-haired man as State Governor Hillmond. At midnight, Spain and Planetta hear the agonised screams of Castle as his inoculation fails, and see the deformed and disappointed Castle shuffling along the corridor in shock. Planetta wants to run, but Spain reminds him that if successful, they'll be part of something strong and powerful for the first time in their lives (in fact, Spain wants to use Planetta for his own purposes). As Planetta settles down, Hillmond's aide, a strange, quiet hunchback, informs them that Castle has become a victim of 'improper attachment', a fate they were warned about as a possibility. Bare-backed, Planetta and then Spain lie on a harsh wooden table to test their inoculations as the bug-like creatures scuttle over them. Later that night Spain sneaks out to meet a contact on the outside. He is, we now learn, an undercover government agent sent to infiltrate and undermine the Invisibles.

*Wiseguy* meets *The Invaders* in this clever allegory of subversive organisations and the two-bit failures who make up their faceless foot-soldiers. *Star Trek—the Next Generation* fans will instantly recognise the inspiration for "Conspiracy", *Wiseguy* fans will recall the Knox Pooley saga. The rest of us will think of innumerable other examples of the genre from *Invasion of the Body Snatchers* to *Alien*.

Officially, it seems the first alien bodysnatching story on film was the delightfully titled *The Purple Monster Strikes*, a 1945 Republic serial, but the notion became a staple theme of the '50s in such classics as *It Came from Outer Space* and *Invaders from Mars* (both 1953), *Invasion of the Body Snatchers* and *It Conquered the World* (both 1956), *Quatermass II* (1957), and *Space Master X-7* and *I Married a Monster from Outer Space* (both 1958), with horrible little parasite creatures first turning up in the dull, lame and cheapo *The Brain Eaters* (1958), most of whose participants—including Ed Nelson and Leonard Nimoy—went on to better things. Most of all, "The Invisibles" shows *The Brain Eaters*, itself based loosely on the Robert Heinlein novel *The Puppet Masters*, what it should or could have looked like. *It Conquered the World* (remade in 1966 as the dreary *Zontar, the Thing from Venus*) and 1958's legendary *Brain from Planet Arous* and *The Space Children* had the humans being taken over by alien 'brains', as did many assorted TV episodes in shows ranging from *Voyage to the Bottom of the Sea* to *Wonder Woman* (*The Outer Limits* will do a 'living brain' story in the second season), but it was this slipshod effort that first had the creepy crawlies actually forcing their way into the human nervous system, a notion popularised in print by Robert Heinlein in *The Puppet Masters* in 1953. Heinlein's novel was legitimately filmed without much fanfare or attention in 1994, starring Donald Sutherland, who had also starred in the 1979 remake of *Invasion of the Body Snatchers.*

Other entries in the 'gloppy creatures take over via the innards' genre have ranged from William Castle's *The Tingler* to the original *Star Trek's* "Operation: Annihilate" as well as *Night Gallery's* "The Caterpillar", and *Stargate SG-1's* Goa'uld, and innumerable less harrowing 'alien takeover' yarns in the various Irwin Allen shows, most notably innumerable *Voyage to the Bottom of the Sea.* But despite all this, and for all its predecessors and descendants, "The Invisibles" is a worthy, and in many ways original addition to the bodysnatching genre that undoubtedly inspired some of its more horrific descendants, a unique take on the oldest plot in the world—the 'bodysnatching aliens' yarn. Like the earlier and similar "It Crawled Out of the Woodwork", the episode makes the most of its gruesome elements, and like that story, itself downbeat and unresolved, there is only a hint that the menace might have been permanently averted. It leaves us with hope, rather than outright assuredness and confirmation.

The episode opens with the three new arrivals at the wet, shabby and spartan hideaway of the Society of Invisibles, where parasitic aliens from outer space are attaching themselves to the highest and lowest members of society in order to quietly invade and overthrow the Earth by covertly—but voluntarily—taking over human bodies in a particularly grisly and gruesome process involving lots of needles, cutting and screaming! Of the three willing joiners, one is typical unquestioning cannon-fodder, the eternal dupe who joins the army in peacetime oblivious to the ulterior motives or politics behind the actions he commits for others; his first question is "Do we get to wear uniforms?", and he pays the price for his naïveté. Later, hideously deformed, we see him peering round a corner like a child... "just to see if they're wearing uniforms". The second is a fragile, terrified neurotic loner who's got himself in too deep to get out, the third the government agent who has infiltrated their ranks. The one false note struck by the proceedings is the unfortunate substitution of GIA for CIA, but even at the time of this dark and cynical tale, the media was still respectful and trusting of government agencies. Spain himself is hardly James Bond, and not too dissimilar from the false identity he has adopted.

George MacReady is excellent as the leader of the alien parasites, himself one of their early acquisitions, but it's Neil Hamilton who steals the show in a single turning point scene that makes the episode, as an alien infiltrator slipping into insane sing-song delight at the thrill and horror of it all, that begs the question—was he an unwilling victim of the alien parasites, or did the aliens simply select and wake up dormant vulnerable targets *Trancers*-style, picking an all-too-willing participant wholly conscious of his deeds? Despite the class that Hamilton brought to the *Batman* show a few years later, one can only regret he didn't work more often during his later years—he's equally good in another *Outer Limits*, "The Bellero Shield".

*Neil Hamilton as Commissioner Gordon in 20th Century Fox's Batman, released on DVD by Warners.*

The story is divided into two equal parts, Agent Spain's experiences at the Invisibles' dreary prison-camp style headquarters, and the lavish lifestyle they aspire to at the General's Washington mansion (the exterior is an MGM set often used in *The Man from UNCLE*) where Spain is assigned as his wife's chauffeur to administer an Invisible parasite to a desired host. Only two minor items flaw the finished product, a heavy-handed indication that Spain's contact is dead (we see

his tell-tale boots three times—okay, guys, we get the message, it's the guy in the last scene), and the Invisibles themselves, pleasing creepy-crawlies, but not terribly convincing, despite director Oswald's admirable attempts to disguise their deficiencies with clever camera angles and quick cuts. They're adequate for the period and quite well designed, and enhanced by the shadowy photography and wonderful panting, growling sound effects.

The episode is further enhanced by the fabulous stock music that became the series' most prominent recurring 'character' in its welcome familiarity and the ingenious and creative shots that inspire and distract the mind when some of the dafter lines of dialogue, or shabbier monsters are being unleashed upon the audience. There is no embarrassing verbiage in "The Invisibles". Stefano, Oswald, and his cast are on top form; the dialogue is exquisite and the performances are without exception superb.

The cast in this episode is uniformly excellent, with Walter Burke suitably sinister as Hillmore's associate, an Igor for the '60s, Dee Hartford a stylish Jackie Kennedy clone in appearance, and Richard Dawson as Clarke's foppish aide, played with just the right degree of restrained effeminacy to avoid the crime of caricature. That he should have spent the rest of his career in a nothing role in the lowbrow sit-com *Hogan's Heroes,* and then as a game show host is a wicked waste of talent nipped in the bud.

Dee Hartford was best known for her work in Irwin Allen's series, most prominently *Lost in Space,* as Verda the android. Also seen in

Burke's Law, Batman, The Time Tunnel (as Helen of Troy) and The Girl from UNCLE, this was a rare adult role as an unfaithful wife, and she shows she could cope with more complex material than beauty queens and robots.

*Dee Hartford as Verda the android in Lost in Space (20th Century Fox).*

Walter Burke's character roles are numerous; also gainfully employed by Irwin Allen, he was "The Toymaker" in Lost in Space, and "The Terrible Leprechaun" in Voyage to the Bottom of the Sea! He returned to The Outer Limits as Dr. Riner in "The Mutant". George MacReady, a familiar screen villain of the '60s (his films include The Alligator People), played a tormented scientist in "Production and Decay of Strange Particles" and another sinister underground villain in "The Recollectors Affair" for The Man from UNCLE. His hoarse but silky voice and natural scar enhanced many films and TV appearances, and it's odd and disappointing that he performs neither the voice on the radio or the scene in the morgue, which is given to a nondescript 'doctor', but he milks what moments he has. Perhaps he was only available for a limited time.

William O. Douglas Jnr., here playing GIA contact Johnny, was often in the creature suits for The Outer Limits, having played "The Galaxy Being" in the pilot, and appearing in "The Human Factor", "OBIT", and "The Children of Spider County". Tony Mordente, fresh from West Side Story, later became a TV director of MTM sitcoms and Stephen Cannell smash-and-crash vigilante actioners. Len Lesser, the security guard, was the luckless convict guinea-pig in the Land of the Giants episode "Brainwash", but is better known today as Seinfeld's Uncle Leo.

*Don Gordon with Janet De Gore in the less impressive "Second Chance".*

The episode's leading man, Don Gordon, whose career was one of hard-nosed cop assistants and heavies (he's excellent in the Steve McQueen classic Bullitt, but otherwise mostly seen on TV), had previously been seen in the dismal "Second Chance", filmed later, but shown earlier. He's much luckier here, and really gets a chance to show what he could do as an actor. Unfortunately, the fun and fluffy

'60s would be the wrong decade for his talents. Nevertheless, he had a good turn in *The Invaders,* in "The Trial", was a favorite of *The Untouchables* and *The FBI,* and the cop shows of the '70s and '80s kept him gainfully employed. He had to pull out of a third *Outer Limits* — the okay "The Premonition" — due to illness.

One of the funniest ideas in the spoof *Austin Powers — Man of Mystery* was the satirising of the endless supply of faceless goons that could be found to populate evil would-be world-conquering organisations like SPECTRE, THRUSH, and SMERSH as little more than bullet-fodder or target practice, as we cut away several times as a stooge is despatched to visit the friends and families of the men so casually and fatally dispensed with (to be fair, some *UNCLE* episodes such as "The Arabian Affair", "The Prince of Darkness Affair", and others did attempt to address this question). As part of the eager schoolboy audience of the spy shows in the 1960s, I felt these hordes to be one of the more incredible aspects of these adventures, but in later years I came to realise that if men could be found to join the mob, or the armed forces, or weird cults, or the legions of mercenaries in illegal bloody wars around the globe, then the possibility of an endless supply of robotic meat for Bond and Solo to pick off wasn't quite so implausible as my child-like logic had suggested.

What makes "The Invisibles" special — besides Stefano's literate and quotable script and Gerd Oswald's shadowy, furtive, off-kilter direction, everyone peeping or skulking — is that it attempts to examine the mindset of 'the joiner', the sort of men who lead such tired,

dull, boring lives that they would risk ending that life in agony, men so lacking in intellectual capacity and aesthetic stimulation that they are unable to draw any meaning from life without endangering that precious commodity.

### Zzzzz

wr. Meyer Dolinsky, Joe Stefano, dir. John Brahm

An entomologist is plagued by a pouty Lolita who is actually a garden bee in human form...

*with Phillip Abbott (Professor Ben Fields), Marsha Hunt (Mrs. Fields), Joanna Frank (Regina), Booth Colman (Dr. Warren)*

*The Outer Limits'* second 'horrible insects' episode is a considerably less hysterical affair than "The Zanti Misfits", but no less creepy. The episode opens with a common or garden ordinary bee metamorphosing into a doe-eyed, shapely young woman in a well-done and clear effects sequence. We know immediately that this young creature and the insect world are one and the same from the opening frames (which incidentally form both the teaser and the opening of the episode, as with "It Crawled Out of the Woodwork"), but it will take Fields, the scientist, until the very last scenes to come to this inevitable and obvious, if bizarre, conclusion.

Openly seductive and manipulative in front of the scientist's likeable and charming middle-aged wife, but wickedly polite, she's every woman's hate figure, the uncaring legal Lolita with an obvious lie for every occasion. She immediately walks into the assistant's role that she brazenly claims she heard the ad for being placed in the shop, even though the wife points out in vain to the besotted fellow that it was impossible for her to have done so.

Stefano's rewrite vastly improves Dolinsky's original take on Stefano's initial idea of a bee-girl (inspired by his meeting the bewitching young actress at his neighbors' home), downplaying the tired and predictable Lolita angle, and making the story about marital fidelity. The episode shies away from the suggestion that Fields is thinking with his dick by having him hungry for fatherhood, and that he sees the girl as a substitute daughter. There's no suggestion of impropriety made in the episode, but it is clear that Regina's indisputable unusual beauty plays a part in his naiveté, and his wife's suspicions and dislike of her. She is understandably dismayed at how little her opinions matter to her husband, or how easily he dismisses her, especially as her fears are entirely reasonable and Regina's so clearly weird.

It isn't long before the flattering little nymphet is excluding and alienating the wife. She plays the role of awestruck student fascinated by his work, and he enjoys playing the wise fatherly scholar. Even Fields eventually tires of her astonishing callow rudeness, but by then it's too late, and the tragedy has unfolded.

Phillip Abbott had previously appeared in "The Borderland", and spent most of the '60s co-starring in Quinn Martin's long-running cop show *The FBI*. He's perfectly cast as the straight-arrow scientist, but the script never falls into the 1950s

stereotype of the boffin too busy for love; Fields is clearly very much in love with his wife, despite his susceptibility to the queen bee right to the end, and it is this that makes the final confrontation with the uncomprehending Regina so poignant. One glaringly obvious foolish line from Dolinsky's original take remains in the finished script and film suggesting that his character is not yet twenty-five, and yet later we are told that the couple had a baby daughter who would now be Regina's age. It is ludicrous that this ridiculous oversight was missed by everyone, to the point of

*Phillip Abbott (right) as he appeared on the long-running Quinn Martin cop show The FBI, with series star Efrem Zimbalist Jnr.*

being rehearsed, performed, and filmed! Unfortunately, director John Brahm, who also worked on *The Twilight Zone* and *Boris Karloff's Thriller*, was, while efficient and competent, also elderly and lazy. He did his job and went home. It was not queried, and one presumes the actor did not want to talk himself out of a job.

After a few minor roles, none so memorable as this, Joanna Frank married actor Alan Rachins, and later played his character's wife on various episodes of *L.A. Law*. Marsha Hunt's credits included *The Twilight Zone* and *Star Trek – the Next Generation*.

The visuals on this extraordinary series are so strong that it's easy to overlook the wonderful quality of the scripts. This episode is beautifully written and observed, with the double meanings at the dinner table particularly clever and eloquent; Stefano may be television's finest writer. The scene in which the wife watches the girl from the bedroom, and the lyrical but strange tranquility of her dancing around the flowers and caressing them turns to horror as she transforms back to bee form to enjoy the nectar, is superb.

But there's always a downside. The talking bees with the *Alvin and the Chipmunks* voices are admittedly hilarious, unfortunate, and unnecessary. When you have a bonkers concept such as this premise right from the start, it's important not to take that one step too far into absurdity. These scenes should have been excised along with the more overt communications between Regina and the bees (we already know what she's up to), but when one thinks of productions like *The Fly* and its sequels, *The Beginning of the End*, and *The Wasp Woman*, all of which were made for the big screen, and then considers that "The Zanti Misfits" and "Zzzzz" were made for television, it puts the lie to the notion that television has only recently superseded cinema as the more sophisticated and mature medium of the two.

## Don't Open Till Doomsday

wr. Joe Stefano, dir. Gerd Oswald

Two under-aged young teens eloping to a dusty small town to evade the girl's authoritarian father are invited to stay at a creepy mansion inhabited by a deranged old woman and a mysterious box housing a malevolent alien life force

*with Miriam Hopkins (Mrs. Kry), Buck Taylor (Gard Hayden), Melinda Plowman (Vivian Balfour/Hayden), John Hoyt (Emmett Balfour), Russell Collins (Justice of the Peace), Nellie Burt (old lady), David Frankham (Harvey Kry), Anthony Jochim (Dr. Spazman), Frank Delfino, Bob Johnson (alien creature)*

Old stagers John Hoyt (a sci-fi veteran of *When Worlds Collide* and *Attack of the Puppet People*) and former beauty Miriam Hopkins have a fine old time working their way through this bizarre Freudian fantasy about a virginal honeymoon couple in the 1920s who have a phallic threatening alien hidden amongst their wedding presents. The groom is absorbed into the evil alien's box, where he survives without ageing, a prisoner until his wife, now completely mad and fluttering around like a crazed Baby Jane, can find a new honeymoon couple who might be tricked into taking their place in this timeless hell.

Thirty years later, the house is a dilapidated ruin, and we cut to two young similarly inexperienced and hapless newlyweds looking for a room. This new honeymoon couple, eloping runaways from the girl's cold and controlling father, are lured to her 'bridal suite' to take the place of the captive groom...

Now on the surface, this is a story about an evil old man who, having been laughed at for saying that he's encountered a flying saucer, captures one of the occupants and takes it to the home of the leading doubter all neatly gift-wrapped for the man's young son, who's holding his wedding reception. He could have taken it to the authorities and been a hero, made history, but he'd rather get petty revenge on the guy who mocked him, by endangering his son. So far, so deranged. But underneath the bare bones science-fiction trappings, which are vague and clearly don't interest Stefano (the creature is a key component of a group of aliens trying to "destroy the universe"), is a story about youthful innocence and the corruption of the soul as people grow older, wiser, and more cynical. Some see themselves as educators and facilitators for the young, encouraging, and passing on their knowledge and experience while trying not to douse the flame of youthful idealism and naivete, others grow bitter, spiteful, jealous, and vindictive as they age. This story embraces the latter group.

While the young groom from 1929, frozen in time, remains idealistic and self-sacrificing, trapped in a stalemate with his tormentor, his 1920s bride, with thirty years in isolated

solitude alone in the empty house and still waiting for marital consummation, has had plenty of time to go completely batty and will sacrifice anyone who is lured into her spider's web to free her now obviously incompatible beau. The elderly couple who send the young elopers to her are mean and corrupted, and the wealthy father searching for the couple is cowardly and selfish (although he mysteriously redeems himself at episode's end without explanation, undergoing a sudden transformation from scared self-interest and arrogance to fatherly love and self-sacrifice; a little bit of exposition here would have been nice). The virginal couple, bland and empty-headed, are utterly innocent to the point of dangerous credulity, and no match for the scheming and manipulative elderly cynics who trample them, while the malevolent, pointlessly evil alien creature resembles a grotesque fusion of the sexual organs, with a leering, single eye! But the beauty of Serling and Stefano's accomplishments on *The Twilight Zone* and *The Outer Limits*, then and now, is that the numb-nuts who run the television industry have no idea what's going on in these series, or what's being said. Serling, Stefano, and, to a lesser extent, Gene Roddenberry (who was a little less subtle) could do and say things in the science fiction medium that could never have got past the gatekeepers of the cop shows, cowboys, and soaps because all the censors saw were the monsters and the spacemen.

It was "Stefano at his most eccentric and daringly experimental, as he translates the loss of virginity into a horror story" observed Show and Frentzen in their *Outer Limits Companion*. "Rife with free associations on marital fidelity, nuptial customs, and sexual dementia, 'Doomsday' is almost the flip side of the repressed attitude that governed 'Zzzzz'".

*One only has to look at the insets in the montage of the publicity pictures showing Melinda Plowman and Buck Taylor posing with the creature suit on the opposite page and compare them with the above image of the alien in the box from the episode to appreciate the huge difference good lighting could make to the credibility of a monster on The Outer Limits. The series' filming in monochrome gave much greater scope to the cameramen and directors to create superb images from the limited options available to them at the time in 1963/4.*

Certainly after the idealistic 'sanctity of marriage' theme of "Zzzzz", "Doomsday" is dark, bitter, cold, cruel, and cynical, despite the later character transformations of the Justice and the runaway girl's father. Yet both stories are about heartless tragedies foisted on the undeserving.

THE BRAINLESS GLOB

*As the photos on page 92 demonstrate, a 'brainless glob' was all ABC had until the creative talents on the first season went to work with everything from story to performance to photography to direction. Pure talent, creativity, and ability from start to finish.*

While linear and intriguing in its storytelling, nothing in "Don't Open Till Doomsday" makes much sense! What are the alien's ill-defined motives for his mad, murderous mission? Why does Kry think the alien will free her husband? Why would this young man still want her, and how has he retained his sanity, trapped in the box with the alien for thirty years? What happiness could they possibly have in a world in which the alien carries out his terrible intentions? How did the Justice of the Peace and his wicked wife (who set the couple up) get involved in all this? Wouldn't the nasty old woman have sought a more profitable outcome from knowing that Mrs. Kry has an alien on the premises?

There's no sense to the horror or the story; it is what it is. It doesn't pay to think too hard about any of it, just succumb to the madness in Stefano's mind and enjoy your excursion to those Outer Limits. It's an hour you won't forget, or regret.

Faded movie star Miriam Hopkins, who that same year played the brothel madame in Russ Meyer's version of *Fanny Hill*, was still

**11.00 Outer Limits**

*Ugh! What a horrible cardigan*

Expanding Human: A university professor experiments with a drug that has the effect of expanding human conciousness. Flip city. What he doesn't know is that it will also change his appearance and give him hypnotic power. Now available on prescription from all good pharmacists.

*This 1990s U.K. listings mag was trying so hard to be funny (and let's face it, succeeding), it's a shame they got the still for the wrong episode... Still, points for trying...*

choosy about her parts, despite her career never really having taken off. To see the delightful Hopkins in her prime, go to the IMDB and play the trailer for Ernst Lubitsch's *Design for Living* ("It's true we have a gentleman's agreement" she sighs languidly about a 'no sex' pact, "but unfortunately, I am no gentleman!"). A former beauty and chorus girl cast in a series of roles that accentuated danger and wit in the 20s and '30s,

*One of sci-fi's finest cold and imperious bad guys, John Hoyt, here in Bert Gordon's B-movie Attack of the Puppet People.*

she would have been quite a catch in Stefano's fictional 1920s, where we see only David Frankham as the unfortunate groom, about to be robbed of his prize and incarcerated for the next thirty years in a bleak limbo.

Buck Taylor, the son of character actor Dub Taylor, usually played in westerns, and was a regular for many years on *Gunsmoke*. He's fine as the dull groom. Melinda Plowman, a standard TV girlfriend type busy on television in the '50s and early '60s, went on to a glittering career in *Billy the Kid vs. Dracula*, after which she seems to

have wisely retired in the mid-'60s. David Frankham had previously appeared in "Nightmare". He can also be seen coming to grief in the *Outer Limits*-ish *Return of the Fly*, and was the equally unlucky in love Larry Marvick in *Star Trek*'s "Is There In Truth No Beauty?", in which he went as mad as he should have gone inside a gift box for thirty years.

John Hoyt's film and TV sci-fi credentials are interminable and invariably memorable. They include the classic shaggy dog story "Will the Real Martian Please Stand Up?" in *The Twilight Zone* (he appeared twice), two other *Outer Limits*, including an alien in "The Bellero Shield", two *UNCLEs*, the *Star Trek* pilot, and two *Time Tunnels*, just a handful of his numerous credits. Nellie Burt made a career out of playing nasty old ladies, and is used to good effect alongside the ever welcome Irene Tedrow in *The Invaders'* "Nightmare". She returns in "The Guests" to play... yes, a nasty old lady. The usual MGM mansion exterior is used in the opening scene (the episode begins after the credits).

*Joseph Stefano on the set of "Tourist Attraction".*

### The Bellero Shield

wr. Arthur Leo Zagat, Joe Stefano, dir. John Brahm

The greed of power-hungry individuals, one a self-serving idealist, the other the wife of a timid but talented young scientist, results in murder and madness when contact is made with extra-terrestrial life

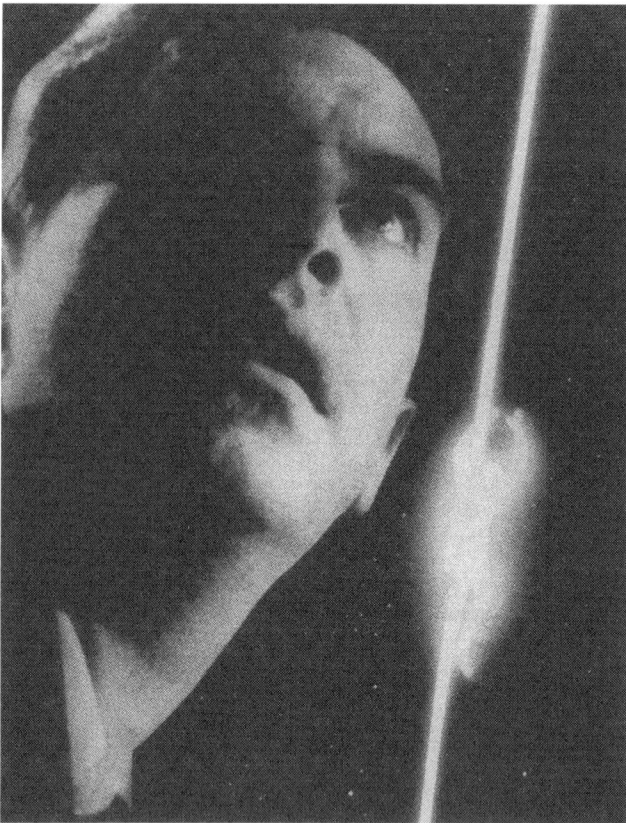

*with Martin Landau (Richard Bellero Jnr.), Sally Kellerman (Judith Bellero), Neil Hamilton (Richard Bellero Snr), Chita Rivera (housekeeper), John Hoyt (alien)*

An innocent, friendly alien becomes a pawn in a power game between a scientist's philanthropic father, living guiltily and vicariously through his son's achievements, and the son's greedy, grasping, malevolent and manipulative wife... who engineers her own descent into a hell of her own making in a chilling climax.

This episode completes a run of eight episodes (interrupted only by the equally strong "Corpus Earthling") either solely written, or rewritten extensively and improved, by Joseph Stefano that began with "Nightmare" and represents this series at its absolute zenith. There had been good episodes earlier, and there were more good ones on the way (culminating in one last solo entry, "The Form of Things Unknown", which Stefano now gave his full attention to, to the detriment of those still to come), but those eight represent the pinnacle of an extraordinary achievement and an amazing body of work—a masterpiece a week. Even *Twilight Zone's* equally overworked and prolific Rod Serling never turned out eight top-notch offerings in a row. And, like Serling, Stefano worked on or oversaw virtually every single episode of the first season.

Yet another old dark house story (Stefano loved his gothic mansions), this superlative yarn adapted from a short story by prolific pulp SF author Arthur Leo Zagat*, offers the unlikely spectacle of seeing Martin Landau, of all people, acted off the screen, blown away by the performances of Sally Kellerman and Neil Hamilton. Kellerman, who had earlier played a nothing role in "The Human Factor", was in the second *Star Trek* pilot, "Where No Man Has Gone Before", and appeared in a superior second season episode of *The Invaders*, "Labyrinth", but as good as she is in both, this is by far her finest moment. Stefano claimed he 'discovered' Kellerman; he didn't really, but he certainly used her to her best advantage. Landau is fine in this, and perfect casting as the weak, frightened scientist, but his *Outer Limits* high point remains "The Man Who Was Never Born".

* I have been unable to identify the title of the story, apparently his only TV or film adaptation, which sadly Zagat did not get to see; he had passed away in 1949.

Neil Hamilton, forever to be known for his superb portrayal of Commissioner Gordon in *Batman*, dished up another superbly knowing, tongue-in-cheek performance here. He had already excelled as the demented General Clarke in "The Invisibles", and he similarly relished his opportunities as Bellero Senior, despite the occasional line of clunky over-explanatory dialogue, some of which he ploughs through valiantly on the doorstep. Dancer Chita Rivera, as the loyal barefoot maid, found herself taking a trip to *The Outer Limits* on account of living next door to Joe Stefano; all the other members of the cast had previously chalked up *Outer Limits* credentials,

Landau in "The Man Who Was Never Born", Kellerman in "The Human Factor", and John Hoyt in "Don't Open Till Doomsday". Hoyt is barely recognisable here, and his alien, introduced sliding down a laser beam like a fireman, resembles the creature in "The Galaxy Being", another self-sacrificing cipher, but there's a great shock twist and a wonderful comeuppance for Kellerman's sci-fi Lady Macbeth.

*John Hoyt in alien costume for "The Bellero Shield". On film, a luminous glowing effect will be added, making all the difference to the final image.*

The dialogue, while needing a rare polish, is still superb on several occasions ("I crawled out of the room. I crawled, Richard", says Kellerman after she's seen the alien arrive, and then later, when she's regained her composure, says to her very own loyal and scheming female 'Igor', the bare-footed maid, "We must show these great men what great men they are"). Relishing his lines as a hypocritical old fool, even when they're overwritten and unconvincing, Hamilton gets the wonderfully assured zinger "Great men are forgiven the sins of their murderous wives!", delivered with the usual bounce on the balls of his feet he reserves for all his best bits. The role isn't quite as efficiently realised as his possessed General in "The Invisibles", but it's a larger one, and all Hamilton's trademark tricks and affectations are in place. Nobody does pompous twits like Hamilton did, and like all the old pros, he doesn't let being seated with his back to the camera do him out of his profile shot.

## The Children of Spider County

wr. Anthony Lawrence, dir. Leonard Horn

Impotent aliens that impregnated Earth women decades earlier to replenish male stocks return to Earth to collect their now teenaged progeny

*with Lee Kinsolving (Ethan), Kent Smith (Aabel), Bennye Gatteys (Anna Bishop), John Milford (John Bartlett), Crahan Denton (Sheriff), Dabbs Greer (Mr. Bishop), Joe Perry (government man), Robert Osterloh (General), Roy Engel (military officer), William O. Douglas Jnr. (alien Aabel)*

Marred by the same laughable grim-faced scenes in the Pentagon to open that hurt the later two-parter "The Inheritors", "The Children of Spider County" starts to look more intelligent and substantial once the scene shifts to one of the wooded, sunlight-filtering off-the-beaten-track nowheres that *The Outer Limits* was best known for. At the end of the day though, and despite the philosophical asides and Wah Chang alien—a glorious bug-eyed incisor-faced horror in a smart suit—the story still belonged to that well-worn genre of aliens impregnating Earth women that takes the theme of *Children of the Damned* from infancy to adolescence, John Wyndham meets James Dean.

*Kent Smith, later of* The Invaders, *plays Aabel in human guise*

98

For all the outside influences though, "The Children of Spider County" is quintessential mainstream *Outer Limits*. Many episodes were worse and quite a few were better, but this is pretty much the archetypal blueprint, representative of the show as the public remembers it—all bug-eyed nightmares, tacky spaceships, lofty liberal ideals, stern-faced authoritarians getting their comeuppance, hicks and rednecks getting zapped, supportive, defiant, but frail women, sunlit woods, second-hand special effects and first rate music.

The two familiar *Outer Limits* themes are well to the fore; the stomping monster march first heard in "The Architects of Fear", and the tinkling weirdness notes purloined by the *Simpsons Hallowe'en Specials* both appear in all their glory, alongside the familiar special effects noises of *War of the Worlds* so frequently employed and the lyrical, romantic music from Lawrence and Horn's previous "The Man Who Was Never Born" used for the series' few idyllic sequences.

The episode has a patchwork quality to it, mostly caused by the editing. Several shots are re-used at different points in the episode, the most obvious of these being one of Kent Smith observing from the cover of a tree, seen when the police first have Ethan in cuffs in the police car (there's a nice silent scene of a spiteful cop pulling on his half of the bracelets to stop Ethan nodding off

—he gets satisfyingly obliterated), and then returned to in a much later scene taking place at a different location. When the alien boards his ship to leave, an earlier close-up of the creature is inserted that, although it looks good, doesn't quite match. There are many wonderful individual shots, for which full credit must be given to the creative Leonard Horn.

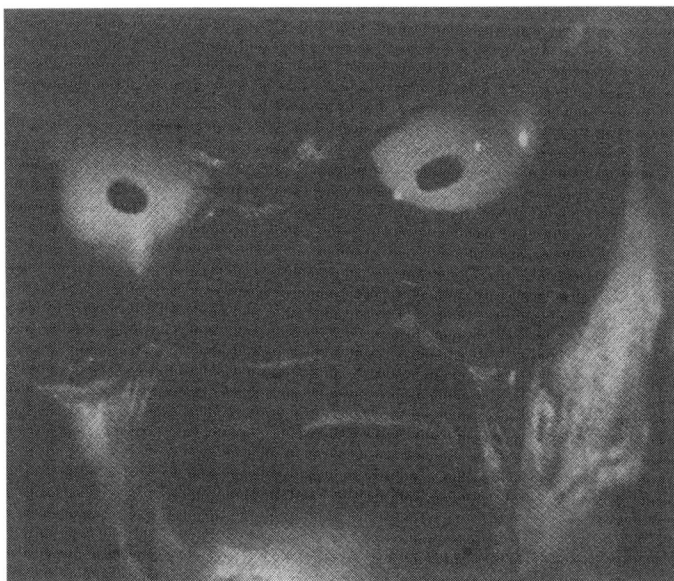

Kent Smith had already appeared in the series as the crazy doctor in "It Crawled Out of the Woodwork". Later, he joined Roy Thinnes in his fight against *The Invaders* as recurring character Edgar Scoville during the second season. His bland, ordinary features, exactly the sort of dignified commanding dullness an alien might choose for human form, made him perfect casting.

Tall and thin, Lee Kinsolving appears in the silly sci-fi j.d. debacle "Black Leather Jackets" for *The Twilight Zone*, filmed that same year. Despite notching up some quality credits, Kinsolving gave up on acting in the mid-'60s, leading a full life in other directions until passing tragically young in the mid-'70s. The oddly named Bennye Gatteys had only a modest TV career, perhaps hindered by her unconventional name in those days, appearing often in westerns. This was her only sci-fi credit.

William O. Douglas Jnr. had played "The Galaxy Being" in the pilot, and played further alien creatures during the series' run. He can be seen in human form as GIA agent Johnny in "The Invisibles". Character actor Dabbs Greer steals his few scenes effortlessly as the leading lady's horrible father, while the dependable John Milford as the investigator is rendered virtually invisible himself by the parade of local yokels, and the mandible-faced monster.

### The Mutant

wr. Ellis St. Joseph, Joe Stefano, Jerome Thomas, Allan Balter, Robert Mintz, dir. Alan Crosland Jnr.

Visiting a remote scientific outpost, an investigator discovers that one of the scientists' number has been transformed into a telepathic mind-reading monster who is keeping his colleagues in subservient terror...

*with Warren Oates (Reese Fowler), Larry Pennell (Evan Marshall), Betsy Jones-Moreland (Julie Griffith), Walter Burke (Dr. Riner), Herman Rudin (Professor LaCosta), Robert Sampson (Lt. Chandler), Richard Derr (Phillip Griffith)*

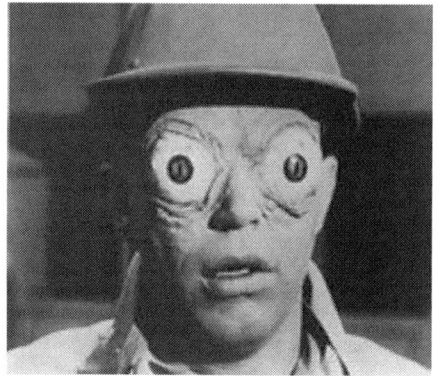

Given that Riner has been trying to work on a cure for Fowler, and bearing in mind the rather drastic change in Fowler's eyes, now consuming half his face, it's really quite remarkable that none of these great learned brains have figured out that Fowler is sensitive to the dark and thus easily disabled—even after this weakness is displayed to Riner in the lab. Still, "The Mutant" is an enjoyable yarn with several nice touches, including a shot of Fowler crying out his name to the silence in a desperate attempt to hold on to his identity in the very scene following Riner's decision to use that name as the unlikely-to-be-heard trigger for Evan's memory, thus instantly exposing the plan for the stupidity it is.

Robert Sampson, who looked very uncomfortable in a minor role in "A Taste of Armageddon" for *Star Trek* and also came to a sticky end in the *Voyage to the Bottom of the Sea* episode "The Enemies", comes to an early demise here but stars in the episode's most chilling and poignant scene as he desperately tries to shield his thoughts from the sadistic Fowler, the ultimate bug-eyed monster (distant relative, perhaps, of the aliens in 1954's *Killers from Space*) (below). Warren Oates puts in an

energetic performance as the mutated madman, writhing like a demon when the rains transform him in a flashback sequence, and Walter Burke, last seen in "The Invisibles", enjoys a rare substantial straight role as Riner that for once is not based on his physical appearance. The romantic leads are typical but adequate cut-outs from a thousand '50s creature features before them; Larry Pennell's main claim to fame is for portraying movie star Dash Riprock, actually Homer Noodleman, in *The Beverly Hillbillies*, while Betsy-Jane Moreland was Roger Corman's *Last Woman on Earth,* and also appeared in his *Creature from the Haunted Sea.* Herman Rudin appeared in numerous bit-parts for *The Untouchables,* always as a gangster.

*Previous page: Oates and Moreland in a pretty lame publicity pose.*

There are certainly enough strong scenes in this episode to make Stefano's criticism of the episode as the first season's worst wholly unfair, despite the army of authors in the credits—always a warning sign. "The Mutant" may be a B-movie BEM-fest, rather than one of the series' more sophisticated contributions, but it's an entertaining hour, and against such first season clunkers as "Second Chance", "Moonstone", and "Specimen: Unknown" it doesn't even qualify for the top three worst. Once the second season is considered, it wouldn't even make the top ten worst.

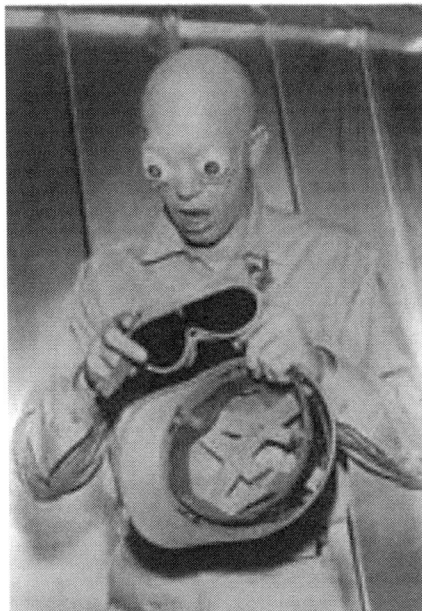

Nevertheless, the episode is littered with the sort of silly irritants that come from scripts with too many cooks and hack directors. Why hasn't Marshall arrived with sunglasses? He knows where he's going. Why doesn't he have a radio on board his ship? A ridiculous oversight. Why should Chandler 'miss dreaming'? Dreaming isn't dependent on darkness, only sleep.

There is also some blatant Irwin Allen-style recycling going on. The spaceship Marshall arrives in is clearly the one from "The Man Who Was Never Born" with a paint job, and absurdly, a faceless refurbished Zanti Misfit shows up in the cave. The corridors in the annexe are actually made up of the backs of the 'flats' (set walls), which is about as cheap as you can get. And the teaser is back, spoiling the Big Reveal of Reese's eyes (although it's entirely likely there were photos all over the place in the promotional media). The climax takes place in dear old Bronson Caverns in Griffith Park, location of the Batcave entrance and numerous sci-fi classics, most notably *Invasion of the Body Snatchers*. See an outdoor, non-studio cave in any western or sci-fi show, and there's a fair chance it'll be this one, the benefits being that it was open to the public, easy to get to, and you could film inside it.

Ellis St. Joseph, who wrote the virtually untouched "The Sixth Finger", had a tendency to come up with ideas that were too big for the budget, and this seems to be what happened here. His work went through several other typewriters before it hit the studio floor, including those of producer Joe Stefano, assistant producer Lou Morheim and story editor Allan Balter, author of "One Hundred Days of the Dragon" and numerous scripts for *Voyage to the Bottom of the Sea* and *Mission: Impossible*. All in all, the episode was nearly a year in production hell.

As already mentioned, St. Joseph has contributed a number of stand-out episodes to other 1960s SF shows besides "The Sixth Finger", including "The Day the Sky Fell In", a superior *Time Tunnel* story, and

"The Weird World", a memorable *Land of the Giants* and perhaps the best after the pilot. He also wrote the disappointing "The Walls of Jericho" for *The Time Tunnel*, the bland "Underground" for *Giants,* and the first version of what became a Catwoman/Sandman team-up for *Batman*. Robert Mintz went on to become a writer and production executive at 20th Century Fox, where he worked on *Batman* and the Irwin Allen shows, among others.

*Warren Oates as he appeared in "Welcome, Stranger" for Lost in Space.*

Warren Oates was an actor with an easy-going, world-weary style, and unsuited to this role, despite carrying it off. Although it was a waste of his talents, a weaker actor may have rendered the episode unwatchable, given the liability of the mutant's appearance, both wonderful but silly. He had been a regular on the short-lived contemporary rodeo show series *Stoney Burke* (the only other TV series by *Outer Limits* producers Daystar), and is best known for his work on the classic Sam Peckinpah films *The Wild Bunch* and *Bring Me the Head of Alfredo Garcia*. Frequently appearing in TV westerns, he was also known to TV SF buffs for "The Seventh Is Made Up of Phantoms", a mediocre *Twilight Zone*, and the *Lost in Space* episode "Welcome Stranger", in which he plays long-lost cowboy astronaut and anachronism Jimmy Hapgood, an ironic prophetic early draft of the sort of roles that would make him an icon in the '70s. A fine actor, he can't do any real acting here with the fragile bug-eyes to keep in place, and Alan Crosland is not a good enough director to do anything clever with the visuals, as Gerd Oswald or Leonard Horn might have done.

### Second Chance

wr. Sonya Roberts, Lou Morheim, dir. Paul Stanley

An alien transforms a fairground saucer ride into a genuine space vehicle to abduct sorry individuals to a new life on another planet, where they might work to save his world from destruction.

with Don Gordon (Captain Crowell), Janet DeGore (Mara Matthews), Simon Oakland (alien), John McLiam (R.J. Beasley), Angela Clark (Sue-Ann Beasley), Yale Summers (Buddy Lyman), Mimsy Farmer (Denise Ward), Arnold Merritt (Tommy Shadbury)

A ridiculous and quite silly piece of theatre (the original script by Sonya Roberts was rewritten by story editor Lou Morheim, and as so often happens, Roberts put a pseudonym on it). Silly, phony dialogue (such as the classic "I'd hate you, Tommy, but you can't hate someone you never liked!" * ), unsympathetic characters, and dreary, uninspired visuals sink this story of alien abduction, which is further burdened by its childish what-if? concept of a fairground simulated spaceship ride that suddenly becomes the real thing.

* Yes you can.

The crucial failure of the premise, the classic sounds-like-a-good-idea-at-the-time, is that when transferred to the screen, the reality looks as fake as the false. As befits such a juvenile wish-dream, we are never enlightened as to exactly *how* the fairground prop is magically transformed into a working flying saucer, and the alien—a bird-like 'Empyrian'—is a stereotypical mix of haughty disdainful superiority and fearsome shock horror. The costume is wonderful, and works primarily because the actor inside is the solid and capable Simon Oakland, *playing* his role beneath the mask rather than simply hiding behind it; the eyes speak volumes, which is more than can be said for the arch romantic novel artifice and hysterical ravings posing as dialogue and failing even as exposition.

The opening scene inadvertently spells out the nature of this episode, when we see the fairground spaceship entertaining a captivated youth; this edition of *The Outer Limits* works on much the same level as a fairground amusement—see the monster, and scream.

The message of the episode, a little more profound, and an interesting nugget of thought hammered home as plainly as possible in the last five minutes, is that some people are quite happy living lives of mediocrity and pettiness and don't have the mental desire or psychological capabilities to want more than they've got. They want what they know, even if it's mundane and very little, rather than have their simple world overturned into the unknown. The Empyrians have hijacked a bunch of losers and no-hopers, thinking they'd appreciate this "second chance" (one of no less than eighty TV episodes listed on the IMDB with this title), not appreciating that they have neither the ability or desire to take it.

Like the Chromoites in "The Mice" who tried to pull a fast one on humankind, and the Luminoids of "A Feasibility Study", who failed to appreciate our stubbornness, the Empyrians are brought down by their lack of empathy for the complexity and contrariness of human beings. They only had to ask for help from humankind (to avert some nebulous tragedy eighty years in the future, their dubious motive for abduction) for their saucer to fill up with starry-eyed Spielberg types and eager, excitable scientists who might be game for a challenge on another planet, whatever the state of their Earthbound lives (we see a variation of this in the similar and slightly better "Counterweight" in the second season, when at least the participants *want* to go into space). Instead, the Empyrians blundered in using force and deceit.

*This page: Janet De Gore poses with Simon Oakland. Previous page: Oakland with future Italian scream queen Mimsy Farmer.*

The Empyrians might be employing misplaced logic to deal with the naturally illogical and contrary Earth people, but there is no logic in their hazy and ridiculous plan, thin hope based on chance—to avert mathematical certainty with the aid of a group of duds and dullards.

Compounding the ill-considered half-assed premise of the idea is the execution of it. The pretentious speeches the actors are burdened with are further scuttled by the shabby special effects for sci-fi cliches, particularly a farcical meteor shower which comes and goes in a few seconds for no apparent reason other than to offer some non-existent spectacle that neither the actors, budget or director have the ability or inclination to fulfil. Add to this the classic whoops-he-fell-out-of-the-door scene. It's unbelievable nonsense from a show with the class of *The Outer Limits*.

The alien has convenient special powers, which emanate from the traditional locket around his neck (of course) and serve no function other than to demonstrate how bizarre those aliens can be; basically, the alien can do anything the plot requires him to be able to do at a given time. If the alien needs to stop a fight—bweee-oop—he's stopped the fight. Unfortunately, he can't magic poor Tom back from outside. But then why would he, when he's shown such contempt for human life in the opening scene. A poor schmuck of a night watchman (who'd be a night watchman in the movies?) gets

zapped in the teaser for the sole purpose of hooking an audience with the promise of horror and menace, pointlessly making the Empyrian a murderer, and later, a knife is conveniently vaporised.

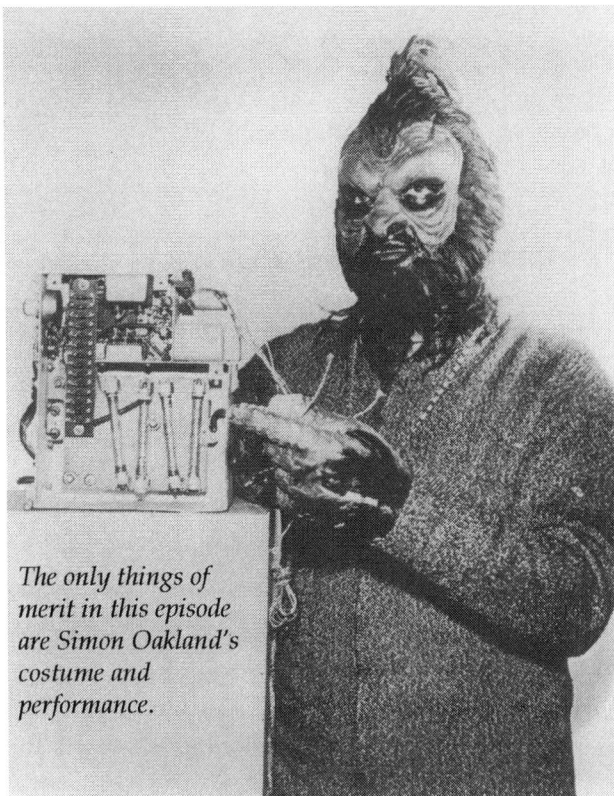

*The only things of merit in this episode are Simon Oakland's costume and performance.*

But the biggest problem is that none of the sights the production offers us to prove the reality of their predicament is any more convincing than the trappings of let's-pretend. One particularly misconceived scene has a girl attacking the alien crying "It's a mask!". Yes it is—so why let the script draw attention to it? She then tears the alien's garb to reveal the evidence of a real extraterrestrial underneath. Sadly, even though the director happily presents us with a close-up, we see nothing to indicate anything remotely more convincing than what we've already seen. Why shouldn't a bodysuit *also* be false?

The usually competent Paul Stanley's direction is also frequently false, from the Empyrian who walks away so that the doofus Beasleys can discuss their free ride, only to pointlessly make a timely sinister reappearance from offstage for dramatic effect when they're done, to Mara's 'silly female' moment in the ship when she tells our hero she feels like she's being watched; both of them only have to look up slightly by a few degrees to see that yes, they are. Against such absurdities, including the usual *Outer Limits* paper spaceship wibbling around in a meteor shower that would embarrass *Torchy the Battery Boy*, the cast struggle gamely.

Immediately after this scene there is a fleeting moment of insight as the cheerleader berates her football hero boyfriend for persuading her to join him on the free ride—"We should have been at the luncheon, but instead we're here!". It's an authentically absurd outburst that has the ring of truthfulness about it in the selfish silliness of its content, a pointlessly vindictive remark that illustrates and defines her self in a

rare moment of character over caricature. A few more moments like that could have made all the difference. Alone, it adds to the general air of silliness.

There are no bad performances, just no opportunities for anyone to shine from behind the stereotypes. Don Gordon, hero of "The Invisibles", gets no chance to define his role as disillusioned academic, in which the defiantly blue-collar actor is miscast anyway, while the ever-wonderful and under-appreciated John McLiam turns in a three-dimensional performance for his one-dimensional old bastard. Angela Clarke is spot-on as his pathetic loyal wife, striving hopelessly to please a man who is never pleased. Everyone else is adequate, but ironically it's the man behind the monster mask who really shines— the measured and distinctive tones of the wonderful character actor Simon Oakland (Tony Vincenzo in the *Kolchak* TV films and series) lend the alien Empyrian a dignity and depth that transcends the script, story, and surroundings. The cast, adrift, deserved much better.

## Fun and Games

wr. Robert Specht, Joe Stefano, dir. Gerd Oswald

A lonely woman and a minor-league gangster are coerced into fighting alien creatures on a hostile world for the salvation of their planet from destruction by deranged extraterrestrial games masters

*with Nick Adams (Mike Benson), Nancy Malone (Laura Hanley), Bill Hart, Robert McQuarry (alien opponents), Ray Kellogg (detective), Bob Johnson (evil alien voice)*

Frederic Brown's short story "Arena" is generally regarded to be the inspiration for both this episode and the *Star Trek* "Arena", and the concept of pitting two people against each other for the gratuitous entertainment of a malevolent third party has never really gone away from either science-fiction or straight fiction. It showed up again in at least two other *Star Trek* stories, "Bread and Circuses" and "The Gamesters of Triskellion", as well as *Lost in Space's* "Deadly Games of Gamma Six" and "Hunter's Moon". It was spoofed, *Star Trek*-style, in *The Simpsons'* "Deep Space Homer".

In the entire run of *The Outer Limits*, this was the only "comic-book" alien, evil just for the sake of it, but the average viewer doesn't know this, they just see a cornball slice of pulp sci-fi where a more thoughtful series was usually to be found. *Outer Limits* aliens were either friendly, misunderstood, or misguided. The Andorran, wearing an Ebonite head from "Nightmare" and Mandarin fingernails, is eloquent, but verbose; his sneering and sniggering gets tiresome

quickly. A malevolent, cackling moustache-twirling alien seems more at home in the likes of 1970s *Doctor Who* than a series of this calibre, and there's way too much of him.

HORROR IN THE WOODS

Whereas Stefano had complained, unfairly and erroneously, that there was too much action while information was being imparted in "The Children of Spider County", "Fun and Games" is the flip side. During a lengthy first act as the alien spells out the nature of their situation, everyone is just standing around. There is then much melodrama of the *Playhouse 90* variety over whether Adams' Benson will take part in the contest, but the teaser has already confirmed he will, so there's no suspense for the second act. The third act—finally, the action—is photographed attractively (if that's the right word given the look of the opposition) on the MGM backlot used for the *Tarzan* films... but still the tedious games master drones on interminably, changing the rules and justifying his fixing like a demented *Big Brother* producer. Everything that happens, every development in the contest, he has a few paragraphs to say about it. At least in the *Star Trek* version, the exposition could be given to the Enterprise crew watching on the ship, or the Captain's Log.

The alien opponents are fearsome and effective, except in the scene before the games, when they scratch and claw childishly at thin air like pantomime cats. One of the masks, slightly customised, is used in *Star Trek's* "The Cage", aka "The Menagerie", when the Talosian telepath takes a ferocious form to force the leading man to release his grip. There's no comeuppance for

*A behind-the-scenes pic from the modern trading cards showing the monstrous Bill Hart, The Outer Limits' go-to guy for towering BEMs, palling around with a member of the crew.*

the alien facilitator, he gets to go on organising his unpleasant activities, and no meaningful resolution for the two Earth people; the ending is botched anyway, with the girl suddenly becoming a perfect shot and a murderer after waiting an absurdly long period of time before acting to save Benson, and the games master suddenly caring about her personal life (!?!).

The alien opponents are actually more interesting than the Earth contestants; the brutal murder of his partner as a simple strategy is the most interesting development in the show. Familiar *Outer Limits* music stings and themes are tracked throughout.

Only the first two names in the cast list have any substantial screen time. Nick Adams was a competent actor who starred in two short-lived series in the early '60s, the western *The Rebel*, and journalism drama *Saints and Sinners*. He was well served by Four Star, makers of the latter, who gave him regular guest roles in *Burke's Law*, but by the mid-'60s his career was struggling, and he died of a drugs overdose in the late '60s. He's well cast here, but his 1950s acting persona was on the way out.

Either side of her appearance here, the very ordinary Nancy Malone, cast as the very ordinary Laura, was a regular player on two series, *The Naked City* and *The Long Hot Summer*, before doing the rounds of the cop shows on the guest star circuit. She also appeared in the *Twilight Zone* episode "Stopover in a Quiet Town".

Writer Robert Specht was a derivative jobbing hack bereft of original ideas (and who has the cheek to take story credit here) who devised *The Immortal* for Quinn Martin (a failed *Fugitive/Invaders* knock-off), scripted the well-remembered TV movie *Night Slaves*, and ended up on the Saturday morning shows *Ark II* and *Space Academy*. He also contributed scripts to *Knight Rider* and *Airwolf*. It looks very much as if the failings in the pacing were in the script and the editing suite rather than the direction, which visually is up to Gerd Oswald's usual creative high standards.

## The Guests

wr. Charles Beaumont, Donald Sanford, dir. Paul Stanley

A young drifter is held captive in an alien construct of a gothic mansion populated by wretched individuals frozen in time by an alien life form studying human nature...

*with Geoffrey Horne (Wade Norton), Luana Anders (Tess), Gloria Graham (Florida Patton), Nellie Burt (Ethel Latimer), Vaughn Taylor (Randall Latimer), Burt Mustin (Dr. Ames)*

*House guest Geoffrey Horne and long-standing tenant Gloria Graham in "The Guests". Next page, the alien intelligence, which was actually a recycled portion of the creature from "The Mice".*

A drifter stumbles onto an isolated house full of hateful individuals frozen in time and all slightly deranged. No wonder — a grotesque glob of an alien parasite is unfeelingly conducting a grim experiment on the poor mad souls trapped in the house, and is penetrating and studying their brains, stripping their souls bare to analyse and intellectualise their emotions. They are convinced that the alien creature will eventually let them go, but having been imprisoned for thirty years without the passage of time taking effect on them, they are all quite mad. The creature has learned about faith, art, destruction, fear, hopelessness, vanity, spite, and hate, but there are emotions to be found within the young man new to it — defiance, and then love for the young girl in the house.

A slightly pretentious but entirely captivating yarn, this is a Stefano story written without him. It has strong elements of "Don't Open Till Doomsday" and indeed all his old dark house gothic sci-fi, but was written by two writers who generally worked on either *The Twilight Zone* (Beaumont) or *Boris Karloff's Thriller* (Sanford). The idea was Charles Beaumont's, the script itself — a town now pared down more logically to a house — was Donald Sanford's. Accreditation for Beaumont's level of contribution is often complicated by the fact that he was very ill at the time with what we now believe was Alzheimers, and had huge medical bills to pay, and about half a dozen very kind writer friends, including Sanford and Richard Matheson, frequently took turns to ghost write for him.

Geoffrey Horne's career never really took off, and he claims on the IMDB to have had a dull life, but he's been married five times, fathered five kids, and had roles in *The Twilight Zone, The Outer Limits,* and *The Green Hornet,* so it can't have been all boring, and he has his niche in cult TV. Luana Anders' life was probably more interesting than any of the minor parts she played throughout her strange career, helping others more than she was helped herself; she started out in Roger Corman films such as *Reform School Girl* and *The Young Racers,* but thereafter had her more substantial roles in television.

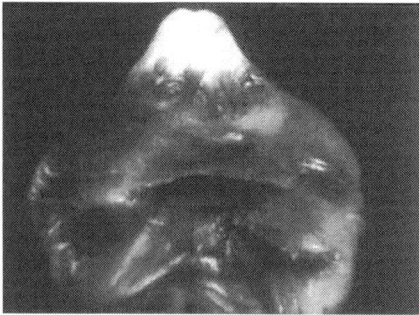

Gloria Grahame's colorful life is in no doubt, and she was a fairly well-known name in the '40s and '50s, when she appeared in numerous films including such major titles as *It's a Wonderful Life, The Big Heat,* and *Oklahoma.* By the time she made her appearances in *Burke's Law* and *The Outer Limits,* her career was well on the slide into television, and her most notable appearances were in the gossip columns. Nellie Burt we saw in "Don't Open Till Doomsday"; she plays a virtually identical role here, and has more to do.

Vaughn Taylor and Burt Mustin were two very busy and familiar elderly character actors; Mustin's career actually began in old age, and he played fragile old timers for

nearly thirty years! A list of his cult TV appearances alone would fill half the page. Taylor's credits are equally extensive over the same period, and include five *Twilight Zones* and eight *Perry Mason* alone. He appears briefly in the pilot for *The Invaders.* As ever, Bob Johnson, later *Mission: Impossible's* taped message voice, provides the voice of the evil alien, which is actually the top half of the Chromoite from "The Mice"!

**The Production and Decay of Strange Particles**

wr. and dir. Leslie Stevens

An accident at a nuclear research station releases alien invaders from another dimension plotting an atomic explosion to bridge worlds permanently

*with George MacReady (Dr. Marshall), Signe Hasso (Laurel Marshall), Allyson Ames, below (Amdis), Robert Fortier (Dr. Pollard), John Duke (Dr. Terrel), Rudy Solari (Griffin), Joseph Ruskin (Collins), Leonard Nimoy (Konig), Willard Sage (Coulter), Paul Lukather (official)*

While undoubtedly visually striking, and an extraordinary piece of television for the period, this episode is a rather empty affair.

Readers impressed by the names in the cast should not get too excited as everyone is obliterated in the first few scenes, leaving Ames, Hasso and MacReady to carry the action throughout the rest of the show. This would not be so bad if we knew who was being destroyed by the aliens and at what time, but with Ruskin, Nimoy, and the others all obscured behind huge radiation suits, it's difficult to follow the action, let alone the science. There are also far too many scenes that just consist of characters frantically calling out each other's names, especially as we often can't tell who's who anyway.

Two things save the episode from being a total disaster. Firstly, MacReady performs what dialogue there is well, some of it (relating to his cowardice) beautifully written, other chunks consisting of impossible scientific gobbledygook. Somehow, he masters both, and gives a fine performance. It's not often we get a three-dimensional mad professor, even rarer to have his defining characteristic being his fear.

The other virtue is the two women. While Ames' character is a typical fluttery female of the period, screaming and carrying on while all the men try to deal with the immediate trouble at hand (although we do feel for her dedication to her lost husband), Signe Hasso's role as MacReady's wife is a wonderful departure from the norm, a strong, resilient woman who shouts sense into Ames and supports her husband and saves the day by forcing him to confront and overcome his fear and insecurity. Without her presence and input, MacReady's careless bungling would literally have destroyed the world, yet not once does she turn into a shrewish or disillusioned nag when he falls apart. Although it's his knowledge that prevents catastrophe, it's her strength that carries the day; it is she, and she alone, who is responsible for that knowledge being deployed. This is a first in science-fiction film and TV of any decade, let alone the early '60s.

If one views the episode for its story, it's a weak one. If one considers it to be about this couple's relationship with each other, it's a strong one. And as ever with *The Outer Limits*, sets, lighting, special effects, and the familiar stomping monster music tracked throughout, do not disappoint. Execution, even of a weak idea and story, is as excellent as ever. This is not the episode you would go to if you wanted to introduce the show to a friend... but it's better than it has a right to be. And it's pro-science. It's twaddle... but it's better twaddle than it's given credit for.

Most of the players in this episode had appeared already in, or would return to *The Outer Limits*. George MacReady had featured memorably in "The Invisibles", and Rudy Solari (later a regular on '60s WWII series *Garrison's Gorillas*) would confront "The Invisible Enemy". Robert Fortier could lay claim to roles in "Controlled Experiment" and "Demon with a Glass Hand", while Leonard Nimoy (*Star Trek's* Mr. Spock) enjoyed a more substantial and rewarding role in "I, Robot". Willard Sage had played bit parts in "Tourist Attraction" and "Nightmare", Paul Lukather for the second season's

"The Brain of Colonel Barham". Allyson Ames was married to Leslie Stevens at the time, and previously appeared in the pilot film for the series, "The Galaxy Being".

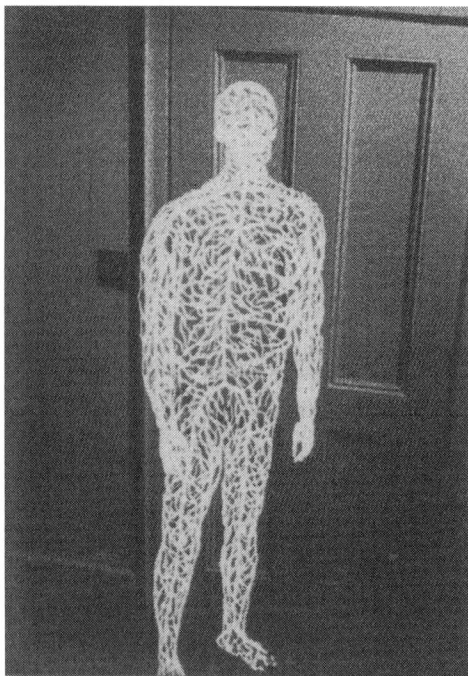

*The highlight of this episode: the alien's arrival and departure effect.*

### The Special One

wr. Oliver Crawford, dir. Gerd Oswald

Aliens planning to infiltrate Earth society send 'tutors' to instruct gifted youngsters... but one young boy rebels

*with MacDonald Carey (Roy Benjamin), Richard Ney (Mr. Zeno), Marion Ross (Mrs. Benjamin), Flip Mark (Kenny), Edward Platt (Mr. Terrance), Jason Wingreen (Bill Turner), Bert Freed (Joe Hayden)*

After a truly horrific opening scene, an alien in human form materialises outside the apartment of the Benjamin family, where he flatters the parents of a talented young boy into letting him participate in a vague educational project for bright youngsters.

The aliens aren't too smart themselves; they impose themselves on the family to such a degree they alienate (no pun intended) the father and mother and create an atmosphere of tension and mistrust. It's completely pointless and unnecessary to drive a wedge between the boy and his family; a little more caution and subtlety and they might have succeeded in their plan, but Zeno is pushy, creepy and rude. Ultimately, the Xenons are defeated by a child, and not surprisingly, although the ending goes on so long it's almost cruel.

Flip Mark is excellent as the boy, but he's working with a cardboard cut-out of a character, and it's not entirely clear how Zeno has such a hold over him. There are lots of spooky goings-on, but ultimately this is a boring entry to the series, more like a second season episode than a first. The special effects are excellent, particularly the arrival and departure of Xeno; given the quality of the average *Outer Limits* spaceship, a few more of the series' alien visitors might have found a different form of transport.

The story goes awry when Benjamin turns up at the office of the education authorities and confirms that they never sent Zeno. Instead of going straight to the police, he starts raving about Zeno being from outer space and describing the impossible things he's seen. He says he can't go to the police and start raving about aliens, which is fair enough, but he can certainly report an impostor who's tricked his way into his son's bedroom! In 1964, it was a little too soon for prime-time TV to be inferring anything more humanly sinister, but modern sensibilities make this episode even creepier than when it was made. And the idea of the young boy saving the day Will Robinson-style makes the series look like a kids show.

### The Chameleon

wr. Robert Towne, dir. Gerd Oswald

A cynical government agent is hauled out of retirement in a bid to infiltrate an alien saucer

*with Robert Duvall (Louis Mace), Howard Caine (Leon Chambers), Henry Brandon (General Crawford), Douglas Henderson (Dr. Tillyard), William O'Connell (alien), Dean Smith (stunt alien), Roy Jenson (enemy agent), Roy Olvera (guitarist)*

This begins as a tamer version of "The Architects of Fear" and ends as a predecessor of *Close Encounters of the Third Kind* by way of "Second Chance". Like "The Special One", it's more typical of the second season than the first, but it has great aliens, a great attitude, and it has Robert Duvall.

The military are in a Mexican stand-off with a flying saucer which has landed in woodland and destroyed an army patrol. All attempts to communicate have been met with silence, and the army are preparing to retaliate. Wiser minds are trying to prevail, pointing out that this may all be a misunderstanding that could

escalate into interplanetary war. It is suggested that a volunteer be found to impersonate and infiltrate the aliens (who have been seen), and the man selected is a washed-up, jaded and compromised agent who's burnt out and tired of life—but crucially, he's loyal. The agency has promised him a "new experience"—to find out what the aliens want, they intend to use what we would now call alien DNA to transform Mace into one of their kind.

Robert Towne was a writer for Roger Corman films who had scripted *The Last Woman on Earth* and *Creature from the Haunted Sea*, both of which had starred "The Mutant"'s Betsy Jones Moreland. In the 1970s he hit the big time when he scripted two acclaimed features, *Chinatown* and *Shampoo*, for the cinema (the latter featuring in the cast Towne's friend, "The Guests"' Luana Anders). Robert Duvall, who also segued into the movies from TV in the '70s, would return to *The Outer Limits* for "The Inheritors", as well as making SF TV appearances in *Voyage to the Bottom of the Sea* and *The Time Tunnel*, the latter in which he excels.

Electric in every scene, and blowing the other performers off the screen, Duvall is a joy to watch. It's unfortunate that his character is transformed into a guy in a monster mask, and one wishes they had taken the John Chambers approach as seen in "The Sixth Finger" and "The Man Who Was Never Born", rather than a Wah Chang headpiece, as impressive as it is. The episode's ending is grim, different, and unusual.

Of the supporting players, Douglas Henderson had previously appeared in "The Architects of Fear", in much the same role. William O'Connell can be seen without his monster make-up in the *Batman* story "Instant Freeze"/"Rats Like Cheese" as a bank clerk. He also appears in *The Twilight Zone, The Munsters, Star Trek* (as another alien, in "Journey to Babel"),

*Mission: Impossible, The Wild Wild West, Kolchak--the Night Stalker,* and *Fantastic Journey*. The guy who gets strangled by Mace is veteran stunt man and tough guy Roy Jenson, a personal favorite bit player of mine, who appeared in virtually every cult TV show of the 1960s and quite a few movies (he's particularly good with Duvall again in 1973's *The Outfit*).

### The Form of Things Unknown

wr. Joe Stefano, dir. Gerd Oswald

Two young women who murder a blackmailing gigolo stumble into a gothic mansion where a fellow fugitive, an odd young man, plays with time and space

*with Vera Miles (Kassia Pane), Barbara Rush (Leonora Edmond), David McCallum (Tone Hobart), Scott Marlowe (Andre Pavan), Sir Cedric Hardwicke (Colas)*

THING FROM MERCURY

THE DEATH RAY

The last episode of Stefano and Stevens' version of *The Outer Limits* to air (the show will get an entirely new production team for the second season, as you'll already know if you've read the main feature), "The Form of Things Unknown" was produced in two slightly different formats, one with the science-fiction elements and one without, but as Stefano pointed out to Schow and Frentzen, the sci-fi element was so small and incidental that it was barely noticeable, and didn't really matter. Initially rejected by ABC as too bizarre even for *The Outer Limits,* the network later reversed their position and asked for the episode to represent a pilot for a proposed supernatural series that would be called, it was decided, *The Unknown.* If they took on *The Unknown* as a series, it would be the first episode; if they didn't, it would then air as an episode of *The Outer Limits* (which, of course, it ultimately did; the significant difference is that in the broadcast version, the time travel element is real, in the other, imagined in madness).

What this about-face meant for the *Outer Limits* series is not really known, or understood, even today. On the one hand, it looked like the network appreciated what they had in Stevens and Stefano, but then at the same time they were talking of moving the show out of its relatively safe 'charmed life' slot against a movie and game shows, and up against killer hit sit-coms, firstly the number one show *The Beverly Hillbillies,* and then the popular lowbrow hit *The Jackie Gleason Show.* This is not how you protect a delicate, middling-rated prestige show, even in the mad hatter world of TV scheduling. As *The Outer Limits* was popular with a young audience, and Gleason was popular with older viewers, in what was still then a mostly one-set situation in most households, with the oldsters paying the bills and setting the program dial, this was a suicidal strategy. In fact, it can't even seriously be called a strategy. It was way too early for what later came to be known, in a multi-set environment some years later, as 'counter-programming'.

In the event, Stevens and Stefano clashed with the network over *The Unknown* to such an extent that they suicided before the network did. In a row with Stevens over Stefano being allowed to direct his baby (that Stefano claimed he was barely aware of), ABC fell out with the duo to such an extent that they took *The Outer Limits,* an ABC property, away from them, handing it to a completely new set of producers for the second season. As for "The Form of Things Unknown", "It was an extraordinary and peculiar piece" Stevens admitted many years later, "but not a coherent thing for an ordinary audience to grab. It was perceived as being far too arty".

Stefano not only lost *The Unknown,* he walked away from

*Outer Limits.* "I love a challenge" he told Schow and Frentzen, "but I also know where a wall is. I just didn't fancy putting in eighteen hour days on a series that was doomed. Monday nights was ideal... but I knew that *Jackie Gleason* was not going to be brought down by *The Outer Limits*".

Byron Haskin, who stayed for the second season and regretted it, put it in his own more typically blunt words. "*The Outer Limits* could have been one of the biggest hits on television" he blustered, "but I don't hold much credence for the network attitude... If you want the truth, they're all fucking idiots. How they can stay out of the way of bicycles I have no idea".

But Stevens was perceived as arrogant and in need of being taken down to size, while Stefano was burnt out and exhausted. As both Stevens and Stefano observed, but made no effort to correct, the network were involved in what they considered a simple power play... one that as executives, they simply had to win... or at the very least not be seen to back down. Perhaps there was more ego involved than art after all. Either way, it was the end of Stevens' and Daystar's ambitions to become show-providers. Unlike the Aaron Spellings and Quinn Martins of the world, they did not play ball; they picked up the bat and took it home with them, and that attitude does not last long in the macho world of executive posturing.

Thus we were left with one final gem from the glittering jewel box that was *The Outer Limits'* first season. What would turn out to be the duo's swan-song was indeed an indulgent masterpiece, based very much on the themes of both Stefano's association with Hitchcock's *Psycho* and its fugitive female (he had adapted Robert Bloch's book for the screen) and the film *Les Diaboliques,* in which two women murder a man, and then lose the body they dumped in a swimming pool. Was their victim still alive, and would he now come after them?

Like Ellis St. Joseph's "The Sixth Finger" and Anthony Lawrence's "The Man Who Was Never Born", "The Form of Things Unknown" had enough originality about it to transcend its very obvious and derivative inspiration, and was unlike anything ever produced for television before, and one can only wonder where *The Outer Limits* might have gone, had it proceeded to a second year under Stevens and Stefano. Cancellation against the big boys of mainstream TV seemed assured, but cancellations came slower in those days; *Outer Limits* lasted another seventeen shows under the new in-house production team, so it seems fair to say it would have done the same with Stevens and Stefano, but would Stefano's old dark house routine have got stale and repetitive, and would—on the evidence of this —the series have disappeared up its own ass in self-indulgent weirdness like the alien in "The Guests"? We'll never know.

We'll also never know how Stefano might have directed this piece, but there's certainly no faulting the end result, and it's doubtful that a neophyte first timer could have pulled off the tricks Oswald tries here. For his part, Conrad Hall lights the old dark house so that shadows precede the players who cast them. Flames crackle, droplets sparkle, silver shines, everything in the frame is enhanced.

Gerd Oswald's direction is wicked and inspired. When the car, a silver Rolls, first careens into view in the opening scene, we see Andre maniacally driving from a side view, as if alone. A second shot allows Vera Miles to lean forward into the frame, imparting new information to the viewer. How many workmanlike directors would simply have shown a full-on master shot of the entire car and its passengers? When the car

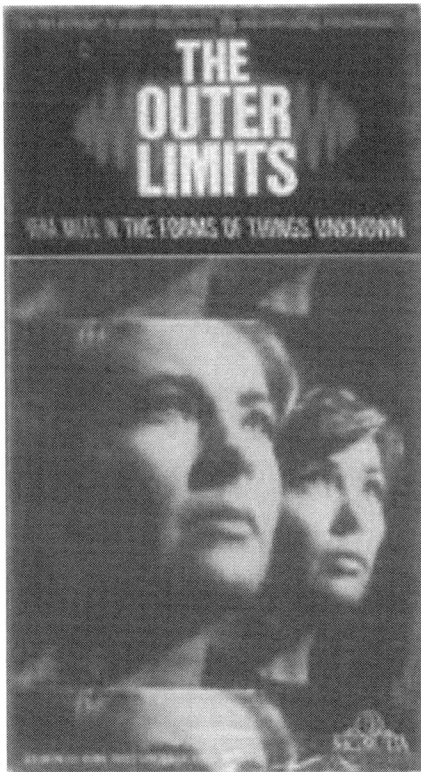

has stopped by the lake, the camera glides along the tranquil scene of the river, with foliage in the foreground. Andre's first appearance in his swim suit is filmed from behind this foliage to make us think for a split second that he is naked. That split second later, we see that he's in trunks, so the network censors can't complain without incriminating

their own perception of the moment. It is only when he steps into the water that we become aware of a third party, the second girl. He stands knee-deep, and demands his drink. It would, of course, be highly erotic, and appropriate, for the girls to join him in the lake naked—but American television can't do that in 1964. So Stefano and Oswald have them join him in the water fully-clothed—making the scene even more perverse and erotic. But Andre is cruel and sadistic; he's already stumbled, and he makes the girls come to him in their high heels. What he doesn't realise is what we have just been cleverly told... that his drink is poisoned. He takes a long time to die. The girls just coldly watch. He was a bully and a blackmailer.

Vera Miles' Kassia is made of stronger stuff than Barbara Rush's Leonora, who is consumed with guilt. I don't think I'm making too much of a Freudian fool of myself if I suggest here that there are strong overtones of a lesbian relationship; there's no other way to interpret the way the two women relate to each other, as they're not sisters, or compatible friends. As Leonora crumbles, several scenes in which Andre seemingly appears alive for more split second shocks are brilliantly executed. "In the night, imagining some fear, how easy is a bush supposed a bear" recites McCallum's Tone Hobart, mockingly, after they've sought shelter from the storm in Stefano's latest and last old dark house. Kassia announces she's going to bury the body. "Do you know why I didn't leave him in the lake? He would have floated into someone's life. Even in death, he'd find a way to betray us. This is the kind of neighborhood I was looking for. A good neighborhood for unmarked graves".

Leonora tries to tell her that the body's gone, but she won't listen, and neither of them know that Hobart has Andre's lifeless form all tied up in his time machine upstairs...

*McCallum and his time machine from "The Form of Things Unknown"*

According to Show and Frentzen, references to that last refuge of the weirdness-peddler, a Rollin-esque clown, were removed as extraneous to requirements, which they surely were. Another scene, filmed but excised, concerned a surrealistic funeral sequence that tortures the troubled Leonora.

As the series' creator, Leslie Stevens was entitled to have his name on the show, and he was working in various capacities on the miserable, lacklustre revamp when he died in 1998. Although he remained active in the medium in between, the original series remained his greatest achievement, and the show itself his claim to fame. He once said that by the time he was 75 he would probably be able to do what he wanted creatively. He died aged 74.

During the 1960s, he worked on the series *It Takes a Thief, The Virginian, The Name of the Game,* and *McCloud.* In the 1970s, he returned to science-fiction of a sort, devising the interesting single season failure *Search,* adapting *The Invisible Man* as a television adventure series with David McCallum, devising its retooling *The Gemini Man,* and then, the saddest indignity, working on early episodes of Glen Larson's *Battlestar Galactica* and *Buck Rogers in the 25th Century.* It was more of a comedown for American television than for Stevens, but that was network TV in the sterile, stifling '70s environment of the three major networks and no alternative venues.

Joseph Stefano finally got his chance to direct when the director of a 1964 TV movie he was producing, *The Ghost of Sierra de Cobre,* aka *The Haunting,* fell ill, and he stepped in. Judith Anderson starred in this ghost story, alongside *Outer Limits* alumni Martin Landau and Nellie Burt. After all that, it was his only directing credit. Following *The Outer Limits*, Stefano dabbled in film and TV occasionally, but to little effect. He wrote a single episode of *Star Trek – the Next Generation,* scripting "Skin of Evil", an episode writing out a regular character with a swift and senseless death, as so many are (upsetting some of the series' fans by not giving her a corny melodramatic goodbye scene), and during the 1990s showed up supervising the production of the *Swamp Thing* TV series. Once again, all future endeavors paled in comparison next to his astonishing achievements on *The Outer Limits.*

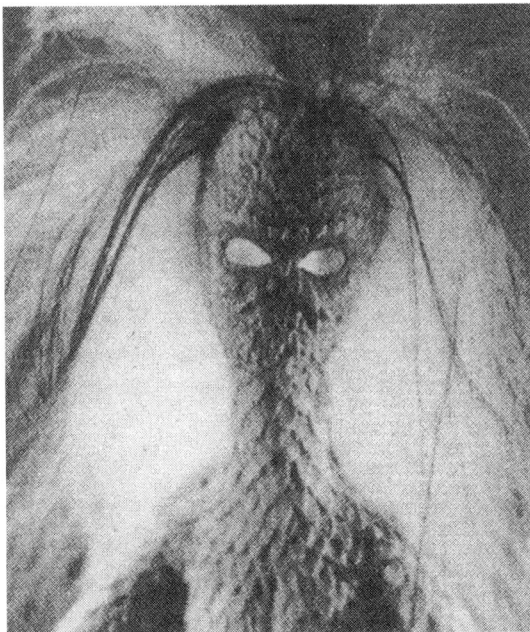

The new producer for the second season of *The Outer Limits* was to be former network executive and well-intentioned, competent, experienced, ladder-climbing yes-man Ben Brady, whose most prestigious credit was producing the formulaic courtroom drama *Perry Mason.* Brady and Stevens did not get along when Brady had been a network executive offering opinions,

and putting him in charge of Stevens' baby was the ultimate insult. It worked as almost certainly intended, and Stevens walked. Stefano had gone to CBS to work on a pilot that wouldn't happen, and scripts were no longer being revised and rewritten by him, but simply filmed as they came in, and it showed, just as it had when he was absent from the series while working on *The Unknown.* Furthermore, the budget had been cut, and that showed too.

Although nothing came of Stefano's *Unknown* pilot, the distinctive 'tearing' of the opening credits (devised by Wayne Fitzgerald) was used some years later for another ABC show, *The Invaders,* as was some of Dominic Frontiere's music for this episode. The producer – Quinn Martin. A safe pair of hands.

**Second Season**

**(1964)**

**Cold Hands, Warm Heart**

wr. Dan Ullman, Milton Krims, dir. Charles Haas

An astronaut returns from a flight to Venus to find that he is inexplicably getting progressively colder

*with William Shatner (Jeff Barton), Geraldine Brooks (Ann Barton), Lloyd Gough (General Claiborne), Malachi Throne (Mike), Dean Harens (doctor), Lawrence Montaigne (construction engineer),*

James B. Sikking (botanist), Henry Scott (electronics engineer), Julian Burton, Peter Madsen (reporters), Hugh Jensen (security), Lou Elias (guard), Ray Kellogg, Patrick Riley (steam bath attendants), Tim Huntley (chairman)

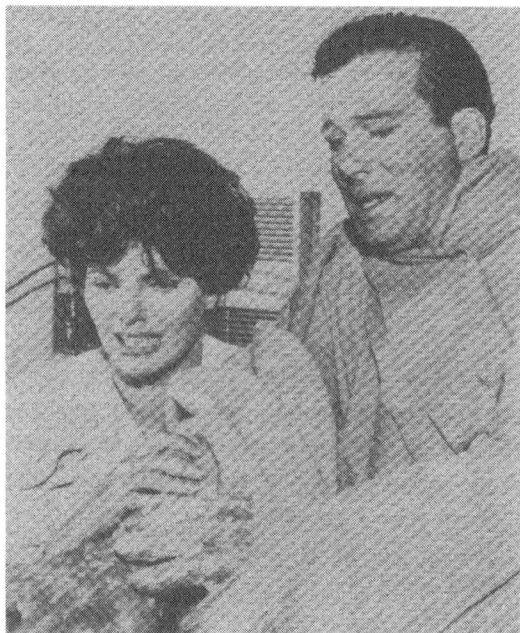

The first episode produced under the new ABC-approved hierarchy had a pre-*Star Trek* William Shatner as a troubled astronaut who witnesses an alien wraith in space and then can't stop shivering. There's not much more to it than that, although if this episode wasn't what suggested Shatner for Kirk it should have been. The entire exercise gets by solely on the charisma of Shatner. When he's on the screen, you look at nothing else. As with *Star Trek*, his *Twilight Zones* and *Thrillers*, all the other actors become line-feeders.

Among Shatner's other pre-Kirk appearances were guest-shots on *The Fugitive*, *Burke's Law*, *The Man from UNCLE* ("The Project Strigas Affair", co-starring Leonard Nimoy),

the two *Twilight Zones* ("Nick of Time" and the extraordinary *tour-de-force* "Nightmare at 20,000 Feet") and the aforementioned two superb *Thrillers* ("The Hungry Glass" and "The Grim Reaper"). He also starred alongside Leslie Stevens' then-wife Allyson Ames ("The Galaxy Being", "Production and Decay of Strange Particles") in Stevens' odd feature *Incubus* in 1965, notable for being filmed in the artificial non-language of Esperanto, and the last Daystar production. Apart from an excruciatingly stupid scene where Shatner's wife shouts at the stars like a schoolgirl possessed by the spirit of Sgt. Ritzig's wife from *Bilko*, this is otherwise quite an efficient time-killer, and a total period piece from the Kennedy era. It's too sixties for the fifties and too early '60s for the late '60s; you could set your watch by it. Shatner gives some stirring pre-*Star Trek* speeches about exploring outer space and rather prophetically is working for Project Vulcan...

*Top: Geraldine Brooks and William Shatner enjoy some histrionics in "Cold Hands, Warm Heart".*

*Right: TV guide ad for the second season.*

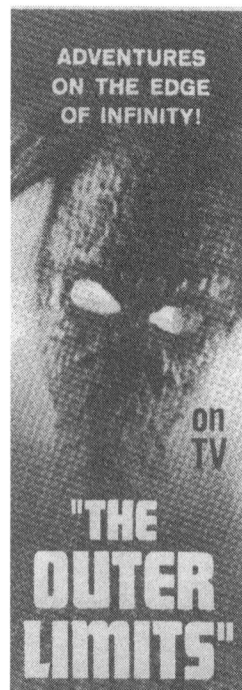

120

An intriguing cast includes two other notable players from the *Star Trek* legend, Malachi Throne, who played Commodore Mendez in "The Menagerie", and is here cast as Shatner's doctor and confidante, and Lawrence Montaigne, who played a Romulan in "Balance of Terror" and a Vulcan in "Amok Time". Both Throne and Montaigne worked extensively in SF TV productions during the '60s. Malachi Throne appeared several times in *Voyage to the Bottom of the Sea,* in the first season in "The Magnus Beam" and "The Enemies", and "The Return of Blackbeard" in the fourth season. He was "The Thief of Outer Space" for *Lost in Space,* and appeared in *The Time Tunnel* as Singh in "The Night of the Long Knives" and as Machiavelli in "The Death Merchant". He was also the man behind False-Face in *Batman,* and a peace-loving official in *Land of the Giants,* in "The Secret City of Limbo". Montaigne has played THRUSH agents in *UNCLE,* aliens in *The Invaders,* a robot in *Batman,* and been on both sides of *The Time Tunnel.* He's also appeared in *Voyage to the Bottom of the Sea, Amos Burke – Secret Agent,* and *Mission: Impossible,* among others.

Busy in television during the 1960s and early '70s, Geraldine Brooks had been the wife in "The Architects of Fear". Lloyd Gough, comic foil of *The Green Hornet,* also appears as a military man. James B. Sikking, best known in the 1980s as Howard Hunter in *Hill Street Blues* and the father in *Doogie Howser,* had previously appeared in "The Human Factor", and was a busy bit player in the 1960s, also chalking up a brief appearance in *The Invaders.*

The creature is a harmless-looking fellow, with only the vaguest sense of menace, and is created through the "Moonstone" method of wires and submerging the puppet in water to make it weave and float. The dreadful spaceship effects hadn't got any better in the second season, but even with a smaller budget, at least they couldn't get any worse.

### Soldier

wr. Harlan Ellison, dir. Gerd Oswald

A soldier from the future is transported to 20th century Earth, where he baffles the authorities while offering no more than name, rank, and serial number

*with Michael Ansara (Quarlo), Lloyd Nolan (Tom Kagan), Tim O'Connor (Paul Tanner), Catherine McLeod (Abby Kagen), Ralph Hart (Loren Kagen), Jill Hill (Toni Kagan), Marlowe Jensen (Sgt. Berry), Ted Stanhope (doctor), Allen Jaffe (enemy), Jaime Forster (news vendor)*

Harlan Ellison, the SF author who was to provide the second season's most acclaimed episode, "Demon with a Glass Hand", is one of the few — if not the one and only

— who considers the second season of *The Outer Limits* superior to the first. In my view, Ellison's episodes are almost the only second season episodes to match the first. Aside of his *Star Trek* episode "The City on the Edge of Forever", which was the subject of much controversy over the circumstances of its delivery and authorship, a situation discussed at length in my book *The Great Desilu Series of the 1960s*, he is best known for his two *Outer Limits* episodes.

A colorful character with acolytes, Ellison wrote "The Price of Doom" for *Voyage to the Bottom of the Sea* (an experience that ended abruptly when he slid along a conference table and punched a network executive in the face) and various episodes of *Burke's Law*, discussed herein. For *The Man from*

*UNCLE* he wrote the *Doctor Goldfoot*-style "The Sort of Do It Yourself Dreadful Affair", a wonderful episode, and "The Pieces of Fate Affair" (with New York playwright Yale Udoff), the latter piece becoming embroiled in a pointless legal controversy after he used parodies of other authors' names for his characters, and one supposed friend took exception.

No stranger to bringing lawsuits himself, he won a celebrated case in the 1970s after claiming his idea for a rejected 'robot cop' series had been stolen for the short-lived *Future Cop,* and in the '80s brought action against the film *The Terminator,* alleging it was a rip-off of this *Outer Limits* episode (in fact, *The Terminator* utilises well-worn ideas from at least four different *Outer Limits* episodes including "Soldier", "Controlled Experiment", "The Man Who Was Never Born", and Ellison's "Demon with a Glass Hand", but most closely resembles Franklyn Adreon's little-known no-budget 1966 feature *Cyborg 2087*). Indeed, as I never tire of pointing out, virtually every fantasy film from the 1980s on can be found to have origins in *Outer Limits* and *Twilight Zone* episodes.

In the 1970s Ellison worked on the short-lived series *The Starlost,* and in the 1980s contributed to the revival of *The Twilight Zone,* walking off the show after CBS broke a 'non-interference' promise to him. His reputation has survived being listed as 'conceptual consultant' on *Babylon 5,* and he contributed the opening narration for *Space Cases.*

Quarlo's arrival on Earth is filmed beautifully, with Ansara briefly looking like a toy soldier before the background materialises behind him (he is in exactly the same place, in the same Paramount backlot street, as Kirk and Spock in Ellison's time travel *Star Trek*). After a dazzling first ten minutes, the episode turns into a dull talk-a-thon intercut with cutaways to Quarlo's opponent trapped in limbo to keep us interested. It takes them a week to figure out that this obvious soldier is giving them name, rank, and serial number (although absurdly, it's in letters, which are not quite so finite; must be a small army). Luckily, it's Ellison's dialogue (mostly), and Michael Ansara's performance is magnificent, award-winning in any other genre. However, everyone is constantly amazed by the obvious, and if it's not obvious it's silly, such as the business with the family cat, which, being just an ordinary cat, could have gone for him at any time, and with a few flicks of his paw sent Quarlo off on a killing spree. But puss aside, who plays an important part in the climax, Kagan is taking a huge risk with his kids. One slip and they're dead. I'd have liked to have seen more dissent from the mother on this, but in *The Outer Limits*, wives are obedient (or, as in the exception "A Feasibility Study", disappointments). A spectacular and superbly executed special effect for the climax as Quarlo's enemy finally arrives, blasting through the wall of the Kagan house, is completely wasted on a bunch of actors who stand there like shop mannequins. The two disintegration effects are equally well-done and the future battleground sets are wonderful.

Often typecast in militaristic roles, Michael Ansara was also a similarly warlike warrior in "The Challenge" during the first season of *Lost in Space*, and a Klingon in "Day of the Dove" for *Star Trek*. He also appeared in the *Voyage to the Bottom of the Sea* feature film, and in the episodes "Hot Line" and "Killers of the Deep". In *Land of the Giants* he was a callous giant scientist in "On a Clear Night You Can See the Earth", and made many other TV appearances during the '60s, including equally ferocious characters in *The Man from UNCLE, The Girl from UNCLE, Bewitched, I Dream of Jeannie,* and *Time Tunnel.*

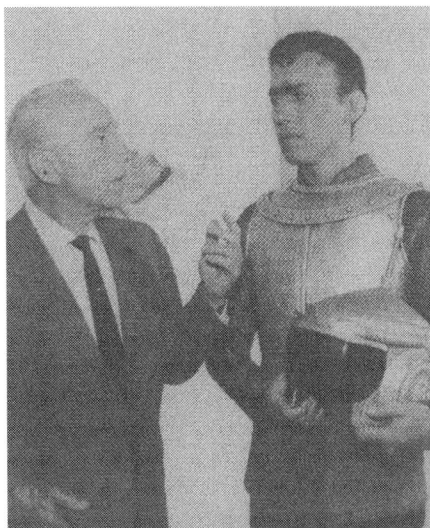

Lloyd Nolan, a veteran of gangster films, is miscast, and apparently cost the producers a small fortune. He would have been far better in O'Connor's part, and vice versa. Tim O'Connor, a fine actor, was previously the best thing in "Moonstone".

## The Invisible Enemy

wr. Jerry Sohl, dir. Byron Haskin

Two astronauts come to grief on Mars in unexplained circumstances after failing to follow procedures. Three years later, with improved technology, another ship sets out to investigate and continue with the original mission to prepare for colonisation. Despite all precautions, people once again start to disappear screaming...

*with Adam West (Major Merritt), Rudy Solari (Captain Buckley), Peter Marko (Captain Lazzari), Robert Do'Qui (Captain Johnson), Joe Maross (General Winston), Chris Alcaide (Colonel Danvers), Ted Knight (Mr. Jerome), Mike Mikler (Captain Thomas), Anthony Costello (Lt. Bowman), James Tartan (technician)*

This is another of the series' good old-fashioned 1950s-style men-in-space type of episodes that always sat rather incongruously with Stefano's gothic horrors during the first season. Melodramatic, pompous, and silly in the grand tradition of *Destination: Moon* and *Conquest of Space* and their imitators, this one has a clever mystery premise given away far too early.

The astronauts in this story may not go by the book, but the episode certainly does. Adam West is the stoic square-jawed safe-pair-of-hands commander, Rudy Solari is the loutish rule-breaking wiseguy who makes cracks about dames, and neither Peter Marko (also a victim in a similar storyline for *Star Trek's* "Galileo Seven") or Robert Do'Qui (later in the *Robocop* films) are around long enough to make an impression. This was Do'Qui's first TV role of many to follow. Among those back on Earth are Joe Maross, wonderful in *Twilight Zone's* "Third From the Sun" and *Time Tunnel's* "Massacre" (as the best General Custer ever put on film), and Ted Knight of *The Mary Tyler Moore Show*, then a bit player with later credits in *The Invaders*.

The monster is fake and ridiculous, a street carnival creation with claws on tentacles that don't even seem to be part of the head (which is quite silly enough on its own), but what really hurts the episode are the minor absurdities that come down to sheer apathy and thoughtlessness rather than budget — the security badges that have nothing but handwriting on them (at first I thought they were someone's lines for a forgetful actor that had come into shot), the astronauts not wearing gloves, and Rudy Solari's character picking a plant specimen by the head, like an infant, rather than by the root (as even a slightly older child would know to do).

And then, of course, there is dear, wonderful Adam West and his equally wonderful trademark mannerisms, which while harmless at the time, are now impossible to take seriously after years of *Batman* and *Family Guy*. West was not to blame for his later casting as the iconic '60s Batman of course, or the manner in which he played it; this was exactly the sort of role he was sending up those few years later, and would continue to do so for the rest of his career.

*Adam West as he appeared in the 1966 Batman feature film.*

## Counterweight

wr. Jerry Sohl, Milton Krims, dir. Paul Stanley

A simulated space flight to test the suitability of hopeful colonists is infiltrated by an alien intelligence

*with Michael Constantine (Joe Dix), Jacqueline Scott (Dr. Hendrix), Larry Ward (Keith Ellis), Charles Hradilac (Michael Lint), Crahan Denton (Dr. James), Stephen Joyce (Captain Branson), Sandy Kenyon (Professor Craif), Shary Marshall (stewardess)*

This is virtually a remake of the first season turkey "Second Chance", and this is only my second viewing of it. I last saw it a quarter century ago (it was never going to be first choice for a random watch!). Based on a published story by "The Invisible Enemy"'s Jerry Sohl, who was justly not very happy with the rewrite, it blows the admittedly guessable twist ending upfront (the simulation was originally a surprise reveal), leaving nothing but a dated character study of cartoon stereotypes. Slow to start, and as dull and depressing as the set and situation, this is not an episode to introduce the uninitiated to the joys of *The Outer Limits* with.

All the participants have solid reasons for going into the experiment, but few seem to have done any research on what the conditions might be, or what they might have signed up for in terms of what is required of them. Did they really not think about food or drink, compatibility, entertainment, or sexual concerns? The Donner party were better prepared.

The experiment seems a little screwy, too—261 days with everyone's hang-ups, in ugly, enclosed surroundings, and an unknown Judas Goat antagonising them… and that's without the alien infiltrator… If the powers-that-be want to experiment with simulated space flight, why not work on habitable surroundings conducive to comfort, and *then* run the tests? This one is built to fail.

Michael Constantine steals the show, while other actors usually given much less to do at least enjoy substantial parts. Nevertheless, the portraits painted are tired, cliched, and offensive. Constantine's builder is a self-made man, blue collar, a striver, and a taker of opportunities, and so of course is portrayed as greedy, ignorant, loud-mouthed, lecherous, and selfish. Like all career women of the '60s, Jacqueline Scott's character is portrayed as unloved and unfulfilled.

TV western veteran Larry Ward did numerous episodes of Irwin Allen shows, and they were all more entertaining than this! The dining room scene (there's no room on board for actual food, but they did bring along a full dining service) is laughable, and the alien Antheon somehow having access to the doll, or a convincing facsimile, is one alien ability too far.

### Behold Eck

wr. Edwin Abbott, William Cox, John Mantley, dir. Byron Haskin

An optician experimenting with lenses discovers the existence of a two-dimensional electrical creature that causes disruptions when it becomes trapped in the third dimension.

*with Peter Lind Hayes (Dr. James Stone), Joan Freeman (Elizabeth Dunn), Parley Baer (Dr. Bernard Stone), Douglas Henderson (Lt. Runyon), Jack Wilson (Sgt. Jackson), Marcel Herbert (Miss Willet), Sammy Reese (George Wilkenson), Taggart Casey (Fire Chief), Paul Sorenson (Grayson), Richard Gittings (newsreader), Lou Elias (electrical creature)*

Arriving at work to find his office mysteriously vandalised, optometrist James Stone finds his own glasses destroyed, and puts on the closest pair available to his prescription, through which he sees the bizarre two-dimensional electrical creature that did the damage. Although he knows where the time warp that brought him to this dimension is, Eck can't see to get back home any more than those humans without glasses can see him. Furthermore, Eck considers the open hole a menace to both dimensions, afraid that if a bird or 'plane flew through it, both worlds would perish. Stone creates the lenses required to enable Eck to find the time warp and return home.

A better title for this episode might be "An Eck-spectre Calls", so primitive and banal is the storytelling. It's not just Eck who's two dimensional. The characters are as flat and as boring as the sets, and the script is riddled with careless unexplained inconsistencies. What is an optometrist doing with quartz from a meteor? Why is it a 'time-warp' that brings Eck to our world? How can Eck steal a list of names in the teaser, but not leave the room with the lens at the end? And if Eck can slide *between* walls, why does he leave a huge hole in the wall at the second client's building? And how trite that the alien just happens to be susceptible to something earthly and simple—if not fire, then water, oxygen, salt or some other element, substance, solid or gas. Somewhere in this unusual yarn is a good idea—a two-dimensional creature that can only be seen with glasses and is in need of them—but the episode is so careless and slapdash that it can only be assumed that all concerned with shaping it before the actors arrived on set were totally disinterested.

Peter Lind Hayes was a vaudevillian, composer, and song-writer with a husband and wife act on the radio and then TV—a very odd choice to play the lead, and apparently quite insecure about the role. Joan Freeman would shortly marry director Bruce Kessler, and much of her later TV was in episodes directed by him. Her main claim to fame while plodding through second-rate TV guest roles was as the leading lady in the Elvis Presley film *Roustabout*. She also had a substantial role in "The Bat Cave Affair" for *The Man from UNCLE*. Like many young women of the period, she looked younger after 1964 than before.

This was the third of three roles in *The Outer Limits* for Douglas Henderson, and by far the most substantial. The most notable performance in the episode is given by the reliable Parley Baer, a veteran comedy actor. Bit player Taggart Casey also appeared in *It Conquered the World* and *The Navy vs. the Night Monsters*. The monster, although it looks like animation, is actually a guy in a suit.

Director Byron Haskin had wanted out at the end of season one, but was being held to his contract. He was missing out on other opportunities, and pissed off about it. He was also admirably cussed enough to take out his grievances on the series. Writer John Mantley was a hack for hire who was working from a discarded script by William Cox, who in turn had taken the idea of a two-dimensional world from a novel by Edwin Abbott. It was the fifth show filmed and the third to air. New producer Brady was already literally just cranking them out with professional journeyman hacks who couldn't give a shit. It was a long way from the naively unattainable ideals of Daystar.

### Wolf 359

wr. Richard Landau, Seeleg Lester, dir. Laslo Benedek

A scientist creates and observes a miniature society evolving on a lab slide, but evil resides there, and escapes

*with Patrick O'Neal (Jonathan Meredith), Sara Shane (Ethel Meredith), Peter Haskell (Peter Jellicoe), Ben Wright (Philip Exeter Dundee), Dabney Coleman (James Custer)*

This clever idea, hampered by a 1964 television budget that can't begin to do it justice, has the honor of being swiped and parodied by both *The Simpsons* and *South Park*. A scientific foundation obtains a chunk of a planet and recreates the conditions that will allow life to develop. Unfortunately, an evil life-form, in the shape of a typical *Outer Limits* creature (a clever little hand-puppet), has also developed.

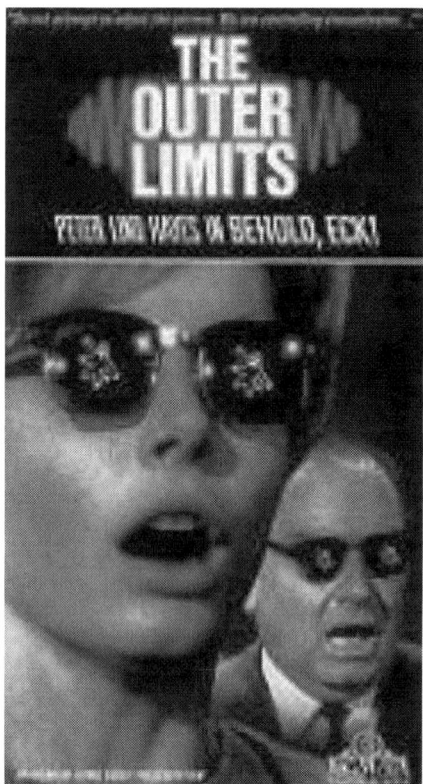

Absurdly, the planet evolves in exactly the same pattern as Earth, and Patrick O'Neal's Meredith becomes obsessed with seeing Earth's future reflected in his microcosm. Ultimately, when the creature breaks into our world, he decides he'd rather live, and aborts the project, although there's no reason to assume the creature will vanish with the destruction of the planet, even though it conveniently

does. The message appears to be that this world they've created is evil, and yet it's also supposed to be identical to Earth. This point of view is never confronted or clarified, although earlier drafts had a religious subtext that apparently posited that the artificial planet was godless, so evil 'moved in'. None of this is developed in the finished form. Also, didn't they just destroy a bunch of living people, literally playing God?

"Wolf 359" is interesting but not exciting, the problem being that O'Neal's character can only talk about what he's seeing, there's no budget to show it. It would work equally well, if not better, as a radio play. The episode never overcomes this fatal flaw, making it a major failure of the second season, despite an amiable cast.

Patrick O'Neal was a bland, capable, and likeable actor who did very little science-fiction during his career, or even cult TV, although he did do a rather poor *Twilight Zone*. Sara Shane also appeared in *Voyage to the Bottom of the Sea* at around this time, but retired shortly after both. Peter Haskell, however, worked regularly until his passing in 2010, but his best roles were all in the first few years of his career; this was his second TV job, and he went on to guest in episodes of *Doctor Kildare, The Man from UNCLE, Ben Casey, The Fugitive,* and *Rawhide*. Then, as the '70s loomed, it was downhill into less prestigious shows, bland cop series, daytime soaps, and short-lived series. Bit player and voice artiste Ben Wright was making his fourth and final contribution to *The Outer Limits*, although only his second onscreen (the other was "Nightmare"). He contributed to several cult TV series, including *The*

*Twilight Zone, Voyage to the Bottom of the Sea, Amos Burke — Secret Agent, The Man from UNCLE, The Time Tunnel,* and *The Invaders.* This was also Dabney Coleman's third of three bit parts.

## Keeper of the Purple Twilight

wr. Stephen Lord, Milton Krims, dir. Charles Haas

An alien anxious to experience emotion offers to absorb those of a frustrated scientist, whose all-too-human feelings are distracting him from his work. In fact, he's the first of an invasion force eager for the scientist's work to be completed, as his colleagues have use for it themselves...

*with Warren Stevens (Professor Plummer), Robert Webber/Mike Lane (Ikar), Gail Kobe (Janet Lane), Curt Conway (Frank Carlin), Edward Platt (David Hunt), Hugh Langtry, Gene Wiley, Leroy Ellis (alien soldiers)*

Behind a completely nonsensical title that sounds like a really bad 1970s progressive rock album is an above average 1950s pulp SF yarn made in 1964. "Keeper of the Purple Twilight" combines the all-time favorite number one and number two classic TV SF cliches and makes them work superbly in a thumping well-crafted monster mash highlighted by aliens straight out of a vintage Stan Lee Marvel comic, atmospheric dream-like camerawork and execution, and — with the exception of a couple of reaction shots that occur before the shot of the incident they are reacting to (a common trap that the original *Star Trek* fell into frequently) — smart editing.

The number one cliche is the insect-like race of all-alike conformist aliens that go against all that the free world stands for, and who would like nothing more than to strip all those individuals of their own personal humanity by bodysnatching or brainwashing.

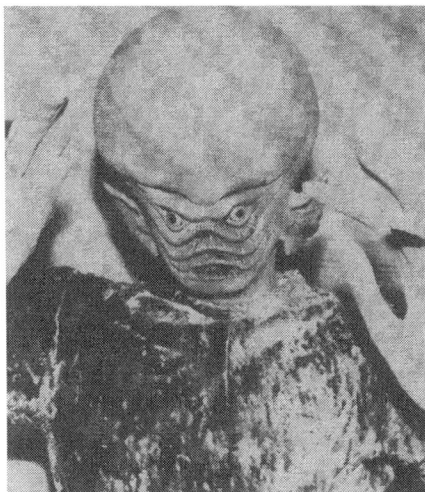

This is the standard sci-fi portrayal of the alien menace, decades later manifesting themselves in the form of *Star Trek — the Next Generation's* Borg, *Sliders'* Kromaggs, or *Stargate's* Gou'ald. Classic TV examples of the emotionless entities waiting to steal our free will include "Monster from Outer Space" in *Voyage to the Bottom of the Sea*, "This Side of Paradise" in *Star Trek*, and every episode of *The Invaders*.

The number two cliche is the emotionless being struggling to understand what it is to be human. Into this category fall Spock and Data of the *Star Trek* franchise (among many others in individual episodes), Rem of the TV incarnation of *Logan's Run*, and the title character of *Starman*. Ikar is one of numerous examples in *The Outer Limits* (see also "The Galaxy Being", "The Bellero Shield", "The Guests",

"Behold Eck", etc. etc.). In fact, if you were to strip TV SF of these two themes, well over half of everything ever produced would blink into oblivion.

This creepy and effective episode was devised by Stephen Lord, who made no secret of his distaste for the finished product, calling it 'junk'. He was then rewritten quite competently by Milton Krims, who he called 'a hack', sending producer Ben Brady a funeral wreath when it aired! All very amusing, but a little rich coming from the guy who scripted first season catastrophe "Specimen: Unknown", which unlike "Keeper" has no saving graces whatsoever and represented the series at an all-time low.

"Keeper of the Purple Twilight" may not be one of the series' more profound exercises in philosophical morality tales, but there is much to enjoy; it is not particularly hindered by the low budgets of the second season, and has some great fish-faced aliens. Cleverly, although they rightly look alike, given the nature of their race, Ikar has a slightly different appearance, with a large

brain, indicating his role in their society. The three thugs, enforcers sent first to aid him, and then to punish him, look like exactly what they are, with weight and mass, and evil appendages with tool-like weaponry in place of their left hands.

There's a wonderfully chilling scene early on, when Ikar sits in the back seat of Stevens' car, and calmly announces to the stressed-out and speeding motorist that "there is nothing to gain by suicide". Stevens is half-way through answering him when he realises there shouldn't be anyone there, and glances nervously into the car mirror to confirm that the car is empty—as indeed it now is!

The few special effects required here are the simplest and most effective in the book, aliens phasing in and out and disintegrator beams. The glowing eyes could have been aligned better, but that's a quibble. One of the most amusing effects shots right at the beginning of the episode shows Carlin going through his elaborate and expensive security system to enter his own building (through the usual over-familiar iron gates from "It Crawled Out of the Woodwork" and "Demon with a Glass Hand" to name but two), and then the alien arriving and stepping right through like a ghost. (One silly scene that could have been cut short quite easily has the alien getting out of a car door manually after walking through walls continuously through the entire episode). I suspect it was never intended to be shown.

Warren Stevens, a familiar face in TV SF after portraying the doctor in *Forbidden Planet,* was an ironic and inappropriate choice as the scientist who loses his emotions in a Faustian deal with extraterrestrials-- he was a stiff, wooden actor and

Robert Webber, a stiff, stocky, dignified-looking character actor with literally hundreds of TV and film roles to his credit, managed to appear in most of the classy TV shows produced from the '50s to the end of the '80s, as well as quite a few

*The heavy mob arrive… "Keeper of the Purple Twilight"*

barely registers any emotion *before* his deal with Ikar, and went on to portray emotionless alien menaces in both *Voyage to the Bottom of the Sea* ("Deadly Invasion") and *Star Trek* ("By Any Other Name"). Other stone-faced bad guy roles came in two other *Voyage,* as well as *Honey West, I Spy, The Man from UNCLE, Wonder Woman,* three *Mission: Impossible* and two *Land of the Giants.* He elicited rare sympathy as a murder victim in *Time Tunnel's* "One Way to the Moon", which saw him cast as the captain's right hand man once more.

others. His credits include *The Rifleman, Maverick, Bilko, Route 66, The Naked City, The Defenders, Ben Casey, The Fugitive, Ironside, Kojak, Mannix, Cannon, McCloud, Quincy,* and several *Rockford Files.* He played Maddie Hayes' father in several episodes of *Moonlighting,* and one of his final roles was in the 1989 SF mini-series *Something Is Out There,* which—while he did relatively little SF—caused him to metamorphose from human to alien once more... but somewhat more graphically than 1964 special effects had allowed!

Curt Conway was in the first season's "Moonstone". Edward Platt had appeared as stuffy bureaucrats in the first season's "Man with the Power" and "The Special One", but his later casting as the long-suffering Chief in Bond/*UNCLE* send-up *Get Smart* put paid to any further dreary straight roles as an authority figure! Gail Kobe plays one of the second season's many cloyingly devoted and supportive *Stepford Wife* figures, always ready with with a drink and an infatuated stare when the hero arrives home to dinner on the table — get a load of the outrageous '50s dress with the giant butterfly bow. These women are almost as scary as Ikar and his goon squad of extraterrestrial bug-eyed Beagle Boys! She had already played a similar role in the first season's pitiful "Specimen: Unknown", and also appeared in three *Twilight Zones*. After spending the '60s in guest-star roles of a similar nature, she later became a successful producer of daytime soaps. Given her immediate mistrust of Ikar, and her understandable terror when Ikar materialises in her bedroom, she seems to adapt to the role of educator in Earth ways with absurd haste, although the way the alien gradually insinuates his way into their lives is done quite well. And yes, she faints away when Ikar reveals his true self — but then who wouldn't? For the best ever whoops-I-just-saw-my-first-alien scene see Candy Clark in *The Man Who Fell to Earth*. She *literally* pisses herself.


### The Expanding Human

wr. Francis Cockrell, dir. Gerd Oswald

Experiments in mind-expanding drugs backfire and create a murderous Mr. Hyde persona...

*with Skip Homeier (Dr. Roy Clinton), Keith Andes (Dr. Peter Wayne), James Doohan (Lt. Branch), Vaughn Taylor (Dean Flint), Peter Duryea (Lee Morrow), Aki Aleong (Mr. Akada), Robert Doyle (Marc Lake), Mary Gregory (Mrs. Merrill/apt. manager), Barbara Wilkin (Susan Wayne), Jason Wingreen (Dr. Leland/ coroner), Troy Melton (Sgt. Alger), Michael Falcon (elevator operator), Shirley O'Hara (receptionist), Owen McGiveney (night watchman)*

This clunker by mystery writer Cockrell was another episode everybody concerned with the show was stuck with — an underdeveloped idea (Jekyll and Hyde meets 1960s LSD drug culture) and no money to do it. It has a wonderful cast with nowhere to go.

Homeier's typical mad scientist is trying to speed up evolution through expanded consciousness, but you can forget about seeing another "Sixth Finger", there's little subtlety here. Once again, Brady's cop show background resulted in another 'investigation' episode from a to b to c, the audience one step ahead as usual, just as in "Soldier" and "Behold Eck". It's another mystery that isn't mysterious.

Skip Homeier appeared in three *Voyage to the Bottom of the Sea* episodes and two *Star Trek*. Keith Andes also appeared in *Star Trek*, in "The Apple" (when it was his turn to look silly in make-up). In this episode they are related by Wayne's marriage to Clinton's sister, but they look so much like actual brothers, it's a shame the script wasn't amended.

The investigating cop is quite a large role for James Doohan at this point in his career, but it's strangely one of his least charismatic. His smaller roles in *Twilight Zone* and *Man from UNCLE* are far superior, despite their brevity. Vaughn Taylor was the henpecked husband in "The Guests", twitchy Robert Doyle was in "The Sixth Finger", and Jason Wingreen dived out of a window in "The Special One".

### Demon with a Glass Hand

wr. Harlan Ellison, dir. Byron Haskin

A visitor to the 20th century from Earth's future is pursued by ruthless hostile alien invaders determined to find the answer to a secret even he doesn't know — where is the population of the future Earth hiding — and why?

*with Robert Culp (Trent), Arlene Martel (Consuelo), Abraham Sofaer, Steve Harris, Rex Holman, Robert Fortier, Wally Rose, Bill Hart (Kyben)*

"Demon with a Glass Hand" was the one episode the series' original team claimed to be jealous of, and it's easy to see why. A cross between experimental theatre and a computer video game, "Demon" boasts the names of Harlan Ellison and Robert Culp, two people who turn anything they touch into gold — or at least manage to sprinkle it with gold dust: Culp, one of the most charismatic, clever and creative actors ever to grace a television screen, Ellison the writer whose plots wriggle on the screen and whose dialogue sings.

To relate the storyline of "Demon with a Glass Hand" in a simple synopsis is not really to do it justice; the detail becomes leaden, the action a formulaic chase (spoilers ahead). Onscreen though, the top-notch acting, script and direction convey desperation, fear, intrigue, despair, resignation, poignancy, fury — a panoply of emotions that dominate and electrify the screen from beginning to end. The whole thing fell together when Robert Justman, eccentric associate producer of *The Outer Limits* and *Star Trek*, came up with the inspired suggestion of location shooting in Los Angeles' baroque Bradbury Building, stylish setting of many a 1930s-based detective show — a chase up and down, rather than along and around the usual string of abandoned warehouses and waste ground. Ellison enthusiastically revised his script accordingly, and the rest was SF TV history.

There has been criticism of the art school appearance of the aliens, but series such as *Buffy* and *Charmed* demonstrate the effectiveness of this simple technique — what are the Grimlocks of *Charmed*, if not contemporary Kyben? The Kyben resemble the equally ruthless aliens of the later series *The Invaders,* in that like so many of TV and cinema's invading extraterrestrials they come in endless, expendable numbers and are always fanatically willing to die for their cause. From Daleks to Cylons to Borg to Gou'ald, their legions are unforgivably evil and unstoppable, so justifying constant,

of 1964 surrounded by the endless array of Ozzies, Beavers, and Harriets of early '60s TV, than to be bundled together into an amorphous multicultural hybrid. And what's with the 20th century guns? Okay, opticals are expensive, but some kind of feeble explanation would have been appreciated.

inexorable slaughter. No matter how many you kill, they just keep on coming and their total and convenient lack of emotion or compassion allows the heroes to keep on killing with equal remorselessness. However, Ellison gives them all different characters, a trait not usually evident in remorseless alien swarms. And then, of course, there was the inevitable network interference, the insistence that Arlene Martel had to be a non-defined all-purpose ethnic type so as not to cause offence, when surely nothing could cause more offence to the invisible multicultural millions

Also, there is far too much exposition in the narration and Culp's dialogue setting the scene; television is a lazily viewed, half watched mass market 'show me' medium, and in 1964 there was no rewind facility for the distracted viewer. "Demon with a Glass Hand" is one of the series' most literate post-Stefano scripts, perhaps the only one, but you have to pay attention, your mind dare not wander. Unlike the theatre—which the pre-Bradbury Building sequence closely resembles (the panda-eyed Kyben look more like performance artists in hairnets than aliens)—the nature of TV viewing doesn't always demand, or receive, total concentration, however much its practitioners might like to think it should. *The Outer Limits* was a show you had to pay attention to, but under Stefano, it was a visual experience as much as a literate one. "Demon with a Glass Hand" requires the audience to listen, rather than watch, but Ellison wisely often gives information twice.

*Arlene Martel as Spock's bride in Paramount's Star Trek; a blue-faced Abraham Sofaer as he appeared in 20th Century Fox's Lost in Space.*

And fortunately, Ellison is brilliant at dialogue, and when his words are given to actors of the calibre of Robert Culp, the fusion of the two is dynamic. Whatever the failings of the episode, and they are few and irrelevant in comparison to what is given in exchange, Robert Culp's intense, driven performance of calm urgency makes the whole thing work in a way that only he and maybe half-a-dozen other small screen actors could. The only

drawback to the sheer three-dimensional humanity of Culp's performance is the ultimate revelation that he's an android. Actors with smooth, ordinary-looking faces (Claire Stansfield as "Alpha" for *The Flash* or James Darren as "The Mechanical Man" for *Voyage to the Bottom of the Sea* spring to mind) make more convincing human-made humans than an actor with the weary humanity of Culp. Of course a more robotic appearance would have wasted Ellison's story, deprived us of Culp's performance, and betrayed the twist ending... but it still feels like a cheat.

As for director Byron Haskin, bad-tempered curmudgeon that he was, the style and skill he puts into this episode shows perfectly well what he could do when he wanted to, and makes his miserable apathetic half-hearted efforts on the likes of "The Invisible Enemy" and "Behold Eck" even more irritating. So he didn't like the scripts, had a beef with the producers—he still had an obligation to the actors and the audience not to cast them adrift.

Arlene Martel's other claim to fame in the annals of TV SF is that she portrayed Spock's scheming bride-to-be in the *Star Trek* episode "Amok Time". She was often cast as exotic untrustworthy types in '60s TV of all shades, and can be seen in *My Favorite Martian*, *I Dream of Jeannie*, *The Man from UNCLE*, *Hogan's Heroes*, *The Wild Wild West*, *Mission: Impossible*, *Bewitched*, *Get Smart*, and *The Monkees*, often as Mata Hari types. Abraham Sofaer was the Thasian minder of "Charlie X" in *Star Trek*, and the warlike Sobram of "The Flaming Planet" (which wasn't flaming) in *Lost in Space*. He also appeared in mortal form in "Revenge of the

Gods" for *The Time Tunnel* and "The Brain Killer Affair" for *The Man from UNCLE.* He has a wonderfully distinctive and funereal voice, perfect for the Kyben leader. Haskin had used him for the role of the wizard in the beautiful adventure film *Captain Sindbad.*

Rex Holman worked mostly in westerns and appeared in *Star Trek's* "Spectre of the Gun". Robert Fortier was an *Outer Limits* regular who appeared in "Production and Decay of Strange Particles" and "Controlled Experiment", as well as portraying the drunken alien in the famous Scotty drinking scene in *Star Trek's* "By Any Other Name". He often played drunks for Robert Altman, notably in *Popeye.* He's excellent as a particularly vicious version of the Kyben species, gloatingly informing Trent he's not afraid to die. "Then why are you whispering?" replies Trent, spitefully.

In a season in which *The Outer Limits* was peopled with an abundance of Joe and Helen Normal types swilling Martinis and mowing lawns, "Demon with a Glass Hand" is immediately different and original, standing out a mile from the rest of the season. It is extraordinary must-watch television, just as you have heard it is.

### Cry of Silence

wr. Louis Charbonneau, Milton Krims, Robert C. Dennis, dir. Charles Haas

A couple have travelled off the beaten track to survey a desert property they've invested in... but find the desert quite literally alive...

*with Eddie Albert (Andy Thorne), June Havoc (Karen Thorne), Arthur Hunnicutt (Lamont)*

One of the series' numerous Mr. and Mrs. All-American average couple types gets trapped in the desert while checking out real estate and they are assailed by a cosmic force from a meteorite that takes over and manipulates the first object it arrives at—tumbleweeds, rocks, frogs, and even the dead zombie form of a local yokel take turns to attack them in an atmosphere of mounting hysteria. Other than being yet another episode on the theme of lack of understanding/communication ("The Galaxy Being", 'The Mice", "Second Chance", etc), a worthy sci-fi topic in itself (perhaps the most important one), the episode has nothing to say on a deeper level, and never overcomes the inherent silliness of the sentient tumbleweeds theme. As ever with dumb ideas, the episode went through a number of writers, ending in the capable hands of speedy hack-for-hire Robert Dennis, a former pulp writer and rewrite man for *The Untouchables* with a good ear for sharp and amusing dialogue. Consequently, the middle aged couple portrayed by a Lucy-ish June Havoc and *Green Acres'* Eddie Albert are at least likably three dimensional, and Dennis gives the absurd visual theme a credibility lesser writers couldn't have hoped for.

A notably clever touch is Andy's constant insistence on logic, and the situation's frustrating lack of it. The desert scenes, in which Havoc's character is already convinced the tumbleweeds have life, and Albert's average joe humors her until he becomes suddenly aware she's right, is particularly well done. These scenes bring to mind the desert-as-ominous-menace ambience of *It Came from Outer Space*, in which once again a skittish female character is frightened by bushes and trees and 'feelings' while the male can't see it. "When we get back to town I'll give up the idea of living on a farm honey" says Eddie presciently, as that was the theme of his future sit-com. Unluckily for her, Eva Gabor, the city wife stuck in rural America with him in his long-running sit-com, didn't have menacing foliage to sway him with.

The only other cast member is Arthur Hunnicutt in another of his dotty old hayseed roles (he was marvellous in *Twilight Zone's* beautiful "The Hunt"). "They didn't act like natural tumbleweeds, so I watched 'em. But I stayed too long. Now do you understand? You, me, your missus, nobody can leave. There just isn't any way of getting out... every night, they scratch at the door, tryin' to get in!". Hunnicutt always acted like he was half-way on the road to being a zombie, and in this episode he gets there (his wife left a few days earlier... he likes to think she got out of the canyon!...). His gradual descent into madness, his decline and then demise, builds the tension to the point of justifying Karen's constant and quite understandable hysteria, in contrast to Andy's desperate attempts to cling onto reason in the persistent face of all absence of it, as tumbleweeds explode and frogs dissolve in the water that should be rejuvenating them. All this builds to the ultimate horror, as boulders slam themselves against the farmhouse and the alien force takes the inevitable step of reanimating Lamont's rock-crushed corpse! It's a much better episode than its reputation would have you believe;

it makes you laugh while your skin crawls. Shame Gerd Oswald wasn't available to direct.

### I Robot

wr. Otto Binder, Earl Binder, Robert C. Dennis, dir. Leon Benson

A reclusive and cynical lawyer can't resist coming out of retirement when a robot is put on trial for the murder of his creator

*with Howard Da Silva (Thurman Cutler), Leonard Nimoy (Judson Ellis), Marianna Hill (Nina Link), Read Morgan (Adam Link, robot), Ford Rainey (D.A. Thomas Coyle), Hugh Sanders (Sheriff Barclay), Peter Brocco (Professor Link), Mary Jackson (Mrs. McCrae, housekeeper), John Hoyt (Professor Hebbel), Robert Sorrells (Fred, handyman), Christine Matchett (Evie Cooper, little girl), Ken Drake (Judge), John Caper Jnr. (Adam's voice), John Hudkins (truck driver)*

For a science-fiction series of the 1960s, there were surprisingly few robots in *The Outer Limits*. Expensive, of course, but there were many ready-made ones out there, including of course the redoubtable Robby from *Forbidden Planet*, who made more guest appearances after his two feature films than many minor human actors manage on the guest-star circuit. The robot here is not immediately recognisable, but it has a Columbia serials look about it, with a wonderful lopsided smile of a mouth, and appears to have been taped together out of existing materials—*literally* taped together, although the tape wouldn't have shown up on 1964 TV sets.

Although they both enjoyed licensed comic-books in their own name, *The Twilight Zone* and *The Outer Limits* both, more than anything, resembled those wonderful five or ten page stories of sci-fi and the supernatural that appeared in the Lee/Kirby/Ditko Marvel comics of the late '50s and early '60s, bite-size twist ending morality tales about alien invaders, stoic scientists, and greedy or selfish men who got their comeuppance in the last panel. Although based on a novel by pulp novelist brothers Otto and Earl Binder (writing under 'Eando'—E and O), the first in a series started in 1937, this little tale more closely resembles such fare more than any other in the series save, perhaps, "Children of Spider County" and "Keeper of the Purple Twilight". *

* In fact, it may even have been done in comic form; the ending seems very, very familiar to me.

As the episode opens, a screaming child points a redneck posse in the direction of her supposed attacker, Adam Link, a lumbering but intellectual metallic robot created by Professor Link. Adam has been accused of murdering his creator, a kindly, benevolent man, and gives himself up to the police without any trouble. Professor Link's daughter Nina opposes the destruction of Adam, claiming that as the sole surviving relative, the robot belongs to her.

Cynical reporter Judson Ellis sends Nina to the irascible and unorthodox retired lawyer Thurman Cutler, knowing that the involvement of such a colorful character will give him a lively story. Although he now lives like a hermit in the woods, Cutler can't resist the chance to humiliate the establishment that rejected him, and comes out of retirement to represent Adam for the dog and pony show of the decade.

What Marvel might have told in five minutes had to be spun out to fill an hour slot, of course, but *The Outer Limits* knew all the tricks. Firstly, Ben Brady was finally on familiar ground with a courtroom story—*those* he understood. Director Leon Benson was, inevitably, a *Perry Mason* stalwart. Secondly, the episode has a wonderful cast, with former blacklisted actor Howard Da Silva licking his lips at such a meaty part as rebel lawyer Thurman Cutler, and bit player Leonard Nimoy, later *Star Trek's* Spock, finally given a role that didn't just involve him standing in the background behind the guy with most of the lines. Nimoy is wonderful as cynical newspaper reporter Judson Ellis, and has not yet developed all those mannerisms he created for Mr. Spock that were so difficult to shake off afterwards and blighted his role as Paris in *Mission: Impossible*. Finally, the dialogue has been provided by one of the sharpest writers of same in the business, Robert C. Dennis. Dennis gives the entire exercise an aura of credibility ("Alright, somebody's coming. What of it?" says Cutler to his dog, instead of the usual "What is it, boy?" anyone else would have written; and the wonderful "Barclay never did have brains enough to pour water out of a boat"). And so, an hour is easily filled.

### The Inheritors (two parts)

wr. Sam Neuman, Ed Adamson, Seeleg Lester, dir. James Goldstone

Government agents hunt down soldiers who have been taken over by an alien intelligence for a mysterious and unknown purpose that even they don't understand...

*with Robert Duvall (Adam Ballard), Steve Ihnat (Lt. Phillip Minns), Donald Harron (Ray Harris), James Shigeta (Captain Newa), Ivan Dixon (Sgt. Conover), James Frawley (Private Renaldo), Dee Pollack (PFC Hadley), Dabbs Greer (Mr. Larkin), Robert Cinder (Mr. Jessup), Ted De Corsia (Secretary of Science), William Wintersole (Professor Whitsett), Leon Askin (shop superintendent), Robert J. Nelson (surgeon), Linda Hutchins (nurse), Sy Prescott (military policeman), Yoneo Iguchi (soldier), Paulle Clark (children's nurse), Jon Cedar (Grainger), Joanne Stewart (Miss Steen), Jan Shutan (Mrs. Subiron), Kim Hector (Johnny Subiron), Suzanne Cupito (Minerva Gordon), David Brady (Daniel Masters)*

As with all these reviews, but particularly this episode, if you don't want to know the big reveal, the punchline, then you must watch the two parts first, because the only way to discuss the story is to reveal the ending.

Government officials discover that four soldiers (played by Steve Ihnat, Ivan Dixon, Dee Pollack, and James Frawley) have been shot in the head while on duty in Vietnam and acquired a set of uniform additional brain waves. When they recover, they become part of an alien intelligence. Robert Duvall, in a far more pedestrian role than he had in "The Chameleon", is government agent Adam Ballard, assigned to locate the soldiers, who have now disappeared (this is another of Brady's a, b, c, investigations). Ballard interviews Lt. Minns, the latest soldier, who is still in the hospital, but learns nothing other than that he is studying finance and that his IQ is rising phenomenally, as did the others' intelligence. Each of the other three soldiers have also been absorbing knowledge on specific subjects.

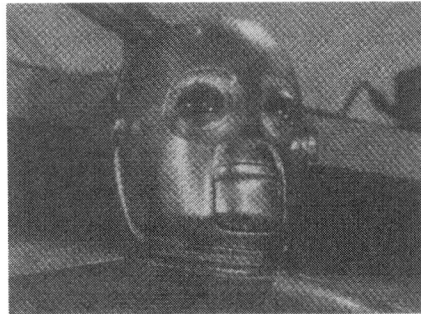

*Adam Link, the misunderstood and persecuted mechanical man of "I, Robot".*

Ballard travels to Vietnam in an attempt to locate where the bullets were made out of an unknown ore, and discovers a meteor. As the scientists in Washington analyse a sample of it, Minns, now a telepath, simply walks out of the hospital to freedom using his hypnotic powers. As the authorities scramble to locate him, Minns is cleaning up at a New York Stock Exchange, making money to send to the other soldiers and finance their mysterious mission. The mission's purpose, slowly being revealed to the four men piecemeal, is on a 'need-to-know' basis for no particular reason that is either given, or makes sense. But it is benevolent, if self-serving.

The message of "The Inheritors" is that we automatically assume that a covert alien plot is for evil purposes, but not that it might be for good. How unreasonable of us. This is all very well, but the episode *plays* sinister, and good deeds don't need to be performed covertly; the Duvall character's suspicions—assumptions, even—that the alien activity is hostile are entirely logical, sensible, and justified. Only a complete fool would assume that all this activity is happening for a good reason on the basis of what we have here. We are dealing with bodysnatching, alien intrusions into the free will of soldiers by way of a bullet, and the four tortured men not even knowing what they're doing, or why they're doing it (there's a beautiful scene with Ivan Dixon in a church, holding a candle, and asking if what he's doing is right, directly to God; another fine scene has James Frawley's tormented Renaldo becoming even more deeply disturbed by the minute, and a moment right near the end when Minns, abducting children, has tears streaming down his face that a blind girl can't see). While Frawley and Dixon's characters are clearly profoundly troubled by their actions, Ihnat and Pollack (until the climax) play out their part as if they *are* evil, behaving in a very sly manner; the scenes of Ihnat making off with the child at the end of part one are even creepier in today's cruel world than they were then.

At no point do the aliens even ask for co-operation. At no point do they make contact and say 'trust us'. At no point do they consider the reactions of the parents to their abducted children. They just behave in a completely presumptuous way. In other words, regardless of the alien intentions, and the wonderful goodness of it all, the authorities are entirely right to be deeply suspicious from start to finish. The message of the episode appears to be that we should just throw up our hands and submit to the extraterrestrial activity and trust that the brainwashed soldiers acting against their will are doing something delightful for humankind while we apologise for being guilt-consumed doubters. This is ridiculous. Not as ridiculous as the spaceship door being held open by string, but *quite* ridiculous.

*Robert Duvall as he appeared in the science-fiction film THX-1138.*

Audiences should not feel guilty about assuming the worst along with Ballard and Harris either. The episode is played with Ballard as the hero and identification figure, and Ihnat plays his role as sinister and suspicious as possible. Everything about the show, from the music, to the casting, to the dialogue, plays the plot as suspect until the big reveal. A speech written for Ballard in which he concedes that the alien activity *may* not be hostile but they can't be sure risked giving the game away, and was rightly removed to make him resolute and certain. But how much anguish might have been avoided if the alien intelligence hadn't deliberately kept everyone in the dark until the last moment? What was the point? The aliens might have been able to take *thousands* of children to better lives, rather than the half a dozen the production could afford (and with permission).

Given the emphasis of the script and direction, all the performances are excellent and perfectly judged, with the single almost inexplicable exception of Donald Harron, who was usually marvellous in everything he went near (see his Australian UNCLE agent in *The Spy With My Face*, or his Robin Hood for *Time Tunnel*). Here, his stiff gimlet-eyed official, self-important but almost bordering on panic, is laughable. Introduced to Ihnat, who says he saw the FBI types stationed outside, he asks "Are they that conspicuous?", and the answer, as filmed, is hell, yes! Hilariously obvious.

James Frawley, later a director, appeared in the *Voyage to the Bottom of the Sea* episodes "The Price of Doom", "The Exile" and "Killers of the Deep" and two *Man from UNCLEs*. Ivan Dixon, also later a director, spent most of the '60s in the sit-com *Hogan's Heroes* in a thankless token role, but also appeared to advantage in guest shots in *I Spy* and *The Name of the Game*. Dee Pollack's numerous TV roles were mostly, but not exclusively in westerns and cop shows. Steve Ihnat was best known as Garth in *Star Trek's* "Whom Gods Destroy" and was the bad guy in the movie *In Like Flint*. He appeared three times in *Mission: Impossible*, and in numerous TV roles in the '60s and early '70s.

"The Inheritors" might have made more sense as the two separate stories it began as.

According to the Schow and Frentzen book, writer Sam Neuman, another *Perry Mason* guy, had come in with the idea of a brain operation in which the surgeons suddenly discover a second brainwave pattern in the patient, but had nowhere else to go with it after that. Ed Adamson, a writer for numerous different series, had come up with a creepy idea for a Pied Piper-like alien who spirited away children (this concept of the mythical figure having been a visiting extraterrestrial turned up many years later in an episode of *Land of the Giants*). It was a difficult and uncomfortable marriage of two intriguing ideas manacled together.

However, Seeleg Lester, who worked so intensely on the project that Brady had to bring in Milton Krims and Robert Dennis to the show to keep the other episodes rolling out, and James Goldstone, who directed it, were both extremely satisfied with the end result. They both saw Duvall's Ballard as a bad guy, rather than a man wrong for the right reasons.

### The Duplicate Man

wr. Clifford D. Simak, Robert C. Dennis, dir. Gerd Oswald

A rogue scientist creates a clone of himself that appreciates life more than he, and starts to take over his identity

*with Ron Randell (Henderson James/Duplicate Man), Sean McClory (Captain Emmet), Constance Towers (Laura James), Steven Geray (Basil Jerichau), Ivy Bethune (Miss Thorson), Alan Gifford (zoo guide), Konstantin Shayne (Murdoch, handyman), Jeffrey Stone (police officer), Mike Lane (creature)*

Like much science-fiction of the '50s and '60s, Clifford Simak's "The Duplicate Man" presumes that the exploration of space has continued to progress after the moon landing. Various animal life-forms have been found during the '80s and '90s, some of them harmless, one or two decidedly not so. A curious combination of intellect and savagery, the Megasoid is a sly, furry alien creature whose ownership is completely banned on 21st century Earth. Naturally, this makes it very desirable to a certain kind of mentality. Scientist Henderson James has been dumb enough to keep one in his cellar, a capital crime, as the creature is virulently murderous, a killer without pause or reason. When it inevitably and easily escapes, he uses another scientific progression, cloning, to make an illegal duplicate of himself to hunt it down, hence the title of the story.

Not a lot of this episode makes much sense. The facts seem to have been decided upon to accommodate the otherwise irrelevant events in the story, to explain the characters', and the monster's motivations, which would otherwise make no sense. Rather than the story being propelled by their actions, events are taking place to justify the story. The monster is silly and tatty, the future/present is amusingly wrong, and the acting is extremely poor. It takes six bullets, all delivered at different times, to kill the creature, yet this is the only weapon anyone attempts to use on it. And there is the small question of the three dead bodies in the garden at episode's end, a problem too great for the incompetent but complicit handyman, I fear. Even the usually excellent Robert Dennis couldn't do anything to help this one, which was more clever and concise in its original form, a solid short story by Simak written in 1951 titled "Goodnight, Mr. James", the punchline.

Credited onscreen as a pedestrian is the ever-welcome Jonathan Hole, whose scene appears to have hit the cutting room floor.

*Ron Randell as "The Duplicate Man"*

### The Brain of Colonel Barham

wr. Sidney Ellis, Robert C. Dennis, dir. Charles Haas

A terminally ill astronaut agrees to have his brain placed in a machine to benefit space exploration... but it begins to grow new cells and assume an identity — and agenda — of its own

*with Grant Williams (Major McKinnon), Anthony Eisley (Colonel Barham), Elisabeth Perry (Jennifer Barham), Douglas Kennedy (General Pettit), Martin Kosleck (Dr. Hausner), Wesley Addy (Dr. Rahm), Peter Hansen (Major Locke), Paul Lukather (Ed Nichols), Robert Chadwick (guard)*

A rehash of *Donovan's Brain* and a dozen others. There are a few good lines of dialogue, as there would be with Dennis on hand, but it's a long, slow haul to the inevitable outcome.

Grant Williams is best known for *The Incredible Shrinking Man*, one of the finest SF films of the 1950s. While that film was worthy of *The Outer Limits* or *The Twilight Zone*, this episode was not such a notable credit, although he does as well as might be hoped in what is essentially the lead role after Barham has been put in the tank and Eisley's bitter egotist is out of it.

Aside of *The Incredible Shrinking Man*, Williams was also in '50s sci-fi films *The Monolith Monsters* and *The Leech Woman*. After a regular role in the early '60s detective series *Hawaiian Eye*, his career declined into occasional guest star parts. Anthony Eisley also featured in *Hawaiian Eye*, had a recurring role in *The FBI*, and appeared several times in *The Invaders*. He also hit the guest star circuit for most of his career, and his B-movie sci-fi credits included *The Wasp Woman*, *The Navy vs. the Night Monsters*, *Journey to the Centre of Time*, and even worse! Douglas Kennedy was a western regular with a recurring role as the sheriff on *The Big Valley*. His B-movie sci-fi credits were *The Alligator People* and *The Amazing Transparent Man*. Martin Kosleck spent his entire career playing Nazis and mad scientists, and he's a bit loopy here too…

**The Premonition**

wr. Ib Melchior,    Sam Roeca,
dir. Gerd Oswald

A couple trapped in a moment in time discover that their daughter is about to be killed or injured in a traffic accident… unless they can think of a way to save her before time resumes at its natural rate…

*with Dewey Martin (Jim Darcy), Mary Murphy (Linda Darcy), William Bramley (General Baldwin), Kay Kuter (man in limbo), Dorothy Green (childminder), Emma Dyson (Janie), Coby Denton (gate sentry)*

This is a weird one, but mostly because it's more like a *Twilight Zone* than an *Outer Limits*. Linda Darcy is on her way to a military air base with daughter Janie to see her husband Jim, a test pilot, land his new experimental aircraft. Leaving the child at a nursery on the base, she instead sees him crash—alive, but trapped in a ten second time rift with her, where everything is frozen. The two of them have been thrown forward in time, with Jim's 'plane in real time still in the sky above them and another car with a frozen Linda at the wheel ten seconds behind hers ("It's my car and I'm in it! Is this some kind of nightmare, or are we dead?"). All around them, animals in motion, birds in flight, everything is frozen in time. First searching for their child, they find her no longer in the nursery, but then encounter her frozen form on a bicycle, with the childminder in frozen pursuit. Making their way to the Flight Control centre, Jim Darcy realises that he's broken the time barrier and "skidded through into the future — jumped ahead somehow into this limbo state". Suddenly his blood runs cold, as he realises a large vehicle has also moved — the brake is off, and the vehicle is inexorably headed for a collision course with his child's bike. They calculate that time is moving by one hour to one second, giving them two hours to save their child's life.

Although produced in haste near the end of the season, with Dewey Martin filling in for the suddenly unavailable Don Gordon (of "Second Chance" and "The Invisibles"), this is a fascinating and fraught story of parental desperation. Sadly, at this point, everyone knew the show's days were numbered, and unfortunately it shows in the production. Inevitably then, there are moments of carelessness. The teaser teases nobody, and could be removed from the broadcast (but don't!) without losing anything — performance, suspense, or information. That old reliable the countdown could have been used to show the set up of the premise — the little girl on her bicycle, the truck starting to roll — but after we see the little girl leave there is no further attempt in the editing process to suggest a dangerous situation. And if the aircraft is "liable to blow" why's Darcy just standing there, fussing about a fire extinguisher? There's nothing to save and nothing's at risk except the wreckage, out in the middle of nowhere.

There are also a few flaws in the script, as there always are when television plays with time, including

the presence of an old science-fiction time travel cliche that never makes any sense and in particular makes no sense here — the couple notice that their watches have stopped. Why? Everything that is with them is unaffected; this is the whole point of the story. Watches are not truly representative of time, they're just man-made mechanical devices; there's no reason for them not to be carrying on regardless. I concede it's a minor point, but it's a recurring silly cliche of science-fiction, where timepieces mysteriously collude and conspire with time itself.

The man in limbo, standing in for the requisite 'monster', is also a curious anomaly. He wants the Darcy's to fail in their attempt to return to reality so that they will somehow take his place (we don't know how he figured out these 'rules' — how does he know all three won't stay trapped in the time warp?), but tells them exactly what they must do to escape. Had the program-makers had, dare I say it, a little more time, they might have created a more meaningful tragic character — he could have been lonely, but persuaded to reveal to them the secrets of departure... or they could have tried to take him back with them, but found only a pile of dust when time resumed, his moment missed long ago. Instead, hr just wanders off, Basil Exposition, back to his eternal misery, a loose thread in the episode's Gordian Knot.

Dewey Martin appeared in the sci-fi feature *The Thing from Another World* and an equally famous *Twilight Zone*, "I Shot an Arrow Into the Air". Mary Murphy's claim to fame was a key part in *The Wild One* with Brando, after which she mostly worked in TV.

### The Probe

wr. Sam Neuman, Seeleg Lester, dir. Felix Feist

Lost at sea after a 'plane crash, a group of people find themselves prisoners in a barren alien environment

*with Mark Richman (Jeff Rome), Ron Hayes (Coberly), Peggy Ann Garner (Amanda), William Stevens (Dexter), William Boyett (Beeman), Richard Tretter (radio operator), Janos Prohaska (microbe creature)*

Filmed on a bare bones set with a dedicated cast for a pittance, this was an intelligently written mystery that gradually escalates into suspenseful hysteria. True to the philosophy of the series as conceived by Stevens and Stefano, it was a suitable and acceptable way to bow out. Unfortunately, the script isn't very kind to the female character, but she is as intelligent, if not more so, than the guys—made up of an intelligent but sexist tough guy, an early victim, and a plank— and she does get to save the day.

"The Probe" could be performed as a stage play. Four survivors of a light 'plane crash find their life craft inside some kind of alien ship; "The 'plane gone, the ocean gone, where are we?".

As we know the players are in an episode of *The Outer Limits* called "The Probe", and they don't, it's easy for us to figure out that they're under an alien microscope; the reveal that they are not at sea in their raft (they assume they're in the calm 'eye of the storm') is brilliantly done. After that, we're one step ahead of them all the way, as everyone stands around figuring out the obvious. Luckily, no-one contemplates the possibility of being dissected, or something equally hideous. In fact, the extraterrestrials are remarkably humanitarian, once they themselves realise what's going on. A nice end for a series like *The Outer Limits,* a series dominated by stories of lack of communication between us and the stars, that ended with a story about those first stumbling steps groping toward successful and positive contact.

The microbe creature, an advantageous and clever addition to the mix, is an early incarnation of the Horta creature from *Star Trek's* famous "Devil in the Dark" episode. Crawling around underneath the costume is legendary monster man Janos Prohaska, of course. For his fascinating story, see "The Architects of Fear" and "The Sixth Finger".

William Stevens had a very minor role in the pilot, thus earning the distinction of appearing in the series' first and last episode! The same could be said of Mark Richman, who also appeared in an early episode, "The Borderland", the first actually made for the series itself. A familiar face in '60s SF TV, he appeared twice in *Voyage to the Bottom of the Sea,* in "The Monster's Web" and "Secret of the Deep", and twice in *The Invaders,* in "The

Leeches" and "Inquisition". He was also in the *Land of the Giants* episode "Panic" and a memorable final episode of *The Man from UNCLE,* "The Seven Wonders of the World Affair".

Peggy Ann Garner was a successful child actress who, like so many, never made the transition to equal adult success. She made various occasional appearances in TV guest shots throughout the '60s and '70s, of which this was one. Ron Hayes spent most of his career in westerns, to which he was well suited, making multiple appearances in shows like *Wagon Train, Rawhide, Gunsmoke,* and *Bonanza.* He had regular roles in three series during his career, *Everglades, The Rounders,* and — for a while — *Lassie.*

William Boyett's career in TV SF has also spanned the decades, from minor roles in *Voyage to the Bottom of the Sea, The Invaders,* *Batman,* and *The Man from UNCLE* to *Amazing Stories* and *Star Trek — the Next Generation.* However, he spent most of his career playing bit parts as cops, military men, or indeed pilots. He had recurring roles in *Highway Patrol* in the 1950s, and, as a favorite of Jack Webb, frequent bits in *Dragnet* during both incarnations, and in *Adam 12* and *Emergency* in the '70s. This was one of William Stevens' larger roles; he also became a cast member of *Adam 12.*

During the cop show glut of the early '70s, and the general blandness of even the sci-fi shows of that decade and on, series with the passion, class, and creativity of *The Outer Limits* were a distant memory. Fortunately, with DVD and other media offering television series of the past on a whim, we now return control of your television sets to you…

series ends

## Burke's Law

The U.S. TV networks CBS, NBC, and ABC all believed that the 1963-'64 season would be remembered for serious, hard-hitting, relevant drama. Those shows are long forgotten. Hindsight shows us that the four most important shows that year in terms of future influence were, as is so often the case, elsewhere in the schedules — two (*The Outer Limits* and *The Fugitive*) believed to be no hopers, the other two (*My Favorite Martian* and *Burke's Law*) inconsequential fluff. The two sci-fi shows were on the fringes of the schedule, the other two considered long-shots in a thin season. All four were far more successful, and have been far more durable and influential, than the social conscience melodramas fussed over at the time.

*Burke's Law* had begun life as a one-off on the *Dick Powell Theatre*. Powell was considered one of the nicer men in the TV industry, and his Four Star Productions had a solid reputation for having found the middle ground between the overwrought so-called 'quality' drama anthologies and the

*Charles Boyer (center), with David Niven (right), two of the founders of Four Star, with co-star Gig Young in publicity for their series The Rogues. The other two of the 'Four Stars' were Ida Lupino and Dick Powell. Powell hired the young Aaron Spelling as first a writer, then producer.*

more entertaining fare the public really wanted. At a time when television was a side activity for the major film companies, Powell had seen the future and started up one of the first independents, with fellow actors Charles Boyer, Ida Lupino, and David Niven. As a company owned and run by actors, it was able to utilise the contacts, gossip, and friendships of four people who had been in the business for years, knew who to hire because they were on the way up, or reliable, and who not to hire (or who to help out if they were on the way down). If you had a reputation, good or bad, one or more of the four knew about it. And most importantly, they knew a good script, knew a good role, and knew their audience. They wanted *stories*, not 'drama'. Even more importantly, they saw the potential and inevitability of television. While none of them had given up their film careers, they didn't regard television as second-rate. Also, all four were pure Hollywood; they had none of the *Playhouse 90* pretensions of New York. They made film, not videotaped stage plays, and they made popular entertainment... but with class. *Burke's Law* epitomised that philosophy more than any other show they made. And from 1952 to 1966, they made a lot of shows.

*The young Aaron Spelling, his then-wife Carolyn Jones, and Dick Powell (as Amos Burke) seated, and surrounded by some of the cast for "Who Killed Julie Greer?", the first episode of The Dick Powell Theater.*

A single teleplay, which aired in September 1961, marked the first edition of *Dick Powell Theatre* and the first appearance of Captain Amos Burke of the LAPD, then a humble Inspector. It had been titled "Who Killed Julie Greer?" and starred Powell himself as the suave and debonair police investigator and a supporting cast of famous faces recruited to launch this new anthology made up of Four Star friends and acquaintances, including Lloyd Bridges, Mickey Rooney, Nick Adams, Jack Carson, Dean Jones, Edgar Bergen, Ronald Reagan,

and producer Aaron Spelling's wife, Carolyn Jones. It was television, but because of the nature of the format it was one day's work and it was publicity, and the tradition continued into the subsequent series. Unfortunately, Powell had since recently passed away, leaving Four Star in disarray (many of their shows are now in the public domain), and when the decision was made to turn the well-received one-off into *Burke's Law*, a regular series for the 1963-'64 season, the casting of Gene Barry as Burke turned the show into not just a more glamorous one, but a campier, frothier confection as well. Former song and dance man Barry, a sort of TV Cary Grant, was one of those oddly effeminate yet heterosexual suave ladies men, a charmer and seducer who was never convincing swinging a fist (although he did on occasion, and had one of the best stunt doubles in the business). He had

previously played western legend *Bat Masterson* as a dandy in an earlier western series, and brought this persona to Amos Burke.

Ludicrously, Burke was a millionaire playboy who inherited his wealth, and just happened to be a police captain in L.A. Imagine the potential political fall-out from that one, I wrote some years ago, but if Donald Trump, a vulgar bully and a moron from the dregs of TV, can be the U.S. President, I see no reason why Amos Burke couldn't be Chief of Police (or, ten years later, Rock Hudson's Stewart MacMillan be San Francisco's Police Commissioner)! Even more absurdly, each episode would open with the fey sophisticate apologetically but willingly ditching a drooling disappointed date on the verge of making love to him when his faithful manservant emerged Alfred-like from the shadows with the important 'phone call that would signal the occurrence of another bizarre murder in high society. And they *were* bizarre. No-one in the wealthy parts of L.A. ever simply shot or strangled someone (in the pilot, the victim is drowned and *then* shot!); the killing was often offbeat and outrageous! A hunter was mounted with his displays, an escapologist drowned in his act, a prolific husband-snatcher buried in a spa mud bath, a millionaire hauled out of the water on his yacht's anchor, a model dumped in a sideshow electric chair. And all episodes were prefaced with the prefix "Who Killed...?".

Co-starring with Barry was Gary Conway, still some years away from his leading role in *Land of the Giants*. Conway's character was clearly part of the trend to create lust objects for the younger audience, and smart hunky wholesome crew-cut lads were a prerequisite of every cop and detective series of the early '60s (*Burke's Law* was one of the few not to be rolling off the *77, Sunset Strip/Bourbon Street Beat/Hawaiian Eye/ Surfside Six* assembly line at Warners). Like fellow young hopefuls and future TV stars Michael Landon and Robert Vaughn, he had first found gainful employment with Roger Corman, where he had paid his dues in such bilge as *Saga of the Viking Women and the Sea Serpent* and *I Was a Teenage Frankenstein* and its sequel *How to Make a Monster*. As Sgt. Tim Tilson, a good-looking younger guy whose similar (and actual) babe appeal made him *persona non grata* with the allegedly sometimes difficult Barry, Conway here had his best role in either TV or film. Despite the onscreen chemistry and compatibility between the likeable regular cast, Conway later claimed that Barry never said a word to him that wasn't in the script during his entire tenure on the show. Surrounded by some of the most beautiful women in Hollywood, most of whom made an appearance on *Burke's Law* during the series' run (it was a resume essential for the Sixties starlet), as well as some of the finest character actors in the business, Conway was not overly concerned, and just lapped up the attention, learning experience, and loot. Playing the older cop, Det. Sgt. Les Hart, was veteran actor Regis Toomey, who carved a career out of playing third cop from the left roles. The fact that these two guys did all the legwork didn't stop Burke from lecturing them both with his wacky witticisms, profundities all concluded with the words "That's Burke's Law!" (less

frequent, and ultimately dispensed with, as the show went on), and the scripts ensured that it was Burke who always pulled the rabbit out of the hat.

The producer of all this delightful nonsense was Aaron Spelling, and *Burke's Law* (featuring far superior scripts to his later 1970s shows) set the pattern for most of the Spelling vehicles to follow — lurid, improbable paperback book scenarios performed by newcomers on their way up or familiar faces on their way down. Aaron Spelling was an actor turned writer who was mentored by Powell, and ended up producing series for Four Star, including Powell's wife's vehicle, *The June Allyson Show*. He had given up acting because he was typecast in depressing weedy weirdo roles (no less than four on *Dragnet*), and taken up producing to protect his scripts.

*Seated, Suzy Parker, Lola Albright, Gene Barry, and Anne Francis, surrounded by some of the other guest stars who adorned the series in the first season.*

The first series he created was for Powell, the western *Johnny Ringo*. Spelling's post-Four Star shows were vulgar and lowbrow, but whatever class they carried came from old Hollywood, and what he'd taken with him from Four Star. The ten years he'd spent with the Powell operation couldn't help but leave some residue.

Now I must be honest here, I couldn't care less "Who Killed..." anybody. The joy of the show is in the guest performances. Dick Powell and his Four Star company were primarily known for their class and their contacts, and he and Spelling virtually invented stunt-casting, that is to say giving cameos and bit parts to look-who-it-is players. Indeed, several old-time movie stars made their final, or near-final appearances before the cameras on *Burke's Law*. These included William Bendix, Sir Cedric Hardwicke, Zasu Pitts, Will Rogers Jnr., Ann Harding, Mary Astor, Gloria Swanson, Edward Everett Horton, Elsa Lanchester, Jane Darwell, Linda Darnell, and Gladys Cooper. Newcomers making early or first appearances included Mary Ann

Mobley, Francine York, Mark Goddard, Marlyn Mason, Stuart Margolin, Celeste Yarnall, Rue McClanahan, and Ken Berry. All the young glamour girls of the period had to be seen in at least three of four venues to claim credibility — *Burke's Law, The Man from UNCLE, Batman,* and an Elvis film.

Aaron Spelling, by his own admission, learned from the master, continuing the tradition of representing 'old Hollywood' and the star system throughout the '60s, '70s, and '80s. In the 1970s, Spelling entered into an exclusivity deal with ABC, and partnered with later network executive Leonard Goldberg, would flood the airwaves with lowbrow mainstream mass-market fluff employing the same mix of youthful beginners and faded faces, including *Fantasy Island, The Love Boat, Vegas,* and in the 1980s, *Hart to Hart, Dynasty* and *Hotel.* He was also the brains, if that's the right word, behind such super-successful confections as *The Mod Squad, Starsky and Hutch, SWAT,* and *Charlie's Angels,* although he was not the creator of any of them. Like number one records, they were incredibly popular at the time, but — with the possible exception of *Charlie's Angels* — while not exactly forgotten, have not endured as 'cult' shows. Once they were off-air, the audience moved on to the next big thing... and it was frequently also from Aaron Spelling! Even into the '90s, he was still turning out hit series such as *Beverly Hills 90210* and *Melrose Place,* which — like his previous endeavors — melted like snow from the public consciousness as soon as they were over. Everyone remembers *Star Trek* and *The Time Tunnel*... but who thinks, and how often, of the more successful and longer running *T.J. Hooker,* which starred those series' leads, William Shatner and James Darren?

*Above: Beauty queen Mary Ann Mobley began her acting career in Burke's Law, later appearing in two Elvis films (here she's in the undoubtedly appropriately named Girl Happy).*

*Right: Gene Barry with British starlet Diana Dors, for Harlan Ellison's first script for the series, "Who Killed Alex Debbs?".*

*Burke's Law* ran for two seasons with reasonable success (curiously, it featured in *TV 21* comic for a while in the U.K., upping its cult status, and Dell retained the comic-book rights in the U.S.). There were paperback books and comic albums and annuals, and the show would probably have run for longer had the network not succumbed to the spy craze of the mid-'60s and turned Amos Burke into a campy Cold Warrior in *Amos Burke – Secret Agent* for his third and very final season. The *Burke's Law* format was revived by Spelling, again with the now silver-haired but still dapper Gene Barry, in 1994 and 1995, but did not last long, sabotaged by network indifference due to change of personnel (new brooms have swept away many potential hits) and constantly changing time-slots. This time, he had a son, played by Peter Barton, but in truth, although watchable, the time had passed. Curiously, the other three 1963 landmarks received weak contemporary revivals too, *My Favorite Martian* as a reasonably amusing Disney film, *The Outer Limits* as a frequently mediocre and undistinguished sci-fi anthology with no particular style of its own (something you could never say of the original), and *The Fugitive* as a movie and then a rather tired-looking and short-lived remake...

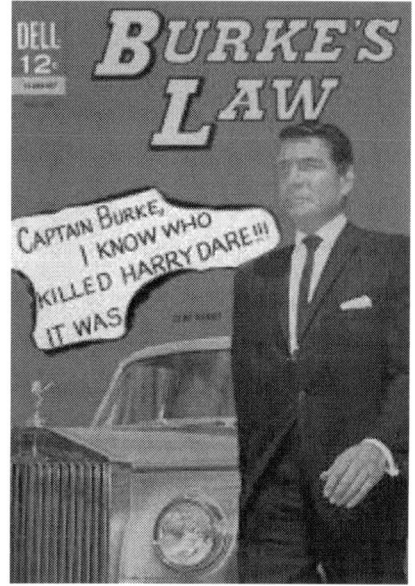

It's important to note that Spelling was not a writer or a creator for any of his numerous series (he had started out writing, but found himself kicked upstairs). People came to him with concepts and formats because he had an extraordinary track record and could do his job, and anyone with a series idea or a property knew that their best chance to get on the air and stay there was with Spelling. And while *Burke's Law* exuded the class and sophistication of the Powell operation, once out on his own, Spelling's lack of same, along with his cynical and low opinion of the mass audience (say it, then show it, then say it again, he told his writers in the '70s) soon dominated the immensely popular dreck he turned out for the next three decades. He threw money around like no other producer in the business, paying the highest fees in television, but the results were shallow, crass, and vulgar. Networks bit the bullet because although he had his fair share of one season flops (the lavish but instantly cancelled *Glitter* in the early '80s being the most prominent disaster), his shows were unashamedly populist and non-controversial, despite their occasional lurid content and unethical characters. Spelling didn't need to be a yes-man, or even kept in line, because—like Glen Larson and Stephen Cannell—he was completely in sync with network thinking. There were no battles to be fought over content, censorship, or storylines where Spelling was concerned.

Like all purveyors of tosh, Spelling was always irked that he never got recognition for his rare forays into upmarket fare, such as the successful soapy drama *Family*, or some of his TV movies that occasionally dealt with more serious subjects. However, the truth is that such programming was heavily outnumbered by his long-running lowbrow rubbish, such as *Love Boat*, *Fantasy Island*, and *Dynasty*, and he was well rewarded in the millions for his efforts.

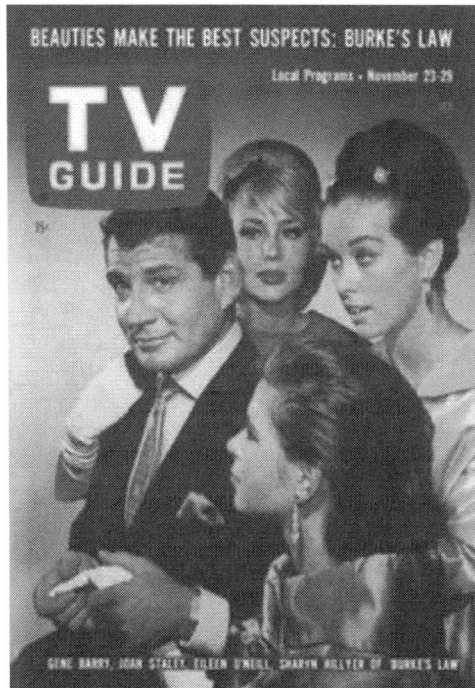

BEAUTIES MAKE THE BEST SUSPECTS: BURKE'S LAW

Local Programs · November 23-29

TV GUIDE

GENE BARRY, JOAN STALEY, EILEEN O'NEILL, SHARYN HILLYER OF BURKE'S LAW

*Three of the 1960s' most beautiful starlets — Joan Staley, Eileen O'Neill, and Sharyn Hillyer — pose with Barry for the cover of TV Guide.*

The true creator of *Burke's Law*, in as much as he wrote the original one-off, was Frank Gilroy, who to be blunt, just got lucky to have his screenplay turned into a series. He never wrote a single episode, but as the creator of Amos Burke, and author of "Who Killed Julie Greer?", was entitled to have his name on both *Burke's Law* and *Amos Burke – Secret Agent*, neither of which he had anything to do with. Gilroy had written for mostly television westerns, and went on to some considerable success on Broadway, but ended up back in TV in the '70s, where he again wrote a TV one-off turned into a series format, *The Turning of Jim Malloy*, a TV movie which was turned into the short-lived melodrama *Gibbsville*.

*Burke's Law* had one other claim to fame besides foisting Aaron Spelling's TV career onto a helpless public, and that was that it was the forerunner of shows such as *Columbo*, *Hart to Hart*, and *Murder, She Wrote* (the latter itself inspired by the *Columbo* episode "Murder By the Book" as much as Agatha Christie's Miss Marple) which offered up bloodless murders and cast lists of familiar faces as suspects. There is no doubt that Richard Levinson and

William Link's *Columbo* (whose first TV appearance offered none other than Gene Barry as the villain) was inspired by *Burke's Law,* and their subsequent more cynical confection *Murder, She Wrote* followed the formula even more closely (the duo wrote for both *Burke's Law* and *Honey West* early in their TV careers).

When *Murder, She Wrote* took off, it inspired at least a dozen similar shows in the same spirit, some by Levinson and Link, some not, some successful, some not; indeed the Silverman/Hargrove operation has used the template successfully ever since, with *Matlock, The Father Dowling Mysteries,* and *Diagnosis: Murder,* to name but three of many (they also revived *Perry Mason* from the same period as *Burke's Law*). And before they made it their own, Universal (who produced *Columbo* and *Murder, She Wrote*) attempted to duplicate it with less success, with the likes of *Mrs. Columbo, The Ellery Queen Mysteries,* and *Blacke's Magic,* among others.

*Gene Barry and Gary Conway look like they might be contemplating their working relationship together… "He never said a word to me that wasn't in the script!" laughed Conway to Filmfax magazine.*

The style of *Burke's Law* also undoubtedly influenced Gene Barry's next series, the superb *The Name of the Game,* in which he played publisher Glenn Howard, lording it over a publishing empire that sent himself, Tony Franciosa, and Robert Stack on adventures in individual rotating style, Franciosa writing 'people' stories and Robert Stack as a crime reporter. So successful was this format of featuring 'rotating' leads who took turns to star that it was carried over into other series of the time, including *Search* (a peculiar short-lived sci-fi marriage of *Man from UNCLE* and *Time Tunnel* presided over by Leslie Stevens), *The Bold Ones* (teams of cops, lawyers, and politicians), and the *Mystery Movies* concept that housed *Columbo, McCloud,* and another series very much in the spirit of *Burke's Law,* the classy *McMillan and Wife,* with Rock Hudson and Susan St. James.

Although, like so many series of the period, *Burke's Law* used the same few sets and locations over and over again, the screen oozed money, and Spelling spared no expense when it came to set decoration and extras. Fashion designer Nolan Miller, who later dressed the casts of *Charlie's Angels* and *Dynasty,* got his start on the show. If the show had a failing, it's that it might have cast its net a little wider for guest stars; many big names showed up between three to six times during what was to be a two year run. It was a great shame the series wasn't made in color as, unlike many other series of the day, such as *The Naked City, The Untouchables,* and *The Outer Limits,* which benefitted from being in black and white, *Burke's Law* would have been greatly enhanced by it. Most of the episodes were satisfying, frothy fun, and oddly uplifting, given that they always opened with a murder, albeit (and crucially) usually of a person nobody much cared was dead. The series got away with murder (ha, see what I did there) because the deaths and discovery of the body were so bizarre that they couldn't be taken seriously, and unlike the many similar, sometimes less polished shows that followed in its wake, the producers almost always ensured the victim was thoroughly unpleasant and deserving of their comeuppance. Series cliche to watch for: "Yes, I hated him enough to have killed him… but I didn't. And I'm *sorry* I didn't!". There were maybe half-a-dozen episodes that were below par, but there were also half-a-dozen that were above average. Although it was their rarity that gave them their strength and power, and the show was rightly light and bright, and full of eccentrics, wealth, comfort, and pretty girls, every once in a while the show would go unexpectedly dark, and when it did, it excelled itself.

*Guest players Quinn O'Hara and Keenan Wynn alongside Gary Conway and Gene Barry in "Who Killed Jason Shaw?". Over the page: publicity pix!*

**Burke's Law**


**episode guide**


**First Season**


**(1963-'64)**


**Who Killed Holly Howard?**

wr. Albert Beich, William Wright, dir. Hy Averback

*with Suzy Parker (Bridget Jenkins), William Bendix (Fred Hopke), Sir Cedric Hardwicke (John Busch; butler), Stephen McNally (Ed Nickerson), Fred Clark ('Mac' McNulty), Zasu Pitts (Mrs. Bowie; landlady), Bruce Cabot (Thomas Matheson), Rod Cameron (Harry Joe Murdock), Will Rogers Jnr. (Vaughn Moore), Elizabeth Allen (party guest), Barry Kelley (Lt. Joe Nolan), John Zaremba (Lt. Charlie Johnson), Michael Fox (George McLeod), Eileen O'Neill (Sgt. Gloria Ames), Jay C. Flippen (Bill; desk sergeant), Buddy Lewis (construction worker), Kathy Kersh (model)*

The body of an ambitious but shy and naive young hopeful model is found on a construction site. This episode marks the first appearance of Eileen O'Neill as Sgt. Gloria Ames, and bit player and sometime acting coach Michael Fox as sometime Coroner, sometime lab man and all-time all-purpose Answer Man George McLeod, both recurring characters. Also recurring, quite pointlessly, Jay C. Flippen as a desk sergeant who just turns up in the corridors of the police department to get star billing. He would make one more equally pointless cameo as this character before turning up at the end of the season in a different (but still cop) role.

More notably, this opener tells us that co-star Gary Conway's Lt. Tilson character has only just joined the team. He is immediately portrayed as a gung-ho eager beaver type who has already actioned everything just before Burke asks him. Burke likes him, but of course he gets to show him up when he makes his inevitable slip, a pattern that would persist throughout the series. When Burke leaves the scene, the construction worker asks Tim why a millionaire is head of the homicide division. Tilson asks him why he's a construction worker. Answer: they're both good at what they do—it's what they do best. It's clunky, but at least it's an attempt to justify an absurd premise. Thus the scene is set for the next 66 episodes. Try finding simple exposition as clear and concise as that in today's television.

The rest of the dialogue consists of the clever quips and snappy patter that defined the exchanges of dialogue in this series. If it wasn't the first, then it was one of the first TV series to have truly sophisticated dialogue of feature film quality. Most dramatic television of the period either took itself painfully seriously, or featured western-style moralising or the "Let's go—and fast!" dialogue of the standard action film. Only *The Man from UNCLE* matched *Burke's Law* in the '60s for sophistication, and *Burke's Law* probably had the edge. Indeed, the series strived for sophistication at every turn; Burke's Rolls Royce had a telephone, radio, tape recorder, and drinks cabinet in the back, all very stylish and unusual for the early '60s. He inherited his wealth from his father, we are told. This episode also introduces the dubious "That's Burke's Law" aphorisms, meaningless Chinese cookie platitudes which, as the series wore on, became less prominent. There are four of the asinine things in this premier.

Shown first, this was clearly always intended to be the series opener. Writer Albert Beich went on to script eight episodes for the series, five of them with William Wright, who whisked him away to work on his own series the following season, the western *Kentucky Jones*. As is often the case with a pilot (see *Batman* for a classic example), the cast is overloaded with extra players being 'tested' for recurring or replacement roles. That way, the network could pick and choose who they wanted. Barry Kelley has more to do than Regis Toomey in this episode, but was not to be seen again (Hart and Nolan had both been characters in the 1961 version, but played by different actors). John Zaremba, later of *Time Tunnel,* also gets some irrelevant screen time, indicating he might be held over.

Ironically, bearing in mind the role she plays here, Suzy Parker, model turned aspiring actress, was once believed to be the most photographed girl in the world at the height of her fame. Perhaps more lasting than any of her magazine covers has been her role in *The Twilight Zone's* iconic "Number Twelve Looks Just Like You", which worryingly predicted today's narrow definition of physical beauty, particularly prevalent in America, but seeping into the rest of Western society too. Parker plays an anxious mother who genuinely can't understand why her daughter won't submit to surgery and choose from the narrow selection of faces and forms available to her. Three attractive performers play all the roles.

*Suzy Parker with Gene Barry*

William Bendix was a cold bastard in an excellent *Untouchables* ("The Tri-State Gang"), and he's equally callous here.

"We have to change models. The girl's dead"

"Oh, that's nice"

"What's nice about it?"

"More overtime"

Another old timer, Zasu Pitts, gives her final performance here as a dotty landlady; she passed away before the episode aired. The dialogue suggests a 'Baby Jane' type, but Pitts plays it as a harmless sweet little old lady ("Is she in trouble?" she enquires of the dead girl/ " Not any more" says Burke, tactfully).

Both Bendix and Hardwicke would pass on the following year, although Bendix would be back in the second season in a more frivolous role, and Hardwicke still had a *Twilight Zone* and an extraordinary *Outer Limits* to leave us. *Burke's Law* was very much about old Hollywood rather than the brave new world of the '60s, and many veteran performers of the '50s, '40s, and '50s would make some of their final or penultimate appearances on this show. Behind them were waiting the young hopefuls (such as Elizabeth Montgomery in the next episode), and many future names of the 1960s also turned up on the series, albeit more often in the end credits rather than the big block letters of the opening roll call (always alphabetically arranged, with no exceptions, even when playing minor roles, as Flippen and Allen do here).

Elizabeth Allen worked steadily, but never made much of an impact. Her main claim to fame was appearing in two classic episodes of *Boris Karloff's Thriller*, both with the up-and-coming William Shatner, "The Hungry Glass" and "The Grim Reaper". She did one more *Burke's Law*, in a slightly more substantial but similar role, and had several parts in episodes of *The Naked City*, *Doctor Kildare* and *The Fugitive*, and regular roles in four short-lived series over the next two decades, *CPO Sharkey,*

*Bracken's World*, *The Paul Lynde Show*, and *Texas*.

Fred Clark was a recurring player in *The Burns and Allen Show* in the early '50s, and played numerous comedic roles in the 1960s sit-coms. It is a measure of his charisma that he is well-remembered as the doctor in *The Beverly Hillbillies,* and yet only appeared in five episodes, including the notorious "cure for the common cold" story.

As well as old-timers like Hardwicke, Pitts, Bendix, Flippen, et al, this opening episode is littered with, to put it impolitely, Hollywood has-beens who never made the big time. Stephen McNally had a single season Four Star series in the 1961 – '62 series melodramatically titled *Target: the Corruptors*. It was okay, but nothing special, with guest stars (Culp, Vaughn, Falk) who overshadowed the uncharismatic lead. He was in movies in the 1940s, but swiftly turned to the TV guest star circuit for the rest of his career from the mid-'50s to the end of the '70s. The Texan businessmen are played by three minor names, Bruce Cabot, best known for his role in *King Kong*, and mostly employed afterwards by John Wayne (in whose films he numbered double figures), Rod Cameron, who had no less than four 1950s TV series under his belt, but was now on the guest star circuit, and politician Will Rogers Jnr., who dabbled in acting and whose final role this was. Suzy Parker provides the glamour in this one (with a brief appearance poolside by starlet Kathy Kersh) and Cedric steals the show as the birdwatching butler. But what sort of birds is he watching?

This was the first of three episodes directed by Hy Averback, who also occasionally produced on series and frequently handled pilots or two-parters for various shows after cutting his teeth on over a hundred episodes of *The Real McCoys*. He wasn't fussy about what he worked on, and rarely stayed with a show he wasn't producing, but did chalk up twenty episodes of *MASH*, so he knew a good thing when he saw it.

### Who Killed Mr. X?

wr. Lewis Reed, dir. Don Weis

*with Elizabeth Montgomery (Stacey Evans), Charlie Ruggles (Mr. Gregory), Soupy Sales (Henry Geller), Ann Harding (Annabelle Rogers), Dina Merrill (Barrie Coleman), Jim Backus (Harold Mason), Barrie Chase (Alison Grahame), Allyson Ames (girl in swimming pool), Hank Grant, Cecil Smith, Vernon Scott, Dan Jenkins (lawyers), Bobby Johnson (butler), Mimi Dillard (secretary), Fred Barry (little boy), Mel Blanc (Edward's voice)*

Lewis Reed had virtually single-handedly written most of Craig Stevens' *Peter Gunn* detective series a few years earlier, and would contribute six episodes in total to *Burke's Law*. He was one of the series' better writers.

This one has a particularly lurid opening, with a body discovered near children (including Barry's son) as they glide past it on a merry-go-round! But what was particularly creepy about the show was the constant references in the dialogue to the death penalty and the gas chamber. Both this episode and the previous one make the point that whoever committed the murder is likely going to pay the ultimate penalty for it.

*Elizabeth Montgomery in Bewitched.*

Director Don Weis directed episodes of anything and everything for forty years, always for TV, and like Hy Averback from the previous episode, showing no preference for any style or genre other than to keep working. He directed thirteen *Burke's Law* in total, and Spelling kept him busy in the late '70s on *The Love Boat* and *Fantasy Island*. In the '80s he worked extensively on the similar-to-*Burke Remington Steele*. The Mr. X of the title is a thinly-veiled Howard Hughes figure with a stable of kept women scattered around Hollywood who are supposedly under contract at his film studio, but never completed a single film.

Elizabeth Montgomery, one year away from *Bewitched* and dominating this episode, is in full Samantha Stevens mode as uptown bimbo Stacey Evans, all mannerisms intact (would you believe she even premieres the frickin' nose twitch?), her character making constant references to Martinis, a silly drink considered the height of sophistication in the early '60s. She's absolutely stunning and thoroughly irritating. Hard to believe that the character she plays hasn't been offered any parts in five years.

Of the other 'kept women' in the episode, all with much smaller parts than Montgomery (they don't appear until the second half of the show), Dina Merrill did mostly guest roles and was married to actor Cliff Robertson, Barrie Chase was a showgirl and dancer, and Ann Harding, giving a marvellous performance here, was a player in numerous melodramas before turning to the TV guest star circuit in the 1950s. Allyson Ames, who has a memorable bit in the pre-credits teaser, was the girlfriend of *Outer Limits* producer Leslie Stevens, and appeared twice in that series, among others. Fred Barry, the little boy, was Gene Barry's ten year old son, and made three appearances in the series during its run, two of them discovering bodies! From hereon, the relationship between Burke and Tim is happily more genial and friendly and less angry and adversarial than it was in the pilot; Tim seems to have lost his embarrassed inclination for a transfer!

Charlie Ruggles, usually cast as blustery con-men types, is great fun as the fussy feather-duster-wielding Mr. Gregory, as is children's entertainer and interminable game show/talk show fixture Soupy Sales in a cameo as another stuffy soon-to-be-unemployed retainer. Jim Backus, of course, went on to '60s sit-com *Gilligan's Island*, and

would be back for a second, and funnier, appearance.

Bobby Johnson worked steadily through the decades in bit parts, invariably cast in typical 'black' roles of the '40s, '50, and '60s — butler, porter, mailman, waiter, doorman, attendant, and so on. Every time a walk-on was needed to hand something to a white guy, there was Bobby. Only in the 1970s did he finally get to play characters with names. He paid his dues to get them.

*Charlie Ruggles and Gene Barry*

### Who Killed Cable Roberts?

wr. Gwen Bagni, dir. Jeffrey Hayden

*with Lizabeth Scott (Mona Roberts), Mary Astor (Florence Roberts), Paul Lynde (Arthur Clark), John Saxon (Bud Charney), Chill Wills (Harry Riggs), Zsa Zsa Gabor (Anna; maid), Charlene Holt (Christy, Burke's date), Alvy Moore (chauffeur), Eileen O'Neill (Sgt. Ames), Tony Regan (Cable Roberts), Karen Flynn (Riggs' wife), June Kim (Henry's date)*

A much-hated Hemingway-esque big game hunter is found murdered and 'mounted' with his trophies. *Bewitched's* Uncle Arthur and '60s sit-com regular Paul Lynde is hilarious as the murder victim's weeping and lovelorn p.a. (but then he's hilarious in everything), while upstairs, husky-voiced Lizabeth Scott as his fit young wife couldn't care less.

"My husband was a very unusual man, Captain. One does not mourn for such a man in the usual way" / "I'd say you've overcome that temptation"

Mary Astor is very good as his ex-wife. She made her first film in 1921, but by the 1950s was mostly in television, this being one of her last roles before retiring. Both she and Scott were in the film *Desert Fury* together. John Saxon had better roles on TV than he did in the movies, *Enter the Dragon* excepted. He's particularly good here as a hostile suspect, although in a later role in the show he gives an appalling performance. Providing the glamour is *El Dorado's* Charlene Holt, coming back in the second season. She also appears in a *Honey West*.

Jobbing director Jeffrey Hayden worked with Donna Reed, Lloyd Bridges, and Andy Griffiths on their shows, and was kept busiest on *Peyton Place*. Writer Gwen Bagni wrote numerous scripts for *Dick Powell Theater* and then, with her future husband, actor Paul Dubov, wrote twelve further *Burke's Law*. When *Burke's Law* ceased production, they wrote ten episodes of *Honey West*. Their dialogue on both series is excellent.

"Alright, you went for a drive, alone. You got home—when?"

"Late"

"Late evening? Late morning?"

"What's time? Who can define it?"

"That timepiece on your hand is no mere bauble"

"It was about two I think, I don't know"

"Anyone see you go out?"

"No"

"Anyone see you come in?"

"I hope not!"

*Gene Barry with Lizabeth Scott*

It's a little disconcerting, and a sign of the times, to see big game hunting glorified in this episode, with only the clearly effeminate p.a. hypocritically taking the opposing view. Everyone other than the p.a. hates the victim, as was the tradition on the show, but not for killing animals for sport. A later episode in the series would be less impressed.

**Who Killed Harris Crown?**

wr. John Meredyth Lucas, dir. Don Weis

*with Lola Albright (Shirley Mills), Gene Nelson (Rick Mason), Juliet Prowse (Amelia 'Angel' Crown), Don Rickles (Lou Kronkeit), Joan Blondell (Ethel Kronkeit),*

Barbara Eden (Marni Lee), Eva Gabor (Lily Bentley), Ruth Roman (Elinor Albrick), Thann Wyenn (Harris Crown), David Renard (Danny; car hop), Charles Lane (Dr. Lusk), Eric Feldary (Prince Thanda), Eileen O'Neill (Sgt. Ames), Susan Flannery (Bentley's secretary), Sandra Donat (Mills' salesgirl), Jackie Loughery (Mason's assistant)

It's a web of womanising and infidelity. Great reveal.

Everyone is cast to type in this one. Cast as dancer and choreographer, Juliet Prowse (Can-Can, G.I. Blues) and Gene Nelson (Lullaby of Broadway, Oklahoma) were indeed dancers, with Nelson moving on to choreography and direction, including such camp classics as Elvis films Kissin' Cousins and Harum Scarum and Star Trek's "Gamesters of Triskellion". Very often, he only directed single episodes of series, but he stayed a while on The Donna Reed Show, and became a regular director on Spelling's Mod Squad. Coincidentally, he also directed Barbara Eden in the earliest episodes of I Dream of Jeannie, with whom he has a scene here. Yet another sit-com queen of the '60s shows up—Eva Gabor of Green Acres, playing (like Montgomery, a couple of episodes earlier) a prophetic facsimile of her character in that. Gabor's sister, the infamous Zsa Zsa, had appeared in the previous episode.

Don Rickles and Joan Blondell are hilarious as a blue-collar couple trapped in a marriage made in hell. When she hit middle-age, former bombshell Blondell created a whole second career for herself as coarse old bags, and she excels here (she will return to the series as a gambling racket floozie). For his part,

club comic Rickles proves he can act. Irwin Allen fan? Blink and you miss Susan Flannery sitting at a desk in Gabor's office.

*Gene Barry with Juliet Prowse*

There's another embarrassing sign of the times when white actor Eric Feldary shows up in the tag, blacked up to play an Indian prince. However, he doesn't play it as a caricature.

As is so often the case when a production resorts to the library, the stock footage used for the crash shows a total conflagration, so there wouldn't have been much left for Tim to study or Angel to identify (I should think he did look different!). Even his wallet and all inside it survived the fireball. Happily, Burke's Law almost never used library footage to represent anything.

Writer John Meredyth Lucas worked in a variety of capacities during his career, mostly on *Zorro*, *Medic*, *Whiplash*, *Ben Casey*, *Star Trek*, *Mannix*, and *Police Surgeon*. He wrote two episodes of *Burke's Law*.

"He sicced the cops on us? His own family? I tell you, Harry's going to pay for this!"

"He paid for it last night, Mrs. Kronkeit. He was murdered"

"Murdered? He's dead? His crummy wife will get everything!"

"I was afraid you'd take it hard"

*The one and only Terry Thomas*

### Who Killed Julian Buck?

wr. William Wright, Albert Beich, dir. Don Weis

*with Ed Begley (James Littlefield), Karl Boehm (Professor Marton), Corinne Calvet (Francesca Bel Ami), Rita Moreno (Margaret Cowls), Terry Thomas (Charlie*

*Hill), Keenan Wynn (Kid Corey), Rebecca Welles (Susan, Burke's date), Michael Fox (Coroner George McLeod), Eileen O'Neill (Sgt. Ames), Dee J. Thompson (nurse), Barbara Pepper (cleaning woman), Barbara Hemphill (drinks waitress), Joe Scott (movie attendant)*

Les — "You look chipper this morning"

Burke (after having his evening at the movies curtailed) — "To bed early with a book"

Les — "What were you reading, *How to Become a Millionaire Without Really Trying?*"

Ed Begley has fun playing against type as a prissy publisher, taking a longer look at Detective Tilson than Sgt. Ames when introduced to them ("Julian had many admirable qualities, but he was as careless with his manuscripts as his choice of friends" he pouts airily. "He left the final draft of *The Foreign Lady* in the dubious custody of one").

Keenan Wynn (who will be back) plays a punchy boxer and Rita Moreno has a lively single scene with co-stars Conway and Toomey, the latter finally given a turn in the spotlight. French-born Corinne Calvet would appear twice more in the series before watching her career plunge downmarket.

Rebecca Welles, this episode's date, was the wife of director Don Weis, and his greatest contribution to television was giving her early retirement. She began her acting career under her given name of Reba Tassell in the early 1950s, and made her last onscreen appearance in 1964 after appearing in numerous shows. She had worked with Gene Barry earlier in his *Bat Masterson* western series.

Terry Thomas is wonderful in everything of course, and very much so here as a bartender who pours himself one for every drink he supplies to the waitress ("I do wish they wouldn't keep mixing my drinks!"). Don't miss him as a British bobby in the *Man from UNCLE* two-parter "The Five Daughter Affair", aka *The Karate Killers*.

A nice clever intriguing story with several twists and turns and strong dialogue from Beich. Gene Barry fluffs a line in the tag, and nobody noticed.

### Who Killed Alex Debbs?

wr. Harlan Ellison, dir. Don Weis

*with Suzy Parker (Angela Pattison), Jan Sterling (Devora Cato), Sammy Davis Jnr. (Cordwainer Bird), Diana Dors (Maxine Borman), John Ireland (Orrin Lashwell), Burgess Meredith (Sidney Wilde), Arlene Dahl (Princess Kortzoff), Michael Fox (George McLeod), Dolores Wells (Burke's date), Sharyn Hillyer, Laura Lynn Hale (Deb girls), Eileen O'Neill (Sgt. Ames), Don Gazzaniga (Tom; cop)*

The infamous Harlan Ellison (watch for the giveaway *Green Hornet* joke in the teaser) offers up Alex Debbs, publisher of naked lady magazine *Debonair*, a thinly-veiled Hugh Hefner type as the usual murder victim everybody hated (nobody nice has been murdered yet, or will be; that was the frothy series' escape clause), and throws in a Grace Kelly pastiche for good measure. He also gives the Bird to Sammy Davis Jnr. — Cordwainer Bird, the name he used on the scripts he didn't want to put his own name on. He puts his name on this one though, and it's as good as any in the series — and of course littered with pop culture references, from Christine Keeler to *Secret Agent X-9*. But for a man who takes such a sniffy tone to *Playboy*-style porn (and despite having written a vast amount of far sleazier fare under pen-

names during this period), it's a little hypocritical to resolve the story with a catfight...

Burke — "Do you read *Debonair*?"

Tilson — "Once in a while"

"How often?"

"Once a month?"

"How often does it publish?"

"Once a month"

Sammy Davis Jnr. steals the show in a single scene as a snappy gag writer who shows up at the police station to provide a list of why he might have done it. However, it's easier to believe Diana Dors as a secret ex-wife than a desk-bound folk singer. Very wisely, she neither sings nor mimes.

The rest of the cast is rather ordinary, even the usually colorful Burgess Meredith (*Batman's* Penguin) as a browbeaten cheesecake cartoonist. And it's a little early for Suzy Parker to be back again, especially in a remarkably similar role. Parker was one of the earliest high-paid super-models during the '50s, and married for the third time in 1960, to actor Bradford Dillman. Third time was the charm, and after a decade in TV guest roles going nowhere, she retired to raise her kids. *Man from UNCLE* fan? Blink, and miss Sharyn Hillyer as a goofy bimbo. This is the first episode to feature a second (and undeserved) killing.

*Sharyn Hillyer in The Man from UNCLE.*

Hillyer: (breathily) "He was a great and wonderful fella. I wouldn't be where I am today if it hadn't been for Alex Debbs"

Barry: "I'll bear that in mind. And what do you think now?"

"About what?"

"Well, about Alex Debbs being murdered"

"Ain't it *exciting?*"

\* \* \* \* \*

"There's another reason I did not like Alex. Would you like to know it?"

"Well, it's four o'clock in the morning. I think that's proof that I'm slightly inquisitive"

## Who Killed Sweet Betsy?

wr. Edith Sommer, dir. Hy Averback

*with Carolyn Jones (Betsy/Meredith/Jane Richards/Olivia Manning), Richard Carlson (Nels Manning), Gladys Cooper (Aunt Harriet), John Ericson (Gil Harris), Michael Wilding (Alan Steiner), Patricia Olson (art gallery date), Stacy Harris (doctor), Mimi Dillard (nurse), Harold Fong (man with earpiece), Janet Clark (nutty old lady), Stuart Margolin (art gallery attendant), Jennifer Gillespie (little girl in art gallery)*

This is a *tour-de-force* episode for Carolyn Jones (soon to be cast as Morticia in *The Addams Family*), who just happened to be Aaron Spelling's wife at the time. Those auditions must have been interesting. She plays no less than four roles, all of them well, as four sisters, the first of whom is the murder victim. Quite a showcase. John Ericson went on to co-star in Spelling's *Honey West,* a series which got its introduction in a second season episode of *Burke's Law.* Naturally, Ericson also appeared. Here, he plays an arrogant and vain surfer, and will return in a similar role later in the series before becoming Honey West's aide. Richard Carlson, that stiff, stuffy fellow from all those 1950s sci-fi films, gets to diversify memorably as a nasty, sleazy alcoholic. He also returns later in the series.

Dividing her time between the U.S. and her native Britain, Gladys Cooper's other cult TV included three *Twilight Zones,* an *Outer Limits,* and a *Girl from UNCLE.* In the U.K., she appeared in cult shows *Adam Adamant Lives, Callan,* and *The Persuaders,* her final role in 1971. She had a regular role in Four Star's *The Rogues,* on which a number of *Burke's Law* personnel worked. Her first film role had been in 1913!

Another British actor, Michael Wilding, has a funny bit as a crazy college professor. He also found time for a *Girl from UNCLE*. Child actress Jennifer Gillespie worked continuously from 1961 to 1964. Mimi Dillard had a bit in "Who Killed Mr. X?" as a secretary. *Rockford Files* fan? Blink and miss Stuart 'Angel' Margolin as a clean-shaven young man who brings Burke the inevitable 'phone message in the teaser.

After paying his dues directing over a hundred episodes of the sit-com *The Real McCoys*, Hy Averback settled into steady work directing film and TV, including the pilot for *Burke's Law* and two further episodes of which this is one. Prestigious work included a couple of *Columbo* and numerous *MASH*. He also worked as a producer on several series, and liked to play small bit parts occasionally; he appears in another *Burke's Law* episode briefly as — what else? — a director.

**Who Killed Billy Jo?**

wr. Tony Barrett, dir. Hy Averback

*with Ida Lupino (Lynn Dexter), Howard Duff (Lou Cole), Laraine Day (Lisa Cole), Phil Harris (Rip Farley), Cesar Romero (Marcus De Grute), Nick Adams (Charlie Vaughn), Tina Louise (Bonnie Belle Tate), Tom Tully (Jethro Tate), Elaine Stewart (Felicia, Burke's date), David Niven (gag cameo), Kelly Gordon (Billy Jo Tate), Marlyn Mason (Julie at party), Ken Berry (Clyde at party), Buddy Garion (Harve, Rip's buddy), Valora Noland (Vicki, Vaughn's girl), Larry Anthony (cop)*

The first dull one. A very loose re-telling of the Elvis story at a time when the pop charts were full of young kids

who wanted to be *next* Elvis (there is, of course, *just* the one!). Billy Jo is one of the deluded hopefuls, but the story is a slow plod through the uninspiring guest performances, led off by real-life husband and wife Howard Duff and Ida Lupino, who a few years later would team up for an embarrassing *Batman*

*Tina Louise with Gene Barry*

episode. The only interest comes during the opening teaser, where Marlyn Mason and *F Troop's* Ken Berry have before-they-were-famous (well, okay, better known) bit parts. Valora Noland, a pretty blonde who later had substantial roles in shows including *The Man from UNCLE* and *Star Trek*, has little more than a background walk-on. And casting Nick Adams as a hanger-on in an Elvis-inspired story is a bit too on the nose, surely?

There's no spark throughout. The usually witty dialogue is reduced to *Dragnet*-style procedural, and the guest stars are not given anything to work with. In most episodes, guest stars were invariably given little bits of business to do while they played their lines, props or professions to color their performances. In this one, everyone sits still to deliver a dull script, and it's the audience that wriggles around. When even Cesar Romero is boring, you know you're in trouble. Writer Tony Barrett would improve.

Bob O'Brien, more commonly a sit-com writer, spent most of the '60s churning out scripts for *The Lucy Show*, one of the best examples of manic, broad comedy. This twisting, turning, surprising and sophisticated story is a revealing departure for him; you'd never know it was the same writer. What a shame he didn't have any more in him. Director Stanley Cherry also worked mostly on sit-coms.

## Who Killed Wade Walker?

wr. Bob O'Brien, dir. Stanley Cherry

*with Dana Wynter (Iris Marlowe), Anne Francis (Suzanne Foster), Rhonda Fleming (Cathy Summit), Martha Hyer (Jerri Vaughn), Frankie Laine (Kelly Rogers), Nancy Sinatra (Jill Stacy), Joan Staley (Laura, Burke's date), Jay C. Flippen (Bill, desk sergeant), Michael Fox (George McLeod), Eileen O'Neill (Sgt. Ames), Jess Kirkpatrick (Cathcart), Harry Lauter (doctor), David Whorf (intern)*

Burke is about to take a break out at his cabin in the woods... with a female companion of course...

"A week of this and I'll feel like a new man"

"I won't"

Then, the inevitable 'phone call.

"Lucky you have that 'phone in the car"

"It's not helping my luck any"

Nancy Sinatra (left) followed her bit part in Burke's Law with her first film role, in For Those Who Think Young, with James Darren (Gidget's 'Moondoggie') and Claudia Martin (Dean Martin's daughter). Can you believe that guy's hair!?

After eight episodes, this is the first story in which the murder victim wasn't hated by all the suspects (although he does have a dark side). On the contrary, the victim is the mirror-image of Burke, a free and easy millionaire with four girls on the go. The fatal difference here is that he was about to make a final choice and marry one... Worse still, the girls all stood to benefit from his will... That's the cue for Burke to work his way through the four female suspects...

Dana Wynter portrays angry nurse Iris, a prudish Brit on the surface, but a phony all the way through... When she's not being too choosy about the interns, she's working her way through the doctors and the patients (this is surprisingly hot stuff for 1964). Anne Francis does a reprise of Elizabeth Montgomery's turn at the beginning of

*Joan Staley, as she appears in Roustabout, dumped by Elvis before the film even starts. Elvis, how could you?*

the series, and it's a pretty accurate study (later she'll be back as Honey West, and then for *Honey West*). Rhonda Fleming made movies from the early '40s to the beginning of the '60s, but then it was TV guest shots until she retired at the end of the '70s. Very much a manufactured Hollywood star (she once spoofed herself as 'Rhoda Fleming'), she never made a classic film, or a memorable TV episode, but she worked constantly. Here, she plays a tough, straight-talking rancher.

Martha Hyer, who also worked steadily from the mid-'40s to the mid-'70s and had a similarly prolific but undistinguished career, plays torch singer Jerri Vaughn. She chalked up an astonishing six appearances in this series. Playing Burke's date is classy Joan Staley, who appeared in three episodes altogether, as well as guest shots in *Bonanza, Perry Mason, The Untouchables, The Dick Van Dyke Show, The Munsters, Mission: Impossible,* and *Batman,* among many others. Early in her career she posed for *Playboy,* had bit-parts in numerous shows such as *Laramie, Bourbon Street Beat, The Detectives, The Tab Hunter Show,* and later two Elvis films, *Roustabout* and *Kissin' Cousins.* She had recurring roles in *77, Sunset Strip,* and the less well-known *The Lively Set,* and *Broadside.* Nancy Sinatra, Frank's daughter, and still dark-haired at this point, has an amusing sub-plot with Tim, who bashfully asks her out. From here, she goes on to such feelgood fare as *For Those Who Think Young, The Swingin' Set, Marriage on the Rocks* (with Dad), *The Ghost in the Invisible Bikini, The Last of the Secret Agents,* and *Speedway* (with Elvis), plus a great guest appearance in *The Man from UNCLE* (as Coco Cool!).

### Who Killed the Kind Doctor?

wr. Edith Sommer, dir. Don Taylor

*with Joan Caulfield (Betty Techman), Susan Oliver (Janet Fielding), Celeste Holm (Helen Forsythe), James MacArthur (Larry Forsythe), Annette Funicello (Dorrie Marsh), Dewey Martin (Dominic Farrow), Sheree North (Myrtle 'Gigi' String), Philip Reed (Dr. Techman), Elaine Devry (Peggy, Burke's date), Sharyn Hillyer, Sonia Sonic (chorus girls), Don Gazzaniga (Jerry, cop), Jakie Deslonde (Joe, cop)*

Burke investigates the murder of a psychiatrist... and the guest players get to go nuts as his patients. Cast and credited, but apparently cut for time, were George Sawaya as a cop, and Jonathan Hole as an airline official; Hole is always funny, and was obviously part of the stolen 'plane sequence with James MacArthur and Annette Funicello as a couple of literally crazy kids.*

* Of course it's possible I viewed an edited print; my source was the Delta DVDs.

James MacArthur was Danny Williams throughout the 1970s in *Hawaii Five-O*, while Annette Funicello was the former *Mickey Mouse Club* kid who made all those beach movies at around this time where she sat and sulked and played hard-to-get while surrounded by up-for-it gyrating beach babes, and all the guys mysteriously chased *her*. Both

manage to get past their bland stereotypes here. Funicello would return to *Burke's Law* later in the series, and made several appearances in Spelling's *Fantasy Island* and *Love Boat* series. Joan Caulfield would also return to the series twice.

Celeste Holm's film career began in 1946, but she swiftly moved into television, doing numerous series and countless guest spots; she was rarely in anything worth watching, but was busier during the 1990s than ever. Sheree North plays the same part she always played, a tired-looking borderline hooker, but appears to enjoy herself, but Susan Oliver steals the show as the doc's equally dotty secretary.

"Didn't you like the doctor?"

"He was like a father to me!"

*James MacArthur, later of Hawaii Five-O, and Annette Funicello, queen of the Beach Party movies, play a couple of worryingly weird young lovers, just two of a deceased doctor's bizarre patients, as Gene Barry tries to figure out "Who Killed the Kind Doctor?".*

"But you hated your father"

"How did you know?"

"Oh, I don't know… it just came to me"

*Susan Oliver as the dotty secretary in "Who Killed the Kind Doctor?"*

Enjoying herself as much as the cast is writer Edith Sommer, who previously wrote the episode about the four sisters who were also a bit wacky, and here has fun with the end chase scene. She went on to become head writer on the daytime soaps *The Guiding Light* and *As the World Turns*. Actor turned director Don Taylor directed eight episodes of *Burke's Law*, appeared in two, and wrote one!

## Who Killed Purity Mather?

wr. Harlan Ellison, dir. Walter Grauman

*with Charlie Ruggles (I.A. Bugg), Telly Savalas (George O'Shea), Janet Blair (Rina Jacobs), Wally Cox (Count Szipesti), Gloria Swanson (Venus Hecate Walsh), Nancy Kovack (Bugg's hooker), Mary Ann Mobley (Sugar, Burke's date), Enid Jaynes (Purity Mather), Michael Fox (George McLeod), Eileen O'Neill (Sgt. Ames), Bill Erwin (fire marshal), Richard Reeves (Gorgo, chauffeur)*

Despite witches, vampires, fakers, fakirs, nudists, Mr. Jinks and Pixie and Dixie, Mary Ann Mobley, a chauffeur named after a Godzilla impersonator, and Harlan Ellison bashing away at his typewriter to mix them all together into the cauldron, this one isn't terribly interesting; the characters are just too weird, the name-dropping references too obvious. And as in all dramas where the body is burned beyond identification… well, you can guess the rest…

Mary Ann Mobley, who made four further appearances on *Burke's Law*, also made numerous appearances on *Love, American Style* and Spelling's *Fantasy Island* and *Love Boat*. She was in two Elvis films and loads of TV shows, but narrowly missed out on two key roles in the '60s, Batgirl and the Girl from UNCLE. This was the young beauty queen's first screen appearance, and she's clearly capable. Wally Cox often played nerds or eccentrics, and was best remembered as Mr. Biddle the birdwatcher on *The Beverly Hillbillies*, a recurring character. He had two series, *The Adventures of Hiram Holliday* and *Mr. Peepers*, and took guest roles in *The Twilight Zone*, *77, Sunset Strip*, *The Dick Van Dyke Show*, *Mission: Impossible*, *I Spy*, *Bonanza*, *The Lucy Show*, *Lost in Space*, *The Girl from UNCLE*, *The Monkees*, *Here's Lucy*, and *McMillan and Wife*, among many. He was best known as the voice of cartoon character *Underdog*, and for his numerous appearances on game show *Hollywood Squares*.

*Janet Blair in a publicity shot for similar fare, the horror film Burn, Witch, Burn.*

Charlie Ruggles' acting career began with the silents. He made four appearances in *Burke's Law*, and his various TV roles included guest shots in *Bewitched*, *Beverly Hillbillies*, *Ben Casey*, *The Andy Griffith Show*, *Wagon Train*, *Bonanza*, *The Munsters*, *Laredo*, and most memorably, *The Man from UNCLE*, in "The Ultimate Computer Affair". Gloria Swanson's acting career also went back to the silents. Other TV roles included

episodes of *Ben Casey*, *My Three Sons*, *The Beverly Hillbillies*, and *Doctor Kildare*. She appeared twice in *Burke's Law*.

Singer and actress Janet Blair did more singing than acting, but also appeared twice in the series. The previous year, she had played a witch in the highly regarded horror film *Burn, Witch, Burn!* Telly Savalas was best known for his film roles and his successful '70s cop show *Kojak*, revived for a run of TV movies in the 1980s and '90s. His early TV roles included episodes of *The Untouchables*, *The Twilight Zone*, *Bonanza*, *The Fugitive*, *Combat*, and two-part episodes of *The Man from UNCLE*, *The FBI*, Spelling's *Love Boat*, and *The Equalizer*. He appeared three times in *Burke's Law*.

This was director Walter Grauman's only episode of *Burke's Law*, and a rather unconventional one, but when he found a series he was comfortable on, he appeared to stick with it. He directed lengthy runs of *The New Breed*, *The Untouchables*, *The Fugitive*, *Streets of San Francisco*, *Barnaby Jones*, and *Murder, She Wrote*, but curiously returned to direct a single episode of the 1990s *Burkes' Law!*

### Who Killed Cynthia Royal?

wr. Jameson Brewer, Day Keene, dir. Charles Haas

*with Stubby Kaye (Joey Carson), Una Merkel (Miss Cartier), Marilyn Maxwell (Eudora Carey), MacDonald Carey (Ken Gardner), Kathy Nolan (Maura), Frankie Avalon (Max), Erika Peters (Miss Miles, Burke's date), Peter Leeds (Lt. Martin)*

Three chorus girls seem to have hit the cutting room floor. And Frankie Avalon appears to be wearing Joan Staley's t-shirt from the "Wade Walker" episode.

Some rather strained humor in this one (Stubby Kaye is pitiful), including the old "filling out a missing person form until realising it's a pet" routine with the amusing Una Merkel (trust me, it's not a spoiler). In fact, just about everything is telegraphed in this one; I defy you to be surprised. Charles Haas directed only this one episode of *Burke's Law*, a pattern that persevered throughout a rather undistinguished career in film and TV, although all credit to him, he kept working.

*Old timers Elsa Lanchester and Edward Everett Horton ham it up as a couple of deranged cheesecake photographers as another silly scheming girl bites the dust in "Who Killed Eleanora Davis?"*

### Who Killed Eleanora Davis?

wr. Don Taylor, dir. Herman Hoffman

*with Elsa Lanchester (Mrs. Ormsby), Edward Everett Horton (Grover Smith), Nick Adams (Harold), Arthur Hunnicutt (Professor Kingston), Jane Darwell (Mrs. Mulligan), Dean Jones (Rudy Davis), Terry Moore (Sarah Kingston), Debra Paget (Juliet, Burke's date), Eileen O'Neill (Sgt. Ames), Bobby Buntrock, Donnie Carter (boy scouts), Tommy Leap (smart kid), Margaret Mason, Carol Merrill, Carolyn Williamson (models)*

Back on form. The guys investigate the death of a pretty model turned photographer and blackmailer. Old timers Edward Everett Horton (who somehow managed to look old all his life) and *Bride of Frankenstein* Elsa Lanchester have a fine old time as an elderly couple in the girlie calendar business, as do Dean Jones and Terry Moore as a couple of quarrelsome lovebirds. Nick Adams is funny as a prudish nerd taking cheesecake pictures. He lives with his mother, who warned him about girls... Deadpan Arthur Hunnicutt, hayseed for hire (see *Outer Limits'* "Cry of Silence" or *Twilight Zone's* superlative "The Hunt") finds the body, and has a fine old time with some of the best lines of his career. This is *Burke's Law* at its best; you could take most of these scripts and film them again today, if only we still had character actors of this calibre and

*Debra Paget as Burke's date.*

anyone capable of making fun, frothy, feel-good TV drama... which, come to think of it, we don't, so you couldn't...

Pre-dating Dirk Benedict's *Battlestar Galactica* double-take in the credits of *The A-Team* by nearly two decades is a gag showing Gene Barry spotting a tombstone for someone who "called Bat Masterson a liar".

### Who Killed Beau Sparrow?

wr. John Meredyth Lucas, dir. David McDearmon

*with June Allyson (Jean Samson), Yvonne de Carlo (Countess Barbara Erozzi), Jack Haley (Victor Hagerty), Agnes Moorehead (Elizabeth Hagerty), Ken Murray (Charles Banner), Rosemary Bowe/ Stack (Ann Martin), Dan Tobin (Dr. Eric McLean), Michael Fox (George McLeod), Celeste Yarnall (Marlene, party guest), Jerry Catron (Beau Sparrow), Hedley Mattingly (Crenshaw, the butler), Jacqueline D'Avril (Paula, the maid), Linda Kennon (Giullietta, croquet player)*

Burke suspects murder when a party guest turns out to be a gigolo with a string of middle-aged women mourning his passing. Amongst them, Yvonne de Carlo (Lily of *The Munsters*) as a self-centred Countess ("like a box of poisoned chocolates") and Agnes Moorehead (Endora in *Bewitched*) marvellous as a wilting wife. Also in the cast is Rosemarie Bowe, a Sally Kellerman lookalike and the wife of Robert Stack.

The male cast is less exciting (although it includes Jack Haley of *The Wizard of Oz* as a hypochondriac businessman). The victim is Jerry Catron, a necessarily good swimmer and

bit player who made several appearances in *Voyage to the Bottom of the Sea* and *Star Trek*. Sci-fi fans can also look out for an equally brief appearance by Celeste Yarnall right at the beginning, who memorably guested in more substantial roles in *The Man from UNCLE*, *Star Trek*, and *Land of the Giants*. Burke goes virtually solo in this one, the second from *Star Trek*'s John Meredyth Lucas. Clever twist at the end, you won't see it coming.

While turning away Rosemarie Bowe and Celeste Yarnell's appealing characters, who both come on to him brazenly, Burke bizarrely pursues middle-aged cold fish and obnoxious hypocrite

CAPTAIN AMOS BURKE, the millionaire cop of ABC-TV's **BURKE'S LAW**, steps out of his Rolls-Royce into a high society party—and a baffling murder.

Starring GENE BARRY

WHO KILLED BEAU SPARROW?

Jean Samson (June Allyson), a deeply unpleasant bad-tempered psycho who we at first assume is simply being pursued for information. But no, he snuggles up with her at story's end, a rare example of bad taste from the debonair millionaire tease. A regular director on *Peter Gunn*, this was McDearmon's only outing on *Burke's Law*.

*Keenan Wynn and the beautiful Quinn O'Hara in "Who Killed Jason Shaw?"*

### Who Killed Jason Shaw?

wr. Lewis Reed, dir. Stanley Cherry

*with Tammy Grimes (Jill Marsh), Keenan Wynn (Hamilton Murphy), Burgess Meredith (Burton Reese), Richard Haydn (Julian Clarington), Oscar Homolka (Janek Cybowski), Joyce Jameson (Lisa Brewer), Marlyn Mason (Marian Wagner), Francine York (Cleo Fitzgerald), Quinn O'Hara (Lois Gordon, "business associate"), Larry Anthony (cue card guy), Milton Parsons (butler), June Kim (housemaid)*

The fully clothed dead body of a businessman who's supposed to be somewhere else is found in a shower, with the water running. Joyce Jameson, a bimbo set up to take the fall, carved a niche career for herself in the '60s playing such scatty babes, with appearances in numerous films, variety shows, sit-coms, and series, but she wasn't always happy about it. Here, she's so dumb, nobody could believe her guilty.

"Did you call about a homicide?"

"I called about a dead man in the shower. If that's a homicide, then you came to the right place"

"Miss Brewer, what do you do for a living?"

"Favors"

"Favors? What kind of favors?"

"Just… favors"

Stanley Cherry's direction is creative and interesting. Lewis Reed previously wrote the episode guest starring Elizabeth Montgomery. Ironically, Tammy Grimes, the guest star in this one, was the first choice for *Bewitched* and turned it down.

This is Burgess Meredith's second role in the series, and it's a bit more colorful than the first—he's a mad botanist. Also making a second appearance is Keenan Wynn, having fun as a used car salesman, Marlyn Mason (who only had a bit part in an earlier episode) as a lovelorn secretary (she'll be back in the second season as a surfer babe), and June Kim, who was previously Henry's girlfriend. Bit player Kim changed her name at the beginning of the '90s to June Kyoto Lu and at time of writing is still working today. Stealing a scene from Keenan Wynn, no mean feat, is gorgeous redhead and beach party movie babe Quinn O'Hara, sadly fully clothed on this occasion. Both O'Hara and Kim will play four roles during the series' run.

## Who Killed Snooky Martinelli?

wr. Gwen Bagni, Paul Dubov, dir. Robert Ellis Miller

*with Janice Rule (Seraphim Parks), Arlene Dahl (Eva Martinelli), Carl Reiner (Binky Fawcett), Cesar Romero (Louis Simone), Broderick Crawford (Carlos Vargas), Hoagy Carmichael (Jango Jordan, pianist), Sandra Giles (party guest), Eileen O'Neill (Sgt. Ames), Joe Scott (bartender), Don Gazzaniga (cop)*

A routine episode. After a deeply embarrassing opening with Barry himself playing the murder victim (this is the episode that would come on if you'd just told somebody how good the show was), the story proceeds with the usual collection of monied cranks and kooks, one of them Carl Reiner, creator of the groundbreaking *Dick Van Dyke Show*. Broderick Crawford is quite funny as a thug turned dandy, "the pedicured palooka" with a head full of rollers who's reluctant to take a swing at Burke because he's just had his nails done. Hoagy Carmichael, cast to type, was a legendary jazz pianist and famous songwriter ("Heart and Soul", "Georgia on my Mind", "Stardust") who dabbled in acting and appeared twice in *Burke's Law* and once in Barry's later series *The Name of the Game*, although not in one of Barry's episodes. Among his less known credits were a recurring role in the western

series *Laramie* and portraying his cartoon self in *The Flintstones*, for which he wrote an original composition.

Bagni (who wrote an earlier episode solo) and Dubov later became regular writers on the equally deeply improbable *Honey West*. Their dialogue was strong, but their stories for both veered well over the line into camp.

## Who Killed What's His Name?

wr. Tony Barrett, dir. Don Taylor

*with Elizabeth Allen (Elizabeth Dunwoody), Dick Clark (Peter Barrows), Andy Devine (Charles Cortland), Reginald Gardiner (Mr. Piggott), Gena Rowlands (Paulette Shane), Virginia Grey (Mrs. Barrows), Spike Jones (Duke), Jonathan Hole (Henry Newbold, bank manager), Elizabeth MacRae (Marcy, Burke's date),*

177

Lennie Weinrib (Cully, bartender), Edgar Bergen (George Smith), Wilton Graff (Victor Barrows, victim), Harry Harvey Snr. (Huggins, bank guard), Michael Fox (George McLeod), Roy Glenn (patrolman), Paul Sorensen (ambulanceman/raider), Hy Averback (director), James Blount ("Igor")

A callous businessman gets his comeuppance; the title actually refers to the second killing. This is a vast improvement over writer Tony Barrett's first effort, "Who Killed Billy Jo?", with the dialogue this time up to standard. An even more sordid selection of the mad, bad, and sad appear.

*David White of Bewitched plays the victim as a crooked lawyer whose guilty conscience gets the better of him fatally, in "Who Killed Madison Cooper?"*

Dick Clark of *American Bandstand* fame is surprisingly good as an actor, and Edgar Bergen shines in a small but significant role. It's also rare to see Andy Devine playing something other than a hick hayseed. Virginia Grey and Gena Rowlands make the most of their single scenes, and Elizabeth Allen vamps it up

again in her second appearance. Reginald Gardiner and Spike Jones give very forced and arch performances as Brits.

The IMDB tells us that Tony Barrett was a pseudonym for Martin Lefkowitz, an actor who turned to writing for the *Peter Gunn* series, to which he contributed extensively. He wrote fifteen episodes of *Burke's Law* altogether, followed by six episodes of *Honey West*, which lead to four *Girl from UNCLE*. Later, he wrote for cop show *The Felony Squad* and wrote for, and produced Spelling's *The Mod Squad*.

### Who Killed Madison Cooper?

wr. Lewis Reed, dir. Jeffrey Hayden

*with Carolyn Jones (Carole Durand), Kevin McCarthy (Elliot Dunning), Jeanne Crain (Amy Booth), Marty Ingels (Wally), Dorothy Lamour (Lovey Harrington), Terry Thomas (Arthur Shelby), David White (Madison Cooper), Louis Quinn (deli owner), Byron Foulger (Howard), Lynn Bernay (Burke's date), Bob Bice (hotel desk clerk), Stephen Chase (judge), I. Stan Jolley (wealthy home-owner)*

A corrupt lawyer with a terminal illness tries to make amends to the clients he sold down the river... but underestimates the strength of their feelings. Which one went so far as to kill him? Lewis Reed was one of the series' wittier writers, and this was his third outing.

Marty Ingels, although primarily a club comic, had an unfortunate habit of turning up in cop shows in dismally unfunny cameos—anything from *The Detectives* to *Adam 12* to *CSI*. He's nowhere near as amusing as he thinks he is. Thirty years later, Ingels turned up in the short-lived 1990s *Burke's Law* revival. Ingels' other claim to fame was providing the animated cartoon voice of *Pac-Man* (in the previous episode, Lennie Weinrib, the voice of the horrendous Scrappy-Doo, appeared!). Carolyn Jones is back, in a single role this time, as is the wonderful Terry Thomas, although not as strong as last time. Kevin McCarthy of *Invasion of the Body Snatchers* appears as a ham actor who tells his story in the flashback format of a bad movie. And the victim is played by David White, Larry Tate in *Bewitched*.

### Who Killed April?

wr. Albert Beich, dir. Lewis Allen

*with Jack Carter (Red Dekker), Hans Conreid (Doctor Bing), Gloria Grahame (Mrs. Decker), Martha Hyer (Clarissa Montgomery), Eddie Bracken (Hatton, diner manager), Mark Goddard (Richard Adams), Irene Hervey (Tim's mother), Francine York (Liz, Burke's date), Michael Fox (George McLeod), Eileen O'Neill (Sgt. Ames), Jean Paul King (hockey players' doctor), Buddy Lewis (workman), Rue McClanahan (waitress), Danielle Aubrey (maid), Stuart Hall (m'aitre d'), Shep Houghton (cop)*

Albert Beich wrote two earlier episodes with William Wright, including the pilot, and this is his first solo effort. Unbelievably, this episode has the gall to use the same opening scene, truncated, as the pilot he wrote. To add to the feeling of *deja vu*, Francine York played Burke's date in an episode a few weeks earlier (but with a different name). The scenes with Tim's mother include so much exposition, it's

quite possible this episode is being constructed around un-used pieces of the pilot. When episode seems cobbled together mid-season, detective Jon suspects attempt to make up time with un-used film — that's Jon's Law. Nevertheless, Mako appear to have hit the editing room floor, so you win some, you lose some. *

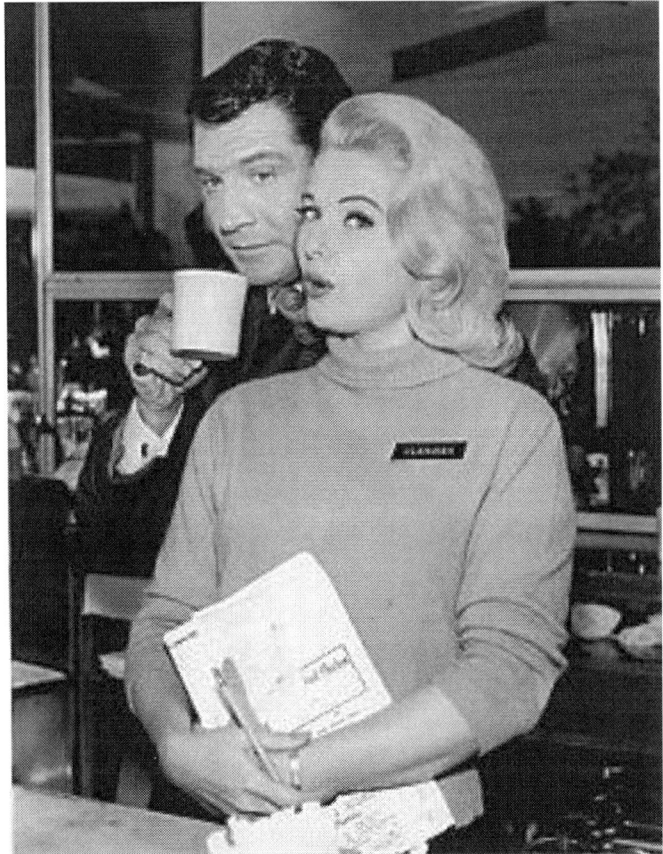

*Martha Hyer appeared in six episodes in total! Here, she's a waitress, helping Burke figure out "Who Killed April?".*

* It's entirely possible that the DVD prints I'm reviewing from are syndication prints cut for extra ads, of course.

Irene Hervey, who appears as Tim's mother, went on to a supporting role in *Honey West*. She had appeared in most of the Warners detective series, and guested on Spelling's *Mod Squad* and *Charlie's Angels*.

Jack Carter looks way too old to be a hockey player. There's a funny scene in a psychiatrist's office, as Hans Conreid (with foreign Euro-voice, of course) analyses Burke's desire for a Rolls. Conreid was rarely funny (he's dire in *The Lucy Show* and *Lost in Space*), but he's okay here.

*Mark Goddard from Johnny Ringo and Lost in Space has a small but strong role in this episode.*

This is Hyer's second of six, and York's second of five. There's a shortage of starlets in Hollywood, you see. Mark Goddard (Major West in *Lost in Space* and a regular co-star in Spelling's *Johnny Ringo*) has a nice substantial role as an angry young man. *Golden Girls* fan? A very young Rue McClanahan is the 'green shrimp' waitress.

### Who Killed Carrie Cornell?

wr. Jay Dratler, dir. Byron Paul

*with Michael Ansara (Big Bwana Smith), William Shatner (Arthur Reynolds),* *Jim Backus (Pork Pie Hannigan), Fernando Lamas (El Greco), Joanie Sommers (Pee Wee Wilson), Diana Lynn (Marian Van Martin), Fred Barry (young cadet), Amzie Strickland (cadet leader), James Secrest (Jennings, unmarried lab man), Percy Helton (girlie mag publisher), Bill Catching (Keeler, manservant), Michael Fox (George McLeod), Maria Tsien McClay (Amiko), Diana Birk (Annabelle), Lou Byrne (party guest), Shep Houghton, Cosmo Sardo (musicians)*

*Fernando Lamas with Gene Barry*

Another selfish and two-faced bimbo bites the dust... the third so far, with more to come. Most of the series' victims are either scheming, heartless women, or greedy, selfish businessmen.

Jay Dratler's dialogue is very good, and it's a shame he didn't do more.

"I didn't like her. But she liked living. And it isn't right that somebody stopped her" / "The police department agrees with you"

180

"I'm a man of many interests, Captain. But I never did anything well until I found myself" / "And where were you when you found yourself?"

"She eats meat. People who eat meat aren't nice" / "We'll have to have the entire department investigated immediately"

*Michael Ansara and William Shatner would be reunited for Star Trek's "Day of the Dove" a few years later. (c) Paramount.*

Captain Kirk (William Shatner) and his adversary Kang the Klingon (Michael Ansara from "Day of the Dove") appear together in this one... and for added cult TV interest, Captain Burton from *Land of the Giants* questions Captain Kirk from *Star Trek*. Yikes. Gene Barry's son finds the body. Jim Backus of *Gilligan's Island* makes a second appearance, this time as a defeatist club owner who keeps trying to turn himself in even though he didn't do it, and the delightful Percy Helton (from *Kiss Me Deadly* and *Land of the Giants'* "Ghost Town" among many more) has an all-too-brief turn.

This was the only contribution to the series from Jay Dratler, story consultant for the psychiatry series *Breaking Point*, and Byron Paul, who worked extensively with television legend Dick Van Dyke.

*Gary Conway with cast members in a publicity picture from his later series Land of the Giants, for 20th Century Fox.*

### Who Killed His Royal Highness?

wr. Gwen Bagni, Paul Dubov, dir. Don Weis

*with Elizabeth Montgomery (Smitty), Mickey Rooney (Archie Lido), Telly Savalas (Charlie Prince), Sheldon Leonard (Ronald 'Touchy' Touchstone), Bert Parks (Gus Leeps), Gale Storm (Honey Feather Leeps), Linda Darnell (Monica Crenshaw), Paul Dubov (Anatole Gregory), Eileen O'Neill (Sgt. Ames), Lurene Tuttle (Amanda), Margaret Mason (Burke's date), David Fresco (desk clerk), Bobby Johnson (butler), Alex Rodine (dancer), Stuart Holmes (Max)*

Burke — "Have you done something to your hair?"

Ames (with new hair-do) — "No sir"

"Are you sure?"

"I'm positive"

"It looks different"

"Don't you like it?"

"Well, if it's the same as it's always been, why shouldn't I?"

"Men!"

*Telly Savalas, later Universal's Kojak, appears three times in Burke's Law.*

Elizabeth Montgomery is as charming and photogenic as ever, and Telly Savalas amusing as a Russian Prince living in a flophouse, but it's Bert Parks and Gale Storm who steal the show as a double act who can barely conceal their loathing for each other during their stage act, a song and dance

performance of 'Baby Face' fraught with tension and ill-disguised hostility, a wonderful bit of improv. Legendary TV producer (*The Dick Van Dyke Show, I Spy*) and professional comedy gangster Sheldon Leonard (after whom the boys in *The Big Bang Theory* are named) goes through his usual routine as a safecracker.

*Gene Barry with Marie Wilson*

### Who Killed Marty Kelso?

wr. Tony Barrett, dir. Don Taylor

*with Luciana Paluzzi (Mia Bandini), Diane McBain (Susan Shaw), Glynis Johns (Steffi Bernard), Herschel Bernardi (Kid McCoy), Marie Wilson (Chuchi Smith), John Ericson (Frank Jorek), Don Taylor (George Hogarth), Mary Ann Mobley (Denise, Burke's date), Michael Fox (George McLeod), Army Archerd (as himself), Henry Corden (Boris, voice coach), Jack Raine (Dunhill, butler), Robert Kenneally, Dana White (secretaries), Harvey Parry (Kelso)*

Writer Barrett, ever the cynical misanthropic reactionary, unimpressed with new trends, has great fun with the French New Wave and pretentious film directors.

Tim — "It was actually a very interesting picture — all that symbolism, especially that scene in the mud. I bet the director talked to you for hours about that scene"

Mia — "No"

Tim — "No? Gee, that complicated motivation, all those subtle shadings… What did he actually say?"

Mia — "He say make love in the mud, and I make!"

Burke (chiming in) — "She make!"

Mia — "Symbolism! Ay-yi-yi!"

Luciana Paluzzi steals the show effortlessly in this one, having great fun with her role as an Italian actress, which of course she was, although not so much in art films as spy films. Best known for *Thunderball*, in a role brutally sent up in the *Austin Powers* franchise, she spent most of the '60s playing treacherous Euro-trash in *UNCLE* episodes and *UNCLE* imitators, although I think this is my favorite of her various appearances. Also on hand, Diane McBain, Elvis babe (*Spinout*) and bad girl of the B-movies (would you believe *The Mini-Skirt Mob?*). She appeared four times in *Burke's Law*, six times in *77, Sunset Strip*, regularly in *Surfside Six*, and two times each in *Batman, The Man from UNCLE, The Wild Wild West,* and *Charlie's Angels*. And fellow Elvis starlet Mary Ann Mobley's back too, again playing Burke's date, but with a new name, in the second of five minor roles that began her career. She went on to co-star with Presley in *Girl Happy* and *Harum Scarum*.

Director Don Taylor cameos as director George Hogarth, voice artist Henry Corden (the second Fred Flintstone and many a boisterous cartoon villain) has a funny bit as a voice coach, and Leon Lontoc finally gets some lines, and struggles with them. John Ericson is back in his swim trunks again playing much the same sort of role as before for the second of three guest shots.

Les — "Anything I can do?" / Burke — "Yes — You tell the boys in the lab if they come up with one more twist, they're fired"

*Right, Luciana Paluzzi; below, Diane McBain with Elvis in Spinout*

## Who Killed Avery Lord?

wr. Lewis Reed, dir. Richard Kinon

*with Felicia Farr (Whitney Kelly), Ed Wynn (Zachary Belden), Chill Wills (Stanton Custer), Broderick Crawford (Hamilton Talbert), Linda Foster (Anne), Lewis Charles (locksmith), Whitney Chase, Milton Parsons, Maureen Dawson (tenants), Jeanne Rainer (Burke's date), John Damler (Avery Lord, victim), Tom Kennedy (charmed warehouseman), Henry Hunter (waiter)*

*Broderick Crawford*

Lewis Reed's episodes always had a slightly jokey tone to them, and after a good start with "Who Killed Mr. X?" his episodes got sillier and sillier in tone. Credibility was not their strong suit. Although *Burke's Law* was a light, frothy series, Reed's episodes tried too hard to be wacky. Sometimes they could be saved by Reed's wit or the guest cast, but not this time. Everything is over-the-top and played for laughs. Comedic actor Ed Wynn has an unfunny bit as a crooked businessman building wobbly tower blocks, Chill Wills is back as another opportunist, a seer before his time, selling 'health food'. "Give everyone time to answer the door" says Burke after a lengthy discourse on the law of illegal entry as he and his men set out to search an apartment building... and then walks right in — twice.

## Who Killed Andy Zygmunt?

wr. Harlan Ellison, dir. Don Taylor

*with Jack Weston (Silly McCree), Ann Blyth (Deidre De Mara), Deborah Walley (Gwenny Trent), MacDonald Carey (Burl Stanley Mason), Aldo Ray (Mr. Harold), Tab Hunter (Barney Blake), Jonathan Hole (art expert), Sandra Warner (Mary, Burke's date), Eileen O'Neill (Sgt. Ames), Jackie Joseph (Peggy), Alvy Moore (Arnie), Michael Fox (George McLeod), Margaret Mason (Dona, poodle girl), Beverly Adams, Kay Sutton (models), Janet Clark (Norman Rockwell admirer)*

*Deborah Walley with Elvis in Spinout. She plays a similar 'tough gal' role here.*

"Accident?" / "Not unless he ran onto those spikes backwards" / "It's invigorating to know that I've got such clear-headed men working for me"

184

Pre-dating Krusty the Klown by thirty years, the scenes with Jack Weston as a creepy and insincere childrens' entertainer are broad, clumsy, unsubtle and heavy handed, as well as featuring a major plot cliche in his exposure as such. Stealing the show are the lovely Deborah Walley (*Gidget Goes Hawaiian, Beach Blanket Bingo, Ski Party, Spinout,* and many more in a similar vein) and recurring player Eileen O'Neill (*Bewitched, The Beverly Hillbillies, Batman, The Munsters, I Dream of Jeannie,* etc.), absurdly called into action when a female suspect ducks into the ladies' restroom, leaving the men powerless outside as if a force field has been turned on. Also on hand, *Little Shop of Horrors'* Jackie Joseph (silly Melody in the *Josie and the Pussycats* cartoons).

Once again, the pop culture references are flying around fast and furious, immediately identifying a Harlan Ellison script, including the *Creature from the Black Lagoon, King Kong, Lassie, Rin-Tin-Tin,* Norman Rockwell, Mickey Spillane, *Nero Wolfe,* and *Have Gun, Will Travel,* alongside an amusing nod to Yves Klein's *Anthropometry* (although sadly, 1960s TV could not present us with nude models).

The theme of the episode is pop art, and Andy Zygmunt (found impaled on one of his own works by the wonderful Jonathan Hole as a snooty lecturer) is, of course, a parody of Andy Warhol, and naturally that old lawyer's trick of mentioning the real Warhol in the script to demonstrate that we're talking about a *completely different person here,* gives the production a legal out if there had been any trouble. This is standard practice in films and TV when someone is being blatantly sent up and might sue, and it's always fun to spot The Line That Must Not Be Flubbed, Changed, or Deleted! (Years later, Ellison had one of his *Man from UNCLE* episodes taken out of the syndication package for several years due to litigation, after he named the characters after parodies of some so-called friends).

And needless to say, Burl Stanley Mason has absolutely *nothing* to do with Erle Stanley Gardner, creator of *Perry Mason.*

## Who Killed the Paper Dragon?

wr. Jameson Brewer, Day Keene, dir. Marc Daniels

*with Barbara Eden (Sylvia Hansen), James Shigeta (Sidney Ying), Ginny Tiu (little girl), Miyoshi Umeki (Mary Ling), Howard Duff (Charlie January), Dan Duryea (Hop Sing Kelly), Ann Tyrell (Ruth Potter, witness), Kathy Kersh (Burke's date), Tura Satana (dancer), Don Gazzaniga (cop), June Kim (hostess), Johnny Silver (Gil, bartender)*

*Howard Duff in The Felony Squad.*

This was the second of Howard Duff's two appearances in *Burke's Law.* A familiar face in American TV, he featured in five ongoing series during his career, *Mr. Adams and Eve* with his wife, actress Ida Lupino, *Dante, The Felony Squad, Flamingo Road,* and *Knots Landing.* He also appeared in several episodes of '70s anthology series *Police Story.*

It was the second of four for Barbara Eden who, despite starring in several other series before and after, will forever be best known for her iconic role in *I Dream of Jeannie.* And it was the first of two guest shots for silver screen villain Dan Duryea, who previously appeared in the threadbare 1950s detective series *China Smith,* set in Singapore. His final work was a recurring role in mid-'60s soap *Peyton Place.*

*Barbara Eden in Flaming Star, with yes, it's that man again.*

After a career spent playing stereotypical roles such as this one, Miyoshi Umeki earned a regular role in the late '60s sit-com *The Courtship of Eddie's Father.* James Shigeta worked constantly throughout a career spanning five decades, but will probably be best remembered for his Elvis film, *Paradise, Hawaiian Style,* as helicopter pilot Danny Kohana, and his appearance in later years as Mr. Takagi, who "won't be joining us for the rest of his life", in *Die Hard.* Ginny Tiu was an accomplished pianist, and demonstrates her skills here.

She was on a number of variety shows of the period, and appeared with Elvis and other members of her family in his film *Girls! Girls! Girls!* Her sister Vicky had a larger and very similar part in Presley's *It Happened at the World's Fair*.

This was also a second appearance for stunning starlet Kathy Kersh, whose TV appearances included three here, several in a *Beverly Hillbillies* storyline, and memorable one-offs in *The Man from UNCLE* and *Batman*. She was married to both Vince Edwards and then Burt Ward for about five minutes each. Her final role was in the low-rent exploiter *The Gemini Affair* with Marta Kristen. Ann Tyrell was Ann Sothern's support in her two 1950s sit-coms *Private Secretary* and *The Ann Sothern Show*. This was her final role before retiring, and she makes the most of it.

Fan of *Faster, Pussycat! Kill! Kill!?* Don't bother. Tura Satana is on early, but briefly, as a dancer who says "Helllooo, Amos"—as they do in this show. Time would be better spent seeking out her two *UNCLE* appearances.

Jameson Brewer previously wrote the lacklustre "Who Killed Cynthia Royal?" episode, also with novelist Day Keene. Frankly, this one is only marginally better because of the cast, and suffers from all the stereotypical Oriental gags of the era, although the script gives short shrift to the cliche that all Asians look alike, commendable for the time. Asians were about ten to fifteen years behind American blacks in ridding themselves of the offensive pop culture stereotypes that littered post-war Hollywood, and unfortunately 1960s film and TV is frequently burdened with embarrassing bits of business based on horribly outdated and ignorant cliches. Ginny Tiu is excellent as the kid Burke gets saddled with, and Shigeta, Eden, and Kersh all brighten up the screen

considerably. The less said about the parts Duff and Duryea were lumbered with, the better. Brewer wrote regularly for *Branded*, *The Guns of Will Sonnett*, and *The Addams Family*, and contributed to other series and film projects including the dumbest *Girl from UNCLE* episode produced, but by the 1970s he was writing mostly for cartoons, notably *The New Scooby-Doo Movies*, a series which paired the dog detective with various guest characters and celebrities in cartoon form. Day Keene was primarily a novelist, who dabbled in television only very occasionally, and always partnered with someone.

Despite lengthy runs on many series, including *I Love Lucy*, *Star Trek*, *Hogan's Heroes*, and the medical series *Ben Casey*, *Doctor Kildare*, and *Marcus Welby*, this was the only episode of *Burke's Law* that Marc Daniels directed, the series joining his list of one-off wonders.

### Who Killed Molly?

wr. Albert Beich, dir. Don Weis

*with Hoagy Carmichael (Carl Baker), Nanette Fabray (Amanda Tribble), Jayne Mansfield (Cleo Patrick), Arthur O'Connell (Dr. Alexander), Marianna Hill (Dr. Goddard), Jay C. Flippen (Lt. Grogan, Vice Squad), Larry Blake (Mr. Taggart, Treasury Dept.), Michael Fox (George McLeod), Eileen O'Neill (Sgt. Ames), Jack Betts (Bucky Martin), Allyson Ames, Sandra Giles, Sandra Wirth (landladies), Rachael Romen, Juli Reding, Carol Andreson, Sharon Cintron (strippers), Joyce Nizzari (Molly Baker), Irwin Charone (funeral director), Breena Howard (waitress)*

Tim—"What do you think about all this?" / Les—"I think that for a sweet little housewife in a rose-covered cottage, she swung like a circus trapeze!"

George—"Not Molly again? What is she, a gang?"

Stripper enters, rubbing her bum: "Watch it girls, there's a juvenile in the balcony with a slingshot"

*Gene Barry and Jayne Mansfield dispose of a pet snake… respectfully, of course…*

It's yet another girl with a secret past, furtive present, and no future, but Beich has come up with a highly amusing and original—yet typical—episode of the series.

The scene at the pet cemetery is particularly funny, with a surprise twist as Burke makes a chance discovery that finally blows the case wide open. Irwin Charone, one of those classic character actors who—like Roger C. Carmel or Jonathan Hole—looks like a human cartoon, appears as the funeral director for doggies and moggies. Arthur O'Connell has a touching single scene as the living embodiment of that old admonishment 'there's no fool like an old fool'.

Nanette Fabray gives the first of two terrible performances in the series; if you think she's over the top here, wait until you see the next one. In fact, wait until you see her in *The Girl from UNCLE* —good grief! Otherwise, everyone is good, and there is plenty of the series' trademark eye candy. Joyce Nizzari was well-cast as short-lived Molly; she had the appearance of a girl-next-door type but worked as a *Playboy* girl and centerfold. Marianna Hill is the discarded date who pulls the time-honored taking-off-her-glasses gag, Jayne Mansfield, one of the 1950s' ersatz second-league Monroes, is obviously well cast as a stripper, and there's three very sexy landladies in a running gag. And how's this for some intriguing trivia? Mansfield's stripper is called Cleo Patrick, in a parody of Cleopatra. A few years later, the punnish name would resurface again, for King Tut's moll in an episode of *Batman…* where Cleo would be portrayed by—Marianna Hill.

### Who Killed WHO IV?

wr. Gwen Bagni, Paul Dubov, dir. Don Weis

*with Lola Albright (Jennifer Carlisle), Steve Cochran (St. John Carlisle), Reginald Gardiner (Pepperill Twill), Patsy Kelly (Agatha Beauregard), Fess Parker (Herman Sitwell), Nancy Kovack (Prudence, secretary), Lisa Seagram (Diana, Burke's date), Eileen O'Neill (Sgt. Ames), Annazette*

188

Williams/Chase (maid), Johnny Silver, Bill McLean (grooms), Larry Anthony (head waiter), Howard Risner (butler)

Just for once, this is Gene Barry's episode rather than the guest players'. Lola Albright returns as a lost love of Burke's who has married a total creep (Steve Cochran enjoying himself immensely as an effete arrogant snob) who's in the frame as the number one suspect. There's an excellent scene of verbal sparring between Barry and Cochran in the first act, and a similarly impressive scene with Albright later. Burke's still bitter about the relationship, and Barry plays it spot on. Furthermore, he's got an excellent script to work from.

A little less successful is a weird and unnecessary dream sequence with Burke as Sherlock Holmes. *Burke's Law* was always entertaining when it offered no more than frothy fun, as the previous episode demonstrated perfectly, but this one and the next showed how readily it rose to the occasion when played for real, with the pointless dream sequence showing the frivolous side of the show at its worst and most indulgent. Patsy Kelly offers classier humor as the proverbial little old lady from Pasadena (who only drives her car on Sundays of course), and Disney's *Davy Crockett* Fess Parker is amusing in his first scene as a wealthy hick. Reginald Gardiner, as opposed to his previous turn, plays his role relatively straight this time to advantage. A good one, with a great one coming up next...

### Who Killed Annie Foran?

wr. Tony Barrett, dir. Lewis Allen

*with John Cassavetes (Eddie Dineen), Don Ameche (Whitman Saunders), Wendell Corey (Milo Morgan), Gena Rowlands (Mitzi Carlilse), Sterling Holloway (Fisk, hotel manager), Jackie Coogan (Coach Crowley), Byron Foulger (Mr. Beldon), Dee Hartford (Cecelia, Burke's date), Seymour Cassell (Artie, car-hop), Sandra Grant (Valerie Van Dyke), Roger Til (Andre, head waiter), John Rayborn (police officer), Gil Stuart (butler), Rachel Romen (Frankie, tipster), Connie Ducharne (secretary)*

*John Cassavetes in his series Johnny Staccato.*

Eddie – "How long do you think a man should live, huh? Seventy? Eighty? My old man died when he was forty-six. There was no cave-in, nothing. He just got tired. I don't think my old man ever had a steak in his life, I have one every night and I have a manicure three times a week"

Burke – "And does that make you happy?"

Eddie – "You bet it does, baby"

Following Duff and Lupino, another husband and wife team guest together in this one – John Cassavetes and Gena Rowlands. Cassavetes, as an

189

arrogant, self-centered ball player, and Don Ameche, as a smooth, vicious gossip-mongering columnist, vie for the dubious accolade of most despicable character in the entire series in this well-played and well-written entry. After his dismal start, this is Barrett's third home-run in a row, an excellent episode with the guest cast superb. A solid script with well-written exchanges played straight allows a great team to bring in a win. The dialogue dances as ever, but lacks the jokey, glib tone that so often sends the series into the category of camp.

Cassavetes as the weasel Eddie, Ameche as the sneering writer, and Wendell Corey as his ill-treated loser assistant are given fine support from a selection of character actors. Byron Foulger is on top form in his usual role of hat-clutching snivelling nobody (which he recreates for a *Honey West,* among many others), the perfectly cast Seymour Cassell makes the most of his lines as a car-hop, Dee Hartford (Verda in *Lost in Space,* Miss Iceland in *Batman*) is Burke's long-suffering abandoned date, Jackie Coogan plays a rare straight role well, Roger Til suffers stoically as a put-upon *maitre'd,* and Sterling Holloway gives his best supporting performance ever as the creepy-crawly hotel manager, a million miles away from his usual cartoonish mad professors. Throughout it all, Cassavetes rants in everyone's face like a frustrated and impotent demon (Conway's Tilson is magnificently unimpressed, stealing the scene simply by being completely unmoved), and Ameche is immaculate as the hateful gossip columnist, trying to look untouched in the face of Burke's withering and well-aimed contempt.

A f*ckin' briliant one, and perhaps the best episode in the series.

## Who Killed My Girl?

wr. Tony Barrett, dir. Don Taylor

*with Richard Carlson (Dr. Carol Smith), Jane Greer (Mrs. Smith), Stephen McNally (Frank Walsh), Gene Raymond (Arthur Wade), Don Taylor (Scubie Baker), Ruta Lee (Laura Jean Cunard), Mabel Albertson (Adrianna Mercer), Barbara Michaels (Diana Mercer), Paul Rhone (Leonard, doctor)*

Burke finally gets to complete one of his own oft-interrupted dates… only to find that when he gets the pre-credits call to action, the victim is the girl he just dropped off. This neat twist on the standard opening scene leads into a second story (following "Who Killed WHO IV?") in which Burke is necessarily a little more grim and a little less flippant than usual. There's a good pay-off, a few twists and turns in the road to get there, and a solid guest cast including returnees Richard Carlson and Stephen McNally. Director Taylor nicks another plum role for actor Don as a creepy jazzman and plays it well, while Ruta Lee has a strong single scene. Ditto sit-com veteran Mabel Albertson, who shows up near the end.

Les—"I hear Acapulco's big this time of year"

Burke—"You've seen one flip, you've seen 'em all"

Les—"Why don't you pack a bag and let us nail this?"

Burke—"You know better"

Les—"I know a walking bomb when I see one"

Tim—"Anything I can do?" / "Make everyone stop walking around on tip-toe and I'd appreciate it"

They should have saved this one for the second season opener.

And for light relief, Leon Lontoc's best line in the whole series.

"Henry, better get that screen fixed" / "Why big hurry? No flies in Beverly Hills! Not allowed!"

## Who Killed the Eleventh Best Dressed Woman in the World?

wr. Edith Sommer, dir. Don Weis

*with Joanna Dru (Solange Kelly), Hazel Court (Constance Dexter), Jeanne Crain (Polly Martin), Martha Hyer (Gloria Vickers), Susan Strasberg (Tawny Hastings), Josephine Hutchinson (Madeleine Vickers), Lisa Seagram (Burke's date), Peggy Rea (Mrs. Lewis), Michael Fox (George McLeod), Betty Barry, Sandra Gould, Emlen Davies, Leoda Richards (spa clients), Gail Bonney, Charlotte Lawrence, Monica Keating, Arlene Anderson (spa attendants), Don Gazzaniga (police officer), Tom Kennedy (repairman)*

"All she wanted was a husband. Everybody's husband"

"Did you know the deceased?" / "No, I've *heard* of her. We're very particular in Pasadena"

A small army of Hollywood grand dames on the slide into television make up the patrons of an expensive beauty spa where the wealthy go to be conned into thinking pain means gain in the eternal youth game. As usual, each one would have loved to have murdered their fellow attendee and victim (body found dumped in a mud bath via wheelbarrow!), but only one got the chance to actually do it ("I refuse to be accused of a murder that I haven't yet had time to commit!" snaps one). It barely matters which one did, but as

usual, it's fun getting there. The journey is a major bitch-fest among the monied sisterhood. The third and final script from Edith Sommer. Smashing.

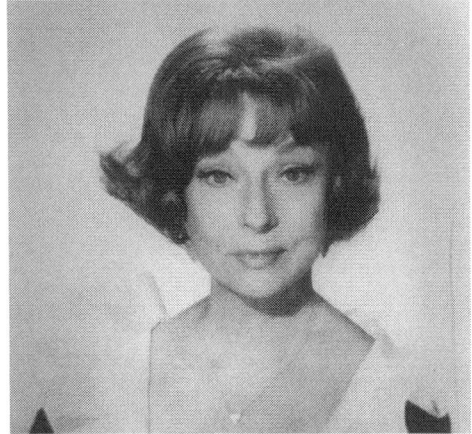

*The wonderful Agnes Moorehead, who made three appearances in the series.*

## Who Killed Don Pablo?

wr. Gwen Bagni, Paul Dubov, dir. Richard Kinon

*with Patricia Medina (Serena Diablo), Agnes Moorehead (Don Pablo's mother), Cesar Romero (Antonio Cardoza), Forrest Tucker (Cyrus Smuts), John Cassavetes (Carlos De Vega), Cecil Kellaway (Brother Flaherty), Joan Staley (traffic cop), Irene Tedrow (librarian), Maureen Dawson (secretary), Marissa Mathes (waitress), Jacqueline D'Avril (maid), Anne Morell, Tina Marsell (girls), Alvira Corona (dancer)*

Rapid return appearances for Cassavetes, Moorehead (above), and Romero, although to be fair, all playing very different roles and always welcome. Last time, Moorehead played a frail sort, here she's a strong woman. Great cameo from Joan Staley as a traffic cop in the opening instead of the usual dodging-a-date routine. Director Richard Kinon helmed six episodes of

*Burke's Law* altogether, and made a career out of handling light-hearted froth, much of it for Spelling. His credits read like a roll call of every cute show on television, and this episode is pretty damn cute.

Burke to Les: "How'd you make out with Mother?" / "Well, either she's confused, or I am" / "Tell your old dad" / "How old would you say Don Pablo was?" / "Oh, I'd say about forty-eight" / "That's what I thought. But she talks about him as though he's a boy" / "Mothers are known to do that" / "She said that he deserved to die" / "Mothers are not known to do that"

### Who Killed One Half of Glory Lee?

wr. Harlan Ellison, dir. Don Weis

*with Gisele MacKenzie (Keekee Lee), Nina Foch (Anjanette Delacroix), Anne Helm (Sable Delacroix), Betty Hutton (Carlene Glory), Buster Keaton (Mortimer Lovely), Joan Blondell (Candy Sturdevant), Jean Carson (photographer), Cheerio Meredith (Mrs. McCree), Michael Fox (George McLeod), Eileen O'Neill (Sgt. Ames), Dawn Wells (Wendy, first date), Jill Donahue (Sherri, second date), Robert Bice (Fergie, pick-up man), Marianna Case (Barbi, elevator girl), Myrna Ross (second elevator girl), Eddie Quillan (elevator supervisor), Milton Parsons (Grippsholm, divorce lawyer), Paul Sorensen (vice cop), Lester Dorr (butler), Sol Gorss (comedy heavy), Patti Pennell (manhandled model)*

By the end of the first season the writers were beginning to have fun with the rigid format of the opening scenes and its inevitable 'phone call to duty, and none more so than Harlan Ellison here, who opens with Burke having two girls on the go. Ellison, Gene Barry, the girls (Wells and Donahue), and Leon Lontoc play the usual interrupted tryst

scene for laughs and it works fine. This time the victim has been found wedged into a stuck elevator in the garment district with a bunch of mannequins... Among the Hollywood old-timers this go-round are Betty Hutton, Joan Blondell, Buster Keaton, and the gravel-voiced Jean Carson. Another strong episode from Ellison, his fourth and unfortunately final contribution to the series.

*Gary Conway as he appeared in his starring role in 20th Century Fox's* Land of the Giants

"Don't feel too badly, Tim. You know they laughed at Da Vinci, giggled at Galileo, and thought Kleinsvogel was a lunatic"

"Who was Kleinsvogel?"

"A lunatic"

"Gentlemen, shall we cool it? We're being observed by the taxpayers, and we wouldn't want them to think we're confused now, would we..."

## Second Season

## (1964-'65)

### Who Killed the Surf Broad?

wr. Tony Barrett, dir. Don Taylor

*with Dewey Martin (Con Murdock), Sharon Farrell (Libby Hale), MacDonald Carey (Franklyn Warren), Dorothy Lamour (Mrs. Romaine), Theodore Bikel (Vic Bates), Marlyn Mason (Maxine, surf shop), Joan Patrick (Cassie, the mechanic), Michael Fox (George McLeod), Kip King (Skins), Barbara Michaels (Tina Romaine), Frank Leo, Mickey Dora Jnr. (surfers)*

"All she had to do was snap her fingers, and they'd come running from miles around" / "Was Con Murdock the four minute mile?"

"What's to care about a bum who'd rather chase a wave than a buck?"

Tim goes undercover as a surfer. Despite the beach scenes being filmed, directed, and acted like a beach movie of the period, Frankie and Annette this ain't. The teenage surfing fraternity doesn't come out of this too well, portrayed by Barrett as shallow, callous, insensitive and empty-headed. He clearly has a major chip on his shoulder about young people, and his low opinion of teenagers permeates the entire episode to its detriment. There's also some pretty lame back projection of background beach scenes. The surfing scenes are filmed the same way they all were in the early '60s, from Gidget to Elvis, with the 'surfer' weaving around against an obvious backdrop in close-up at the studio and cut in with long shots of library footage. It wasn't convincing then, and it's even less so now.

### Who Killed Vaudeville?

wr. Gwen Bagni, Paul Dubov, dir. Gene Nelson

*with William Demarest (Charlie Who), Gene Nelson (Danny Swift), Jim Backus (Herkimer Witt), Gypsy Rose Lee (Miss Cathcart), Gloria Swanson (Miss Lily Boles), Eddie Foy Jnr. (Claude Jester), Phil Harris (Gus Watt), Shary Marshall (Alpha Zeta), Paul Dubov (Rags McGuire), Eileen O'Neill (Sgt. Ames), Kitty Kover (waitress), Joni Webster (stripper), Bob Bice (delivery man), Phil Arnold (Billy, pickpocket)*

How's this for contrast? From fresh air and fit and healthy beach bums to motheaten, decaying vaudeville; the series is certainly more at home with old Hollywood than the drive-in's world of Katzman, Asher, and AIP, as the presence of Lee, Demarest, Swanson, Foy, and Harris demonstrates. Not too many fruggin' surfers in this one. Co-writer Dubov nicks the role of the victim for himself this time, and dancer and director Gene Nelson gets a return engagement and dances around Burke's office.

Highlight is the school for strippers (inevitably run by Gypsy Rose Lee, the acceptable TV face of sanitised sauce), a finishing school in reverse—enter classy, leave brassy. Return appearances for Jim Backus and Gloria Swanson; William Demarest (*Viva Las Vegas*) went on to a regular role in *My Three Sons*.

"I'm just here between engagements. Just for laughs"

"How long you been laughing?"

"Twelve years"

### Who Killed Cassandra Cass?

wr. Lorenzo Semple Jnr., dir. Jerry Hopper

*with Lola Albright (Eve Chapin), William Bendix (Harrison Weems), Shelley Berman (King Dimitri), Elsa Lanchester (Bessie Mopes), Louis Nye (Hooper, butler), Nehemiah Persoff (Jason Flonder), Nancy Kovack (Athelstone Scone), Shelby Grant (abandoned diner), Fritz Feld (head waiter), Hedley Mattingly (Dimitri's butler), Annella Bassett (Cassandra Cass), Judith Boyle, Patricia Scott (society girls), Bob Bice (waiter with 'phone)*

Lorenzo Semple, the guy primarily responsible for realising the *Batman* show developed by William Dozier a few years later, comes on board with the second season and gets the measure of the show and its format immediately. Unfortunately, he tries way too hard. He will write three more episodes before moving on to launch the Adam West *Batman* and write the scripts for Raquel Welch's secret agent film *Fathom* and the mid-'60s *Batman* feature film.

Bendix, Berman, and, naturally, Nehemiah Persoff are all way over the top under the direction of another new arrival, Jerry Hopper, while Lanchester and Feld were not known for their subtlety in the first place. Louis Nye, another very broad player (he was the Drysdale's effete pampered son in *The Beverly Hillbillies*), does a funny turn as an inebriated butler. This is the third of five appearances on the show by Lola Albright. Bendix, Lanchester, Kovack, and Mattingly are all making second appearances.

*Nancy Kovack, who appears in four episodes.*

Director Jerry Hopper had been working since 1946, and clearly just took work where he could get it. After lengthy stints on *Bachelor Father* and *Wagon Train* in between one-offs, he directed nine episodes of *Burke's Law* altogether, plus two of *Amos Burke—Secret Agent*, simultaneously working on such diverse shows as *The Addams Family*, *Perry Mason*, and *The Fugitive*. He could turn his hand to seemingly any type of show, and lengthy stays with *It's About Time*, *Gilligan's Island*, and *Voyage to the Bottom of the Sea* followed before retirement. There's a silly ending that doesn't match what we see.

### Who Killed the Horne of Plenty?

wr. Tony Barrett, dir. Richard Kinon

with Vera Miles (Claudia Sutton), Terry Moore (Felice Knight), David Wayne (Al Devlin), Ed Platt (Captain Metcalfe), John Saxon (Gil Lynch), Richard Devon (Errol Fuller), Claire Kelly (Samantha, Burke's date), Susana Contreras (Meredith, secretary), Beverly Adams (swimsuit model), Linda/Lori Saunders (polo girl), Anthony Eustrel (polo snob), Byron Morrow (Charles Horne)

This is less about the murder mystery and who killed Charles Horne (prolific bit player Byron Morrow) and more about who framed Tim Tilson. Unfortunately, what could have been a special and uniquely memorable script is simply infuriating. Barrett's script has Tim behaving like a complete idiot, not once but twice, so it's very difficult to stay sympathetic. Vera Miles (The Outer Limits, I Spy, The Man from UNCLE) romances Burke, John Saxon embarrasses himself as a would-be Southern lug, David Wayne is a phoney Wolfman Jack-style d.j. (Barrett really hates youth culture!), Terry Moore plays a treacherous vixen, and Ed Platt (Chief in Get Smart) is internal affairs.

A dramatic actress of beauty but limited range, Vera Miles appeared in most of the major western series and drama series of the '60s, and many police dramas in the '70s. She also appeared in the John Wayne film The Man Who Shot Liberty Valance and Hitchcock's Psycho. She's excellent when cast as cold women (see The Outer Limits' "The Form of Things Unknown" or The Man from UNCLE's "Bridge of Lions Affair"). Terry Moore is best known as the female lead in Mighty Joe Young and to TV buffs for a three-part Batman. Beverly Adams appeared three times in Burke's Law and three times in Doctor Kildare. She had minor roles in three Matt Helm films with Dean Martin, an episode of Bewitched, and several feelgood films of the '60s, including Winter A-Go-Go and two with Elvis

(Roustabout and Girl Happy). Linda aka Lori Saunders went on to regular roles in Petticoat Junction, The Beverly Hillbillies, and Dusty's Trail.

Vera Miles in a publicity picture for The Man from UNCLE's "Bridge of Lions Affair", aka One of Our Spies is Missing.

### Who Killed Everybody?

wr. Richard Levinson, William Link, dir. Richard Kinon

with Susan Silo (Phoebe McPhee), Alan Mowbray (Butterfield), Margaret Leighton (Connie Hanson), Corinne Calvet (Felice De Marco), June Havoc (Miranda Forsythe), Arlene Dahl (Gloria Cooke), Joan Huntington (Burke's date), Bob Kanter (Eddie Jordan, waiter), Michael Fox (George McLeod), Norman Leavitt (intern), Bobby Johnson (John, the butler), Bob Bice (desk sergeant), Fred Barry (Norman, little boy), Army Archerd, Hank Grant, Lonnie Fotre (irate parents)

"Well, I'm not one to spread rumors, but, er…"

"That's a very interesting sentence, Mr. Butterfield. Finish it!"

"We're almost there" / "I hope so. This was a new car when we started"

Although best known for creating the legendary *Columbo,* perhaps the greatest television murder mystery series of them all (the first and best episodes of which aired between 1971 and '78), Richard Levinson and William Link were also responsible (alongside Leonard Stern with *McMillan and Wife* and Aaron Spelling with *Hart to Hart),* for reviving the *Burke's Law* format of multiple guest star murder mysteries, with the long-running *Murder She Wrote* and several less successful attempts to duplicate the format, such as *The Ellery Queen Mysteries* and *Blacke's Magic,* following on. Here then, we see them at the beginning their television careers, working for Four Star and others (on such series as *Johnny Ringo, The Rogues, Burke's Law,* and *Honey West*), which would segue into the standard two-fisted detective series *Mannix,* which they created with *Mission: Impossible's* Bruce Geller, before returning to their roots, as it were, for the extraordinary *Columbo* and its imitators. Incidentally, both Gene Barry (as a perpetrator) and Gary Conway (as a victim) would appear on *Columbo* during its run (Barry, in fact, was in the very first episode, at that time a one-off TV movie from a stage play titled *Prescription: Murder*).

Their main achievement in this first outing is coming up with perhaps the dumbest bimbo Burke ever dated, in the shape and form of Joan Huntington's breathy, brainless actress. They counteract this dubious achievement by having the bodies discovered by an angry young actress (Susan Silo) who opens the show bawling out her idiot agent for booking her a bursting-out-of-a-cake gig. Her humiliation and outrage is short-lived when she springs from the cake into a room full of dead men!

The story has the four men at an exclusive country club murdered by a poisoned bottle of wine; Burke naturally pursues the four wives as potential suspects, all played—of course—by Hollywood divas Calvet, Dahl, and Havoc, and British stage actress Leighton. The problem is that while all four women have good cause to murder their own husbands, they have no reason to take out all four... except for the obvious one, an old chestnut which provides the episode's resolution. Happily, as ever, the show is less about solving the murder—a mere formality on *Burke's Law*—than about watching the various players do their party pieces. Leighton is wonderful, but Silo and Mowbray steal the show between them. Silo spends most of the show with Conway, and Alan Mowbray, as the pompous club historian, is hilarious.

Butterfield, on being club historian —"It's very rewarding—tournaments, marriages, births..."

Les—"Murders"

Butterfield—"I don't believe I like you! (pause) Actually, there's no precedent for murders here (pointedly looking at Les). So lower middle class!"

Burke enters a hospital room in tuxedo:

"Well—visiting hours are improving. Don't let me keep you from your date, Doctor."

"You're my date. I'm Captain Burke, of Homicide. I'm sorry to bother you this late"

"Oh, don't give it a thought. The nurse just woke me to ask me how I was sleeping"

and later:

"What do you expect, crocodile tears? My husband liked to win arguments. He had an endearing habit of knocking me down stairs to make his points"

Having segued into providing cartoon voices at the end of the '60s, Susan Silo appeared in quite a few guest roles in late '50s and early '60s TV, most notably in *Wagon Train, Hawaiian Eye, Doctor Kildare, Batman,* and *The Man from UNCLE.* She had a regular role in the short-lived sit-com *Harry's Girls.* Bob Kanter, rather unfairly uncredited given the size of his part, went on to a few appearances in television war series, but appears to have abandoned his career after writing himself a part in the teen movie *Winter A-Go-Go.*

### Who Killed Mr. Cartwheel?

wr. Gwen Bagni, Paul Dubov, dir. Don Weis

*with Diane McBain (Xenobia, town sheriff), Nick Adams (Sonny Dancer), Fred Clark (Jackson Trade), Patsy Kelly (Big Mouth Annie), Sheldon Leonard (Chicasaw Pete), Charlene Holt (Cecily Channing), Jonathan Hole (Mr. Swift, auctioneer), Fred Krone (rider on horse), Ella Ethridge (lady at auction), Annazette Williams/Chase (auctioneer's assistant), Janet Clark (Sonny's mother), Chuck Hayward (deputy in shoot-out), Bill Hart (Tex, cowboy actor)*

They say that Hollywood is a very small place. For proof of that old saying, one needs go no further than *Burke's Law.* These are return appearances for almost everybody in this extremely silly western-themed episode, which is painfully and remorselessly over-the-top and hard going.

Portraying a succession of tiresome wild west cliches are a selection of previous guest stars, including Nick Adams (third of five), Diane McBain and Ed Begley (both second of four), and Patsy Kelly, Fred Clark, and Sheldon Leonard (all second of two). All but Clark and McBain are horrendously over-acting for non-laughs (although to be fair, there wasn't much else they could do with the material). Even the date Burke dumps is making her second of two. The Cartwheel name, of course, is a play on top-rated TV western *Bonanza's* Cartwrights.

Among the supporting players, Jonathan Hole has yet another funny turn at the murder scene (his fourth of six bits). Hole played different roles (but always the same part) in numerous episodes of such 1960s sit-coms as *Bewitched, The Lucy Show, The Farmer's Daughter, Green Acres, Petticoat Junction,* and *I Dream of Jeannie,* to name but just a few, westerns and cop shows (with multiple bits in *Dragnet, Maverick, Rawhide* and *Perry Mason*), and including episodes of *Honey West* and *Amos Burke – Secret Agent.* Anytime a casting director needed a nervous, pompous or officious minor public servant or department manager, Jonathan Hole seemed to be first choice. And he was always perfect in the part.

Bit player Annazette Chase/ Williams (in her third of five), discovers the body this time. Stunt player Bill Hart takes a break from playing towering monsters and aliens on *The Outer Limits* to play cowboy Tex.

## Who Killed Cornelius Gilbert?

wr. Lewis Reed, dir. Don Taylor

*with Barbara Eden (Linda Murray), Edgar Bergen (Horton Galbraith), Dane Clark (Milton Yeager), Nanette Fabray (Rowena Coolidge), Martha Hyer (Adrienne Shelton), Eileen O'Neill (Sgt. Ames), Alvy Moore (Ralph Baskin), Bara Byrnes (Millicent), Bob Bice (Hanson, patrol cop), William Baskin (Bruce, minion), Steve Carruthers (Gilbert)*

Bergen, Eden, Fabray, Hyer, and Moore are all making return appearances; Hyer and Eden will return again. This episode, a routine investigation spiced up by the kidnapping of Tim Tilson and some classic dialogue from the ever reliable Lewis Reed, features a first for the format. Instead of being reunited with the girl he ditched at the beginning of the story when the murder is solved, Burke nips off with one of the guest stars.

"If you're looking for suspects, start with the A's in the telephone book" / "Nothing between you and Gilbert but space?"

'Captain, I have to do some investigating" / "Oh that's fine, Tim, keep your hand in. The old days might come back"

"Why did you kill Gilbert?" / "A line was starting to form. I didn't want to miss my chance"

## Who Killed Lenore Wingfield?

wr. Leigh Chapman, dir. Don Weis

*with Anne Helm (Effie Mae Porter), Charlie Ruggles (Charles Wingfield), Ida Lupino (Meniletha Calhoun), Dean Stockwell (Jay Boy Calhoun), Victor Jory (Jim Clover), Mary Ann Mobley (Nancy's friend), Dub Taylor (Lenore's companion), Eileen O'Neill (Sgt. Ames), Quinn O'Hara (Rebecca), Hank Patterson (Lukey), Annazette Williams/Chase (elevator girl)*

Both this episode and the previous one have babes just turning up at Burke's front door for a date out of the blue—just as they do in real life, of course. Despite some broad performances, this one is amusing, entertaining, and eye-catching in the usual manner.

Charlie Ruggles makes his third appearance, this time as a lecherous photographer and ex-husband of the victim, while Dean Stockwell and Anne Helm play a couple of hicks from the sticks (Helm does an Elly May Clampett routine that makes the 'real' Elly of *The Beverly Hillbillies* look like a boy). Victor Jory is a comic strip Southern colonel straight out of the cartoon shows (gorgeous Quinn O'Hara plays his daughter).

Ida Lupino is hilarious as an obsessive prude with a hidden cache of scandalous erotica from which she selects, all the time appalled of course, spicy segments to read aloud in disgust ("You can see what we're up against, Captain! Believe me, you can be an invaluable aid in stamping out sex!" / "Well, I appreciate your faith in me, but I think I'd like to decline... on the grounds that I might have a slight conflict of interest"). Mary Ann Mobley is back as Burke's date, in a third identity (he really does go for the same type).

Ruggles as photographer: "Now remember what I told you dear, we want our products to stand out"

(model pushes chest forward)

Tim — "Products?"

"The shoes! Beautiful, aren't they? Plastic (rolls eyes)"

"Yeah, I've never seen a better made pair"

Ordinarily, Leigh Chapman was on the other side of the camera as a dumb dolly, as she was in such shows as *The Man from UNCLE,* but in fact she was an excellent screenwriter, specialising in tough, hard-as-nails action; among her credits, *Truck Turner* and *Crazy Larry, Dirty Mary,* two of the most violent of early '70s crime thrillers. For TV, she wrote six episodes of *The Wild Wild West.* She's quoted on the IMDB as having said "I wrote action-adventure. I couldn't write a romantic comedy or a chick flick if my life depended on it. I could write a love story, but it would have to be a *Casablanca* type of love story, and some people would have to die!"

## Who Killed the Richest Man in the World?

wr. Stephen Kandel, dir. Gene Nelson

*with Ricardo Montalban (Nicholas Amenor), Tom Smothers, Dick Smothers (the Rafer Brothers), George Hamilton (Clint Perry), Diana Lynn (Elaine Truscott), Karen Sharpe (Dana Prentiss), Pilar Seurat (Sakito, bodyguard), Troy Melton (Lesage), Army Archerd, Vernon Scott, Hank Grant (reporters), Joy Harmon, Edy Williams (party girls), Barbara Michaels (artist's model)*

Rather unusually, Burke gets assistance from the murder target in this episode, as the killer shoots down the accountant/bookkeeper of Nicholas Amenor, the 'richest man in the world', a superbly magnetic performance by Ricardo Montalban (in full Khan mode), who literally gets everything he wants with a snap of the fingers. The suspects are three other millionaires all trying to do the same deal with the Satanic Amenor, and — as usual — all despise him. And with just cause; who wouldn't? The solution to the crime is fairly apparent to seasoned viewers.

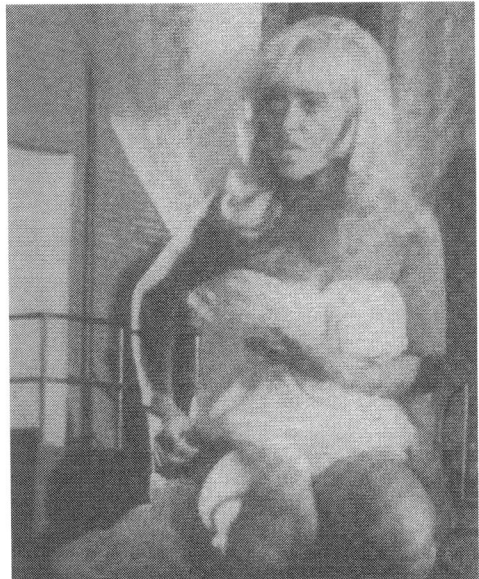

*Joy Harmon, as she appeared in Village of the Giants. She's not so keen on the towel in this one…*

"Three minutes later and I would have been in that automobile"

"Three minutes plus half a second and you'd have been right out again"

"I am not amused"

"I assigned a man to guard you. You dodged him and walked right into a bomb. I cannot protect you against your own stubbornness"

New to the series, writer Stephen Kandel gave TV another familiar face from the *Star Trek* universe, Harry Mudd. Bearing in mind the script comes before the players are chosen, he is as equally lucky with the casting here as he was with *Star Trek*. The Smothers Brothers comedy duo, who made a lame sit-com for Spelling before finding fame and notoriety in the late '60s, guest as a couple of moron millionaires with a mansion full of junk; Tom Smothers is particularly funny as the one marginally dumber than the other — who's still pretty dumb. George Hamilton is a Texan with a twist, and Diana Lynn is another representative of the era's unfortunate predilection for big game hunters, although this time the episode takes a less impressed view. We also get to see Tim mobbed by sexpots Edy Williams and Joy Harmon, two of the '60s most fun starlets, shortly after Pilar Seurat has thrown him across the room. And *Johnny Ringo's* Karen Sharpe's on hand too.

Girl — "You sure are a smart one! If you get out of here in one piece, stop by the pool. Maybe we can take a dip together" / Tim — "I'm sorry, I didn't bring a bathing suit" / Girl — "Oh, it's a *private* pool"

"As you may have noticed, I'm a woman" / "I have 20/20 vision"

### Who Killed the One in the Middle?

wr. Tony Barrett, dir. Don Weis

*with Diane McBain (Lana De Armand), Juliet Prowse (Renee De Armand), Stanley Adams (Lou Manzini), Eduardo Ciannelli (Dominic De Armand), Hal March (Yates Dudley), Steve Cochran* *(Phil Ross), Peter Leeds (Don Kyles), Mary Ann Mobley (Cindy, Burke's date), Barbara Horne (Alicia De Armand), Jackie Joseph (trainee singer), Tracey Butler (audition singer), Jimmy Cross (vaudeville performer), Chuck Couch (hood)*

Burke is dating yet another Mary Ann Mobley lookalike (this time called Cindy) when he gets the call to investigate the murder of one of the De Armand Sisters, a singing trio... and as the girls on either side of her are guest stars Juliet Prowse and Diane McBain, it's bad luck for the one in the middle (who has no other credits to her name!). For once, the series dispenses with the

parade of wackoes to instead give us a good, solid drama built around real, credible people. Excellent performances from Eduardo Ciannelli, Steve Cochran, and Stanley Adams, and quite a sad tale. Some good action scenes too.

### Who Killed Merlin?

wr. Richard Levinson, William Link, dir. Richard Kinon

*with Nick Adams (Max the Mysterious), Janet Blair (Violet the ventriloquist), Paul Lynde (Doctor McCoy), Paul Richards (the Great Grindle), Charlie Ruggles (O.B. Danberry), Jill St. John (Pinky Likewise), Joan Huntington (Doctor Johnson), Michael Fox (George McLeod), Eileen O'Neill (Sgt. Ames), Robert Easton (hopeless magician), Ralph Moody (cemetery caretaker), Gil Frye (Merlin), William Woodson (TV host), Anthony Eustrel (florist)*

With Richard Kinon directing, and a guest cast like this, we can be fairly sure we're back in the land of froth and fun for this one (Barry even sings—painfully). It's murder at a magician's convention.

Robert Easton ('Phones' in *Stingray* and frequently cast as hicks in '60s shows like *The Man from UNCLE, The Lucy Show,* and *The Munsters*) has fun as a useless magician, and Paul Lynde is a hoot as an equally hapless and befuddled doctor (TV's first Dr. McCoy, no less!). Joan Huntington, who played a major league bimbo in a previous episode, is cast as a doctor-come-date this time. It's Jill St. John's turn to play the bimbo this time, as a magician's assistant, first seen levitating above the stage; she never gets any of Burke's jokes ("You'd better come down from there, you're liable to be arrested for vagrancy" / "How come?" / "No visible means of support").

Nick Adams makes the fourth of five appearances, this time as 'Max the Mysterious' ("So I do the bullet-catching trick—is that against the law?" / "Depends on who catches the bullet"), while Charlie Ruggles is back unfeasibly soon. William Woodson was the narrator of *The Invaders*.

### Who Killed 711?

wr. Gwen Bagni, Paul Dubov, dir. Sidney Lanfield

*with Hans Conreid (Pepe Van Heller, manager), Burgess Meredith (Harold Harold), Rhonda Fleming (Clarissa Benton), Broderick Crawford (Tristram Corporal), Dan Duryea (Sam Atherton), Mamie Van Doren (Aurora Knight), Eileen O'Neill (Sgt. Ames), Lisa Seagram (hypnotist), Susanne Cramer (Cindy, Burke's date), Lou Krugman, Allyson Ames (couple waiting for elevator), Marianna Case (dance studio receptionist), Buddy Lewis (cabbie), Henry Hunter (doorman)*

Another stuck elevator, another dead body, but the same set. 711 is a room in a plush hotel; Burke and the boys go undercover as hotel waiters. It's quite silly, of course—everyone knows Burke by sight, especially the swanky monied sort staying in the hotel—but as this episode is playing purely for laughs, and the episode gets them, we can forgive. As ever at this point in the series, quite a few returnees in the cast, including Conreid, Duryea, Fleming, Crawford, Seagram, Ames, Hunter, and Lewis, but it's Burgess Meredith, in his third and final turn in the series, who steals the show as the guiltiest-looking innocent suspect in the series.

Directing since 1930, this was Sidney Lanfield's only episode of *Burke's Law,* but he worked lengthy runs on *Jane Wyman Fireside Theatre, M Squad, Bachelor Father, The Deputy, The Tall Man, McHale's Navy,* and *The Addams Family.* He directed numerous Bob Hope films before turning to television, but curiously also directed the very first Sherlock Holmes film with Basil Rathbone, *The Hound of the Baskervilles.*

### Who Killed Super Sleuth?

wr. Lorenzo Semple Jnr., dir. Lawrence Dobkin

*with Thomas Gomez (Caligula Foxe), J. Carroll Naish (Mr. Toto), Carl Reiner (Chief Inspector House), Ed Begley (Bascule Doirot), Zsa Zsa Gabor (Commissar Ilona Buda), Eileen O'Neill (Sgt. Ames), Francine York (Nurse Brown), Art Lewis (O'Hara, reporter), Eve Brent (English maid), Margaret Sullivan (girl at lake), Bebe Louie, Miko Mokusho (geisha girls), Robert Bice (cop), Tom Kennedy (bartender)*

Lorenzo Semple's second of four scripts for the series is at first glance tainted by several embarrassing stereotypes typical of the period that we have since happily left behind. Naish, who more forgivably played an Oriental cliche in 1943's post-Pearl Harbor serial *Batman*, is even worse here, and particularly offensive, the rest are just unfunny, other than Carl Reiner, who plays a Holmesian buffoon with discordant violin and ridiculous presumptions. The storyline has a highly regarded police official murdered within the vicinity of a bunch of his peers, equally highly regarded renowned visiting detectives (all heavy-handed send-ups of famous fictional sleuths), who came to honor him and have now become the suspects. Begley has fun as a Poirot parody, while Gomez is supposed to be Nero Wolfe (Naish is actually supposed to be Mr. Moto, a condescending but more rounded and complex figure from detective literature than played here).

Begley, Gabor, and Reiner are returnees, and the scenes between Burke and Gabor's Communist officer are amusing, highlighting the hypocrisy and absurdity of communism with humor rather than getting on a soapbox:

"Alright, arrest me. Throw me in your dungeons! What can a poor working girl like me expect from a millionaire police captain like you?"

"I admit it might be fun to seize you, but we have strange customs, darling. We never arrest people for murder unless they did it"

*Zsa Zsa Gabor in her most famous film, Queen of Outer Space; in that one, she was the revolutionary!*

"Don't call me darling. I fully realise that in your decadent culture you despise women... What do you want me to be, a plaything in some millionaire's hands? Do you kiss all your suspects? How do you know I'm not the murderer? I could even give you the motive, beautiful Captain. I might have killed him simply to prove that I could do it"

"That would make me very sad, beautiful Commissar... It would mean you were insane"

"Look into my eyes, beautiful Captain"

"There's a woman in there, trying to get out"

"Does she look to you insane?"

"No, not insane, just mad. Mad that she's not drinking champagne out of a slipper. Mad that she was born when and where she was".

### Who Killed the Swinger on a Hook?

wr. Tony Barrett, dir. Lewis Allen

*with Gloria De Haven (Connie French), Janis Paige (Sharon McCauley), Don Rickles (Frank Cross), Dick Clark (Gil Knox), Leif Ericksen (Jason Hayes), Jean Ingram (Lucinda, plumber), Gil Stuart (Grosvenor, butler), Bek Nelson (party girl), Joe Higgins (Charlie the drunk), "The Great John L", Gene Le Bell (wrestlers)*

Burke finds himself next on a list found on a body—a list of people who are turning up dead ("If this is let's kill six people week, where's my list?"). While one appreciates why Burke refuses to run and hide while the boys tie up the case, it is rather absurd that he has absolutely no protection at all. However, dialogue and performances are excellent. After a bad start, Barrett became one of the series' most reliable names in the credits; he managed to get the tone of the series just right, keeping it light but giving the audience real people with real emotions, without the camp excesses of some of the other episodes (those by Bagni and Dubov, for example).

This was bit player Gil Stuart's second appearance as a butler in this series. Working since 1940, and usually sporting a Hollywood Brit accent, he turned up several times in *77, Sunset Strip, Honey West, Twelve O'Clock High, The Invaders,* and both *UNCLE* series.

Les — "You have enough on your hands, why don't you take it easy?"

*Gene Barry with Dick Clark*

Burke—"Why don't you just stop finding bodies?"

Wrestling trainer—"Pain, pain! Scream a little! What do you think the little old ladies at ringside came for?"

### Who Killed Davidian Jonas?

wr. Gwen Bagni, Paul Dubov, dir. Sam Freedle

with Ruta Lee (Ulla Swenson), Reginald Gardiner (Putzi Voltran), Sheree North (the Maharini), Broderick Crawford (Milhew Court), Cesar Romero (Gregorio Jonas), Dennis Day (Harvey Haight), Lisa Seagram (Pandora Shriner), Peter Bourne (Captain's mate), Walter Janowitz (yacht captain), Naji Gabbay (maitre'd), Tania Lemani (exotic dancer), Raul Martin, Papita Funez (gypsy dancers)

*Gene Barry with Ruta Lee*

"Whose floating palace?"

"The late Davidian Jonas, shipping magnate"

"How late?"

"Well, his watch stopped at twelve fourteen. Presumably when he hit the water"

Cesar Romero, Reginald Gardiner and Ruta Lee are returnees, with Crawford and Seagram making speedy return visits. On a weekly basis this may not have been so obvious as when the series is stripped daily or watched in a marathon today, but it must have given, even subliminally, a sense of sameness to the show, especially given the rigidity of the format. That said, just for a change, Burke is spirited away not from a date, but a daytime TV show.

This episode is so light, it almost floats away, although there's a nice bit with Cesar Romero as a proud, arrogant gypsy, and some knife-throwing one-upmanship. Ruta Lee pretends to be Swedish (badly), and dominates the episode. Other frothy stereotypes include Sheree North as a New Joisey princess, Reginald Gardiner as a finagling boozehound, and Broderick Crawford as a sea captain who plays with toy boats. The hotel clerk and the fortune teller are uncredited. Sam Freedle was a script supervisor and jobbing director who later worked his way down to become an assistant director and then production manager. He directed four episodes of *Burke's Law*, three of which aired consecutively.

**Who Killed the Strangler?**

wr. Larry Gordon, dir. Sam Freedle

with Robert Middleton (Rocky Mountain), Annette Funicello (Anna Najensky), Frankie Avalon (Ralph Hirt),

Jeanne Crain (Lorraine Turner), Una Merkel (Mrs. Barrett), Michael Fox (George McLeod), Eileen O'Neill (Sgt. Ames), Mary Ann Mobley (Teri, Burke's date), Quinn O'Hara (Sally Lou), Sharyn Hillyer (Rosie Belle), Michelle Breeze (Cora Lee), Joy Harmon (Barbara Sue), Margaret Muse (ballet school teacher), Margaret Nelson (receptionist), Shari Lee Bernath, Teri-Ann Lee (go-go dancers), Gene Le Bell (the Strangler), Robert Bice (butler)

Avalon and Funicello made the 'beach party' movies for the teen audience at this time, although *Burke's Law* had an older demographic, and was probably more likely watched by the parents, particularly with the likes of Tony Barrett writing the scripts. Both had guested in the series previously, but in different episodes.

This was Larry Gordon's first of two scripts for the series (he also wrote for Spelling's other reasonably good '60s show, the western *Guns of Will Sonnett*). Gordon's attitude to youth was slightly more compatible with the times; he worked for AIP and later created the ambitious but of-its-time short-lived *The New People*, a rare Aaron Spelling flop about a bunch of teenage air crash survivors starting a 'new society' on a desert island (Rod Serling wrote the pilot, but apparently—it's one of the few U.S. series to have completely escaped me—took his name off it). What the *Burke's Law* series did have in common with the beach party genre was an abundance of pretty starlets of the period, and this episode alone offers Sharyn Hillyer, Joy Harmon, Quinn O'Hara, and the ubiquitous Mary Ann Mobley, an Aaron Spelling favorite who later made more appearances on his *Fantasy Island* series than anybody.

We first see Burke playing Monopoly with Mobley before the inevitable interruption. "Now look what you've done, you've taken away all my

assets" she pouts, pushing her tits in his face as she rises. "Honey" replies Burke, "You've still got plenty in the bank". Ahh, anybody else remember flirting?

*Frankie and Annette in their Beach Party days…*

The Strangler of the title is a professional wrestler who gets into the ring that night, but doesn't get to leave (it's Gene Le Bell, an actual former wrestler, and TV's go-to guy whenever one is needed). Unusually, we see many of the guest players (in the audience) before their names come up in the credits, a rarity. The five suspects, one of whom killed the wrestler with a poisoned dart from their seat, are man-eater Crain, bitter sister Funicello, sports journo Avalon, little old lady from Pasadena Merkel, and portly piggy rival Middleton.

### Who Killed Mother Goose?

wr. Richard Levinson, William Link, dir. Sam Freedle

with George Hamilton (Little John Lester), Lola Albright (Peggy Frost), Ann Blyth (Valerie), Jan Murray (Dr. Abernathy), Walter Pidgeon (Mr. Perkins), Suzanne Cupito (Lolita), Kathy Kersh (TV repair girl), Eileen O'Neill (Sgt. Ames), Alvy Moore (creepy photographer), Dave Willock (helicopter pilot), Eddie Quillan (Mr. Jellybean), Jimmy Gaines (Tommy, patient), Todd Baron (Skippy, reader), Anzanette Chase/Williams (Abernathy's secretary), Madge Blake (Mrs. Hubbard/ Mother Goose)

A children's author who hated children (hard to imagine Madge Blake hating anyone!) is found strangled with her own typewriter ribbon, and a precocious little girl saw four potential suspects go into the house. They are her publisher, a psychiatrist, a bearded beatnik, and a TV performer and rival.

George Hamilton is cast against type as a pretentious beat poet, while Lola Albright is a supposedly sexually repressed p.a. Jan Murray has a funny turn as a useless child psychologist. Dave Willock was also the helicopter pilot in It Came from Outer Space. He also

appeared in the sci-fi films Revenge of the Creature and Queen of Outer Space, but more notably provided the narration for the legendary cartoon classic Wacky Races.

Jimmy Gaines was a freckle-faced kid who did the sit-com circuit throughout the '60s, as did young Todd. Between them, they appeared in every 1960s sit-com that needed a precocious kid to show up. Suzanne Cupito, who also appeared in The Outer Limits and The Twilight Zone, grew up to be Morgan Brittany, best known for '80s super-soap Dallas. Brittany then turned up in an episode of the brief '90s revival of Burke's Law, a nice touch.

And what a waste of a wonderful character actress it at first seems to cast Madge Blake (Batman's Aunt Harriet, left) as the murder victim. But there's a method to such seeming madness; Mrs. Hubbard comes back to life via earlier TV recordings, Blake's familiar, lilting melodic voice reciting nursery rhymes in her distinctive and unique manner... Perfect casting after all... Blake can also be seen in episodes of Bewitched, The Lucy Show, and The Man from UNCLE. Films include Singin' in the Rain and Elvis' Loving You.

### Who Killed the Toy Soldier?

wr. Lorenzo Semple Jnr., Andrew McCullough, dir. Jerry Hopper

with Joan Caulfield (Psyche Jones), Martha Hyer (Dr. Serena Standish), Abbe Lane (Melissa Hammer), Louis Nye (James Stock), Chill Wills (General Harder), Richard Hale (Granny Grabber), Julie Parrish (Tanya), Elisa Ingram (party guest/ Burke's date), Dave Loring, Jon Sargent (special boys), Bill McLean (Philby, Harder's valet), Breena Howard (Harder's secretary), James Secrest (young scientist), Don Gazzaniga (sentry)

After the dark side of children's entertainers, the dirty world of Santa's elves. I'm not sure why this one wasn't more obviously called "Who Killed Granny Grabber?"; perhaps it was too close to Mother Goose. Chill Wills, in his third and final appearance in the series, is amusing as an army general who wants to "get 'em while they're young" by selling little kids war toys, while Joan Caulfield plays a simpering psychologist who mollycoddles louts. Louis Nye, in his second of two guest shots, plays to his strengths alongside *Paradise, Hawaiian Style's* Julie Parrish. This is Hyer's fifth of six, Caulfield's second of three, Howard's second of two. Good performances from all, but Abbe Lane, back in *Amos Burke – Secret Agent*, steals the show as a typical *Burke's Law* babe.

### Who Killed Rosie Sunset?

wr. Tony Barrett, dir. Paul Wendkos

*with Russ Tamblyn (Maximillian), Sheree North (Cleo Delaney), Dennis Day (Waldo Fleischacker), Hans Conreid (Leonid Borodny), Eddie Albert (Arthur Poindexter), Lisa Seagram (Mathilde, tax accountant), Michael Fox (George McLeod), Eileen O'Neill (Sgt. Ames), Torben Meyer (Mr. Lobbermacher), Jonathan Hole, Alice Backes (tourists), Francine York (Vanya), Phil Arnold (Harry, printer), Margaret Nelson (Colette, model)*

An eccentric old lady who sold maps showing the locations of Hollywood stars' homes is found murdered, dead in her usual roadside spot. It quickly transpires that there was more to her than met the eye; she was a secret do-gooder with a ton of money, covertly doing good deeds by being kind to those who were kind to her. But there's a twist…

This is Sheree North's third and final appearance in the series as a floozie. Kept busy mostly in television, her films include such jewels as *Lawman, The Outfit, Charley Varrick,* and *The Shootist.* It's also Hans Conreid's third and final appearance in the series as a nutcase. Eddie Albert was best known for his role in the long-running sit-com *Green Acres,* although he had memorable guest shots in *The Outer Limits* and *The Man from UNCLE* at around this time.

*Gene Barry, clowning around on the set with his son Fred, who appeared in three episodes in minor roles.*

Dennis Day previously appeared in the episode "Who Killed Davidian Jonas?", which also included Sheree North and Lisa Seagram in the cast. Lisa Seagram worked until the mid-'70s, making guest appearances in such cult TV as *Bewitched, My Favorite Martian, The Beverly Hillbillies, Amos Burke – Secret Agent, Honey West, Batman,* and *The Girl from UNCLE.* This was her fifth and final appearance in *Burke's Law.*

### Who Killed Wimbledon Hastings?

wr. Leigh Chapman, dir. Jerry Hopper

*with Nick Adams (Clayton Newman), Marie Wilson (Ramona Specks), Nancy Wilson (Choo Choo), Debra Paget (Helen Harper), Gale Storm (Nonnie Harper), Edgar Bergen (Clyde Olsen), Vic Dana (Forrest, ball boy), Teri Lee (Gloria, Burke's date), Army Archerd, Hank Grant (sports reporters), Alan Caillou (announcer), George Atkinson (Wimbledon Hastings)*

Leigh Chapman's second script for the series. Nick Adams makes his fifth and final guest appearance on the show, Edgar Bergen his third and final. Vic Dana was a cabaret singer who got his start in Sam Katzman's *Don't Knock the Rock*. Singer and occasional actress Nancy Wilson gets her first major role here, and a lengthy sequence performing. Marie Wilson and Gale Storm were both film actresses who turned to TV sit-coms in the '50s (Wilson in *My Friend Irma*, Storm in *My Little Margie* and *The Gale Storm Show, aka Oh Susannah*), and both were making their second appearances in *Burke's Law* here. This was also Debra Paget's second and final appearance on the show, and her last role before her third marriage and retirement. She co-starred with Elvis in *Love Me Tender*.

### Who Killed the Fat Cat?

wr. Gwen Bagni, Paul Dubov, dir. Jerry Hopper

*with Billy De Wolfe (Artemis Newpenny), MacDonald Carey (Waldo Nicely), Diana Hyland (Laurel Peachey), Martha Raye (Beulah Brothers), Don Rickles (Swifty Piedmont), Michael Fox (George McLeod), Joe Higgins (Monty Crippen), Claire Kelly (lingerie model/ Burke's date), Bambi Hamilton (lingerie model), Shannon Farnon, Marianna Gaba (girls at mansion), Kitty Kover (Laurel's receptionist), Chuck Hicks (Atlas, Laurel's heavy), Don Gazzaniga (cop)*

Four phoney corporations, four phonies running them, four suspects. Diana Hyland's twenty year career in television included guest appearances in numerous series, including *The Twilight Zone*, *The Fugitive*, *The Invaders*, *The FBI*, *The Green Hornet*, and *The Man from UNCLE*. She was a regular player in *Peyton Place*. Rather amusingly, her musclebound heavy Trojan from the Venus and Adonis health spa has been re-named Atlas… but the name stays in the credits. A network censor stepped in, I suspect (Trojan is a prophylactic brand name).

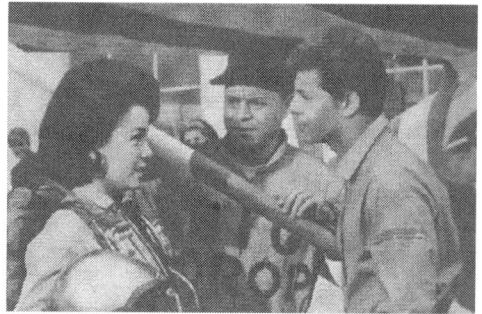

*Don Rickles with the Beach Party duo in Beach Blanket Bingo.*

Comedienne Martha Raye was a regular on various American variety shows in the '50s, '60s, and '70s. This was fellow club comic Don Rickles' third and final appearance on the series. He did the rounds of the 1960s sit-coms, as well as episodes of *I Spy*, *The Wild Wild West*, and the movies *Kelly's Heroes* and *Casino*. MacDonald Carey is making his fourth of four; Bagni and Dubov have the cheek to recycle their one-upmanship scene from the earlier "Who Killed WHO IV?". Carey does it great though. Cabaret drag act Billy De Wolfe tones down for an uncharacteristic turn as a pompous futurist who turns street for a knife fight when Burke riles him. Busy bit player Joe Higgins, the victim, had regular roles on *The Rifleman* and *Arrest and Trial*.

## Who Killed the Man on the White Horse?

wr. Berne Giler, David Giler, dir. Allen Reisner

*with Fernando Lamas (Kelly Mars), Virginia Mayo (Terry Foster), Robert Middleton (Ragnar Windsor), Telly Savalas (Richard Goldtooth), Barbara Eden (Vanessa Barrett), Michael Fox (George McLeod), Nancy Kovack (Alistair, Burke's date), Alvy Moore (bartender), Bob Bice (butler), Frank Scannell (rodeo announcer)*

"Vanessa Barrett?"

"Well, that's my given name"

"Now I'll give you mine—Captain Burke. I'm with Homicide"

A web of romantic intrigue to boggle a soap addict, but not terribly interesting. The characters are all too obnoxious to be entertaining, and this is is really "Who Killed the Lone Ranger?", but it's not really obscure enough not to be offensive, as there's no resemblance to the reality of either the serials or TV series in this slur. Telly Savalas as an embittered Tonto is a bad joke, as is the parodic pseudonym of Clayton Steele. Clayton Moore should have sued!

Barbara Eden is appearing in her fourth and final *Burke's Law*, Lamas and Middleton in their second of two, Savalas in his third of three. Virginia Mayo (left), in her only appearance in the series, is surely best remembered for her role in the iconic James Cagney film *White Heat*. Nancy Kovack, who appeared in numerous cult TV shows of the 1960s including *Bewitched, Star Trek, Batman,* and *The Man from UNCLE,* is also in her fourth of four.

Berne and David Giler were father and son writers, but they collaborated on only four scripts, including this single episode of *Burke's Law* and a really bad *Girl from UNCLE*, "The Low Blue C Affair". Berne Giler had worked in the Warners factory in the '50s, and in the '60s wrote acceptable episodes of *Voyage to the Bottom of the Sea* and *The Man from UNCLE*. Shortly after his father's death in the late '60s, son David (having written on his own what was one of the worst episodes of *The Man from UNCLE* ever filmed, "The Matterhorn Affair") had considerable success writing feature films, most notably co-creating what became the *Alien* franchise, and later producing for television.

## Who Killed the Thirteenth Clown?

wr. Charles Hoffman, dir. Jerry Hopper

*with Joan Caulfield (Alexis Raff), Betty Hutton (Rena Zito), Corinne Calvet (Ariella Martell), Terry Thomas (Gideon Auerbach), Jack Weston (Gogi Zito), Eileen O'Neill (Sgt. Ames), Grady Sutton (Hubie), Fred Krone (police officer)*

*Batman* writer Charles Hoffman makes his debut on *Burke's Law* with a yarn about a clown impaled in a trick car. Beginning almost exactly the same way as the previous episode, with the victim showing up dead after making an entrance before a huge crowd waiting to see him perform, the intro at least dispenses with the dumped date routine; Burke skips out on reluctantly rehearsing a speech with Sgt. Ames.

Gene Barry shows a genuine flair for comedy in this episode, quite literally clowning around during the second half in clown costume. Hoffman, a writer who played *Batman* for outright comedy (the secret of the show's unique style, as fellow *Burke's Law* writer Lorenzo Semple continually pointed out, was to play it straight), writes in a classic slapstick chase through the streets, but the director and editor stage it with no flair at all, so it falls a little flat, coming across as clever rather than amusing (although a cop does a lovely double take when he tries to nick Barry).

This was Hoffman's only script for *Burke's Law,* and it's probably for the best. He could only go downhill from here, and didn't have the knack of writing the show's smart-mouth dialogue. Had the show gone on through the '60s, Hoffman might well have written further episodes, and the show—in the manner of other '66-'67 series—might well have got sillier, but one of the intriguing characteristics of *Amos Burke — Secret Agent* was that when Burke moved into the spy business with season three, the show got colder and darker, and was shorn of its quirky banter.

The cast is dull. Former model and minor film actress Joan Caulfield makes her third of three appearances, one only a few episodes ago, while Betty Hutton, who had an almost identical career (former model turned actress, single

season sit-com in late-'50s, retired mid-'70s after brief TV guest star run) makes her second of two (both finally retired after guest-starring in *Baretta,* I don't know what that says about Robert Blake!). Corinne Calvet, a French import more famous for being famous than for any of her film roles, also retired in the mid-'70s after working her way through four husbands. This was her third of three (episodes!).

*Gene Barry with recurring co-star Eileen O'Neill as Sgt. Gloria Ames.*

Working in the middle of all this is Terry-Thomas, in *his* third of three, wearing a ridiculous Cyrano-style false nose and given nothing to work his magic on, and 'sad slob' specialist Jack Weston in his second of two. Weston's numerous roles, invariably as a small, hateful type or down-and-out loser, included episodes of *Boris Karloff's Thriller* and *The Twilight Zone* (also two each, including the famous "The Monsters Are Due on Maple Street"), *The Untouchables, The Fugitive, Bewitched,* and *The Man from UNCLE.*

Grady Sutton, also given nothing to work with, was a prolific bit-player, also usually cast as comical nobodies, who was active from the mid-'20s to the mid-'70s, working with everybody from Laurel and Hardy to Elvis and *Batman*.

## Who Killed Mr. Colby in Ladies Lingerie?

wr. Tony Barrett, dir. Jerry Hopper

*with Arlene Dahl (Maggie French), Bert Parks (Ernie Webb), Paul Lynde (Guy Hawthorne Jnr.), Joan Bennett (Denise Mitchell), Edd Byrnes (Davey Carr), Jonathan Hole (Mr. Larchmont), Eileen O'Neill (Sgt. Ames), Michael Fox (George McLeod), Chris Noel (Miss Larchmont), Beverly Adams (Angela, second model), Gunilla Hutton (first model), John Neris (fashion show customer), Lorri Scott (Burke's date), Don Diamond (tour bus passenger), Irwin Charone (Mr. Fitzell, landlord)*

Just for once, Burke refuses a case... not for a date, but a convention. Barry is obviously unable to appear in this episode, filming brief inserts later, but the show must go on. Toomey and Conway are clearly playing Barry's lines, but naturally Burke must make the 'phone call that solves the case. Eileen O'Neill moves forward to the opening credits for her one and only time.

Joan Bennett, working since the silents, went on to appear in the gothic daytime soap *Dark Shadows*. Edd Byrnes was best known for his role as teen heart-throb Kookie the car-hop in the early '60s detective series *77, Sunset Strip*, after which he hit the guest star circuit. This was Arlene Dahl's fourth of four. Beverly Adams appeared in several Elvis films and similar fare, and played the ridiculous Lovey Kravezit in the Dean Martin *Matt Helm* films. She later married hairdresser Vidal Sassoon.

Gunilla Hutton appeared as Billie Jo in the early episodes of sit-com *Petticoat Junction*.

A wonderful collection of comical character actors includes spots from Paul Lynde as a man rich enough to have his servants do his exercising for him (Lynde is on top form here; he gave his best performances on *Burke's Law*), Bert Parks as a thieving toy salesman, the ubiquitous Jonathan Hole as a camp window dresser, and Irwin Charone as a sleazy landlord.

## Who Killed the Rest?

wr. Lorenzo Semple Jnr., dir. Sam Freedle

*with Lisa Gaye (Sam Scott), Cesar Romero (Captain Alvaro), Steve Cochran (Fletcher Seamway), Eartha Kitt (Witch Lady), Theodore Bikel (Senor Gonzalez), Janice Rule (Mimsy Cohen), Gonzales Gonzalez, Bern Hoffman (comedy cops), Inger Stratton (Brunhilde), Nestor Paiva (Padre), Pepe Callahan (Trino, first witness), Rafael Lopez (Filipe, second witness), Linda Rivera (dancer)*

It had to happen—Burke is himself accused of murder, while on vacation in Mexico. Fortunately, his female companion is a little smarter than most, and is able to break him out of jail with Henry to clear his name. Steve Cochran, in his third and final appearance in the series, is a Hemingway-esque author, Eartha Kitt is a college professor gone native, and Theodore Bikel, in his second of two, a cartoon Nazi war criminal hiding out while he waits for the Fourth Reich. He insists his name is Gonzalez, but has an Aryan female aide called Brunhilde who keeps forgetting to call him by his alias, and there's a massive picture of Hitler on the wall. So far, so Semple.

Cesar Romero, in his last of five appearances, plays the local police chief, and Janice Rule is a knockout as a tomboy sailor in her second of two turns in the show. Rife with outdated stereotypes, but fun.

The basement/cellar set with all the steps down would be a regular fixture on *Amos Burke – Secret Agent*, where it was in almost constant use. Semple and Romero, and Romero and Kitt (who have no scenes together here), would be reunited on *Batman*.

*A light moment on the Batman set with Cesar Romero and Eartha Kitt as Joker and Catwoman.*

### Who Killed Cop Robin?

wr. David P. Harmon, dir. Murray Golden

*with Hal March (Paul Anders), Susan Strasberg (Melinda Drake), James Whitmore (Joe Piante), Ricardo Montalban (Armand Dubovier), Terry Moore (Nikki Manners), Eileen O'Neill (Sgt. Ames), Herbie Faye (Mr. Jacobson, druggist), Monica Keating (Beatrice Anders), Michael Fox (George McLeod), James Flavin (Danny Robin), Debbie Butler (dancer)*

Burke investigates the murder of his mentor. Hal March, Susan Strasberg, and Ricardo Montalban are making their second appearances, Terry Moore her third. Strasberg is particularly good. This was prolific TV writer David Harmon's only contribution to *Burke's Law*. He wrote for anything and everything, from *Gilligan's Island* to *Star Trek*. It was also the only episode directed by Murray Golden, but he became a regular director of *Honey West* and *Amos Burke – Secret Agent*. Speaking of the latter, if you'd rather forget that series ever existed, save this one as your 'last in the series'. It's got the perfect ending.

### Who Killed Nobody Somehow?

wr. Gwen Bagni, Paul Dubov, dir. Jerry Hopper

*with Lola Albright (Dee Dee Booker), Rory Calhoun (Ashton De Witt), Kevin McCarthy (Chukker Curtis), Diane McBain (Cissy Davenport De Witt), Tom Ewell (Leander Clement), Steve Brodie (Graham Tree, victim), I. Stanford Jolley (Thomas, the butler), Julie Reding (secretary), Michelle Breeze (maid), Stephen Chase (Dr. Harris), Clifford Kawada (referee), John Roseboro (male nurse), Ray Weaver, Lonnie Fotre (party guests)*

Burke goes undercover to investigate the attempted murder of a muck-raking author who revives in the morgue.

This was Lola Albright's fifth of five appearances in the series. She was a regular player in the 1950s *Peter Gunn* series, and retired in the early '80s after a number of TV guest star roles, including memorable *Man from UNCLE* and *Incredible Hulk* two-parters. This was Diane McBain's fourth of four; she was a regular on the early '60s detective show *Surfside Six*, and appeared in numerous Warners series several times. Noted for bad girl roles, she guested several times in such cult '60s shows as *77, Sunset Strip, Batman, The Man from UNCLE,* and *The Wild Wild West.*

*Terry Moore and Gene Barry in "Who Killed Cop Robin?"*

Rory Calhoun's private life was far more colorful and interesting than any of his mediocre film and TV roles. He was served up to *Confidential* magazine on a plate in the '50s by his agent, in exchange for their silence on Rock Hudson's sexuality. He starred in the late '50s western series *The Texan,* and this was his only appearance in *Burke's Law.* Same for Broadway actor Tom Ewell, who appeared in three TV series during his career, the single season *Tom Ewell Show* in 1960, a recurring role in early '70s cop show *Baretta,* and the short-lived *Best of the West* in the '80s. Kevin McCarthy appeared in anything

and everything, but is best known for the film *Invasion of the Body Snatchers* and a wonderful *Twilight Zone,* "Long Live Walter Jameson". Tough guy Steve Brodie was a regular on the *Wyatt Earp* TV series, and appeared in two Elvis films as a boorish thug who picks a fight with our hero, in *Blue Hawaii* and *Roustabout.* Michelle Breeze was a bit player who worked regularly on *Gunsmoke.* Both she and fellow bit player Juli Reding were making their second appearances on *Burke's Law.*

## Who Killed Hamlet?

wr. Albert Beich, Lewis Reed, dir. Don Weis

*with Basil Rathbone (Milo James), Agnes Moorehead (Pauline Moss), Edward Everett Horton (Wilbur Starlington), John Cassavetes (Stephen Collins), Eddie Foy Jnr. (Mr. Dugan), Susan Bay (Eileen, reporter), Nina Shipman (Sandra Prentiss), Bobby Darin (Roland Trivers, victim), Monica Keating (mother with baby), Valora Noland, Joyce Nizzari (beat girls in bar), Ami Luce (guitarist), Gene Bayliss (apartment manager), Ray Weaver, Arline Anderson (replacement actors), Paul Micale (maitre'd)*

Pop singer Bobby Darin joke-cameos as a dismal Shakespearean actor who is knocked off while rehearsing Hamlet. "Did Trivers have many enemies?" asks Burke. "Only those that knew him" sniffs guest star Basil Rathbone, stealing the show as an insufferable snob.

After Agnes 'Endora' Moorehead gets it, Burke replaces the third target on stage.

"Captain, you don't wear a breast-plate there"

"Timothy, this happens to be my breast-plate, and it also happens to be my..."

"Sorry, sir"

This is Cassavetes' fourth appearance (spoofing *West Side Story*, painfully), Moorehead's third, Horton and Foy's second, and sadly, Rathbone's one and only. Blink and you miss Valora Noland and Joyce Nizzari, a line each.

## Who Killed the Rabbit's Husband?

wr. Tony Barrett, dir. Jerry Hopper

*with Gloria Grahame (Doris Landers), Una Merkel (Clara Lovelace), John Ireland (Bullock), Paul Richards (Lennie Krull), Sal Mineo (Lew Dixon), Lyle Bettger (Captain Donohue), Lou Krugman (Art Sanders), Lennie Weinrib (Maddox), Vaughn Taylor (Dr. Schneider), Joanne Ludden (Gina Landers Holt), Jimmy Garrett, David Alan Bailey (kids), Francine York (Francesca, Burke's date), Eileen O'Neill (Sgt. Ames), Phil Arnold (Barney, pawn shop owner), Stafford Repp (Cody, barman), David Fresco (flop house manager), Don Gazzaniga (station house cop), Robert Bice (butler)*

A rabbit is, we're told, police slang for runaway. What makes a rabbit run? Could be almost anything says guest

Lyle Bettger. Amos Burke sits listening so long, so still, and so patiently to this interminable *Dragnet*-like waffle that I smell test footage for a backdoor pilot. Ditto Vaughn Taylor's scene as a psychiatrist.

"They come to me for solace... and so I reach out my hand, in love" chants lonely hearts specialist Merkel theatrically, a cynical operator. "Palm upwards" notes Burke.

"No sparks?" / "Sparks are fine when you can afford to pay the electric bill"

Agnes Moorehead's wicked witch Endora transforms Francine York's statue of Venus into a mortal in Bewitched.

This is Francine York's fifth and final appearance in *Burke's Law*. She made numerous appearances in cult TV over four decades, memorably appearing as the goddess Venus in *Bewitched*, villain's moll Lydia Limpet in *Batman*, and Amazon queen Neolani in *Lost in Space*. Jimmy Garrett was about to be cast as Viv's son in *The Lucy Show*.

## Who Killed the Jackpot?

wr. Gwen Bagni, Paul Dubov, dir. Richard Kinon

*with Anne Francis (Honey West), John Ericson (Sam Bolt), George Nader (Chris Maitland), Jan Sterling (Vera Selby), Steve Forrest (Jocko Creighton), Nancy Gates (Elizabeth Friendly), Louis Hayward (Stacy Blackwell), Michael Fox (George McLeod), Jim Turley, Jan Brooks (hotel patrons), Gordon Doversola (judo opponent), Arline Anderson (voice)*

This is the backdoor pilot and test footage for the wonderful *Honey West*, starring Anne Francis and John Ericson. So wonderful, that there's full coverage of the thirty episode show elsewhere in this book.

"Selby converted everything into cash. Theory — he was running away from something"

"Yeah, I just met her"

There's a notable lack of cheesecake in this episode, as all eyes are supposed to be on Francis. And boy, are they. Not a traditional '60s sexpot, Francis had a certain something that transcended mere surface beauty, which she took with her to the *Honey West* series, a sort of sluttish sophistication, pure pulp paperback. Les, Tim, and even George, are all under her spell. There are only two other major female roles (and one bit part), and even Burke's date is offscreen; Jan Sterling plays an over-the-hill gold-digger superbly and Nancy Gates is a sympathetic lovelorn secretary. Burke spends the entire episode following in Honey's tracks, giving Francis centre stage to make her mark, which she does, effortlessly. Writers Bagni and Dubov, *Burke's Law* regulars, developed the series and wrote many of the *Honey West* half-hours, both before and after it went campy.

Burke and West spar enjoyably and easily on equal terms, and there are several good exchanges to make this one of the great television team-ups, right up there with *Batman* and *The Green Hornet* and *Man* and *Girl from UNCLE*. The character of the over-protective Maitland looks suspiciously as though intended for the series. If so, he was wisely dropped, giving Honey her all-important independence. Irene Hervey's Aunt Meg is not here (perhaps for the best, as she earlier appeared as Tim Tilson's mother), but John Ericson, who had played a couple of gigolo roles in the series, is to hand as the delightfully named Sam Bolt.

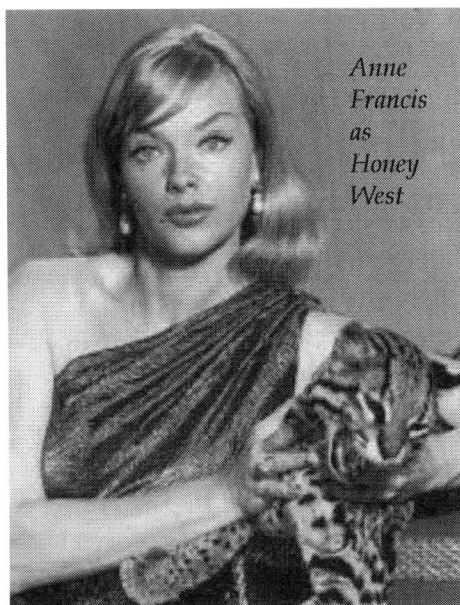

*Anne Francis as Honey West*

As well as appearing in numerous western series one-offs, Steve Forrest effortlessly flitted from hero to villain roles throughout his career, spent mostly in TV. He starred in two series, the British syndicated series *The Baron*, in which he was cast as a Burke-like adventuring antiques dealer, and Spelling's stupid and lowbrow *SWAT*. He had recurring roles on *Dallas* and *Team Knight Rider*, and played a bad guy in a 1979 *Captain America* pilot.

A former child star, Nancy Gates was busy in TV in the 1950s, but work dried up in the 1960s, and she retired to married life. Jan Sterling made a career out of playing bad girls and trash, and worked until the end of the '80s. Louis Hayward starred in two forgotten series, *The Lone Wolf* and *The Pursuers*. He retired in the early '70s and has some great lines here as a callous sleaze. George Nader also retired in the early '70s, and starred in *three* forgotten series from the early days of TV, as well as various B-movies. He was Ellery Queen in the '50s, and the oddly named Jerry Cotton in a series of German Eurospy films in the '60s.

concert appearance in Los Angeles" / "And his last"), and there's seventy-five suspects, but at least it gives Burke the chance to get away from his annoying Uncle Patrick (also played by Barry, with that curious combination of Scots and Irish that the Americans always put on when they're playing someone either Scottish or Irish). Cassavetes would later play a murderous concert pianist on *Columbo*.

Apparently bearing no grudge for the earlier Ellison episode in season one, Hugh Hefner of *Playboy* fame puts in a cameo as a manager of a bunny club. Marianna Case and Joyce Nizzari are both making their third of three appearances in minor roles.

## Who Killed the Grand Piano?

wr. Larry Gordon, dir. Fred De Cordova

*with John Cassavetes (Robert Algernon), Marilyn Maxwell (Maria Groovy), Nehemiah Persoff (Wilhelm Kasimer), Ed Begley (Morgus Ghoul), Martha Hyer (Bunny Mother), Michael Fox (George McLeod), Eileen O'Neill (Sgt. Ames), Chris Noel (Patience Stevens), Marianna Case (Spring), Trish De Brea (Misty), Hugh Hefner (cameo as Bunny Club manager), Milton Parsons (Kasimer's butler), John Hubbard (Kasimer's manicurist), Tom Cassidy (M.C.), Joyce Nizzari, Bonnie Beecher (bunnies)*

The old exploding piano trick... A concert pianist is blown up Yosemite Sam-style ("He was making his first

*Barry plays a pointless dual role in this episode as his 'Uncle Patrick'. Perhaps he was getting bored... but not as bored as he was about to get, thanks to ABC...*

Gordon's got the ear for the dialogue (assuming he hasn't been rewritten), but his sledgehammer satire is borderline *Batman*; Boris Karloff and his buddies and a Maria Callas routine are among the bits of business bludgeoned into the storyline.

Frederick De Cordova, director of the infamous *Bedtime for Bonzo*, inevitably ended up in TV, directing numerous runs of 1950s and 1960s sitcoms, including 108 episodes of the mechanically directed *My Three Sons*, before becoming producer of *The Tonight Show*.

### Who Killed the Card?

wr. Gwen Bagni, Paul Dubov, dir. Jerry Hopper

*with Jill Haworth (Ambrosia Mellon), Eddie Bracken (Simeon Quatraine), Les Crane (Holton Rocket), Wally Cox (Doctor Handy), Hazel Court (Goody Handy), Monica Keating (interior decorator), Eileen O'Neill (Sgt. Ames), Quinn O'Hara (Rocket's secretary), Michael Fox (George McLeod), Hugh Sanders (Lt. Ellison), Don Gazzaniga (Charlie, cop in drag), Bob Bice (waiter)*

Barry returns to his roots to do a song and dance routine for what would be the final episode. For the only time in the series, the killer taunts Burke with a series of messages (in greetings cards). Eddie Bracken, Hazel Court, and Wally Cox are all making second appearances. Quinn O'Hara is making her third. Monica Keating made several appearances in minor supporting roles during the show's run, and also did a *Honey West* and an *Amos Burke – Secret Agent*. Les Crane was a game show host.

series ends

*Happy days. Gene, Gary, and Regis gather with some of the big name guest stars of the first season. Note Anne Francis and Leon Lontoc on the right.*

BURKE'S LAW
THE COMPLETE FIRST SERIES
DETECTIVE
STARRING
GENE BARRY

BURKE'S LAW
TELEVISION STORY BOOK

BURKE'S LAW
Annual
Based on the popular
TV. programme
Starring GENE BARRY as
Captain Burke

BURKE'S LAW
Jigsaw    SIZE 17"x11"

DELL 12
BURKE'S LAW
Captain Burke
Investigates
Dock Homicide
YACHT CREWMAN
FOUND DEAD
MILLIONAIRE DETECTIVE
NABS SUSPECTS

INSTRUMENTAL THEMES FROM THE ORIGINAL SOUNDTRACK RECORDING OF
BURKE'S LAW
GENE BARRY

*Captain Burke examines the merchandise…*

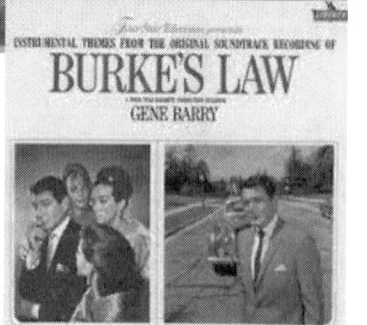

# Jonny Quest

## September 18th, 1964 — March 11th, 1965

William Hanna and Joe Barbera turned to television cartoon production during the infancy of the medium after the closure of the MGM cartoon department where they had made 114 *Tom and Jerry* cartoons. MGM later realised their mistake, and started cartoon production up again, but by that time H-B were firmly established in television, having had huge hits with *Huckleberry Hound, Yogi Bear,* and *The Flintstones. Jonny Quest* was a brave attempt to create a prime-time animated adventure show, and not only was it the first TV cartoon to entirely feature reality-based characters (figures based on the actual human form), it was only the second continuing animated series to do so (following the Max Fleischer *Superman* cartoons made for the cinema in the war years). Both Fleischer and Disney had experimented with the human form, often rotoscoping their characters (drawing over filmed actors), but *Jonny Quest* had to be produced at the rate of thirty minutes a week like all TV cartoons and could not afford such luxuries. The results were extraordinarily good.

*Jonny Quest* was a boys' adventure comic come to life on the TV screen. It was fast, creative, action-packed, and beautifully animated (from the start, but improving as it went on). The series was originally proposed as an animated version of *Jack Armstrong, All-American Boy,* a syndicated comic strip adventure, and test-footage of same can be seen as the end credits begin, with a ginger-haired lad in what became the famous Quest flying saucer. The artist involved with the character design was a guy named Doug Wildey.

Jonny Quest was the brave and curious son of widowed scientist Doctor Benton Quest. While the bearded scientist involved himself in the work of the scientific community, Jonny was usually in the company of bodyguard Race Bannon, who doubled as his teacher.* Making up the all-male foursome (because it was 1964, there were no gurls allowed!) was Indian boy Hadji, who despite a passion for exotic and somewhat inexplicable magic tricks, was a pleasingly non-stereotypical best buddy for Jonny (one wonders why he didn't use such powers as levitation a little more often in times of danger!).**

* The question of where Jonny's mother is has been a bone of contention for some time! In a 1986 comic book, the writers decided she had died of an incurable disease, but in a 1993 animated cable TV movie one-off it was announced that she had been bumped off by recurring villain Doctor Zin. While the first was unpleasant, the second was cliched. Her name was also changed, from Judith to Rachel. Then, in 2017, all this was ignored and revised in the DC comic *Future Quest,* a rare enjoyable reboot that now had her killed in an explosion caused by Doctor Zin *and* FEAR, the evil organisation from the *Birdman* cartoons. Oh, and her name was Emma.

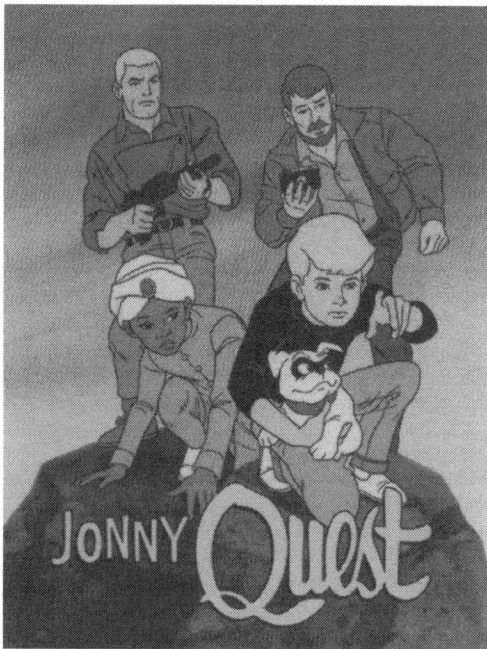

** In "The Invisible monster", one of the series' best episodes. Hadji's flying belt fails, and Jonny and Race have to rescue him. And yet, in another episode, he mysteriously levitates Jonny into the air!

The one concession to traditional cartoons was Bandit, Jonny's pet bulldog, so-named because of his mask-like face, and drawn in greeting card style as a mischievous comic relief figure. This addition later became a traditional inclusion in all similar cartoons (the Great Dane added to 1969's Mystery Inc. later took over the show and it's title—Scooby-Doo), and while older viewers winced, the fact is that these funny animals were much loved and appreciated by the younger target audience (in fact, I quite enjoy Bandit's antics now).* And, like the rest of the show, Bandit is beautifully animated. Otherwise, *Jonny Quest* took itself relatively seriously, and there were clearly drawn boundaries regarding credibility that were not present in later animated adventure series such as the flood of colorful super-hero cartoons that invaded Saturday morning U.S. TV a couple of years later.

* The inclusion of a cute animal for comic relief in Hanna-Barbera's adventure cartoons later became such a traditional ritual that it was wickedly sent up in *South Park's* "Korn's Groovy Pirate Adventure", a cynical but funny spoof of *Scooby-Doo,* with a pet chick called Niblet.

The adversaries in *Jonny Quest* had one foot in the world of science and the other in the world of comic-books. Blobs, robots, electrical monsters, and scientific experiments gone awry were featured alongside Bond-ish super-villains and secret societies of evil-doers of the sort favoured by the pulps. One memorable episode featured an Egyptian mummy come to life, others included pirates, mercenaries, mad scientists, and prehistoric creatures.

If the story ideas were unavoidably formulaic, the execution of them was not. And not only were the stories genuinely suspenseful (and the writers unhampered by budgetary considerations for sets, locations, special effects and props), but the dialogue was surprisingly and gratifyingly literate; there were no concessions for dumb schmucks and seeing them today one immediately spots the gulf between this series and anything written for animation since the beginning of the 1970s—imagine *Josie and the Pussycats* with long words and no chases and you've got it. Imagine the Famous Five meets *The Outer Limits!* That was *Jonny Quest*. It was a cool show.

*A rare case of a tolerable 21st century update – DC Comics' Future Quest, featuring Jonny alongside Hanna-Barbera's 1960s super-heroes*

And here's a dirty word. It was *wholesome*. Jonny and Hadji were good kids. They were not foul-mouthed and disobedient, but they *were* child-like and mischievous. The show was not 'dark and gritty', it was light and bright, and the kids had a great time, despite the dangers they faced. To the show's young audience, it was an enviable scenario. The boys had the sense to know when they were in trouble, and when they'd done something wrong, but they were never scared or terrified, and neither was their audience. They were typical kids, and the real adventuring was left to Dr. Quest and Race. Jonny and Hadji were lucky and privileged, and they knew it… and so did the envious kids watching in the audience. The boys travelled all over the world, and got to ride aeroplanes, submarines, flying saucers, rocket-belts, hydrofoils, jet-skis, and almost anything that moved without the need for feet!

Jonny was voiced by child actor Tim Matheson, who went on to numerous films and TV shows in adult life, including runs in *The Virginian* and *Bonanza*. As a young man, he had a short run in his own show, a western ironically called *The Quest*, with fellow former child actor Kurt Russell, but it had the misfortune to be scheduled against the first season of *Charlie's Angels*. Best known for *National Lampoon's Animal House* and a recurring role in *The West Wing*, Matheson (then billed as Matthieson) also did voices for *Sinbad Jnr.*, *Young Samson and Goliath*, and Jace for *Space Ghost*. Child actor Danny Bravo, who voiced Hadji, did minor parts in live action shows before and after *Jonny Quest*, but retired from the business at the end of the '60s.

Doctor Quest was initially voiced by John Stephenson, and then replaced after the first few episodes by the equally familiar tones of Don Messick. Both continued to provide other voices for the show, and worked ceaselessly for Hanna-Barbera. A Warners contract player with numerous appearances in their western and detective series, Mike Road still played occasional live action parts afterwards, but found it more profitable to provide voices for animated series, Race Bannon being his most well-known. His distinctive baritone was so easily recognised that when he did other voices in the *Jonny Quest* series, they were too obviously by the same performer!

Many voice artists went uncredited on *Jonny Quest*, but the IMDB lists as recurring names *The Outer Limits'* Vic Perrin (who was also Doctor Zin), *Augie Doggie's* Doug Young (Augie's dad), veteran voice man Henry Corden (as many of the rougher types), character actors Tol Avery (in virtually his only cartoon voiceover work), Will Kuluva (ditto), Nestor Paiva, Keye Luke, and most surprisingly, stage actor Everett Sloane.

One of the nicer elements about *Jonny Quest* was that while it was never boring, and always exciting, there was none of the mindless, manic non-stop hysteria of other cartoons, even high quality ones like *The Herculoids*. The series had a very laid-back feel to it (dare we say cool?), and we always saw plenty of scenes of everyday life, sports and recreation (ya-hoooo!), bedtime and/or studies (*booo-oo!*). Seeing Jonny and the others regularly at play gave the show a grounded sense of reality to youngsters amid the monsters, mercenaries, and cartoon dogs, and the kids were always doing something active or exciting. There was always a new country to explore (in one episode, the boys discuss their favorite locale), and a new amazing experimental flying disc, submarine, or rocket belt to try out. In many ways, the series was aspirational; kids envied Jonny and Hadji, while at the same time knowing that such a life of adventure, activity, and exploration when they were older was not unattainable. And if Race or Doctor Quest said no, it was never arbitrary, fearful, or unreasonable. There was parental caution, but never fear. Common sense and rational presumption ruled the day for the science-based Quest party, not paranoia, psychotic villains, or violence. Hope for the future, but not naivete. Bad guys got what was coming to them, and were pitied, but went unmourned. No other animated adventure series had such high standards as *Jonny Quest*. It set a bar that has never been reached again in animation.

*Jonny Quest* went out on Friday nights at 7.30. and there is little to explain its failure unless one blames the dads for preferring the seventh season of *Rawhide*. Apart from *The Addams Family*, Friday nights were a bust for all three networks that season. However, those that liked *Jonny* loved him, and the series—like fellow H-B one season wonders *Top Cat* and *The Jetsons*—flourished in syndication and on Saturday mornings, where several other networks screened the re-runs regularly throughout the next twenty years. In Britain, the series enjoyed a couple of runs on the BBC before fading into oblivion, marked only by the release of a paltry couple of episodes on video during the 1980s, at which time thirteen new episodes were produced, succeeding only in demonstrating how far standards in animation had fallen. A handful of re-runs on Boomerang followed in the 1990s before the inevitable arrival of a charmless late-90s update not to be confused with the 1964 original, which, unlike its ham-fisted and already dated remakes, which made all the mistakes so nimbly avoided thirty years earlier, is still watchable for all ages today.

*note: all episodes other than the pilot (which was written by Walter Black) are credited to William Hamilton. This may well be the case, but it may also be the case that the series has used just one set of the end credits on all episodes in syndication, something Hanna-Barbera or its distributors have been known to do before. While remaining faithful to the format, so many episodes are variable in approach that it seems likely to me that there were several writers, some better than others. However, there are few people left around to trust or to ask for a straight answer, so the authorship of the Jonny Quest adventures may be the biggest mystery of them all.*

## Mystery of the Lizard Men

Hadji is missing from this opening episode (but not the opening credits), which otherwise introduces the main characters and the premise of the show. This story was used for the one and only comic book based on the series for Gold Key (although there have been subsequent comic book series since), and reprinted in the British *Jonny Quest* Christmas annual of the period from World Distributors.

The lizard men of the title are actually minions of the bad guy in scuba-diving kit, and the menace is a deadly beam operated from within the wrecks of the Sargasso Sea. The absence of a cackling fool rubbing his hands with glee was a welcome change from the usual standard

Hanna-Barbera bad guy as seen in *Atom Ant, Secret Squirrel,* and *The Impossibles et al.*

There's a strong educational element in this episode which, it has to be said, gradually disappeared from the show as it went on. There are also speedboats, hydrofoils, and laser beams. Hanna-Barbera followers will recognise background music from *The Jetsons* every time Bandit is at play, a tradition generally followed throughout the series.

### Arctic Splashdown

A pleasant, leisurely adventure in the Arctic. How jealous were we in 1964 as we watched Jonny take a turn driving the Snow Skimmer.

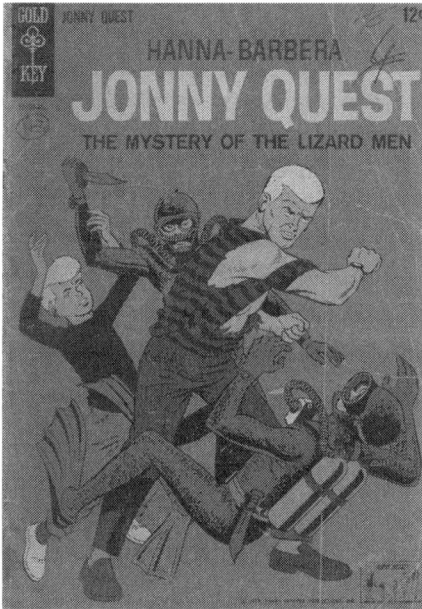

Hadji turns up without explanation in this story (complete with his "Sim Sim Salabim" routine), in which the Americans rush to retrieve a downed missile from the Arctic before foreign powers get there. It's that simple. This is a good one for fans of Bandit; there are quite a few laugh-out-loud moments with the little guy in various gag sequences.

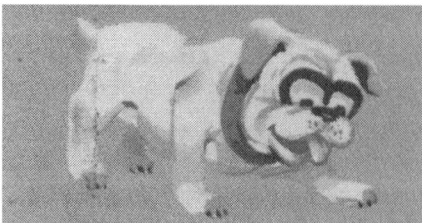

In between watching bad guys get blown to tiny little bits, that is.

### The Curse of Anubis

The Quests skootch off to Egypt this time, but it's a trap. Although the story includes a revived mummy in the traditional Universal films manner, the creature is used sparingly, as an incidental feature, rather than as the focus of the story. Nevertheless, this is a rare excursion into the supernatural for the normally fact-based pro-science show, and this extends to Hadji's own magical abilities, which include snake-charming! Despite all this, it's a noticeably adult script and dialogue, despite a lengthy slapstick chase in the middle. Jonny is centre stage in this one, and he and Hadji save the adults... with a little help from Bandit of course.

### Pursuit of the Po-Ho

Dr. Quest goes to the rescue of a friend who has been captured by a hostile primitive native tribe, who intend to make a human sacrifice to their Fire God. Some of the more blinkered politically correct have worried themselves over Race constantly referring to the tribesmen as 'savages' in this episode, but as their behavior most clearly is savage, this seems a little silly. There are plenty of friendly primitives and natives in future episodes who aren't trying to burn humans alive, and they're treated with friendship and respect. Quest's own escape is very cartoony, and probably not survivable!

# BEGINS TODAY! JONNY QUEST

*The first page of a British Jonny Quest strip for Britain's Huckleberry Hound Weekly. For some reason, Jonny seems to think his father's flying saucer vehicle belongs to Hadji! Writer and artist unknown. Huckleberry Hound Weekly featured strips drawn in the U.K. style by the Dell/Gold Key artists which were later reprinted in the U.S. in Whitman books. This strip, which ran only a few weeks, appears to be an exception.*

## Riddle of the Gold

The Quest party go to India to investigate a gold mine producing fake gold. It's recurring bad guy Dr. Zin, making his first appearance. With this episode, Don Messick takes over the voice role of Dr. Quest. The idea of a tiger hunt is a little outmoded today, but rest assured the tiger gets the best of it. Visually, this is a very good-looking episode, with several good action scenes and striking backgrounds.

## Treasure of the Temple

Fairly straightforward adventure involving a search for Mayan treasure. Not that it's dull though, it ain't. And the canoe chase at the end is a highlight, but you have to wonder why Race didn't just steal or sink their pursuers' canoe, he overturned it twice, so he had two opportunities! The bad guy is a rather dull and overdone British Cockney, but it makes a change from the Russians and Chinese.

## Calcutta Adventure

Doctor Quest is asked to investigate a suspected enemy establishment producing nerve gas. We never find out who, or why, but the Bond-like operation manned entirely by faceless minions is duly closed down with extreme prejudice. The IMDB suggests this was to have been the second episode, as it introduces Hadji in flashback form, but this is debatable, as it features Don Messick as Quest, and they didn't bother to re-dub him in the delayed first, "Double Danger", which is still to come. This one's a bit of a dud for several reasons, not least because Jonny and Hadji are written out of the action in the second half entirely (who else thought they were hiding in Pasha's sled?).

There's way too much of 'hilarious' scoundrel and opportunist fixer Pasha Peddler, but at least they didn't bring him back. He has a whole stupid bit where he gets Race into the enemy installation with a dumb comedy salesman routine, even referring to the secret laboratory as a secret laboratory. Obviously, he would have been shot right there, but the guard behaves like a human version of Bandit. On the other hand, more bullets miss their targets in this episode than in a whole season of *The A-Team*; nobody even gets winged, so even from that close range, he'd probably have missed. The bad guys, however, expendable mercenaries all, do ultimately get burned, boiled alive, and buried alive. What nobody gets, despite extensive expenditure of ammunition, is shot.

226

### The Robot Spy

One of the series' most fondly remembered episodes, this story features a stylish spider robot with a single eye and spindly stick legs that is a masterpiece of spartan animation. Although it arrives in a flying saucer, the menacing device, a large black ball with a big roving eye and thin mechanical legs, is actually of Earth origin, a creation of recurring bad guy Doctor Zin. It has a monitor relaying pictures back to

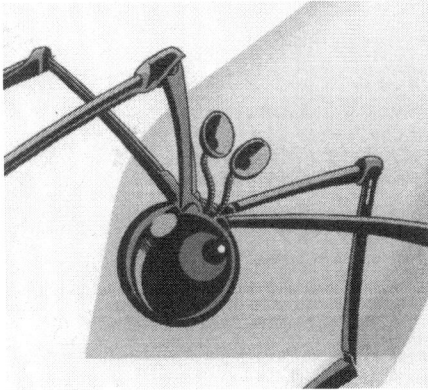

base, a neat paralysing attack ability, and can be seen in the series' magnificent opening credits montage taking on the massed forces of the military. It features in the packaging of the Warners DVD release of the series, and it was a joy to see it turn up again in the 2017 comic series *Future Quest*.

### Double Danger

As is often the case, the first episode actually produced is often buried later in the series after the bugs have been ironed out. That's the case with this story, which concerns a double of Race Bannon

being planted in the Quest household by Doctor Zin (thus making this technically his first appearance). The idea of an evil double of a regular character is a very routine and familiar storyline, handled here in a very routine and familiar way, and rightly held back. Consequently, John Stephenson provides the voice of Doctor Quest again for this one, and the rather mature character of Jade, Race's exotic girlfriend, makes her first of two appearances. Jade's method of discovering the fake Race is surprisingly self-evident, even for 1960s primetime, let alone an animated cartoon!

With social engineering and demographic box-ticking not having yet started in television during the '60s, the show had little use for female characters, making this very much a 'boys' only' adventure show (and interestingly, a favorite with female fans!), and Jade was used only when necessary rather than for any trendy box-ticking reasons. She was a typical mid-'60s *femme fatale* type of the sort that adorned most of the secret agent adventures of the period. I don't suppose women like to be patronised any more than any other section of society, and can spot a 'token girl' character a mile off, I'm sure (see the lame 1990s revival with predictable inevitability).

### Shadow of the Condor

After a tense emergency landing in the Andes on a mystery airstrip, the Quests realise they've stumbled onto the mountain hideaway of a deranged WW One war veteran who wants one last dogfight. The 'planes are beautifully animated.

## Skull and Double-Crossbones

This is one of the series' more cartoonish offerings, and might better be sub-titled 'the adventures of Bandit', as Jonny's comic relief dog, usually used sparingly and sensibly, takes centre stage and is seen both putting on his own breathing apparatus and riding on the back of a porpoise! Flipper and Lassie eat your hearts out as the scientific party are menaced by another bunch of modern-day pirates.

## The Dreadful Doll

Commendably fake voodoo is the theme of this episode, in which a local charlatan is aiding a slobbish mercenary (voiced by second Fred Flintstone Henry Corden, a regular on the series) to operate a hidden submarine for a foreign power. The series' scientific bent is very much to the fore in this one; there's no hocus-pocus nonsense about the voodoo element, Dr. Quest announces outright that it's all hooey, and so it is seen to be. Although the lead bad guy is a rather dull creation, the supporting characters are very well done and three dimensional.

## A Small Matter of Pygmies

Race and the two boys crash-land in hostile jungle territory, and are pursued by cruel and violent pygmies.

A contentious episode with what the writer P. J. O'Rourke called "the professionally indignant", this episode includes the shooting of a black panther (to save the life of a human character, and showing Jonny flinching as the creature is finished off) and the dispatching of numerous babbling native attackers.

The prolonged battle between the guys and the natives is interesting in that their attack strategies don't magically work perfectly the first time, a story characteristic quite rare in adult entertainment, let alone children's animation. When the cavalry arrives in the form of a swarm of helicopters lead by Doctor Quest, the episode takes on a more traditionally fantastic cartoonish tone as the natives are gusted away or bumped rather than decapitated by the rotor blades, but by then we're won over.

### The Dragons of Ashida

Straightforward Bondish/*Enter the Dragon* type of adventure with a mix of judo and lizard monsters and a *Dr. No*-style scientist gone bad. Very nicely animated. It takes a while for the Quest party to figure out that Ashida is nuts, although to be fair they never seem too taken in that he isn't.

### Turu the Terrible

The Quests are searching for the source of a rich vein of an element in rock form valuable to the space race. They find a crazed old man on the top of a mountain who thinks the rocks are silver, and is forcing local natives to work as his slaves to mine it by threatening them with a trained and supposedly extinct pteranodon. The monstrous bird creature is accurately rendered and brilliantly animated. When the murderous old bastard follows his prehistoric creature into bubbling lava at episode's close, the Quests are sorry, but not that sorry. After all, he's spent the entire episode screaming "Kill! Kill!".

### The Fraudulent Volcano

This is the one with the Steranko-ish cylindrical flying machines big enough for two armed stooges shown in the closing credits in a particularly stylish piece of test footage for the series. The mercenaries' green outfits also resemble the Kirby/Steranko *SHIELD* comics of the 1960s, although of course it should be remembered that *Jonny Quest* preceded the *Nick Fury* comic by a year. The villain is the *Dr. No*-inspired Doctor Zin again, and with his headquarters in a volcano and a poisonous spider menacing Dr. Quest in his bed, there are numerous other Bond-style influences in this story. The animation here, already regularly of a high standard, is excellent in this one.

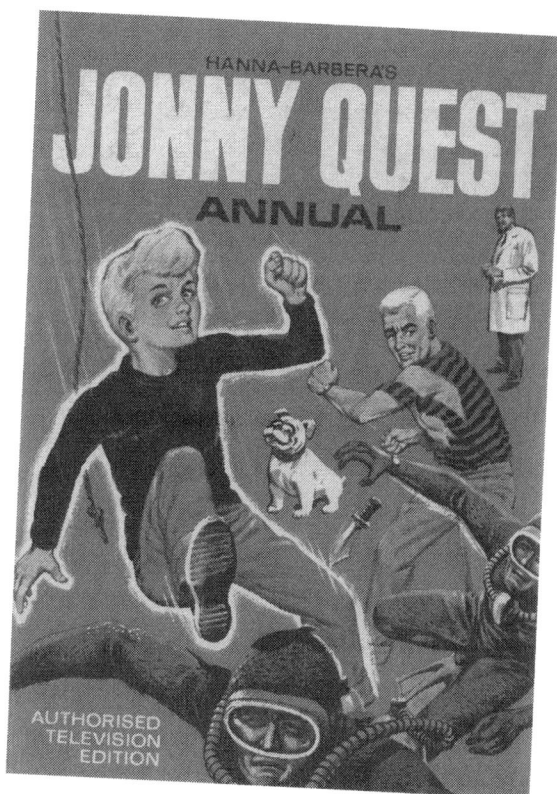

## The Werewolf of the Timberland

This is quite possibly the worst episode in the series. The Quests are on a research expedition in Canada's forests, which for the boys means a camping trip, when a bunch of gold smugglers moving their loot from a logging camp decide to draw attention to themselves by rattling on about a local werewolf... which is, of course, their leader in a silly suit. There is absolutely no reason for this guy to be running around in a Hallowe'en outfit and attracting attention to themselves, but no-one seems to question his leadership or his sanity.

Then the boys get lost in the woods and run into a mystical warrior with a pet wolf and the rather obvious voice of Race Bannon's Mike Road; with the character sounding so much like Race one would almost suspect a reveal if it wasn't for the fact that Race is there too.

This is a rare lapse of this science-based show into mystical twaddle — and stupid Native American tourist trap twaddle as well. It's all a bit *Scooby-Doo*, not helped by French-Canadian voices that sound like *Huckleberry Hound's* Powerful Pierre... Had these mugs left the happy campers alone to whizz around in their hovercrafts until they found what they came for, they'd still be trading today...

## Pirates from Below

While Doctor Quest tests a new underwater exploration vehicle, Race and Jonny are kidnapped by Bond-ish pirates with an undersea base who want the new submarine (they already seem to have Quest's flying saucer vehicles!).

There's a beautifully animated opening sequence with a stationary seahorse surrounded by fish. More fish swim into the foreground and then they all scatter except for the seahorse as Quest's submarine disturbs them. Less welcome is another cliched foray into supernatural powers for the sake of a cheap laugh, as Hadji does his 'Sim Sim Salabim' routine and levitates Jonny into the air. Shame he never seems to use these tricks when they're in trouble! Once again, superb art and animation.

*The Jonny Quest series, while sci-fi, was admirably science-based, but bizarrely made an exception to indulge in the cliche of Indian tourist trap mysticism. Hadji's powers were only ever employed for comic relief, and curiously never manifested themselves when the boys were in danger!*

## Attack of the Tree People

A good solid adventure story as Jonny and Hadji are stranded on an island after their vessel catches fire accidentally. As Quest and Race search for them, the boys fall into the protective company of some comedy apes, and the story goes a bit ape itself. Also on the island some nasty Brit gun-runners, who fall afoul of everybody... The comedy apes help to negate some of the scary unpleasantness of the scary Cockneys, no relation to the guy from "Treasure of the Temple".

## The Invisible Monster

This is perhaps the most fondly remembered episode of the series, featuring an invisible energy monster similar to that found in the 1956 feature *Forbidden Planet.* They expose the creature by covering him in paint (right).

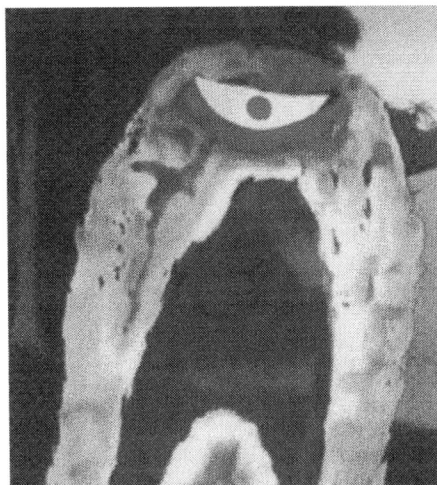

With open-top flying saucers for transport, coupled with flying belts, what more could an eight year old boy have wanted back in 1964? Come to think of it, what more could a grown man today want for a toy? The basic premise was re-used a couple of years later in *Space Ghost* as "The Energy Monster".

## The Devil's Tower

In Africa, at the top of a mountain known as the Devil's Escarpment because it is impossible to access by foot, the Quest party encounter a tribe of German-speaking primitives while trying to retrieve the valuable instrumentation on a stray balloon. Using the primitive throwbacks as slave labor to dig out diamonds is a Nazi war criminal (this is 1964, remember), who now has a way to escape the escarpment in the Quest 'plane... leaving them stranded with the cavemen. After a slow start, the action picks up when the Nazi uses the Quest 'plane to attack the escaping group with grenades. He gets an amusing and well-deserved comeuppance. This one's very similar to both "Shadow of the Condor" and "Turu The Terrible", but without the pteranodon.

## The Quetong Missile Mystery

No-one could ever accuse me of being "politically correct", but unfortunately this one is a little, uh, unfriendly in its portrayal of China, which you will recall back in 1964 was as Red as the blood spilled by Mao. Today, it's not suitable for children because of some of the coloring and dialogue, although it should be available for viewing. It's also unusually brutal, with several deaths and some harsh sentiments. Politically, the writer is deliberately vague about what the wicked General Fong was up to, we only know the police would like to have a word. They won't be able to,

## Cast of Characters

**JONNY QUEST...**
AN ELEVEN-YEAR-OLD BOY WHO
BECOMES INVOLVED IN ACTION-
PACKED ADVENTURES THE WORLD
OVER.

**DR. BENTON QUEST...**
JONNY'S FATHER, A TOP GOVERN-
MENT SCIENTIST WHO USES HIS
BRILLIANT MIND AS A WEAPON
AGAINST ENEMY GROUPS AND
NATIONS.

**ROGER "RACE" BANNON...**
GOVERNMENT-ASSIGNED BODY-
GUARD FOR JONNY AND DR.
QUEST. BETWEEN ADVENTURES HE
ACTS AS JONNY'S TUTOR AND
COMPANION.

**BANDIT...**
JONNY'S BULLDOG, HE GETS HIS
NAME FROM THE MARKINGS ABOUT
HIS EYES, AND HE SHARES IN HIS
MASTER'S THRILLING ESCAPADES.

*Above, early promotional materials for the show from 1964 (and before Hadji). Right, promotional art for the superb Future Quest comic.*

because he's blown himself up! Oops.

Story-wise, there's not much to it, although the animation is as excellent as always. As Jonny says himself, he slept through all the action!

### The House of Seven Gargoyles

The Quests are in Scandinavia, to see a demonstration of an anti-gravity device. Far from sleeping through the action, this time Jonny's having waking nightmares, teased because he's seeing submarine periscopes and moving statues.

This one's great fun, and quite scary and creepy, with a gargoyle coming to life, climbing down off the ledge and attacking people. The seventh of the six has been replaced by a circus acrobat, you see. Note the use of shadows in the animation. "Get back to your perch!".

### Terror Island

The Quests are in Hong Kong for Chinese New Year when Dr. Quest is kidnapped by a mad scientist who is growing insects and sea life into giant deadly monsters. Exactly why we never find out, and the monsters do very little but stalk around. And Jezebel Jade returns from "Double Danger".

This one manages to avoid most of the unintentional racism in "The Quetong Missile Mystery", although the ghost of "Bugs Bunny Nips the Nips" resurfaces cruelly in a surprising sequence where Race merrily throws a grenade into the lap of a jeep driver and his passengers with a comical quip, ducking round a corner to the sound of the offscreen explosion. Only the most pedantic purist would complain if that were excised, although is it really that much different to any act of comedy violence in a Stallone or Schwarzenegger film?

### Monster in the Monastery

While visiting Nepal, the Quest party are trapped in a village under siege from yeti. Split up from the adults, Jonny and Hadji discover a distinctly human element to their attackers... not to mention that, once again, they're exceedingly bad shots. A nice grim ending for all the bad guys. The carnival monster is the same one that just appeared in the Chinese New Year parade in "Terror Island".

### The Sea Haunt

A Dutch ship is attacked by an amphibious prehistoric monster. When the Quests board the ship, they find it smashed up and abandoned, and the creature still aboard. This is a genuine creature, rather than a guy in a suit, which makes the laid-back attitude to the creature rather bizarre. The Quests are on a small ship with a rampaging, murderous monster, and behave with no sense of urgency, as though they have all the time, space, and freedom in the world. Most of us would be crapping bricks. The problem, I think, is that having assembled everyone on the boat with the sea monster, the writers don't seem to have anywhere to go with it. And sadly, this was where the series ended, a victim of its own costly quality.

series ends

## Honey West

**September 17th, 1965 — April 8th, 1966**

Filmed in black and white, the gloriously pulpy *Honey West,* with the perfectly cast Anne Francis as the title babe, was the last gasp for the prestigious Four Star Studios, and it was a return to the half-hour format they favored in the '50s. It was a stylish but B-movie-ish detective show with spy trappings, a sort of American paperback rack mix of Emma Peel and Modesty Blaise. Based on a series of private eye novels with a hint of eroticism by Skip and Gloria Fickling, and developed for television by *Burke's Law* writers Gwen Bagni and Paul Dubov (who wrote ten of the thirty episodes), it had a distinct 1940s ambience in the opening credits that oozed past the austere, conservative 1950s and into the swinging '60s with a vengeance, as the producers jazzed the show up with Bondish gimmickry, including tear gas earrings, sunglasses with radio transmitters, a very conspicuous listening device, and my favorite personal bugbear, the magic hidden camera that supernaturally films, cuts, edits, and zooms according to the story's requirements. There were also some excellent cars and car chases. Fortunately, like *Top Cat,* no-one ever occupies the streets except the cast (and, if backlot streets, a handful of extras).

The half-hour format means that some potentially elaborate plots are wrapped up quite quickly sometimes, but mostly the format worked to the show's advantage. The pace never drags; there's not much time for filler or even exposition, making it a great show to binge-watch. We were back to the era of *Peter Gunn, Richard Diamond,* and *Johnny Staccato.* No sooner have episodes started, than they've finished, but unlike many half-hour shows, *Honey West* was an hour's worth of plot crammed into a half-hour. This has its virtues and its disadvantages, but generally the format works because the dialogue and direction is zippy. Certainly, there's more story in a half-hour of *Honey West* than most of Spelling's 1970s and '80s series! And a jazzy score to rival *The Man from UNCLE.*

The stunt doubling is fairly obvious, and it was at the time. There weren't too many female stunt players in the '60s, although fortunately there were some. Usually, Anne Francis' stunt person is female, although in an obvious wig, but occasionally, and hilariously, a guy stands in.

However, above all, *Honey West* was a great series to actually *watch.* There were excellent chase sequences and fight scenes of the karate chop and judo variety), and the cars and locations were super-cool. Francis was always dressed (or undressed — episodes included bubble baths and numerous opportunities for swimwear) beautifully by Nolan Miller of *Charlie's Angels* and *Dynasty* fame, and fresh off *Burke's Law,* the first of Spelling's glamorous series that he wardrobed.

*Honey West* ran throughout the 1965–66 season, which means it ran straight into the camp craze head first. Although the series always had an inevitable air of disbelief about it due to the crazy collection of gadgets in the back of Sam's van (John Ericson was back from "Who killed the Jackpot?" as her short-tempered techie tough guy, Sam Bolt), the stories had always been reasonably credible by TV standards. However, the moment the series entered 1966, the series slipped noticeably into excess, with the same type of ridiculous, gimmicky, and deliberately silly stories as the other shows of the period. And as the story ideas became more absurd, there was less attempt to explain things away. Suddenly, we had a guy in a gorilla suit, a guy in a bear suit, a guy in a Robin Hood suit, a guy in a Saturday morning serials robot suit. In one episode, Honey solved a mystery by dreaming it, in a series of movie parodies. At this point, the series was on the verge of going down the same psychedelic road to excess as *The Girl from UNCLE* and the *The Avengers,* but in general, Honey kept her cool and her credibility. Had the show proceeded to a second season, it would undoubtedly have been in color and completely bonkers, but the series ended on a relatively sane note after a run of sillies, and as such is remembered favorably and with affection by the clued-in few. Cool TV? You betcha.

The case of the kissing killer

A GUN FOR HONEY

featuring Honey West, the sexiest private eye ever to pull a trigger

G. G. FICKLING
author of THIS GIRL FOR HIRE

HONEY WEST

STARRING ANNE FRANCIS
THE COMPLETE SERIES OF THIRTY EPISODES
FOUR DVD VIDEO BOX SET   Bonus Feature: Honey West's Debut In "Burke's Law"   PG

Honey West

episode guide

(1965-'66)

*regular cast: Anne Francis (as Honey West), John Ericson (as Sam Bolt), Irene Hervey (as Aunt Meg)*

## The Swingin' Mrs. Jones

wr. Gwen Bagni, Paul Dubov, dir. Paul Wendkos

Honey poses as a wealthy wife to stop blackmailers who prey on married women by seduction

*with Ray Danton (Sonny), Winnie Coffin (Mother), Marvin Brody (private eye), Louise Arthur (Mrs. Mainwaring/ victim), Thann Wyenn (waiter/driver), Don Gazzaniga (greedy gang member)*

In her first appearance following her debut in *Burke's Law*, Honey slinks around a tourist resort trying to tempt Ray Danton's heartless gigolo into making a play for her—not too difficult, as she looks amazing, as if she stepped off the front cover of, oh, say a *Honey West* paperback. Great dialogue, great ambience, great start to the

series. Bruce the ocelot and Aunt Meg are introduced in the tag (they won't be seen in every episode), and we get to see transmitters in sunglasses and tear gas in earrings. Honey's most ridiculous gimmick, a two-way radio in Martini olives, would resurface to hilarious effect in the wonderful spy spoof *The Glass Bottom Boat* the following year. Honey was definitely ahead of the game!

Despite appearing in the single season of *The Alaskans*, Ray Danton is best known for his lead role in gangster flick *The Rise and Fall of Legs Diamond* and subsequent string of television guest appearances as smooth bad guys. One of the best is in the *Man from UNCLE* episode "The Discotheque Affair". Winnie Coffin was the mother of actor Frederick Coffin, and despite all her numerous character roles under this name, and just one, presumably in error, as Collins, the IMDB insists on listing her under that name! Stereotyped as a tough old battle-axe type, this may have been her most unusual credit. Don Gazzaniga was a regular background player on *Burke's Law*, usually as a uniform cop. He plays five different background roles in this series. Here he's mis-credited as Dan; hear that, IMDB? Mis-credited.

## The Owl and the Eye

wr. William Bast, dir. Paul Wendkos

Honey and Sam accept a job to test the security of a museum... but there's more to the assignment than they suspect

*with Lloyd Bochner (Guy Patterson), Richard Loo (Tog), William Bramley (Mortimer), John McLiam (Gordon), Guy Lee (houseboy)*

This is the second episode in a row that begins with Honey and Sam screwing up their initial assignment. This tended to be *Honey West's* go-to formula plot for the first few episodes—mess it up in the teaser, make amends, win conclusively. Adventure shows with female leads always seemed to feature more bungling during the story than those with two males, although of course the leads in *The Man from UNCLE* and *I Spy* needed to mess up once in a while to advance the story. Nevertheless, you got the impression that Honey West, April Dancer and Tara King were always considered to be winging it until the guys arrived. Fortunately, *Honey West* rarely fell into that trap of employing the cliche of having her wait to be rescued by Sam all the time. Otherwise, only *The Avengers'* Emma Peel, even though constantly in *Perils of Pauline* situations, gave the impression she was still in charge when in jeopardy!

Once again, Honey uses her feminine wiles to seduce a sleazy charmer... and who better to sleaze away than Lloyd Bochner? Best known for his straight role in *The Twilight Zone's* classic twist ending yarn "To Serve Man", his extensive credits as a sly villain are alluded to in the *Green Hornet* section. He was a great sweaty, furtive, fretful bad guy, and always enhanced any show he was in.

With fifty years of roles as Chen, Chang, and Tanaka, Hawaiian-born Richard Loo must have been resigned to his Hollywood fate, and at least had a more varied career than some alongside his bad guy parts of enemy agents and wartime adversaries. He was never short of work, albeit always bit parts, and his credits in cult TV alone include *Maverick, Hawaiian Eye, The Outer Limits, Burke's Law, I Spy, Voyage to the Bottom of the Sea, The Wild Wild West, I Dream of Jeannie, The Man from UNCLE, Bewitched, Hawaii Five-O, Kung Fu,* and his final role in *The Incredible Hulk.* Guy Lee was less fortunate; he spent most of his career playing bellboys and valets.

William Bramley began his TV career alongside Sergeant Bilko, but was most gainfully employed thereafter in westerns and cop shows. His cult TV roles include episodes of *Bewitched, Star Trek, The Invaders, The Girl from UNCLE,* and *Land of the Giants,* but his two most notable roles in cult TV were voices, for the Robotoid and Mr. Nobody in first season *Lost in Space!* He was in a number of 1970s 'youth films' as the fall guy authoritarian, including *Suppose They Held a War and Nobody Came?, Bless the Beasts and Children, Getting Straight,* and *Revenge of the Cheerleaders.* Veteran chameleon character actor John McLiam, one of

the best in the business, has a couple of lines as the museum boss.

Writer William Bast was a jobbing hack who flitted from one show to another in a lengthy career mostly in TV. He later developed the *Dynasty* spin-off *The Colbys* for Spelling, and was also known for capitalising on his relationship with James Dean.

Modern technology betrays the unfortunate stunt man who had to drag up in the scene where "Honey" smashes a window and climbs through it. Girls, if your fella is ogling Anne a little too much, just freeze-frame this scene for him...

### The Abominable Snowman

wr. Gwen Bagni, Paul Dubov, dir. Paul Wendkos

Warring factions pursue a snowman paperweight

*with Henry Jones (Reedy Comfort), Leon Askin (the Count), George Keymas (mystery man), Barry Kelley (Lt. Stone), Henry Hunter (Mr. Lucas/client), Paul Stader (chauffeur)*

Sounds like an exciting storyline, doesn't it? But actually it is. Henry Jones and Leon Askin make a fine pair of villains, and familiar faces George Keymas and Paul Stader are the henchmen in this drugs smuggling escapade in which the highlight is an early and lengthy car chase.

Jones' credits as slimy villainous weirdoes include *Boris Karloff's Thriller, Lost in Space, Bewitched, The Man from UNCLE, Amos Burke – Secret Agent, Voyage to the Bottom of the Sea, Night Gallery, Kolchak,* and *The Six Million Dollar Man.* He's particularly creepy here, leching all over Honey! Leon Askin appeared in *The Man from UNCLE* several times, but is best remembered as the nasty General Burkhalter in *Hogan's Heroes.* His TV and film roles as Russian agents were well into double figures.

This was the third and last of three early episodes directed by the stylish Paul Wendkos, king of the TV movies during the '70s, '80, and '90s. In the '60s, he also directed multiple episodes of *The Untouchables, The Detectives, Doctor Kildare, I Spy,* and *The Invaders.*

### A Matter of Wife and Death

wr. Tony Barrett, dir. John Florea

Honey discovers that protecting a friend of hers from death threats is a more complex case than she imagines

*with Dianne Foster (Maggie Lynch), James Best (Vince Zale), Michael Fox (Lt. Kovacs), Henry Brandon (Alexander Sebastian), Henry Beckman (Fred Cody)*

This was the first of six episodes written by *Burke's Law* writer Tony Barrett. He wrote more episodes than anyone other than series' developers Bagni and Dubov, and while they weren't quite up to the same standard they were acceptable, and undoubtedly got him a similar gig at *The Girl from UNCLE* a couple of seasons later.

A film actress in the '50s, Dianne Foster did a ton of television in the early '60s before retiring to raise her family. James Best was a wonderful but undistinguished performer in mostly westerns whose big break as comic relief in *The Dukes of Hazzard* was also his downfall as a serious actor. It must have been a nice early pension though, and came along just as the western was a spent force. Although mostly in westerns, his cult TV appearances included *Amos Burke – Secret Agent, The Green Hornet, I Spy,* and several *Twilight Zones.* Michael Fox had a recurring role on *Burke's Law* as George the all-purpose answer-man, which followed a similar recurring role on the *Perry Mason* series, and he played dozens of bit parts from the early '50s to the mid-'90s. Henry Brandon's cult TV included *The Outer Limits, Get Smart, Mission: Impossible, Kolchak,* and *Night Gallery,* while Henry Beckman played dozens of invisible bit parts in anything and everything over five decades, including four series.

A competent but undistinguished director and sometime producer, John Florea handled three episodes of *Honey West*, and it was probably the most interesting show he worked on during a routine and mundane career spanning three decades directing mostly rubbish. Honey's gimmick in this one is a sort of supernatural CCTV often seen in U.S. TV, whereby a hidden camera is able to pan, zoom, cut, and edit... amazing for today, let alone 1965. It excels itself in this episode; despite being attached to the bottom of a chair, it records at waist height from two different directions and even knows when to cut from one to the other! However it's Sam who dominates this episode.

### Live a Little, Kill a Little

wr. Tony Barrett, dir. Murray Golden

Honey and Sam are hired to protect a young woman from a bitter ex-lover

*with Warren Stevens (Arthur Strickland), Harry Millard (Charles French), Mary Murphy (Vicky), Maureen Dawson (Karen), Herb Edelman (Phil Moody)*

The series' first weak episode guest stars the wooden Warren Stevens, a close friend of *Voyage to the Bottom of the Sea's* Richard Basehart, and Harry Millard, a friend of his co-star David Hedison. And that's the most interesting trivia about this one, which unusually features a lot of padding, mostly action carried along by the music and nothing else. The best scene is between Honey and *The*

*Wild One's* Mary Murphy, but it's not the episode to show your friends to convert them.

Director Murray Golden, who most often flitted from one series to another on single assignments, directed three *Honey West*, four *Amos Burke – Secret Agent,* and six *Batman.* "Massacre", a memorable *Time Tunnel*, was probably his best moment.

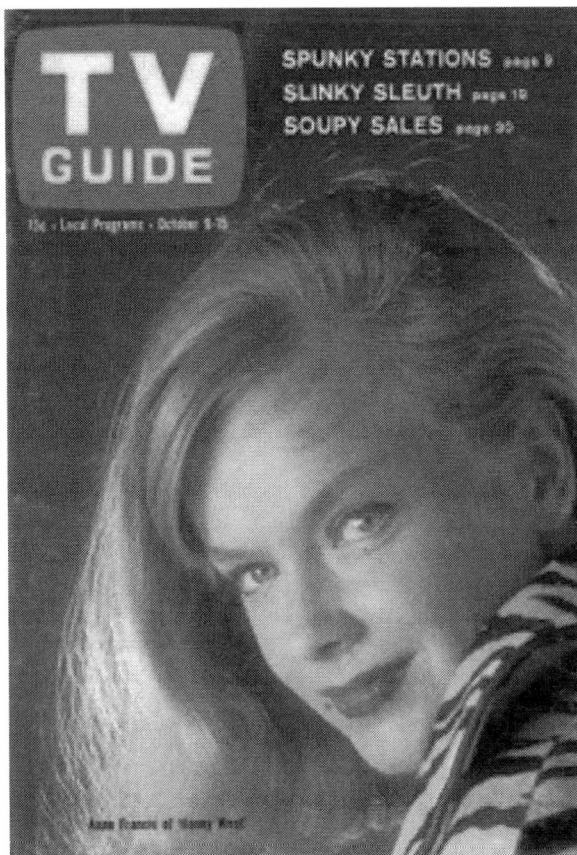

TV GUIDE

SPUNKY STATIONS page 9
SLINKY SLEUTH page 19
SOUPY SALES page 99

Local Programs · October 9-15

Anne Francis of Honey West

### Whatever Lola Wants

wr. William Bast, dir. John Peyser

Honey and Sam stumble onto an elaborate mob operation at a mansion *with Richard Angarola (Ramon Vargas), Audrey Christie (Lola Getz), Johnny Haymer (Manuel Rodriguez), Horst Ebersberg (Gunter), Jerry Brutsche (Carlos), Don Gazzaniga (butler)*

A peculiar episode, with a diamond-smuggling spy-fi villainess with a punnish name (see episode title) who rather bizarrely blows up her mansion lair when captured, presumably with all her party guests still in it!

This was director John Peyser's first of two *Honey West*. He had previously had lengthy runs on *The Millionaire, Cain's Hundred* and *The Untouchables,* and went on to equally lengthy stays on 1960s war series *Combat* and *The Rat Patrol. Honey West* appears to be a series directors took, rather than sought, an aberration on their resumes.

**The Princess and the Paupers**

wr. Leonard Stadd, dir. Virgil Vogel

A rock group arrange a phony kidnapping, but the plan goes wrong

*with Phil Ober (Mr. Van der Hyden), Stanley Adams (Tobias Quinn), Michael J. Pollard (Jingles), Bobby Sherman (Nicky Van), Nino Candido (Marv), Bern Hoffman (lech at river), Don Gazzaniga, Joe Perry (kidnappers), Richard Crane (m.c.)*

This is one of the oldest plots in the book, even in 1965, and the rotten music and obvious plot developments don't help. For once, the episode doesn't begin with Honey and Sam already on an assignment that they blow, but it doesn't take long for them to start messing up. Virgil Vogel puts no thought into the direction of Leonard Stadd's already careless story, and so sequences such as the botched pick-up stake-out and the tainting of the money are handled really poorly. The thugs may have been hired to make it look real, but as no-one else is present when the band are beaten up, what's the point? Pollard's Jingles has killed two people, so why is he simply making a run for it rather than killing everyone else? Watch also for a hilarious brief fight sequence with a male stunt double for Francis, and Honey talking into her sun cream bottle.

Pop singer Bobby Sherman gives a really poor performance both acting and singing, Michael Pollard coasts through his role sheepishly, with none of the effort he put into his *Lucy Show* or his *Lost in Space,* and Nino Candido looks ridiculous in an obvious beatnik wig. Only Stanley Adams (*Star Trek's* Cyrano Jones) walks away with his dignity as a sleazy promoter; he's excellent.

The title of the episode makes no sense at all; was the pop singer originally intended to be female? The dialogue throws in a few lame references by Quinn to Honey as 'princess', but it seems forced, an afterthought to justify the title.

Both Vogel and Stadd have done much better work than this. Stadd's episodes of *Man from UNCLE* and *Time Tunnel* were really creative, while either side of his single *Honey West* episode, Vogel had an extensive career on westerns and cop shows that makes his amateurish efforts here inexplicable.

## In the Bag

wr. Gwen Bagni, Paul Dubov, dir. Seymour Robbie

While safeguarding an obnoxious little girl, Honey and Sam stumble onto a jewel smuggling operation

*with Everett Sloane (Mr. Bartholomew), Robert Carricart (gem smuggler), Len Lesser (air passenger), Gene Darfler (henchman), Maureen McCormick (Margaret Mary), James Donohue (father), Don Gazzaniga (treasury agent)*

A good one. Guest player Everett Sloane, in his final work, has a plum role in this yarn, playing three very different parts, something he loved to do. Robert Carricart (*The Untouchables'* Lucky Luciano) and Len Lesser (*Seinfeld's* Uncle Leo) are the familiar faces in this episode, although not as familiar as bit player Don Gazzaniga, who turns up yet again. Bit player Gene Darfler, usually cast

as guards and cops, has his best scene in a brief career here as a dumb goon. Child actor Maureen McCormick went on to feature in *The Brady Bunch.*

This was Seymour Robbie's only *Honey West*. He worked extensively for Quinn Martin on his various detective series, and later had lengthy runs on *Remington Steele* and *Murder She Wrote.*

## The Flames and the Pussycat

wr. George Clayton Johnson, dir. James Goldstone

Honey suspects a series of elaborate arson attacks to be an inside job *with Sean McClory (Mr. Booth), Harry Basch (Mr. Flowers), Ken Lynch (Lt. Barney), Liam Sullivan (Mr. Canby), R.J. Nelson (police officer)*

Author George Clayton Johnson was a regular contributor to *The Twilight Zone,* and wrote the memorable "Man Trap" episode of *Star Trek,* but had the greatest financial success with the feature films *Ocean's Eleven* and *Logan's Run.* Despite the paint-by-numbers story, the dialogue is excellent.

"Perhaps you girls should stay around the house, don't you think?"

"Wouldn't that be rather dull for little boys?"

"Good day, Miss West"

"It was when I came in"

The story is less impressive. The audience will be one step ahead of the heroes throughout most of this adventure, never a good thing for their credibility. Every episode at least one of them gets hit over the head, and in this one both of them get it. And Sam really thinks Honey stayed home?

Ken Lynch of *I Married a Monster from Outer Space* and *Star Trek's* "Devil in the Dark" is this episode's angry cop, and although the series never settled on a regular station house adversary/ally for the duo, his Barney Keller, if not exactly the go-to guy, became the most frequently used. As with *Land of the Giants'* recurring Inspector Kobick, other 'inspector' roles were occasionally given to him, resulting in odd closing credits discrepancies, such as the series' final episode, where an Inspector Wyman is still listed against his name.

## A Neat Little Package

wr. Gwen Bagni, Paul Dubov, dir. Murray Golden

Honey and Sam help an amnesiac with a suitcase full of money and gangsters on his trail

*with J. Pat O'Malley (Mr. Grady), Arthur Batanides (Mr. Chico), Roy Jenson (Mr. Stashall), Val Avery (Roger), Sydney Smith (Charles Addison), Harold Fong (custodian), Clarence Lung (maitre'd), Charles Wagenheim (fleapit desk clerk), Gil Stuart (fancy hotel clerk), Barbara Morrison (indignant woman)*

No stand-out performances, but great action scenes with stunt man Roy Jenson as the bad guy and a climactic punch-up in a river. Second of three from Murray Golden.

## A Stitch in Crime

wr. Gwen Bagni, Paul Dubov, dir. John Peyser

When valuable gowns are stolen from Honey and Sam while in transit to a San Francisco fashion show, Honey masquerades as a high-class model

*with Charlene Holt (Gloria), Laurie Main (Mr. Antoine), James B. Sikking (Valentine), David Pritchard (Frankie McGovern), Herbie Faye (Mr. Kessler), Nino Candido, Seymour Cassell (henchmen), Marjorie Bennett (diner owner)*

Somewhat less convincing than Honey's masquerade as a fashion model is the duo's turn as a couple of shades-wearing hipsters. Charlene Holt is excellent as the series' second scheming manipulator of gullible men following "A Matter of Wife and Death", but *Hill Street Blues'* James Sikking, still playing bits way down the cast lists in the '60s, steals the show as a treacherous fashion photographer. *Bilko's* Herbie Faye is less entertaining as a stereotypical Jewish tailor, but character actress Marjorie Bennett is fun as an elderly coffee diner proprietor. There's a very satisfying punch-up in the opening scene, and another to close.

**A Million Bucks in Anybody's Language**

wr. Tony Barrett, dir. John Florea

When a fellow private eye is killed by a counterfeiting ring, Honey and Sam inherit the case

*with Steve Ihnat (Garth), Ken Lynch (Lt. Barney Keller), Harry Bellaver (Charlie Neeley), Sarah Selby (Dora Neeley), Percy Helton (engraving expert), Frank Scannell (pick-up man), Judy Kane (Dottie/waitress)*

Honey goes to work in a fur swimsuit in this one, which features Steve Ihnat as the villain, with the same bad guy name he had in his *Star Trek* episode. As in the earlier "A Matter of Wife and Death", Sam enjoys his work as a legitimate peeping tom a little too much.

Harry Bellaver had a recurring role as a cop in the classic early '60s series *The Naked City*. Ken Lynch returns as the inevitable belligerent cop. Percy Helton's scene as a fake bills expert is all too brief.

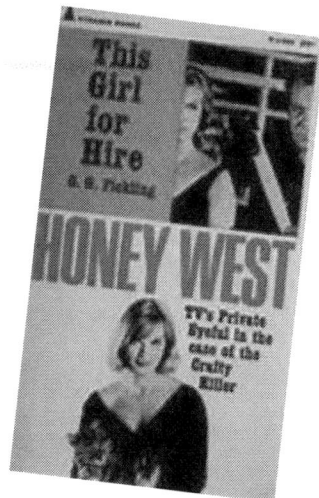

### The Gray Lady

wr. Richard Levinson, William Link, dir. Walter Grauman

Attempts to apprehend a jewel thief stealing from celebrities are hindered by a publicity-hungry actress

*with Cesare Danova (Abbott), Kevin McCarthy (Jerry Ivar), Pat Collins (Babs Ivar), Fred Vincent (Lt. Keith), Nancy Kovack (Nicole), Bert Parks (television host), Jon Sargent (Charlie/parking valet), Bambi Hamilton (nurse), Jason Wingreen (room service), Dana White (photographer)*

"Look what she's wearing"

"Zsa Zsa must have missed one"

Richard Levinson and William Link will go down in pop culture history as the creators of the legendary *Columbo*, the best detective murder mystery series ever to grace the medium. However, before that, they pottered around in television for some years, viewing the medium with disdain, but seeing it as easy money. It more than fulfilled their expectations when they later created the cynical confection *Murder, She Wrote*, but in their days as jobbing hacks, they contributed scripts to Four Star's *The Rogues, Burke's Law,* and *Honey West.* Fortunately, despite their attitude, they were usually unable to write bad television.

The Gray Lady is a valuable gem sought by stereotypical jewel thief Cesare Danova, wonderful as always. Pat Collins is amusing as the gem's vulgar, bossy owner, but

Kevin McCarthy steals the show as her pussy-whipped husband ("Thank you, ma'am... I mean sir", says Sam, accepting a tip). There's a not entirely unexpected but well played reveal as everyone's plans unravel. Levinson and Link's dialogue races along, and is performed well by all.

"You mean you actually said that to him?"

"He went a very satisfying shade of magenta"

Honey's magic hidden camera gimmick, last seen in "A Matter of Wife and Death", is this time somehow inside a television that—get it?—watches you. Once again, it is able to pan, zoom, cut, and edit.

And although the name Abbott *oozes* sexual and intellectual sophistication in an almost subliminal way of course, it was a poor choice for the Eurotrash jewel thief's name once the wonderful Cesare Danova (*Viva Las Vegas, Mean Streets*) had been cast.

Kevin McCarthy remains best known for *Invasion of the Body Snatchers*. His cult TV credits include *The Twilight Zone, Burke's Law, Amos Burke – Secret Agent, The Invaders, The Man from UNCLE, The Wild Wild West,* and *Mission: Impossible.* He did a fair bit of work for Spelling, and had recurring roles in both *Dynasty* and *The Colbys*. Nancy Kovack's cult TV credits were extensive, and included *Bewitched, Burke's Law, Voyage to the Bottom of the Sea, Batman, I Dream of Jeannie, The Invaders, The Man from UNCLE, Star Trek,* and *Get Smart.*

### Invitation to Limbo

wr. Richard Levinson, William Link, dir. Tom Gries

Honey pursues a hypnotist who is using innocent dupes to steal business secrets and take the rap

*with Louise Troy (Darlene), Wayne Rogers (Jerry), Peter Leeds (Lt. Sherman), Stacey Harris (Charles Kenyon), Dan Frazer (Harold Sutter), Judy Lang (Miss Christie), S. John Launer (Mr. Tyler), Lonnie Fotre (Tyler's wife), Cal Bolder (motorcycle cop), Will J. White (security guard), Danny Reese (juggler), George Atkinson (police officer)*

"Alright, Miss West... who would want to kill you?"

"Oh, about a dozen people, including Sam sometimes"

motorcycle cop writing ticket: "Afternoon, ma'am, you figurin' on bein' the first lady astronaut?"

Oddly, Pat Collins, who was in the previous episode, had a nightclub act exactly like the one shown in this episode (which she ran through in a *Lucy Show*, "Lucy Meets Pat Collins"). Nevertheless,

she was well cast in "The Gray Lady", and Louise Troy is perfect here as the series' third beautiful femme fatale (fourth, if you want to count the older Lola Getz).

Wayne Rogers, later of *MASH*, is suitably thuggish as her crass colleague. Sam has his magic CCTV running again.

247

Stacy Harris was busy in the '50s and '60s, and as a close friend of Jack Webb, appeared numerous times in Webb's cop show productions. He also played in many western series. Dan Fraser went on to co-star in *Kojak*, as the title character's standard harassed boss. Cal Bolder was in fact a moonlighting traffic cop who frequently played massive muscle-bound heavies. He made several appearances in *UNCLE*, and played the monster in *Jesse James meets Frankenstein's Daughter*.

In a kangaroo-like career hopping from films to TV and writing to directing to producing, Tom Gries managed to stop off at *Batman* and direct one of the best in the series, a dark Riddler two-parter, an enjoyable and typical *Voyage to the Bottom of the Sea*, "The Menfish", one of the silliest episodes of *Mission: Impossible* ("Wheels"), and while on *I Spy*, one of the best *and* one of the worst! Ducking between trash and treasure throughout his whole career, he won an Emmy for his work on social conscience drama *East Side, West Side*, and then went and created and wrote for *The Rat Patrol*, one of TV's dumbest war series. After struggling, and succeeding, to direct his script for his highly praised western *Will Penny*, he then spent the 1970s working on trashy TV movies before his death in 1977, an enigma to the last.

### Rockabye the Hard Way

wr. Gwen Bagni, Paul Dubov, dir. Bill Colleran

Honey and Sam try to help out a trucker who has lost his high-security cargo to a hijacking ring

*with Vincent Beck (John Raven), Larry D. Mann (Tripp), Joe Don Baker (Rocky), Paul Sorensen (Swetlow), Ivan Treisault (Lazlo Shatzi), Gil Lamb (diner owner), Pepe Callahan (Mexican man), Bella Bruck (Mexican woman), Jonathan Hole (chemist)*

Honey and Sam trade quips and slick dialogue while posing as truck stop waitress and trucker. The half-hour format makes this one fairly swift and straightforward, but there's not enough meat on the bone for an hour show anyway. A very young Joe Don Baker (*Junior Bonner, The Outfit, Charley Varrick*), mostly in westerns during the '60s, has his first TV role here, and he's a guy who looked better as he aged. Several familiar faces include Vincent Beck and Larry D. Mann as the bad guys. Beck's numerous bad guy roles include Megazor in *Lost in Space* and the Viking leader in *Time Tunnel*, as well as bits in both *UNCLE* series, while Mann, a henchman here, was boss bad guy in *The Man from UNCLE, My Favorite Martian, The Green Hornet* and a dozen more. He made numerous appearances in *Bewitched* and *Hogan's Heroes* and in the '80s switched sides to become a judge in a recurring role in the exemplary cop show *Hill Street Blues*.

Bill Colleran was a very odd choice to direct an episode of any drama series, as he was otherwise a director and producer of big name variety shows for the likes of Judy Garland, Frank Sinatra, and Dean Martin, so there's obviously a story there. He shortly afterwards retired, so perhaps he was trying to begin another career and failed.

## A Nice Little Till to Tap

wr. Tony Barrett, dir. Jerry Hopper

Honey poses as a bank teller to capture some bank robbers and their inside accomplice

*with Anthony Eisley (Peter Sutton), Peter Leeds (Lt. Coombs), Howard McNear (Tweedy), Marvin Brody (Mears), Lou Krugman (Durant), William Benedict (Farley), Chuck Hicks (Crowley/stunt)*

Anthony Eisley (not long off *Hawaiian Eye*) plays the smooth seducer who is pumping undercover Honey for information until he discovers her true identity and she becomes a hostage; one of his motley crew recognises her. He's caught only because he rather absurdly insists on going ahead with his plan; if he'd abandoned it, he'd have got off scot free. Howard McNear plays the same nervous little guy he always does; Peter Leeds from "Invitation to Limbo" makes a second appearance as the house cop, but with a different name. Marvin Brody, Lou Krugman, and serials veteran Billy Benedict make up a sleazy shower of henchmen.

Jerry Hopper was a regular director on *Burke's Law* (more about him there). This was his only *Honey West*.

## How Brillig O Beamish Boy

wr. Don Ingalls, dir. Ida Lupino

Sam is held captive by villains who want a package in Honey's possession

*with John McGiver (Brillig), Norman Alden (Ben Fancher), Howard Dayton (Ardo), Monte Hale (Sheriff), Leon Lontoc (Wong), Charles Horvath, Bill Hart (henchmen)*

John McGiver carved a career out of playing pompous asses and scoundrels, and was particularly good in memorable episodes of *Voyage to the Bottom of the Sea* ("The X Factor") and *The Man from UNCLE* ("The Birds and the Bees Affair"). He was a regular in the short-lived super-hero spoof *Mr. Terrific*. The meaningless title is a mish-mash of nonsense words originated by poet Lewis Carroll for *Through the Looking Glass*, his sequel to *Alice in Wonderland*. Leon Lontoc, Henry in *Burke's Law*, has a minor role.

Don Ingalls was a producer and very mediocre sometime hack writer on the series he produced for (and some he didn't), who was associate producer on *Honey West* for two thirds of the series. He had previously served in the same capacity on two westerns, *Have Gun, Will Travel* and *The Travels of Jamie McPheeters*, and left *Honey West* to work on *Twelve O'Clock High*. As a producer, he worked on *The Virginian*, *Fantasy Island*, and *T.J. Hooker*. Ida Lupino was an actress who became one of the very first woman directors by writing and producing her first two features; thus, she cleverly broke through the glass ceiling by hiring herself. She subsequently divided her time between acting and directing, although she rarely directed more than one or two episodes of the various TV series she worked on. One exception was Ingall's *Have Gun, Will Travel*. She was, of course, one of the four stars who founded Four Star, producers of *Honey West*.

It's McGiver who makes this episode work, along with a routine involving a radio transmitter in a pair of glasses. Without him, there's nothing here. Familiar heavy Charles Horvath makes his first of two appearances as a henchman.

### King of the Mountain

wr. Jay Simms, dir. Thomas Carr

Honey poses as the private nurse of a wealthy man to find out who killed her predecessor

*with David Opatoshu (Mr. King), Dennis Patrick (Carson), Charles Lane (Ash), Richard Kiel (henchman), Allyson Ames (nurse), Troy Melton (guard)*

Writer Jay Simms was a Z-movie hack who flitted from one TV assignment to the next, his longest stays being on *The Rifleman, Have Gun, Will Travel,* and *The Big Valley.* This was his only *Honey West.*

Thomas Carr, whose previous similar fare included *Richard Diamond, Private Detective* and *The Detectives,* and close to his retirement after a career that began as a child actor in the silents, directed three episodes of *Honey West.* He had been a director of Columbia's serials, which gave him an entry into early TV, where he ploughed through numerous episodes of *Dick Tracy* and *Adventures of Superman.* After dozens of low budget cowboy films for the sticks, he had no trouble securing work on numerous TV westerns, including a fair number of *Trackdown, Stagecoach West, Wanted: Dead or Alive, Laramie,* and *Rawhide.* Thus, this former bit-player in the 1930s worked with Robert Culp,

Steve McQueen, and Clint Eastwood.

Richard Kiel, in his usual role as a henchman, gets to show more intelligence than usual, and is surprisingly good, while a still dark-haired Dennis Patrick, a few weeks away from his role as "The Golden Man" in *Lost in Space,* smarms as Opatoshu's aide. Patrick later had recurring roles on *Dark Shadows* and *Dallas.*

David Opatoshu, a familiar face in cult TV with memorable roles in such shows as *The Twilight Zone, The Outer Limits, The Time Tunnel, The Man from UNCLE,* and *Star Trek* among many, many others, plays the dual role of kidnap victim and impostor.

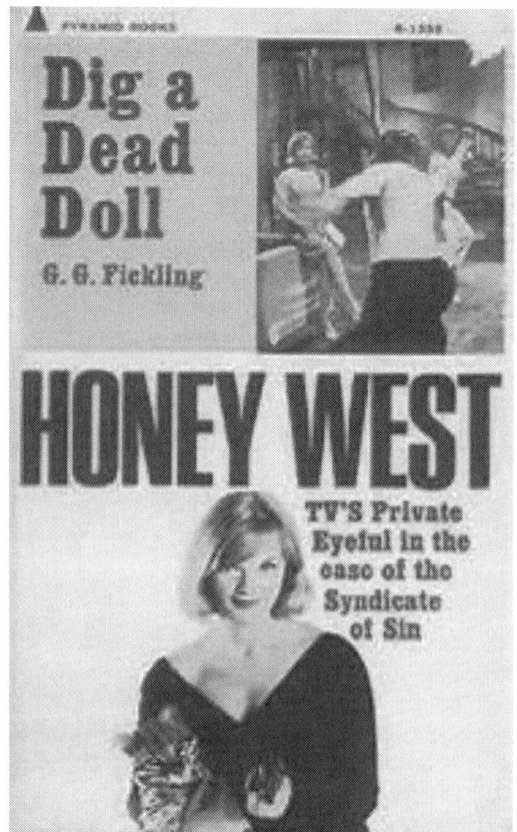

**It's Earlier Than You Think**

wr. Marc Brandel, dir. James Brown

Honey encounters a variety of eccentrics when a messenger arrives in her office to announce the assassination of President Abraham Lincoln!

*with Maurice Dallimore (first Conrad), Leonid Kinsky (second Conrad), James Griffith (third Conrad), Ken Lynch (Lt. Keller), Bill McLean (Mr. Pringle), Bill Catching (Wycherly), Paul Sorensen (cop)*

"You know, Miss West, you're a very pretty young girl. *Now.* I know you've never seen one of these before, because it's the only one in the world. In fact, I invented it"

"Congratulations"

"Ponce de Leon spent years searching for the Fountain of Youth. This machine has exactly the opposite effect. It produces instant old age!"

"It changes the isotope of carbon fourteen"

"How did you know that?"

"Oh everybody's talking about isotopes these days. They're really in"

This is a rather silly one with an under-exploited sci-fi theme of an ageing device, by *Amos Burke – Secret Agent* writer Marc Brandel. Magic televisions and spy gizmos aside, it's the series' first slip into outright fantasy.

James Brown worked as an assistant director on numerous series, mostly westerns, before finally getting his chance to shine on six episodes of *Honey West*.

One of Hollywood's professional Brits-for-hire, Maurice Dallimore's cult TV included *Amos Burke – Secret Agent, Batman, I Dream of Jeannie, The Monkees,* and *Bewitched.* Leonid Kinsky, invariably cast as mad professors, racked up cult TV credits in *My Favorite Martian, Amos Burke – Secret Agent, Batman, The Man from UNCLE,* and *The Girl from UNCLE.* James Griffith's numerous credits include bits in *Batman, The Man from UNCLE, The Monkees,* and *Kolchak.* Maurice Dallimore's picture is shown over James Griffith's credit. Ken Lynch returns as Lt. Keller.

**The Perfect Un-Crime**

wr. Ken Kolb, dir. Sidney Miller

Honey helps a repentant accountant return the fortune he stole before it's discovered missing

*with Byron Foulger (Arthur Bird), David Brian (Rockwell, store manager), John Harmon (elevator engineer), James Secrest (store assistant), Bob Stephenson (watchman), Max Wagner (vagrant)*

At this point, the heady influence of camp is starting to permeate the series, and the stories are starting to get a bit silly. Tellingly, Sidney Miller mostly worked on comedies, and Ken Kolb, although formerly a writer for such sober 1950s series as *Dragnet* and *Have Gun, Will Travel*, was not averse to writing for some of the more outlandish series on TV (he wrote several *Wild Wild West,* and ended his career with one-off scripts for *Future Cop* and *Fantastic Journey*). Here, Honey endangers her entire business and reputation, not to mention becoming an accomplice in crime, by helping a 'loveable' nerd who's having second thoughts about the perfect crime he's just committed, and wants to return the money. However, none of this really matters, because the manager *knows* what he's done and intends to let him take the fall while making off with the cash himself. Even *this* doesn't matter, because the episode is being played for laughs... and while David Brian and John Harmon are accomplished at playing their roles spot-on, it's an unfortunate change of pace for what was a lively action series on the right side of absurdity.

Byron Foulger played variations of Arthur Bird throughout his entire career. He appeared in *Burke's Law* twice in such roles, was in countless sit-coms, and was memorable in *The Time Tunnel* as a terrified and treacherous saloon keeper menaced by aliens. He had recurring roles in *Captain Nice* and *Petticoat Junction*.

The highlight of the episode features the little-seen Aunt Meg character. Irene Hervey comes into her own with an enjoyable scene posing as a difficult customer while casing the store owner's office ("Why is there no fire escape out there?" / "Because I do not allow fires in this office").

"If anything goes wrong, I'll come to see you on visiting day" she jokes later to Honey and Sam. Exactly.

## Like Visions and Omens and All That Jazz

wr. Tony Barrett, dir. John Florea

An unemployed actor finds a new career as a fortune teller who ensures that his predictions come true

*with Nehemiah Persoff (Faustini), June Vincent (Victoria Tilson), Fred Beir (Pete Lynch), Mimsy Farmer (Tina Tilson), Norman Alden (Artie Dixon), Benny Rubin (Marty, talent agent)*

Cult TV regular Nehemiah Persoff eats up the cliche role of the crooked fortune teller Faustini, flouncing around in a cape like Lugosi as the series gets campier into 1966. The bad guy who predicts crimes because he or she is the one committing them is an old favorite that also got an airing in both *Batman* and *The Green Hornet* at around this time, to recall but two. It was even the plot in the same producer's unsold pilot for *Dick Tracy.*

June Vincent as the society woman who's the mark for the scam had a lengthy career playing well-to-do upmarket types, and rarely left her safety zone. And while he had more varied roles, including a silver-skinned alien on the same *Time Tunnel* as Byron Foulger, and a victim of ghostly possession on *Kolchak,* Fred Beir was always at his best as a sleaze. Mimsy Farmer soon moved on from such cutesy fare as *My Three Sons, The Donna Reed Show, Lassie,* and *Ozzie and Harriet* to sleazy B-movies in the late '60s, and Italian horror films in the '70s.

Anonymous but busy supporting player Norm Alden is making his second appearance in the series. He had a recurring role in the legendary *Electra Woman and Dyna Girl* series of the early '70s, and a regular gig as the voice of Aquaman in the *Super-Friends* series.

A nice action scene with a lecherous bookie is let down by a comically obvious male stunt man. But there's a genuinely amusing tag.

## Don't Look Now But Isn't That Me?

wr. Gwen Bagni, Paul Dubov, dir. James Brown

Arriving at a party to guard the wealthy visitors' furs, Honey discovers that a double of her has already been at the venue for a while... and stolen them!

*with Alan Reed (Chick), Monica Keating (Mrs. Carter), Jonathan Hole (Mr. Gruder), Louis Quinn, Charles Horvath (henchmen), Paul Sorensen (cop)*

Impersonators, doubles and lookalikes of the heroes, almost always with evil intent, were a popular plot-line in TV series during the '60s, with *The Man from UNCLE*, *Batman*, *The Avengers*, *The Green Hornet*, *Lost in Space*, *Voyage to the Bottom of the Sea*, *Star Trek*, *The Prisoner*, and *I Spy* all among those to take on this storyline. It was still being used in the 1980s (*The A-Team* and *Knight Rider* come to mind). All is forgiven though, because this one is nicely done. Anne Francis has fun as her floozie impersonator, and then turns the tables by having Honey impersonate her impersonator.

Alan Reed had just spent the first half of the '60s as the voice of Fred Flintstone, and was now returning to guest star work. During the run of *The Flintstones* he had taken small roles on *The Dick Van Dyke Show*, *The Lucy Show*, *My Favorite Martian*, and *The Addams Family*, and following *The Flintstones*, guested on *The Beverly Hillbillies*, *Petticoat Junction*, *Batman*, and *Mothers-in-Law*. He continued to do cartoon voices into the 1970s, including Fred Flintstone in various follow-ups. Monica Keating, seen here as a society woman, worked extensively for Four Star Productions, including four appearances on *Burke's Law*.

Always welcome character actor Jonathan Hole, also frequently used on *Burke's Law* and busy throughout the '60s in everything, milks his single scene as ever. Louie Quinn had a supporting role in cult series *77, Sunset Strip*, and often portrayed minor hoods and petty criminals. He turns up in *Burke's Law, Amos Burke – Secret Agent*, and *Batman*, among others.

Charles Horvath was previously a henchman in "How Brillig O Beamish Boy", Paul Sorensen returns as the cop from "It's Earlier Than You Think", and the creepy house returns from "In the Bag".

With this episode, the series acquires a new associate producer, former *Burke's Law* production manager Bruce Fowler Jnr. Fowler worked extensively for Four Star, moving on to 20th Century Fox when they folded. From *Honey West*, he would go on to *Voyage to the Bottom of the Sea* (from the third season) and *Land of the Giants*.

### Come To Me, My Litigation Baby

wr. Gwen Bagni, Paul Dubov, dir. Thomas Carr

Honey and Sam investigate a disparate trio of insurance swindlers

*with Ellen Corby (Mrs. Peedy), James Brown (Buster Macon), Michael Fox (insurance agent), Army Archerd (announcer), Ron Lerner, Kami Stevens (dancers), Chuck Couch (gym attendant), Bill Shannon (witness)*

This episode, the start of the series' camp phase in earnest, and revolving around a gang that stages fake accidents for insurance swindlers, certainly gave the stunt people plenty to do. It still ran short, and so features a typical 1966 extended dancing sequence in the tag, as Honey and Sam are invited to watch, and then participate in, a new dance craze—the Honey West. Yeah, you're right, it was never heard of again! In fact, it looks rather similar to every other 1960s dance sequence!

Texan actor James Brown, no relation to the *Honey West* director James Brown, had a leading role on *Adventures of Rin Tin Tin* in the 1950s. On the guest star circuit, he switched allegiance to *Lassie* for three episodes and made numerous appearances on *Route 66* and a fair number of westerns, securing a recurring role in the mid-'80s on *Dallas*.

A bit player in films since the early '30s, and in TV from the early '50s, Ellen Corby was best known for her long-running role as the grandmother on *The Waltons* during the 1970s, but it sometimes seems she was born an old lady. Often cast as busybodies, she played several sinister or crooked parts, including this one and a murderous alien in the pilot for *The Invaders*. Michael Fox had a recurring role on *Burke's Law*.

**Slay Gypsy Slay**

wr. Tony Barrett, dir. James Brown

Honey disguises herself as one of a colorful band of gypsies suspected of kidnapping a prominent citizen

with Michael Pate (Darza), Ralph Manza (Putzi), Byron Morrow (Mr. Buckley), Arline Anderson (Mrs. Buckley), Papita Funez (Lida), Jack Perkins (Szabo, henchman), Bobby Johnson (waiter), Janos Prohaska (gorilla)

Now we're really getting silly. This one is a corny, campy and confused collection of romantic gypsy cliches in the tradition of *From Russia With Love* and others, with Honey posing briefly as a gypsy, and John Ericson getting a rare chance to spread his wings masquerading as a grizzled old prospector, Hollywood-style. Ralph Manza's turn as a karate-chopping comic relief clue-giver recollects Barrett's stint on *Burke's Law*.

For the second half, we're in more familiar territory as Honey and Sam sit poolside talking into their sunglasses. Little disappointing that nobody took a swan dive into that underground river at the end...

In between a fair number of roles in westerns, usually as a Native American, swarthy, heavy set Michael Pate played numerous villainous roles in the 1960s, in episodes of *Amos Burke – Secret Agent*, *Get Smart*, *The Man from UNCLE*, *Batman*, *The Time Tunnel*, *Tarzan*, *The Wild Wild West*, *Mission: Impossible*, and *Voyage to the Bottom of the Sea*, before returning to his native Australia in the early '70s, no doubt exhausted from being so wicked. Papita Funez was a speciality dancer who appeared in several early '60s series in that role, including *Burke's Law* and *I Spy*. Arline Anderson was a regular bit player on *Mission Impossible* and *Mannix* at Desilu.

Bit player Byron Morrow, cast alternately as a military man or a businessman, had extensive cult TV credits, and turns up in virtually everything from this period sooner or later. Janos Prohaska gets his gorilla suit out of mothballs again...

## The Fun-Fun Killer

wr. Art Weingarten, dir. Murray Golden

Honey investigates strange goings-on at a toy factory after a man is killed by a rampaging robot

*with Marvin Kaplan (Byron Manners), Woodrow Parfrey (Ronald Neuwirth), John Hoyt (Professor Von Kemp), Ken Lynch (Inspector Keller), William Keene (Granville Manners)*

"Your situation is hopeless, Miss West. Why not end it quickly?"

"I'm the long-suffering type"

With *Batman* taking the industry by storm in the month this aired, the gloves were off. This one is as camp as Christmas. As well as writing for *The Addams Family* and *It's About Time* the same year he wrote this, Arthur Weingarten later wrote for *The Man from UNCLE*, *The Wild Wild West*, *The Girl from UNCLE*, *The Green Hornet*, *The Six Million Dollar Man*, and *Wonder Woman*. Weingarten's episodes were always fun to watch, but there's no denying how silly they were, and indeed were often the silliest in the series (his *Wonder Woman* featured an evil living brain in a tank, his *Green Hornet* was the infamous "Invasion from Outer Space", and his *Girl from UNCLE* credits include the notorious giant toaster trap).

We're well into the camp phase of the series here, as Weingarten's presence suggests; there's a beach ball that emits knockout gas, an unexplained super-magnet in the toy factory warehouse, conveniently and clearly labelled and with a handy control switch, and Bruce the ocelot is watching wildlife shows on TV. A sure sign of camp excess is that no-one bothers to explain things — is the robot a prototype? Why is there a giant magnet on hand? What was the point of the beach ball? Why was the professor killed? Where did Byron and the body go? These weren't mistakes or plot-holes, they could easily be explained, but the point is, it was the fashion not to bother.

There is one cute gag. In the toy factory, Honey is browsing and spots one of the period's now highly collectable *Honey West* dolls!

According to the IMDB, the robot in this episode later turned up on *Gilligan's Island*, in the episode "Gilligan's Living Doll", and photos confirm this. It looks like a cut-price version of *Tobor the Great*, and is a long way from Anne Francis' *Forbidden Planet* playmate, who although presumably still for hire at this time might have been too on the nose! Fortunately, this clunky fellow is supposed to be a mere toy, and the storyline resembles the Cybernauts yarns in *The Avengers*, the first of which appeared at around this same time with much the same premise. Still, despite looking like a refugee from a Columbia serial, that's some Christmas present. Especially if it comes with the bad guy inside (there's two of them in the climactic confrontation, so who's in the second one?).

Old sci-fi stagers Woodrow Parfrey and John Hoyt were on familiar ground in this episode, cast to type in their usual roles of sleazy schemer and lab-coated sinister scientist. An unusually subdued Marvin Kaplan (*Top Cat's* Choo-Choo) rounds out the cast.

Woodrow Parfrey's cult TV credits included memorable turns in *The Man from UNCLE*, and *Voyage to the Bottom of the Sea*. Numerous other TV roles included *My Favorite Martian*, *Batman*, *Lost in Space*, *The Munsters*, *Get Smart*, *Bewitched*, *I Dream of Jeannie*, *Mission: Impossible*, and *Planet of the Apes*. John Hoyt's most memorable turns in cult TV were probably his roles in *The Twilight Zone*, *The Outer Limits* and *The Time Tunnel*. He was also in numerous sci-fi films, and episodes of *Voyage to the Bottom of the Sea*, *The Munsters*, *Amos Burke — Secret Agent*, *I Spy*, *The Man from UNCLE*, *Star Trek*, *Get Smart*, *The Wild Wild West*, *Kolchak*, *The Six Million Dollar Man*, and *Battlestar Galactica*. Bit player William Keene, the robot's victim, had small roles in *The Twilight Zone*, *The Addams Family*, *Get Smart*, and *Mission: Impossible* among his credits.

### Pop Goes the Easel

wr. Gail Allen, Chris Christensen, Lila Garrett, Bernie Khan, dir. James Brown

When a pricey piece of Warholian pop art finds its way onto the shelves of the supermarket with the other tin cans, Meg's purchase of it leads Honey and Sam into a bizarre and bohemian environment that hides some typically establishment motives...

*with Larry D. Mann (Willis Van Wyck), George Furth (Sandy Corbin), Robert Strauss (Barry King), Anthony Eustrel (Mr. Leopold), Bill Quinn (police lieutenant), Howard Curtis (motorcycle thief), Beau Hickman (waiter)*

Pop art was a favorite and frequent target for mockery in 1960s TV, and the villains were always using the trend as a ruse to get their mitts on something more traditional — either money, or some Old Masters (I covered this topic in my review for *Batman's* "Pop Goes the Joker" in the first *Cool TV* book, and also in *The Elvis Films* under *Easy Come, Easy Go*, so I won't go into it again). Variations on this plot turned up in *Top Cat, Batman,* and *The Man from UNCLE,* among others.

Here, George Furth (hilarious during this period in *The Girl from UNCLE* and *The Monkees*) is cast as an obvious parody of Andy Warhol, one of the leading practitioners of pop art, whose notorious straightforward painting of a Campbell's soup can changed the way the world thought about both art and advertising. The writers' heavy-handed joke is that Sandy Corbin's masterpiece is an actual facsimile of a can of soup. Needless to say, the whole episode is played for laughs from start to finish.

The first two writing credits are for the story, the second two for the script. This is the only known credit for Allen and Christensen, but the prolific Garrett and Kahn wrote separately and together, always on light-hearted fare, and mostly on sit-coms, including *My Favorite Martian, Petticoat Junction, The Addams Family, The Lucy Show, My Mother, the Car, Get Smart, Love, American Style,* and predominantly *Bewitched.*

"I made a sketch of the thief" says Corbin, and emerges with a cardboard cut-out of a photograph of the guy. Later, art dealer Leopold announces that it's painted with Corbin's technique and tries frantically to buy it. Later, the thief turns up dead... dressed exactly the same way as the sketch/photo/painting.

Poorly done is the climactic comeuppance for the obvious villain of the piece. If he truly thought Honey and Sam were destroying his art collection in the vault, he wouldn't have been standing there looking perplexed and uncertain, he'd have been hysterical.

Portly Larry D. Mann's cult TV credits include *My Favorite Martian, Get Smart, Captain Nice, I Spy, The Green Hornet,* three each of *The Man from UNCLE* and *Hogan's Heroes,* and five *Bewitched.* In the '70s, he switched sides, and started playing judges, doctors, and police lieutenants! Robert Strauss toured the sit-com circuit of the 1960s playing dodgy characters. He also made films with Marilyn Monroe and Elvis Presley.

Bill Quinn appears to be taking on Ken Lynch's lines as recurring character Lt. Keller, as an un-named police lieutenant. Four Star's make-up man, Robert 'Beau' Hickman, plays the waiter in the tag. He began his career working at Universal on the iconic monsters for *The Creature from the Black Lagoon* and *This Island Earth*.

### Little Green Robin Hood

wr. Ken Kolb, dir. Sidney Miller

When a weirdo is discovered running around a wealthy private estate convinced that he's Robin Hood, Honey and Sam discover he's the patsy for some less idealistic thieves

*with Edd Byrnes ("Robin Hood"), Severn Darden (Dr. Ames), Eleanor Audley (Mrs. Murdock), Francoise Ruggieri (Annette, the French maid), Allen Jenkins (Max, the gate guard), Peter Leeds (police lieutenant)*

Singer, bit player, writer, gag man, cartoon voice, why shouldn't Sidney Miller direct sit-coms as well? And who's to say he can't throw in a couple of *Honey West* episodes? Especially with a story this loopy. This was his second of two, and as with the previous episode, it's played for laughs. Sledge-hammer style. Unfortunately, the biggest laugh is the performance of the miscast Edd Byrnes. Given that 77, *Sunset Strip* had only just gone off the air, it was a pretty sharp steep drop to the bottom of the barrel. Severn Darden 'phones his performance in, while Eleanor Audley shines as ever.

Of course, it's the Sherwood Forest Park estate. We are asked to believe that Honey and Sam can't apprehend this guy when they spend half the episode standing right next to him. There's quite a good punch-up at the end, but the stunt doubles are obvious, as is the identity of the bad guy. And Honey tries to put out an electrical fire with soda stream water... and does.

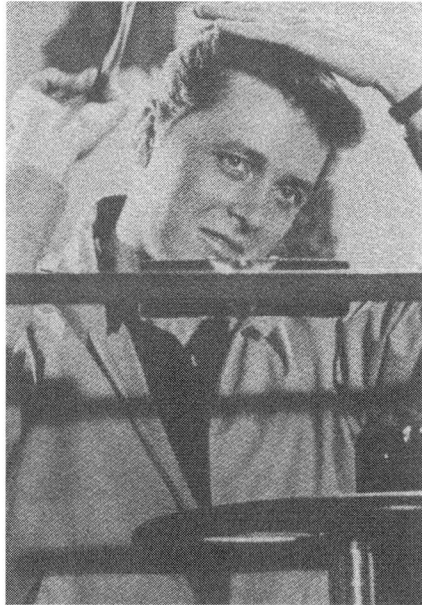

*Edd Byrnes and ever-present comb as Kookie the car-hop in Warners' 77, Sunset Strip.*

Severn Darden often played psychiatrists, usually Hollywood ones that looked like Sigmund Freud. Other cult TV included *Kolchak, Night Gallery, Wonder Woman,* and the Bigfoot episodes of *The Six Million Dollar Man* and *The Bionic Woman*. Nevertheless, he always looked like he should be somewhere else. Anywhere else. He played his roles as if he was in another room.

Eleanor Audley, always the society dowager with a snooty air, had recurring roles on *The Dick Van Dyke Show, The Beverly Hillbillies, Green Acres,* and *My Three Sons.* She also provided voices for the Disney films *Cinderella* and *Sleeping Beauty.*

Edd Byrnes played teen idol Kookie the car-hop for five years in the long-running detective series *77, Sunset Strip,* and the role haunted him throughout the rest of his career, which consisted mostly of guest appearances, often Kookie-related. His most frequent employer turned out to be Aaron Spelling, and Byrnes is one of a handful of performers to have appeared in both the original *Burke's Law,* and the 1990s revival— the latter alongside Anne Francis as 'Honey Best' in "Who Killed Nick Hazard?".

*The voice cast of Top Cat; Allen Jenkins is on the left, Marvin Kaplan in the middle at the top.*

Gate guard Allen Jenkins was the voice of Officer Dibble on *Top Cat,* and in earlier years, appeared in numerous Warners gangster films. Other 1960s bit parts were for *Bewitched, Batman,* and *The Man from*

UNCLE (he was also in 1964's *Robin and the Seven Hoods!*). Bit player Francoise Ruggieri had minor roles in episodes of *Lost in Space, Voyage to the Bottom of the Sea, Mission: Impossible, The Wild Wild West,* and *Night Gallery.*

Peter Leeds might be Lt. Coombs from "A Nice Little Till to Tap", or he might be Lt. Sherman from "Invitation to Limbo". Perhaps wisely, he's un-named in his third and final role as token cop.

Ken Kolb described himself as a 'dependable hack', and that about sums him up. His interview in the Tom Weaver book *Earth vs. the Sci-Fi Filmmakers* is a delight, and worth hunting down by those who want to know what a writer's life is like, and how TV works. If only he'd put some of his anecdotes into his scripts, they're a darn sight better than what he handed in.

**Just the Bear Facts, Ma'am**

wr. Gwen Bagni, Paul Dubov, dir. James Brown

Honey and Sam investigate the death of a stuntwoman... and find themselves in show business

*with Frank Wilcox (Mr. Burgess), Richard Carlyle (Twilly), Mousie Garner (horror film actor), Don Gazzaniga (Jago), Frank Gerstle (film director), Marvin Brody (bear trainer), Lonnie Fotre (actress), Robert Kenneally (actor), Bill Catching (henchman)*

Few will be fooled by the cornball teaser, which is the old trick of pulling back to show that the scene we've just witnessed is a play, or in this case, a film. Of course, stunt girls are stand-ins, they very rarely, if ever, play the role or take the lead. The film company also get their cameras from the same company that supplies Sam and Honey with their magic hidden CCTV; the raw footage has been neatly cut and edited inside the camera. Neat trick. I've heard of directors editing inside the camera*, but this is ridiculous… as is the entire episode (complete with a dumb mystic dream sequence; Honey hopes for a clue, and just dreams it up).

\* editing inside the camera means the director has forced the editor to edit in a certain way by shooting scenes without coverage, in other words they can't choose which shot to use because he only gave the one option. Although this gives the director greater control of his work, it can get producers' backs up and result in less future assignments.

## There's a Long, Long Fuse A'Burning

wr. Gwen Bagni, Paul Dubov, dir. Thomas Carr

Honey and Sam pursue a mad bomber who is using the m.o. of a retired villain

with Dick Clark (Mr. Payton), Lennie Bremen (Maxie Bripp), David Fresco (Mousey), Paul Dubov (Lt. Badger), John Holland (Piccadilly Charlie), Richard Hoyt (henchman)

Before he became famous for playing himself as an American icon, Dick Clark of American Bandstand and America's New Year's Eve countdown guy for decades put in some fairly good performances as a straight actor. He was very good in two different roles for Burke's Law, and also put in appearances in Stoney Burke, Ben Casey, Perry Mason, Branded, and Coronet Blue.

David Fresco usually played bit parts as elderly men, and did so in both Batman and The Man from UNCLE. Paul Dubov, co-writer and also an actor, gives himself a supporting role, maybe standing in for an unavailable actor as it's a very ordinary nondescript bit.

## An Eerie, Airy Thing

wr. Richard Levinson, William Link, dir. James Brown

While attempting to dissuade a broken man from jumping off a ledge to his death, Honey uncovers a complicated web of lust, lies, and murder

*with Lisa Seagram (Connie Phillips), Adam Williams (Gordon Forbes), Ken Lynch (Lt. Keller), Lou Krugman (Stuart Bell), Jan Arvan (Mr. Rush, hotel manager), Bill Quinn (Lt. Curtis), Michael Harris (TV cameraman), Fred Murphy (Bell's aide)*

For the final episode, future *Columbo* creators Levinson and Link turn in a relatively sober and quite clever yarn about a suicidal man on a ledge. He won't come in until his wife shows up, but she's already shown up somewhere else... dead.

Lisa Seagram has one of her more substantial roles as the man's self-interested and callous bit on the side. After the usual '60s starlet roles (*Burke's Law, The Beverly Hillbillies, Bewitched, The Girl from UNCLE, Batman*, etc.), she moved to Italy in the early 70s to make exploitation films before retiring in the mid-'70s. Adam Williams, a bland and undistinguished actor usually in invisible roles, has his moment in the sun here as the potential suicide.

series ends

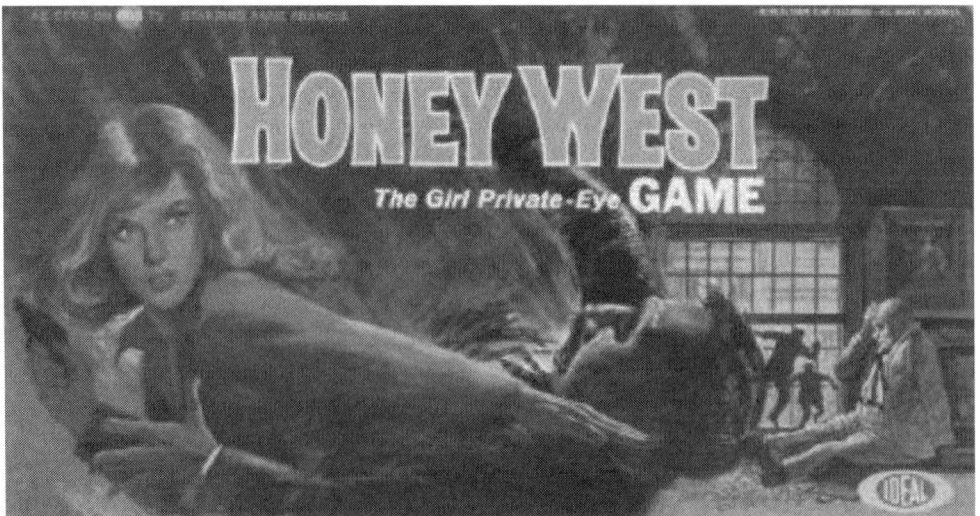

## Amos Burke — Secret Agent

### September 15th, 1965 — January 12th, 1966

As the 1965-'66 season opened in September, and with *Thunderball* in cinemas alongside a slew of imitators, *The Man from UNCLE* was a bona-fide hit show, perhaps in general terms, the most successful TV show of the 1960s. Spy-mania, and also UNCLE-mania, was rampant across not just the U.S., but the world. And *UNCLE*, which had far surpassed and transcended its origins as a mere Bond cash-in thanks to the inventiveness and inspiration of creator Sam Rolfe, deserved its success. It may not have had the longevity or numbers of *Lucy*, *The Beverly Hillbillies*, or the westerns, but in terms of impact, significance, and influence it was matched only by *Batman*, which flashed and crashed within two years, and *The Monkees*, which touched only a small and specific teen audience. All this, of course, was discussed in detail in the first volume of *Cool TV*.

*Robert Vaughn contemplates his between-seasons movie assignment at the height of the spy craze in the mid-'60s. So popular was UNCLE, that a mere TV series graced the cover of the ABC cinema chain's Film Review not once, but twice... despite the rivalry between the mediums.*

As *UNCLE's* ratings shot skyward in the first few months of 1965, programmers were not slow to see which way the wind was blowing for the new season. Within a week at the start of the 1965-'66 TV season, five new series directly owing their existence to Bond's box office success and the *UNCLE* ratings premiered — two directly against each other in the schedules, another two on the same evening as *UNCLE!* The spy frenzy had started in earnest.

First off the starting block was *I Spy*, which aired its first episode on September 15th, 1965 and ran for three seasons (although the perfectly fine pilot was held back until mid-season). This was a classy and sophisticated series starring Robert Culp as tennis player Kelly Robinson and Bill Cosby as his trainer Alexander Scott... but the truth was that this was just a cover, and they were both American government spies. This was the most intelligent and grown-up of the '60s spy series, featuring serious stories and ideas and adventures in real countries. It was also unique among '60s spy shows for being filmed on location; each season, the show would travel to two different locales for a run of episodes. The writing and direction was superb, with no Cold War histrionics or laser-beam-wielding world conquerors, just several layers of complexities and ambiguities.

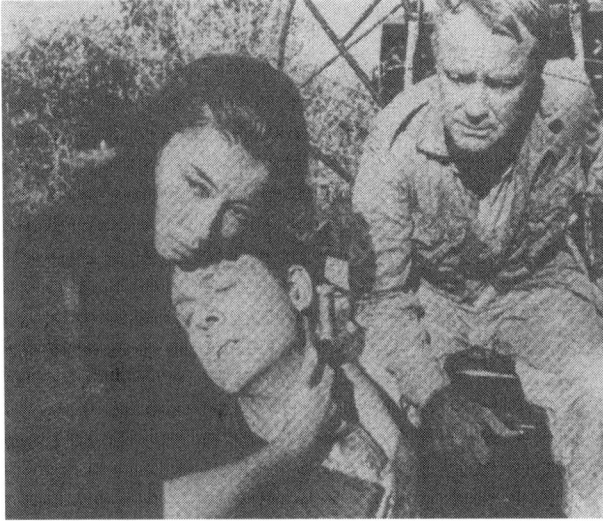

*Robert Culp with future wife France Nuyen and Lew Ayres in the I Spy episode "The Tiger"*

The series encountered some problems with Cosby being the first black man to co-star in a television series (extraordinary to realise that), but the producers, the network (NBC), and notably Robert Culp to his eternal credit, all stuck to their guns (Culp's rule for the show was that color was never mentioned, never an issue positive or negative, no preaching, no jokes; "the statement was the non-statement"), and Cosby went on to become one of America's most successful TV stars just twenty years later with the hit sit-com *The Cosby Show*. Culp, infuriatingly, was less successful, his enormous talent wasted in a succession of guest roles in lame murder mystery series over the years, although he has three wonderful *Outer Limits,* three superb *Columbos,* several fine 1970s TV movies, and the early '80s gem *The Greatest American Hero* to his name, not a bad body of work. And he brought something, anything, to every role he played. He was magnetic, spellbinding to watch at his craft. *I Spy* remains his finest work, and he frequently wrote and directed on the show, too.

*Culp with Susan Oliver in the I Spy episode "One Thousand Fine"*

264

Playing directly opposite *I Spy* on NBC was *Amos Burke – Secret Agent* on ABC. This disastrous and ill-judged revamp of *Burke's Law* was everything *I Spy* wasn't. An absurd premise (former devil-may-care police chief Burke was now a hard-nosed ruthless spy working for the government agency MX-3 and a pre-*Charlie's Angels* mysterious contact known only as 'the Man') was married to standard spy movie plots trying to cash in on Bond and/or *UNCLE* and every dumb spy cliche in the book. It was amazing that the show was as good as it was.

But ABC had ruined one of their hit series to get it; *Burke's Law* might well have run for five seasons if it had been left alone, and the anger of the audience hung over it like a cloud. Series star Gene Barry was furious when the inevitable cancellation notice came, and there was a very public and heated altercation in the press about it (I remember one quote of the "he'll never work in this town again" variety; three years later he was top-lining the highly prestigious *The Name of the Game!*). "I hated it, Gene hated it, we all hated it" said Spelling, later. No-one was happy, and so it is to the credit of both Spelling and Barry that so much genuine effort was put in by both of them to make it work. At no point did anyone involved throw their hands up, shrug, and try to create a self-fulfilling prophecy; Spelling and his people did everything they legitimately could to make the show a success.

If disassociated from the loss of *Burke's Law,* a big ask which few people, myself included, were able to fully accommodate, the series is actually better than it is often given credit for. If the show had existed as a single entity, with Barry in a different role, the ratings outcome would most likely have been the same against *I Spy,* but the series would have a different reputation, most likely as a lost classic. I'd even go so far to suggest that if *Amos Burke* had aired first, and been replaced by *Burke's Law,* the pendulum of popular opinion and received wisdom might well have swung the other way. Indeed, had the show had been filmed in color, it would often have looked like a feature film.

Nothing was done half-assed or short-changed. The viewer was never just *told* something had happened. We always saw it. Yes, the storylines were quite mad, but that was par for the course in the '60s spy genre, and yes, it is bonkers that the former suave, debonair, chauffeured-everywhere softie who strolled around L.A. sneering at the eccentrics while his assistants did all the legwork has suddenly morphed into a fightin' super-skilled secret agent to give Solo and Bond a run for their money, but Gene Barry carried his new role far better than the series deserved (and he had a stunt double who actually looked like him, which is more than can be said for *The Avengers,* and boy, does he earn his money; this is very much an action show, too).

*Burke's Law's 'Sgt. Ames', Eileen O'Neill, nabs a guest role in the new format... and a beverage!*

Given that his forte was light-hearted easy-going sophistication, and bearing in mind he didn't want to do the show, Barry gave some of his best performances in the series, notably "Nightmare in the Sun" when a friend is killed, and "Peace—It's a Gasser", when he believes he's murdered a fellow agent in cold blood. Ironically, *Amos Burke—Secret Agent* may have been his best work. It was certainly his most serious. And whether being cold and cruel, or witty and heroic, Barry gave a perfectly judged performance. Yes, there was some pretty poor back projection now and again, but generally the sets were very good, with Spelling and his people throwing money around like a drunken sailor on background and extras. When the bad guys raided somewhere, there would be a small army of a couple of dozen extras, not the usual five or six you got on other series. The politics and settings for the shows were more varied and creative than the holiday destination locations of *I Spy* and *UNCLE,* even though the series was still filmed on the backlot. Only one episode sent Burke to a comic-book Russia; otherwise, the bad guys represented a variety of nationalities... and when Burke went to Britain, it was neither fog-and-cobblestones Ripper-land, or swingin' London. His second trip took him to Cornwall! Best of all, the guest casts were a role call of every wonderful character actor available in Hollywood at the time, including the small army of usual suspects who seduced square-jawed heroes or practiced super-villainy in all the other espionage series of the day. Also, several Hollywood Brits pass through as MI5 types.

It's interesting to observe which of the spy cliches different series latch on to. *Amos Burke* seems to have taken from Bond the idea of the ill-fated female! While the guest female lead usually survives, being the second female lead in this show is a bit like wearing the red shirt on *Star Trek!* The show is surprisingly dark right across the board — not as serious or as sensible as *I Spy,* but not as light or as silly as *Man from UNCLE.* There were some quite cruel killings of innocents, and some sad disposals of likeable characters, as well as some chilling well-deserved demises for the bad guys. Had *Amos Burke* not carried the baggage of formerly being *Burke's Law,* it might have lasted longer — but putting it up against *I Spy* was borderline insanity. Not only was *I Spy* marginally the better series, it was in color.

*Hi-tech '66! "Operation Long Shadow"*

Premiering the same Friday night together two evenings later, and with series leads carrying the same surname, were ABC's *Honey West* (ironically, a *Burke's Law* spin-off) at 9.00. and CBS' *The Wild Wild West* earlier at 7.30. (the same evening *The Man from UNCLE* began its second season with part one of the superb "Alexander the Greater Affair", aka Europe's *One Spy Too Many*). As UNCLE faced the threat of Rip Torn's megalomaniac world conqueror, the two Wests were facing their first foes too, but in monochrome that first year. *The Wild Wild West* audaciously shoe-horned the trappings of James Bond — advanced science, mad villains, and zany schemes — into, as the title suggests, the western, and featured a tough guy and disguise expert duo who travelled around the

*Ross Martin and Robert Conrad in The Wild Wild West.*

267

west on board a classy locomotive, where they took their orders from the U.S. President himself. Dreary sets and dull direction sometimes made the series a lacklustre effort, but it was popular enough to run as long as *UNCLE* itself did, so they must have been doing something right. Robert Conrad was James T. West, Ross Martin his Watson-like second banana Artemus Gordon, and the duo met some quality guest stars during their four year run. What the series did have going for it was the presence of *Star Trek's* Gene Coon as a story editor, some good writers, enthusiastic leads, bizarre villains, and a bunch of familiar faces from 1960s film and TV, including the usual array of show-hopping starlets, although sadly bereft of their mod fashions or bathing attire, given the 1880s setting.

The very next night, as if sensing the need, came *Get Smart*, the inevitable comedy send-up. *Get Smart* was a play on words; the series was the creation of Buck Henry, Mel Brooks, and Leonard Stern and concerned the misadventures of the oafish but eager Maxwell Smart, a well-meaning buffoon who succeeded in his secret agent shenanigans with the bad guys more by luck than skill.

Playing Smart was comedian Don Adams, who had refined the Smart persona on *The Bill Dana Show* while playing the similar role of hotel detective Byron Glick. He brought with him a legion of catch-phrases which the devoted audience sat on the edge of their chairs waiting to hear — "Missed it by that much!", "I have an alternate plan!", and the famous "Would you believe it?" routine, which began with a proud boast along the lines of (for example) "Would you believe there's a huge army waiting for you out there?", followed by the more hopeful "Would you believe a small army?" followed by the despairing "Would you believe my mother and a very angry poodle?" or some such crack. My personal favorite of the many catch-phrases was "And loving it!" — as in "But Max, you'll be all alone on an enemy infested desert island with only a penknife for protection"... to which he replies heroically, "And loving it!". Adams never escaped the role of Maxwell Smart, and to a certain extent, never tried to, reviving the character numerous times in unsuccessful comeback formats.

During the course of the series, which ran from 1965 to 1969 on NBC and then a further season on CBS, *Get Smart* lampooned numerous films and shows of the time in episodes with punnish titles and wacky plots ("Bronzefinger","House of Max," "Pussycats Galore", "Die Spy," "Dr. Yes," "The Mild Ones", "The Apes of Wrath", "Smartacus", and so on) and inevitably got round to most of the spy shows (including gag cameos from *I Spy's* Robert Culp and *Mission: Impossible's* Martin Landau), but mostly its obvious main target was *UNCLE* and its direct copies. Max worked for CONTROL and the long-suffering 'Chief' (an exasperated and weary-looking Ed Platt) and was accompanied by his beautiful and devoted Agent 99 (Barbara Feldon). The bad guys were the evil KAOS, who — like *UNCLE's* THRUSH — were evil just for the sake of it, seeking nothing less than world domination (the producers of *UNCLE* had admitted that the use of THRUSH as all-purpose bad guys was purely to avoid having to keep coming up with mad reasons to rule the world! It's just THRUSH! It's what they do!). *UNCLE's* producers soon got the hint, and after the excesses of *UNCLE's* third, maddest over-the-top season (1966-'67) the memo went out that fourth season *UNCLE* should be "more like James Bond and less like *Get Smart!*". Ironically, *UNCLE* did not survive its fourth season, while *Get Smart*, which had moved beyond parasitic parody to take on a life of its own, lasted into the 1970s! The only other survivors to make it into the 1970s were *The Wild Wild West*, which ended, with *Get Smart*, with the 1969-'70 season, and *Mission: Impossible*, which survived until 1973 by revising its format, and had joined the throng late, the following year, in 1966.

Later in the season, *The Avengers* had a brief early run beginning in March, and by September '66, for the start of the 1966-'67 season, the show was firmly in the ABC schedule, where it would stay for the next three years (bumping *Honey West*). Less fortunate was the bona fide *UNCLE* spin-off, *The Girl from UNCLE,* which opened and closed the same season, a victim of overkill and incredibly silly scripts (a huge shame, as casting, credits, and guest players were all superb).

Three nights after the premiere of this inevitable *UNCLE* spin-off, and a day after the premiere of *The Man from UNCLE's* third season, came *Mission: Impossible,* the most parodied spy show of them all. The series even made its debut on September 17th, the same date as *Honey West* and *The Wild Wild West* a year earlier (if anyone ever decides there ought to be a National Spy Day to celebrate secret agent shows, then September 17th should be it!).

The memory of all these series lives on, but *Amos Burke – Secret Agent* is long forgotten, forever tarred with the curse of having killed off *Burke's Law.* This is a shame, as for all its flaws, it was a worthy addition to the second stringers who followed in the wake of Bond and *UNCLE.* And of all the Bond copyists, it was the closest in approximation. The bottom line—it was a good show. Cool TV.

episode guide

(1965–'66)

## Balance of Terror

wr. Robert Buckner, dir. Murray Golden

Burke infiltrates a private army planning violence in Latin America by intercepting and replacing the American traitor working as their liason in Switzerland.

*with Will Kuluva (General Baratta), Michele Carey (Bianca Andrade), Susanne Cramer (Elsa), Gerald Mohr (Paul Schriner), Theo Marcuse (Hugo Sihler), Arthur Batandides (Baratta's aide), Lawrence Montaigne (Franz), Michael St. Clair (Volkers), Peter Mamakos (Delgado), Lisa Bernay (Teresa), Carl Benton Reid (American contact), Ben Wright (Interpol agent)*

As already detailed, Gene Barry was quite vocal about the change in format, and he looks thoroughly pissed off in the pre-credits sequence! There is the briefest mention of the police department and his new role, and off we go.

Suzanne Cramer, Gene Barry, and Michele Carey poolside in premiere episode "Balance of Terror"

Here was a show starting as it meant to go on. Just look at that cast. A whole bunch of familiar faces from cult TV, and spy shows in general. Gone are the Hollywood has-beens, Spelling's next-door neighbors and best friends, the fizz and the froth, the glitz and the glamour. In come a small army of the usual suspects from 1960s adventure shows, and a poker-faced, played-straight Ian Fleming atmos. And all credit to Spelling and Four Star, there's been no snapping of the purse when it comes to supplying cars, helicopters, extras, and enough stunt players to pitch a good battle when the cavalry charges in at the end.

Will Kuluva was the original UNCLE boss in the *Solo* pilot, before being replaced by the Waverley character. Here, he plays the Latin American recipient of Red Chinese gold being supplied by an American traitor (Gerald Mohr in full sleaze mode) via Switzerland to fund a private army.

Kuluva was in two *Man from UNCLEs* and *It Takes a Thief*, and four *Mission: Impossibles*. He also appeared in episodes of *I Spy* and *The Wild Wild West*. Mohr was a bad guy in numerous early '60s Warners series, and also Spelling's *Johnny Ringo* and Gene Barry's *Bat Masterson*. In the '60s, he was a bad guy in *Lost in Space*, *Voyage to the Bottom of the Sea*, and both *UNCLE* shows. In animation, he was on the right side of the law, voicing super-heroes Green Lantern for Filmation, and Mr. Fantastic for Hanna-Barbera's *Fantastic Four*.

Sexy Michele Carey, always welcome, is the sultry *femme fatale*, while Suzanne Cramer (who appeared twice in *The Man from UNCLE*) is the helpless waif out of her depth. Carey was in spy shows *The Man from UNCLE*, *THE Cat*, *The Wild Wild West*, and *Mission: Impossible*. Although she made films with Elvis, Sinatra, and John Wayne, her career was pretty much over by the early '70s.

Cramer also appeared in a spy spoof episode of *My Favorite Martian*, and episodes of *Get Smart*, *THE Cat*, and *The Girl from UNCLE*. Heavies Theo Marcuse, Arthur Batanides, Lawrence Montaigne,

Michael St. Clair, and Peter Mamakos are all straight from central casting, regular players in similar fare throughout the '60s. It would be quicker to list the shows they *didn't* appear in, Marcuse and Montaigne being particularly active in the spy genre. At one point, someone tries to gas Burke in the shower, which is exactly what happened to Solo in one of the earliest *UNCLE* episodes, "The Iowa Scuba Affair". The secret agent genre is already starting to repeat itself, even without this series' flagrant Bond steals.

Elderly warhorse Robert Buckner was the man chosen to launch *Amos Burke – Secret Agent*. It was his only script for the series. He was a writer of action films for Warner Brothers for nearly twenty years starting in the early '30s, although his best known title was James Cagney's *Yankee Doodle Dandy*. He moved to 20th Century Fox and television in the mid-'50s, where he wrote the screenplay for *The Reno Brothers*, the western that would ultimately become Elvis Presley's film debut, *Love Me Tender*, and created and worked on the Rod Taylor adventure series *Hong Kong*. His credits were thin on the ground during the '60s, and he retired at their close.

Buckner had written a few episodes of *The Rogues* for Four Star, but his career was well on the wane at this point, and he was a curious choice to launch the series. Possibly no-one wanted the poisoned chalice of signing off *Burke's Law*. Murray Golden later directed multiple episodes of *Batman* and *Mission: Impossible*, and his resume includes *Burke's Law*, *The Fugitive*, *Honey West*, *Get Smart*, *Green Hornet*, *Time Tunnel*, *The Invaders*, and *Star Trek*.

### Operation Long Shadow

wr. Albert Beich, William Wright, dir. Don Taylor

The kidnapping of the son of an Algerian ally in the Middle East leads Burke to a plot to kill the Prime Minister of France

*with Antoinette Bower (the Countess), Berry Kroeger (the General), Francoise Bellini (Claire Plouvier), Maurice Dallimore (British Contact), Carl Benton Reid ( American contact), Thann Wyenn (Mohammed Bassa), Dan Tobin (Homer Franklin), Rosemary De Camp (Mrs. Franklin), Bartlett Robinson (U.S. Ambassador), Dick Caruso (Ahmed Bassa), Jacques Roux (Gilbert), Guy De Vestel (Pierre), Chuck Couch, Allen Jaffe (thugs), Jamie Farr (telephone lineman)*

*Gene Barry with Antoinette Bower*

Utilising the same opening footage of Barry getting off his 'plane and being taken to his American contact (Reid), this episode gets off to a very grim start with the callous murder of a French girl (uncredited) thrown from the observation deck of the Eiffel Tower by a thug (Couch) working for bad guys Bower and Kroeger. She was an unsuspecting dupe used by them to lure a young and smitten Algerian prince to his own kidnapping, their plan being to frame him for murder and instigate a military coup that will unite Algeria and France under their command. His father is "one of the men we're relying on to keep the Middle East facing West", says Burke's U.S. commander.

Absurdly, Burke goes 'undercover', taking on the identity of a playboy, but of course the millionaire Burke would be mixing with exactly the sort of people who would instantly recognise him. As it is, he's recognised by a couple of wealthy tourists who know him from the police department. Burke tells them he's now just a simple jet-setter (sigh). Naturally, they keep turning up throughout the episode, to make increasingly 'hilarious' observations.

All attempts at subterfuge now squashed, Burke plays cat and mouse with the Countess Marton (Antoinette Bower, shortly to appear in both *Star Trek* and *The Invaders*)... although which is the cat and which the mouse is debatable.

It's British import Maurice Dallimore though (*Batman, Bewitched, The Monkees, I Dream of Jeannie,* etc.) who steals the show in both his scenes, comic and tragic, as Burke's British contact in Paris. Having played Basil Exposition, as he takes his leave, he casually hands Burke a card.

"This is the telephone number of a good friend of mine, a very, very discreet undertaker"

"Now why would I need a discreet undertaker?"

"There's a dead girl in a swimsuit on your terrace"

Albert Beich and William Wright wrote the pilot for *Burke's Law* and several other episodes; Don Taylor also worked on the series' previous incarnation. The episode keeps moving, and there's a clever scene in a freight car. For the grand showdown, however, the production uses exactly the same tunnel as in the opening episode's first scene!

### Steam Heat

wr. Marc Brandel, dir. Virgil Vogel

A gangster in exile from America plans a conspiracy to loot New York by launching a massive sleeping gas attack on the city

*with Nehemiah Persoff (Albert Indigo), Jane Wald (Miss Prince), James Best (Tucson), Kipp Hamilton (Silky), John Hoyt (Otto Veidt), Joan Huntington (Victoria Rose), Carl Benton Reid (American contact), Jack Lambert (Charlie Segar), Jonathan Hole (Mr. Digby), George Greco (JoJo)*

Story consultant Marc Brandel turns in his first script (his contributions are the weakest, by the way), and sends Burke after gangster Nehemiah Persoff (who played quite a few on *The Untouchables*). He's his usual histrionic self, and John Hoyt is in his comfort zone as a mad scientist. Although the episode moves along, it's not quite as engrossing as the previous two. There's an element of *Goldfinger* to the plot, which involves knocking out the entire city of New York for a night of looting. It's quite silly, and the even sillier tag, possibly featuring Madlyn Rhue and Monty Margetts, although, like several other players, they're not credited, is real *Get Smart* stuff, with Burke playing a flapjack like a vinyl disc. After the intense scenes that had preceded it, involving the two lead women and played exceedingly well by Barry, it was poor.

James Best enjoys himself as the cowboy-hatted heavy Tucson, and George Greco makes such a great thug, it's a mystery why this was his last of just a handful of early '60s roles.

Joan Huntington's career lasted into the early '70s. She appeared twice in *Burke's Law,* and twice in this series, as well as spy shows *The Man from UNCLE* and *I Spy* and three episodes of *The Wild Wild West.* Kipp Hamilton worked throughout the '50s and '60s, and also appeared in *The Man from UNCLE* and *The Wild Wild West.*

Rock-faced Jack Lambert worked throughout the '40s, '50s and '60s, almost always as a heavy, and mostly in westerns. Married with kids, Jane Wald's career fizzled after a few minor roles in films and a few more significant guest shots in TV, including this and a *Batman*.

Marc Brandel flitted from England to America throughout his career, working mostly on syndicated series. After his inevitably short stint on *Amos Burke – Secret Agent*, he returned to British television for ten years.

Unlike many of his contemporaries, Virgil Vogel never retired, and was still working right up until his death at 76. He directed three *Amos Burke* episodes during its short stay on the air, either side of extensive runs on *Wagon Train*, *The Big Valley*, *The FBI*, and *Streets of San Francisco*.

### Password to Death

wr. Marc Brandel, dir. Seymour Robbie

*with Janette Scott (Jennifer Robbins), Joseph Ruskin (Sir Tristran Voss), Michael Pate (Assassin), Bill Glover (Captain Aldington), Patrick O'Moore (General Pierce-Rivers), Horst Eberseberg (Max), Lisa Pera (Anna), Lyse D'Anjou (Carla), Brendan Dillon (Kossler), Martin Kosleck (Basalon), Carl Benton Reid (American contact), Sharyl Locke (little girl)*

Burke is in London, but this must be one of the few American TV episodes not to indulge in all the standard cliches—no fog, steam trains, Scotland Yard, Trooping of the Colour... The bulk of the story revolves around a tin mine in Cornwall that is not what it seems. Deep underground is a typical spy set-up of computers and corridors where fave 1960s heavies Joseph Ruskin and Michael Pate plan to trick the Americans and Russians

into going to war. It doesn't make a lot of sense, but it holds the attention, the cleverest of the action revolving round a two-way mirror. It was Brandel's best script for the show.

British actress Janette Scott had made a series of unmemorable films and was about to slide into TV. Despite her perky middle-class prim and proper voice and demeanour, her real name was Thora, and she came from Morecambe oop North. She appeared in this before throwing in the towel and getting married instead. Child actress Sharyl Locke also opted for a normal life after this and a *Bonanza*. Bill Glover, Patrick O'Moore, and Brendan Dillon were all Brits working in Hollywood.

Lisa Pera worked until the mid-'70s, usually playing European girls of various nationalities in spy shows and war series. She was on this show twice, and was particularly good as another ill-fated amateur in *Mission: Impossible*. Continuing the tradition of this series in offing women, this episode manages to bump off two pretty young girls, the latter in a *From Russia With Love* scenario.

Seymour Robbie worked mostly for Quinn Martin and Universal on their detective series, but dabbled briefly in such cult series as *The Man from UNCLE*, *Honey West*, *The Green Hornet*, *Lost in Space*, *Bewitched*, and *Wonder Woman*. He directed two episodes for this series.

### The Man With the Power

wr. Stuart Jerome, dir. Murray Golden

with John Abbott (Conrad Jaeger), Herb Andress (Ehrberg), E.J. André (Dr. Brenner), Fred Beir (Tony Scott), Horst Ebersberg (Batton), Steven Geray (Dr. Crystal), Thomas Gomez (Herr Kraus), Lisa Pera (Heidi Schaefer), Carl Benton Reid (American contact), Leslie Perkins (Maggie), Ilse Taurins (Paula), Albert Szabo (Weiss), Ivan Triesault (Wexler)

This is the one episode of this series that I have not been able to track down a copy of for review, so there is little I can say about it, and the cast information comes from the IMDB. Very frustrating. It, and the later "A Very Important Russian is Missing" were missing from the U.K. screenings, although I located the latter on You Tube, where a number of these public domain items can be found. I won't deal with pirates.

My almost-namesake John Abbott made several appearances in cult TV at around this time, including *Bewitched*, *The Munsters*, *Lost in Space*, *Star Trek*, and *Land of the Giants*. He did well out of the spy craze, and also played assorted scientists and villains in *Get Smart*, *The Wild Wild West*, *I Spy*, and a particularly good *Man from UNCLE*. Horst Eberseberg and Lisa Pera had both appeared just weeks ago in the episode "Password to Death".

### Nightmare in the Sun

wr. Tony Barrett, dir. James Goldstone

Burke attempts to prevent the assassination of a Mexican union leader which will be blamed on the U.S.

with Edward Asner (Pablo Vasquez), Barbara Luna (Consuela), Larry D. Mann (Maximillian Darvas), Elisha Cook (John Wyatt), Nico Minardos (Pepe Delgado), Joan Staley (Chrissy Keller), Mari Blanchard (Maria Vasquez), Carl Benton Reid (American contact), Alex Montoya (Paco), George Keymas (Arturo), Jan Arvan (bartender), Nadia Sanders (salesgirl)

A superb cast, with excellent action scenes. And another pretty girl comes to grief in a quite shocking scene (and she's not the only one).

Ed Asner (above), best known for his long-running role as Lou Grant in *The Mary Tyler Moore Show* and *Lou Grant* in the 1970s, played cops or heavies throughout the '60s. His SF roles included appearances in *Voyage to the Bottom of the Sea*, *The Outer Limits*, *The Man from UNCLE*, *The Girl from UNCLE*, *The Wild Wild West*, and *The Invaders*. He was a favorite of director James Goldstone, and always delivered the best performance possible with the material given.

Both playing to type here, the substantial contributions of Barbara Luna and Larry D. Mann to cult TV are discussed elsewhere in this book, ditto the lovely Joan Staley, who has one of her more substantial showcase roles here and would have made a good recurring character.

A character actor best known for his gangster roles in the 1930s and '40s, including *The Maltese Falcon* and *The Big Sleep* with Bogart, Elisha Cook (often billed as Jnr.) was mostly in television from the 1950s on, including *Batman*, *The Man from UNCLE*, *The Wild Wild West*, *I Spy*, and an appalling *Star Trek*, although he still occasionally landed supporting roles in prestigious films. He had an occasional recurring role in the long-running *Magnum p.i.* as the informer Icepick.

B-movie queen Mari Blanchard (*Abbott and Costello Go to Mars*, *She-Devil*) was in TV by the 1960s, although she did get to make a later film with John Wayne, *McLintock*. Nadia Sanders, under the name Nadine, was in Italian sword and sandal films during the '50s, and was trying to break into Hollywood at the time she appeared here. She never progressed beyond bit parts and retired in 1970.

Tony Barrett was a regular writer on the original *Burke's Law*, and managed to knock out three scripts for the series' new incarnation before the axe fell. James Goldstone, an excellent director who managed to direct the same number, also worked on *Voyage to the Bottom of the Sea*, but should be best known for his work on *The Outer Limits* ("The Sixth Finger", "The Inheritors"), and *Star Trek* (the second pilot "Where No Man Has Gone Before" and "What Are little Girls Made Of?").

## The Prisoners of Doctor Sin

wr. Gilbert Ralston, Marc Brandel, dir. John Peyser

A greedy mercenary exploits vulnerable people by offering them false sanctuary for their wealth and secrets

*Gene Barry poses next to the 'plane where he meets 'the Man'.*

with Michael Dunn (Mr. Sin), Robert Cornthwaite (Waldo Bannister), France Nuyen (Zini), Margaret Muse (Lady Constance), Leonid Kinsky (Juan Bagulesco), Mako (Happy Tuava), Greta Chi, Fuji (Chinese agents), J. Pat O'Malley (Flynn), Roy Jenson (Biggs), Carl Benton Reid (American contact)

A wonderful cast piles in, all doing what they do best. J. Pat O'Malley is being shifty, France Nuyen is being seductive, Leonid Kinsky is being sinister, and Mako is being Mako.

Writers Ralston and Brandel have done their homework well. A Bondish scene has a cobra dropped into Burke's bedroom while he's sleeping, and when he and Nuyen's treacherous Asian encounter a rather phoney-looking skeleton hanging from the branches, Burke again flashes his Bond credentials by quipping "Someone work themselves to the bone?". The ever-welcome Fuji plays an Oddjob-style killer.

But one Bondish element doesn't ring true. Burke is told that if scientist Bannister won't return with him, he is to be killed. The Amos Burke of *Burke's Law,* or even indeed this show, was never a cold-blooded assassin, that's one Bond imitation too far. Mr. Sin's island fortress looks a lot like the location for Spelling's later *Fantasy Island.*

*Right: Amos Burke guest stars Michael Dunn ("Mr. Sin") and Barbara Luna ("Nightmare in the Sun") as they appeared in fellow '60s spy show The Wild Wild West.*

Lead guest player Michael Dunn was best known as recurring villain Dr. Loveless on *The Wild Wild West* at this time. Here he plays a combination of *Austin Powers'* Dr. Evil and Mini-Me merged into one. An actor of restricted height, he played bad guys in *Get Smart* and *Voyage to the Bottom of the Sea,* and also appeared sympathetically in *Star Trek,* but was always irritated that the roles he was cast in were always specifically due to his appearance... but, he told people, casting agents always "think of Mike" for such roles, because he's "the only dwarf who can act"...

*Dunn, as he appeared in Voyage to the Bottom of the Sea's "The Wax Men"*

278

Character actor Robert Cornthwaite's career in film and TV spanned fifty years, and he was particularly good stealing scenes in episodes of *The Twilight Zone, Voyage to the Bottom of the Sea*, and *Batman* at around this time. Exotic France Nuyen did well out of the spy craze, appearing in episodes of *I Spy* (during which she married the star, Robert Culp) and *The Man from UNCLE*, as well as a memorable *Star Trek* as "Elaan of Troyius" (although she more closely resembled 'Cleop of Ejo'). During the 1980s, she had a recurring role in the quality drama *St. Elsewhere*.

What can you say about an episode that offers all three cult TV heavies Mako, Fuji, and Roy Jenson in the same story? TV heaven.

Gilbert Ralston wrote for both *Star Trek* and *Land of the Giants*, the memorable episodes "Who Mourns for Adonais?" and "Ghost Town". This makes three cult TV treasures from his typewriter. He also wrote for *The Wild Wild West* and *I Spy*. John Peyser's direction is excellent.

### Peace—It's a Gasser

wr. Palmer Thompson, dir. James Goldstone

Idealistic kids are duped by enemy agents into employing a mind control gas to ultimately be used against Washington

*with Paul Carr (Paul Stark), Ruta Lee (Margo Davis), Henry Jones (Mr. Fillmore), Brooke Bundy (Suzanne), Jill Hill (Emily), Richard Hoyt (Jeff), Larry Thor (General Corning), Deanna Lund (Sergeant), Carl Benton Reid (American contact), Robert Sorrells, James Secrest (Corporals), Hal Lynch (Captain)*

The standard Hollywood take on the youthful idealism of the '60s —at a time when the vast majority of the television script-writers were middle-aged—was that the kids were naive dupes, conned by people with a political agenda beyond their knowledge or comprehension. To a certain extent, this was true; they had posters of Che and Mao on their dorm walls, after all. But the feelings of the young were beyond *their* knowledge or comprehension, too. It was a two-way street, but on television, the traffic was all going in one direction. This too was discussed in the first *Cool TV* book, as *Batman* and *The Man from UNCLE* (with guest star Henry Jones, as it happens) were both among those shows that followed this line, as were *Star Trek* and *Mission: Impossible*, covered in my *Desilu* book, which is a *Cool TV* entry (of quality, but perhaps less trendy shows) in all but name. Consequently, all that needs to be added at this point, is that this episode of *Amos Burke* does at least acknowledge that the feelings of the peace protesters were at least genuine, and it is this that the evil conspirators Fillmore and Stark take advantage of. Fillmore is a simpleton, but Stark is a psychopath.

Palmer Thompson flitted from one series to another during a writing career that lasted throughout the '50s and '60s. He rarely stayed long anywhere, but had just settled into *Hawaii Five-O* when he passed away. He did most of his work on the Four Star series *The Rifleman, The Detectives* and the bizarre little-known two-fisted lawyer series *The Law and Mr. Jones*.

In *Goldfinger*, in 1964, the bad guys put an entire army base to sleep. In 1965's *One Spy Too Many*, made up from the two-part "Alexander the Greater Affair" it's a will gas sapping same. In this episode, an entire army base is reduced to a state of childlike laughter and play by the same process. The episode itself, however, is no laughing matter. The callous and careless killings in the pre-credits teaser bring to mind the Clint Eastwood film *The Enforcer*, made ten years later. And there are more to come. Burke is told he's expendable in this one. Once again, this is not the Amos Burke of *Burke's Law*. It's a shame the network didn't just make him a new character. The result would have been the same in the ratings, but the series could have been judged as a separate entity — which it is.

Henry Jones made numerous appearances in cult TV playing a variety of eccentrics and oddballs, including *Lost in Space, Voyage to the Bottom of the Sea, Honey West, The Man from UNCLE, Night Gallery, Kolchak, The Six Million Dollar Man,* and *Project UFO*. His role here is very similar to that in "The Neptune Affair", the first of his UNCLE appearances (it's "The Cap and Gown Affair" I refer to above). Paul Carr had a similarly impressive list of cult TV credits, including *Star Trek, Time Tunnel, Voyage to the Bottom of the Sea, The Invaders, The Green Hornet, Mission: Impossible, Land of the Giants, The Six Million Dollar Man, The Amazing Spider-Man, The Incredible Hulk,* and *Buck Rogers in the 25th Century*. He could play good guy or bad guy with equal skill (he plays both in *Time Tunnel*, only weeks apart). Brooke Bundy also appeared in episodes of *The Man from UNCLE, Voyage to the Bottom of the Sea,* and *Mission: Impossible*. Ruta Lee appeared twice in the original *Burke's Law* format.

Watch for Deanna Lund of *Land of the Giants* in an early role hula-hooping on a desk!

*Deanna Lund in a Fox promo shoot for Land of the Giants*

**The Weapon**

wr. Tony Barrett, dir. James Goldstone

A powerful businessman possesses a formula which compels rivals to reveal their business secrets and then take their own lives

*with Dyan Cannon (Francesca Zsabo), David Sheiner (Alexis Zsabo), James Frawley (Lucien Garth), Bernard Fox (Colonel Drummond), Elisa Ingram (Inga Ernst), Richard Angarola (Anton Povlanyl), Jack Perkins (Janos), Carl Benton Reid (American contact), Jason Wingreen (Gunther Ernst), Louis Mercier (Duprez), Max Dommar (Perineau)*

David Sheiner, who conducted the raid in *The Man from UNCLE* referred to in the last episode's details, is similarly wonderfully nasty as his own man in this fun episode from Barrett and Goldstone. Usually the chief heavy for the bad guy, Sheiner has James Frawley as his aide, both actors being firm favorites of the director.

Sheiner played some great sleazy thugs at around this time, notably here and in the aforementioned *UNCLE* adventure and *The Invaders*, but he wasn't always the bad guy. Other roles in cult TV included *The Twilight Zone, Voyage to the Bottom of the Sea, I Spy, The Six Million Dollar Man, The Amazing Spider-Man, Automan, Manimal*, and numerous *Mission: Impossible*. Frawley, later to become a director and producer, appeared in *The Outer Limits, My Favorite Martian, The Man from UNCLE, I Spy*, and *Voyage to the Bottom of the Sea* (once for Goldstone) at around this time.

This was one of Dyan Cannon's last forays into television series work for thirty years, as she then segued into films and TV movies. She later had recurring roles in the shows *Ally McBeal* and *Three Sisters*. Britisher Bernard Fox, always a treat to see, had been persuaded to try his luck in Hollywood after spending the 1950s in British TV, and soon acquired recurring roles on *Bewitched* as Doctor Bombay and *Hogan's Heroes* as Colonel Crittenden at this time. He frequently enjoyed plum roles on the two *UNCLE* series. Elisa Ingram's spy show resume included *The Man from UNCLE, Get Smart, The Wild Wild West*, and *Mission: Impossible*.

This episode takes place in Britain, again cliche-free. Some minor characters are not credited. Great comeuppance scene.

## Deadlier Than the Male

wr. Albert Beich, William H. Wright, dir. John Peyser

The power-crazed wife of a Spanish General disposes of anyone who knows her dictator husband is dying, so that she and her lover can return to their country and take power.

*Burke with his two-way communications watch*

*with Julie Adams (Carla Cabral), Lisa Gaye (Florita), Alizia Gur (Carmen), Felice Orlandi (Captain Tony Lasada), Arnold Moss (General Pedro Cabral), Nestor Paiva (Doctor Pepe Gonzalez), Alan Caillou (Jamieson Willoughby), Nacho Galindo (Doctor Torres), Richard Loo (Chinese General), Carl Benton Reid (American contact), Lisa Seagram (fake Princess)*

This is a good one in itself, but it has a few of the cornier spy trappings of the '60s—a morse code message stamped out by a Flamenco dancer, a cuff-link with a handy knife inside for cutting free, a Matt Helm style gun that switches from real bullets to blanks, and so on. Julia Adams gives an excellent performance as the deadlier of the title, Felice Orlandi is less convincing as her lover and co-conspirator. There are plot holes, too. Why does a woman as cold and ruthless as Carla let her sister live once she knows? Her drunken state is the perfect opportunity for an unhappy accident. For some reason, the episode is written, and Barry plays, in the style of the old Amos Burke. And no-one is taking it seriously (the Chinese General's code name is the childishly offensive 'Grass Slipper', which Gene Barry cleverly undermines).

Julie Adams extraordinary career ranged from B-westerns and *The Creature from the Black Lagoon* to Elvis and John Wayne films, Dennis Hopper's drugs-addled appropriately named *Last Movie*, and being cast as the young wife of the doddery star of the schmaltzy feelgood *Jimmy Stewart Show*. She was also in a *Girl from UNCLE* at this time. Arnold Moss was a great villain, and appeared in such roles in several series at around this time, with memorable turns in *The Man from UNCLE*, *Time Tunnel*, and *Star Trek* (he was Kodos in "Conscience of the King"). He has little to do here. Lisa Gaye was in the same *Time Tunnel* ("The Walls of Jericho"). Veteran character actor Nestor Paiva appeared in the Mexican-based episode of *Burke's Law* as a padre. He also frequently provided voices for various supporting characters in the *Jonny Quest* cartoon series.

More familiar faces from the spy genre turn up in this one. Alizia Gur was in *From Russia With Love* (in the gypsy fight) and episodes of *The Man from UNCLE*. She even gets to do another gypsy fight in this one, presumably as a gag tribute for those who recognise her. Alan Caillou was also a regular guest on *UNCLE*, and wrote for the series. Here, he does a Q routine, providing coincidentally exactly the right tools for the forthcoming mission. Hawaiian-born Chinese-American Richard Loo was a familiar face on TV at this time, turning up in *The Outer Limits*, *The Man from UNCLE*, *Voyage to the Bottom of the Sea*, *Honey West*, *I Spy*, *The Wild Wild West*, and *I Dream of Jeannie*.

This was the second of three scripts from *Burke's Law's* team of Beich and Wright. It was also the second and last directed by John Peyser, who went on to war series *Combat*, *The Rat Patrol*, and *Garrison's Gorillas*.

## Whatever Happened to Adriana, and Why Won't She Stay Dead?

wr. Warren Duff, dir. Seymour Robbie

An arms dealer has a Sicilian police chief in his pocket by kidnapping a fiery Italian girl to cover up a scandal; Burke makes a counter-offer...

with Albert Paulsen (James Keraback), Jocelyn Lane (Angelina Brascia), Richard Angarola (Colonel Lashi), Joan Patrick (Lola Redmond), Rodolfo Hoyos (Colonel Metaxa), Lee Delano (Lashi's aide), Carl Benton Reid (American contact), Sandra Williams (travel agent), Sandra Harrison (nurse), Charles Horvath (heavy)

There's another cruel and unnecessary killing in this one.

Albert Paulsen appeared numerous times on *Mission: Impossible*. His foreign accent invariably cast him as the foreign scientist or diplomat target of bad guys, or the leader of them. Countless TV appearances included *The Man from UNCLE, I Spy, Search Control, Kolchak, Wonder Woman, Charlie's Angels, Automan, Manimal, Knight Rider,* and *Airwolf*. He retired from his two stereotypes in 1986.

Working in the industry since the 1930s, Warren Duff had written for *The Rogues,* and would later provide scripts for *The Girl from UNCLE* and *The Invaders.*

Beautiful Jocelyn Lane, seen at her best in the Elvis film *Tickle Me* and the biker travesty *Hell's Belles,* was also in both *UNCLE* series during their run, as well as spy shows *The Wild Wild West* and *It Takes a Thief.*

Jocelyn Lane with Elvis in Tickle Me

Richard Angarola had appeared only a couple of episodes earlier in a minor role as a victim of "The Weapon". He was one of those actors blessed/cursed with an unrecognisable face, so could slap on a moustache and a foreign accent, as he does here, and play a different role. This particular talent also allowed him to appear in four *Mission: Impossibles* and five *Man from UNCLEs!*

Joan Patrick's career ended with *The Astro Zombies.* Who could blame her? She made TV appearances in series including *Burke's Law, It Takes a Thief, Get Smart,* and *I Dream of Jeannie.*

Lee Delano had minor roles in *Voyage to the Bottom of the Sea, The Man from UNCLE, Star Trek, Batman,* and *Mission: Impossible.*

### The Man's Men

wr. Albert Beich, William H. Wright, dir. Jerry Hopper

A list of all Burke's fellow MX-3 agents has been stolen... and it looks like an inside job...

*with Nancy Gates (Sylvia Kellogg), Vaughn Taylor (Mr. Moody), Louis Quinn (Hank Cassidy), Kit Smythe (Louise Hovey), Norm Alden (Mark Hodges), Bartlett Robinson (Ralph Benbow), Carl Benton Reid (American contact), Whit Bissell (Dr. Freestone), Lincoln Tate (Peterson/ Moody's aide), Clinton Sundberg (Charles/maitre'd), Army Archerd (Press Secretary)*

"There's ten million here! Five of it's yours!"

"I've *got* five"

Yeah, how *do* you buy off a millionaire?

Burke's American contact as a secret agent was referred to in the credits as "The Man", and was played with grim unpleasantness by Carl Benton Reid. He was a blunt bastard, referred always to Burke by his surname, spoke to him like a schoolboy, had no faith in him, and was all business. There was none of the avuncular humor of M or Waverley, nor any of the fawning subservience of Flint or Helm's harried bosses. In fact, had the series lasted long enough to be retooled, he should have been the first thing replaced.

Rather absurdly, we see Burke's mansion from the previous series as a location in this episode. Our memories aren't that short, guys! Equally absurdly, Burke discovers and pursues one of the traitors he's identified without telling anyone his identity. And as things are being wrapped up in such a devastating mission, why on earth is Burke on his own? However, all is forgiven for the way in which the third traitor is identified, a brilliant idea from the writers.

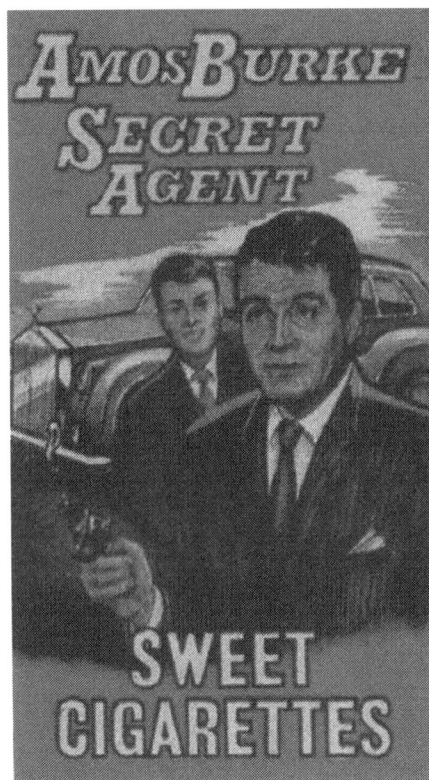

*Sign of the times. Today they're called candy sticks; back then, they were given a red tip to look as though they were lit! Note the picture clearly represents Burke's Law, illustrating the haste of the sudden format change. The trading cards enclosed showed standard Bondish action scenes.*

Once again, as with "Steam Heat", a powerful ending is spoiled by American television's need at this time in its history to have a funny, jokey little tag at the end that negates all the drama and poignancy of the story's conclusion. It's okay for adventures like the following two, with a relatively happy ending, but it really spoils the mood of the darker tales.

### Or No Tomorrow

wr. John and Ward Hawkins, dir. Virgil Vogel

A madman in India obtains a chemical fungus that can destroy the world's rice crops, leading to mass starvation.

*with Abbe Lane (Tashu Amil), Lee Bergere (Dana Ransputa), Eileen O'Neill (Betty Hamilton), Milton Parsons (T. Mena), John Holland (Maurice Glenden), Tommy Nello (Mr. Jacobus), Ziva Rodann (Shani), Anthony Eustrel (hotel manager), Carl Benton Reid (American contact), Gloria Manon (Rosana)*

Gene Barry looks as bored making this episode as I was watching it. Almost all the performances bar a couple are really poor. We are also in the era of blacking up white people to play Indians.

Abbe Lane was much better in her *Man from UNCLE* from this period. Lee Bergere is a dull, uncharismatic adversary. He also appeared in *UNCLE,* and fellow spy series *THE Cat, The Wild Wild West, Get Smart, It Takes a Thief,* and *Mission: Impossible.* In the 1980s he had a recurring role on Spelling's *Dynasty.*

The presence of Eileen O'Neill simply serves to remind us of the superior format we'd lost; it was foolish to guest a former recurring character from the previous format.

Ziva Rodann appeared in *UNCLE* and *Batman* at around this time. Character actor Milton Parsons appeared four times in *Burke's Law*, and four times in the two *UNCLE* series, one of them Abbe Lane's episode, "The Come With Me to the Casbah Affair".

*Eileen O'Neill plays a ditzy female agent in "Or No Tomorrow", one of the era's more tiresome cliches*

John and Ward Hawkins were brothers who wrote mostly for western series such as *Bonanza* and *The High Chaparral,* although they did contribute four fun episodes to *Voyage to the Bottom of the Sea.*

### A Little Gift for Cairo

wr. Ben Starr, Tony Barrett, dir. Jerry Hopper

In Spain, Burke must prevent a weapons shipment of missiles reaching a sheik who wants to take power in Cairo.

*with Jeanette Nolan (Agatha), Ariane Quinn (Jasmine), Ron Whelan (Farid), Fernando Roca (Santos), Paul Genge (Van Zandt), Rico Cattani (Rachid), Rick Traeger (Karoum), Carl Benton Reid (American contact), Jan Arvan (head waiter), Natividad Vacio (bootmaker)*

It's another dull one, but at least the performances are better. There's quite a good finale too. Ron Whelan is very good as the lead villain, but sadly died shortly after filming. He had already appeared on *The Man from UNCLE, I Spy,* and *The Wild Wild West* when he appeared here. Paul Genge went on to two iconic roles as hit-men in the early '70s thrillers *Bullitt* and *The Outfit.* And Rick Traeger is always fun, whatever his role.

Bizarrely, Jeanette Nolan, who isn't nearly as funny as she thinks she is, played exactly the same sort of character on a couple of episodes of *I Spy,* this series' time-slot rival. She was in television guest roles for sixty years, and married to fellow actor John McIntire for over fifty; they even played husband and wife while running the Shiloh ranch for a couple of seasons of *The Virginian.*

Even more bizarrely, Ben Starr was a sit-com writer who wrote numerous episodes of *Bachelor Father* and *Mister Ed,* wrote for *All in the Family* in the '70s, but had his greatest success with *Diff'rent Strokes, Silver Spoons,* and *Facts of Life* in the 1980s. Right in the middle of all this drivel and much more like it he wrote the feature film spy spoof *Our Man Flint!* And this.

## A Very Important Russian is Missing

wr. Samuel Peeples, Tony Barrett, dir. Virgil Vogel

*with Phyllis Newman (Comrade Alexia Sarrov), Donald Harron (Paul Kimbrell), Nina Shipman (Felicia Knight), Parley Baer (Colonel Pavlov), Ben Astar (Boradin), Marvin Brody (Werner Kurtz), Jamie Farr (Zava), John Zaccaro (maitre'd), Madeleine Taylor Holmes (maid)*

"Comrade Burke?"

"Well, at least you got the last name right"

Burke finally goes to Russia in this episode, and all your favorite cliches are here… probably courtesy of Tony Barrett, who rewrote Sam Peeples' script. Between them, they manage to include everything except the old reliable of a Russian diplomat taking off his shoe and banging it on the table.

As was the common fear in the '60s, the Americans and Russians are having to work together because of the activities of the Red Chinese, a far greater worry during that decade. While Red China in the '60s was portrayed as sinister and shadowy, Russia, as was the norm at this time in pop culture, was considered a joke of the 'Boris and Natasha' variety, and this episode is a perfect example. Throughout the episode, Burke is trailed by a humorless bumbling nitwit of a girl who slowly melts under the light of his charm. Curiously, the brighter, lighter, *Burke's Law* did a far better dissection of the miseries of Communism in the otherwise silly "Who Killed Super Sleuth?".

Also on hand, although sadly only in the pre-credits scenes, is Jamie Farr of *MASH,* who does a great turn as an even greater bumbler alongside Ben Astar's cliche Boradin. As with James Best, who ended up on *Dukes of Hazzard,* Farr did many odd bits at the bottom of the cast before becoming the cross-dressing Corporal Klinger. It's a shame he wasn't written as Burke's unhappy ally and comic relief instead of the unconvincing Phyllis Newman.

Newman played a number of brash, broad, loud parts at this time, notably as a 'Princess Sophie', a New York girl in a harem in *The Man from UNCLE* ("The Arabian Affair") and a 'Princess Wanakee' in *The Wild Wild West* ("The Night of the Raven"). She has a hard time with an impossible part, but she still seems miscast, coming across as far too American to be Russian. It's the sort of part to freeze up the Cold War again. Parley Baer, who plays Pavlov, was also more often cast in comedy than drama, although he plays his part relatively straight.

Canadian chameleon Donald Harron, discussed in the *Outer Limits* section, plays a British agent, Nina Shipman (also seen in *Burke's Law*) has the secondary female role as an American agent in Switzerland. Naturally, these roles are played straight. "James Bond would have got both of them", says Harron's agent after dispensing with an uncredited Fred Carson as a Russian agent. "Sure, but do you know how much he gets for a picture?" replies Burke.

Despite writing dozens and dozens of western novels and TV scripts, writer Sam Peeples is probably destined to be best known

for writing the second *Star Trek* pilot, "Where No Man Has Gone Before". The credit stood him in good stead when westerns went out of fashion, and he found himself writing for sci-fi cartoon shows in the 1970s. This cliched secret agent caper was certainly a one-off in his career, but he also contributed a single script to *The Girl from UNCLE* at around this time, so perhaps he just fancied a slice of the spy-fi action. Whatever the story behind the diversion, he swiftly went back to westerns, creating both *The Legend of Custer* and *Lancer.*

**Terror in a Tiny Town (two parts)**

wr. Marc Brandel, dir. Murray Golden

A security officer at an atomic research station goes berserk in a bar and the investigation takes Burke to the small town of Sorrel, where the population is being slowly but surely brainwashed by a right-wing radio station.

*with Lynn Loring (Anna Rodriguez/Ann Rogers), Robert Middleton (Judge Jed Hawke), Kevin McCarthy (D.A. Bill Adams), Patricia Owens (Sharon O'Brien), Joan Huntington (Joan Lineker), Skip Homeier (Paul Lineker), Carl Benton Reid (American contact), Harry Basch (Harlan O'Brien), John Qualen (Richard Prince), James Edwards (John Norton/shoeshine contact), Robert Donner (Ross Stanton), Monica Keating (Ruth), Martin Blaine (Wilson), Troy Melton (Taylor), Don Haggerty, Paul Sorenson (police officers), Don Gazzaniga (agent)*

Apart from a cluttered and complicated cast of characters, there doesn't seem enough here for a two-parter. As it's obvious what's going on and how it's being done, where's the incentive to come back for a second part? However, the producers presumably knew that the series was done for at this point, and perhaps were just finishing off their obligations. On the other hand, the absence of a 'to be continued' sting at the end of part one, and no 'last time' resume, plus the use of the episode title without a 'part one/part two' designation suggests that this might not even have *been* a two-parter initially, but a double-length episode. Was the network going to start the series after the Christmas break with a double-length story to give it a boost in a new time-slot, and then decided to cancel after all? We can only guess. But it's a very clumsy break.

Although the two 'taken-over' towns in *Mission: Impossible* were both Communist cels, the 'enemy within' storyline of a mad right-wing General or politician planning a coup, as here, also occasionally turned up in films and TV over the years; various examples that come to mind would be "The November Plan" for Stephen Cannell's *City of Angels* (he often used this storyline), the *Airwolf* episode "Firestorm", and the feature films *The Manchurian Candidate, Seven Days in May* and *Twilight's Last Gleaming*. The story also has the feel of an *Invaders* episode, particularly with Kevin McCarthy of *Invasion of the Body Snatchers* as one of the chief participants. Skip Homeier also appeared in a similar storyline in *Voyage to the Bottom of the Sea* ("The Day the World Ended"), as a Senator who hypnotises the entire crew of the submarine.

Burke's boss at MX-3 is a complete disbelieving moron in this one, without explanation. Why wouldn't he trust Burke's judgement, particularly when there's an atomic research establishment involved? He's *so* stupid and obstructive that you begin to wonder if he's part of the conspiracy himself, but it turns out to be just bad scriptwriting. On the subject of stupid, couldn't anybody go check out the actual radio station? Sabotage it, even?

Director Golden uses a curious and clever trick to hammer home when the citizens of Sorrel are spouting pre-programmed thoughts — he stops the background music cold and goes in for a close-up. It's a clever and effective conceit in an episode that is almost all talk. One exception is an excellent sequence that even *The Invaders* or its predecessors never pulled off, as Burke is jostled, intimidated, pursued, and ultimately beaten up by dozens of the townspeople on a street set often used in *Honey West*.

The 'seconds to spare' countdown ending is a bit corny, okay, a lot corny, better suited to kiddie classics like *Stingray* or *Thunderbirds*, although there's a good tag this time, as we note that not *all* bigotry is down to brainwashing.

series ends

## The Green Hornet

**September 9th ,1966 — March 24th, 1967**

With the phenomenal overnight success of the *Batman* TV series, producer William Dozier looked around, at the request of the network, for further crimefighting super-heroes to bring to television. After abortive attempts to create *Dick Tracy* and *Wonder Woman* series, with a dreary pilot and disastrously misconceived test footage respectively, Dozier settled on *The Green Hornet,* a creation for radio by George Trendle and Fran Striker (the Hornet actually predates *Batman's* creation in 1939 by three years). Trendle and Striker had brought the more famous Lone Ranger to radio and TV, and the Green Hornet was actually conceived as a descendant of the legendary western icon. Whereas the Lone Ranger rode the range on trusty steed Silver and with faithful ally Tonto at his side, the Hornet sped around the crime-infested streets of an unidentified big city in his "rolling arsenal" the Black Beauty (in the series, a customised Ford Chrysler Imperial) driven by faithful aide Kato. Publisher and media magnate Britt Reid (the '60s series was updated to give the newspaperman a TV station too) was the true identity of the Hornet, and the son of Dan Reid, the Lone Ranger's nephew (so eliminating the thorny subject of who Lone Ranger John Reid might have sired a son with).

*Van Williams and Bruce Lee as the Hornet and Kato in action with the Black Beauty*

The significant item about the Green Hornet was that he was a vigilante, and worse still, a criminal in the eyes of the outside world. Like Batman, the Hornet had a dual identity, but unlike Batman, was assumed by the world at large to be a super-criminal--he fought crime by betraying the criminal operations he muscled their way into by striking up an unwanted alliance with the hoods through force and then betraying them at the first opportunity. These collusions were brought about by intimidation, with the wicked Hornet's sting to show the boys meant business. If you were really unlucky--and many mob goons were—you'd be on the receiving end of a swift kung-fu kick from the Hornet's black-clad chauffeur, the loyal Kato (the legendary Bruce Lee). All the Hornet's plots to bring down gangsters and murderers were built around the false notion that he wanted to blackmail the murderers or grab a piece of the gangsters' action for himself. In fact, he only wanted justice... and Reid was not averse, in several episodes, to using the media toward his own crimefighting ends--planting false stories to deceive gangsters or bring murderers out into the open, for example. As the series' rather simplistic stories had the Hornet and Kato treating the bad guys in exactly the same way a super-hero crimefighter would, posing as a bad guy himself rarely made much sense.

To further complicate matters, the city's district attorney was in collusion with him, one of the series' many unintentionally amusing moments coming from Walter Brooke's D.A. Frank Scanlon--a character invented for the TV show to legitimise the Hornet's activities--smartly nipping around deserted alleyways to sneak into the Hornet's hideaway, a suspicious and furtive activity for a prominent public servant that would have made a meaty front page story--had the media not already been under the control of the Green Hornet's alter-ego anyway, of course! Also in on the secret was Reid's loyal secretary Lenore (Casey) Case, portrayed by Wende Wagner, and of course Kato, his chauffeur and manservant, portrayed by 1970s kung-fu icon Bruce Lee. Lee, who actually had to slow his martial arts moves down because the camera couldn't pick them up, learned to act on the *Green Hornet* show, and it cost a lot of stunt men a lot of medical bills! The only person rather unkindly out of the loop was the Hornet-hating and perpetually enraged crime reporter Mike Axford, played with popping veins by Lloyd Gough, whose ignorance of Reid's dual identity provided the series with a number of suspenseful moments when the crusading newshound blundered into the Hornet's scams, and relegated the poor fellow to comic relief for the wrap-up scenes at the end of each adventure. Beneath the living room of Britt Reid's townhouse was a green-hued garage which hid the Hornet's slick black slab of a car with rockets between the headlights and guns behind 'em, plus a mobile spy satellite

*Van Williams as Britt Reid, with Wende Wagner as Lenore Case (inset: Bruce Lee kicks bad guy butt as Kato)*

in the back. Other gimmicks included a device that spread ice on the road in their wake, and brushes that swept away their tyre tracks. Whereas the Lone Ranger had a mere six silver bullets in his gun, the Hornet's car was a veritable armored tank, and the Hornet himself carried a gas gun and painful-looking zapper known as the Hornet Sting.

The infamous Hornet Sting was one of those delightful props--like the Bat Cycle and the UNCLE car--that never worked the way it was supposed to, and the device was forever flying out of the cane and embedding itself in the set; eventually, Williams resorted to discarding the trigger and operating it manually! Filming on location in Malibu was also no picnic for Williams, who--clad in the Hornet's overcoat, hat and mask--shed pounds of weight in fight scenes (he had no fight double, and neither of course, did Lee) and inside the baking hot car he nicknamed "Black Ugly".

Like Batman at Columbia, the Green Hornet had also already been immortalised in two early movie house serials, but for Universal, *The Green Hornet* in 1939 and *The Green Hornet Strikes Again,* in 1940. Consequently, costuming was never a problem, as this had already been decided by the pulp magazines and the serials. Kato continued to wear his chauffeur's uniform and mask; the Hornet simply ditched his full face mask for a more actor-friendly eye mask. Like Batgirl's mask, this underwent a few changes for practicality; after the first episode was shot ("Programmed for Death", which ran third), the mask was revised and reformed from a

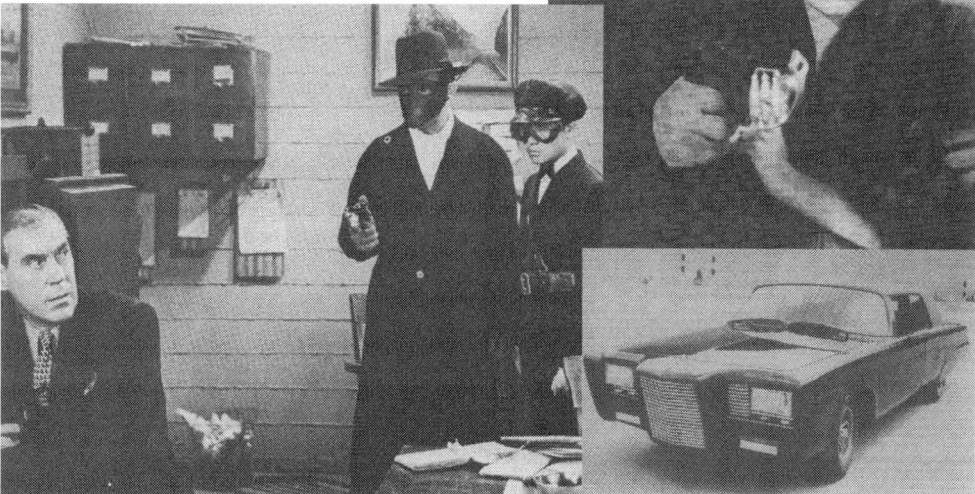

cast of the actor's face to keep it comfortable and secure. Oddly, given the instant success of the 1960s *Batman* and television's tendency never to buck a winning formula, the decision was taken to play *The Green Hornet* straight, with no campy villains, no colorful sets and bizarre camera angles, and no cliffhanger endings... and this, confounding audience expectations, among other factors such as the show's scheduling and cheapness of budget, was perceived as why the Hornet never caught on in the same way as the Caped Crusader.

Batmania died relatively quickly (ratings were high only for a year or so before dropping sharply), but the *Batman* series still outlived *The Green Hornet*, which lasted only a single season of 26 episodes. Despite the obvious and intentional clash of styles, Dozier still had the Hornet and Kato put in a cameo appearance in the ongoing window gag on *Batman* (episode 41, "The Spell of Tut"), and--in a desperate attempt to boost the Hornet's ratings--initiated a memorable and enjoyable team-up episode in March 1967, with the Hornet and Kato plunged head-first into the wacky *Batman* universe for an encounter with Roger C. Carmel (*Star Trek's* Harry Mudd) as freaky philatelist Colonel Gumm (episodes 85 and 86, "A Piece of the Action"/"Batman's Satisfaction"; legend has it that Bruce Lee terrorised Burt Ward on set). Opinions differed as to whether *The Green Hornet* should have followed the *Batman* formula more faithfully, with Trendle

surprisingly for, and series star Van Williams emphatically against. Indeed, Williams looks much more comfortable as an actor when playing wealthy womaniser Britt Reid than the stiff trench-coated Green Hornet; and Williams and Lee particularly disliked doing the *Batman* crossover. "Trendle complained about the lack of humor" series lead Van Williams told *Starlog* magazine twenty years later in 1988. "Instead of doing it like the radio show, he thought it would have been better to have done it like *Batman*. I didn't agree with that. We tried to make it as truthful as you could be with a guy running around in a mask. I feel proud about that, and I don't care what anybody says".

Although each episode was complete in itself, *The Green Hornet* featured two-part stories occasionally in a vain attempt by Dozier to convince the ABC network to expand the show to an hour (had the *Batman* series not been flagging in the ratings by now, he might have got his wish). By far the most bizarre of these two-parters was "Invasion from Outer Space", one of the last stories filmed, and signalling a very definite change of direction into more fantastic storylines. This features poor Larry D. Mann, thanklessly clad in full B-movie regalia as a silver-suited would-be space invader in outfits that look like they've been swiped from the neighboring Irwin Allen productions (and almost certainly were). In fact, he is not an alien invader at all, but mad Doctor Mabuse, a hoaxer who, with his similarly garbed henchmen and golden girl Vamma (game starlet Linda Gaye Scott), manages to cause offscreen Wellesian chaos before his ulterior motives are revealed. It's marvellous trash, reminiscent of the Republic serials and, paradoxically, the Jack Schiff 1950s *Batman* comics, and an amusing diversion from the usual gangland capers. When the series was cancelled, Van Williams had mixed feelings; it had been an uncomfortable show to film, and he saw the series going in wilder directions that he didn't approve of.

There was much to like about *The Green Hornet*, but also much that disappointed. One of the most obvious characteristics of the show, and the one factor that united all the show's failings, was its cheapness. The bargain basement budgets meant that no-name actors stood on shabby sets reading lame dialogue for famously cheap and fast directors, and less forgivably, the montage that accompanied the wonderful theme music was slapdash and careless; the pictures could and should have been much better. The writers, although competent providers of pulp fiction for paperbacks, film and TV, were the cheapest available, many of them authors of little-known B-westerns from the '50s. The directors likewise, even including the notorious William 'One-Shot' Beaudine, a Poverty Row hack given his nickname for never reshooting a scene, no matter what went wrong; at the same time he was working on *The Green Hornet* he turned out the infamous Z-movies *Billy the Kid vs. Dracula* and *Jesse James meets Frankenstein's Daughter!* These contributors were so used to working with budgets that didn't allow them to do much that this habit permeated the stories. Many of the functions that had been built into Dean Jeffries' customised *Green Hornet* vehicle--the 'rolling arsenal' the Black Beauty--were never even employed in the series as the writers didn't know they were there! Even those devices that were used were not employed often enough. And when the show did manage to secure the services of quality performers, fine character actors like Lloyd Bochner, Victor Jory, and Robert Strauss were given nothing to work with. The show did not need high camp scripts or deranged super-villains (although it might have helped), just a little more care and imagination.

Still, the show had several things working in its favor as well--a dazzling theme, with saxophonist Al Hirt rendering a jazz version of *Flight of the Bumblebee* (swiped to great effect by Quentin Tarantino for his Tokyo motorbike sequence in *Kill Bill*), wonderfully sleazy, jazzy background music from Billy May that differentiated it from most other shows on the air, and the perfect casting of Van

Williams and Bruce Lee as the Green Hornet and Kato. There were memorable moments—Lee's dazzling kung-fu displays that sent several of Bennie Dobbins' stunt men to casualty; the Black Beauty under attack from a ray gun; a waterfront assault by frogmen; an aerial bombardment of the Black Beauty by gangsters dropping mortars from a helicopter; and the aforementioned alien invasion hoax by a disgruntled scientist with bottle glasses and silver-suited henchmen, aided by a blonde bombshell who shoots electrical bolts from her fingertips (the only episode to move from gangland action into outright fantasy).

Among other guest players of interest were John Carradine as a Jack the Ripper style wax museum murderer, Ralph Meeker, Raymond St. Jacques, and Paul Carr as angry war veterans, Cesare Danova, Jason Evers, Richard Anderson, Michael Strong, Mako, Lynda Day George of *Mission: Impossible, Star Trek's* Jeffrey Hunter and Angelique Pettyjohn, and Barbara Babcock of *Hill Street Blues* in one of her earliest roles as one of Britt Reid's ladyfriends. However, few of these welcome faces had much to do. The series was also graced with some remarkably silly pseudo-pulp magazine episode titles, including "Eat, Drink, and Be Dead", "Corpse of the Year", and--my favorite—"The Frog is a Deadly Weapon".

Somewhere along the way, someone decided the Hornet worked best as a creature of the night, but unfortunately the wafer-thin budgets didn't allow for expensive night shooting. Consequently, the series always had a muddy and distinctly phoney look, as studio shots of the Black Beauty whizzing round the backlots were mixed with awful back projections of an entirely different city inside the car, and hopelessly ineffectual day-for-night shooting everywhere else; just turning on the car's striking green headlights and putting a filter over the lens didn't alter the fact that the sun was clearly shining away brilliantly and throwing shadows everywhere, and these incongruities, mixed with the night time stock shots of the Black Beauty used every time the crimefighters left the garage, made for a blatantly obvious mish-mash of unmatched shots whenever the car--the series' ace-in-the-hand--was featured. This shoddy day-for-night shooting, and the way the shots often didn't match up, obscured the actors, costumes, and actions. In daylight, the car looked less impressive, having been repainted a dirty grey when the original black gloss proved too restrictive for the

studio lighting. With many Americans still using black and white sets in the mid-'60s, the filtered lenses must have made the pictures even worse. The green-hued garage, which did look good, was concealed behind a mock advertising billboard in an alleyway (a device brazenly ripped off by the 1980s series *Streethawk*), and many of the locations used will be readily familiar to regular viewers of 1960s TV; the first street the Black Beauty turns into after leaving the garage, for example, is clearly the European street used in the *Time Tunnel* episodes "Secret Weapon", "Invasion", and "Reign of Terror".

Of the cast, Bruce Lee is of course legend. He appeared as "the little dragon" in a number of films in his home country of China before travelling to America and securing his roles in *The Green Hornet* TV series and the 1969 James Garner movie *Marlowe*; during the 1971-'72 TV season he had a recurring role in the detective series *Longstreet*, with *The Naked City's* James Franciscus, in which he appeared in four episodes. The first of his famous kung-fu movies was dated 1972, and he knocked out a non-stop parade of them before his untimely death in 1973 from a tragic mixing of medicines, including *Fists of Fury* (aka *The Big Boss/The Chinese Connection*), *Enter the Dragon*, and *Return of the Dragon* (aka *The Way of the Dragon*). His final film, *Game of Death*, was completed with little taste or compassion after his death with a body double, unleashing a slew of opportunistic imitations in the months that followed. His son was the ill-fated Brandon Lee, who died in a props accident during filming of another dark comic-book project, the feature film *The Crow*. Bizarrely, this film was completed with a double as well.

Attempts were made to cash in on Lee's later superstar status in the 1970s by sticking episodes of *The Green Hornet* together into two feature-length travesties titled *Kato and the Green Hornet* and *Fury of the Dragon*, and these were later released on video and DVD. *Kato and the Green Hornet* consisted of the episodes "The Hunter and the Hunted", "The Preying Mantis" and "Invasion from Outer Space", while *Fury of the Dragon* was cobbled together out of "Trouble with Prince Charming", "Bad Bet on a 459 Silent", "The Ray is for Killing", and "The Secret of the Sally Bell". To add insult to injury--Lee is of course toplined over true series' lead Van Williams--fight scenes from other episodes were inserted to pad out the action scenes, including clips from "Programmed for Death", "Ace in the Hole", "Hornet Save Thyself", and "The Frog is a Deadly Weapon" among others, which rendered the entire storyline temporarily incomprehensible. Almost inevitably, some video and/ or DVD jackets further confused the issue by relating the wrong plot-lines.

Lloyd Gough was corny but fun as the show's blustering comic relief, apoplectic crime journalist Mike Axford, the only regular cast member unaware of Reid's dual identity (on the radio show, Axford had been Reid's bodyguard, a pointless role with Kato around), and Wende Wagner was beautiful as eye candy and resourceful damsel in distress Lenore (Casey) Case. Only Walter Brooke's potentially intriguing D.A. Scanlon, introduced by the producers to legitimise the Hornet's dubious activities for TV sensibilities, was dull. As with the show's gimmicks and gadgets, none of these characters were utilised with as much imagination as they should have been.

Van Williams (real name Van Zandt Jarvis Williams), a Warner Brothers contract player of the '50s and early '60s who previously appeared in the detective series *Bourbon Street Beat* and its spin-off *Surfside Six* before donning the Hornet's mask, has no regrets. With the demise of *The Green Hornet,* he decided to retire from acting (although he did try his luck again in the 1979 Stephen Cannell pilot *The Night Rider*). "I never liked the business, even though I spent 25 years in it" he told an interviewer. "I grew up on a ranch and dealt with people who were very honest. Your word was your bond".

Williams was a reserve deputy for the L.A. sheriff's office, had worked undercover for the government, taught skin-diving, spent time as a salvage diver for the Navy, and worked in mountain rescue; he was hardly going to miss the supposed glamor of acting. It is also often overlooked, because of the inevitable dominance of Bruce Lee, that Van Williams performed his own fight scenes.

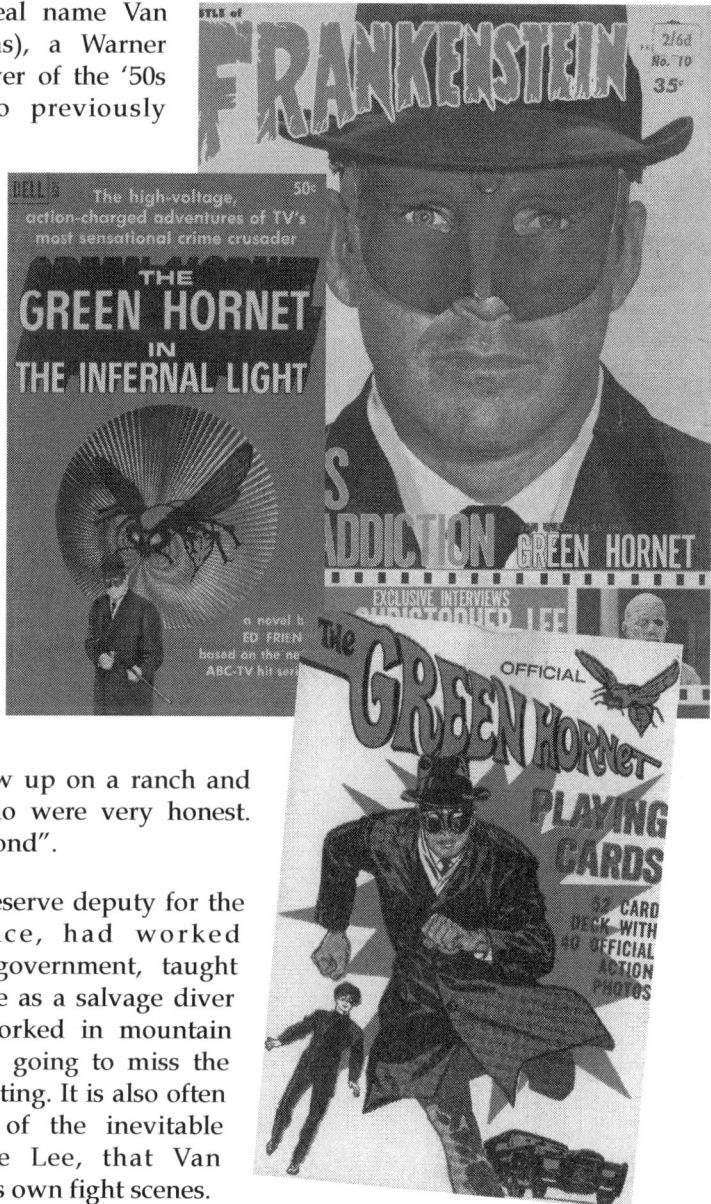

Like many actors in supposedly forgotten old TV shows, Williams is amused and intrigued by his new-found celebrity thanks to cable and satellite re-runs, and like others of that period who had either dismissed or resented their '60s TV careers, Williams has adjusted his attitude to the show, and although still disappointed with the failings of the series, is proud to be associated with the legend. "I get all sorts of fan mail now" he said in the year 2000. "More now than I ever did thirty years ago. I don't know what's going on out there. I think what it might be is a little nostalgia. Most of the mail is from people who are too young to have remembered the radio show. So they saw the TV show, and liked what they saw". With his money from acting, he started one of the first cellular 'phone businesses, still finding time to work as a deputy reserve sheriff (imagine being arrested by the Green Hornet) and oversee a number of cattle ranches in Texas! Lloyd Gough and Walter Brooke were veteran jobbing actors who both worked steadily in bit parts before and after *The Green Hornet.* Wende Wagner's films included *Rio Conchos, Destination Inner Space, Rosemary's Baby,* and *Guns of the Magnificent Seven.*

All the supporting cast have since passed on. Van Williams did, however, briefly return to acting in 1993 for a cameo role--as a film director in a scene for *Dragon--the Bruce Lee Story* in which he was seen directing a fictitious scene for... *The Green Hornet!* "Of all my shows" said Williams in 2000, "ninety percent of the fan mail I get is for *The Green Hornet,* and it was the least successful I did!".

## The Green Hornet

### episode guide

### (1966-'67)

*regular cast: Van Williams (as Britt Reid/The Green Hornet), Bruce Lee (Kato), Walter Brooke (D.A. Frank Scanlon), Wende Wagner (Casey), Lloyd Gough (Mike Axford)*

## The Silent Gun

wr. Ken Pettus, dir. Leslie Martinson

The Green Hornet pits two murderous gangsters against each other for possession of a gun that makes no noise or flash at all when fired...

*with Lloyd Bochner (Dan Carley), Charles Francisco (Al Trump), Kelly Jean Peters (Jackie Cameron), Ed McCready (Sgt. Olson), Max Kleven (heavy), Al McGranary (minister), Breland Rice, Bob Harvey (police officers)*

Alongside Victor Jory, Robert Strauss, and John Carradine, Lloyd Bochner was one of the few then well-known names to appear on *The Green Hornet*, and was a familiar face throughout the '60s and '70s as a

cowardly bad guy. He made several appearances on the two *UNCLE* series, and enhanced episodes of *Voyage to the Bottom of the Sea, Honey West, Mission: Impossible, Six Million Dollar Man, The Bionic Woman, Charlie's Angels, The Amazing Spider-Man, The A-Team, Manimal,* and *Superboy* with his villainy. Here, he plays Dan Carley in much the same manner as his more aspirational hood in the gangster classic *Point Blank*. Kelly Jean Peters also appeared on cult shows *The Monkees* and *The Invaders*.

Ken Pettus wrote more scripts for *The Green Hornet* series than anyone, and appears to have been the rewrite man of choice. He totals nine episodes, including two two-parters —"The Silent Gun", "Beautiful Dreamer" (with Lorenzo Semple

Jnr.), "The Preying Mantis Kills" (with *Batman's* Charles Hoffman), "Deadline for Death", "Freeway to Death", "Corpse of the Year", and "Trouble for Prince Charming", before moving on to script numerous episodes of *The Wild Wild West* and *Mission: Impossible*. He would tackle any genre, but wrote most extensively for westerns.

Leslie Martinson was a prolific TV helmsman, formerly with MGM and Republic, where he directed Roy Rogers films; he then spent the vast bulk of his career at Warners, directing episodes of virtually all their westerns and detective series. He directed the *Batman* story "The Penguin Goes Straight"/"Not Yet, He Ain't", and then the *Batman* feature film, followed by two episodes of *The Green Hornet* ("The Silent Gun" and "The Frog is a Deadly Weapon") and the Raquel Welch spy thriller *Fathom*. After a stint on *Mission: Impossible*, he continued his association with comic-book fare, helming episodes of *The Six Million Dollar Man, Wonder Woman, Buck Rogers in the 25th Century, The Powers of Matthew Star, Manimal*, and *Airwolf*.

Although not the first episode filmed (that is clearly "Programmed for Death" as it features an early discarded design of the Hornet mask), this is very much the blueprint for the majority of episodes.

### Give 'em Enough Rope

wr. Gwen Bagni, Paul Dubov, dir. Seymour Robbie

The Green Hornet and Kato pursue a black-clad assassin while breaking an insurance scam.

*with Diana Hyland (Claudia Bromley), Mort Mills (Alex Colony), Jerry Ayres (Pete), Joe Sirola (Charlie), David Renard (Joe Sweek), Ken Strange (heavy)*

After an intriguing opening scene (after which the charismatic Joe Sirola, a familiar hood from numerous 1960s and '70s crime shows and three times *UNCLE* guest player, is never seen again), this episode turns into a rather banal insurance scam episode. The story promised, featuring a tall, rope-swinging black-clad assassin who's a sort of cross between Spider-Man and a ninja, never unfolds. Diana Hyland, another *UNCLE* guest star, brightens up proceedings as a shallow lawyer.

Mort Mills, who plays the insurance swindler, appears to be performing his own stunts as the assassin, as he makes the same moves out of costume in the closing fight. He also had credits in episodes of *My Favorite Martian, Bewitched, Mission: Impossible, The Wild Wild West, The Invaders,* and *Land of the*

*Giants.* After years of bit-parts, including *Star Trek* and *The Invaders* at around this time, Jerry Ayres had lengthier stays in the soaps during the late '70s and 1980s. Bit player Ken Strange returns in "Crime Wave" and "Hornet, Save Thyself".

This is the first of four episodes directed by Seymour Robbie, whose numerous directing credits also include episodes of *The Man from UNCLE, Honey West, Amos Burke--Secret Agent,* and *Wonder Woman.* Writers Gwen Bagni and Paul Dubov were regular contributors to *Burke's Law* and fellow pulp crimefighter *Honey West.* This was their only contribution to *The Green Hornet.*

**Programmed for Death**

wr. Lewis Reed, Jerry Thomas, dir. Larry Peerce

A Sentinel reporter meets a bizarre end when he is forced out of a window to his death by a leopard. The trail of his murderer takes the Green Hornet to a man who can make diamonds.

*with Signe Hasso (Yolande de Lukens), Richard Cutting (Professor Miller), Don Eitner (Pat Allen), Norman Leavitt (zookeeper), Sheila Leighton (Scanlon's secretary), John Alvar (de Lukens' aide), Gary Owens (newsreader), Pat Tidy (cleaning woman)*

A perfect example of why the show should have filled an hour slot (de Lukens has no sooner been introduced than is defeated--offscreen), the episode highlights are the scenes with the leopard and the sequence in which the Hornet is locked in a freezer and blasts out with his Hornet sting.

This episode also features a prime example of that ridiculous contrivance of all masked crimefighter fantasies where Axford is not only face to face with his boss Britt Reid, a man he's known for years and sees every day, and not only doesn't recognise him under the flimsy Hornet mask, but actually discusses Reid with him! (He also emerges remarkably unscathed after his tussle with the leopard, not a spot of blood or single tear in his clothing!).

Signe Hasso's other appearances in cult TV include *The Outer Limits*, and the bizarre transexual of *The Girl from UNCLE* episode "The UNCLE Samurai Affair". Don Eitner also appears in episodes of *Star Trek, The Invaders, Lost in Space*, and *Mission: Impossible*. Norman Leavitt usually played hick roles, including bits in *Boris Karloff's Thriller, The Twilight Zone, The Addams Family, The Man from UNCLE*, and *Lost in Space*. Sheila Leighton also appeared in *The Man from UNCLE, Get Smart*, and *Star Trek*.

This was the first episode written by Jerry Thomas, also the series' assistant producer, working from a premise by *Peter Gunn* and *Burke's Law* writer Lewis Reed. He wrote two further, "The Hunters and the Hunted" and "Seek, Stalk, and Destroy", and later wrote single episodes of *The Wild Wild West, Land of the Giants*, and *Mission: Impossible*. Larry Peerce divided his time between directing episodes of *Batman* ("The Bookworm Turns/ While Gotham City Burns", "The Spell of Tut/Tut's Case is Shut", and "The Devil's Fingers/The Dead Ringers") and *The Green Hornet* ("Programmed for Death" and "Crime Wave").

## Crime Wave

wr. Sheldon Stark, dir. Larry Peerce

who mysteriously predicts crimes that he, of course, is committing, with a view to eventually sending the cops in the wrong direction while he pulls off The Big One, as seen in Dozier's unsold *Dick Tracy*

The occupants of an airplane are gassed, and the Hornet framed for the theft of valuable jewels. It's all part of an elaborate plan to steal a gold bullion shipment by exploiting the talents of a computer operator.

*with Peter Haskell (Abel Marcus), Sheilah Wells (Laura Spinner), Ron Burke (Joe), Gary Owens (newsreader), Jennifer Stuart (stewardess), Dee Carroll (woman on 'plane), Wayne Sutherlin (party guest), Breeland Rice (cop), Jack Garner, Ken Strange (security guards)*

This is the first episode filmed after the pilot, and features all the scenes from which stills are taken for the lazy and scrappy opening credits. It also features one of Dozier's favorite plots, the bad guy

pilot and the *Batman* King Tut story "The Unkindest Tut of All" (Victor Buono the villain in both). This fellow, clad in a devil costume for the Hornet's confrontation with him at a costume party, purely to add some comic-book color to the proceedings, is using a super-computer which, at the time, couldn't possibly have predicted anything (information has to be put into a computer in order for information to come out, something the villain's innocent dupe computer expert, the girl of the show, should surely have known). Perhaps in recognition of this absurdity, the background score suddenly breaks into horrendous discordant comedy music of the sort that plays in cartoons when wacky 'futuristic' things are happening.

Peter Haskell was a nondescript jobbing actor who also appeared in episodes of *The Outer Limits, The Man from UNCLE, Land of the Giants, Mission: Impossible,* and *The Bionic Woman.* In 1979, he appeared in the unsold pilot for another vintage crimefighter, *Mandrake the Magician.*

Sheldon Stark was a former comic book writer now providing similar fare for TV. His credits include *Voyage to the Bottom of the Sea, The Man from UNCLE, Batman, Land of the Giants,* and *Mission: Impossible.*

**The Frog is a Deadly Weapon**

wr. William Stuart, dir. Leslie Martinson

When a small-time detective is dragged into the water and drowned by frogmen, the Hornet is put on the trail of a wanted criminal hiding out at the docks under a new identity.

*with Victor Jory (Charles Delaclaire), Thordis Brandt (Nedra Vallen), George Robotham (Nat Pyle), Barbara Babcock (Elaine), Rudy Hansen (fisherman), Roger Heldfond (attendant)*

Victor Jory was at the end of his career when he began doing television in the 1960s, his most memorable appearances being for two quite deranged Irwin Allen episodes, "Fires of Death" for *Voyage to the Bottom of the Sea* as a crazed immortal, and *The Time Tunnel's* "Pirates of Dead Man's Island" as a cruel, demented pirate. He made a meal of both, and next to these, slighter, more sober roles on *I Spy* and *The Green Hornet* didn't really do him justice. Nevertheless, it was good to see a real actor on *The Green Hornet,* and Jory lights up the screen whenever he's on.

Beautiful Thordis Brandt was usually background decoration in '60s spy fare, making several appearances in *The Girl from UNCLE,* and enjoys good exposure here as the scheming ill-fated Euro-starlet.

Busy stunt man George Robotham's career goes all the way back to the Columbia serial *Atom Man vs. Superman.* A big man, he often doubled for Rock Hudson.

This is the first appearance of Barbara Babcock as Britt Reid's spoilt but patient romantic interest. Wende Wagner has a little more to do than usual in this episode, the highlight of which is the attack by the frogmen.

## Eat, Drink and Be Dead

wr. Richard Landau, dir. Murray Golden

Britt Reid's campaign against modern-day bootleggers puts him in their firing line.

*with Jason Evers (Henry Dirk), Harry Lauter (Brannigan), Harry Fleer, William McClennan, Eddie Ness, Shep Sanders (hoods and heavies), Jo Ann Milam (secretary)*

Jason (formerly Herb) Evers was a nondescript jobbing actor of the period with credits in *The Invaders, The Wild Wild West, Star Trek, Mission: Impossible,* and many westerns, who has little to do here but drop explosives from a helicopter, the main showpiece of the episode. It's a rather noisy and conspicuous way to protect your secret distillery, especially as it's disguised as a dairy. Supporting player Harry Lauter, one of the best, appeared in numerous serials, westerns, and '50s sci-fi films, and is here the nervous bartender. At around this time he was seen to best effect in *Time Tunnel's* "Billy the Kid" and "Pirates of Dead Man's Island" episodes. As a half-hour diversion, this episode is fine, but with the already over-used cliche of Mike Axford's kidnapping occurring offscreen, we see yet again the value of a hour slot.

Richard Landau wrote low-budget movies in the '50s to order, before turning to television in the 1960s, where he wrote for *Voyage to the Bottom of the Sea, The Outer Limits, The Wild Wild West,* and in the '70s, *The Six Million Dollar Man.* Murray Golden directed for such '60s gems as *Honey West, Amos Burke--Secret Agent, Batman, The Time Tunnel, The Invaders,* and *Star Trek,* as well as handling five *Mission: Impossible.*

## Beautiful Dreamer (two parts)

wr. Ken Pettus, Lorenzo Semple Jnr., dir. Allen Reisner

A mysterious 'phone call leads the Hornet to a murder scene, and then to a health club where the clients are being brainwashed into committing crimes for the owner.

*with Geoffrey Horne (Peter Eden), Pamela Curran (Vanessa Vane), Maurice Manson (Mr. Cavenaugh), Jean-Marie (Dorothy), Victoria George (Harriet), Marina Ghane (Helga), Barbara Gates (Mary), Henry Hunter (Professor Wylie), Gary Owen (newsreader)*

Geoffrey Horne gave perhaps the best performance of his brief television career as the smarmy Peter Eden, and two times *UNCLE* guest star Pamela Curran (see *The Invaders* section for credits) flounces about floridly as the socialite millionairess Vanessa Vane, a very *Batman*-like name. Not only did the *Batman* series swipe this already well-worn brainwashing storyline for the final episode in the series the following year, but it appears to have been one of the earliest scripts, if not the first, to be written for the *Green Hornet* series, as scenes from it were used in auditions and test reels (in non-broadcast test footage, Jan Murray plays Reid and a more dashing, less laid-back Hornet, Cindy Wood is Casey, Richard O'Brien works his buns off as Mike Axford, and Jeff Corey pitches in as the bad guy, with only Bruce Lee already cast as Kato). Presumably, the original was written by Semple, who provided the *Batman* pilot script and much early inspiration, and then revised by *Hornet* regular Pettus to fit the series once in production. If so, then the decision to avoid camp and do the *Hornet* series straight, was not a foregone conclusion when the series was in pre-production. Some decidedly *Batman*-style dialogue remains in the script, particularly when Scanlon discusses the crime wave.

Allen Reisner directed another four stories after this two-parter, making a grand total of six episodes.

### The Ray is for Killing

wr. Lee Loeb, dir. William Beaudine

The Black Beauty must face a powerful laser beam head on when Britt Reid becomes the victim of a costly art theft.

*with Robert McQueeney (Thornton Richardson), Grant Woods (Steve), Bill Baldwin (science editor), Mike Mahoney (detective), Bob Gunner (police officer), Jim Raymond (driver)*

A routine story, the highlight being the nonsense with the laser beam burning up the police car and hospital room, and later taking on the Black Beauty. Bizarrely, Richardson and his goons deal face to face with both the Green Hornet and Britt Reid, and despite the exact same facial features and voice, never make a connection. Mike Axford complains about the science editor getting a raise over him, neatly overlooking a previous episode where he gets a fifteen percent raise! Note Wende Wagner's very '60s Op Art outfit when she sets off to deliver the ransom.

Robert McQueeney was a Warners contract player who worked his way through most of their cop and western series before appearing regularly in the short-lived and now forgotten war series *The Gallant Men*.

Grant Woods frequently turned up as a crewman on *Star Trek*, and also appears in episodes of *Batman* and *The Man from UNCLE*.

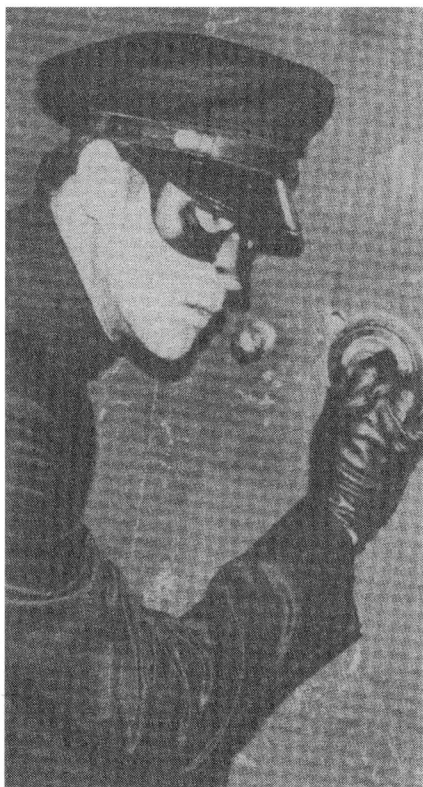

William Beaudine's reputation is discussed in the main feature, but there's an odd loud noise that may have been an accident, or may have been supposed to be replaced in post production as the bad guys burst in on McQueeney, whose look of confusion may or may not have been acting!

## The Preying Mantis Kills

wr. Charles Hoffman, Ken Pettus, dir. Norman Foster

The Hornet moves in when seedy thugs try to extend their protection racket into Chinatown.

*with Mako (Low Sung), Tom Drake (Duke Slate), Al Huang (Jimmy Kee), Lang Yun (Mary Chang), Keye Luke (Mr. Chang), Allen Jung (Wing Ho), Gary Owens (newsreader)*

This one, predictably enough, is Bruce Lee's episode, although one still wishes he had done more. Nevertheless, this is one of the better episodes, and an early pop culture reference to '70s fad kung fu.

Lee's adversary, Mako Iwamtsu, often simply billed as Mako, was frequently seen as a gimlet-eyed bad guy in 1960s TV, including classic *Amos Burke--Secret Agent* episode "The Prisoners of Doctor Sin" and to excellent effect in three editions of *I Spy*, particularly "Court of the Lion". The same year as his *Hornet* guest shot he turned up in a memorable *Time Tunnel* appearance, "Kill Two by Two", and in the 1970s kept super-heroes *The Incredible Hulk* and *Wonder Woman* busy. In short-lived and belated late-'70s spy entry *A Man Called Sloane* he appeared in an episode titled "Samurai", later appearing in episodes of *Fantasy Island, Voyagers, Greatest American Hero,* and the two *Conan* films. One of his more bizarre assignments was to provide the melodramatic opening narration for the *Dexter's Laboratory* cartoons! Still working in his later years, he played a book publisher in an early episode of *Frasier*, a series that often employed veteran '60s performers for small roles.

Keye Luke, acting in films since the 1930s, was the original Kato in the 1940 Columbia *Green Hornet* serials. During the 1960s, he also appeared in cult series *I Spy* and *Star Trek*, and provided voices for *Jonny Quest* and *Space Ghost*. In the 1970s, he took on his best known role, as Master Po in the *Kung Fu* series. Tom Drake's credits include episodes of *The Wild Wild West*, *Land of the Giants*, and *Kolchak--the Night Stalker*.

Familiar heavy Allen Jung also notched up three appearances in *I Spy*. The comedic closing scenes with Lloyd Gough's boorish Mike Axford are rapidly getting tiresome, but at least this one is amusing.

Charles Hoffman was one of the head writers on *Batman*. Norman Foster, appropriately enough, had directed numerous episodes of *Zorro* with Guy Williams in the '50s.

## The Hunters and the Hunted

wr. Jerry Thomas, dir. William Beaudine

A group of big game hunters looking for a new challenge decide to pick off gangsters... but their leader has a secret agenda.

*with Charles Bateman (Quentin Crane), Robert Strauss (Bud Crocker), Frank Gerstle (Mel Hurk), Douglas Evans (Stone), Rand Brooks (Conway), Bill Walker (barman), Dick Dial, Gene Le Bell (heavies)*

One of the more violent episodes, and--according to James Van Hise and his 1988 fan publication *The Green Hornet Book*--originally even more so, the filmed episode being considerably toned down from the original script, which had rifles replacing the bow-and-arrow wielding hunters, and Bateman dying impaled on spikes in a hidden pit.

The presence of veteran films and TV gangster specialist Robert Strauss raises the bar for this episode; Strauss was doing quite a bit of TV at this time, essaying no-goods in episodes of *The Munsters, The Man from UNCLE, Honey West, Bewitched, Get Smart,* and *Mister Terrific.*

Douglas Evans had appeared in the original Columbia serial version of *The Green Hornet* in 1939, as well as Republic's *King of the Rocket Men!*

Stunt player Dick Dial had appeared in *The Man From UNCLE's* "The Minus X Affair", and would be back for "Bad Bet on a 459 Silent". Stunt player Gene Le Bell was also a boxing match referee, and appears in episodes of *The Munsters, Mission: Impossible, I Spy, Land of the Giants, Kolchak--the Night Stalker, The Bionic Woman, The Gemini Man, The Man from Atlantis, Fantasy Island,* and *Knight Rider.*

## Deadline for Death

wr. Ken Pettus, dir. Seymour Robbie

Crime reporter Mike Axford is accused of a series of robberies and murder... but is reluctant to accept who framed him.

*with James Best (Yale Barton), Linda Day George (Ardis Talston), Jacques Aubuchon (Tubbs), Annazette Chase/Williams (telephone operator), Pat Patterson, Kirby Brumfield (cops), Glenn Wilder, Roy Clark (crooks)*

Before being saddled with the profitable but dead-end role of the corrupt comedy relief Sheriff Rosco in the gormless *Dukes of Hazzard* series in the late-'70s, James Best was an undistinguished, unrecognised, but talented actor in numerous roles--usually westerns, and usually lowlifes. Here he's on his usual top form as a sleazeball thief and murderer who has seduced a weak-willed friend of Mike's to betray him.

This one could easily have been a two-parter. Once again, the half-hour format denies any extrapolation or development of the characters, who become ciphers to take the Hornet and Kato to their rendezvous at the airport, where the showpiece is the Black Beauty taking on a departing aircraft. Absurdly, the Hornet calls Kato to rescue him from a locked door first, before an attempt is made to stop the 'plane, something Kato could easily have accomplished with the car on his own.

Lynda Day, soon to be billed as Lynda Day George, was a regular on some of the later episodes of *Mission: Impossible,* and also appears in episodes of *The Invaders, Wonder Woman,* and numerous *Fantasy Island* stories. Jacques Aubuchon frequently played shifty characters on such shows as *Voyage to the Bottom of the Sea, Bewitched, The Man from UNCLE, The Monkees,* and *Land of the Giants.* Annazette Chase/ Williams was a bit player frequently on *Burke's Law.*

**Secret of the Sally Bell**

wr. William Stuart, dir. Robert Friend

A courageous nurse is kidnapped when only a comatose crook knows the whereabouts of an illegal shipment of drugs on board a boat.

with Beth Brickell (Dr. Hannah Thomas), Warren Kemmerling (Bert Selden), Jacques Denbeaux (Gus Wander), Timothy Scott (Honey Boy), Ann Rexford (nurse), James Farley (police officer), Dave Perna, Greg Benedict (hoods)

This is one of the few occasions the half-hour format was right for the show. Dull, undistinguished performers and a simple, rather silly premise (for a stash of drugs known to be aboard a small vessel, the authorities would simply systematically dismantle the boat rivet by rivet, assuming they hadn't already found the cursory hiding place even a child could locate) make this a straightforward romp enlivened only by William Stuart's dialogue.

This is the second of four *Green Hornet* episodes by Stuart, the other three being "The Frog is a Deadly Weapon", "The Firefly", and "Alias the Scarf". He was probably the best writer the series had, in terms of ideas, although his stories were weak. Had anyone been supervising the series with care, Stuart would have made a good rewrite man. He also wrote three episodes of logic-free cult sci-fi series *Land of the Giants*.

As was so often the case in this series, the best scenes are the fights, the Hornet confronting the criminals, and the sequences with the Black Beauty. Often a dull episode was helped considerably by the big black car—"The Ray is for Killing", "Eat, Drink and Be Dead", "Deadline for Death", "Freeway to Death", etc.--and the highlight of this one is the Black Beauty attacking the assassin on auto-pilot.

**Freeway to Death**

wr. Ken Pettus, dir. Allen Reisner

Mike Axford must reluctantly ally himself with the Hornet to smash a phony insurance scam. The Hornet and Kato then confront a battalion of earth-movers at a construction site when they go to Axford's rescue.

with Jeffrey Hunter (Emmet Crown), John Hubbard (Clinton Giles), David Fresco (Wiggins), Reg Parton, Harvey Parry, Fred Krone (heavies)

A routine story about corruption in the building trade, with a strong central performance by Jeffrey Hunter. Absurdly, once again Axford fails to realise that the Hornet is his boss, despite sitting right next to him and discussing Britt Reid. For his part, the Hornet makes no attempt to disguise his voice or turn his head. The highlight of the episode is the Black Beauty's confrontation with the earth-diggers.

His career cut short by an early accidental death, Jeffrey Hunter's main claim to fame is as the first Captain of the Enterprise in *Star Trek*, where he appeared in the unsold pilot "The Cage", and later, in that same footage, the composite two-parter "The Menagerie". Although that was only two years earlier, he already looks older and fuller here. Bit player David Fresco's credits include episodes of *Honey West, Batman, Mission: Impossible, The Girl from UNCLE*, and *Night Gallery*. Harvey Parry would be back for "Seek, Stalk, and Destroy".

**May the Best Man Lose**

wr. Judith and Robert Guy Barrows, dir. Allen Reisner

When D.A. Scanlon is up for re-election, his opponent's ambitious brother ensures an explosive campaign.

*with Harold Gould (Calvin Ryland), Linden Chiles (Warren Ryland), Bill Phipps (Starkey), Stuart Nisbet (Quincy), Gary Owen (newsreader), Jim Drum (security man), Troy Melton, Robert Hoy (heavies)*

An interesting episode, well-written, and another that would have benefitted from the hour format that Dozier wanted. Scanlon is up for re-election as the D.A., but ironically the one thing that goes against him is the idea that the Green Hornet is a successful criminal that he hasn't been able to apprehend. Consequently, the Green Hornet could cost Scanlon the election. As the entire series hinges on the fact that the Hornet works alongside Scanlon to keep the city secure, the operation may be brought down by a too successful

cover story--a nice twist. Scanlon's opponent himself in a good man with good intentions, but his criminal brother is the liability that saves Scanlon's job. The scene where he is exposed is great fun.

This is one of Harold Gould's larger roles in the 1960s, after smaller bits in *The Man from UNCLE, Get Smart, Mission: Impossible*, and *The Invaders, The Wild Wild West*, and *I Dream of Jeannie* all twice. In the '70s, as he aged he looked warmer, and found a career in comedy roles; he was Rhoda's father in *Rhoda*, Rose's suitor in *Golden Girls*, and worked with both Woody Allen and Mel Brooks. Linden Chiles, by contrast, was busiest in the 1960s, appearing in *The Twilight Zone, The Munsters, My Favorite Martian, The Man from UNCLE, Land of the Giants*, and in the '70s, *The Six Million Dollar Man, The Bionic Woman, Logan's Run*, followed by *Buck Rogers in the 25th Century, The Incredible Hulk, Knight Rider, V*, and *Werewolf* in the '80s. He was Tony Newman's father in the classic Pearl Harbor episode of *The Time Tunnel*, and saucer-spotting David Vincent's angry, sceptical brother for *The Invaders*.

Troy Melton was one of television's busiest stunt men, and would be back for "Invasion from Outer Space". Stunt man Robert Hoy frequently appeared on *The Man from UNCLE*. Stuart Nisbet played several bits in *The Man from UNCLE*. Jim Drum played police officers in two early episodes of *Batman*.

Husband and wife writing team Judith and Robert Guy Barrows wrote together throughout the 1960s, but when Judith passed away in 1970 at just thirty-six, her partner stopped writing at that time.

They wrote cop shows, westerns, and medical dramas during their partnership, with *Green Hornet* something of an aberration. They would be back with "Bad Bet on a 459—Silent".

## The Hornet and the Firefly

wr. William Stuart, dir. Allen Reisner

Reid leads a suspected arsonist to investigate his own crimes under the ruse that the Green Hornet is the suspect.

*with Gerald S. O'Laughlin (Ben Wade), Russ Conway (Commissioner Dolan), Buff Brady (guard), Gary Owens (newsreader)*

This rather straightforward and simplistic story goes the only way it can in twenty minutes, with just one suspect for the mystery arsonist. Gerald O'Laughlin later became a regular cast member on short-lived super-hero crime show *Automan* in the '80s. Russ Conway frequently played authority figures and officials, and is doing the same here. He had a recurring role on *I Spy*. Gary Owens, who appeared in several episodes as a news reader, is best known as the voice of *Space Ghost*. He was also the announcer on *Rowan and Martin's Laugh-In*.

Wade's actions show little logic, particularly keeping Axford prisoner. Today, Wade wouldn't have to become the Firefly to get revenge for being given a desk job, he could simply launch a disability discrimination lawsuit!

## Seek, Stalk and Destroy

wr. Jerry Thomas, dir. George Waggner

Three embittered Korean war veterans steal a tank to break their former platoon leader out of jail, where he awaits execution for a murder he didn't commit.

313

*with Ralph Meeker (Earl Evans), Raymond St. Jacques (Hollis Silver), Paul Carr (Eddie Carter), John Baer (Brad Devlin), E.J. Andre, Harvey Parry (gate guards)*

The third and final episode written by associate producer Jerry Thomas (and the only one directed by *Batman* director George Waggner) is an unusual offering that veers from the usual--but welcome--Hornet vs. gangland scenario. A change of pace was welcome occasionally (but only occasionally), and this story--predating the theme of *The A-Team*--has three veterans of Korea (the producers weren't brave enough to say Vietnam) going to the aid of their former officer, accused of that old chestnut the crime he didn't commit. This gives Fox the chance to get a bit more mileage out of their surplus army tank, and the Black Beauty a worthy adversary. Note that it's Kato's unerring aim that does the job though. This is the only episode in which Scanlon takes an active part in the mission instead of just making dopey leading comments at home base to make Britt Reid look clever.

*The Green Hornet* was not known for its thoughtful or adventurous direction, so Waggner's creative shot showing silhouettes of the Hornet and Kato when they appear in Carter's workshop is both welcome and indicative of what the series might have achieved more often with a little more effort. It's interesting that the selling point of *Batman* was that his appearance supposedly struck terror and dread into the hearts of criminals, when this so rarely was the case in the *Batman* series, but was a regular component of *The Green Hornet*. Many of the series' *frissons*--perhaps the only ones--came from the

Hornet's sudden arrival in the villain's lair, and it's ironic that one of the best comes from a visiting *Batman* director.

This is one of the episodes to be graced with real actors instead of bit-players. Although his film career was about to resume with *The Dirty Dozen* and *The St. Valentine's Day Massacre*, Ralph Meeker, a busy 1950s leading man in various tough guy roles (the best known being Mike Hammer in the legendary *Kiss Me Deadly*), had found himself in lean years when he took the guest role here. Raymond St. Jacques, on the other hand, after appearances in such series as *I Spy, The Girl from UNCLE, The Man from UNCLE,* and *The Invaders,* was on the verge of starting a film career in various movies aimed primarily at the black audience, where he would make his name in *Cotton Comes to Harlem* and its sequel. Completing the trio of war veterans was the competent and capable Paul Carr, mostly prolific in TV, where he gave three dimensional guest performances in such series as *Voyage to the Bottom of the Sea, Star Trek, Time Tunnel, The Invaders,* and many others.

### Corpse of the Year (two parts)

wr. Ken Pettus, dir. James Komack

The Hornet and Kato must put an end to the career of a bogus Green Hornet who really does have criminal intentions... and a powerful duplicate of the Black Beauty.

*with Joanna Dru (Sabrina Bradley), Celia Kaye (Melissa Neal), J. Edward McKinley (Simon Neal), Cesare Danova (Felix Garth), Tom Simcox (Dan Scully), Barbara Babcock (Elaine),*

*Nora Marlowe (Annie), Jack Garner (doorman), Sydney Smith (butler), Sally Mills (secretary), Angelique Pettyjohn (party girl)*

Bizarrely, with so many *Hornet* episodes truncated and making the case for an hour format, this two-parter seems padded. The theme is a good one, albeit a familiar one, with a bogus Green Hornet and duplicate Black Beauty on the loose. Although the car chase between the two vehicles is exciting, the shots don't match, with nighttime stock shots intercut with sequences shot in broad daylight, a common flaw in this series.

Joanna Dru is best known for her role in the classic western *The Searchers*.

J. Edward McKinley usually appeared in sit-coms, and was frequently seen in episodes of *Bewitched*.

Cesare Danova's credits can be found in the section on *Honey West*. Barbara Babcock makes her third appearance as Britt's girlfriend, and a second one as Elaine.

Jack Garner was the nondescript brother of James Garner, and frequently played invisible bit parts on Garner's series *The Rockford Files*. *Star Trek* legend Angelique Pettyjohn has a one line moment —"It's the Green Hornet!".

## Bad Bet on a 459 Silent

wr. Judith and Robert Guy Barrows, dir. Seymour Robbie

Two crooked cops raid a jewelry store and frame the Green Hornet after wounding him in a shoot-out.

with Bert Freed (Clark), Brian Avery (Dixon), Nicolas Coster, Barry Ford (patrol car cops), Jason Wingreen (doctor), Bud Perkins (dispatch officer), Dick Dial (reporter)

*Universal's 1940 serial The Green Hornet Strikes Again*

Bert Freed has a more substantial role than usual here as a corrupt cop bullying his younger partner into criminal ways. More interesting than this storyline is the sub-plot that has a wounded Green Hornet unable to get medical treatment without exposing his identity. This would have been an ideal opportunity to bring back the friendly Dr. Hannah from "Secret of the Sally Bell", but instead Kato turns up at the Sentinel and takes a pot shot at Reid (does no-one ever see Kato at Reid's residence?). The flaw here is that the two shootings occur several hours apart, something a doctor would notice from the condition of the wound. Still, the scene with Kato at the Sentinel is unusual, unexpected and exciting. So exciting, in fact, that it was swiped wholesale for the light-hearted *Green Hornet* film of 2011. One feels that if this had been a two-parter there was more to be explored than what we get on the screen in a half-hour format, particularly where the two crooked cops Clark and Dixon are concerned.

Nicolas Coster, whose career developed more fully in the '70s, is seen here briefly as a fellow cop. In the years to come he would have more substantial roles facing *The Amazing Spider-Man, Wonder Woman, The Incredible Hulk,* and *Buck Rogers in the 25th Century.*


### Ace in the Hole

wr. J.E. Selby, Stanley Silverman, dir. William Beaudine

The Hornet's plans to break up a blossoming mob alliance are complicated by crime reporter Mike Axford, who interrupts a crucial meeting.

*with Richard Anderson (Phil Trager), Richard X. Slattery (Steve Gant), Tony Epper (Gant's henchman), Percy Helton (Gus), Chuck Couch, Bill Hampton (Trager's men)*

This convoluted plot setting two mob bosses against each other is a fairly routine escapade with no memorable scenes and a few poor ones. Axford is pointlessly freed to blunder around as usual, whereas he should have been kept under wraps, as he naturally jumps straight back into the frying pan; the gangsters turn up at Reid's apartment and encounter Kato in his manservant role, but still fail to figure out who the Green Hornet is; a fight scene is accompanied by comedy music, and yet up until then the episode has been played completely straight with no attempt at humor. It might be kind to suggest that Selby and Silverman had a completely different set of images in their minds' eye when they wrote this episode next to what eventually appears on the screen. It was their only work on the show (Selby was a pen-name for HUAC-blacklisted writer Robert Lees).

Richard Anderson, busy in guest roles during the 1960s, including two turns in *The Man from UNCLE,* went on to play Oscar Goldman in *The Six Million Dollar Man* and *The Bionic Woman* in the 1970s. Tony Epper, one of several members of the Epper family involved in stunt work, also appeared in three *Batman* stories —"Hizzonner the Penguin/Dizzonner the Penguin", "That Darn Catwoman/Scat, Darn Catwoman", and "I'll Be a Mummy's Uncle".

## Trouble for Prince Charming

wr. Ken Pettus, dir. William Beaudine

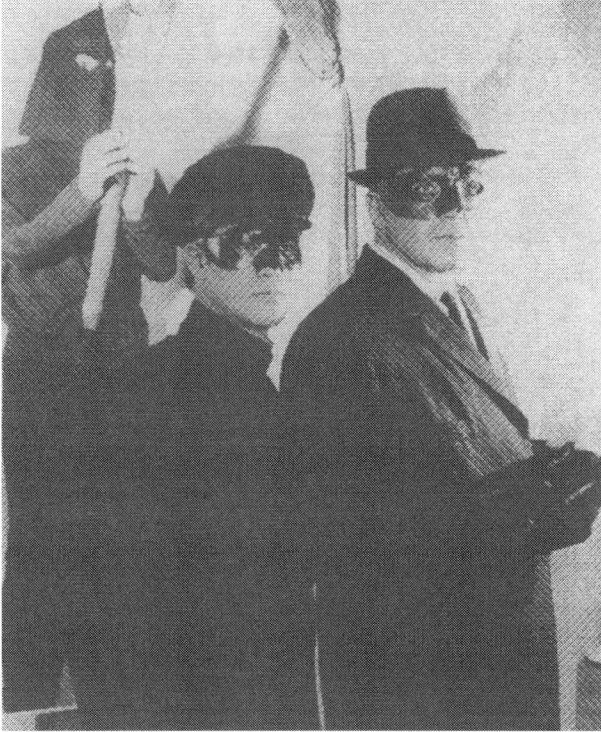

The Hornet kidnaps the ruler of a foreign country visiting the U.S. when his American bride-to-be is kidnapped by conspirators in an attempt to force him to abdicate the throne.

*with Edmund Hashim (Prince Rafil), Susan Flannery (Janet Prescott), Alberto Morin (Abu Bakr), James Lanphier (Colonel Sarajek)*

The Hornet's only foray into international affairs has him involved in the usual plot concerning a friendly prince's treacherous aides. Edmund Hashim has one of his more substantial roles here as the Charming Prince. Other appearances in 1960s TV include *The Man from UNCLE, Get Smart, I Spy, The Wild Wild West,* and *Mission: Impossible.* Susan Flannery was an underused actress in the 1960s, with a very naive and childlike acting style, perfect here for the lovestruck society girl who can't quite believe her luck in landing a royal suitor. Other roles include episodes of *Voyage to the Bottom of the Sea* and *The Time Tunnel.*

James Lanphier, with little to do here, but often cast as a sinister figure, also appeared in episodes of *The Wild Wild West, Get Smart, Mission: Impossible, The Time Tunnel, Captain Nice,* and *Batman.* Alberto Morin also appeared in *The Wild Wild West* and *Batman.*

Having announced he's "something of a romantic", the Hornet takes his leave... while Kato pauses behind him to get in two vicious last kicks!

## Alias the Scarf

wr. William Stuart, dir. Allen Reisner

Midnight at a wax museum where the Green Hornet and Kato are the latest exhibits in the Chamber of Evil... and the model of a long-vanished, never-caught killer seems to have to come to life to commit new crimes.

*with John Carradine (James Lancourt), Patricia Barry (Vena), Ian Wolfe (curator), Paul Gleason (assistant), Brenda Benet (girl in street), Jack Garner, Danny Costello (cops)*

An attempt to do something different from the usual gangster stuff has horror film veteran John Carradine, at this time doing anything and everything from TV to Z-movies, stalking a suddenly foggy city as an obvious Jack the Ripper clone, the mad strangler the Scarf--who apparently doesn't much care *who* he strangles. With the villain basically motiveless, and the mystery of his identity foiled by the casting of Carradine and the unavoidable evidence that the wax dummy looks exactly like him, there isn't really anywhere for this story to go. Most *Green Hornet* stories are over far too quickly to bother with fake leads and red herrings, and the brief early introduction of Paul Gleason--much busier in the '70s and '80s--in a one-line walk-on presumably to furnish at least one slim possibility for a second suspect is completely undermined by the above. Had the Scarf's wax image been a concealed face--say, *by a scarf*--then there might have been more of a mystery. Continuing the Jack the Ripper motif, future soap actress Patricia Barry plays a stripper, and dancer and Elvis movie starlet Brenda Benet plays a potential victim. Patricia Barry appears in *The Girl from UNCLE* this season; Benet, married to Bill Bixby, later appeared in *The Incredible Hulk*. Ian Wolfe's many TV and film appearances include two *Star Trek* and the second *Wonder Woman* pilot. The Scarf, of course, is ultimately trapped in the wax museum by the Hornet and Kato posing as their own entries in the Hall of Infamy.

**Hornet, Save Thyself**

wr. Don Tait, dir. Seymour Robbie

Britt Reid becomes a fugitive from the law for real when a birthday party turns into an elaborate frame for murder.

*with Michael Strong (Dale Hyde), Frank Marth (police lieutenant), Jack Perkins (desk sergeant), Marvin Brody (Eddie Rech), Ken Strange (cop)*

Once again there is only one obvious suspect to be exposed for framing Britt Reid for murder. A rather contrived resolution has Casey belatedly and conveniently remembering something blatantly obvious on cue, and the bad guy pointlessly leaving evidence behind. On the plus side, the Hornet's raid on the police station is excellent.

Michael Strong, memorable as the luckless used car salesman in the classic gangster film *Point Blank,* and as the tormented Dr. Corby in "What Are Little Girls Made Of?", an early *Star Trek,* was doing much TV at this time, and also appears in episodes of *The Man from UNCLE, I Spy,* and no less than four *Mission: Impossible.* Busy bit player Frank Marth also had run-ins with TV super-heroes *The Six Million Dollar Man, The Bionic Woman, Captain America,* and *The Incredible Hulk.*

## Invasion from Outer Space (two parts)

wr. Arthur Weingarten, dir. E. Darrell Hallenbeck

Casey is abducted by a mad scientist and his men, who are masquerading as alien invaders in order to capture a nuclear missile.

*with Larry D. Mann (Dr. Eric Mabouse), Linda Gaye Scott (Vama), Arthur Batanides (Shugo), Christopher Dark (Martin), Joe Di Reda (Joe), Brett King (Air Force Major), Frank Babich (Air Force Sergeant), Lloyd Haynes (driver), Troy Melton, Jerry Catron (henchmen), Tyler McVey (Police Chief), Richard Poston (Air Force Captain), Bennie Dobbins (Air Force Colonel)*

Apparently inspired by the infamous hoax radio broadcast of a Martian invasion that turned out to be a radio production of *War of the Worlds*, this has a small army of empowered extraterrestrials dressed in Irwin Allen hand-me-downs. This was not Larry D. Mann's finest hour, although he stoically gives one hundred percent in an impossible role. His numerous 1960s credits are covered in detail in the *Honey West* section.

Linda Gaye Scott was one of those 1960s starlets who started out promisingly with guest roles in series like *My Living Doll, My Favorite Martian, Bewitched, Lost in Space, Batman,* and *The Man from UNCLE* (the latter two and this her largest parts) but then gradually found herself playing smaller and less significant parts until eventually she was girl number three or whatever. 1966, however, was definitely her fifteen minutes of fame; she had a major role on *UNCLE*, played Moth, the Riddler's moll on *Batman*, was clearly having a fine old time as a biker babe on *Lost in Space*, and will forever be remembered by cult TV aficionados for the electrically-charged Va-Va-Vama!

Arthur Batanides, Christopher Dark, and Jerry Catron had numerous roles in cult TV of the 1960s, particularly on the Irwin Allen shows. Lloyd Haynes played roles on *Star Trek* and *Batman* before taking the lead in high school drama *Room 222.*

Bennie Dobbins was in charge of stunt fights on *The Green Hornet.* The Arnold Schwarzenegger film *Red Heat,* on which he worked second unit, and during which he died of a heart attack, is dedicated to his memory. E. Darrell Hallenbeck was assistant director on the third season of *The Twilight Zone,* and then directed numerous episodes of *UNCLE.*

series ends

## The Invaders

**January 10th, 1967 - March 26th, 1968**

*"How does a nightmare begin? For David Vincent, architect, returning home from a business trip, it began at a few minutes past four on a lost Tuesday morning, looking for a short cut he never found..."*

In many ways Quinn Martin's *The Invaders* is the forgotten sci-fi show of the '60s, overlooked and overshadowed by the sheer mass of Irwin Allen's series and the legend of *Star Trek*. And yet, in many ways it *is* well-remembered. Those who have seen the show readily remember the show's infamous visual gimmick of the aliens having stiffened little fingers, the manner in which the aliens disintegrated when killed, and the sonorous introduction by William Woodson, telling how only David Vincent knows that the aliens are here...!

*The Invaders* began as an addition to a relatively new television genre at the time—the man-on-the-run show. It's a familiar TV premise today... but when TV producer Roy Huggins (*Maverick, The Rockford Files, Alias Smith And Jones, Hunter*) first suggested the idea of a man-on-the-run show—*The Fugitive*—to 20th Century Fox back in the 1960s, they thought the idea was such a non-starter they gave him the sack! No-one, they said, wanted to watch a show where the authorities were the villains and the hero was a man wrongly accused of murdering his wife. Ultimately, other opinions prevailed, and Huggins' idea was given over to successful TV producer Quinn Martin (*The Untouchables, The FBI, Streets Of San Francisco, Cannon*) for development. ABC owed Martin a series commitment, and they were extremely happy for it to be this one, which they were obliged to air, or pay him off. "This will finish you" gloated one executive's telegram. Nice.

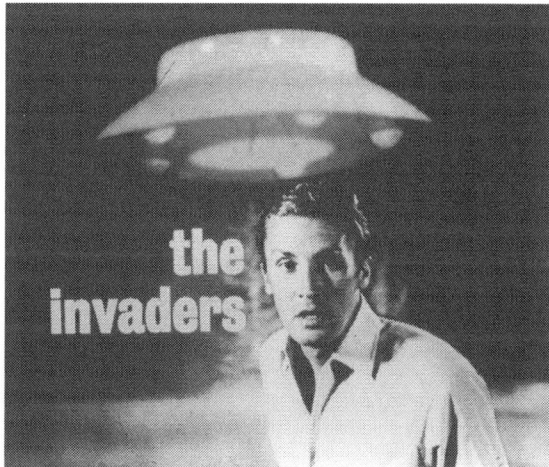

The concept became *The Fugitive*, made a star of David Janssen, heroes of Huggins and Martin, and a big screen movie hit thirty years later in the 1990s. The final episode of *The Fugitive*, which resolved the saga, cleared streets around the world and was for many years the most-watched TV episode ever aired (until the final episode of *MASH* in fact). Since then, the man-on-the-run format has become a staple of American TV series, with a different variation on the theme turning up in over two dozen different series since. Consequently, when future film maker Larry Cohen presented the same network with the idea of a paranoid fantasy about a man who both fights against and flees from emotionless aliens quietly and covertly invading the Earth in human form, a chastened ABC presented Martin with the task of turning *The Invaders* into what they hoped would be another *Fugitive*, with *Fugitive*-style ratings to match.

*David Janssen making his solitary way across America in The Fugitive, just as Roy Thinnes would in The Invaders, its sci-fi equivalent...*

Only one man initially knew that these beings were attempting to take over the Earth in human guise... architect David Vincent... and they knew that he knew. A deadly game of cat and mouse followed over the next two seasons, with the alien forces trying to discredit Vincent and brand him a flying saucer nut while he tries to delay and expose their grand master plan. "How many chances do you think we're going to get... before they wipe out the human race?" asks Vincent in "The Betrayed". The answer turned out to be 43... 43 variable episodes, some so astonishing, inventive and exciting they made you tingle, others so disappointing they made you despair.

Although it began airing in January 1967 as a mid-season replacement, *The Invaders*, a stylish, garishly colored pastiche of almost every invasion-from-space/ bodysnatchers film of the '50s was actually made in 1966, a golden year for TV SF (*Star Trek* and *The Time Tunnel* also premiered). It was Quinn Martin's hit man-on-the-run show *The Fugitive* with a sci-fi slant taken from the mass of cheap paperback fiction about flying saucers that proliferated in the '50s and '60s, the lights in the sky given substance. The premise was superb, paranoia incarnate: What if the nuts who claimed they had seen men from Mars were actually telling the truth, and not nuts at all? This was the show's brilliant conceit.

Roy Thinnes was the luckless David Vincent, "a man too long without sleep" who stops at a roadside diner for a rest and sees a flying saucer landing. From that moment on, his life becomes a waking nightmare, as Vincent realises that the Earth is infested with alien infiltrators burrowing their way into every area of power and influence around the world, and he becomes a single-minded obsessive intent on avenging the death of his partner and ruin of his former life. Disguised in slowly degenerating human forms that need periodic recharging at special alien regeneration bases to keep up the deceit, the alien foot-soldiers can only be identified by their slightly deformed fingers, although some of the alien ringleaders have mysteriously conquered even this giveaway (or was it just lazy or obstinate directors?). The invaders are heartless in every sense of the word, and without pulse, sweat, or blood, which makes identification easy for the series' writers and directors but leaves a few holes in some of the plots (in many episodes, one wonders why immediate players aware of his claims aren't simply offered a physical).

Like many movie aliens, the invaders consider their lack of human emotions an attribute and consider themselves often shockingly expendable for the cause (invaders are quick to suicide for the greater good), but when they die they burn

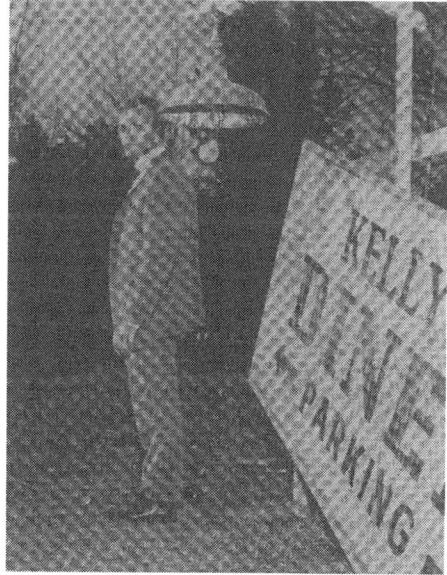

*Vincent in the pilot at the subtly altered abandoned roadside diner where he first sees an alien saucer land...*

up instantly, leaving nothing but a small spread of ashes, and thus, no evidence that they were ever there at all (it also gave Vincent free rein to obliterate as many of the bastards as he liked; to soften such murderous if justifiable inclinations, the aliens were not only equally cavalier with their own lives, but those of the Earth's—they were brutally and horrendously ruthless). Their weapons include a small disc that can cause plausibly explained sudden death, hypnotic devices that turn brains to mush, and deadly incinerator guns that leave virtually no trace of anything or anyone. Although they are often reluctant to try to kill David Vincent for fear of giving his claims credibility, they will blithely dispense with all other unfortunates who get in their way, and all associates and converts of Vincent's are ruthlessly disposed of, making him a guy to steer well clear of. Each episode, Vincent investigates sightings, seeks allies, and follows aliens in the hope of exposing their existence to an understandably sceptical world. Unfortunately for him, the invaders are everywhere, and he never knows whether the people he meets on his travels across country are humans, aliens, or alien stooges, duped into helping them... Every time they attempt to ridicule or even, occasionally, eradicate him anyway (not all the aliens appear to be 'on-message')... while he in turn tries to throw a spanner into the works of their various schemes to corrupt and subdue humanity... At the end of each episode, Vincent would have the rug pulled from underneath his feet while winning a "small victory" or delaying tactic for an unknowing and ungrateful humankind...

The beauty of the show was that no sane person would believe David Vincent's story... but it just happened to be true. And *The Invaders* took place in the real world —our world, not a comic-book universe where alien visitations were a common occurrence to be seen off by super-heroes. One of the obvious storylines the show never followed up was to have Vincent encounter frauds, hoaxers, fantasists and opportunists; every bizarre story he followed up turned out to be a genuine alien encounter, unless it was a trap set by the aliens, which happened a couple of times.

Sometimes Vincent will scour newspapers for clues of alien activity (strange occurrences, UFO sightings, etc.) and follow them up himself; other times, as Vincent's dubious reputation has grown, other terrified people with fears, suspicions, or evidence will seek him out in the hope that he is as genuine as they. There's a wonderful ambiguity in the pilot about who the aliens really are that was missing from subsequent episodes, in which--in a series of revelations throughout the story--extraterrestrial origins would be confirmed or denied. In the pilot "Beachhead", we're never sure whether J.D.

*J.D. Cannon, archetypal TV cop, as he appeared in Universal's McCloud... and indeed here.*

Cannon's Holman is just an angry, pragmatic cop reacting naturally toward a man he perceives as a dangerous nut, or whether he's an alien stooge when he threatens Vincent angrily in the final scene, fuming "This is the final word, Vincent, the bottom line. For your own sake, let it end here. Whatever you're planning, let it end here!". Happily for us, Vincent ignored this ominous warning!

"I think that people like to be scared out of their wits, but they're no longer frightened by three-headed monsters" said producer Alan Armer to the press. "So we've made the invaders look just like the folks next door. Any one of them might be an invader from outer space... the new neighbors across the street, the substitute teacher, that too-pretty secretary in the office... Always they are without pulse or heartbeat--for they possess no hearts! What we're after, quite simply, is fear!".

Author of the pilot was Anthony Wilson, one of the unsung heroes of '60s SF. Although the writer of a very poor *Twilight Zone* ("Come Wander With Me"), Wilson was the story editor of *Lost in Space* and *Land of the Giants,* where he was responsible for what little character delineation there was in those wacky and wonderful series, and developed *Planet of the Apes* for television. It was Wilson who added Doctor Smith and the Robot to the Robinson party of *Lost in Space,* seeing the need for an agent provocateur, and *Land of the Giants* fans owe him a particular debt; the half dozen or so episodes he oversaw were the only ones that gave the Spindrift passengers any dimension or depth at all.

Creator Larry Cohen, who had initially pitched the idea to ABC, specialised in series about tortured loners (the western *Branded* was also his), and later went on to sacrifice the high production values of the major studios for the personal pleasures of low-budget film-making, where he made warmly received schlock horror films like *It's Alive* and *Q--the Winged Serpent,* and perhaps his best effort, the paranoiac *The Private Files of J. Edgar Hoover.* He dabbled in television with reluctance, solely to work his way into film-making, and had no desire or intention to stay with the series past development. In the event, he didn't even stay that long. When ABC took his man-on-the-run concept to Quinn Martin Productions on the strength of their success with *The Fugitive,* Cohen departed the project with little ill-feeling, although of his story ideas he noted twice, both to Gary Gerani and Michael Doyle, that "Quinn Martin said they were discarding all 22... They then proceeded to film every one of them!".

Which of the 43 episodes were built around Cohen's dozen-or-so plot-lines has never been revealed (we know two of them were "Nightmare", one of my personal favorites, and the chilling "Storm", 'comic-book plots' said Armer), and he received no story credits on any of them, having been paid off long before the series went into production. It's impossible to say whether *The Invaders* would have been a better show had Cohen stuck with it, but in a lengthy series of interviews with Michael Doyle for the excellent book *Larry Cohen – The Stuff of Gods and Monsters,* he offered a number of misguided and wrong-headed criticisms alongside changes he would have liked to see, some far too costly, none expedient, and many of them over-complicating and diminishing the concept, so it would certainly have been a very different show.

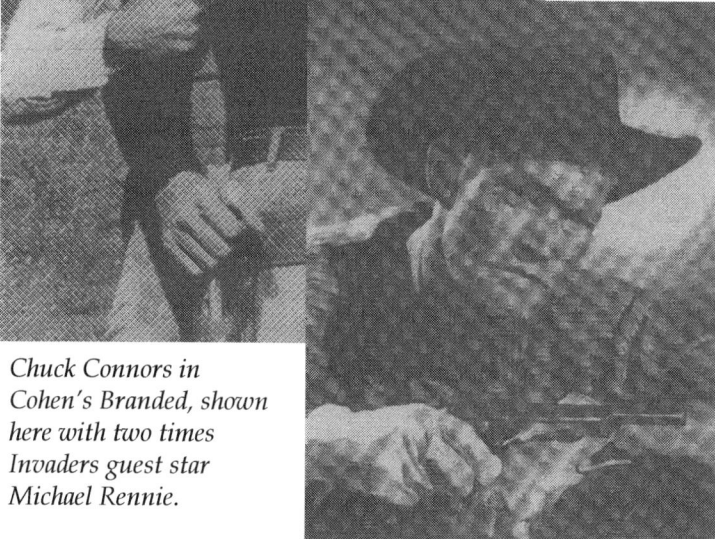

*Chuck Connors in Cohen's Branded, shown here with two times Invaders guest star Michael Rennie.*

He was particularly down on the number of aliens in each episode, the look of the saucers, the quality of the burning-up effects, and the performance and casting of Thinnes, most of them aspects of the show I personally felt enhanced it. Similarly, many of those later working on the show, including writer Robert Sherman and directors William Hale and Robert Butler (the latter of whom thought *The Invaders* superior to *Star Trek*) felt that Cohen's giveaway visual device of the extended fingers was a gimmick too far, although again, I personally feel that—as the first thing many people remember about the show—it was a fun idea, and useful storytelling shorthand. Suggestions from Cohen such as an eye in the palm of their hands (made in his interview with *Starlog*) and the burning or charring of their surroundings when they burnt up (made to Doyle) would have been costly production nightmares, even today, let alone in 1966. Other potentially ruinous ideas by otherwise intelligent contributors that were never acted on included showing what the aliens really looked like, a steady girlfriend for Vincent (no doubt adding instant paint-by-numbers jeopardy) and a youthful assistant! Lucky escapes, all.

Under the guidance of Martin and his usual collaborators from *The Untouchables*, *The FBI*, and *The Fugitive*, *The Invaders* was a rare creature indeed... a science-fiction series with a strong human element to it, an adult drama emphasising realism over special effects, human foibles over *Flash Gordon* heroics, real-life fear and paranoia over rubber monsters, and aliens mounting a slow but sure invasion of earth through subversion and infiltration rather than fleets of flying saucers swooping over Washington. While the image of a fleet of airborne saucers hurling forth death rays while cities crumble and the military are blown to oblivion is one of the staples of sci-fi, there were far fewer actual outright overt alien invasion movies than you might think, at least from Hollywood-- putting aside Japanese contributions such as *The Mysterians* and *Battle in Outer Space* and their like, the truth is that there were only three: the superb *War of the Worlds*, the low-budget but impressive *Earth vs. the Flying Saucers*, and the inane *Plan Nine from Outer Space*. *I Married a Monster from Outer Space* featured a memorable shot of an alien fleet waiting patiently in space to invade (but was actually another 'taking human form' yarn) while *Invasion of the Saucer Men* gave us some classic pulp aliens, but no fleet of saucers. There had also been a conspicuous and very public landing of a single saucer in *The Day the Earth Stood Still*. All other movie saucer landings had been out in the boonies, as with *Saucer Men*, all other alien invasions have been covert rather than overt, and all other mass destruction sci-fi had involved dinosaurs or giant creatures. Although there is a pop culture image of dozens of flying saucer attacks in the 1950s, the majority of it is from pulp sci-fi mags, comic books and bubble gum cards. There were, on the other hand, numerous space invasion films of the 1950s that dealt with aliens either taking

*From the pilot, the aliens in their regeneration tubes. As the tubes start to rise, and we realise, with Vincent, that they are about to emerge, we see one of the few moments in the series where Vincent is in a total panic!*

over human bodies or taking human form, for the simple reason that it was cost-effective as well as sneaky and logical. It costs a fortune to blow away Washington, Moscow, Paris, London, and New York all before lunchtime, especially without CGI, but much less to scuttle in subversively, especially if you're doing it in human form...

The show drew heavily on 1950s sci-fi influences--hardware and a visual look resembling that of *This Island Earth*, sound-effects from *War of the Worlds*, surreal off-kilter visuals and an innocent-looking cerebral haemorrhage death for those who had served their purpose inspired by *Invaders from Mars*, and the bodysnatching paranoia of a dozen different sci-fi spookers, specifically the small-town menace of *It Came from Outer Space* and the suburban sexual tension of *I Married a Monster from Outer Space*. Cohen freely admitted he was inspired by the likes of *Invaders from Mars* and *Invasion of the Body Snatchers*, and virtually every theme from

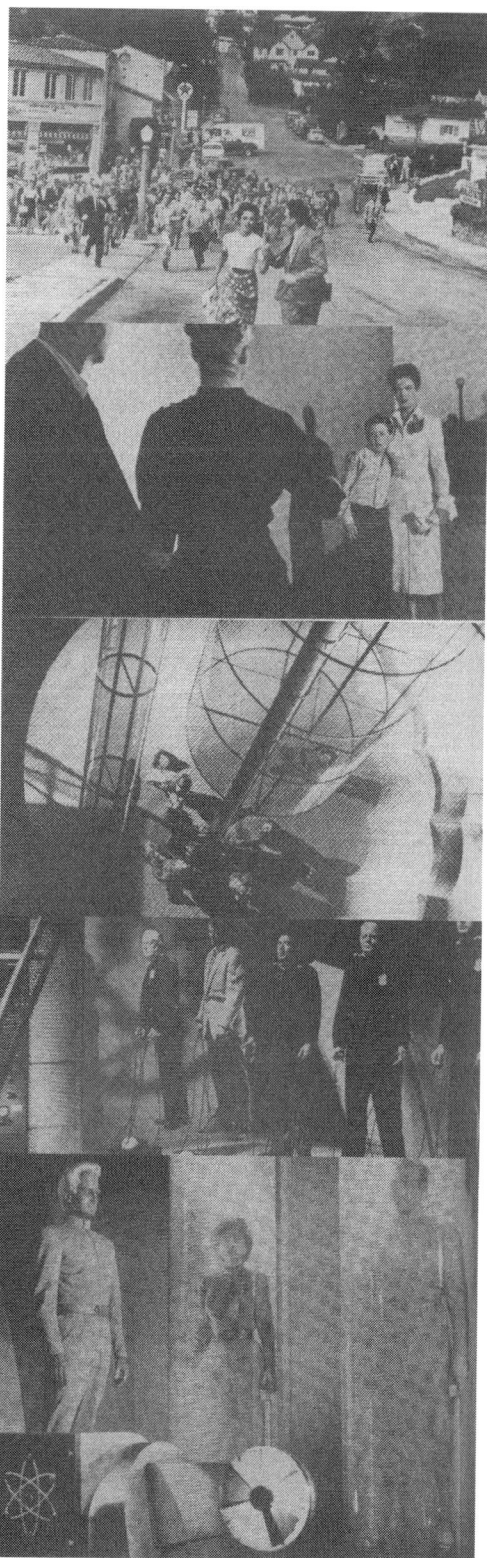

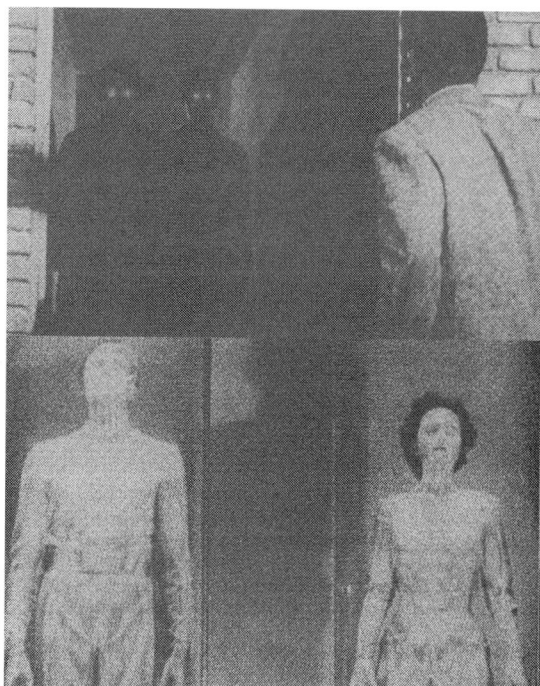

*1950s influences on the series included top to bottom, Invasion of the Body Snatchers, Invaders from Mars (x2), I Married a Monster from Outer Space, bottom (x2) This Island Earth, It Came from Outer Space.*

every 1950s SF film reared its head during the 43 episodes, including many of the players from those films (Kevin McCarthy, Dana Wynter, Peter Graves, Charles Drake, Anne Francis, John Zaremba, Whit Bissell, Arthur Franz, Anthony Eisley, Ross Elliott, Robert H. Harris, and Michael Rennie all made guest appearances).

Film critics have always been divided over whether the 1956 feature *Invasion of the Body Snatchers* was a parody of the obsession of 1950s America with Communist infiltration, warning against witch-hunts, or an uncritical reflection of the mood of the time, a subject about which director Don Siegel kept suspiciously vague, often giving interviewers the answer they were looking for, it seems. Hindsight is a wonderful thing. Cohen, however, when approached by ABC for series ideas, made no secret about the fact that *The Invaders* was inspired by Cold War paranoia, later claiming that QM Productions never really grasped this... although one episode, "The Ivy Curtain", was classic Red Menace hooey, while a couple of second season stories made references to Vincent "finding aliens under every bed", so the point, while not exactly hammered home, wasn't entirely lost. QM were much too network-savvy to be as unsubtle and heavy-handed as Cohen.

As a continuing series, *The Invaders* did what a self-contained feature film couldn't, often the strength of television. It carried on from where the other films--particularly *Invasion of the Body Snatchers*--left off, with a lone, desperate man single-handedly trying to warn a sceptical world about a covert invasion from outer space. The Red Menace subtext *was* there, and it was cleverly presented in such a way that viewers could take it as seriously as they cared, depending on their politics and level of sophistication! Martin's series ranged from unquestioningly reactionary (*The FBI*) to cautiously liberal (*Streets of San Francisco*) in content, and his series are object lessons in mass market fence-sitting; he told interviewers Alley and Newcombe for their book *The Producer's Medium*, that he'd run a story with a corrupt cop, but not a corrupt department. It seems fair to say that *The Invaders* was not so much belatedly adding its voice to the Cold War cacophony of the '50s as simply adhering to the established rules and conventions of the form. *The Invaders* deliberately and unapologetically modelled itself on the heady fear of those enemy-in-our-midst films of a decade earlier, but more from a search for style rather than any deliberate attempt to return to the simplistic politics of that era. During the course of the series, the invaders tried to infiltrate industry ("Vikor"), the military ("Doomsday Minus One"), NASA ("Moonshot"), the U.N. ("Summit Meeting"), politics ("The Vise"), religion ("The Prophet"), defence ("Condition: Red"), and the media ("Task Force").

Astute viewers will recognise in the pilot and early episodes background music from the earlier *Outer Limits* series also on ABC and scored by Dominic Frontiere (note the sequence of Vincent trying to escape the hospital at the close of Act One in the pilot); it even turns up in episodes of Cohen's ABC western *Branded!* In many ways, *The Invaders* is the full-color step-child of *The Outer Limits*, and not only because it was made for the same network, and utilised the unique talents of Frontiere--it was equally strong on scaring the viewer silly through powerful music, manipulative visuals, convincing performances that were neither wooden nor hysterical, and a paranoia-inducing sense of impending menace. *The Invaders'* distinctive spotlight and jagged-edged graphics had been designed for an *Outer Limits* spin-off series to be titled *The Unknown* that never happened, and *The Invaders* also inherited it's trademark sinister music from that busted pilot, which can be heard in the regular *Outer Limits* episode it became, "The Form of Things Unknown". In many ways, it was a spin-off series in every way but factual!

Significantly, *The Invaders* was blessed with well-drawn, realistically-portrayed supporting characters who displayed honest human behavior and reactions (a distinct boon in a genre famous for cardboard cut-out characters and stereotypes, as in evidence in the interminable *Star Trek* spin-offs and rip-offs). Many of the actors were, of course, the same as those appearing in the other shows of the day, but given more to work with. In a genre dominated by the special effects monster-fests of Irwin Allen and the point-making preaching of Rod Serling and Gene Roddenberry (all enjoyable in themselves), *The Invaders* was unique in its tendency to build stories around real earth-bound people leading ordinary, often humdrum lives, caught up against their will in events they wanted no part of. This was a characteristic of Martin's *The Fugitive* and his cop shows, and the series benefitted from it.

Martin's involvement also ensured network support for the duration of the series (even as ratings gradually eroded during the first season, with quality diminishing during the second and final season), and guaranteed a succession of top-notch television actors, writers, and directors, many of them among the best in the business. "The Quinn Martin organisation was a prestigious company" said story editor Anthony Spinner to Mark Phillips in a 1994 interview for *Starlog* magazine. "It didn't do schlock, and actors respected that. Actors knew that if they were in the QM stock company, they could move from one show to another. They could get three to four acting roles a year just on Quinn's shows. Quinn himself never stepped on the set. He wasn't comfortable with actors. He ran QM Productions like a movie mogul. It was his company, it was his money, and what goes on today in television, with actors making demands... would never have gone on with Quinn. And most of the writers and directors who worked on *The Invaders* were better than average for weekly series TV".

Portraying the tortured David Vincent was newcomer Roy Thinnes, a jobbing actor trying to grab the brass ring of a continuing series who had done little before *The Invaders,* and would do little of note afterwards. Cohen, along with a few other commentators, criticised the casting of the stoic, steely-eyed Thinnes as Vincent, claiming he wasn't emotional enough, but 43 episodes is a long time to behave like the hysterical Kevin McCarthy in the closing scenes of *Invasion of the Body Snatchers!* (In many ways, *The Invaders* as a series picks up where *Invasion of the Body Snatchers* left off). Others, like myself, felt Thinnes was a perfect choice to portray what came across as Vincent's remorseless, robotic determination to pursue these extraterrestrial critters across the cities and small towns of America. This, after all, was a man who had lost everything that one fateful night--his business partner (murdered by the aliens), his career, and his credibility. Everyone Vincent encounters is either dead, endangered, or doomed. Everyone he meets either dies, betrays him, or takes him for a madman. Eventually, he expected to lose his life. It would have been absurd, if not downright tasteless, for Vincent to have been played any other way. So Vincent never smiled--no kidding!

Director William Hale considered Thinnes "underrated". "Roy made the series work" agreed Paul Wendkos, another regular director on the show. "When you looked at him, you knew that he believed he was seeing something that could happen, and did happen. He wasn't manufacturing something". Robert Butler also felt he was right, as did writers Norman Klenman, Laurence Heath, William Blinn, and Barry Oringer.

Writers Robert Sherman and Don Brinkley disliked Thinnes' approach, as did directors Gerald Mayer and Robert Douglas. Producer Alan Armer felt he should lighten up, in order to gain audience sympathy. But he never seemed short of it; despite its short run, QM received more mail on *The Invaders* than any other show they produced... some of which ran four to eight seasons against *The Invaders'* one-ands-a-bit's-worth. And Vincent could hardly be glib and jokey in his situation, with such high stakes and equally high body counts. Interviewed for a second *Starlog* retrospective by Mark Phillips in 2009, second season assistant director Bob Rubin said "Roy was blamed for not properly developing the character (but) he lived the part of David Vincent twenty four hours a day. It would have been different if he'd 'phoned the part in, but he arrived early and left late. The bottom line is, he worked his ass off to make the series work".

Whether Thinnes was a wooden actor or playing it down deliberately, it was the

*Roy Thinnes as David Vincent poses with the aliens' regeneration machines during the making of the pilot.*

right attitude for the role--and so was he the right person for it. Unashamed to be doing science-fiction, he took the part, and the premise, seriously — so much so that if visiting actors or directors made too many jokes about the material, it would irritate him. David Vincent shouldn't have looked like Mr. Family Man--he had to seem a bit strange for the role to work, and his piercing blue eyes and pushy, brusque demeanor gave him that strangeness. However it was achieved, Thinnes gave a perfectly judged performance as a grim, numbed, obsessed, resolute loner, a driven and determined man winning small victories for a lost cause.

Anyone who claimed that Thinnes simply couldn't act has only to look at the bitter, haunted visage of David Vincent at the close of "The Pursued". His guest appearances in *The Untouchables* proved that he was capable of a more emotional performance if he'd chosen to give it. In fact, Vincent's own humanity often worked against him--in several episodes he relinquished valuable gains against the invaders to save the lives of single, often undeserving individuals. In some episodes ("Wall of Crystal", "The Saucer"), it was difficult to sympathise with such a decision, especially when other, better people had given their lives.

All Martin's series were devised very deliberately with a distinctive visual style (Martin has spoken of a wide-angle approach to evoke the solitude of *The Fugitive*, and low-angle and tracking shots to heighten the bustle and movement of *The Streets of San Francisco*), and *The Invaders* was given a very deliberate *outre* form of camerawork, with tilted angles, distorted lenses, and a clever exploitation of light, shadow, and color to create a menacingly claustrophobic and dreamlike aura around the aliens vaguely reminiscent of Conrad Hall's stunning monochrome camerawork for *The Outer Limits*. Sadly, as the series stumbled in its second season, the more outrageous camera angles, odd visuals and dreamy, lurid background music were abandoned--either through laziness, apathy, or misguided policy--and the show became much more conventional in style. The series' hands-on producer was Alan Armer, who for the first season worked alongside Anthony Spinner, who departed the show after the first season to work on the doomed revitalised but ill-fated fourth and final season of *The Man of UNCLE*.

Replacing him for a more scattershot, less completely satisfying second season alongside Armer was David Rintels, who went for more contemporary scenarios, chose to take many--but not all--of the stories out of the small towns of the first season and into the city, and sadly dispensed with the series' more adventurous imagery and camera angles (a visit to an alien lair in the second season would be a small room with a few banks of computers; in the first season it would be the full bells and whistles job with colored light effects, sweeping, tilting cameras, distorted lenses and booming, leery music). There was also much more cop show-style gunplay rather than alien weaponry. Many late second season episodes are quite slow and stodgy in places, despite the occasional flash of brilliance, such as the alien boardroom in "Task Force", or the hallucinations of "The Pit").

There is no denying that as a continuing series *The Invaders* lost its way during the second and final season (Anthony Spinner joked that the series was in trouble direction-wise after the pilot!), or that the format resulted in a certain sameness and predictability as the show wore on. However, this is true of every continuing television series, and although the series had a rigid premise (Vincent had to keep moving, had to seek allies, had to lose the war each week while winning small battles), it did not indulge itself with repetitive formula plots. There is a tendency for people to remember the series' failings and gimmicks more than its virtues. The pilot, most of the first season, and some of the second remains essential viewing for every fan of TV SF, and an object lesson in evoking horror and mystery through style and substance. "I think the reason it didn't last long was because it was too *sophisticated* for the audience" mused Spinner.

Interviewed by sci-fi buff Bill Warren for *Starlog*, Thinnes had nothing but praise for Quinn Martin. "He was a gentleman, and generous. Every script that came in was finished; rarely did you see a color change (last minute alterations). Those were polished scripts when we filmed, and they were good well-structured stories. His shows had great production values... and that was achieved by going on location, four or five days out of seven. (I was) invited to all the story conferences".

Cohen had conceived the series as a Red Menace allegory in serial form, complete with recurring villains and cliffhanger ending; ABC were not brave enough, or indeed foolish enough, to try the *Peyton Place/Batman* format with *The Invaders*, and with Martin on board and in charge it became an hour show with no continuity whatsoever, a major flaw in an otherwise superb series that will be discussed shortly. Every episode featured a single, self-contained story of alien infiltration into society, not through gimmicky devices (although there was usually an alien McGuffin, something either Vincent had and the aliens wanted, or the aliens had and Vincent wanted, or an evil plot built around such enjoyable tomfoolery as carnivorous insects or a hurricane machine) but through the manipulation of Earth people themselves, by exploiting their hopes, fears and dreams. As earlier pointed out, unlike many producers of filmed SF, Martin's programs placed top priority on characterisation and motivation, and this was his greatest contribution to the series.

In "Vikor", for example, guest star Jack Lord (later best known as super-cop Steve McGarrett in the long running crime series *Hawaii Five-O*) gives a superb performance as a deluded army man turned industrialist who has been promised a return to his military glory days by the aliens in return for the use of his factories. The sequence where Lord, as George Vikor, parades around his office to a recording of cheering multitudes from the past in a perverse ritual of self-deception is poignantly chilling (it was one of Lord's favorite roles). In "The Experiment", Roddy McDowall plays the son of a scientist valuable to the aliens who is kept supplied with addictive drugs by the aliens in return for his collaboration. In "The Innocent", William Smithers plays a frightened fisherman paralysed with fear after witnessing a saucer landing and hiding out in a waterfront warehouse while the invaders try every trick in the book to flush him out. "The Ivy Curtain" features Jack Warden as Barney Cahill, an ageing, cash-strapped private pilot coerced by smooth manipulator Murray Matheson and the desire to hold on to his attractive but fickle young wife Susan Oliver into ferrying newly arrived invaders to Matheson's indoctrination centre. Sex was rarely a factor in sci-fi TV of the '60s, or indeed in any decade; that is to say, real adult sexual emotions and complications, rotten marriages, jealousies, and infidelities, as opposed to space-bunnies or macho posturing, but *The Invaders* took place in the real world. As with *The Twilight Zone, The Outer Limits,* and *Star Trek, The Invaders* slipped a lot of complex stuff through by coating it in SF trappings. When Vincent persuades the pilot of the true nature of his not-so-human cargo, Cahill angrily dumps himself, his plane, and his helpless cargo onto the bogus college in fiery retribution.

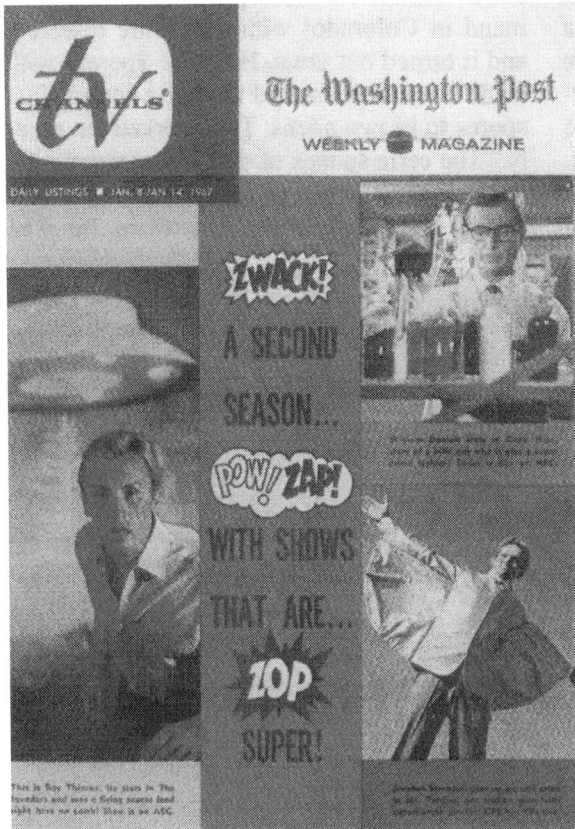

*The Invaders, an intelligent show of quality, has the misfortune to share its network debut cover announcement on this contemporary TV guide with the insipid Batman cash-ins Captain Nice and Mr. Terrific, unfairly making it look like just another 'comic-book' show*

Vincent also experiences bizarre encounters with individual aliens. Robert Walker Jnr., so excellent in "Charlie X" for *Star Trek* and "Billy the Kid" for *Time Tunnel* that same year, plays an invader with an uncanny alien ailment that gives his touch a fatal freezing effect, in "Panic". The aliens want him dead before he gives the game away, and the frightened creature is forced to seek a deal with Vincent. "The Enemy", which threatens a shadowy, tantalising glimpse of the invaders' real appearance, but barely delivers, has Richard Anderson as a desperate alien seeking shelter with a pacifist nurse who has seen too much killing in Vietnam (an early TV reference to the conflict years before it became prominent in drama) and refuses to believe the creature is evil. In "The Mutation", Suzanne Pleshette plays an alien with troubling human emotions, a role she later repeats in a virtual remake, "The Pursued", the last but one episode to air.

Individual storylines resemble the plots of *Earth vs. the Flying Saucers* ("Moonshot"), *I Married a Monster from Outer Space* ("Condition: Red"), *Invasion of the Body Snatchers* ("The Spores"), and *Invaders from Mars* ("The Possessed") to name just a few. Other gems include "The Leeches", "Genesis", "Nightmare", there are many more. "Valley of the Shadow", having painted itself into a corner, is seriously flawed in resolution, but tough not to like... In the second season, "Condition: Red" and "The Saucer" stand out early in the run. Dependable, established veteran writers and a list of directors that reads like a role-call of excellence (Robert Butler, James Goldstone, Paul Wendkos, Sutton Roley) were accompanied by some of the most familiar favorite faces and finest character actors in American television. A number of performers destined for the big screen made appearances on *The Invaders,* including Gene Hackman, Pat Hingle, Strother Martin, Dabney Coleman, Karen Black, Raymond St. Jacques, and Barbara Hershey. Destined for small screen fame were Jack Lord, Ed Asner, Peggy Lipton, Suzanne Pleshette, Jack Warden and Wayne Rogers.

What hurt the credibility of *The Invaders* badly was a total disregard for continuity and the irritating re-use of admittedly fine actors who had already appeared in the series in other roles. This one nagging flaw was something which may not be noticed during a series' original run, when episodes are shown once a week and separated by a summer break, and 1960s networks and producers alike felt that viewers would watch once and forget, but it becomes glaringly obvious and confusing when episodes air daily and/or seasons are shown altogether without interruption. And no-one in the 1960s realised the potential longevity of these shows; they were considered to be disposable entertainment, which makes their commitment to quality even more extraordinary and admirable. *The Invaders* was not alone in this practice, and every show had overlapping talent pools of favored guest players and bit part people, many of them sufficiently anonymous to get away with it, but Quinn Martin programs were particularly notorious for this, and it was very prevalent in *The Invaders,* where the absence of character continuity ultimately hurt the series. In many ways, this practice was understandable--producers and directors liked to use people they'd worked with before and could trust to deliver, and no actor was going to turn down work. The same names crop up repeatedly in television, and this can often enhance the viewing experience for TV buffs who enjoy seeing familiar faces. Unfortunately, Quinn Martin Productions took this tradition to extremes, and it was precisely because they used charismatic actors, giving powerful performances in strong scripts, that the repetition stood out.

Actors who had played victims or innocents returned as aliens. Aliens who had been disintegrated showed up again. Often, actors who had played characters who conceivably *could* have turned up again in new stories--who, in some cases, had made themselves available to Vincent should they be needed—turned up in new roles, so rendering the previous open ending redundant. Memorable, and often poignant roles performed by J.D. Cannon, Laurence Naismith, Harold Gould, Suzanne Pleshette, Peter Mark Richman, Susan Oliver, Tim McIntire, Diana Hyland, James Callahan, William Smithers, Patricia Smith, and Joanne Linville were undermined by their return appearances as someone else. Kent Smith and Anthony Eisley managed to return as different characters and take on recurring roles! Even James Daly and Linden Chiles, who had portrayed David Vincent's business partner and brother (in the pilot and "Wall of Crystal" respectively), returned with new identities.

Equally annoying were the missed opportunities to feature recurring characters. Michael Rennie had played a major role as an alien in "The Innocents", as the wicked Magnus, and had escaped to fight again another day. It was a very significant and traumatic encounter for Vincent. Now, here he was again, in "Summit Meeting", as someone else, and Vincent didn't bat an eyelid. There was no reason this couldn't be Magnus again. Similarly, Alfred Ryder, the sinister Mr. Nexus in "Vikor" returned twice as an (unidentified) alien, with no indication as to whether he was the same alien, or another one. He could easily have been Nexus, who again had survived his original appearance. Logic dictated that an alien who lived to fight another day would immediately become involved in another operation, so why was this simple notion never exploited? It would have brought much-needed depth and significance to Vincent's fight, given that the format already dictated he could never win. In both cases, a flick of the pen could have made Rennie and Ryder returning adversaries.

A TV show that does well in the ratings is generally left alone, and a series that bombs is cancelled, but a series that is so-so is constantly meddled with, and that was the fate of *The Invaders*. The show was popular with college kids and young adults, but older viewers, who flocked *en masse* to Martin's comforting detective shows, simply couldn't suspend disbelief. Consequently, ABC's attempts to boost it seemed to mostly involve watering it down, perhaps because there was no way to ramp it up. When the second season started, the stories were much the same, but the series' beautiful distinctive score was barely used. When no visible improvement was seen, the sci-fi trappings were diluted, a ridiculous decision. "Quinn Martin's real world was cop shows" said Spinner. "He did them better than anyone else. But he got burned by *The Invaders'* cancellation. He really wanted the show to succeed. Quinn was more comfortable with *Barnaby Jones*, *Cannon*, *The FBI*. That was the genre he understood". He added, "My assistant bought an episode into the office. I said, get it out of here! I didn't want to be reminded of those days. It only reminds me that television was better back then. Today, you don't have the Quinn Martins, the Aaron Spellings, the Grant Tinkers. The golden years aren't coming back".

The worst episodes come at the series' end. The last thirteen give David Vincent the support of a group of "believers", and it's at this point the series starts to unravel. "I saw some of the Believers episodes, and I understood what they were trying to do" Anthony Spinner said to Mark Phillips for his *Starlog* retrospective.

"But they needed to work on David Vincent, not invent ten other characters". Kent Smith was cast as benevolent millionaire and friend-in-high-places Edgar Scoville (oddly, at exactly the same time, the series suddenly remembered Thinnes was an architect, and in "The Captive" and "Counter Attack" actually showed him at work). Scoville and his team of Believers (always announced as numbering seven after three of the original ten were gunned down in the opening scene of their debut episode, despite casualties and new members coming and going) at first seemed to be an attempt at continuity, but the concept very swiftly switched from a roomful of collaborators to Scoville on the end of a 'phone.

Three further recurring characters were dispatched during their second appearances, only increasing the air of hopelessness; ironically, this concept was supposed to introduce the idea of David Vincent winning a few and making progress. Instead, it increased the feeling of despair.

Despite this misfire, in the last few episodes, Vincent *was* starting to make noticeable progress. As well as his allies, he was starting to accumulate evidence, witnesses, and in one story, peaceful aliens.

*Roy Thinnes with Carol Lynley in "The Believers", a format change for the worse*

However, Vincent--or rather, his writers--were starting to get sloppy. Despite the scripts being apparently checked and checked again by executive producer Quinn Martin and his staff, the other fatal flaw of the series was not why the aliens didn't try to kill him, as many critics claimed in retrospect, but Vincent's offhanded carelessness with alien evidence and, by extension, other people's lives. Several characters throughout the series' run are killed or seriously injured because of Vincent's misjudgements or carelessness after they helped or listened to him. It may be argued that these errors of judgement made Vincent more human and the scripts more realistic, but in "The Experiment", "The Saucer", and "Labyrinth", Vincent is quite careless with evidence that could bring the aliens down. The absurdities and ironies of real life, where people really do behave illogically or make stupid mistakes, aren't necessarily dramatically correct, where TV heroes have to be near-perfect to be credible. More significantly--and bluntly--the hero has to not be seen as stupid. During the second season, Vincent's trickle of errors and misjudgements became a torrent. Events in "The Pursued"--in which Vincent seems closest to ending his nightmare--result in disaster, and Vincent only has himself to blame as the entire string of events he unleashes is caused by two catastrophic but fundamental errors. First, he asks directions to the summer resort hideaway and so leaves a trail to follow, when all he had to do was buy a fifty cent map, and secondly he leaves an ally alone with someone prone to violent episodes. As with so many series that slowly slip and slide into decline, many second season episodes are perfectly serviceable, and it's only when you revisit the earlier episodes that you notice the obvious decline in quality.

*Kent Smith as Edgar Scoville, leader of the Believers, with Thinnes looking thoroughly pissed off as David Vincent, and guest star Ahna Capri in "Counter Attack".*

Martin did not repeat the mistake he made with *The Fugitive,* where a ratings smash finale killed the show stone dead in syndication. *The Invaders,* like most U.S. series, closed open-ended. Each week, Vincent won small minor victories slowing down the alien assault... but his was a lonely, ultimately futile struggle against insurmountable odds, and he was never to win a final battle. We were left to assume that poor David Vincent is still out there somewhere, fighting his solitary, obsessive war, saving the world single-handed in the quiet horror that his task is hopeless... and he knows it.

## The Invaders

## episode guide

*regular cast: Roy Thinnes (David Vincent)*

*recurring cast (as from "The Believers"): Kent Smith (Edgar Scoville)*

*also: Dick Wesson (narrator — opening credits), William Woodson (narrator — premise and episodes)* \*

\* This is a perfect example of Quinn Martin's commitment to quality. Most producers would simply have the same narrator read out the guest credits. Martin wanted a different voice for the guest credits, and thought nothing of paying to have one. A tiny detail, unnoticed by most, but he cared about it.

## First Season

## (1966-'67)

## Beachhead

wr. Anthony Wilson, dir. Joseph Sargent

Travelling late at night, architect David Vincent stops his car at a deserted diner and witnesses the landing of a flying saucer. From that moment on, his life becomes a constant ongoing nightmare as he tries to warn the Earth of impending invasion while the invading aliens pursue both him and their aims in human form...

*with James Daly (Alan Landers), Diane Baker (Kathy Adams), J.D. Cannon (Lt. Ben Holman), John Milford (Lou Carver), Ellen Corby (Aunt Sarah), Vaughn Taylor (Mr. Kemper), James 'Skip' Ward (John Brandon), Bonnie Beecher (Mrs. Brandon), Mary Jackson (nurse)*

Sleeping in his car, Vincent is woken by a strange whirring sound and colorful lights. To his astonishment, he witnesses the landing of what can only be a 'flying saucer'.

When Vincent reports what he's seen to the local police department, they assume he's stressed and overworked, and contact his partner, Alan Landers, to take him home. Vincent demands the police accompany him to the landing site, and with great reluctance, the cynical and irritated Lt. Holman drives out there with Vincent and Landers, where they find no evidence of any UFO landing, and-- to further discredit Vincent's credibility--that the deserted 'Bud's Diner' was in fact 'Kelly's Diner'.

Final confirmation that nothing bizarre has been happening comes from the Brandons, two young marrieds who claim to have been living in their trailer by the deserted diner for the past two days, and say they were awake and saw or heard nothing. When the young man shows Holman his driving licence for identification, Vincent notices for the first time what will eventually become a tell-tale sign of one of the extraterrestrial invaders in human form — a stiff and protruding little finger.

That night, Vincent drives back to the scene and begins aggressively questioning the honeymooners. He's greeted by the wife, carrying a shotgun, but then the husband emerges from the camper looking agitated—they need to leave quickly. Vincent tries to restrain him, and they fight. As the young man prepares to finish Vincent with a rock, both combatants react in horror as the man's hands begin to glow brightly. As they flee, Vincent is hit a glancing blow by the camper, and wakes up in a hospital room. "Do you remember anything?" asks the nurse. "Don't try and remember any more!". She then tries to administer medication, but Vincent notices to his horror that the name on his i.d. tag isn't his. For an awful moment, Vincent suspects the ultimate betrayal, a grand conspiracy, but Landers reveals that he was found unconscious by the roadside and signed in to the hospital by his colleague under an assumed name-- to protect his reputation.

Recuperating, Vincent desperately tries to convince Landers that the campers were in on the plot to discredit his sighting and conceal an extraterrestrial presence on Earth, but everyone is understandably convinced he's deluded. As the despairing Landers leaves, his departure is watched by an elderly lady in a wheelchair... who awkwardly cleans her spectacles with the disadvantage of two stiff little fingers!

When Landers collects Vincent from the hospital that evening, he has obtained the address of the honeymoon couple in an effort to placate his anxious friend-- they live in the small town of Kinney. That night, Vincent's hotel room is engulfed in flames... and through the haze, Vincent spots the little old lady--standing--and peering into his room.

Vincent travels to Kinney, where he finds the town nearly deserted, and the only hotel closed. The owner, Kathy Adams, is a recent widow who tells Vincent that the town, abandoned when the local hydro-electric plant closed down, is in the process of being bought up by the Kogan corporation. In the meantime, the local sheriff, Carver, has 'phoned Lt. Holman and left a message that "he was right--the psycho did show up here".

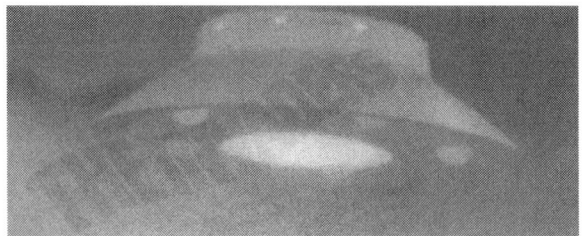

Vincent snoops around the deserted hydro-electric plant and discovers an alien stronghold, full of what he will discover in subsequent episodes is their regenerating equipment. However, he triggers a silent warning system, and as a task force of aliens speeds to the town, Vincent hides out in a local coffee bar, where he 'phones Alan Landers and begs him to witness what he's discovered. Reluctantly, Landers agrees to come to Kinney, where Vincent will meet him at Kathy's hotel. Unfortunately, Vincent is unaware that the 'Aunt Sara' Kathy has asked to inform them of his arrival is none other than Vincent's not-very-disabled geriatric firebug!

When Landers arrives, he is intercepted by the old lady and told to meet Vincent at the plant... where he is ambushed by aliens. Meanwhile, the unsuspecting Vincent, reassured by Kathy's lack of deformed fingers and the suspicion that her husband may have been disposed of by the invaders, confides in her that he feels his high profile noisemaking about an invasion from space will dissuade the aliens from delivering a similar fate to him. However it soon becomes dismayingly evident that Kathy is deliberately keeping him occupied, and standing revealed, makes a last-ditch attempt to seduce Vincent into submission. Vincent flees, and finds Landers' car, but delayed by Sheriff Carver, is too late to save him, who's discovered the truth to his cost. The hydro-electric plant is now, of course, completely empty.

The next morning, surrounded by silently watching aliens in human form he can't expose, Vincent is escorted out of town with the body of his friend. "What a shame" says the old lady. "He looked and talked so normal... You just never know..."

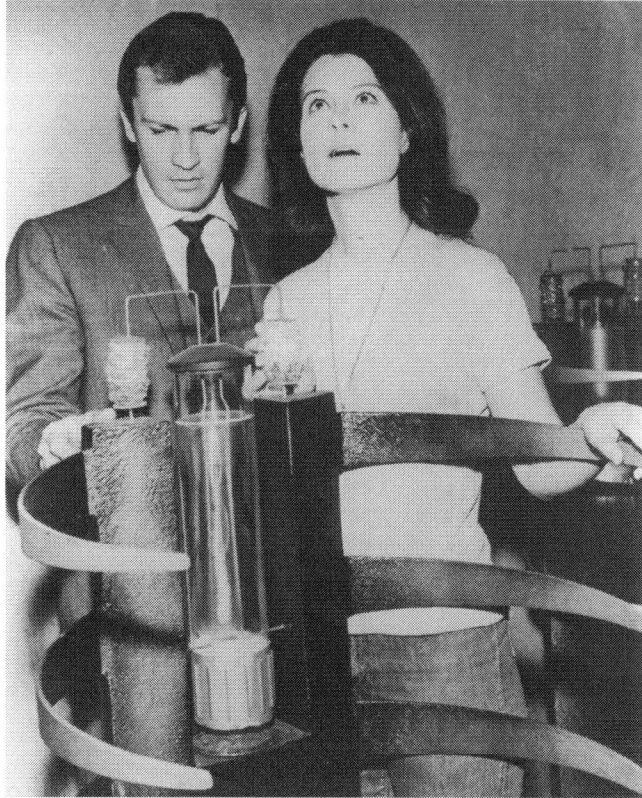

*Roy Thinnes and Diane Baker pose for a publicity shot in the regenerating centre (in the episode, Kathy never actually goes there)*

end result: poor. Kinney colony closed down, but no alien casualties; Adams, Carver, Sarah, and the Brandons still out there; David's partner killed.

The pilot, directed by Joseph Sargent, is wonderful--the performances were uniformly excellent, and included James Daly from the tragic *Twilight Zone* "A Stop at Willoughby", and Ellen Corby, Grandma in *The Waltons,* superb

341

here as the malevolent old woman who haunts Vincent's trail. J.D. Cannon's sceptical cop is a delight-- after a decade of playing villains, he later became a familiar face in the '70s as Chief Clifford, a delightful portrayal of the snarling harassed boss stereotype in Glen Larson's *McCloud*.

Perfectly structured, particularly at the end as David fights in vain to rescue his friend, Landers' doomed advance into the power plant played against Vincent's desperate struggle to find him. There was a nice sense of irony and humor in this one, too; the old lady's remark that Vincent, dragged away as a loony, "looked so nice and normal, but you never know" when in fact she's an alien, and Holman's ambiguous warning to Vincent at the end—is he an alien making a knowing threat, or just an angry cop upset at a needless death?

There's a wonderful ambiguity in the pilot about who the aliens really are that was missing from subsequent episodes, in which--in a series of revelations throughout the story--extraterrestrial origins would be confirmed or denied. In "Beachhead", we're never sure whether Holman is just an angry, pragmatic cop reacting naturally toward a man he perceives as a dangerous nutter, or whether he's an alien stooge when he threatens Vincent angrily in the final scene, fuming "This is the final word, Vincent, the bottom line. For your own sake, let it end here. Whatever you're planning, let it end here!". Happily for us, Vincent ignored this ominous warning, and 42 more episodes followed.

What to make of Anthony Wilson? He worked in a variety of genres throughout his career in the '60s and '70s, and made only weak and modest contributions to *The Twilight Zone* and *Voyage to the Bottom of the Sea*, and yet his contribution to sci-fi TV was incalculable. He came up with the idea for Doctor Smith in *Lost in Space*, and worked as story editor on the entire series; he wrote two of the best TV SF pilots in the history of the medium, this one, and "The Crash" for *Land of the Giants*; he was responsible for making all the characters on *Land of the Giants* three-dimensional, and all depth of characterisation disappeared when he unfortunately left to work on the western *Lancer*; he also came up with story ideas for some of the most memorable episodes. He also developed *Planet of the Apes* for TV, executive produced *The Immortal*, and wrote the pilot for *Future Cop*. In mainstream TV, he created the series *Cade's County* and *Banacek*.

On the one hand, he comes across as a jobbing hack, flitting from one series or genre to another, and over-reliant on the man-on-the-run formula and stock plots; on the other, he was responsible for getting and keeping three legendary and much-loved sci-fi series on the air, and stuck his fingers in several others. At the very least, we should salute his memory.

*One of the many symbolic composite publicity pics produced showing Roy Thinnes with the alien saucer.*

Followers of *The Outer Limits* will hear some of Frontiere's stock music for that series in the opening teaser, at the close of Act One, when Vincent is running through the h o s p i t a l  c o r r i d o r s ,  a n d apprehended, and again, when he loiters outside the power plant. A clever touch by the aliens is the alteration of the diner sign to discredit Vincent—if he got that wrong, he was probably mistaken about everything else, right?

Beginning an annoying trait of the series right from the off, James Daly will return as a guest star, albeit late in season two and heavily made up. Later returnees would not be so well concealed. J.D. Cannon

also returns late in the second season.

Kinney was in reality, the town of Temecula, according to Jonathan Etter's *Quinn Martin Productions* for McFarland. "Today, Temecula has vineyards and resort hotels" said a production assistant. "When we shot there, there was nothing". The power plant scenes were shot at the Fox Ranch in Malibu and the El Segundo sewage plant.

### The Experiment

wr. Anthony Spinner, dir. Joseph Sargent

Vincent's race against the invaders to secure a terrified elderly scientist's evidence of the alien presence on Earth is hampered by the man's drug-dependent son, the victim of the invaders' experiments in brainwashing...

*with Roddy McDowall (Lloyd Lindstrom), Laurence Naismith (Dr. Curtis Lindstrom), Harold Gould (Dr. Paul Mailer), Dabbs Greer (The Minister), Lawrence Montaigne, Max Kleven (government men/aliens), Roy Sickner (Minister's aide/driver), Stuart Lancaster (apartment superintendent), Jackie Kendall (landlady), Willard Sage (Lt. James), Mel Gallagher (male nurse), John Ward (State Trooper), Soon-Teck Oh (alien valet)*

end result: grim. Alien brainwashing centre destroyed, along with alien leader and several minions; but several alien survivors and 43 known human casualties--the Lindstroms and Mailer, plus the air passengers.

and inspired direction. Joseph Sargent's constantly dipping, swerving, tilting camera and some extraordinary exploitation of color — particularly in the chapel and the alien brainwashing centre — lends the episode a sweeping disorientating tone heightened by the carefully choreographed assaults on McDowall's mannered but disintegrating addict Lloyd, a clear anti-drugs allegory. Naismith is superb as the terrified doomed scientist, and Gould dependable as the disbelieving doctor; Sargent, who also directed the pilot, plays the audience like a maestro.

As in the best episodes of *The Invaders*, the minor roles are made the most of, too--the leering smug villainy of Roy Sickner (an actor able to put on an extraordinarily evil face!) and Lawrence Montaigne (smirking when Lindstrom realises he is not in the company of government agents), the venality of the lonely hotel landlady and the apartment super (who, taking Vincent's bribe, trails off with a pathetic 'you've got an honest face'!), and the inspired casting of rent-a-rube Dabbs Greer, playing against type as the sinister minister (although he went on to play a more genial Minister in the long-running *Little House on the Prairie*), burning in allegorical fire in his alien pulpit at episode's end.

The only weakness is in the too clear sight we get of the all-important proof that Vincent is so excited about--actually, not much at all. Lindstrom has nothing really, little more than the average saucer sighting, with affidavits from the standard farmer and military man, and a few shots of alien bric-a-brac and inevitable saucer... just another day at Bluebook, and hardly the

stuff of a government meeting. Lindstrom would surely have been laughed off the podium by his peers after all...

*Thinnes with Roddy McDowell*

Anthony Spinner was a producer, and produced (with Alan Armer, who stayed for the whole run), the first and best season of *The Invaders*, with most of the best episodes. His m.o. was essentially to work on a different show each season, usually but not always for Quinn Martin, and whether or not it went on, the only exception being *Cannon*, on which he worked for two. He was also a writer, and usually did something for each show he worked on, but not much. This, in common with his usual practice, was the only episode he wrote for the show. It was a good one, but the actors and director steal the show to such an extent, it's difficult to assess his input. He was, nevertheless, as much as he despaired of the difficulties inherent in the format, at the helm of the series when it was at its height. The show he moved on to from here was *The Man from UNCLE*, with which he did a phenomenal job of restoring it

344

to its former glories before its thoughtless and foolish cancellation (for the full details behind that debacle, see the first *Cool TV* book).

wr. David Chandler, George Eckstein, dir. Paul Wendkos

An elaborate plot is staged to keep Vincent and the Air Force away

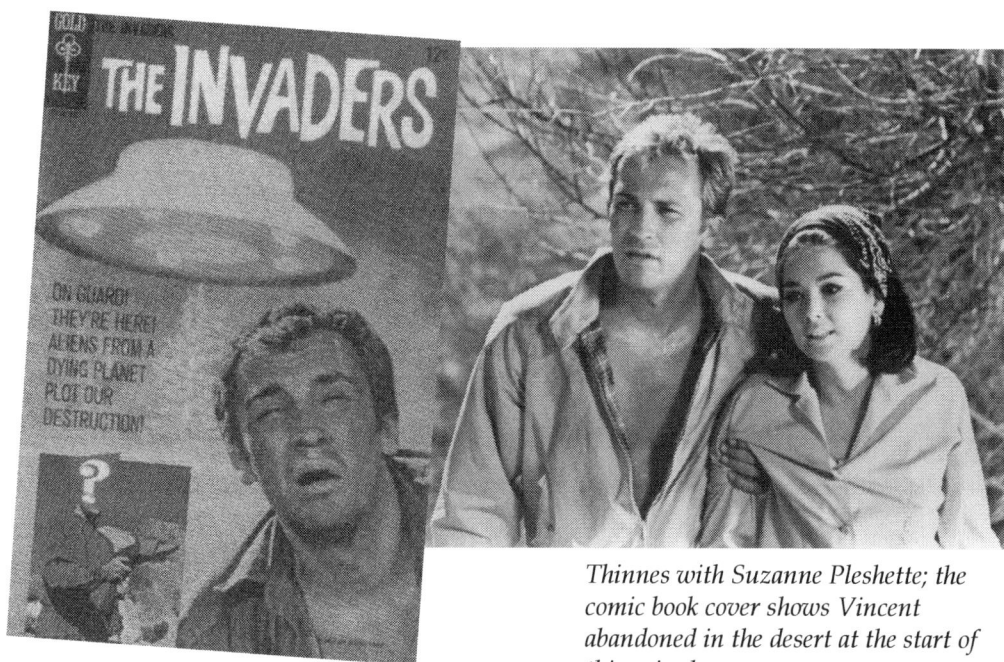

*Thinnes with Suzanne Pleshette; the comic book cover shows Vincent abandoned in the desert at the start of this episode.*

Following *UNCLE's* close, he then moved to Burt Reynolds' *Dan August*, *The Mod Squad*, *The Banana Splits* (!—as a writer only), the interesting failure *Search*, *The FBI*, the short-lived QM disaster *Caribe*, the safe port of *Cannon*, the notorious minefield of *Baretta*, the instant cancellation *Supertrain*, and finally, as QM closed, to Britain, for *Return of the Saint*.

This is the first episode to use the sinister cerebral haemorrhage device, and introduces much of the superb background music that will haunt the first season.

**The Mutation**

from a downed UFO in Mexico until it can be repaired

*with Suzanne Pleshette (Vikki), Edward Andrews (Evans), Lin McCarthy (Fellows), Roy Jenson (lead alien), Rodolfo Hoyos (rancher), Argentina Brunetti (rancher's wife), Val Avery (strip club manager), William Stevens (Cobbs), Tina Menard (mother), Tony Davis (boy), Roberto Contreras, Pepe Callahan (bandits), Pedro Regas (beggar)*

end result: not bad--Evans and the saucer got away, but Fellows is almost converted to the cause, the rest of the aliens are dead, and the Mexican family survived.

This is the episode in which we--and Vincent--first learn that the aliens glow red and dissolve into ash when killed.

David Chandler was one of the regular writers on *Adventures of Superman, Big Town,* and *Richard Diamond, Private Detective* during the '50s. For such a simplistic resume, this is a surprisingly strong and complex episode. George Eckstein was a producer on *The Fugitive, The Name of the Game,* and *Banacek,* and a writer for numerous series, including *The Untouchables, The Fugitive,* and *The Invaders.* He divided his time mostly between Universal and Quinn Martin, and when QM closed its doors, he spent the late '70s and 1980s producing TV movies and mini-series.

Paul Wendkos would go on to direct nine episodes of *The Invaders* in total, all good ones. He also directed around a dozen or so episodes of *The Untouchables* and *I Spy,* two other quality shows of the '60s. He also became king of the TV movies in the 1970s for the next three decades, only occasionally returning to series TV in favour of TV films and mini-series.

This episode has a great cast. Edward Andrews was a polished and professional character actor who could play comedy (he was good at bluster, confusion, and verge-of-panic), and sweaty, sleazy villainy. Suzanne Pleshette was a tough, ballsy actress who spent the 1970s profitably but unchallenged in *The Bob Newhart Show.* She played several different roles in *Doctor Kildare, Bonanza, The FBI, The Fugitive,* and *The Name of the Game.*

Lin McCarthy worked regularly for Quinn Martin, notably in *The Invaders, The Fugitive,* and *The FBI.* Roy Jenson, as regular readers of my work must know by now, is my favorite heavy, and he's been in everything. His largest role, in *Star Trek's* "Omega Glory", was his least impressive, but he was golden in *Batman, The Man from UNCLE, Voyage to the Bottom of the Sea,* and numerous films, working regularly with John Wayne, Clint Eastwood, and Sam Peckinpah.

Mexican-born Rodolfo Hoyos specialised in South-of-the-border roles and appeared in *Amos Burke – Secret Agent, The Wild Wild West, The*

*Time Tunnel, I Spy,* and *The Man from UNCLE,* among many others. Argentina Brunetti and Tina Menard played countless bit parts as mothers and maids throughout their careers. Ditto bit players Roberto Contreras and Pepe Callahan who played an assortment of ethnic roles from humble workers, to bandits, to corrupt police officers and Generals over the years.

*Peter Mark Richman stands in front of the helicopter he and Vincent take to the skies in to search for "The Leeches".*

Young Tony Davis played numerous similar roles throughout the 1960s, including both *UNCLE* series, and plenty of westerns, including the feature film *Guns of the Magnificent Seven,* also directed by Paul Wendkos.

Perhaps cop show regular Val Avery's best role was as a gangster in Cohen's finest work, the early '70s exploitation film *Black Caesar.*

**The Leeches**

wr. Dan Ullman, dir. Paul Wendkos

When the invaders kidnap leading figures in science and industry to drain their brains, an industrialist suspects he'll be next and sets himself up as bait to trap them. The plan is hampered by the unrequited love of his neglected wife and best friend

*with Arthur Hill (Warren Doneghan), Peter Mark Richman (Tom Wiley), Diana Van der Vlis (Eve Doneghan), Robert H. Harris (Hastings), Theo Marcuse (Markham), Peter Brocco (Millington), Noah Keen (psychiatrist), William Wintersole (alien project leader), Hank Brandt (cruel gloating alien), Ray Kellogg, Craig Chudy, Ron Nyman (alien henchmen)*

end result: good--Vincent has a powerful ally in Warren Donegan, and the brain drain scheme and accumulated information is destroyed. Several aliens are killed, with just two known human casualties.

This is the first of many stories in which the aliens wilfully destroy themselves rather than let their presence on Earth be exposed. It's also the first of many to feature that familiar *Invaders* cliche, the neurotic, drippy wife forever standing in the way of the men, who act while they react. To be fair, it was probably truthful for the time, as women had few options in the '60s once they'd chosen a man, and were frequently patronised and excluded—and to be fair a second time, *The Invaders* does also feature its fair share of strong women.

One minor goof has Donegan saying he'll put the radio transmitter in a St. Christopher... but when the aliens pull it from around his neck, it's a standard disc-shaped device, and fairly obvious in its purpose. The self-destruct device the invaders use in this early episode is rather more traditionally explosive than the instant disintegration we'll see in later episodes such as "Nightmare", "Wall of Crystal" and "The Betrayed". This gives Vincent and the scientists a chance to get out as the place crumbles around them that they couldn't have had in later episodes, and provides an exciting conclusion. All things considered though, the instant immolation of buildings that we later see is a quite a sight, and exclusive to this particular series.

For whatever reason, Arthur Hill (who specialised in being the 'surprise' bad guy so often that it wasn't much of a surprise when he was unmasked), didn't do much sci-fi, although when he did, it was a lulu—the scientist controlled by an evil disembodied brain from outer space in "Monster From the Inferno", a classic *Voyage to the Bottom of the Sea*. Here, he's a bona-fide good guy for a change. Peter Mark Richman, Theo Marcuse, Peter Brocco, and Robert H. Harris were, on the other hand, veterans of this sort of stuff, with credits in almost every major sci-fi show of the '60s.

William Wintersole would be back in "Dark Outpost", and did several *Mission: Impossible,* being particularly good in an opportunity in the first season's "Old Man Out", in which he plays a guard mentally tortured by his duties.

Ron Nyman was an often uncredited bit player who appeared as aliens four times in *The Invaders,* and was also often a caveman in *It's About Time* this year! He also made numerous uncredited appearances in shows such as *The Rogues, Bewitched, Batman,* and *Mission: Impossible.* Craig Chudy also made numerous appearances on *Mission: Impossible,* and is instantly recognisable as an alien in at least six different episodes of *The Invaders.* He also appeared on *Lost in Space* and *The Man from UNCLE.*

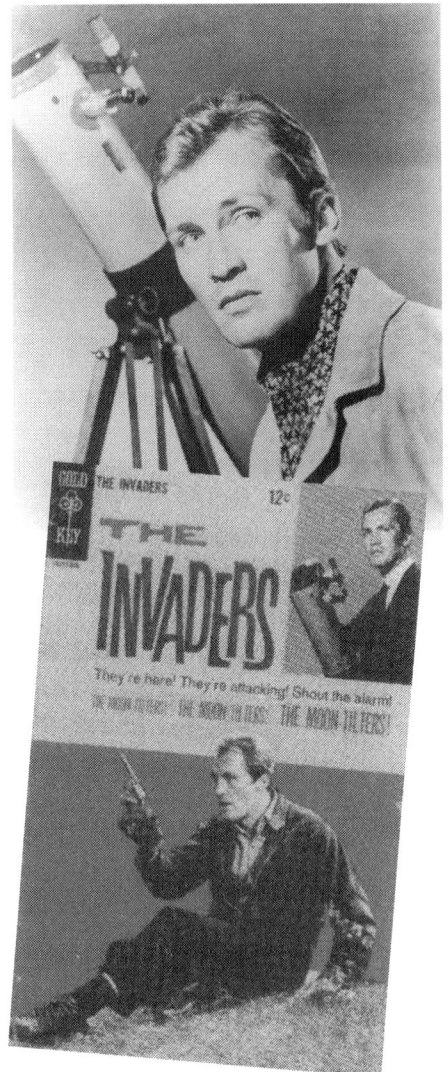

## Genesis

wr. John Bloch, dir. Richard Benedict

When a motor cycle cop goes mad after seeing a degenerating alien, Vincent and a sceptical police lieutenant discover sinister goings-on at an oceanic research centre where only two human staff remain

*with John Larch (Lt. Greg Lukather), Carol Rossen (Selene Lowell), William Sargent (Dr. Ken Harrison), Frank Overton (Dr. Grayson), Louise Latham (Joan Corman), Phillip Pine (Hal Corman), Tim McIntire (alien teenager), Jonathan Lippe (alien in garage), Dallas Mitchell (Andy/cop), James Devine (Jimmy/lab alien), Bill Erwin (building manager), Dani Nolan (nurse)*

*William Sargent in "Genesis" returns for "Dark Outpost"*

end result: good, but at the price of Corman's life; Vincent gains another convert, the hard-nosed incorruptible cop Lukather, the alien experiment is destroyed, and all the known aliens are killed.

This is the only time in the series anybody survives the alien disc experience. It's never explained why Hal the cop is still alive. But once again with this series, it's the chilling unspoken sub-text which is most unnerving... that Ken and Selene were the only human beings unwittingly and unknowingly working alongside work colleagues who were all of them deceitful, inhuman evil aliens!

John Larch was the archetypal TV cop, playing around two hundred roles from the earliest days of TV until the end of the '80s, almost all of them various levels of the law and order hierarchy, from the lowliest detective, to police chief, and up! One rare exception was as a *Man from UNCLE* villain, a THRUSH mad scientist in "The Man from THRUSH Affair".

Carol Rossen is the daughter of writer/director Robert Rossen, and worked her way through a variety of nondescript TV roles including five different parts on *The Fugitive*.

Frank Overton memorably appeared as the father of Martin Sloane in the classic *Twilight Zone* episode "Walking Distance", and shortly before he died, the mellifluous tones of his extraordinary voice graced both this exemplary episode of *The Invaders* and the *Star Trek* favorite "This Side of Paradise". William Sargent and Tim McIntire would both appear together again in the episode "Dark Outpost".

Louise Latham appeared to have cornered the market in tragic wives, many for QM, and she's filling that function here too.

Phil Pine's cult TV credits include *The Untouchables, The Outer Limits, Voyage to the Bottom of the Sea, The Wild Wild West, Star Trek, Mission: Impossible, Police Story, Lou Grant*, and numerous appearances in QM series, frequently more than once or twice. Throughout the '60s and '70s, Dallas Mitchell played cops, reporters, and occasionally military men over fifty times in popular series.

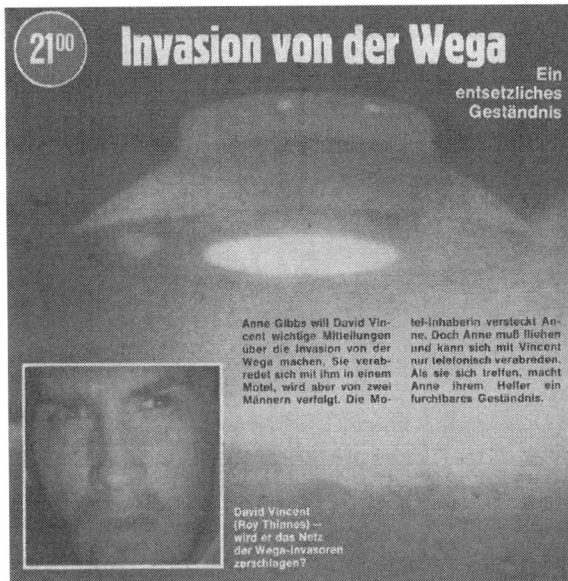

Invasion von der Wega

James Devine also mostly appeared in QM series during a brief career in the '60s.

John Bloch wrote six episodes of *The Invaders,* all good ones, but no other SF TV. He seems to have preferred contemporary series to westerns, and stayed with few shows past one or two episodes, but wrote more of *The Invaders* than anything except *Run For Your Life,* a *Fugitive* clone that ran for three seasons but is virtually forgotten today. He seems to have preferred stories that tried to say something, and stayed on *The Young Lawyers* as a story consultant throughout its short run.

Former actor Richard Benedict found directing more profitable, and like any television director, took work where he could get it. He started out at the Warners factory of the early '60s, and then found most of his assignments on the aforementioned *Run For Your Life,* alongside *Police Story* and *Hawaii Five-O.* Working until his death in the early '80s, he also occasionally took bit parts, a common practice among semi-retired actors to maintain their medical insurance.

Acting under the name of Lippe throughout the '60s and '70s, and Goldsmith thereafter, Jonathan Lippe played a number of recurring roles, and was frequently used by QM.

Looking elderly throughout his entire career (and living to 96!), Bill Erwin played over two hundred minor roles in numerous dramas and comedies on U.S. TV from the earliest days to his final credit in 2006. Dani Nolan also played dozens of bit parts in U.S. TV, a huge number of them in Quinn Martin productions. She was briefly married to producer William Asher.

### Vikor

wr. Don Brinkley, dir. Paul Wendkos

Vincent finds an egotistical and embittered war veteran with a grudge aiding the aliens by manufacturing components for the devices at his factory in return for the promise of power.

with Jack Lord (George Vikor), Diana Hyland (Sherri Vikor), Alfred Ryder (Mr. Nexus), Richard O'Brien (police sergeant), Sam Edwards (Hank/linesman), Joe Di Reda (Phil/linesman), Larry Duran (valet), Hal Baylor, Max Kleven (guards)

end result: successful disposal of manufacturing plant for alien regeneration centres; Nexus escapes, but all other aliens disposed of; two known human losses — the poor linesmen whose discovery of a regeneration centre first alerted Vincent to the entire operation.

Jack Lord, later to spend the 1970s as leading man of the hit series *Hawaii Five-0*, considered Vikor one of his best roles, and he was absolutely right. He plays George Vikor brilliantly, making the most of such scenes as when he abandons his wife to her fate, and earlier, when alone in his office, he stalks around listening to a recording of his hero's welcome, gently lifting the stylus on the record player and moving it back to lengthen the cheers. Prior to his iconic cop show (for which Wendkos directed the pilot, securing them both a comfortable decade ahead), he had guested in episodes of *The Untouchables* and *The Man from UNCLE*.

Diana Hyland's cult TV roles included *The Twilight Zone*, *Burke's Law*, *I Spy*, *The Green Hornet*, and *The Man from UNCLE*. She had a regular role on *Peyton Place* at around this time for a while, and returns for the two-parter "Summit Meeting".

Sinister-looking Alfred Ryder is best remembered as the Phantom in two episodes of *Voyage to the Bottom of the Sea* and Professor Crater in *Star Trek's* "Man Trap". He played the leader of the aliens in *The Invaders* three times. He also villained the place up in *The Outer Limits*, *The Man from UNCLE*, and *Land of the Giants*.

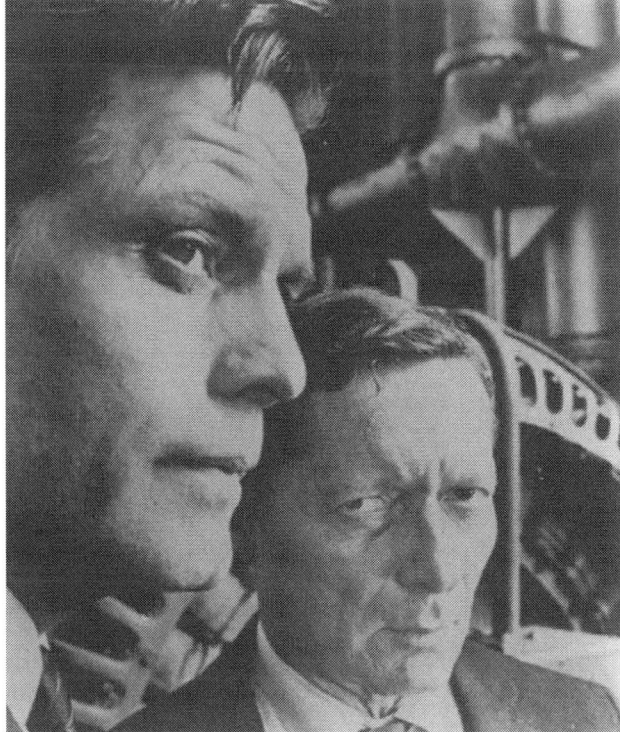

*Jack Lord and Alfred Ryder looking suitably sinister and suspicious in this wonderful promo pic for "Vikor". Ryder went on to make two more appearances in the series as bad guys!*

Equally sinister-looking stunt man Larry Duran's numerous credits include thugs and henchmen in *The Man from UNCLE*, *I Spy*, *THE Cat*, *Batman*, *Get Smart*, *The Wild Wild West*, *The Six Million Dollar Man*, *The Bionic Woman*, and *Buck Rogers in the 25th Century*.

### Nightmare

wr. John Kneubuhl, dir. Paul Wendkos

A nervous, stressed schoolteacher stumbles onto an alien experiment to create a plague of flesh-eating insects across the U.S. from a farm in Kansas.

*with Kathleen Widdoes (Ellen Woods), James Callahan (Ed Gidney), Robert Emhardt (Oliver Ames), Jeanette Nolan (Miss Havergill), William Bramley (Constable Gabbard), Logan Field (Carl Gidney), Irene Tedrow (Clare Lapham), Nellie Burt (Lena Lapham), John Harmon (diner owner), Wayne Heffley (Deputy Walton), William Challee (Ira Danielson), Jim Halferty (Fred Danielson), Carey Loftin (Hank Braden)*

end result: a great success--all aliens either driven out of Grady or destroyed, with no known human losses; invaders Ames and Havergill destroyed with the silo.

A superb episode, great fun. A personal favorite, and the series at its best.

This episode, like the pilot, demonstrates the series' concept of the aliens gradually moving into town and taking it over by degrees, as in '50s classics *Invasion of the Body Snatchers, Invaders from Mars*, and *I Married a Monster from Outer Space*. The only mystery is why the aliens waited so long to dispose of the schoolteacher, unstable enough to be written off as a suicide, especially with the principal and the police spoken for. But the images... oh, the images!

The butterflies devouring the meat, Nellie Burt and Irene Tedrow as the fluttery old women fussing over Ellen, Ellen suddenly realising that all the men working at the farm are out to get her, Ellen and Vincent fleeing the bugs, Ames and Havergill scuttling around the silo like panicky cockroaches themselves, desperately trying to destroy all the evidence of their work... wonderful.

This has been the only sci-fi work by stage actress Kathleen Widdowes, who only occasionally did films and TV before eventually taking a regular role on daytime soap *As the World Turns* from the mid-'80s to 2010. James Callahan, a familiar face on TV, returned in the second season, and had another strong SF role in *Time Tunnel's* "One Way to the Moon".

The supporting cast is wonderful from top to bottom. Professional old biddies Irene Tedrow and Nellie Burt are on top form, Jeanette Nolan is another of the series' aliens-as-wicked-witches (she played actual witches in *The Twilight Zone, Boris Karloff's Thriller*, and *Night Gallery!*), and familiar face William Bramley is solid as the alien police officer.

Robert Emhardt played many different roles during a career in TV from the beginning of the '50s to the mid-'80s, but he was always best employed as a villain, and he outdoes himself here as the horrible Ames, a *noir*-ish monster who's stepped into the small-town color world of *The Invaders* to infiltrate another simple community of the sort the invaders targeted in the early episodes, before second season producer David Rintels moved the stories less effectively into the city.

## Doomsday Minus One

wr. Louis Vittes, dir. Paul Wendkos

Vincent is called in undercover by the security officer at a military base where the commanding officer is in league with the aliens to create an atomic disaster with an anti-matter bomb

*with William Windom (Major Rick Graves), Andrew Duggan (General Theodore Beaumont), Wesley Addy (Mr. Tomkins), Robert Osterloh (Carl Wyeth), Tom Palmer (Charlie Spence), Lee Farr (alien Justice Dept. agent), Lew Brown (military officer), Rick Murray (parking attendant), K.L. Smith, Dan Kennedy (guards), Dave Armstrong (military policeman)*

end result: success--major nuclear disaster averted, with all known aliens destroyed; there are four known human casualties-- Spence, MacIntyre, Beaumont, and his driver.

In the earliest and best episodes of the series, the show put great emphasis on the weaknesses of individual human beings — Vikor, resentful of his treatment by the banks as a 'bad risk' after being hailed as a hero, the drugs-addled nephew of the Professor who's seen the aliens, Ed Gidney, a small-town thug without the guts to report what he's seen, and later, Nat Greeley, the fisherman who's seen too much and is cowering in the dark. Sometimes, like Tom Wiley, and later Barney Cahill, they were initially weak and self-centred, but then rose to the occasion. Here, we have a combination of both, the alien dupe who sees the light right at the end.

Tall, silver-haired Andrew Duggan was a powerful actor, perfectly suited to the tense, sweaty human interest-centred melodrama of the Quinn Martin studios, and was the archetypal Patton-esque 1950s-style butt-clenched military hardass. He was also a good friend of series creator Larry Cohen, who used him several times in his films. Here, he plays — brilliantly — a General driven so mad by the death of his son in Korea that he is the perfect foil for the aliens. He entertains the ridiculous fantasy that a single nuclear disaster will cure the world of warfare and that he can then expose the aliens to the world (which you would imagine would then make everyone re-arm even more!). The scenes where Vincent and Graves desperately try to snap him out of his illusions, and then shock, make for a tense and exciting conclusion.

Louis Vittes was a regular writer on *Rawhide*, and wrote for various shows during the '50s and '60s. More significantly, he was the writer of *I Married a Monster from Outer Space*. (Less significantly, he also wrote *Monster from Green Hell*). There is no indication of either the themes or the style of either film in his single sci-fi TV episode, but it's a good one, and a shame he didn't write more. Once again, as in several early episodes, despite supposedly being unemotional, in the opening scenes disposing of Spence, the aliens appear to be taking a sadistic delight in tormenting their victims. This element of spiteful evil and horror, also seen in "The Experiment", "The Leeches", and "The Innocent", to name but three, would disappear in the second season, as the aliens become simply and coldly pragmatic.

## Quantity: Unknown

wr. Don Brinkley, dir. Sutton Roley

When the aliens lose a valuable cylinder of data, Vincent encounters a man even more driven than he is

*with James Whitmore Jnr. (Harry Swain), Susan Strasberg (Diane Oberly), Milton Seltzer (Mr. Richards), William Talman (Colonel Griffiths), Barney Phillips (Walt Anson), Douglas Henderson (Lt. Farley), Ernest Sarracino (Leo Rinaldi), Byron Keith (Air Crash investigator), Michael Harris (Mail Truck Driver), Raymond Guth (guard), Melville Ruick (Minister), Ron Doyle (rescuer)*

end result: a major debacle; Vincent is brutally fooled, there are numerous human casualties, many aliens go unpunished, and the valuable evidence is destroyed.

This one feels like a bit of a cheat, but if you haven't watched it yet, don't read on until you have— major spoilers as we discuss it.

We have established in most episodes that the invaders are clever, but unemotional, which is their giveaway flaw. Diane Oberly, for example, is a good red herring because she seems cold and aloof, and is a potential alien. It's a good twist that she isn't. Douglas Henderson's pissed-off cop could also easily go either way. However, Whitmore (so memorable in the iconic sci-fi giant bug monster movie *Them*) plays Harry Swain with such great emotion and conviction that the big reveal at the beginning of Act Four seems like a deception too far. His character, as written and played, was far too 'human' to suddenly be

exposed as an award-winning performance by an alien. It's a disappointing development because his human identity was so well drawn, and original. This is, or would have been, the only episode where Vincent encounters a man as driven and tortured as he is, and for an even more powerful motive—the casual immolation of his whole family.

Also, we've earlier seen Swain bloodied and beaten; aliens aren't supposed to bleed. This can be explained away as faked, but it still seems unfair to the audience. The fun of *The Invaders* is that although the aliens are masquerading as humans, they always *look* like they could be aliens. William Talman's granite-faced Griffiths is a perfect example of this casting. Whitmore's performance is far too realistic and lifelike, and moves the goalposts. He's just too good in this powerful gift of a role; the fault is not with him, but the premise.

The episode also suffers from another kind of cheat, the scene where a character does something unrealistic and ridiculous just to create the next situation. When Vincent is in Griffith's office, and the deception is revealed, Vincent shoots and disintegrates Griffiths, but after overpowering Swain, fails to destroy him as well, despite having a clear shot. Instead, he just turns and runs, and then removes the cylinder from its hiding place *right in front of the alien*, who is now naturally in pursuit. This facilitates both the exciting chase, and the inevitable destruction of the cylinder... all very good for the show, which would otherwise have ended with this episode, but what a stupid thing for Vincent to do after being smart enough not to have it with him in the office. I've said it before and I'll say it again—the leading man *must* be a credible hero who acts credibly, otherwise it's impossible to believe in him or the series. Vincent cannot be cavalier with other people's lives or careless with his evidence just to keep the series rolling along, otherwise it ceases to roll and grinds to a halt. You cannot get away with careless direction or bad writing in a series like *The Invaders*. If the aliens can be this clever, and Vincent can be this dumb, they can never be defeated, and the entire format crumbles. We have to believe that Vincent has a chance to beat these things, which means *he* has to be perfect and the aliens have to be vulnerable. That means no alien method actors.

## The Innocent

wr. Norman Klenman, Bernard Rothman, John Bloch, dir. Sutton Roley

While pursuing a fear-stricken fisherman who has an alien device in his possession and is in turn being hunted by the invaders for it, Vincent is abducted and discredited in the eyes of his military contact after experiencing a pleasurable hallucination on board an alien saucer to attract him to the alien cause

*with Michael Rennie (Magnus), William Smithers (Nat Greely), Patricia Smith (Edna Greely), Paul Carr (Billy Stearns), Katherine Justice (Helen), Dabney Coleman (Captain Ross), Robert Doyle (Sgt. Ruddell), Frank Marth, Harry Lauter (alien pursuers), Erik Holland (alien military policeman), Johnny Jensen (young Nat)*

end result: neither a win or a loss for Vincent or the aliens, just an emotional roller-coaster for Vincent.

This is one of the most memorable episodes in the series, with a great premise and a wonderful cast to realise it. It's also the second and last of two directed by Sutton Roley, an adventurous director and one of the few whose work was often recognisable and distinguishable from other TV directors, something very rare.

Roley did his most memorable work on *Lost in Space, Voyage to the Bottom of the Sea,* and *The Man from UNCLE,* but the visuals on *The Invaders* were so offbeat anyway, he simply blends in! That said, some of the shots of Vincent's hallucination, and the composition of the scenes on the saucer are exceptional. The scene at the fishing boat with the aliens also features many of his innovative trademark shots, noticeably the aliens walking toward, and into, the camera.

Several aspects shine — the terrible dilemma of the fishing family, simple people who were in the wrong place at the wrong time, and whose lives are now spiralling out of control into a never-ending nightmare; the various torments of David Vincent; the pure, remorseless evil of the invaders; and the notion of the aliens trying to buy him off — what do you most want? It can be yours.

Greeley as soon as he leaves. And why did Vincent not pre-arrange a code word for contacting Ross that would tip him off his call is coerced.

The dream sequence, where David realises his architectural ambitions, now taken cruelly away from him by his crusade against the aliens, was filmed at the futuristic Rossmore Leisure World, says Jonathan Etten's QM book... much

*On board the alien saucer. On the far left, one of my favorite character players, Harry Lauter. In the centre, wearing glasses, Frank Marth. And on the far right, Michael Rennie.*

The theme — Earth people's humanity against the invaders' inhumanity. Fighting for the survival of our entire race, we probably needed a stronger, colder, more ruthless man than Vincent, who caves in to protect the Greeleys when the actual stakes are much higher than either of them. Although Thinnes plays it beautifully (as does Smithers), the script is flawed, as Vincent has no reason from past experience to believe that Greeley's wife and kid are still alive at all. He should also know by now that the aliens can't let them live anyway (we actually never see them again), and sure enough, they try to kill

to the irritation of the elderly residents (how long could they have been there, a day?).

Every time Michael Rennie turned up on screen , it was to make a memorable contribution to cult TV and film — the smug and superior Klaatu in *The Day the Earth Stood Still*; the miserable shamed Lord Roxton in *The Lost World*; the sinister creepy Keeper in *Lost in Space*; the tortured stoic Captain of the Titanic in *The Time Tunnel*; the smoothly seductive Sandman in *Batman*; and his slimy, smarmy villains in *The Invaders* and *The Man from UNCLE*.

In a rare sympathetic role, William Smithers is very good as the frightened fisherman. He usually played gangsters and sinister slimeballs, and would return in the second season. In sci-fi, he had two strong villainous roles in *Star Trek* ("Bread and Circuses") and *Voyage to the Bottom of the Sea* ("The Plant Man").Two great bit players, everyman chameleon Harry Lauter, who always brought more to the camera than was in the script, and granite-faced Frank Marth, play the aliens searching for him with superb friendly menace.

Paul Carr was in most of the major sci-fi series of the 1960s, notably *Star Trek*, *Voyage to the Bottom of the Sea* several times, *The Time Tunnel* twice, and *Land of the Giants*. He was also in episodes of *Amos Burke – Secret Agent*, *The Green Hornet*, *Get Smart*, *Mission: Impossible*, *The Six Million Dollar Man*, *Logan's Run*, *Time Express*, *The Amazing Spider-Man*, *The Incredible Hulk*, *Buck Rogers in the 25th Century*, and *Airwolf*.

Both Katherine Justice and Patricia Smith return in the second season, as do many of this episode's players. Robert Doyle was in two *Outer Limits*, three *Voyage to the Bottom of the Sea*, both *UNCLE* series, and no less than seven episodes of QM's *The FBI*.

### The Ivy Curtain

wr. Don Brinkley, dir. Joseph Sargent

Vincent follows an alien he has recognised to a teaching academy fronting for an indoctrination centre for newly arrived aliens who are being shipped in by a private 'plane

flown by a middle-aged pilot eager to hold on to his pretty young wife with the money from his new-found wealthy clients

*with Jack Warden (Barney Cahill), Susan Oliver (Stacy), Murray Matheson (Mr. Reynard), David Sheiner (Burns), Barry Russo (Lt. Alvarado), Clark Gordon (Nova), Byron Morrow (Gilbert), John Napier (alien teacher), Ted Markland, Laurie Mock (alien students), Paul Pepper (dispatcher), Jacqueline Mayo (crying woman), Garth Pillsbury (intern), Bud Perkins (bartender)*

end result: despite the fate of poor old Barney, who finally did the right thing, a major win. Numerous aliens polished off, and a major operation put out of business.

Another story about the greater good, but this time the initially weak and self-interested man makes the ultimate sacrifice, and very satisfying to see it is too, as the aliens flee like vermin. The strength of *The Invaders* was always the human interest side – real, ordinary flawed people with real self-interested agendas and emotions, something rarely seen in even the best SF, and then, for whatever motivation, rising to the occasion – and Susan Oliver's selfish rubbish Stacy is beautifully drawn, as is Cahill's understandable desperate obsession with her. It makes perfect sense for the aliens to use a private 'plane to reach the populated areas they needed to infiltrate, as we all know flying saucers only land out in the middle of nowhere...

The wild scenes in the classrooms, where the aliens are being taught to behave like typical average Americans bring to mind a similar exercise in paranoia, "The

Carriers", for *Mission: Impossible* the previous year, but make more sense here. The *M:I* story was 'Reds under the beds' stuff with real Reds, and had Communist agents 'learning' the hedonistic, indulgent ways of the West, but Socialists have the same feelings and desires as anyone else; that's the madness of Communism, that it goes against human nature, and so has to be enforced. But in *The Invaders,* there had to be a way of instructing these cold emotionless beings in how to mimic human behavior, and these scenes are a useful add-on to the premise.

Smoothie Murray Matheson as a dapper piece of shit and thuggish spy show standby David Sheiner as his gloating aide are both well cast in their usual speciality roles. "It was a great show, an interesting show" said writer Brinkley, who also wrote for *Star Trek,* for which Oliver played Vina in the pilot. "It had a great concept—paranoia unlimited. You could do wild things because of that. Making them believable was where the problems came in". But in this well-crafted, carefully considered story, everything locks creepily into place.

### The Betrayed

wr. Theodore Sturgeon, John Bloch, dir. John Meredyth Lucas

A computer tape giving landing sites for alien saucers leaves a trail of tragedy and death in its wake when Vincent takes a job at an oil refinery

*with Ed Begley (Simon Carver), Laura Devon (Susan Carver), Nancy Wickwire (Evelyn), Norman Fell (Neal Taft), Victor Brandt (Joey Taft), Bill Fletcher, Max Kleven (Evelyn's goons),* *Ivan Bonar (alien operations leader), Ron Stokes (alien seated at controls), Joel Fluellen (Henry/valet)*

end result: alien plans set back by a couple of years, but at quite a cost—Carver's daughter and Taft's brother have died, as have two watchmen; Carver's a broken man, and Vincent and Taft are both discredited.

"There was never a story bible that dictated the approach to the aliens" writer John Bloch told Mark Phillips for his coverage of the series in *Starlog* magazine. "Nor were we told that they were evil. They were *threatening*, and that's a big difference. Because of this, you could feel some sympathy. To me, the aliens were pioneers from space. We were the Indians they found". I'm not sure quite how much more specific Anthony Spinner's opening narration had to be, or how many people had to die, for Bloch to figure out the format of the show he was supposed to be scripting for... I think we must put these comments down to age and memory factors, particularly as this is one of the most callous scripts in the series!

Laura Devon as Susan is a shapely but bland actress here; her hairstyle mysteriously changes from scene to scene. Vincent blunders by repeating out loud the meeting place with Joey in front of Susan. The callousness of the aliens is brutally illustrated by the casual execution of Evelyn. It's not made particularly clear what killed Laura as she was only exposed to the same hypnotic device as David Vincent and many others in the series; the tanker, unlike anything else in the course of the series, obligingly destructs slowly and in segments for David to rescue her... unlike, for example, the large building in "Wall of Crystal", which disappears rapidly.

Theodore Sturgeon was a well-regarded science-fiction novelist who dabbled in SF TV, and contributed to *Star Trek*. He wrote the novelisation of Irwin Allen's *Voyage to the Bottom of the Sea* film. Bloch was handed the idea to turn into an *Invaders* episode, and did not believe it was written specifically for the show. It does, however, fit the format perfectly, and I can't quite see it as an episode of *The Fugitive* or *The FBI!* John Meredyth Lucas also contributed to *Star Trek*, as a producer for a few weeks, and also a writer and director. In later years he worked on *The Six Million Dollar Man*, *Planet of the Apes*, *Logan's Run*, *Fantasy Island*, and *Beyond Westworld*.

### Storm

wr. John Kneubuhl, dir. Paul Wendkos

Infiltrating a small coastal town, the invaders set up base in a church from where they operate a device to create deadly hurricanes to batter major U.S. cities...

*with Joseph Campanella (Father Joe Corelli), Barbara Luna (Lisa), Carlos Romero (Luis), Dean Harens (Dr. MacLeuen), .Simon Scott (Dr. Gantley), Paul Comi (Danny), Edward Faulkner (alien leader), Allen Emerson (Organist/alien), John McLiam (hotel clerk/alien), John Mayo (weather reporter)*

end result: one known human casualty, plus storm victims, but a major plot foiled, even though Corelli lets two invaders escape to kill again

There is, in fact, a similar *Untouchables* episode ("The Canada Run"), in which a kindly Father (played by Arthur Hill) is fooled and exploited by gangsters (lead by Simon Oakland) into letting them use his church as a base, but it was in the third season, after Quinn Martin had departed. John Kneubuhl, who also had nothing to do with it, was a regular writer on *The Wild Wild West*.

This is one of the wilder, science-fiction-y plots, with a weather machine that whips up storms to order, but there is also a strong all-too-human element to it too, not the least being Vincent being accused of sexual assault, an extremely rare occurrence on 1960s TV of any genre (one of those other rare moments was, of course, on another sci-fi series, *Star Trek's* "Enemy Within").

Barbara Luna is best remembered for her role in *Star Trek* favorite "Mirror Mirror". Paul Comi also appeared in *Voyage to the Bottom of the Sea*, *Star Trek*, and *Time Tunnel* at around this time. Simon Scott was also a murdered medic in *The Green Hornet* this season. Dr. Gantley is referred to in the episode by the first name of Ed, but listed in the end credits as Malcolm.

### Panic

wr. Robert Sherman, dir. Robert Butler

Vincent captures a callous and devious alien infected with a deadly freezing virus, but both are pursued by invaders anxious to dispose of him

with Robert Walker Jnr. (Nick Baxter), Lynn Loring (Madeline Flagg), R.G. Armstrong (Gus Flagg), Ford Rainey (George Grundy), Len Wayland (Deputy Wallace), Rayford Barnes (alien deputy), Ross Hagen, Don Eitner (alien pursuers), Robert Sorrells (gas station owner), Helen Kleeb (Molly/ shopkeeper), Joseph Perry, Don Ross (truck drivers), Mercedes Shirley (woman outside diner), Ralph Thomas (deputy)

there no need to kill the shopkeeper and most of the others, but the doofus is leaving a trail of bodies for everybody to follow.

This was one of three showcase sci-fi roles for Walker during this TV season. He was equally excellent in *Star Trek* as "Charlie X" and *The Time Tunnel* as "Billy the Kid". Lynn Loring—then Thinnes' wife—played a similar role in a fourth season *Man*

end result: poor—although the alien responsible is killed, no alien plot is exposed or delayed, no gains are made, and at least ten innocent people are dead

A former actor turned writer, story consultant, and producer (of *Barnaby Jones*), Robert Sherman wrote mostly but not exclusively for Quinn Martin. This is the first of his two okay episodes of *The Invaders*. Poor David Vincent runs himself ragged in this episode trying to help a bunch of country folk way out of their depth and aliens swarming all over the place trying to do in one of their own. Given the haste with which these creatures knock themselves off for the good of the cause, the alien Baxter seems remarkably keen to live but just as eager to senselessly kill. Not only is

*from UNCLE* story, "The Test Tube Killer", within months of this episode. Director Robert Butler said she was "one of the finest actresses I ever worked with". However, the greatest acting challenge was given to R.G. Armstrong, who was afraid of heights; he valiantly climbed to the top of a water tower for his character's demise.

### Moonshot

wr. Rita Lakin, John Bloch, dir. Paul Wendkos

The invaders infiltrate a moon mission to cover up covert activities on the surface of the moon, where they have built some sort of structure, discovered too soon *with Peter Graves (Gavin Lewis), Joanne Linville (Angela Smith), John Ericson (Navy Cmdr. Hardy Smith), Strother Martin (Charlie Coogan), Kent Smith (Stan Arthur), Anthony Eisley (Lt. Col. Tony La Cava), Paul Lukather (Officer Correll), Richard X. Slattery (Riley/Lewis' aide), John Carter (Owens/medic), John Lupton (Major Banks), Robert Knapp (Lt. Col. Howell), Ross Elliott (McNally/PR man), Steve Cory (car valet), Charles A. McDaniel (Roberts/control technician), Steve Ferry (launch technician), Morgan Jones, Lee Millar, Bob Duggan, Ollie O'Toole (reporters)*

end result: success in exposing the alien impostor and probably scuttling the activities on the moon, but the aliens have been at work a while creating victims...

The first of two episodes built around the *I Married a Monster from Outer Space* scenario. This episode, possibly unintentionally, creates a one-off precedent for the series as it is the first time the invaders have actually replaced and impersonated an existing person, something they did only twice in the series (the other time was "The Watchers"). "Moonshot" is also unusual for being one of the first of only a very few U.S. TV drama series to make specific reference to Vietnam while the war was still in progress. Note also that no-one is saying that this is the first moonwalk...

Peter Graves, only months away from being cast in his long-running role as Jim Phelps in *Mission: Impossible*, is Jim Phelps in all but name as head of security Lewis. John Ericson, just off his regular co-starring role in *Honey West*, is excellent as the fake Hardy, and Strother Martin is as wonderful as ever in his bit as the old

beachcomber who witnesses the oddly high profile and unusual alien murder. What's with the alien mist attack anyway (reminiscent of the opening of *The Incredible Shrinking Man*)? Couldn't they just more credibly *sink* the ship?

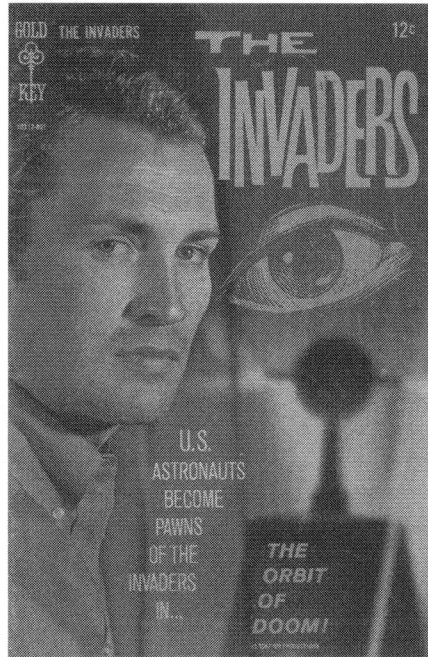

Joanne Linville struggles gamely with a typical 1960s female role as the troubled and traumatised wife of the bogus astronaut, but it's an honest script and she is strong in the part, holding her own in the face of a barrage of strong, confident, self-assured and occasionally patronising men. Kent Smith and Anthony Eisley will both be back in the second season as 'believers', and next time Eisley won't have such a lucky escape...!

Richard X. Slattery frequently played bits as cops, sheriffs, and military men, and was often seen in various roles on *Bewitched*. He held regular supporting roles in three series, *The Gallant Men, Mr. Roberts,* and *CPO Sharkey*. This was one of bit player John Carter's earliest roles, one of many in the decades to follow. He had recurring roles in *The Smith Family,* and Quinn Martin's *Barnaby Jones,* trying his hand at directing on the latter.

The meagre pre-credits role of Banks was a small one for John Lupton to accept, although he would take smaller in the years to come. Even though he was no big name actor, he usually enjoyed larger roles than this, and the same year had played significant roles in *The Time Tunnel* ("The Alamo") and *Voyage to the Bottom of the Sea* ("The Lost Bomb"). He was also Jesse James in the infamous B movie *Jesse James Meets Frankenstein's Daughter*. Ross Elliott, another familiar supporting player from the period, has also taken a smaller role than usual here, and will take an even smaller one in "Summit Meeting". He also has two strong roles in *The Time Tunnel* this season.

Robert Knapp's career went all the way back to the beginning of the '50s, and he appeared numerous times in *Dragnet, Gunsmoke,* and *The FBI.* He would be snuffed out twice by the invaders, back in the second season as an ill-fated congressman in "The Saucer".

## Wall of Crystal

wr. Don Brinkley, Dan Ullman, dir. Joseph Sargent

When David Vincent secures a poisonous suffocating alien crystal, he tries to enlist the aid of a powerful media commentator to expose the aliens--who then threaten the life of Vincent's brother...

with Burgess Meredith (*Theodore Booth*), Linden Chiles (*Dr. Bob Vincent*), Julie Sommars (*Grace Vincent*), Ed Asner (*Taugus/alien leader*), Lloyd Gough (*Joe McMullen*), Russ Conway (*Detective Harding*), Peggy Lipton, Jerry Ayres (*honeymoon couple*), Mary Lou Taylor (*Mrs. Endicott*), Karen Norris (*Miss Johnson*), Ray Kellogg (*police officer*), Fred Waugh (*alien*)

end result: aliens defeated, but at great cost in lives, and whose to say they can't--indeed must--try again?

This is a deeply unsatisfying episode, as it puts David Vincent in a bad light and highlights the futility of his mission and the flaws in the series. In it, Vincent is prepared to abandon his main goal of exposing the alien plot to secure the safety of his brother and sister-in-law, which in itself is understandable, if not exactly admirable (after all, the deaths of the luckless honeymoon couple in the teaser that set up the story have demonstrated all too clearly the size of the bigger picture).

Presumably, the point in stories and incidents such as these (Vincent letting aliens win to guarantee the immediate safety of an individual innocent) is to demonstrate Vincent's humanity against the behavior and actions of the soulless, emotionless aliens. Understood. However, if all the aliens have to do in stories such as "The Innocent" and "Wall of Crystal" is threaten the lives of one or two individuals to cause Vincent to surrender, then he can never win; callous military generals have sacrificed entire platoons of men and written off civilians in their hundreds to secure military aims for far less justifiable victories.

Making matters worse in "Wall of Crystal" is that poor Booth has thrown in his lot to assist Vincent in his mission, and pays with his life. Morally, one understands Vincent's actions, and individually we might even find ourselves making the same choices... but factually, should the lives of Vincent's friends and relatives be worth more than those of the anonymous honeymoon couple or the brave, committed Booth?

Happily, the episode is bolstered by a strong cast. Burgess Meredith is excellent as the pompous, sanctimonious newsman Theodore Booth, and Linden Chiles turns in yet another solid performance in 1960s sci-fi. Julie Sommars played a certain type of fluttery, timid, sheltered and selfish woman well throughout the 1960s and early '70s, and delivers the usual here as the tremulous wife. Peggy Lipton, the luckless young bride, would shortly become the female lead in the long-running period piece *The Mod Squad*; her unfortunate groom Jerry Ayres would wear a red shirt on *Star Trek*.

Ed Asner is at his leering best as the villainous Taugus (named only in the credits, not the episode). When Asner played the villain in 1960s TV (before becoming indelibly associated with the long-running character of another dedicated newsman, Lou Grant, in *The Mary Tyler Moore Show* and then spin-off *Lou Grant* throughout the 1970s), he always played the same slimy character the same way; other villainous turns included *Voyage to the Bottom of the Sea*, *Amos Burke — Secret Agent*, and *The Girl from UNCLE*. Given a different kind of role, however, he was quite capable of turning in a different

performance; he's superb in a single scene bit in *The Untouchables* episode "The Night They Shot Santa Claus" as a despondent informer resigned to his fate. His other 1960s stereotype was the bluff cop, as seen to perfection in his *Outer Limits*.

The seriously under-used Lloyd Gough, at this time a regular on *The Green Hornet* series the same season, has a small but strong part as Booth's boss, with some good lines.

This episode reveals that the invaders need to regenerate primarily because of our planet's atmosphere, ultimately fatal to them, hence the plot to adjust it, suffocating the Earth's occupants in the process. As this must be accomplished before they colonise, the writers and producers have somewhat casually upped the ante with this episode, making Vincent's qualms about his brother seem even more trivial. We are also told that Vincent has approached Booth before without success (the assumption by one and all that Vincent is deranged is one of the series' great strengths and saving graces in the otherwise often compromised credibility department), and is trying again out of desperation, having failed to interest the police or FBI.

Given the known depths of invader penetration in these forces, wouldn't it make more sense for Vincent to take his proof to the ever-growing stream of reliable trusted allies he has accumulated in previous episodes? Men in the military, media, or government just waiting for another crack at the invaders they now know exist? In the military, we have Fellows ("The Mutation"), Major Graves ("Doomsday Minus One"), Captain Ross ("The Innocent"), in the police, Lt. Lukather ("Genesis"), and later Ernie in "The Spores", industrialists Warren Doneghan ("The Leeches"), A.J. Richards (in "Quantity: Unknown") and Simon Carver ("The Betrayed"), reliable witness Father Corelli ("Storm"), and Gavin Lewis at NASA ("Moonshot"). But every episode, the series seems to start with a clean slate--Vincent is forever alone and friendless (until the disastrous addition of "The Believers", to be discussed in due course).

The story is by Don Brinkley, a regular writer on *Highway Patrol* and *Bat Masterson* in the '50s, and later to contribute to *Voyage to the Bottom of the Sea* and *The Man from UNCLE*. Although he was a hack, and more at home on medical shows, Brinkley did his best work on *The Invaders*, having provided the previous episodes "Vikor", "Quantity: Unknown", and "The Ivy Curtain", while Ullman had provided the superb "The Leeches", and for the second season, "The Saucer" (which also has Vincent putting the safety of two of the planet's less impressive occupants over the lives of others lower down the cast list).

Dan Ullman was a pulp novel writer who scripted B-movies in the '50s before moving into 1960s TV,

and his skills with simple but strong dialogue are on display here. He wrote three episodes each for *The Invaders* and *Land of the Giants*, and also wrote one-offs for *The Outer Limits, The Wild Wild West, Mission: Impossible, The Bionic Woman, Fantasy Island,* and *Wonder Woman,* but could turn his hand to anything and everything, and did. His last work was for *The Incredible Hulk.*

**The Condemned**

wr. Robert Sherman, dir. Richard Benedict

A little girl witnesses the invaders incinerate a truck, drawing David Vincent to the aid of a businessman who has unwittingly leased his property to the invaders...

*with Ralph Bellamy (Morgan Tate), Marlyn Mason (Carol Tate), Murray Hamilton (Lewis Dunn), Larry Ward (Detective Carter), Garry Walberg (Detective Reagan), John Ragin (John Finney), Wright King (Ed Tonkin/lawyer), Harlan Warde (Ed Peterson/Tate's aide), Paul Bryar (D.A. Brock), Kevin Burchett (drugstore kid), Stuart Nisbet (coroner), Seymour Cassell (cab driver), Gordon Westcourt, Geoffrey Deuel (teenagers at beach), Debi Storm (little girl)*

end result: three known human casualties if we include the unidentified body from the sea, but otherwise a major victory to end the first season--one alien outpost lost, plus nearly a dozen high-ranking infiltrators around the world.

A fairly standard episode, mostly covering ideas already explored, which is probably why it ran last in the season. Not a bad one though, just undistinguished.

Ralph Bellamy is very good as the industrialist who realises his new tenants are aliens, and Murray Hamilton is suitably sleazy as the leader. He makes a great bad guy. The scene of all the aliens speaking in different languages is quite effective and sinister, and the announcement that aliens are to land in Bournemouth caused much amusement to the station announcer in the Southern region of ITV when this one first aired, who decided to introduce the episode with the news! Happily, a *War of the Worlds*-style scenario did not occur among the seaside town's elderly populace.

Ward and Walberg are the cliche cops, Walberg and Ragin having both later gone on to play recurring characters in the 1970s *Quincy* series. It's not clear at the end of this episode just how the second disappearance of Morgan Tate is going to be explained... or, indeed, why no-one missed his poor colleague Ed, lost in the truck. It's possible that Ed lived alone, and with his employers not missing him, no-one would--but the issue is never touched on.

Larry Ward was a regular in the western series *The Dakotas*, and made sci-fi show appearances in *The Outer Limits*, *Lost in Space*, *The Time Tunnel*, and *Land of the Giants*. Among his last appearances were roles in *Wonder Woman* and *Buck Rogers in the 25th Century*.

The little girl who played the child who sees the truck melt "like a glob of butter" was in several TV series at around this time, and got her start in the SF film *Village of the Giants*. Kevin Burchett, the boy in the drug store, was similarly busy in the '60s, but retired in 1971.

## Second Season

## (1967-'68)

## Condition Red

wr. Laurence Heath, dir. Don Medford

Vincent discovers that a female alien has married an intelligence officer at a NORAD base where the invaders plan to spirit a fleet of saucers past Earth's defences

*with Antoinette Bower (Laurie Keller), Jason Evers (Major Dan Keller), Mort Mills (Arius), Simon Scott (General Stanhope), Forrest Compton (Captain Albertson), Robert Brubaker (General Winters), Burt Douglas (Captain Conners), Roy Engel (Dr. Rogers), Jim Raymond (technician)*

end result: a major victory, with the Pentagon in denial but many at NORAD knowing the truth; unfortunately, the cost in human tragedy has been high for Keller and his wife and the doctor...

The series' second and more blatant attempt to do *I Married a Monster From Outer Space* (after "Moonshot"), complete with rather grim implications for poor Keller and his first wife. Odd, given invader policy, that the fleet didn't just self-destruct rather than brazenly turning round and going back. However, the writer had plainly just seen the aforementioned B-movie, which ends with exactly the same visual.

## The Saucer

wr. Dan Ullman, dir. Jesse Hibbs

Vincent captures a saucer, but his attempts to hold on to it are complicated by two fugitives from the law, and the aliens will stop at nothing to get it back

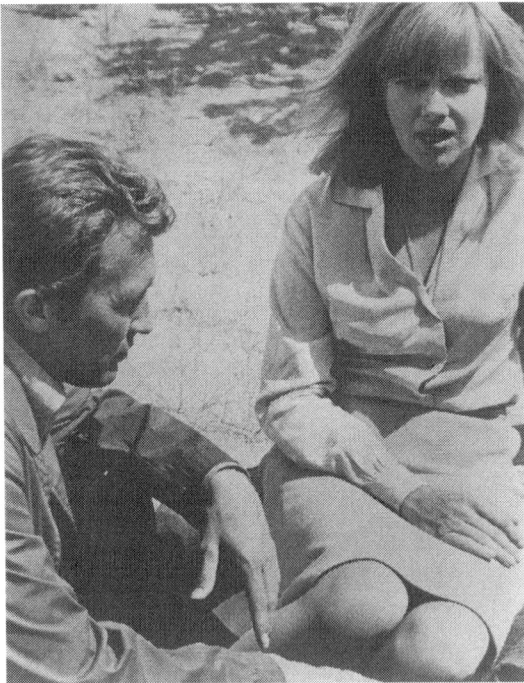

with Dabney Coleman (John Carter), Charles Drake (Robert Morrison), Anne Francis (Annie Rhodes), Robert Knapp (Joe Bonning), Kelly Thordsen (Sheriff Sam Thorne), Sandy Kenyon (boy's father/alien leader), Christopher Shea (alien boy with frisbee), John Ward (alien), Robert Dulaine (gas station attendant), Tina Menard (maid), Glenn Sipes (medic)

end result: a major loss, and frankly a deserved one. Four good men killed and a saucer destroyed so that two wasters can live happily ever after... Really?

Vincent exchanges the fate of the entire world for a pair of thieving losers, while four good men (let's not forget the mechanic) give their lives up for nothing. Ullman's earlier "Wall of Crystal" also had Vincent giving up the world for a couple of threatened lives, although with better reason, and that incident cost the life of a man more committed than himself. It was never the formula that ultimately did for The Invaders, it was implausible behavior provoked by bad writing. Given everything that Vincent had been through, it was absurd that he could, would, or should surrender the saucer for Rhodes.

*Thinnes with guest star Anne "Honey West" Francis in "The Saucer".*

Even more unlikely though was the idea that the aliens couldn't either call for other saucers to assist them, self-destruct the one Vincent had, or simply disintegrate it with their ray-guns. Previous episodes had shown them to be suicidal at the drop of a hat; they would think nothing of destroying the saucer, and themselves if they had to. The entire hostage scenario was quite preposterous from a variety of angles. To further aggravate the situation, although well cast, Anne Francis and Charles Drake had played a pair of romantically involved embezzlers only a year earlier, in "The One That Got Away", a fourth season episode of Quinn Martin's The Fugitive. Although the story and outcome was somewhat different, as the premise of The Invaders was similar to The Fugitive in the first place, this was repeat casting of the clumsiest kind.

On the plus side, we get lots of effects shots (although the saucer is a little ropey) and another trip to sci-fi shrine Vasquez Rocks and its famous slanting rock formation; "The Mutation" and "Dark Outpost" were also filmed there, plus numerous other SF classics including *Outer Limits'* "The Zanti Misfits", and *Star Trek's* "Arena".

Both lead players have places in the SF hall of fame. Charles Drake was the sheriff in *It Came from Outer Space*, Anne Francis (TV's *Honey West*) was the female lead in *Forbidden Planet*.

Dabney Coleman previously appeared in "The Innocent", and had minor roles in episodes of *The Outer Limits*. This is the second time Robert Knapp's been offed by the aliens; he was an unlucky astronaut in "Moonshot". Kelly Thordsen, usually cast

*Right: Vincent steals some vital alien technology to prove the existence of "The Saucer"*

as small town cops, had a turn at being an alien in *The Time Tunnel's* "Town of Terror", completely concealed by the creature's mask.

This is one of two episodes with an alien as a child. The idea of an alien in child form was an intriguing one left unexplored. Was it an actual alien child in human form, or an adult alien in child-like form? If the latter, they could have had a bit of fun with the concept. But we don't see the kid (one of

three acting Shea brothers) again after the teaser.

## The Watchers

wr. Meyer Dolinsky, Earl Hamner Jnr., Jerry Sohl, dir. Jesse Hibbs

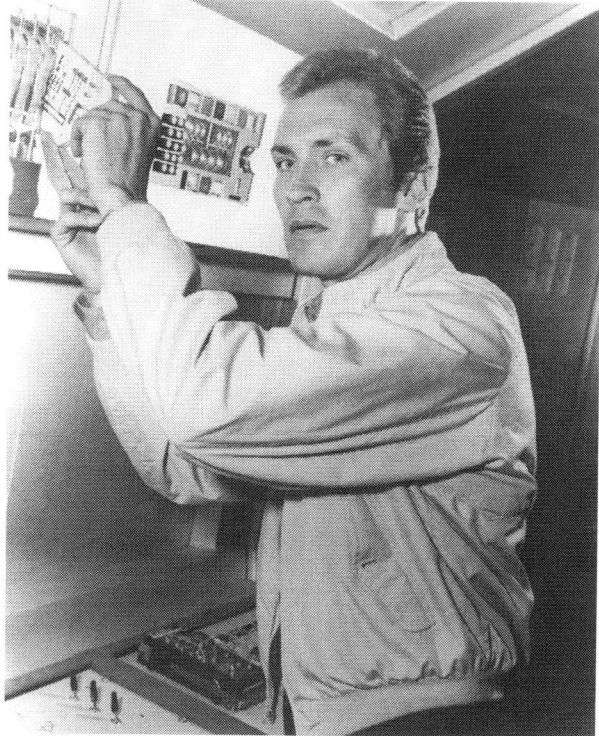

Vincent investigates strange goings-on at a resort lodge after the manager commits suicide after claiming his guests "aren't human"... The players—a reclusive, bitter electronics genius responsible in part for the U.S. missile defence system, and his young, blind niece

*with Shirley Knight (Margaret Cook), Kevin McCarthy (Paul Cook), Leonard Stone (Ramsey), Robert Yuro (Simms), Walter Brooke (Mr. Danvers/ new owner), Harry Hickox (Mr. Bowman/airport manager), James Seay*

Grayson/former owner), Paul Sorensen, Marlowe Jensen (aliens at airport), John Zaremba (General)

end result: success in diverting another alien plot, but at quite a cost of human life--at least four innocents in the wrong place at the wrong time.

*Shirley Anne Knight as Margaret Cook, with Roy Thinnes as David Vincent in "The Watchers".*

It was probably inevitable that someone was going to think of casting Kevin McCarthy, the leading man from *Invasion of the Body Snatchers,* in the series sooner or later; Siegel's 1956 film about 'pod people' assuming human form was a major influence on this show's concept, although *The Invaders* was more (pardon the pun) down to earth and realistic (there were an

awful lot of pods to ship around the country). This story, however, had little else to do with that film (the closest *The Invaders* came to do doing *Body Snatchers* was with "The Spores" a little later). This episode is very much a replay of the first season's "Vikor", with McCarthy as a brusque, self-obsessed and self-important figure in U.S. defence who has apparently sold out to the aliens. In this case though, he's innocent, and the aliens plan to replace him with a double. Meyer Dolinsky's use of a pen-name, and the presence of two other writers (one of them the rewrite-averse Jerry Sohl) suggests the story went through a number of revisions.

This usually results in inconsistencies in logic, and one slightly annoying irritation is that the double has a few minor differences to his appearance that are pointless, even though nobody's seen him since the car accident that scarred him and blinded her; he has no scars, and a slightly different hair-style, both of which the duplicate could easily fix. Plainly this has been done to help the audience figure out which character they're watching, but it's not that difficult to follow the plot, and Margaret still has her sense of touch.

Walter Brooke was the bland D.A. Scanlon in *The Green Hornet,* and is quite scary in his short scene at the end. Why Vincent shot the double after he shot Danvers is a mystery. Danvers was the one with a gun, the fake Paul Cook was his evidence, his proof.

Sci-fi veteran John Zaremba (*Earth vs. the Flying Saucers, Twenty Million Miles to Earth*, etc.) had just completed his year as a cast member on *The Time Tunnel*. Busy bit player Paul Sorensen's name comes up several times in this book, and no doubt in my others. Instantly recognisable, he was frequently cast as cowboys, cops, and blue-collar workers, usually of the aggressive type.

Shirley Knight, still working at time of writing, has done much mainstream TV, but her only other sci-fi credit was a gem—the tragic Noelle in "The Man Who Was Never Born" for *The Outer Limits*.

### Valley of the Shadow

wr. Howard Merrill, Robert Sabaroff, dir. Jesse Hibbs

An entire town is doomed to be destroyed by the invaders after an alien disintegrates in full view of the population

*with Nan Martin (Maria McKinley), Harry Townes (Will Hales), Joe Maross (alien Captain Taft), Ron Hayes (Sheriff Clements), Hank Brandt (alien in cell), Jon Lormer (minister), Mark Roberts (Doctor LaRousse), Ted Knight (alien leader), James B. Sikking (real Taft), Wayne Heffley (alien Sergeant), Don Eitner (real Sergeant), Robert Sorrells (Jimmy/deputy), Claudia Bryar (McKinley's patient), Phil Chambers, Jimmy Hayes, Richard Gardner (townspeople)*

end result: over a thousand townspeople saved, three lost—but a highly implausible get-out of an impossible situation.

Given that the aliens had a dam they could burst, offering a perfectly plausible natural catastrophe, and think nothing of hatching plans to kill thousands, it just doesn't ring true that they would spare the town to save awkward questions. The writers had a great premise—an alien disintegrates in front of dozens of witnesses—but had painted themselves into a corner they couldn't credibly get out of.

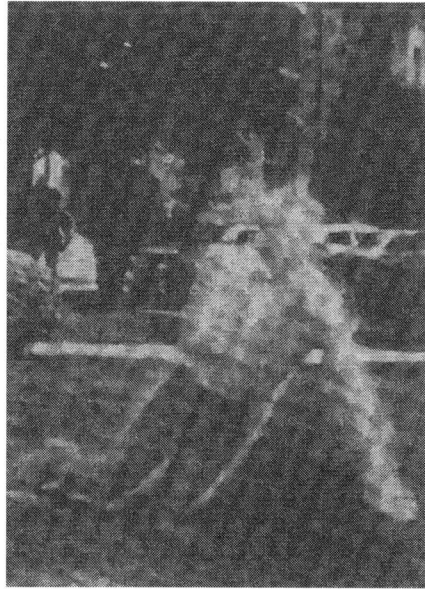

Still, it's a compelling episode to watch unfold. There are a number of chilling scenes—the murder of the doctor, the *Day the Earth Stood Still* swipe as everything stops and the automobiles glide to a halt, the earthquake, and the bizarre spectacle of the townspeople running to the military with joy when they arrive, when in actuality, these are the alien death force come to gas them. And the scene of the alien fleeing and dying in front of dozens of witnesses (David Vincent's most fervent desire) is a lulu.

With a few tweaks, "Valley of the Shadow" would have made a great final episode, had QM decided to film one. However, the realisation that such a perfect hand as an alien dissolving in front of dozens of witnesses will do him no good whatsoever is another nail in the series' coffin. If every time Vincent gets irrefutable evidence, all the aliens have to do is threaten anywhere between two and a thousand people, Vincent can never win. Episodes such as "Wall of Crystal", "The Saucer", and this one, paradoxically three of the most gripping and entertaining human stories, render Vincent powerless and the series' format seriously flawed.

There's only one way out, and it's a massive cheat—the idea that the day never happened. The alien leader, through an elaborate hypnotic brainwashing procedure, tells the entire town that the next day is in fact the previous day. But for how long is this deception to continue? At some point these people will turn on a radio, switch on a TV, pick up a calendar. And at that point, they cannot fail to notice that they've lost a day. The alien leader was right the first time when he said that mass hypnosis would be useless, and yet this is exactly what they do. And the first thing Vincent does after the event is introduce himself needlessly to Dr. McKinley, and so risk jogging her memory!

Never mind, there's a wonderful cast. Harry Townes is excellent as the sleazy opportunist newspaper man, as is Joe Maross as the cold-eyed false Captain Taft. James Sikking has a nice bit as the real Captain Taft, creating a character in just a few minutes who we're sorry to see meet an offscreen end. Robert Sorrells is also effective in his role as the hick deputy, Jon Lormer is, of course, as ever, the minister, and Ted Knight, through no fault of his own, delightfully corny as the lead alien. It must be the greatest fear and irritation for the writer, producer, or director of a drama meant to be taken seriously that, sometime in the future, one of your cast will become instantly recognisable from another, completely incompatible comedic role. Knight's performance and recognition factor as the ludicrous and much loved Ted Baxter from *The Mary Tyler Moore Show* is so great that it becomes impossible to take him seriously in his earlier roles ever again, and renders an already dubious sequence of events even more foolish.

Hank Brandt previously appeared as an invader in "The Leeches", and Wayne Heffley in "Nightmare".

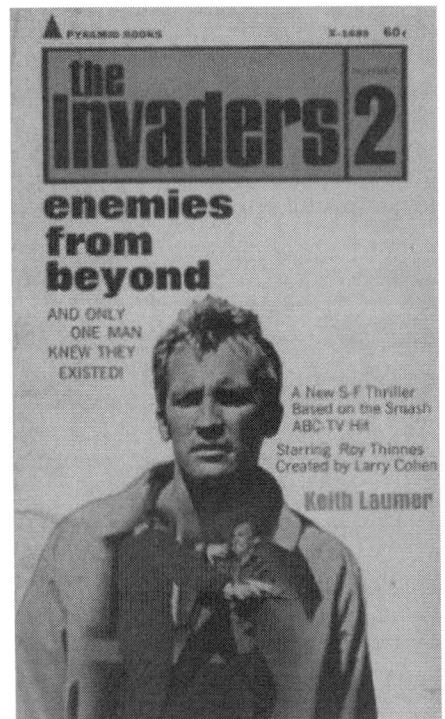

370

## The Enemy

wr. John Bloch, dir. Robert Butler

A compassionate nurse returned from Vietnam ignores David Vincent's pleas when she treats and shelters the victim of a crashed saucer, an alien reverting back to his natural form

*with Barbara Barrie (Gail Frazer), Richard Anderson (Blake), Paul Mantee (Vern), Russell Thorson (Sheriff), Gene Lyons, George Keymas (alien contacts)*

end result: the big loser here of course is poor old lovestruck Vern, the life sacrificed by Frazer for her ideals. One can't help noticing Vincent might have tried to save the ray gun to avoid the incident being a complete loss.

The main problem with this one is that Barbara Barrie's character is completely unlikeable and unsympathetic. Even after poor Vern's callous murder, Frazer seems more concerned about Blake than a real, live human who genuinely cared about her. Gail Frazer provokes anger rather than compassion. It has been suggested by the director that Gail is falling in love with the alien, and that the alien is somehow becoming more mortal as he approaches death. I have to say that I see none of that anywhere in the production; Gail appears to be driven solely by ethics over pragmatism, and Anderson's alien shows no signs of compassion at all, until his sudden change of heart right at the end. In this case, the production's failure to achieve those cliches worked in the episode's favor. However, to be fair, Vincent doesn't argue his case very well; Frazer has all the best lines.

This was one of Barbara Barrie's more complex roles. Her frail middle-aged appearance and worried looks frequently typecast her as a tragic wife or mother, although Louise Latham usually had that cliche covered at QM. A regular Quinn Martin player, Richard Anderson co-starred in his single season cop show *Dan August*, but was best known for his role as Oscar Goldman in *The Six Million Dollar Man* and *The Bionic Woman*. His sci-fi credits include *Curse of the Faceless Man* and *Forbidden Planet*. Gene Lyons was the Ambassador who fouled up in *Star Trek's* "A Taste of Armageddon". George Keymas frequently made appearances in minor roles in '60s and '70s TV, often as guards or gangsters. This, and a role in *The Man from UNCLE*, were among his larger parts.

The image of the crashed saucer, broken in half and then destroyed by the alien, is beautifully done (Anderson's alien does what Kenyon's should have done in "The Saucer" before the opening credits have even run). However, the footage of the saucer in the sky just before it crashes is as ropey as all the others in the series. The saucers, when flying, were the series' weak spot; and yet the images of the aliens dissolving when shot were never less than excellent.

This might be a good time to ask awkward questions about the aliens' physiology. It's been established that the aliens have no pulse or heartbeat, and that when they're cut, they don't bleed—so what exactly is Frazer injecting into Blake, how is she doing it, and what exactly is it doing?? The aliens must be similar to humans in some way, as whenever Vincent fights them, he uses strategies that presume human nerve systems and responses.

And just to put the tin lid on it, why is Blake asking Vincent to finish him when he's standing there with a ray gun in his hand? And why didn't Vincent tell him to drop it, so he could hang on to it as evidence—not to mention a useful weapon. Ah well—a good atmospheric episode when all's said and done.

### The Trial

wr. George Eckstein, David Rintels, dir. Robert Butler

Vincent helps an old friend defend himself of murder, knowing that the victim was an alien—but there are very human complications

*with Don Gordon (Charlie Gilman), Linda Day George (Janet Wilk), Harold Gould (Allen Slater/ prosecution), Russell Johnson (Robert Bernard/defence), Malcolm Atterbury (Judge), James McCallion (Detective Brennan), Bill Zuckert (Bert Wisnofsky), Selette Cole (waitress), John Rayner (Fred Wilk), Richard Hale (Mr. Wilk), Amy Douglass (Mrs. Wilk), Sid McCoy (John Lovell), Bob Duggan (officer), Jason Wingreen (clerk)*

end result: three high profile witnesses to an alien burning up and nothing to show for it--except the body of poor old Brennan, who has a target painted on his neck from the minute he puts in an appearance.

"This isn't *Perry Mason*" says Lynda Day George at one point... but it kind of is—it's *Perry Mason* with aliens. Ordinarily, when regular series do their inevitable 'murder trial' episode, the result is a major snooze. Several things work in the

favor of this one, written and filmed in a hurry, although you'd never know it. First, the defendant keeps surprising us with new information. Second, the writing and dialogue is good. Third, it's a strong cast, not a dud player among them. And fourth, there's a great twist that I didn't see coming—and I usually see 'em coming. One minor detail niggles, though. The scene where the phoney Wilks parents calmly suicide, job done, is a doozy--but why on earth didn't Vincent insist they be called back, and why didn't he have their heartbeats and pulses looked for while they were in court?

*Lynda Day George of Mission: Impossible fame.*

### The Spores

wr. Al Ramrus, John Shaner, Ellis Kadison, Joel Kane, George Eckstein, David Rintels, dir. William Hale

Three teenagers foolishly steal a suitcase full of invader spores from an alien courier, and a frantic search ensues as the case is passed around...

*with Gene Hackman (Tom Jessup), John Randolph (Officer Ernie Goldhaver), Wayne Rogers (Lt. Mattson), James Gammon (teenage delinquent), Judee Morton (teenage girl), Kevin Coughlin (teenage boy), Patricia Smith (Sally Palay), Mark Miller (Jack Palay), Brian Nash (Mike/ good boy), Joel Davidson (Earl/naughty boy), Stephen Liss (Archie/Earl's pal), Christine Matchett (Elizabeth/Earl's sister), Noam Pitlik (highway patrol cop), Vince Howard (police sergeant), Norma Connolly (waitress)*

end result: a rather vague alien plot spoiled or delayed, only one known casualty, the poor dumb kid.

An early role for future movie star Gene Hackman, toiling away in television at this time and just a few months away from his breakthrough role in the awful *Bonnie and Clyde*; classic 1970s films like the superb *Prime Cut*, the overrated *French Connection*, and the underrated *Night Moves* lie in the future, as did 1978's *Superman*.

This episode clearly came about when someone realised the series hadn't yet ripped off *Invasion of the Body Snatchers*. There were deadly alien spores all over the place in 1960s SF (*The Outer Limits, Lost in Space, Voyage to the Bottom of the Sea, Star Trek,* and *Land of the Giants* all had a go), so why not here?

The presence of a small army of writers is usually a bad sign, an indication of an episode that went through several desperate rewrites. There's quite a bit of narrative exposition in the introduction, another sign of trouble. And the second hefty chunk of narration as Vincent arrives tells us nothing new and is completely unnecessary.

The end result here isn't so bad as the roll call of writing teams suggest it ought to be, but the aliens' intentions are vague and the episode inevitably has no direction or vision. There are several plot holes, as you might expect with six writers. Why does the invaders' van turn tail in the teaser? If they can't bluff their way past the cops, there's four of them and only two officers, so no need to run? Just arrange another of their nasty little accidents. And why not hypnotise the boy, rather than just killing him? As we see in this episode and the next, the aliens have fewer qualms about leaving a trail of bodies behind them this season.

At one point, Vincent has an alien being met by more aliens, as he hears over the 'phone. Instead of calling in the authorities, he clumsily tries to steal the briefcase; he makes a similar impulsive goof in the next episode too. And Ernie checks up on Mattson, and finds out the real Mattson was killed over a year ago. But invaders usually create new identities for themselves, they don't take previous ones.

Never a dull moment though, including during the filming; according to Jonathan Etter's interviews for his book on QM, the show had its very own *Italian Job* moment when instead of blowing out a couple of panes of glass, the effects team managed to obliterate an entire greenhouse, the blast apparently causing some minor fender benders on the nearby highway... It's a great story, but it doesn't really match up with what's on the screen though, a clumsy gunfight and a fire, at night.

Nevertheless, explosions were apparently not the series' safest moments; similar conflagrations apparently occurred during the filming of "Doomsday Minus One", which ill-advisedly tried to replicate an atomic bomb going off, and "Storm", which managed to immolate a boat.

## Dark Outpost

wr. Jerry Sohl, dir. George McCowan

Vincent accidentally takes a ride in a saucer to an alien hospital researching Earth diseases, where a professor and his students become implicated in a grim charade

*Roy Thinnes with Tom Lowell*

*with William Sargent (Dr. Devin), Whit Bissell (Colonel Harris), Tim McIntire (Hal), Andrew Prine (Vern), Dawn Wells (Eileen), Tom Lowell (Steve), Kelly Jean Peters (Nicole), William Stevens (alien sentry), Walter Reed (alien Major), Susan Davis (Mrs. James/witness), William Wintersole (civilian alien), Sam Edwards (alien patient), Ron Doyle (clerk), Brad Stevens, Patrick Riley (ambulance medics), Mark Allen (mechanic)*

end result: three innocents dead, including the professor, with little achieved

Filmed at Vasquez Rocks. George McCowan frequently directed for Quinn Martin and Aaron Spelling, but fortunately he only came to *The Invaders* the once, as he makes several irritating mistakes, including showing audiences in a master shot that a wire fence doesn't go all around the army base when Vincent confronts a sentry. What a dink.

There are several holes in Jerry Sohl's plot as well as the fence, and only him to take the blame this time. Firstly, the aliens leave not one, but two bothersome ambulance-men lying in the road with cerebral haemorrhages when the obvious thing would have been to create a far less suspicious road accident with the bodies. And secondly, and more seriously, Vincent acts absurdly when he steals the alien device from the invaders' hospital, getting poor old Doctor Devin killed in the process. Once he knew the aliens were at the abandoned army camp (they had no idea *he* knew they were there), all he had to do was alert one of his various allies in the military or the media, and have them swarm in to wrap up the base and the series. Instead, as ever, the army arrive after the event, and find the usual abandoned and deserted locale the invaders always leave behind them when they've been discovered and thus bolted.

Still, as always, there are several memorable moments that help us forgive such carelessness, including Devin's horrible death as all the aliens pile onto him, the creepy morphing scene where the fake Devin transforms before their eyes into the alien Major, and the earlier saucer ride (during which Vincent sneaks around the ship with amazing good fortune not to be discovered, even blindly descending a ladder into who-knows-what at one point).

William Sargent and Tim McIntire both appeared in the first season episode "Genesis". McIntire's mother, Jeanette Nolan, was an invader in "Nightmare".

Whit Bissell appears in his familiar General role (see also *The Outer Limits, Voyage to the Bottom of the Sea,* and his regular *Time Tunnel* gig), but is creepier when operating the alien machinery. Dawn Wells, best known for *Gilligan's Island,* appeared many times in the early '60s Warners detective shows, and episodes of *Burke's Law* and *The Wild Wild West.* Andrew Prine would be back in an alien environment for *V — the series.*

## Summit Meeting (two parts)

wr. George Eckstein, dir. Don Medford

The invaders exploit a naive but well-intentioned spokesman for world peace to call a world summit meeting that is in fact an enormous mousetrap to gas to death the world leaders and pave the way for full scale invasion

*with William Windom (Michael Tressider), Diana Hyland (Ellie Markham), Michael Rennie (Per Alquist), Eduard Franz (Thor Halvorson), Ford Rainey (General Blaine), Ian Wolfe (Knut Rosmundson), Jay Lanin (Alquist's aide), Martin West (alien Lt. in Ellie's office), Peter Hobbs (alien Colonel who kidnaps Tressider), Richard Eastham (Carl Vanders/ security), Ben Wright (alien negotiator), Lew Brown (Jim/alien sergeant), Vic Perrin (alien hypnotist), Don Lamond (TV newsreader, part one), Hank Simms, Troy Melton, Albert Carrier (radio newsmen, part two), Ross Elliott (man in hotel lobby), Victoria Hale (girl in art gallery), Don Ross, Gil Stuart (print media), John Mayo, Lee Farr, Morgan Jones, Hal Riddle (aliens), Ted Knight (observation room voiceover)*

end result: many aliens killed and a major plot foiled, four known human casualties, plus the traitor Blaine.

As the series' only two-parter, the excellent second season story

"Summit Meeting" expertly demonstrates both the strengths and the weaknesses of *The Invaders*. In a genre that peoples its stories so often with the most two-dimensional cardboard stereotypes, *The Invaders* offered characters who lived and breathed in the real world, individuals who had careers, romantic affairs, ambitions, agendas, fears, flaws, and jealousies before, during and after the science-fiction trappings of the invading aliens touched their lives. William Windom's character illustrates this beautifully—the scene between Tressider and Blaine in the factory is

a gem. Whereas the mighty *Star Trek* and the Irwin Allen series provided viewers with the traditional heroic adventurers established in the '50s SF feature films and TV series, individuals who did not exist outside of their science fiction escapades, *The Invaders* was the only continuing series that took up the gauntlet thrown down by *The Twilight Zone* and *The Outer Limits* and told stories about the sci-fi world touching real people, rather than extraordinary people populating a sci-fi world.

These were not bold explorers venturing willingly into alien environments like Brick Bradford, Flash Gordon, or Buck Rogers, they were people with ordinary, everyday aims and priorities who had suddenly found that an alien environment had thrust itself into theirs. Again nodding to realism, most of them couldn't handle it—they were sceptics, or in denial, or corrupted, or selfish, or terrified, or a combination of any of the above.

Roy Thinnes is at his icy, detached best in "Summit Meeting". We even see him lose his cool and kill an alien in cold blood when an ally dies. There's a wonderful cold and telling line where Tressider snaps "Suspecting our friends isn't going to get us anywhere", and Vincent coldly replies "Well, it's kept me alive for the past two years". This statement also interestingly spaces his exploits out a bit, as we now know in this episode that Vincent has been on his mission a little longer than the series has been airing in real time, which makes sense.

As was often the case with *The Invaders*, there are careless plot holes. Nitpickers might question why Markham's shooting of the alien proves her allegiance when previous episodes have demonstrated the invaders' willingness to sacrifice themselves and each other for the grand plan. Blaine is named Jonathan in the official cast list, but called Jake in the episode. The invaders' desire to take Earth in pristine condition hammers a further nail into the coffin of the hamfisted 1990's TV movie revival to be discussed later. However, in earlier episodes, there was talk of the invaders' incompatibility with Earth, and preparing the atmosphere for their arrival and wiping out humanity in the process.

The chauffeur is left dead on the beach, highly suspicious; it would have made more sense to disintegrate the body and leave the poor guy a missing person. Despite easily hypnotising Tressider to take a pot shot at Vincent, instead of doing the same to dispel the doubts of Halvorsen's aide they clumsily murder the poor sod. Luckily for them, Halvosen is dumb as only a politician can be, and doesn't add two and two.

Michael Rennie of *Third Man* and *Day the Earth Stood Still* fame was making the transition from suave good guy to slimy baddie expertly shortly before he died, and he's at his villainous best here. He was wonderful also in "The THRUSH Roulette Affair", a *Man from UNCLE* that aired the very same week as the first part of "Summit Meeting". The previous year he had appeared as the Sandman in *Batman*, "The Keeper" in *Lost In Space*, and the captain of the Titanic in the *Time Tunnel* pilot.

With appearances ranging from *The Twilight Zone* to *Airwolf*, William Windom's roles in *The Invaders* are among his best work, but he will be forever remembered by SF fans as the tragic Commodore Decker in the classic *Star Trek* "The Doomsday Machine". Although the closest he came to a hit series was the long-forgotten *The Farmer's Daughter*, he made well over two hundred guest appearances in various shows.

A number of familiar faces from numerous minor SF roles appear in bit parts, including Ben Wright, Vic Perrin, William Boyett, and Ross Elliott. Elliott appeared twice in *The Time Tunnel*, as a traitor in "One Way to the Moon" and a western town sheriff in "Visitors from Beyond the Stars". Ben Wright appeared in *The Outer Limits*, *The Man from UNCLE*, *Voyage to the Bottom of the Sea*, and *The Time Tunnel*, among many others. Vic Perrin's numerous sci-fi credits include *The Twilight Zone, Star Trek,*

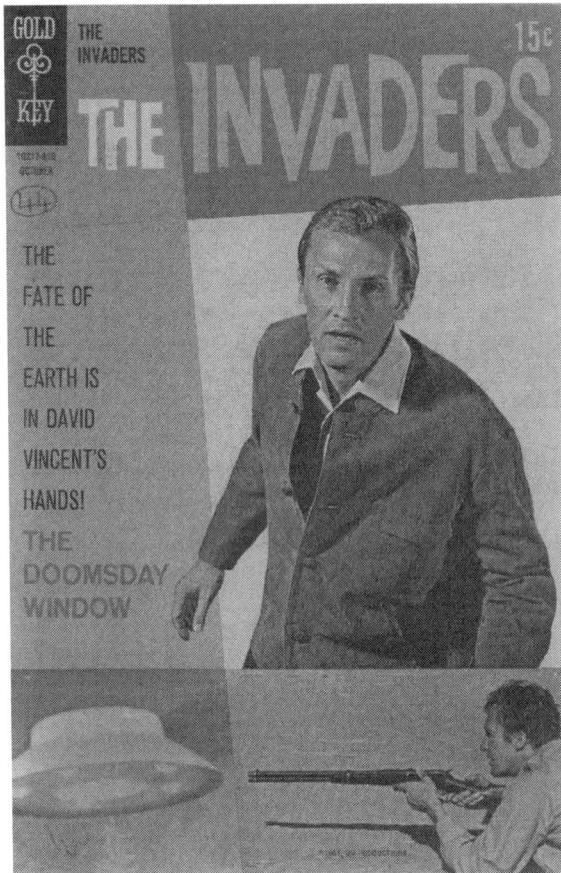

*Land of the Giants,* and *Wonder Woman,* also among many others. Bill Boyett's credits span the decades, from *The Outer Limits* to *Star Trek – the Next Generation.*

Diana Hyland previously appeared in "Vikor". Ian Wolfe was in *Star Trek* twice, as a rebel in "Bread and Circuses" and as Mr. Atoz in "All Our Yesterdays". Richard Eastham was General Blankenship in the first and best season of *Wonder Woman.*

Ted Knight, best known as Ted Baxter in *The Mary Tyler Moore Show,* was the narrator of *Super Friends* and similar fare, and previously appeared in "Valley of the Shadow", also as an alien.

Given that we are nearly at the end of the worthwhile episodes, this would have made a good two-part finale in the manner of Quinn Martin's *The Fugitive.* Instead, the series would shortly be rebooted in an inferior format with "The Believers" and disappear quietly into the night. On the other hand, giving *The Fugitive* a proper conclusion did kill it in re-runs for a while, whereas *The Invaders* carries on…

### The Prophet

wr. Jerry De Bono, Warren Duff, dir. Robert Douglas

Vincent is intrigued by a dubious traveling evangelist boasting a magical red glow and preaching about the coming of a "host from the skies"…

*with Pat Hingle (Brother Avery), Zina Bethune (Sister Claire), Roger Perry (Bill Shay), Richard O'Brien (Brother John), Byron Keith (Brother James), Dan Frazer (reporter), Ray Kellogg (guard)*

378

end result: no known human deaths, but lots of aliens gone up in smoke along with a very clever plan.

This is the first of two episodes with a religious subtext, with faith being an easy option for the invaders' schemes. It's a little slow to start, with a good turn by Roger Perry in a well-written scene as a sceptical but intrigued journalist.

*Thinnes with Ed Begley in "Labyrinth"*

Perry is perhaps best remembered as the jet pilot brought aboard the Enterprise when the ship time travelled back to the '60s in *Star Trek's* "Tomorrow is Yesterday".

Lots of aliens burn up in this one, with good optical effects, although a supposedly bullet-shattered car window is poorly done with animation. Sadly, the great character actor Pat Hingle has little to do as the alien evangelist, despite being perfectly cast. It should have been a meaty role for him, but the episode never really picks up steam. In small roles, Byron Keith, the mayor from *Batman,* and Dan Frazer, the harassed boss of *Kojak*.

## Labyrinth

wr. Art Wallace, dir. Murray Golden

Having secured x-rays taken of an alien's insides, Vincent takes them to the head of a university UFO research project — with the invaders in anxious pursuit

*with Ed Begley (Dr. Samuel Crowell), Sally Kellerman (Laura Crowell), James Callahan (Dr. Harry Mills), John Zaremba (Prof. Edward Harrison), Martin Blaine, Ed Peck (alien pursuers), Virginia Christine (Mrs. Thorne), E.J. Andre (Dr. Thorne), Bill Quinn (police lieutenant), William Sumper (cab driver), Wilhelm Von Homburg (injured alien)*

end result: a continuous succession of mistakes and misjudgements on Vincent's part causes the careless loss of two sets of x-rays and the death of the poor doctor to become meaningless.

This is almost a dry run for "The Believers", and they're a more likeable group too. Unfortunately, plot-wise it's a real groaner. This is one of those episodes (by Art Wallace, author of *Star Trek's* "Assignment: Earth") where the viewer is constantly one step ahead of the protagonist, even though the writing plays the episode's cards close to the chest. That said, Sally Kellerman (who had two *Outer Limits* to her credit, including the magnificent "The Bellero Shield", as well as the second *Star Trek* pilot) has a beautifully written part as the sarcastic daughter of the scientist, a role summing up perfectly the glory of the series concept, which is that it's ridiculous to believe Vincent— we viewers just happen to know it's all true. Von Homberg's alien, by the way, is deliciously evil.

For all the carelessness of Vincent in this episode, who has the best evidence he's ever had, and is completely cavalier with it, the story itself is suspenseful, cleverly making us doubt every so often the obvious villain and never letting up on the tension and suspense. A solid cast helps, too, although Begley, Callahan, and Zaremba had all appeared previously in different, memorable and significant roles.

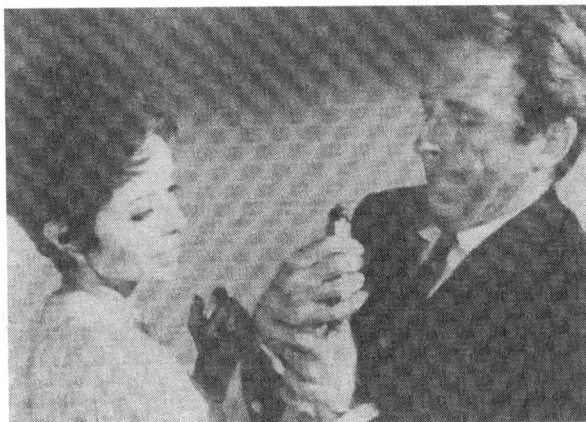

However, with all the main players aware of the situation and initially sympathetic to Vincent, a lot of misery could have been avoided by subjecting the immediate players to a physical examination before things got out of hand. Once through the door, Vincent should and could have asked for physical examinations, especially given the nature of the evidence. No-one in this story would have objected, except any alien infiltrators! The fact that the aliens could be so easily cornered and exposed was one off the loose screws in the series' delicate construction. Let's all draw blood or take pulses, guys!

### The Captive

wr. Laurence Heath, dir. William Hale

When an alien intruder is caught rifling a safe in an Iron Curtain embassy, Vincent tries to prevent the invaders' inevitable proposed retribution being seen as a U.S. act of aggression

*with Dana Wynter (Dr. Katharina Serret), Fritz Weaver (Peter Borke), Don Dubbins (Wesley Sanders), Lawrence Dane (Josef Dansk), Tom Palmer (alien leader), Douglas Henderson (alien cop), Dallas Mitchell (Rogers/federal agent), Alex Rodine (gate guard)*

end result: stalemate--no gain for either side, but a friendly fed gets dead

Appropriate, perhaps, that *Mission: Impossible* regular Laurence Heath should write the series' only Iron Curtain episode... and that everybody's favorite special guest fascist Fritz Weaver should be the villain. Weaver was the totalitarian face of *Twilight Zone's* "The Obsolete Man", the *Man from UNCLE* pilot "The Vulcan Affair", and four different *Mission: Impossible* including the memorable "Operation: Rogosh". Other roles include *The Name of the Game, Night Gallery, Kung Fu, Wonder Woman,* and the mini-series of *The Martian Chronicles.* In the 1990s, still working, he appeared in *L.A. Law, Star Trek: Deep Space Nine, Law and Order,* and *Frasier,* the latter of which has given roles to many old-timers from the '60s and '70s.

As is so often the case at this point in the series, there are holes big enough to fly a saucer through. It doesn't make sense that the invaders should blow up the embassy in a blatantly hostile attack, when something more mundane — such as a gas explosion or similar — could accomplish the same thing and preserve their anonymity. Why are the aliens being so blunderingly heavy-handed? Also, speaking of anonimity, note the non-specific names of the Iron Curtain characters. This is also one of those rare episodes where we see Vincent at his work as an architect.

### The Believers

wr. Barry Oringer, dir. Paul Wendkos

Having made several allies, Vincent survives an alien attack and is taken to a secret compound, where he meets a young woman with equal reason to despise the invaders, and claiming knowledge of a huge alien offensive

*with Carol Lynley (Elise Reynolds), Donald Davis (Harland/ alien leader), Thann Wyenn (Torberg/ alien deputy), Kent Smith (Edgar Scoville), Rhys Williams (Professor Hellman), Anthony Eisley (Bob Torin), Maura McGiveney (Mary Torin), Byron Morrow (Colonel Newcomb), Kathleen Larkin (Lt. Sally Harper), Hal Baylor (apologetic killer), Ed Long (security guard in corridor), Warren Parker (Arthur Singeiser), Richard Karlen (Charles Roselli), Tim Burns (alien student), Ed Barth (cabbie), Mark Tapscott, Frank Reinhardt, Allen Emerson, Mark Russell, Walter Reed (aliens)*

end result: a dispiriting lack of progress made and much endured for no gain and many deaths.

It was at this point that a wonderful series lost the plot. It's tempting at this point to bring up the old phrase "don't fix a hit", or "if it ain't broke, don't fix it", but the truth was that *The Invaders* was in need of a fix, or at least a bit of a paint job, and in ratings trouble. The premise was wearing thin, story ideas were running dry, the writers were getting careless and eroding audience sympathy for Vincent's credibility, and as is so often the case (*Burke's Law, Get Smart, Mork and Mindy, Buck Rogers in the 25th Century, The A-Team, Moonlighting*), efforts to inject new life into the show simply made it worse. Several babies were thrown out with the bathwater.

The introduction of the dull and wooden Kent Smith as Edgar Scoville and his "believers" was a bad move and a disappointing one that heralded the beginning of the end for the series, which was no longer about one man's paranoia but built around the cliche of having him regularly report back to a desk-bound boss figure. As well as spoiling the format, it also highlighted the series' two biggest flaws, which were the re-use of familiar actors who had played large, memorable roles in new, different parts, and the fact that up until now we never saw any of Vincent's valuable converts to the cause from previous episodes again. To do this would have given a far better sense of hope and gain than seeing Scoville's foot soldiers join the casualty list every week, but the series had already shot itself in the foot by re-using guest actors in second or third roles.

How, for example, could you bring back William Windom's Major Graves from "Doomsday Minus One", when he'd already returned and been killed as Tressider in "Summit Meeting", or Linden Chiles as Vincent's brother, when he would be back shortly as a newspaper publisher's son? Far from proving Vincent wasn't alone, "The Believers" simply highlighted the hopelessness of their efforts.

*Carol Lynley and Roy Thinnes in "The Believers"*

In the opening scene, one of his newfound friends optimistically suggests this is "the beginning of the end". Vincent melodramatically replies "Or the end of the beginning". They were prophetic lines for the series, for which "The Believers" was indeed both.

Although she was never in *Burke's Law*, Carol Lynley did a lot of work for Aaron Spelling, including no less than eleven episodes of *Fantasy Island*, including the pilot. This same year, she also appeared in an excellent *Man from UNCLE* two-parter "The Prince of Darkness Affair", which became the feature release *The Helicopter Spies*. Anthony

Eisley previously appeared in "Moonshot". Byron Morrow had also previously appeared in *The Invaders*, but then he'd appeared in everything—admirals, generals, colonels, doctors, judges, politicians, crooked businessmen, you name an authority figure, he'd played it half a dozen times. Allen Emerson escaped Vincent in "Storm".

## The Ransom

wr. Robert Collins, dir. Lewis Allen

When Vincent captures an alien leader at a regeneration centre, he finds himself under siege in the home of an elderly man and his granddaughter.

*with Alfred Ryder (alien leader), Laurence Naismith (Cyrus Stone), Karen Black (Claudia Stone), Anthony Eisley (Bob Torin), Lawrence Montaigne, John Ragin (alien hunters), Kent Smith (Edgar Scoville), Christopher Held (army lieutenant/alien), John Graham (Colonel Gentry), Ron Husmann (sentry), Joe Quinn (police officer)*

end result: once again empty-handed due to occasional careless lapses, one of which costs Torin his life. Not a good start for Vincent's seven dwarves, now down to six.

"The Ransom" is a routine entry, saved by some good guest performers. Laurence Naismith had previously appeared in the early episode "The Experiment", where he had met a memorable end as the haunted Dr. Lindstrom—an event now belittled by his reincarnation as pompous poet Cyrus Stone.

Alfred Ryder had previously appeared in the early episode "Vikor" as the alien leader Nexus. Here, he plays much the same role, only is not given a name. John Ragin also played a surviving alien in "The Condemned", but of course there is no effort to tie this in with his previous appearance. Lawrence Montaigne was an alien in Naismith's earlier episode! It's a mystery why the aliens simply leave after regaining their leader when the evidence of all previous episodes would have had them obliterate the house and everyone in it.

Naismith went on to play the Scoville-like boss of adventurers *The Persuaders* in the trans-Atlantic adventure series made for export by the British ITC company. Karen Black went on to become a significant movie star in early 1970s feature films, notably the wonderful *Five Easy Pieces*.


**Task Force**

wr. Warren Duff, dir. Gerald Mayer

When a powerful news magazine publisher is persuaded to join the battle to expose the invaders the term 'hostile takeover' acquires a whole new meaning

*with Linden Chiles (Jeremy Mace), Nancy Kovack (June Murray), Martin Wolfson (William Mace), Frank Marth (Eric Lund), John Lasell (Bob Ferrara), John Stephenson (John Niven), Barney Phillips (Emmet Morgan), Kent Smith (Edgar Scoville), Walter Woolf King (alien executive)*

end result: although Vincent and Scoville cause the death of Mace by approaching him in the first place, they can't be blamed for seeking to utilise the power of the media, and they do end up with the news group on their side--so a considerable triumph. However, once again, as with "Labyrinth", having laid their cards on the table with the story about alien invasion, much early progress could have been made by giving the immediate staff physical examinations.

The episode is enhanced by a strong supporting cast, but Nancy Kovack struggles with some appalling dialogue; director Gerald Mayer only comes to life in the alien boardroom. The aliens appear to have ditched their ray guns and saucers for regular guns and helicopters, but it's good to hear Dominic Frontier's music from the first season again. Frank Marth had previously played an invader in the first season episode "The Innocent", and had survived, so--in the series' non-existent continuity--could have been the same creature again. More importantly, Linden Chiles, already a familiar face in TV SF, had played the significant part of David Vincent's brother in "Wall of Crystal" (where his other fantasy credits are listed). Nancy Kovack, who later married noted orchestral conductor Zubin Mehta of Three Tenors fame, was also a 1960s TV SF stalwart, with a string of credits including *Burke's Law*, *I Dream of Jeannie*, *Honey West*, *Batman*, *I Spy*, *Bewitched*, *Voyage to the Bottom of the Sea*, *Star Trek*, *Get Smart*, and *The Man from UNCLE*, as well as Quinn Martin's *The FBI*.

Martin Wolfson was in the classic *Outer Limits* "The Architects of Fear". John Stephenson was a familiar voice on 1960s Hanna-Barbera cartoons, notably on *The Flintstones* (as Mr. Slate, among others) and *Top Cat*, (as Fancy-Fancy, among others), and as almost all the bad guys on *Josie and the Pussycats!* Onscreen roles included *The Beverly Hillbillies, Hogan's Heroes,* and numerous other sit-coms. Almost all his credits from the '60s on are for cartoon show voices, with a sprinkling of bit-parts. Barney Phillips was in the first season episode "Quantity: Unknown". Frequently cast as cops, he was best known as the punchline of a famous *Twilight Zone*, and was the voice of the cartoon genie *Shazzan*.

### The Possessed

wr. John Bloch, dir. William Hale

Aliens infiltrate a sanitarium to carry out experiments in behavioral control

*with Michael Tolan (Ted Willard), Michael Constantine (Martin Willard), William Smithers (Adam Lane), Katherine Justice (Janet Garner), Charles Bateman (Burt Newcombe), Kent Smith (Edgar Scoville), Lyn Hobart (alien nurse), Booth Colman (coroner), Matt Pelto (coroner's clerk), Rose Hobart (housekeeper)*

end result: the successful termination of an alien enterprise, the three other human casualties having occurred before Vincent and Scoville's involvement (Believer Burt must lead a charmed existence, he's one of the few allies Vincent acquires who walks away with his life at the end of the episode!).

Michael Constantine, later to star in 1970s drama series *Room 222*, had previously appeared in *The Twilight Zone, The Outer Limits,* and a memorable first season *Voyage to the Bottom of the Sea,* "The Indestructible Man". A new generation now knows him, in his nineties, for the *My Big Fat Greek Wedding* films and short-lived spin-off TV series.

William Smithers had previously appeared in the first season episode "The Innocent", in the memorable and important role of Nat Greeley. His other TV SF credits included *Voyage to the Bottom of the Sea,* in the infamous "The Plant Man", and the Roman world episode of *Star Trek,* "Bread and Circuses" as Merrick. He had recurring roles in *Peyton Place* in the '60s, *Executive Suite* in the '70s, and *Dallas* in the '80s.

Katherine Justice had played Vincent's old flame in "The Innocent", which must have given viewers already struggling to place Smithers an even greater sense of *deja vu*. Michael Tolan had appeared in the memorable *Outer Limits* episode "The Zanti Misfits". Charles Bateman was Captain Decatur in *Time Tunnel's* classic "Pirates of Dead Man's Island", and also played roles in *The Munsters* and *The Green Hornet*.

All the named SF episodes above are vastly superior to this, which is little more than a time-killer.

### Counter Attack

wr. Laurence Heath, dir. Robert Douglas

Vincent and his newfound allies decide it's time to launch an offensive against the invaders, but Vincent is accused of murder and appears to fall apart...

with Anna Capri (Joan Surrat), Donald Davis (Lucian), Lin McCarthy (Col. Archie Harmon), John Milford (Jim Bryce), Ken Lynch (Lt. Connors), Kent Smith (Edgar Scoville), Ross Elliott (Eliot Kramer), Ed Prentiss (Stanley Leeds/contractor), Pamela Curran (Louise/alien barfly), Don Chastain (Blake/alien cop), Warren Vanders (Earl/alien), Charles J. Stewart (Robertson), Walter Baldwin (night watchman), Orwin Harvey, Craig Chudy (aliens)

end result: a major success, with Vincent and Scoville obtaining valuable film and eye witness testimony of alien disintegration; major casualty is Kramer, done in by his own carelessness.

It's not very clear how much of the plan is intentional and how much is improvisation until Vincent is abducted, but this episode covers three aspects of the series rarely touched on— why Vincent regularly gets away with 'murder', why the aliens have never tried to buy him off, and why we 'never' see him working as an architect. In this episode, we see all three, although he had been arrested for murder in "The Condemned". The special effect of the alien disintegrator gun is interesting, but why don't they just obliterate the whole building, "Wall of Crystal"-style?

This is Ross Elliott's third *Invaders* bit part, after "Moonshot" and "Summit Meeting", while John Milford had previously appeared in the pilot. Lin McCarthy had previously appeared in "The

Mutation". Anna Capri's other cult TV roles included episodes of *Voyage to the Bottom of the Sea*, *The Man from UNCLE*, *I Spy*, *The Wild Wild West*, and a minor part in the 1970s classic *Enter the Dragon*, as well as countless cop shows in the '60s and '70s. Despite the series' recent half-assed attempts at continuity with the Believers, Donald Davis, an alien in the "Believers" episode, returns swiftly here as a different leader!

*Roy Thinnes with Anna Capri in "Counter Attack"*

Ken Lynch, a familiar face in supporting character roles, did little TV SF, but also appeared in the *Star Trek* episode "Devil in the Dark" and 1950s gem *I Married a Monster from Outer Space*. He was recurring cop character Lt. Keller in *Honey West*.

Pamela Curran appeared in numerous 'vamp' roles in the '60s, including episodes of *Surfside Six*, *Boris Karloff's Thriller*, *My Favorite Martian*, *I Dream of Jeannie*, *Branded*, *Garrison's Gorillas*, *Hogan's Heroes*, *The Green Hornet*, and *The Man from UNCLE*. She appeared in the sci-fi films *The Blob* and *Mutiny in Outer Space*, and the Elvis film *Girl Happy*. Don Chastain, a regular player on *The Debbie Reynolds Show* in the 1970s, had bit parts in *The Man from UNCLE* and *The Girl from UNCLE* and was one of the lead villains in black action film *The Black Godfather*.

Orwin Harvey was a bit player turned stunt man who started out with Irwin Allen on *The Time Tunnel* and *Lost in Space*, worked with Lucille Ball, and appeared at least three times on *The Invaders* as an alien. Craig Chudy had a similar career, appearing in bits on *Lost in Space* and *The Man from UNCLE*, working at Desilu on *Mission: Impossible* and *Mannix*, and appearing as aliens in five of six *Invaders* episodes.

### The Pit

wr. Jack Miller, dir. Lewis Allen

Vincent is put in the position of the disbeliever when an old friend has a nervous breakdown and claims that the invaders are sabotaging science projects at the research centre where he works...

*with Joanne Linville (Pat Reed), Charles Aidman (Julian Reed), Donald Harron (Jeff Brower), Simon Scott (John Slaton), Kent Smith (Edgar Scoville), Bartlett Robinson, Noah Keen (fellow scientists), Johnny Jensen (the Reeds' son), Lisabeth Field (alien secretary), Dort Clark, Michael Harris (security), Pat O'Hara (alien scientist)*

end result: a success--no known human fatalities and much alien interference with scientific research nipped in the bud

This was one of writer Jack Miller's earliest writing assignments, but he came to the series too late to become a recurring contributor. He later wrote mostly, but not exclusively, for western series, including numerous episodes of *Gunsmoke*.

Here, he comes up with a neat if obvious idea to put Vincent into the same position he puts everyone else—to believe the impossible. By now, many people know that David Vincent travels around the country looking for aliens, including everyone who ever knew him. Charles Aidman plays a scientist friend who goes off the deep end and hallucinates that he's seeing David's saucers and aliens. Just as David is about to dismiss his stories as a genuine breakdown (there's a clever bit with an alien 'heartbeat'), a chance accident reveals that yes, the invaders are interfering in the projects at the research centre. This is one of the few episodes in which Edgar Scoville actually proves to be useful to Vincent, as opposed to just a reassuring voice on the 'phone as 'Basil Exposition'. Not only does he get David through the door at the research station, but he comes to the rescue at the end. The one loose end is that the security guard who accompanies him shoots two aliens and sees them die. Usually, any poor schlub who can corroborate Vincent's story doesn't get out alive! And by what authority was he killing people, anyway? As far as he knew, he was shooting bullets into a secretary and a scientist.

Joanne Linville had played the Romulan commander in the *Star Trek* episode "The Enterprise Incident". She had previously appeared in the first season's "Moonshot", and was very good in an early *Hawaii Five-O* as a medical fraud. Here, she's stuck with another 'tragic wife' role typical of the period.

The chameleon-like Donald Harron never played the same role twice. He was Robin Hood in *The Time Tunnel*, and also appeared in *Voyage to the Bottom of the Sea* ("Doomsday") as a panicky crewman and *The Man from UNCLE* ("The Four Steps Affair" aka *The Spy With My Face*), as an over-confident Aussie UNCLE agent. Charles Aidman appeared in several episodes of *The Wild, Wild West* and the famous *Twilight Zone* "Little Girl Lost". Busy bit player Simon Scott had previously been disposed of by the invaders in the first season's "Storm". Johnny Jensen had

previously played Nat Greeley's son in the first season episode "The Innocent".

One of the pleasures of this entertaining episode is to hear Dominic Frontiere's superb background music from the first season running throughout it. Many second season episodes did not always feature this distinctive and important plus.

## The Organisation

wr. Franklin Barton, dir. William Hale

Apprehended while boarding a ship at the docks to search for alien wreckage from a destroyed saucer, Vincent is under the impression he has been abducted by aliens until he realises he is in the hands of gangsters trying to retrieve a missing drugs shipment

*with J.D. Cannon (Peter Kalter), Chris Robinson (Mike Calvin), Larry Gates (Weller), Roy Poole (Cort), Barry Atwater (Dorcas), Kent Smith (Edgar Scoville), John Kellogg (Dom), Ross Hagen (Perry), Nelson Olmstead (Foster)*

end result: no win for anybody--some heroin is put out of circulation though.

A clever idea—aliens vs. the mob. J.D. Cannon had previously appeared in the pilot as the sly is-he-or-isn't-he cop, but there's no such hope of any such subtleties here. He had a memorable role on an early *Voyage to the Bottom of the Sea* as a grandstanding glory hound scientist in "The Condemned", and was wonderful in the *Untouchables* episode "The Man in the Cooler",

387

but is best known as the colorful Lt. Clifford--one of the best of TV's snarly cop show superiors--in *McCloud*. Chris Robinson had bland guest roles in *Voyage to the Bottom of the Sea* and *The Man from UNCLE* and was a regular player on war series *Twelve O'Clock High* at around this time. Many of his TV guest shots were for Quinn Martin. John Kellogg had a recurring role on

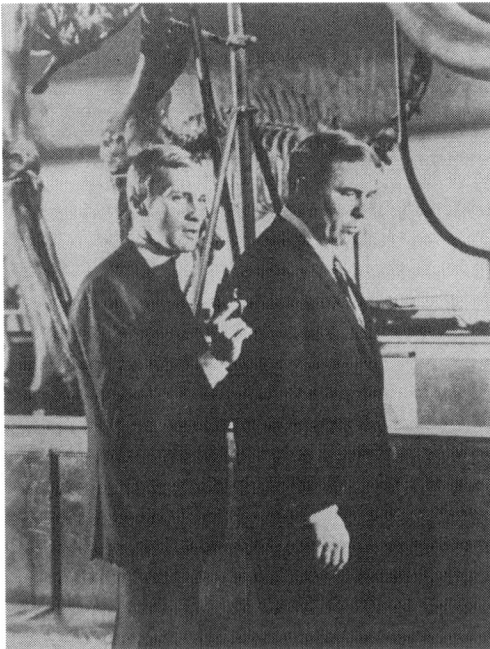

*Peyton Place*. Barry Atwater gave strong performances in *The Man from UNCLE* ("The Sort-Of-Do-it-Yourself Dreadful Affair") as a THRUSH boss and the TV movie *The Night Stalker* that spawned the *Kolchak* series as a modern-day vampire.

Ross Hagen had previously played an alien in "Panic". After an undistinguished career in small TV roles, he became king of the Z-movies. This episode's one-off writer, Franklin Barton, went on to work on cop shows *The Felony Squad* and *Hawaii Five-O*.

## The Peacemaker

wr. David Rintels, dir. Robert Day

Vincent and Scoville finally prove the existence of the invaders to a high-ranking military man only to discover that he's quite mad...

*with James Daly (General Samuel Concannon), Lin McCarthy (Col. Archie Harmon), Kent Smith (Edgar Scoville), Alfred Ryder (alien leader), Jan Merlin (alien aide), Phyllis Thaxter (Sara Concannon), Pat Cardi (Billy Concannon/kid), Larry Thor (Doctor Jacobs), Byron Keith (General Cullenbine), Craig Huebing, Jack Bannon (aliens), Ed Deemer (air policeman)*

end result: disappointing--an excellent opportunity for progress spoiled by the mental state of the man they were relying on--and the loss of Harmon.

James Daly (father of actors Tim and Tyne) played a key role in the pilot as David Vincent's business partner and best friend, but for once the producers have made the effort to make him look completely different here. A silver-haired and moustached Daly gives a superb performance as the deranged world-saver that blows everybody else off the screen... as indeed his character tries to.

That said, most of the other players in this episode are very bland, with the exception of Jan Merlin, who is delightfully evil as the main alien, and Alfred Ryder, who has little to do in his final appearance as an alien leader, but was always magnificently sinister even when just standing around.

Bizarrely, Thinnes calls the alien leader "Mr. Ryder" in one scene, and later, in another scene, the alien is again referred to as Ryder suggesting either that it was oddly decided to use Ryder's real name originally, or that rather than re-film the earlier scene, they would employ it to cover the mistake. Ryder certainly looks briefly taken aback. All very strange, and this is Ryder's third appearance as an alien leader, after "Vikor" (in which he was named Nexus) and "The Ransom", in which he was not named at all.

Phyllis Thaxter's few TV roles mostly came from Quinn Martin Productions. She portrayed Martha Kent in the 1978 *Superman* film, and her daughter Skye Aubrey (who was married to *Superman* producer Ilya Salkind) appeared twice in the 1966 *Batman* series, and twice in Salkind's 1990 *Superboy* series. Pat Cardi was a child actor who featured in the short-lived sci-fi sit-com *It's About Time* and guest-starred in episodes of *77, Sunset Strip, Gunsmoke, Rawhide, The Fugitive, Ben Casey, The FBI*, and *Branded*, among others.

## The Vise

wr. Robert Sabaroff, William Blinn, dir. William Hale

With civil rights tensions high, a black government official incurs the anger and dismay of his wife when Vincent persuades him to further investigate the background of a likeable but too smooth black politician suspected of being an alien

*with Raymond St. Jacques (James Baxter), Roscoe Lee Browne (Arnold Warren), Janet MacLachlan (Celia Baxter), Austin Willis (Warren's alien aide), Kent Smith (Edgar Scoville), Joel Fluellen (Warren's 'father'), Lou Gossett (Ollie/bar owner), D'Urville Martin (Casey/bar patron), Pepe Brown (the Baxters' son), John Ward, Mark Russell (cops), Red Boyd Morgan (station attendant), James Devine (TV reporter)*

end result: no gain for civil rights or the fight against the aliens, but a dangerous infiltrator put out of action

The aliens play the race card, a brilliant idea. In this episode, it's the aliens who are careless. Clearly, none of them ever saw the Nixon/Kennedy TV debate, then only a few years earlier, as they are willing to let their candidate go on the air sweaty and nervous. Storywise, could nobody be found in Warren's fake life resume to testify he was never there? If he was, then the aliens have been on Earth far longer than we have so far been lead to believe. Joel Fluellen previously appeared as Henry the butler in first season episode "The Betrayed".

## The Miracle

wr. Norman Herman, Robert Collins, dir. Robert Day

A troubled and confused young girl who sees an alien burn up near a religious shrine refuses to part with an alien crystal he gave her as he died, convinced she's seen a vision

*with Barbara Hershey (Beth Ferguson), Ed Asner (Harry Ferguson), Christopher Shea (Johnny/orphan kid), Robert Biheller (Ricky/teen), Arch Johnson (Father Paul), Marion Thompson (alien nun), Rayford Barnes (alien courier), Wayne Heffley (deputy)*

end result: a happy ending for the kids, but no gain for Vincent

Ed Asner, later to become familiar to TV viewers in the 1970s as Lou Grant in both *The Mary Tyler Moore Show* and *Lou Grant*, spent the 1960s playing cops and heavies. He previously appeared in the first season episode "Wall of Crystal". Other cult TV guest roles include *The Outer Limits*, *Voyage to the Bottom of the Sea*, *Amos Burke – Secret Agent*, *The Wild Wild West*, and *The Girl from UNCLE*.

Barbara Hershey had a regular role on the previous season's western series *The Monroes*, and went on to an award-winning film career. One of three acting child actor brothers, Christopher Shea was best known as the first voice for Linus in the early *Charlie Brown* cartoon specials. He had a regular role on the western series *Shane*, and had previously appeared in "The Saucer". Wayne Heffley previously appeared as a deputy sheriff in "Nightmare". He appeared in several episodes of *Voyage to the Bottom of the Sea* as one of the series' recurring ship's doctors.

### The Life Seekers

wr. Laurence Heath, dir. Paul Wendkos

Vincent encounters two persuasive aliens who ask him to get them safely to a departing saucer, claiming they want peace and have been marked for death because of it

*with Diana Muldaur (Claire), Barry Morse (Keith), R.G. Armstrong (Captain Battersea), Stephen Brooks (Officer Joe Nash), Arthur Franz (Captain Trent), Kent Smith (Edgar Scoville), Paul Comi (Sgt. Leeds), Morgan Jones (Lt. Rawlins), Herb Armstrong (Doctor Stark), Barry Cahill, Scott Graham (alien hit-man)*

end result: possible major progress, but at great cost in human life; several police officers are callously killed off

*Barry Morse with Roy Thinnes*

A nice idea, and another entertaining episode, but the flaw is that the aliens seeking peace tell Vincent that if he exposes them, they'll be forced to move forward the invasion, and make it overt rather than covert. If that's the only outcome if Vincent ever proves his case, then his mission has been futile since day one. When he proves his case, Earth loses.

Barry Morse co-starred in Quinn Martin's *The Fugitive*. In the 1970s, he co-starred in the first season of *Space: 1999*. Diana Muldaur's many credits include two guest appearances on the original *Star Trek*, and a regular role in the second season of *Star Trek – the Next Generation*. R.G. Armstrong previously appeared in "Panic".

Stephen Brooks, a regular on Quinn Martin's long-running series *The F.B.I.*, also appeared on *Star Trek* in the episode "Obsession". Arthur Franz was a lead player in *Invaders from Mars*, a 1953 film that was very much a predecessor of this series, as well as several other sci-fi films of the '50s. Paul Comi previously appeared in "Storm". His numerous sci-fi credits include *The Twilight Zone, Voyage to the Bottom of the Sea, Star Trek, The Time Tunnel, Get Smart, The Wild Wild West,* and *Voyagers.* Bit player Morgan Jones previously appeared in "Moonshot" and "Summit Meeting", and had minor roles in *The Twilight Zone, Bewitched, Star Trek, Land of the Giants, Project UFO, The Six Million Dollar Man, The Gemini Man,* and *Knight Rider.*

### The Pursued

wr. Don Brinkley, dir. William Hale

Experimentation with human emotions has caused the invaders to turn one of their own into a homicidal psychopath who endangers their covert activities. Knowing her life is endangered, she contacts David Vincent, offering evidence in exchange for protection...

*with Suzanne Pleshette (Anne Gibbs), Will Geer (Hank Willis), Dana Elcar (Sheriff Tom Halloway), Gene Lyons (John Corwin), Richard O'Brien (Dr. Charles MacKay), Kent Smith (Edgar Scoville), Mary Jackson (Hattie Willis), Orwin Harvey (Corwin's aide), Eldon Quick (antiques dealer), Mike McGreevey (Eddie MacKay), Barry Williams (alien boy)*

end result: disastrous, and Vincent only has himself to blame as the entire string of events he unleashes is caused by two catastrophic but fundamental errors. First, he asks directions to the summer resort hideaway and so leaves a trail for the aliens and Willis to follow, when all he had to do was buy a fifty cent map, and secondly he leaves MacKay alone with the alien when he knows she's prone to violent episodes.

An extraordinary episode, blatantly remaking an earlier premise with the same actress. Not content with re-using the same actors in different roles, the show now reuses the same plots too; this is a rehash of early first season episode "The Mutation", with a dash of "Panic" thrown into the mix. However, instead of running around Vasquez Rocks, Thinnes and Pleshette are scurrying around the suburbs, and there are enough other differences—plus a genuine and brilliant twist ending—to give the episode its own identity. The cast is uniformly excellent, particularly Will Geer's tortured has-been and Dana Elcar's delightfully dimwitted sheriff, not the usual heavy-handed *Dukes of Hazzard*-style redneck, just a bit slow. A couple of speaking parts are not credited.

There is a curiously odd and uncharacteristic private joke in the credits, with the duplicitous and effeminate antiques dealer-- charming one minute, grasping for bribes the next--referred to in the cast list as 'nice young man'! Very strange. As I'm not in on the joke, I've credited him more conservatively. And this is the second and last episode to include an alien in the guise of a child; you have to wonder why they didn't do it more often given the numerous psychological advantages.

### Inquisition

wr. Barry Oringer, dir. Robert Glatzer

Vincent and Scoville are framed for the murder of a senator and pursued by a zealous and blinkered public prosecutor while trying to prevent a major alien attack

*with Peter Mark Richman (Andrew Hatcher), Susan Oliver (Joan Seeley), John Milford (Jim Bryce), Robert H. Harris (Stanley Frederickson), Kent Smith (Edgar Scoville), Stewart Moss (Hadley Jenkins), Alex Gerry (Senator Breeding), Mary Gregory (secretary), Ernest Harada (maitre'd), Lincoln Demyan, George Robotham (hotel aliens)*

*other unidentified roles: Bill Egan, Burt Douglas, Richard Merrifield, Allen Joseph, Michael Harris*

end result: a major attack prevented, but at the loss of at least three good people

All four of the lead players had already played major roles in the series, and the story, while entertaining, offers nothing new. The series ends with a major attack prevented, but we are never told exactly *why* the aliens are planning a major attack. With this episode and the previous one (in which a bunch of official-types see an alien disintegrate) we appear to be building to a conclusion, a final episode that never arrives. But given how *The Fugitive* struggled in syndication after the public got their final episode, perhaps that's for the best. For some reason, even though in those days a series was definitely over with no chance of a reprieve when it was cancelled, audiences would not return to a series that had concluded its storyline for repeats. In their minds, it was over.

Anyone who still maintains that Roy Thinnes couldn't act, or was 'wooden' as David Vincent, needs to look at his face in that final scene at the end of Act Four of the previous "The Pursued", a better final episode.

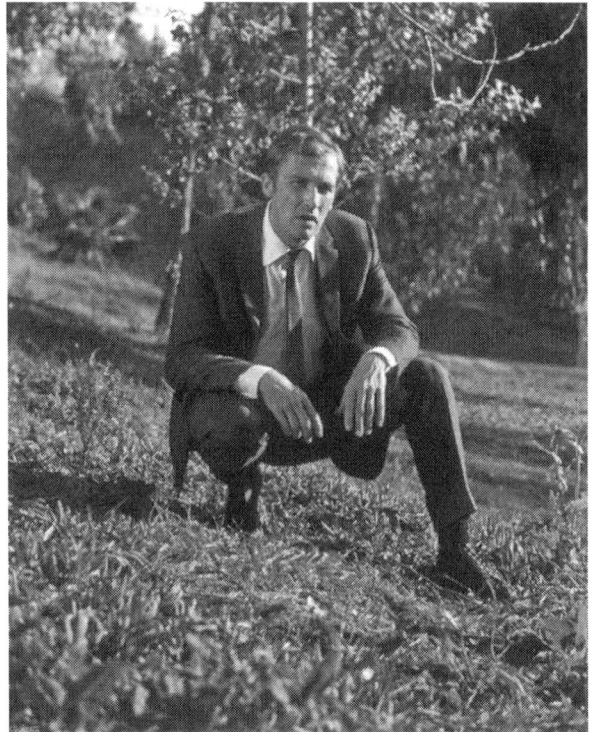

series ends

392

# Afterwards...

Although *The Invaders* was unfortunately the one and only SF series from Quinn Martin Productions, there have been several attempts to revive the formula, including "The Nomads", an episode of *Quinn Martin's Tales of the Unexpected,* the unsold pilots *The Aliens Are Coming* (1980, also QM) and *The Annihilator* (1985, from *Otherworld's* Rod Taylor), and the series *Beyond Westworld* (1980), *V – the series* (1985), *War of the Worlds* (1988-90), *Nowhere Man* (1995), and *First Wave* (1998), all of which plainly owe a debt. None of them lasted, with the most promising, *Beyond Westworld* (a fun but juvenile and shallow retread, not of the movies, but *The Invaders'* premise of guess-who's-a-bad-guy), lasting only a mere five episodes. With that level of commitment, all concerned must have wondered why they bothered; the ratings weren't even in. All the others stunk on ice. However, in the late 1990s, a deliberate attempt to exploit the title and premise of *The Invaders* was made by the Fox network with TV fantasy veteran James Parriott (*The Bionic Woman, The Incredible Hulk, Voyagers, Misfits of Science, Forever Knight*) at the helm.

This 1996 version of the 1966 TV series dispensed with most of the established mythology of the original (yeah, I know… *why??*), and--as covert alien invasion was hardly the most original premise in the world anyway--the result was just another low budget invasion movie among dozens. In sequences eerily reminiscent of the 1970 TV movie *Night Slaves,* the two-part TV movie opened with busloads of alien-absorbed people being integrated into society to slowly but surely wreck our green and pleasant globe until it's disgusting enough to suit the lifestyles of the gross and horrible aliens, now identified by their grubby habit of smoking. These are supposedly the same guys the luckless David Vincent fought for two seasons in the '60s, and Vincent--again played by Roy Thinnes--shows up midway through this story (although we glimpse him earlier a couple of times) reduced to the role of Basil Exposition to clue in mini-series star Scott Bakula (of *Quantum Leap/Enterprise* fame) about things which even *he* shouldn't logically know about... although thirty years is a long time, I guess, in which to find out more.

But what galls most is that this isn't *The Invaders.* It's a fraud masquerading under the same name, and that's a shame, because the original series, despite being a deliberate homage to the '50s movies (and occasional steal), managed to be distinctive in its own right and find a voice and style of its own. Although moderately watchable in a seat-shifting sort of way, the *Invaders* revival was just another bodysnatching yarn, of which there have been dozens. The famous red glow disintegrations of the series occur offscreen, the tell-tale little fingers have been replaced by unexplained swarms of flies, and most criminally of all, instead of coming to Earth disguised as humans, they are now bodysnatchers, which is a completely different premise entirely. It seems to this writer that if you are going to call your project *The Invaders,* and deliberately associate it with the original, then you should at the very least try to stick the original format, flexible though it was.

This version isn't a bad concept in itself (it's more like a Larry Cohen film than the original!), and might have made a reasonable series if unrelated to the '60s show, a ploy which rather than giving the show strength forced it to carry unwanted baggage. The concept of a covert invasion quietly encouraging us to destroy ourselves and slipping in agitators to make people paranoid and despondent, while not new, is a good one rarely seen on TV, and Bakula would have made a good 'new David Vincent'. Even the notion of undermining society with fear is fudged though, with the invaders' adversary being a scaremongering ecology doomsayer (Jon Cypher, *Hill Street Blues'* Chief Daniels, well-suited to the role of phoney bandwagon-jumper). Given the ecology bandwagon's lack of legitimate science, dismissal of uncomfortable facts, and panic-spreading qualities, combined with its economy-damaging aspects, it would have been a far more intriguing and original concept to have alien troublemakers deliberately propagating blatantly false science and scare stories through influential doomsayers of the Al Gore variety. It would have been a much cleverer and more intriguing premise (and totally original) if the aliens had been behind the outbreak of anti-science eco-fascism that has blighted government policy over the last twenty years and wasted the time and money of gullible politicians and well-meaning do-gooders. After all, what could be more disruptive to the Earth than a media-assisted panic that is scientifically unsound and damaging to the global economy? *

* Before anyone starts snapping at me in the Amazon reviews, I'm not a 'climate change denier' or some such loaded term, any more than I'm a Holocaust denier. What is in dispute and open to debate, or would be if contradictory voices were not silenced so quickly, is whether *industry* is to blame for climate change. Climate change has always been with us, ever since the dinosaurs were wiped out. Industrial pollution, while it should obviously be eradicated as much as possible, has only been around for about a hundred years. What creeps me out is the certainty with which certain views as to the cause of climate change are unquestioningly embraced, to the exclusion of all other scientific opinion, to the extremes of, some say, manipulating data. It's too important an issue for one side to be silenced. Who are the real deniers here? My mind remains open to all viewpoints. If we've got it wrong, it will cost us dearly. That's my point. So no hanging me out to dry, please!

Another problem with the *Invaders* reboot was that someone decided to make a three-hour mini-series out of what should have been a 90 minute pilot. Judicious trimming of each scene, many of which go on much too long, would have made a reasonable TV movie; the padding is obvious. These aliens smoke all the time and breathe pollution, a nice touch--but there are other sillier visual gimmicks that aren't explained properly and seem to have been slipped in just for the sake of weirdness. A missed opportunity for *The Invaders* then (was this it? the series' only chance for a comeback?), and a very ordinary TV movie with flashes of unrealised greatness with or without the David Vincent connection. Standing alone, we might have said, hmm, could be a good show, reminds me of *The Invaders*. Instead, we just say hey, this *isn't The Invaders...!*

The same applies to the revival of *The Outer Limits*, which is *The Outer Limits* in name only, and will be discussed further on.

Gene Barry reprised his TV role as Amos Burke for a six-episode order of a revived *Burke's Law* that eventually ran to 27 episodes! Regis Toomey, already quite old when the original series was made, had of course passed on, and Gary Conway once said in an interview that he and Barry didn't get along, and that Barry once went six months without speaking to him, so he wasn't likely to either return, or be asked (Chief Tilson? Commissioner Tilson?)!

Co-starring in the new version was Peter Barton, lead of the short-lived SF stiff *The Powers of Matthew Star,* but who had more recently been a stalwart of daytime soap *The Young And The Restless.* Barton played Burke's son, and the apostrophe in the title made a subtle and mostly unnoticed move one space along. Now it's the son who turns down sex to investigate murders (there's clearly a reason why the family name is 'burke', British slang — as 'berk' — for idiot\*), while the now silver-haired Mr. Barry, looking well ready for the rest home, was reduced to making coy sexual innuendo. The pretentiously named Bever-Leigh Banfield was on hand to feed the boring bits of information to the audience while the Burke boys trade quips. If there was no production date on this revival, you'd place it late '70s alongside *Charlie's Angels* and *Three's Company,* not early '90s. At least no-one was talking about making it 'dark and gritty'. The only giveaway was where contemporary production values come into play — the backgrounds are cluttered and unclear, the picture is fuzzy instead of sharp, and the gorgeous, bold and grand '60s theme had been replaced by a tacky and forgettable substitute.

\* I'm being polite — the full Cockney rhyming slang is 'Berkeley Hunt'!

The series retained the original show's formula of semi-celebrities as eccentric suspects interviewed in zany locales; the first episode alone offers a movie shoot (which naturally affords a chase around the sets), a lobster restaurant, a suspect who insists the young berk accompany him on a bungee jump to interview him (I can just imagine the *NYPD Blue* cops' response to that one!), and a synchronised swimming sequence. We are later treated to the spectacle of the elder berk boogieing away on a rock video after being 'accidentally' swept away among the extras. This is so painful to watch you can only laugh, although not perhaps in the way the series' producers intended... Among the guest stars were Morgan Brittany of *Dallas,* who appeared in the original series as a precocious child actress, and Anne Francis, who shows up in a detective-themed episode as 'Honey Best'...

James L. Conway (*Paradise, Buck Jones, Bodies of Evidence*) was in charge for original producer Aaron Spelling. None of Conway's dull and bland series lasted very long, made much of an impact, or were remembered two weeks after they'd gone off the air, and despite following the original format and not being an embarrassment, it was, like all his shows, a non-event, proving that even when a remake is done respectfully, you can't go home again.

Initially the ratings weren't too bad, but musical chairs with network executives caused the series to be mishandled and moved around; the 27 episodes had five different time-slots, and each time some genius moved it, it lost a few more ratings points. Spelling called it "his greatest disappointment" during his career. It was one thing to have the occasional flop, quite another thing to have a hit series sabotaged by network stupidity. Twice, thirty years apart. Who were the real berks?

An utterly banal and undistinguished remake of *The Outer Limits* appeared in the 1990s, attracting very little attention at all, and simply exploiting the name and prestige of the original. Possessing only a handful of episodes during its run worthy of bearing the name ("A Stitch in Time" is superb), the best place to look for a contemporary equivalent is in the films of Guillermo del Toro (*Chronos, Pan's Labyrinth, The Devil's Backbone*), who cites a childhood devotedly watching the original as his major source of inspiration. And it shows.

As with the numerous reboots of *The Twilight Zone,* the revived *Outer Limits* served only to embarrassingly illuminate just how seriously standards had fallen in the intervening years. Sharp and crystal clear photography of stand-out performances, inspired aliens, and original interpretations of sci-fi standards had been replaced by dull, dreary and unclear images of tired and unoriginal ideas with predictable endings and uninspired acting by bland and uncharismatic performers. Episodes consisted of very routine and predictable stories with a vast number of flaws and few new interpretations of old ideas. A few of the names associated with the original understandably turned up to collect paychecks, but the finished product did the original no favors at all. It says much that the only episodes that had anything going for them at all were remakes of episodes from the original. Leonard Nimoy, who had played a small role well in the original version of "I, Robot" had in the interim become Spock of *Star Trek* of course, and played a lead role in the new version directed by his son Adam, while David McCallum, who appeared twice in memorable classic episodes of the original, took the lead in a reboot of an episode he hadn't played in, "A Feasibility Study". Sadly, while special effects advances allowed us to see things only implied in the original, and no harm was done, none of the obvious flaws of that original were addressed thirty years later.

The idea that a series like this could have turned out an episode to match the likes of "The Invisibles", "The Bellero Shield", or "The Form of Things Unknown" was laughable, but eventually the law of averages kicked in with a single entry titled "A Stitch in Time". Here's me, writing about it in my hopefully forthcoming and long unpublished *Time Travel Television and Movies,* the next project on my 'to do' list…

* * * * * * *

Some time travellers don't need to hide. As grim in theme as *Timescape,* with its natural disasters, and *Millennium,* with its air crash disasters, is the superior "A Stitch in Time" (1995), an episode of the otherwise weak 1990s *Outer Limits* reboot which, despite its serial killer theme, is remarkably intelligent and non-exploitative, unlike the glut of serial killer films and TV episodes that polluted the 1990s and on, and which revel in the horror.

Robert Beck (David Longworth) is the seventeenth victim of a serial killer —"the same gun, the same killer, and maybe one a year since 1956. What does a two-bit sugar pimp have in common with a construction worker, a real estate broker, and a minister?". The answer lies with Doctor Theresa Givens (a superbly defined performance by Amanda Plummer), a strange, frail, destroyed woman whose adult fingerprints were found at the scene of one of the decades-old murders, and now match those taken routinely at a bomb scare at the university where Givens works and teaches. The problem--Givens was a pre-schooler at the time of the murder where her fingerprints were retrieved.

Feeling foolish, FBI agent Jamie Pratt (Michelle Forbes) follows the lead, and Givens seems to have a surprisingly good memory where Pratt's last case is concerned--the apprehension of serial killer Jerome Horowitz (Samuel Khouth), whose victims included Jamie's best friend, the life-loving, love-giving Alison (Kendall Cross). Givens' responses to the agent's questions are revealingly appropriate--told that the only link between the murdered men was that six of them had been arrested for 'minor sex crimes' Givens perceptively enquires "Is there really such a thing?"--and she seems to revel in the obvious incongruities of the evidence. Otherwise, Givens' only offence besides gloating like the cat who got the cream, seems to be that she's a bit strange, with that scarecrow style of clothes and hair so beloved of those people who insist on compelling the world to confirm their own low opinions of themselves. The answer lies in the *Sliders/Stargate*-like time travel device in her laboratory, and after Pratt has departed, Givens materialises in the apartment of the killing and wipes the offending prints from the lamp, safe again. However--even as the report on Givens vanishes from Pratt's grasp--the trail is heating up again. This time, the FBI have unearthed the *gun* that was used in the crime, a weapon constructed in 1988 and acquired by Givens in 1989. And the bullets from 1956 to the present all match. All they have to do now is figure out how a weapon made in 1988 could have been fired in 1956...

Pratt is not a happy woman herself--she's haunted by the death of her friend at the hands of Horowitz, now set to be executed for his crimes, and her FBI partner (Andrew Airlie) is jealous of her relationship with a selfish, two-timing caveman of a cop (Adrian Hughes), who has no interest in her other than sex. Meanwhile, watching Horowitz on TV, manipulating the media with a sob story, Givens darkly notes the date of his first killing... and selects her next victim. Givens has been travelling in time executing serial killers, but she's no crazy militant feminist out for revenge on 'all men'--she's been killing the guilty *before* they commit their crimes, so saving the lives and miseries of the women they killed... and so when Horowitz is executed for his crimes--an act which gives Pratt none of the vengeful satisfaction or sense of closure she had hoped for--Givens slips back in time to February 16th, 1988 and blows away the baffled dweeb before his murders can be committed. "I haven't done anything!" he bleats, as Givens administers the final, fatal shot.

Back at Pratt's office, where a photo and details of the fresh eight year old crime now join the other unsolved mysteries on the board, it has been discovered that Givens spent a year in hospital after being abducted, imprisoned, and raped for five days when she was fifteen. Everything fits--except the time-line. By now though, Givens--a serial killer herself after all—is becoming increasingly unhinged by her deeds and no doubt by her time travelling ("A Stitch in Time" is one of the few time travel stories to contemplate the psychological trauma of time travel). Confused, she refers to having met Pratt before, and to Pratt's persistence ("That must be how you caught Horowitz"), even though in this latest timeline, Horowitz is a victim and Pratt is meeting her for the first time.

At the end of her tether, she spills her guts ("I am so tired... of trying to fix things...") and proudly announces that she "killed all twenty monsters, and because I did, 83 women are all alive... but there is only one problem. The time traveller remembers not only the changed timeline, but the original one as well. Every time I use the technique, another universe of possibilities slams into my head *and my mind cannot handle it any more*".

Givens sees Pratt as her successor, but Pratt sees only one mission ahead of her--to face the one monster Givens couldn't, until today--the man who tortured her on October 28th, 1976. As Givens devastatingly confronts her tormentor (William McDonald), this time at the moment of the crime, Pratt materialises behind her. After a harrowing confrontation resulting in the death of the adult Givens but the escape of the child (Corrie Clark), Pratt returns to the present, where the secret time machine now ceases to exist in its previous locale. With Givens having averted her own nightmare her murderous do-gooding is undone, and Pratt--with the memory of two timelines herself, realises to her horror that Horowitz's victims were to include her best friend. Elsewhere, a vibrant, happy, healthy, attractive and well-adjusted Theresa Givens—only vaguely recognisable as the former haunted scarecrow of her 'past'--entertains her students with the delightful and more traditional possibilities of time travel.

"Imagine witnessing Lincoln deliver the Gettysburg address... or actually being in Paris when Lindbergh landed...!"

She is interrupted by the arrival of Jamie Pratt--who she recognises as the woman who saved her life nearly twenty years ago.

"You built it, didn't you? The time machine. I don't care why you did it--for yourself, for the government... I just need to know that you did it".

Now it's Jamie Pratt who materialises at the park bench of the bitter and miserable Jerome Horowitz...

"A Stitch in Time" is a near-perfect time travel story. There are no silly flaws or paradoxes, as in the similar *Time After Time* or *Running Against Time*, the story is complex but simply and straightforwardly told, beautifully directed (by Mario Azzopardi, who reveals the time machine to us slowly and cleverly) and very well written by Steven Barnes. The characters, from the leads to the smallest three-line roles, are keenly and sympathetically observed, played out to an undercurrent of the sexual tensions exhibited between men and women all day and every day. The morality on display is thoughtful and philosophical rather than vengeful and emotional, and Barnes has been lucky indeed to have such flawless performances from everyone involved to bring his ideas to fruition. The first season of the 1990s *Outer Limits* was uniformly cliched and predictable, but episodes like this justify the entire dreary project, and ensure that the reputation of the original series has at least not been taken in vain for nothing.

\* \* \* \* \* \* \*

If the rest of the series had matched the quality and originality of this, we would still be talking about the revived *Outer Limits* today, and with the same reverence held for the original.

## sources and bibliography

Alley, Robert S., Newcombe, Horace,

        *The Producer's Medium*, Oxford University Press, 1983

Bradley, Matthew, interview with Anne Francis, *Filmfax*, Winter, 2008

Burbey, Mark, interview with Robert Culp (and Harlan Ellison),

        *Ultra Filmfax*, no. 63/64, October 1997

Counts, Kyle, interview with Gary Conway, *Starlog*, February 1990

Doyle, Michael, *Larry Cohen: The Stuff of Gods and Monsters*,

        Bear Manor Media, 2016

Etter, Jonathan, *Quinn Martin, Producer*, McFarland, 2003

Etter, Jonathan, interview with Gerald Mayer, *Filmfax*, April, 2008,

Graham, Jefferson, and Spelling, Aaron, *Aaron Spelling: A Prime-Time Life*,

        St. Martin's Press, 1996

Levinson, Richard and Link, William, *Stay Tuned*, St. Martin's Press, 1981

Lisanti, Tom, profile of Wende Wagner, *Drive-In Dream Girls*, McFarland, 2003

Murray, Will, interview with Van Williams, *Comics Scene* no. 15, 1988

Murray, Will, interview with Van Williams, *Starlog*, October 1988

Phillips, Mark, *Invaders* retrospective, *Starlog*, September, October 1994

Phillips, Mark, *Invaders* retrospective, *Starlog*, March 2009

Sandler, Adam, Lost and Found: Van Williams, *Variety*, May 17th, 1993

Schow, David, Frentzen, Jeffrey, *The Outer Limits Companion*,

        Ace Science Fiction Books, 1986

Tagliaferro, Linda, profile of Bruce Lee, *Outre* no. 20, 2000

Van Hise, James, *The Green Hornet Book*, 1988

Van Hise, James, interview with Van Williams, *Outre* no. 20, 2000

Warren, Bill, interview with Roy Thinnes, *Starlog*, February, 1996

Weaver, Tom, interviews with Gene Barry, Gary Conway, Ken Kolb,

        *Earth vs. the Sci-Fi Filmmakers*, McFarland, 2005

**about the author**

Jon Abbott was born in Lambeth, London, England, and has lived in Brighton on the South Coast since he was five years old. He has been writing professionally for over thirty years, having started out in 1982 by writing brief previews and reviews for the London listings magazine *City Limits*. For two years he contributed an annual report on the U.S. TV season to the trade paper *Television Weekly* before it was amalgamated with *Broadcast*. Since then, he has written over 400 articles and features for around two dozen different trade, specialist, and populist publications, including numerous regular columns and features.

In 1983, he wrote his first article for the British science-fiction and fantasy media magazine *Starburst*, on the cult series *The Prisoner*. This was followed by features on *The Outer Limits, Danger Man, Voyage to the Bottom of the Sea, The Man from UNCLE, V, The Greatest American Hero, Blue Thunder, Knight Rider, Airwolf, Streethawk, Otherworld, ALF, Batman, Battlestar Galactica, The Time Tunnel, Fantastic Journey, Land of the Giants,* and *The Invisible Man*. For the companion title *TV Zone*, he has written about *Misfits of Science, Beauty and the Beast, Planet of the Apes, Fantastic Journey, Quantum Leap,* supernatural anthology shows, *Starman, Man from Atlantis, The Incredible Hulk, Spider-Man, Logan's Run, The Invaders, The Avengers,* and *Hercules--the Legendary Journeys*.

For six years he wrote TV news and individual features for *Video Today* in the popular column *Time-Shift*, which he proposed in 1984 and which became one of the most well-received features in the magazine. These pages included previews of new shows, retrospectives on popular old series, genre pieces, and regular updates on the U.S. TV scene. He wrote individual features on *Night Gallery, Dallas, Dynasty, Soap, The Mary Tyler Moore Show, Hill Street Blues, Mike Hammer,* Britain's Euston Films, producers Donald Bellisario and Quinn Martin, *Bilko, V, The Invaders, Cheers, Police Squad, Lou Grant, The A-Team, Crazy Like a Fox, The Equalizer, The Prisoner, The Twilight Zone, Lost in Space, L.A. Law, Moonlighting, Mission: Impossible, Star Trek--the Next Generation, The Time Tunnel,* supernatural anthology shows, the anti-violence-on-TV lobby, and the arrival of satellite TV. He also reviewed video releases. Particularly successful were the occasional TV Index features listing the status of then-current American shows both in the U.S. and the U.K.

Between October 1984 and March 1986 he wrote a regular column of criticism and comment on U.K. scheduling policy for the highly regarded industry journal *Stills*, and from September 1986 he had a number of features on program planning developments in British, American and satellite TV published in *Media Week*. These features covered such issues as the program scheduling strategies of ITV, the birth and growth of Sky Television, a comparison of the original SuperChannel and Sky satellite services, the U.S. TV seasons, video releases of popular television series, merchandising spin-offs from television series, how British broadcasters used imported American programmes in their schedules, the perils of sponsorship and the American experience, television censorship, the merger of satellite broadcasters Sky and BSB, and the purchase of MTM by U.K. broadcaster TVS.

In 1988 he began contributing to *What Satellite* magazine, writing features on such shows as *The Legend of Custer, Hawk, Lost in Space, 21, Jump Street, St. Elsewhere, Murphy Brown, The Flash, Melrose Place, Beverly Hills 90210,* Steven Bochco's *Civil Wars,* Stephen Cannell's *Stingray, The Simpsons, Land of the Giants, Tom and Jerry, Taxi, Cheers, Frasier* and *The Twilight Zone.*

For *The Dark Side,* a horror and sci-fi magazine, he has provided features on *Alien Nation, The Outer Limits, Werewolf, Land of the Giants, Star Trek, Star Trek--the Next Generation, Voyage to the Bottom of the Sea, Lost in Space,* the Stephen King mini-series *It, The Flash,* and *The X-Files.*

For *Video Buyer* he covered the video release of *Star Trek, V, The Avengers, Robin of Sherwood, Doctor Who,* the Marvel Video Comics, '50s sci-fi films, the early *Superman* serials and TV shows, the output of the Hanna-Barbera and Warner Brothers animation studios, *The Outer Limits, The Twilight Zone,* and *Twin Peaks.* For *Video World* he covered the video release of *Lost in Space, Cheers, The Simpsons,* and *Twin Peaks* and wrote their *Satellite Preview* column, which has included features on *Beverly Hills 90210, The New Avengers, Charlie's Angels, MASH, Twin Peaks,* Robin Hood films, *Quantum Leap, Lou Grant, Star Trek--Voyager, Earth 2, The Invaders, Kolchak--the Night Stalker, Planet of the Apes, Alien Nation, Automan, Manimal, Starsky and Hutch, Murder One, The X-Files,* modern westerns, *Space--Above and Beyond, Bewitched, Star Trek: Deep Space Nine, Starman, Strange Luck,* and *Hercules--the Legendary Journeys.*

In November 1989 he was awarded a special commendation for his writing on American TV and satellite TV in *Media Week* from the first *Broadcast Journalist Awards,* sponsored by TV-am.

During 1990 and 1991 he produced the column *Broadcast News,* a monthly collection of strange stories, anecdotes, and comment and criticism on television for *What Video* magazine.

In 1995, he was asked to contribute a monthly TV news column for *Home Entertainment,* and also wrote additional features on the U.S. TV season, the Cartoon Network and TNT, and Bravo's 'Weird Worlds' strip. He was also invited to join the writing team of *SFX,* for which he reviewed *Robocop--the series, The X-Files, Sliders, Highlander,* and *Space: Above and Beyond.* For 'Yesterday's Heroes', a regular monthly feature in the early issues of *SFX,* he featured *The Six Million Dollar Man, Wonder Woman, Blue Thunder, The Invisible Man, Randall and Hopkirk (Deceased), UFO, The Time Tunnel, Manimal, Max Headroom, The Man from UNCLE, Voyage to the Bottom of the Sea, Starman, V, Batman, Mission: Impossible, The Incredible Hulk* and *Land of the Giants.* For another then-new publication, *Cult Times,* he wrote about *Earth 2, The Six Million Dollar Man, Kolchak--the Night Stalker,* and *Sliders.*

In 1996, he was invited to write for the SF media magazine *Dreamwatch* and the new publications *Infinity* and *Comedy Review.* For *Comedy Review,* he prepared features and episode listings for the series *Soap* and *MASH.* For *Infinity,* he wrote a monthly *Cult TV* column and contributed articles on *The X-Files, War of the Worlds--the series, Space-- Above and Beyond, V, Star Trek: Deep Space Nine, Dark Skies* and *Lois and Clark: New Adventures of Superman.* For *Dreamwatch,* he wrote about *The Green Hornet,* the *Fantasy Worlds of Irwin Allen* documentary, *The X-Files,* sci-fi in *The Simpsons, Fantastic Journey, The Man from Atlantis, Fireball XL-5,* the 1950s *Superman* series, and *The Pretender.* His exclusive reviews of *Millennium* and *Dark Skies* were the first published in the U.K.

Over a five year period between 1997 and 2001, he covered over forty episodes of different vintage sci-fi series for the *'Fantasy Flashback'* series for *TV Zone*, which featured an individual episode of a classic TV fantasy series examined in detail. Shows covered included *Star Trek, The Outer Limits, The Time Tunnel, Lost in Space, Batman, Voyage to the Bottom of the Sea, Mork and Mindy, Battlestar Galactica, The Greatest American Hero, Once a Hero, The Flash, Land of the Giants, Otherworld, The Man from UNCLE, The Wild Wild West, Airwolf, Kolchak--the Night Stalker, The Invaders, Thunderbirds, Quantum Leap, Mission: Impossible, Bewitched, The Flintstones, The Twilight Zone, Streethawk,* and *I Dream of Jeannie*. He also reviewed third season *Stargate* for *TV Zone*, and later wrote a *'Retro TV'* column for *TV Zone* covering all aspects of classic TV.

In 2006, American publishers McFarland published his book *Irwin Allen Television Productions 1964-1970*, a detailed critical review of the 1960s sci-fi series *Lost in Space, Voyage to the Bottom of the Sea, The Time Tunnel,* and *Land of the Giants*, and in 2009 *Stephen J. Cannell Television Productions: A History of All Series and Pilots*, a critical study of 22 detective and action adventure series from this prolific producer, including *The Rockford Files, The A-Team,* and *Wiseguy*. Also in 2009, the Irwin Allen book was reprinted in softback.

Now concentrating solely on 20th century film and TV, and self-publishing on Amazon's Createspace platform, he has published *The Elvis Films* in 2014, *Cool TV of the 1960s: Three Shows That Changed the World,* and *Strange New World: Sex Films of the 1970s* in 2015, and *One Hundred of the Best, Most Violent Films Ever* and *The Great Desilu Series of the 1960s* in 2016. Two more *Cool TV* volumes are planned for the future, and with luck, the long-shelved and updated *Time Travel Television and Movies of the 20th Century*.

*Free Reading: See my lists on the Internet Movie Data Base,*

*all under the pre-fix DISCOVER...*

*See my Amazon Author's Pages for*

*Jon Abbott*

*and Americana: Jon Abbott for a planned collection of reprint titles*

# index

Armstrong, Dave 353,

Armstrong, Herb 390,

Armstrong, R.G. 360, 390,

Arnold, Phil 193, 207, 214,

*Arrest and Trial* 208,

Arthur, Louise 237,

Arvan, Jan 262, 276, 286,

*As the World Turns* 172, 352,

Asher, William 350,

Asimov, Isaac 34, 71,

Askin, Leon 139, 239, 240,

Asner, Ed 28, 81, 82, 276, 335, 362, 363, 389,

"Assignment: Earth" 379,

Astar, Ben 286, 287,

Astor, Mary 150, 161, 162,

*Astro-Zombies, The* 283,

Atkinson, George 208, 247,

*Atlantis – the Lost Continent* 80,

*Atlas* 82,

*Atom Ant* 223,

*Atom Man vs. Superman* 304,

"Attack of the Monster Plants" 61,

*Attack of the Puppet People* 95,

**"Attack of the Tree People" 231,**

Atterbury, Malcolm 372,

Atwater, Barry 75, 77, 387, 388,

Aubrey, Danielle 179,

Aubrey, Skye 389,

Aubuchon, Jacques 309, 310,

Audley, Eleanor 259, 260,

*Augie Doggie* 222,

*Austin Powers – International Man of Mystery* 89, 183, 278,

*Automan* 281, 283,

Avalon, Frankie 173, 204, 205, 208,

*Avengers, The (U.K.)* 236, 238, 254, 257, 266, 270,

Averback, Hy 157, 160, 166, 167, 178,

Avery, Brian 315,

Avery, Tol 222,

Avery, Val 345, 347,

Ayres, Jerry 300, 301, 362, 363,

Ayres, Lew 264,

Babcock, Barbara 295, 304, 314, 315,

Babich, Frank 319,

*Babylon 5* 52, 74, 122,

*Bachelor Father* 194, 201, 286,

Backes, Alice 207,

Backus, Jim 160, 161, 180, 181, 193, 194,

**"Bad Bet on a 459 Silent" 315 – 316,**

*Badlands* 74,

Baer, John 314,

Baer, Parley 126, 127, 286, 287,

Bramley, William 143, 238, 239, 352,

*Branded* 28, 187, 261, 324, 325, 329, 389,

Brandel, Marc 251, 274, 275, 277, 278, 287,

Brandon, Henry 113, 240,

Brandt, Hank 347, 348, 369, 370,

Brandt, Thordis 304,

Brandt, Victor 358,

Bravo, Danny 221,

"Bread and Circuses" 107, 357, 378, 384,

Breaking Point 181,

Breck, Peter 26, 71, 72,

Breeze, Michelle 205, 212, 213,

Bremen, Lennie 261,

Brent, Eve 202,

Brewer, Jameson 173, 186, 187,

Brian, David 252,

Brickell, Beth 311,

*Bride of Frankenstein, The* 174,

"The Bridge of Lions Affair" 195,

Bridges, Lloyd 148, 162,

*Bring Me the Head of Alfredo Garcia* 103,

Brinkley, Don 331, 350, 354, 357, 362, 364, 391,

Brittany, Morgan 206, 395,

*Broadside* 169,

Brocco, Peter 137, 347, 348,

Brodie, Steve 212, 213,

Brody, Marvin 237, 249, 260, 286, 318,

Brooke, Walter 290, 297, 298, 299, 367, 368,

Brooks, Geraldine 45, 48, 119, 120, 121,

Brooks, Jan 215,

Brooks, Mel 268, 312,

Brooks, Rand 308,

Brooks, Stephen 390, 391,

Brown, Frederick 107,

Brown, James (actor) 254, 255,

Brown, James (director) 251, 253, 255, 258, 260, 261,

Brown, Lew 353, 375,

Brown, Pepe 389,

Browne, Roscoe Lee 389,

Brubaker, Robert 51, 365,

Bruck, Bella 248,

Brumfield, Kirby 309,

Brunetti, Argentina 345, 347,

Brutsch, Jerry 242,

Bryar, Claudia 369,

Bryar, Paul 364,

BSB 18,

*Buck Jones* 395,

*Buck Rogers in the 25th Century* 28, 70, 83, 118, 280, 300, 312, 316, 351, 357, 365, 381,

Buckner, Robert 271, 272,

*Buffy the Vampire Slayer* 133,

"Bugs Bunny Nips the Nips" 233,

*Bullitt* 88, 286,

Bundy, Brook 279, 280,

Buntrock, Bobby 174,

Buono, Victor 303,

Burbey, Mark 48,

Burchette, Kevin 364,

Burke, Ron 303,

Burke, Walter 27, 84, 87, 88, 100, 101,

*Burke's Law* 32, 33, 39, 88, 108, 110, 120, 122, **147–218,** 235, 237, 239, 240, 246, 247, 249, 252, 254, 255, 256, 260, 261, 262, 265, 267, 273, 274, 277, 278, 280, 282, 283, 285, 287, 301, 302, 310, 351, 375, 381, 383,

*Burke's Law (1990s series)* 152, 178, 206, 260, 394, 395,

*Burns and Allen Show, The* 159,

Burns, Tim 381,

Burt, Nellie 91, 95, 109, 118, 352,

Burton, Julian 120,

Butler, Debbie 212,

Butler, Robert 325, 331, 335, 359, 360, 371, 372,

Butler, Tracey 200,

"By Any Other Name" 51, 131, 136,

Byrne, Lou 180,

Byrnes, Bara 198,

Byrnes, Edd 211, 259,

Cabot, Bruce 157, 159,

*Cade's County* 342,

"The Cage" 23, 46, 108, 312,

Cagney, James 209, 272,

Cahill, Barry 390,

Caillou, Alan 208, 281,

*Cain's Hundred* 242,

Caine, Howard 113,

**"Calcutta Adventure" 226,**

Calhoun, Rory 212, 213,

Callahan, James 335, 352, 379, 380,

Callahan, Pepe 211, 248, 345, 347,

*Callan* 166,

Callas, Maria 216,

Calvet, Corinne 164, 195, 196, 209, 210,

Camden, Joan 51, 81, 82,

Cameron, Rod 157, 160,

Campanella, Joseph 359,

*Can-Can* 163,

"The Canada Run" 359,

Candido, Nino 242, 245,

Cannell, Stephen J. 47, 88, 153, 288, 297,

*Cannon* 131, 321, 336, 344, 345,

Cannon, Dyan 280, 281,

Cannon, Glenn 54,

Cannon, J.D. 324, 335, 339, 342, 343, 387,

"The Cap and Gown Affair" 280,

Kneubuhl, John 64, 352, 359,

*Knight Rider* 29, 64, 108, 254, 283, 309, 312, 391,

Knight, Shirley 65, 66, 68, 367, 368, 369,

Knight, Ted 124, 369, 370, 375, 378,

*Knots Landing* 186,

Kobe, Gail 59, 129, 132,

*Kojak* 131, 173, 182, 248, 379,

Kolb, Ken 252, 259, 260,

*Kolchak: the Night Stalker* 54, 77, 106, 114, 240, 251, 253, 257, 280, 308, 309, 388,

Komack, James 314, 315,

"Korn's Groovy Pirate Adventure" 220,

Kosleck, Martin 142, 143, 275,

Kovack, Nancy 172, 188, 194, 209, 246, 247, 383,

Kover, Kitty 193, 208,

Krims, Milton 119, 125, 129, 130, 136, 141,

Kristen, Marta 187,

Kroeger, Berry 273,

Krone, Fred 197, 209, 311,

Krugman, Lou 214, 249, 262,

Kuluva, Will 222, 271, 272,

*Kung Fu* 239, 308, 380,

Kuter, Kay 143,


*L.A. Law* 91, 380,

**"Labyrinth"** 42, 97, 337, **379—380**, 383,

Laine, Frankie 168,

Lakin, Rita 360,

Lamas, Fernando 180, 209,

Lamb, Gil 248,

Lambert, Jack 274,

Lambert, Paul 52,

Lamond, Don 375,

Lamour, Dorothy 178, 193,

Lancaster, Stuart 43, 343,

*Lancer* 287, 342,

Lanchester, Elsa 150, 174, 194,

*Land of the Giants* 28, 40, 48, 61, 64, 75, 88, 101, 121, 123, 131, 141, 146, 149, 175, 181, 192, 239, 244, 254, 276, 279, 280, 301, 302, 304, 308, 309, 310, 312, 324, 342, 351, 357, 364, 365, 373, 378, 391,

Landon, Michael 149,

Landau, Martin 22, 28, 29, 30, 65, 67, 68, 96, 97, 118, 269,

Landau, Richard 127, 305,

Lane, Abbe 206, 207, 285,

Lane, Charles 163, 250,

Lane, Jocelyn 283,

Lane, Mike 129, 141,

Lanfield, Sidney 201,

Lang, Judy 247,

Lang Yun 307,

Langley, Jane 41,

Langtrey, Hugh 83, 129,

McKinley, J. Edward 314, 315,

McLean, Bill 206, 251,

McLiam, John 103, 106, 238, 239, 359,

McLuhan, Marshall 13, 17,

*McMillan and Wife* 154, 173, 196,

McNally, Stephen 59, 157, 159, 190,

McNear, Howard 249,

McQuarry, Charles 37,

McQuarry, Robert 107,

McQueen, Steve 250,

McQueeney, Robert 306, 307,

McVey, Tyler 319,

*Mean Streets* 246,

"The Mechanical Man" 135,

Medford, Don 365, 375,

Medic 164,

Medina, Patricia 191,

Meeker, Ralph 43, 44, 295, 314,

Mehta, Zubin 383,

Melchior, Ib 143,

*Melrose Place* 151,

Melton, Troy 132, 199, 250, 287, 312, 319, 375,

*Men in Space* 42, 60, 69,

"The Menagerie" 108, 121, 312,

Menard, Tina 345, 347, 366,

"The Menfish" 42, 248,

Mercier, Louis 280,

Meredith, Burgess 165, 176, 201, 362, 363,

Meredith, Cheerio 192,

Merkel, Una 173, 174, 205, 214,

Merlin, Jan 388,

Merrifield, Richard 392,

Merrill, Carol 174,

Merrill, Dina 160, 161,

Merrill, Gary 40, 41, 42,

Merrill, Howard 369,

Merritt, Arnold 103,

Messick, Don 221, 226,

Metcalfe, Burt 37,

Meyer, Russ 94,

Meyer, Torben 207,

MGM 219,

Micale, Paul 213,

**"The Mice"** 25, 26, 44, 59, **83—84,** 104, 110, 136,

Michaels, Barbara 190, 193, 199,

Mickey Mouse Club 171,

Middleton, Robert 204, 209, 287,

*Midsummer Night's Dream, A* 48,

*Mighty Joe Young* 195,

*Mighty Thor, The* 28,

Mikler, Mike 77, 124,

Milam, Jo Ann 305,

Miles, Vera 27, 28, 114, 117, 195,

Milford, John 98, 100, 339, 385, 392,

Millar, Lee 361,

Millard, Harry 241,

446

Quillan, Eddie 192, 206,

*Quincy* 131, 365,

Quinn, Ariane 286,

Quinn, Bill 258, 259, 262, 284, 379,

Quinn, Joe 382,

Quinn, Louie 178, 253,

*Quinn Martin Productions* (book) 343,

*Quinn Martin's Tales of the Unexpected* 393,

Rachins, Alan 90,

Ragin, John 364, 365, 382, 383,

Raine, Jack 182,

Rainer, Jeanne 184,

Rainey, Ford 137, 360, 375,

Ralston, Gilbert 277, 278, 279,

Ramrus, Al 372,

Randell, Ron 141, 142,

Randolph, John 373,

**"The Ransom" 382—383,** 389,

*Rat Patrol, The* 242, 248, 282,

Rathbone, Basil 213, 214,

Ravel, Francis 43,

*Rawhide* 128, 146, 197, 222, 250, 353, 389,

Ray, Aldo 184,

**"The Ray is for Killing" 306—307,**

Rayborn, John 189,

Raye, Martha 208,

Raymond, Gene 39, 190,

Raymond, Jim 306, 365,

Rayner, John 372,

Rea, Peggy 191,

Reagan, Ronald 148,

*Real McCoys, The* 160, 167,

*Rebel, The* 108,

"The Recollectors Affair" 88,

*Red Heat* 320,

Reding, Julie 187, 212, 213,

Reed, Alan 253, 254,

Reed, Donna 162,

Reed, Lewis 160, 176, 178, 184,

198, 213, 301, 302,

Reed, Phillip 169,

Reed, Walter 374, 381,

Reese, Danny 247,

Reese, Sam 71, 72, 126,

Reeves, Richard 172,

*Reform School Girl* 110,

Regan, Tony 161,

Regas, Pedro 345,

Reid, Carl Benton 271, 273, 274, 275,

276, 277, 279, 280, 281, 283, 284,

285, 286, 287,

Reiner, Carl 177, 202,

Reinhardt, Frank 381,

Reisner, Allen 209, 305, 306, 311, 312, 313,

Reisner, Dean 43, 44,

*Remington Steele* 160, 243,

also available from the same author

## Irwin Allen Television Productions, 1964—1970

Before establishing himself as the "master of disaster" with the smash hit 1970s films *The Poseidon Adventure* and *The Towering Inferno,* and before there was even CGI, Irwin Allen created four of the most exciting and enduring television sci-fi series of the 1960s—*Voyage to the Bottom of the Sea, Lost in Space, The Time Tunnel,* and *Land of the Giants.*

Filmed within yards of each other on the busy sound stages and backlots of 20th Century Fox, Allen's shows were one third Jules Verne and Conan Doyle, one third Saturday morning serials, and one third 1950s bug-eyed monster movies. He also had a "house style" created through using the same actors, writers, directors, sets, props, locations and even aliens and monsters that made them 100 percent Irwin Allen. His tricks and techniques, sometimes adapted from earlier sources, others devised by himself and his award-winning special effects teams, have influenced other productions from *Star Trek* through to the present day.

Allen's imprint is everywhere on fantasy TV. Every SF TV show owes him something, and yet none have matched his series for pace, excitement, innovation, or originality. If it was eloquence, scientific accuracy, or profound commentary on the meaning of life you were looking for, then it was best not to look in Irwin Allen productions—but for superb special effects of the day, excellent sets, superior guest performances, action and adventure, hard-nosed heroes, horrible monsters, sinister villains, and sheer escapism, then Irwin was the go-to guy. When Irwin Allen's series were good, they were great. And when they were bad (and sometimes they were)—they were great fun.

This book—a critical history, written by a lifelong fan—documents and examines in detail the premise and origin of each show, and discusses fairly and objectively all 274 episodes of his four fantasy TV series, all of which promoted and perpetuated the traditions and trademarks of pulp sci-fi on film.

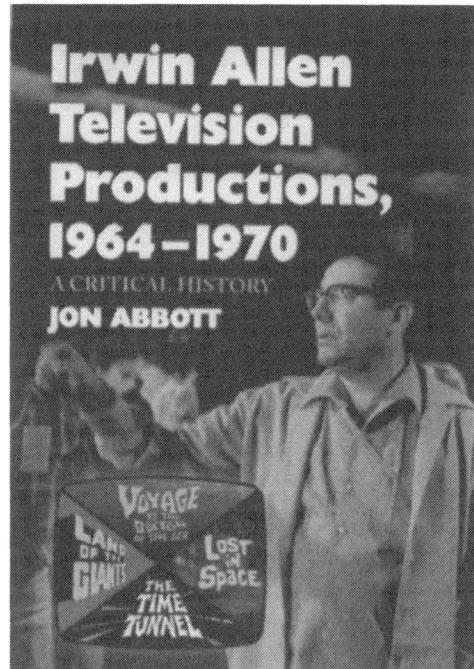

## The Elvis Films

When a man single-handedly changes the course of popular music with one of the most pure and passionate original sounds of the 20th century, it's tough to care about his sideline occupations. But Elvis Presley wanted to be an actor as much, if not more, as he wanted to be a singer. Many Elvis fans didn't like his movies, and neither did Elvis, very much. And yet, the vast majority of them were box office smashes, sure-fire money making hits. *Someone* was buying tickets. In the 1960s, it seemed *everyone* was buying tickets.

This book considers Elvis Presley's films not as an unwelcome intrusion into the insular Presley universe, even though this is how Presley and his associates usually viewed them, but as a significant part of the late 1950s and primarily 1960s pop culture they represented. Elvis Presley, after all, loved film and TV. *The Elvis Films* puts these guilty pleasures into context with not only Presley's life and circumstances at the time, but looks at how they related—or in some cases did not relate to—the other popular culture of the period.

Jon Abbott has been writing about popular culture for over thirty years in a variety of specialist and trade publications, and his kaleidoscopic knowledge of his subject leaves no stone unturned in this provocative and fact-filled analysis of the Elvis movies and the arts and media environment that surrounded them. He is the author of *Irwin Allen Television Productions 1964-1970, Cool TV of the 1960s,* and *Stephen J. Cannell Productions: A History of All Series and Pilots.*

# Cool TV of the 1960s: Three shows that Changed the World

It was perhaps synchronicity, everything in the right place at the right time. After Prohibition, the Depression, WWII, and McCarthyism, mainstream America wanted some fun—in color. The post-War world was ready for a New Age and new ideas, for which Elvis and JFK had paved the way. When pop music, the art world, and the fashion world told the rest of the world to lighten up and loosen up, the timing was right. Television followed other aspects of popular culture just as enthusiastically as the public did—and the buzzword of 1960s popular culture and media was NEW! NEW! NEW!

The 1960s was an extraordinary time of creativity for television, with over thirty classic shows on the air in the mid-1960s simultaneously. September 1964 had seen the debut of secret agent show *The Man from UNCLE*, which in 1965, soared up the ratings to become an all-media phenomenon, influencing toys, books, comics, film, fashion, satirical comedy, and advertising.

Although its beginning was a little more complicated, *The Man from UNCLE* was conceived quite bluntly as a TV version of James Bond. It became an entity in its own right when development fell to the enormously creative Sam Rolfe, who single-handedly devised the complicated, multi-faceted organisation that was the United Network Command for Law Enforcement—UNCLE. The end result was the most dynamic, complex, fast-paced, action-packed, sexy, and exhilarating adventure show of the 20th century; as the first television series to employ the hand-held camera, the faddish, youth-orientated shows that preceded it moved at a snail's pace in comparison. And with the casting of a co-star who became the most popular MGM actor of all time, *UNCLE* thawed the Cold War and created the buddy movie.

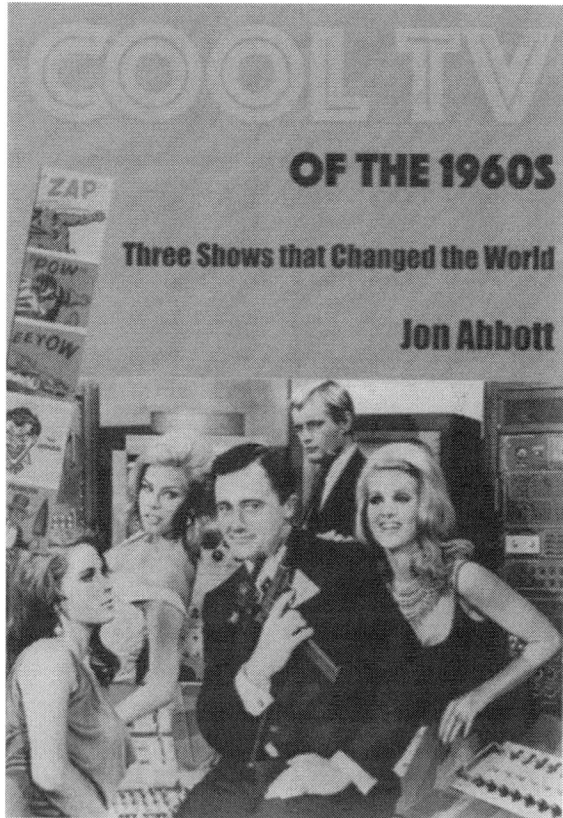

But with the death of President Kennedy, the brave new world of youthful hope and co-operation that the *UNCLE* franchise represented had taken a severe blow. As a result, *The Man from UNCLE* became less of a hopeful dream and more an escapist fantasy in the years to follow. *UNCLE* wanted global peace too, but instead of growing its hair long and throwing flowers around, it wore a dinner suit and used smoke bombs and bullets!

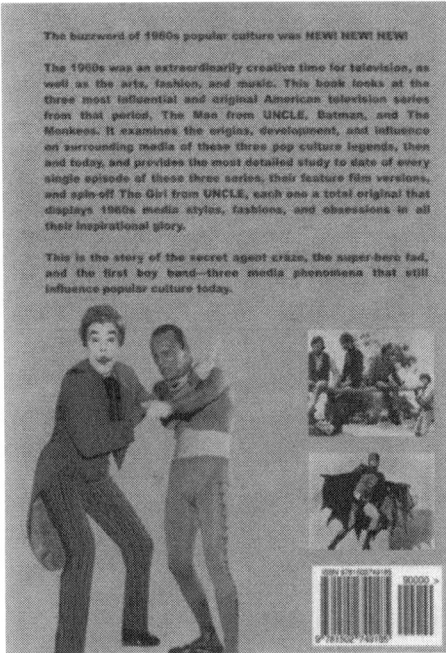

The buzzword of 1960s popular culture was NEW! NEW! NEW!

The 1960s was an extraordinarily creative time for television, as well as the arts, fashion, and music. This book looks at the three most influential and original American television series from that period, The Man from UNCLE, Batman, and The Monkees. It examines the origins, development, and influence on surrounding media of these three pop culture legends, then and today, and provides the most detailed study to date of every single episode of these three series, their feature film versions, and spin-off The Girl from UNCLE, each one a total original that displays 1960s media styles, fashions, and obsessions in all their inspirational glory.

This is the story of the secret agent craze, the super-hero fad, and the first boy band—three media phenomena that still influence popular culture today.

But 1966 was to get wilder still. The *Batman* TV series had arrived in January, 1966 as a mid-season replacement that, following dire test screenings, ABC had no great hopes for. This colorful and stylish parody of the comic-book character delighted kids and adults alike with its bizarre confrontations between the preposterous cowled boy scout Batman and his obnoxious do-gooding student Robin and marvellous performances from familiar Hollywood character actors as the heroes' eccentric adversaries. It became television's second major fad of the 1960s.

The primary legacy of the *Batman* TV series was to give everybody in film and TV permission to go completely loopy, and late '60s film and TV still looks quite bizarre because of it. Nowhere was this more evident than in the wacky TV series *The Monkees*, a half-hour freestyle sit-com imitating the madcap style of the Beatles' feature films. The show was the precursor of the pop video, and the birth of the manufactured boy band, and the onscreen spot gags, parodies, and imaginings of the four leads pre-date series such as *The Simpsons* and *Family Guy* by decades. There had been nothing like these three series before. It would be well over twenty years before anyone dared attempt such levels of creativity again.

These three shows are unique among most television series of any decade in that their influence spread beyond television to affect all aspects of other arts and media as well—books, film, comics, toys, music, satire, fashion, and advertising.

This is the story of the secret agent craze, the super-hero fad, and the first boy band—three media phenomena that still influence popular culture today.

# Stephen J. Cannell Productions: A History of All Series and Pilots

For twenty years, Stephen J. Cannell was in the hero business. Or perhaps, the anti-hero business. Whatever the case, his heroes were on the side of the slightly tarnished angels.

During the late 1970s and early 1980s, Cannell was the single most influential figure in populist action/adventure television. His series range from the smart, wry humor of *The Rockford Files* to the comic-book exploits of *The A-Team*. In between, he has created, co-created, and overseen such productions as the pacifist but macho war series *Black Sheep Squadron,* super-hero spoof *The Greatest American Hero,* the beach boy bromance *Riptide,* the outrageous vigilante show *Hardcastle and McCormick,* and the Eastwood-inspired anti-cop show *Hunter.* In the late '80s, he produced the critically acclaimed *21, Jump Street,* and the quietly horrific, grim, dark mob show *Wiseguy.*

In the 1970s, his marriage of B-western plots and values to the post-Watergate cynicism of 1970s cinema refreshed popular culture, drawing from themes explored and avenues opened by Robert Altman and Clint Eastwood, perhaps the two most influential film-makers of the period. His knowing, self-parodic approach to a tired and weary action/adventure genre permeated all of American television throughout the 1980s, and much cinema thereafter.

On the surface, Cannell's heroes are traditional conservative icons of Hollywood myth, cops, judges, vigilantes, military men, tough guys--but they are also renegades and rebels, individual malcontents at odds with the injustices of the world. And despite producing shows featuring handsome but flawed male heroes (or perhaps because of it), his shows were phenomenally popular with the female audience as well as the intended men, displaying a satisfying progressive attitude towards women both in front of, and behind the camera.

This book discusses in detail the programs of this writer-producer (and sometimes director and actor), and lists every episode of his 1970s and 1980s series, with storylines and writer, director, and cast credits for 22 shows. With extensive quotes and research, it discusses Cannell's methods of working, his critics, his recurring themes and

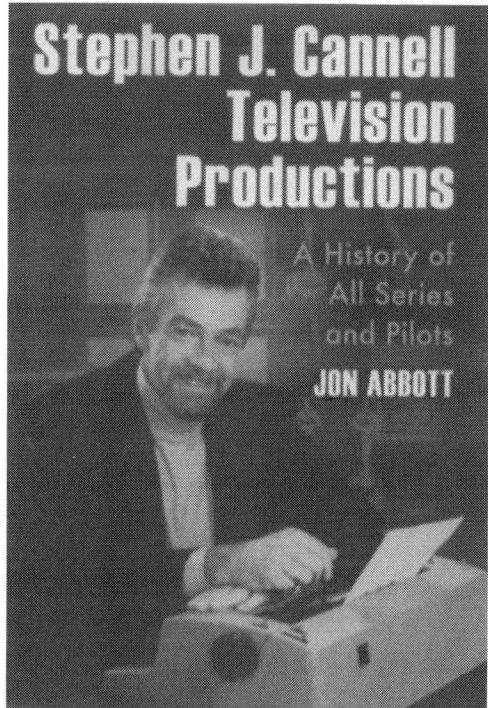

obsessions, and his successes and failures, and includes publicity materials, information on unsold pilots, and a four-page bibliography and ten pages of sources and quotations to support the author's observations and opinions. Every statement is backed up by cross-referencing numerous examples not only of specific episodes of Cannell shows, but other producers' series as well. There is a 38 page index.

The book features: Part One: Beginnings--*The Rockford Files; Baretta; City of Angels; Black Sheep Squadron; Richie Brockelman; The Duke; Stone;* unsold pilots (one); Part Two: The Golden Years--*Tenspeed and Brownshoe; The Greatest American Hero; The Quest; The A-Team; Hardcastle and McCormick; Rousters; Riptide;* unsold pilots (two); Part Three: From L.A. To Canada--*Hunter; Stingray; The Last Precinct; 21, Jump Street; Wiseguy; J.J. Starbuck; Sonny Spoon; Unsub;* unsold pilots (three); The Wrap-Up (his later series, including *Renegade*); sources of quotations; bibliography; index (all featured series chapters include episode listings).

"Outstanding" (e-mail to publishers, Cannell Entertainment)

# The Great Desilu TV Series of the 1960s:

## a critical celebration of four classic shows

Desi Arnaz and Lucille Ball's imprint is all over television history. The Desilu company that was formed by Lucy and Desi to produce and market Lucy's TV series *I Love Lucy* and *The Lucy Show* was later sold to Paramount, handing them three of the biggest cash cows in television history--for it was Desilu that produced and financed *The Untouchables, Mission: Impossible* and *Star Trek,* three of the most admired and respected television series ever made.

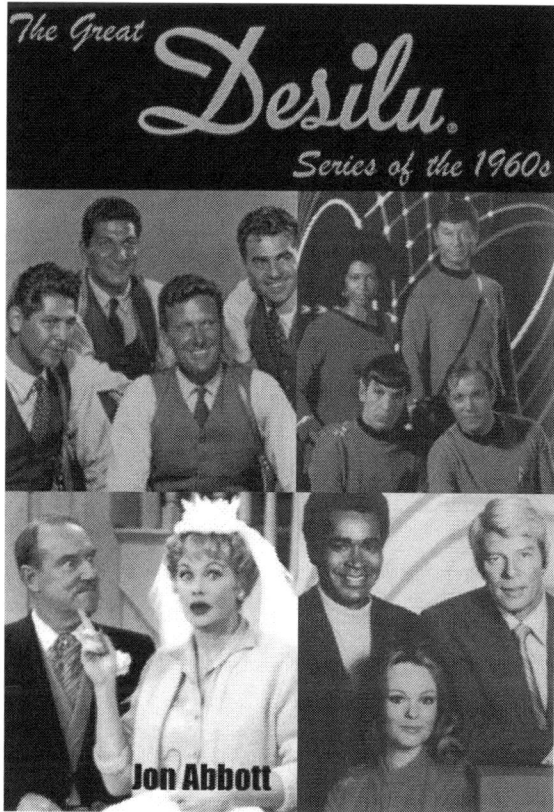

All three would never have made it to air without the power, influence and support of Desi Arnaz and Lucille Ball. It was Lucy who took television out of New York theaterland to Hollywood; she financed the pilot for *I Love Lucy* with her own money; she was the first to film before a live audience; her show pioneered the three camera system of filming sit-coms; her onscreen pregnancy forced American television to grow up a little when it was written into her series. It was Desi who protected *The Untouchables;* it was Lucy who bullied *Star Trek* and *Mission: Impossible* onto the air.

This book examines the four major Desilu legacies of the 1960s in detail--*The Untouchables, The Lucy Show, Mission: Impossible,* and *Star Trek.*

Controversial mob show *The Untouchables* ran for four seasons (1959 to 1963) until TV's censors and professional complainers finally finished it off. It set the bar so high and created such controversy (albeit media-manufactured) that it was twenty five years before gangster shows of comparable quality appeared, and to this day there has not been a gangland show as successful. It was a pulp paperback brought to life, the American trash magazine as live action TV. The slam-bang rapid pace, the justifiable but shameless voyeuristic violence, and the staccato machine-gun-like narration was unique and exciting in the more slower-paced environment of early-'60s TV, and the list of guest stars giving top-rate performances of mostly first-rate scripts is as long as it is distinguished.

*The Lucy Show* ran for six seasons, featured wonderful physical comedy, numerous staple sit-com formula plots, and dozens of celebrity guest stars as a significant and popular part of Lucille Ball's twenty year TV career. Her co-stars, Vivian Vance and Gale Gordon (as Mr. Mooney) achieved career highs.

*Mission: Impossible* was the longest running and most parodied spy show of the 1960s, and is today a major movie franchise. With its dazzling theme, self-destructing taped messages, convoluted schemes, drop-jawed disbelieving villains, and iconic characters, it became a genuine pop culture item.

*Star Trek,* also a major movie franchise, presented pure science-fiction concepts to a mature and wide-ranging mass audience for the first time in television's history, by brilliantly transposing the western formula to futuristic space adventure, and becoming one of the most significant and revered television series in the history of the medium. Desi and Lucy were barely aware they were producing it, but Lucy got it on the air by securing another television first--a second pilot.

**The Great Desilu Series of the 1960s** is a fascinating, fun-filled, fact-filled story of four famously loved television series--related in the context of each other and discussed together for what I believe to be the first time.

Presented in the same popular format as *Irwin Allen Television Productions* and *Cool TV of the 1960s.*

# One Hundred of the Best, Most Violent Films Ever

If it's hypocritical to thoroughly enjoy lurid, violent films yet abhor real violence (as I do), then it seems even more hypocritical to deny the *frisson* one gets from a violent movie. This book has been written for the pleasure of the audience that shares my enjoyment of the Stallone/Schwarzenegger style of film and their predecessors, and that laughs and hoots along with me as bullet-riddled thugs dance and fall, and buildings and cars explode. I attempted to produce it with the same honesty that I did with *Strange New World,* my study of 1970s sex films, another frowned-upon genre that I enjoy and examined with a complete absence of self-imposed guilt.

Here, we look at the very best violent movies and their follow-ups before CGI ruined everything and turned action films into second-rate animated computer games. From Cagney and Corman to Jackie Chan and Chow Yun Fat, from *Coffy* and *Black Caesar* to *Kill Bill* and *Pulp Fiction,* from Republic serials to the *Die Hards* and their clones, from *Shaft* and *Get Carter* to Schwarzenegger and Stallone, these are films faked the hard way, with real stunts, real explosions, real muscles, real imagination, strong scripts, serious carnage, and real cars on real roads.

Here are one hundred of the best, most violent movies ever. Where they came from, why they're great, and what's in 'em that makes them great.

If one picture is worth a thousand words, what are this lot worth?

# Strange New World: Sex Films of the 1970s

**(Adult content and strong language)**

To look at the world of the past through films can be a sobering insight into how things have changed, but to look at the world of the 20th century through sex films is to witness a world that is almost inexplicable. In no decade is this experience more bizarre than the 1970s, and yet it is less than half a century in the past. Was society really so strange and different only forty years ago?

JON ABBOTT, born in 1956 and a teenager in the 1970s, looks back at the era through over two hundred films exploiting sex and nudity, some of which he loved, and some of which he... liked a little less!

This book looks at films from all around the world, including America, Britain, France, Italy, Sweden, Germany, Spain, Czechoslovakia, China, and Japan, at sci-fi, horror, crime thrillers, comedies that weren't funny, and serious-minded films that were hilarious.

Some of the best-known masters of sexploitation are well represented--Stanley Long, Greg Smith, Joe Sarno, Russ Meyer, Mac Ahlberg, Jess Franco, Jean Rollin, Tinto Brass--as are some of the sex films' most beautiful and prolific practitioners--Sylvia Kristel, Gloria Guida, Lina Romay, Maria Forsa, Edwige Fenech, Felicity Devonshire, Christina Lindberg, Joelle Coeur... and such mainstream movie names as Jane Fonda, Jenny Agutter, Julie Christie, and Pam Grier.

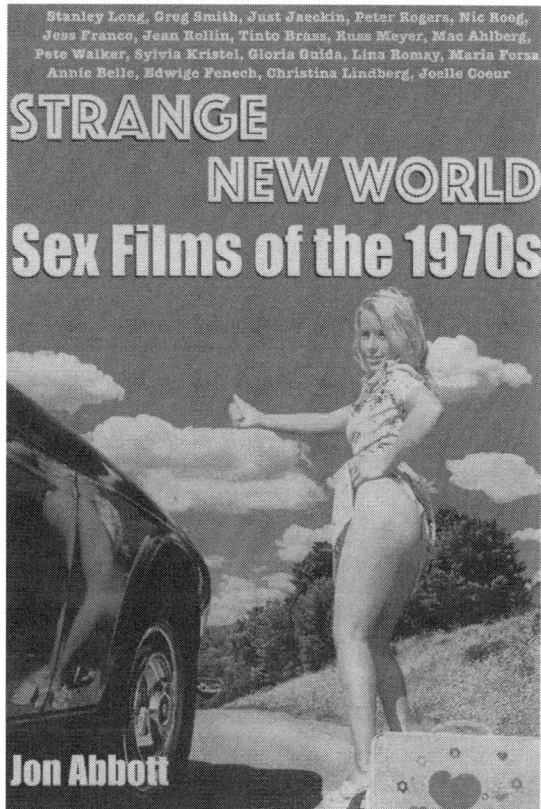

These films were often not pornography, as we understand the term. But what were they? Who made these films and why, and who were they made for? What did they say then, and what do they tell us now? In some cases, what were we thinking?? But in others, what have we lost? Nothing even remotely like these films is being made today. What has replaced them, and how, and why?

This opinionated and fact-filled history looks at the strange new world that adults of both sexes and all ages found themselves in during the 1970s and surrounding decades, from the 1950s to the present day.

Jon Abbott is a freelance writer on 20th century pop culture with over four hundred articles on TV and film published in over two dozen different magazines, trade, specialist, and populist. He self-publishes, has had two previous books published by McFarland in the U.S., and lives in Brighton, England.

\*   \*   \*   \*   \*

# Preview:

# The Secret Unseen History
# of a Television Robin Hood

Okay, now that I've got your attention with a come-on title, here's what this really is.

What we have here are some random behind-the-scenes photographs taken during the production of what clearly appears to be the 1955 British television series *The Adventures of Robin Hood*. I stumbled upon them during one of my periodic rambles around the boot fairs and collectors' markets, and as a baby boomer TV and film buff immediately recognised them for what they are.

I've put them together into a 138 page book without superfluous comment or guesswork, as seen, as a social and historical document for pop culture enthusiasts, TV archivists and social historians, and — if you're the right age — as a nostalgic trip down memory lane.

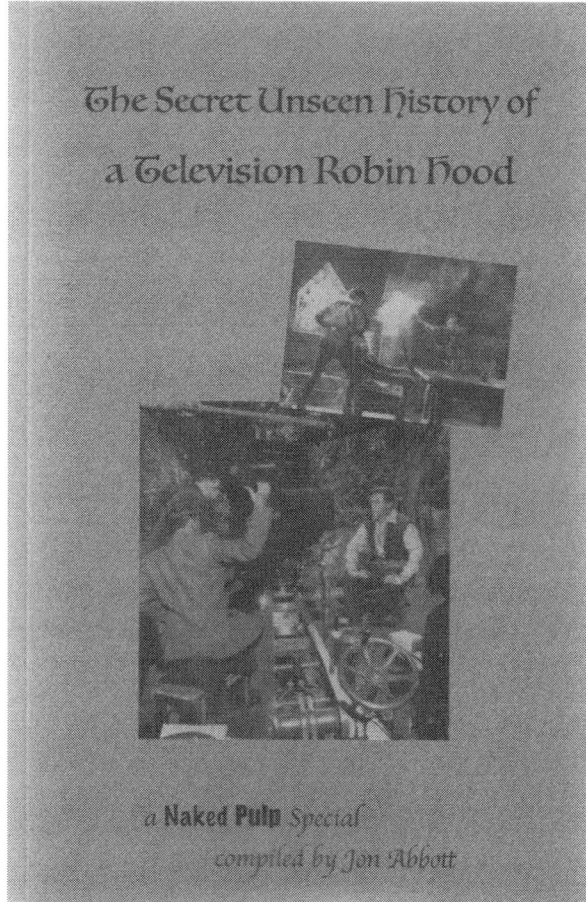

You may have a better idea of what and who the pictures show than I do, as I'm not a personal fan of the show, but as a general enthusiast for the period's television, I remembered and recognised Richard Greene, Alexander Gauge, Archie Duncan, and Alan Wheatley. The only captions I could offer would merely state the obvious, so make of them what you will. A few episodes might be identifiable, but not enough for me to attempt chronological sequencing. There is no intent to breach anyone's copyright; if I hadn't purchased these they'd probably have ended up blowing around a car park somewhere. At best, this book might draw a few more people to buy the DVD set. Those who already have the DVDs will find it fascinating. Those

ISBN 9761545480823

90000 >

9 781545 480823

who haven't yet will probably find it even more so. I cherry-picked as many of the best of them that I could afford, and if sales are modest, which is the best I can hope for with a series this old and obscure, I might even break even in three or four years! But, as a TV historian (this show is sixty years old, and still watchable!), I felt they deserved—needed—to be preserved and seen as a valuable record of a part of U.K. TV history and its production process, so I did my duty, rescued them from the damp cardboard box they were scattered in, and present them here as found history. This is a mere taster of well over a hundred photos of filming and waiting to film (the reproductions in the book are bigger, one or two to a page). They are what they are. Enjoy.

**interview with Jon Abbott, by Nigel Patterson**

**for The Elvis Information Network, June 2015**

**to see the full interview, and all things Elvis, go to elvisinfonet.com**

**EIN:** Jon, it's great to talk with you today. Before we discuss your books including *The Elvis Films* and your passion for pop culture please tell us a little about the Jon Abbott story.

**JA:** It's a familiar one — like Elvis himself, and like a lot of British kids in the 1960s and subsequent decades, I was immersed in American popular culture, loved the music, the comics, the films, the TV shows, as I said in the book. I tried to get into writing either comics, or about TV, the comics stalled, and the TV writing took off, so I never looked back. There's more to it than that, but that's the short version. What I will say is that unlike most people who get into writing about film and TV, I had absolutely no interest in meeting "the stars". It was the end product that interested me, and I was mostly motivated by the desire to a) keep the stuff being shown in Blighty, and b) spread the word. No DVDs or internet in those days, of course. We were entirely at the mercy of the broadcasters' whims. Even when we could finally home-tape, the show had to air.

What younger readers have to appreciate is the complete and utter lack of information back then, no IMDB, no Wikipedia, no Google, nothing. My generation literally clipped cuttings out of listings mags. I knew nothing about how American TV worked, but I wanted to learn. So when I had the chance, I read everything, talked to everyone.

The episode guides in the book *Fantastic Television,* the first ever, were a revelation. My God, running orders, number of episodes, seasons! So I sought out program buyers and program sellers, made friends and contacts, rifled their files (with permission of course!), became the go-to guy for press offices or private individuals in the business for ideas and information, stuck my nose in everywhere, shot my mouth off in private and in print, wrote articles and TV news columns about what was being made, where and when we might see it. There was a three month lead time for monthlies in those days, which was just about right. You'd find something out in February, it'd be in print in April, the show itself could turn up anytime between March and December! It was ridiculously hard to get anyone to publish episode guides, which I had access to and knew everybody else like me wanted, so as well as my magazine work I ran a newsletter with guides throughout the '90s.

The internet eventually killed my TV news business (I used to get it the hard way, ringing up, calling in...), so I've made it work for me, rather than against me. My books are available worldwide, thanks to Amazon.

## Part A: The Elvis Films:

**EIN:** Your recent book, *The Elvis Films,* is a delightfully fresh and off-centre approach to discussing the Elvis film canon. For me it worked so wonderfully because of your ability to weave together an abundance of facts, opinion and anecdote into an entertaining and informative examination of Elvis' celluloid output. How have other Elvis fans reacted to your book?

**JA:** Thanks. Actually there's been a deafening silence mostly, if the Amazon reviews are anything to go by, but then I don't seek out responses, I just go on to the next project. I should send out review copies, but I don't. Fortunately, the books move anyway... well, all except the Cannell one, which just lies there like a dead fish! I only found *your* review because I clicked on my book cover on Google images out of curiosity!

If the books are selling, and they are, I figure I must be doing something right. Books sell, or don't sell, by word of mouth, and no amount of advertising or hype will work as well as someone saying to a friend "have you seen...?" or "hey, read this". People are buying it, they're just not reviewing it. I get the occasional idiot, as we all do, but when people get what I'm doing, it's a joy.

The weird thing about the reviews is that when people like my stuff they usually give reasons and examples, but the complainers say 'oh, he got it wrong' or 'he made mistakes' but rarely say where or how. That sort of criticism is useless, because you can't respond to it. Why is it wrong? Maybe I can explain myself, or fix it, but often, what they mean is "I don't agree".

I used to get some lovely letters to the magazines I wrote for, often asking for me by name to cover specific shows, but I only ever saw them if they were printed! Editors don't like you to know how popular you are, for various obvious reasons, but it did slip out in a careless moment that my TV column in *Video Today* got more letters than the rest of the mag put together! I was always quite chuffed about that.

**EIN:** Not surprisingly, given their teen focused/pop culture/'B grade' status, Elvis' films featured many actors who were prominent in 1960s TV shows. Who were some of your favourites?

**JA:** What we don't have today is all those wonderful character actors, that's what I love about the '60s and miss the most. There's the chameleons, the guys like John Crawford, George Mitchell, Donald Harron, Harry Lauter, who the average punter doesn't even realise they're watching, and then there's the specialists who they would go to if they wanted a certain kind of role filled, people like Joseph Ruskin, George Macready, Reta Shaw, Kathleen Freeman, Roy Jenson, Jonathan Hole, or Michael Ansara and Theo Marcuse of course! These are off the top of my head, there were hundreds! Remember all that corny vaudeville stuff that Guy Raymond and Stanley Adams did in *Star Trek's* "Trouble with Tribbles"? They both turned up in the Elvis films. Stanley Adams was paired with Walter Burke, another great character, in *Double Trouble*. There's no-one like them now. For about the last thirty years, with just a handful of exceptions (*Seinfeld*,

*Frasier, Friends,* a few others), it's been the handsome guy, the pretty girl, the best buddy (often the ethnic role), and the bald-headed boss who's a bleep, over and over again, clones of clones. And nobody over forty! Where are the Mr. Mooneys, the Endoras, the Mr. Waverleys, the Doctor Smiths, the Miss Hathaways, the Colonel Klinks, the Aunt Harriets and Commissioner Gordons? All gone. It's paint by numbers.

**EIN:** When reading *The Elvis Films* I really liked the tangents you veered off in, informing the reader of the non-Elvis film and TV careers of many of his co-stars and the back story to his films. In my review I mentioned these diversions were both a strength and a weakness of the book.

I see their strength being your adeptness at placing their context relative to the social and popular culture landscape in which they were made. I was concerned though that at times, e.g. in reflecting on *King Creole,* you wrote vociferously and most interestingly about the political, cultural and personnel back story but less about the film itself, and to me this resulted in an imbalance in the narrative. What is your response to my observation?

**JA:** Fair comment. If I've nothing to say I don't say it, but I'd rather include too much information than leave it out.

It's interesting, one recurring criticism of my books is that I give too much information about the actors' other credits, some people said that about the Irwin Allen book. But for me, that cross-pollination is the fun of it. I love it that the same people will turn up in an Elvis, a John Wayne, a *Batman,* a *Star Trek,* a *Lucy Show,* a *Time Tunnel…*

As you said, and as I made a big deal of in the introduction to the book, the USP was that it was about how the films slotted into the environment of the '60s and surrounding media, rather than just about the films themselves. I never like to do what's already been done, I'm always looking for a different angle. I've turned down several suggestions from McFarland and Scarecrow because of that. Silly really, but there's no great money in this, so if I'm going to spend at least a year, maybe two or three, on something, I've got to care. I'd dance like a drunken whore if it was big bucks, but it's not, it's pocket money, whether its mainstream publishing or self-publishing, so it's my way or the highway. I can afford my principles!

With Elvis, there was more to say about some films than others, I don't deny it. There was virtually nothing to say about *Kid Galahad! King Creole,* in terms of content, is basically the middle ground between *Loving You* and *Jailhouse Rock,* it's all been done. What makes *King Creole* is the musical content, with *Loving You* a close second. It's pure Elvis at his peak.

The buzz for me was that the bulk of the films are so similar, yet so eclectic. I was able to write about so many different aspects of 1960s pop culture, and yet still stick to the subject — sex, race, pop art, TV, the generation gap. I mean, where else will you find so much completely useless but, to me, fascinating trivia about *Tickle Me!?* I mean, who cares? Not your average Elvis researcher, or your general film buff. They either know all about Elvis, or all about films. Not often both. What Elvis fan knows or cares about Jocelyn Lane's spy shows or *Hell's Belles!?* Only me. But I think the detail on say, Sam Katzman, really helps you understand where *Kissin' Cousins* came from, puts it in perspective. And

I love that *Harum Scarum* went out in a double-bill with a King Ghidora film. I could be the only person who would have enjoyed both films equally!

I had a ball doing *The Elvis Films*, the words just flowed. It's not for everyone, I accept that, but my Amazon page makes it absolutely clear what you're getting. People who want everything sealed into separate little boxes are not well served by my books. I embrace everything, not one show, genre, or category, that's the joy of it. My forthcoming book on 1970s sex films takes in everything, comedies, comics, dramas, arties, sci-fi, horror, mainstream, the lot. It's not just about plain old porn. *Cool TV* is as much about the '60s as it is about the three TV shows. They may not all like my books, but there's nothing else like 'em.

**EIN:** There are so many interesting pieces of information in *The Elvis Films*. One is that a title song was written for *Tickle Me*. Could you share the back story to this and do you know who the songwriter(s) was (were)?

**JA:** It's been a while, but I'm fairly sure that information came from the Guralnick book. It only skims the movies, but it's absolutely essential reading for anyone interested in Presley, I mean, start here, you know? As I recall, they dropped the song, but kept the now meaningless title because all the publicity stuff had been prepared! I love that, classic Colonel Tom! I'd say go to Guralnick, and if I'm wrong, I apologise. Generally, if it ain't in there, it ain't anywhere.

**EIN:** You also mention that the '60s most popular sitcom, *The Beverly Hillbillies*, seems to haunt the book. Please tell our readers why you said this.

**JA:** Well, it was one of those shows that just kept cropping up in the research. *Follow That Dream* is very similar in spirit and appears at exactly the same time, Max Baer played football with the guys, there's Donna Douglas, Raymond Bailey, Phil Shuken...

*Bewitched, Burke's Law, Batman* and *UNCLE* kept turning up as well, as you might expect... and *Star Trek*, bizarrely, given its niche status at the time.

**EIN:** As I mentioned in my review of *The Elvis Films* you and I disagree on the final phase of Elvis' film career, the late '60s releases (*Charro, Stay Away Joe, Live a Little, Love a Little, The Trouble with Girls* and *Change of Habit*). I view them favourably (due to their attempt to reinvent, admittedly unsuccessfully, Elvis' flagging film career through an 'adult makeover') while you term them "the dreadful mistakes". What is it about the films in this phase that you don't like and do any of the films have redeeming features?

**JA:** They all had something going for them, and I mentioned those few things in the text. But "admittedly unsuccessfully" is not a description of a good time.

I tried to be fair, but it's not just the Elvis films, the whole of American cinema seemed to be lost during the late '60s, absolutely clueless and out of touch. Then you get that artistically wonderful but financially poor early '70s period, and then along come Spielberg and Lucas. Yuk. Have you read Peter Biskind's *Easy Riders, Raging Bulls* covering this period? It's a revelation.

**EIN:** What alternative approach would you like to have seen adopted to try and reinvent Elvis' film career or was it a case that Elvis should have gone back to live performing earlier than he did?

**JA:** I think *Easy Come Easy Go* proves conclusively that the traditional Elvis movies were over, but I loved the so-called *Comeback Special* when it was just him and the boys and I think that was the way to go. But the '70s was the decade of bad taste, and Elvis was a part of that, there's no denying it. He made some terrible musical choices, and some terrible lifestyle choices, and the colonel lost the plot when the movies ended, let's face it. But Elvis was a big sheltered man-child who could have anything he wanted, and frankly it was a hell of an achievement that the colonel kept him alive into his forties. Look how much earlier all the other icons went.

**EIN:** The mid-70s appeared to provide Elvis an opportunity to resurrect his film career when he was offered or at least had discussions about co-starring with Barbra Streisand in *A Star Is Born*. Do you think this was a missed opportunity? Would Elvis have been up to the challenge?

**JA:** When you look at what the colonel said no to (in terms of film projects), I'm totally with him on all counts. It's in my book somewhere. First of all, I can't stand Streisand, but personal opinions aside, look at the plot. Elvis gives up his career to protect hers? Really!? And that biopic about a C&W singer... that's like asking John Wayne to portray Roy Rogers. And Mae West in *Roustabout?* He protected Elvis far more than people acknowledge.

**EIN:** The visuals in *The Elvis Films.* I was disappointed that there weren't a lot more, preferably also in color and of a higher visual quality. What was the reason you didn't include a greater range of visuals?

**JA:** I agree, but there are some great pics in there. And I love the cover, if I say so myself. As I said in the book's introduction, *The Elvis Films,* as a relatively small project, was the ideal guinea pig for me to try self-publishing. I went from using an archaic word processing system (WP5.1) on discs and a box-sized computer and screen to Apple MacBook Air and Createspace overnight, jumping completely over the last twenty years of the infuriating Microsoft, which I dreaded facing working on when Old Faithful finally crashed (which it never did), so it was a huge learning curve. In the last year, I've formatted three existing texts into three self-published books, and (with the aid of my tutor, obviously, a miracle worker who solves every damn silly thing I throw at him) I've done everything myself—designed the interiors, picked the art, selected the fonts, formatted the text, designed the covers, proofed and indexed... it's been a massive and quite exhilarating experience. As proud as I am of *The Elvis Films,* inevitably, my subsequent two books, one 500 pages, the other 700 pages, do look better. To re-do *The Elvis Films* would be terribly unfair to the people who have already bought it, and I think it's okay as is. I've never yet had a book out there I've been ashamed of or embarrassed by.

I have considered color, but my writing is already highly specialised (non-fiction doesn't sell as well as fiction), and I don't want to price myself out of the market. There are also, of course, copyright issues as to what I can legitimately use. I have, for example, some wonderful magazine pictures of Elvis filming supposed exteriors of *Fun in Acapulco* in the studio, but I don't have the right to use them. I have to restrict myself to freely available promotional materials, and can only use it for its specified purpose, which is to illustrate and promote. I mustn't exploit or infringe, and color might be pushing it.

Quality of the visuals, well, there are limitations with self-publishing, but Createspace are getting better all the time, I'm getting better all the time, but we can only go as fast as the engine. I'm learning new tricks every month, and so are the guys making the technology. Apple's support service is phenomenal, they don't just sell you a computer and kick you out of the door. To be honest, I'm in awe of it all, if only I could have accessed this technology ten, twenty, forty years ago, my god, what I could have achieved!

**EIN:** It has been suggested by some analysts that because of Elvis' status as the first mega-teen star in an increasingly mass production/profit driven/lowest common denominator entertainment industry, his film career was never going to be allowed to evolve like the film careers of Bing Crosby and Frank Sinatra did. Is this a valid observation?

**JA:** Did their film careers evolve? Crosby did the same reliable shtick every time, and who can name a Sinatra film that wasn't a musical? *Ocean's Eleven* maybe, but who remembers *Tony Rome* or *Dirty Dingus McGee?* Elvis surely had a more varied career, and as you know, I and the mass audience preferred the formula stuff.

I must say I hate "film studies" where the writer pretends he or she's above the subject and looks down on the audience as if they're mice from Mars. Popular culture is us. I tried to analyse why people went to see *G.I. Blues,* because I hated it. But "we" wanted *Blue Hawaii* and *Girl Happy* too, and so did I. So it's a "mass production/profit driven/lowest common denominator entertainment industry". Good! So it should be! Doesn't he or she like movies? These so-called analysts talk about the entertainment industry in this sterile, derogatory way you describe, but *we* are the audience, the industry is us, all of us. If the industry is the horse and instead of looking at the beauty of the animal we're following it with a bucket and a shovel, whose fault is it if we look in the bucket and see crap? And who's to say it's crap if people like it, want it, choose it? People flock to reality TV, *The Da Vinci Code,* Jeffrey Archer, Barbara Cartland, *Fifty Shades,* even though "everyone" agrees it's crap.

Having said that, the popular culture that endures isn't always what is popular at the time. The classic pop music that has survived is not made up of all the trashy long-forgotten number one records. A lot of great tracks we revere never made it to the top ten. But the good stuff endures, the flash in the pan burns out. That's not just true of music, it's true of films, TV, books, comics, everything. I find that immensely encouraging. It's nothing new, either. Look at the Impressionists. They were reviled. People wanted cows in fields, portraits of fat men and plain women. But quality will out.

Popular culture, music, TV, film, whatever, is defined by what we want. Then we re-evaluate it over the years and decide what we want to keep. There are basically two forms of 'word of mouth'. One is advertising and media, which generates interest and makes people feel they ought to see, hear, or read something, and which dies when the hype ends. Look at *Avatar*, it broke box office records. Who cares now? The other is friends telling friends, relatives telling relatives, dads and mums telling their kids, where interest is generated and perpetuated because something is good. *That's* the stuff that's timeless. Kids watching *The Flintstones, Batman, Star Trek,* or *The Simpsons* with their dads. The media says hey, look in the bucket, everyone else is… but eventually we look up and see the horse, not the horse's ass…

**EIN:** What is your view on the Colonel's role in Elvis' film career? I ask this question in the context that in *The Elvis Films* you quote Memphis Mafia member Lamar Fike who said "This isn't a popular view but the Colonel's formula was correct. The serious stuff — the movies that didn't have many songs in them — flopped".

**JA:** It's like Frasier and Bebe, his agent. The Colonel was a dreadful, awful man, but he protected him, kept him alive for twenty years. It was a strange relationship, they both needed each other equally, but it worked. He was the father figure. Imagine Vernon in charge. And I quoted Lamar in the summing up because he's so right. Everyone says the films are awful, but everyone went to see them. If the films had died, if the fans had rejected them, Elvis would have been straight back in the recording studio. But in the '60s, they went to see Everything. Everything. So this is either the riddle of the ages, or the paradox to end them all, or somebody's lyin'. My book addresses this at length. People say, oh the fans would have watched him in anything, they just wanted to see Elvis so they tolerated the films. Really? 31 of them? For fifteen years? Could the market sustain 31 bad Bond films in a row, 31 bad Disney/Pixar, 31 bad John Wayne films? Rubbish. Fool

me once with *Blue Hawaii,* and shame on you… but fool me repeatedly with *Spinout, Speedway, Clambake…?* What would, or should, Elvis have been doing? The answer appears to be, exactly what he was doing. Box office doesn't lie, but people do. If people came out of the cinemas griping, it was probably the quality of the songs that disappointed. Everyone agrees they were one third good, two thirds poor.

**EIN:** And what about the role of Elvis in his own career? You note in *The Elvis Films* that there is no known record of him choosing scripts, rewriting lines, changing dialogue on the set or wanting to direct. If Elvis hadn't been acquiescent could his film career have been materially different?

**JA:** But should it have been? At the height of his success, when he was making these supposedly awful films, they were making three a year! They couldn't churn them out fast enough! He was working for three or four studios at a time. Some people paint him as this rock and roll rebel, but you know, the truth is — he wasn't. He loved his family, the church, and the flag, and ironically, he hated the drugs culture. I covered this in the introduction and the early films segment. The fact is, his teen audience grew up alongside him. They settled down, had kids, went to the family films, dreamed of holidays in Hawaii, bought the MOR stuff in the '70s. There's a few frazzled old rockers out there who can't accept that. What we do know, and I said this in the book, is that Elvis hated some of the songs he was given. But that's the one place where he could have put his foot down, and he didn't. You have to ask why, and none of the answers are pretty.

**EIN:** Will Elvis' body of film work simply be an artefact of 20th century teen culture or can it survive as an area of interest for future generations?

**JA:** Who knows? He has a wonderful voice, that's the bottom line. It's recorded, on film and on disc, and it's out there. At three o'clock in the afternoon, or three o'clock in the morning, it can melt you.

In the '80s a new generation of kids found *Bilko, Thunderbirds, The Munsters, Lost in Space...* and took from them different things than the original audience. They watched them in a different way. *Thunderbirds* and *Lost in Space* weren't futuristic and forward-looking any more, they were kitsch, camp, and retro. Sky's original MD, who came over from Australia, told me that when they re-ran *The Munsters* over there, the kids thought it was a new show. They thought it was in black and white to emulate the source material. The BBC have kept piles of stuff which they flagged as important and that no-one wants to see, and wiped forever recordings that we're now desperate to retrieve — Hancock, *Dr. Who*, Peter Cook and Dudley Moore, all gone. We have to preserve everything, because nobody, but nobody, knows, including me. If you had told me in the 1980s that in the 21st century I would have *Charlie's Angels* on DVD, but wouldn't be bothered about *Lou Grant*, I'd have thought you were insane. But *Charlie's Angels,* which insulted my intelligence at the time, now looks kitsch and quaint and campy, while *Lou Grant,* despite its undeniable craft and quality, now seems irrelevant, preachy, heavy-handed, and dated.

The Adam West *Batman* is rightly revered and frequently revived, but nobody cares about *UNCLE,* only the die-hard fans. That breaks my heart. But if Tarantino had made his *UNCLE* film, who knows? My daughter frequently goes to see films based on old TV shows and doesn't even realise it.

21st century cinema bores me to tears, but they seem to be giving the public what they want. And "the public" is the under-forties, and I'm now in my fifties, so no mystery there. But I don't get *Star Wars,* which came out when I was in my early twenties. So banal and derivative next to absolutely everything else in pop culture from *Buck Rogers* onwards, yet it's bigger than anything. From 1936 to 1976, what wasn't superior to *Star Wars*? But then I was born in 1956, so I grew up with Lee and Kirby Marvel Comics, Weisinger's *Superman* family, Gerry Anderson, Irwin Allen, *Doctor Who* and the Daleks, the original *Star Trek, UNCLE, Batman, The Outer Limits, The Twilight Zone, The Invaders,* all the 1950s pulp sci-fi films... If I'd been born ten years later, in 1966, I'd have grown up in a sci-fi drought. To those kids, raised on Tom Baker and the bionic man, *Star Wars* obviously blew them away. To my eyes, it was a cynical, inferior, one-dimensional rip-off of a dozen things that were better. To other people, it's the meaning of life.

So whether something is wonderful or rubbish can be based purely on personal perspective. I was ten years late to Elvis, so I like the movies. A wise man once said "the golden age of anything is when you're twelve years old". Still, the ongoing adulation for *Star Wars* reminds me of that wonderful Jerry Seinfeld joke about Chinese food — they've *seen* the knife and fork, but they're sticking with the chopsticks!

I write about this stuff because I want to keep it alive. I love it, and I want other people to find it and love it. I'm very fond of pointing out at the moment that old TV is everywhere *except* on TV (in Britain, at least). Collectors' fairs, t-shirts, mugs, posters, books, comics, coasters, DVDs, retro this and that, all over the internet, Amazon, You Tube, e-bay, Google Images, you name it, but not on TV. Even the Elvis films aren't on TV any more (here in the U.K.). Bond, the *Carry Ons,* John Wayne, the tiniest handful of often ill-chosen off-peak re-runs, and that's it. Sixty years of television, but the people in charge can't remember anything earlier than *The Simpsons.* They don't know the history of their own industry, they watched *The A-Team* when they were toddlers. That's when I *started* writing professionally. They don't know *Hill Street Blues,* let alone *UNCLE.* I don't know of any industry so ignorant of its own history as television.

But… the kids don't actually watch TV on TV any more. Marshall McLuhan, the guy who predicted the global village, said back in 1952… 1952!… that's before *Adventures of Superman* aired… that one day television would be considered an art form, but it would no longer be on TV. How right he was.

I'm running on, but here's a couple of anecdotes if you've got the space or the inclination to use them. I carry my office around with me on my computer in a bag with *Top Cat* on it. All the time I get warm comments, at least once a week, and it's always "why isn't it on TV any more?". And I laugh and say treat yourselves to the DVDs, look on the net. When my Apple guy was helping me with *Cool*

*TV of the 1960s,* my follow-up book after *Elvis,* he asked me about *The Man from UNCLE* and I was telling him how big it was in its day… As we spoke, he leaned over to his keyboard, and called up every episode onscreen, legally available, and sampled the first few minutes of the pilot to see what I was on about. So there's the future. You've just got to do what I've been doing since 1983, and spread the word. By the way, my wife is five years younger than me, so she completely missed the *UNCLE* phenomenon. When I was nine in 1965, she was four. When she first saw a still from *UNCLE* in the early '80s, she said "That's *The Invisible Man!*". A completely forgotten half-season run in 1975, plus repeats, and that was her reference point. Five years difference.

About ten years ago, pre-internet (for me), I went into HMV, a high street DVD shop currently in dire straits, and asked if they had *The Man from UNCLE* on DVD. The guy said maybe, but you'll have to tell me who he is! No, I said, that's the title! So we've got our work cut out for us. In fact, it was when *Tickle Me* came out on DVD that I discovered Amazon.

HMV said they weren't going to stock it, but they could order it for me, ten days, come in and get it. *Not stock an Elvis film!* I knew my daughter used Amazon, so I asked her to look for it for me. She said give me your wants list dad, and within half an hour I'd ordered forty films I'd been desperate for, gladly spent a hundred quid. So after that there was no looking back, and it was goodbye HMV, goodbye high street, goodbye region two only. All because they weren't going to stock *Tickle Me!* So there's the future. It's up for grabs.

**EIN:** After watching and re-watching Elvis films have you formed a view on which directors got the best out of Elvis?

**JA:** Well Siegel didn't want Elvis, and Elvis certainly didn't need him. Elvis was always polite and professional and prepared, we know that. But all he needed was traffic cop directors, no shame in that. But only Wallis got the formula right. When they copied him, they got it right. Those were the money makers, so those were the ones that worked.

**EIN:** Jon, what are your favourite Elvis films and why?

**JA:** I hate to keep saying it's in the book, it's in the book, but it's in the book! From *Blue Hawaii* to *Speedway* and *Clambake*. All the fun stuff. *Viva Las Vegas* is probably my favorite non-sf film. Jonathan Harris of *Lost in Space*, one of my TV idols, said that the audience expects you to do the same thing every week, and woe betide you if you forget it. He didn't mean it quite so literally, but I know what he meant, and he's right. People go to see an Elvis film, or a John Wayne, or a Doris Day, or a *Dirty Harry*, or a *Die Hard*, and you had bloody well better give 'em what they came for. Disappoint them at your peril.

**EIN:** And what do you regard as the worst Elvis film or films and why?

**JA:** Sorry, Nigel, you know the answer to that one! I'm afraid I won't be changing my mind. The very worst has got be *Change of Habit* though… That one stinks on so many levels…

**EIN:** Elvis films as "guilty pleasures". Why is it OK to enjoy watching an Elvis movie?

**JA:** We call them "guilty pleasures", and I'm "guilty" of using that term too, usually when I'm sitting in front of a Godzilla film, or something smutty, but you know there's no prizes for sitting in front of a 24 hour news channel and getting depressed, and a good game show is "better" than a bad documentary. I love Italian opera, but it's better experienced through earphones or seen on a stage than on TV, especially as the BBC pander to the snob element. If everybody who said "Oh, my husband likes the sport, and I only watch the wildlife documentaries and the news" was telling the truth, why is the TV top thirty here in the U.K. dominated by twenty-five episodes of soaps and freak shows for morons?

But I don't think people are so snobby as they used to be. We don't defend ourselves so much these days, we just indulge. People openly discuss the dumbest reality shows round the water cooler. My personal criteria for non-fiction, because obviously this doesn't apply to Bond villains or Basil Fawlty, is that I don't want to watch anybody on TV who I wouldn't have in my house… so I'll watch *QI* and all the similar panel shows, anything with David Mitchell or Jimmy Carr, but not car crash TV, Jeremy Kyle, or the Kardashians. But these days you're more likely to be mocked for saying you *don't* watch the Saturday night crap. But I really don't. On the other hand, I'm a grown man watching *Space Ghost* or *Fireball XL-5*. So it's all relative. Each to his own.

A better question would be why is it *not* okay to watch an Elvis movie? Why is it okay to have sex? Why is it okay to eat a splendid meal? Put it like that and you realise what a strange question that is.

### Part B: 1960-70s Pop Culture

**EIN:** Jon, let's move on now to something which is a real passion for you—pop culture. Your books on

1960s and 1970s film and television have been critically acclaimed for their insight and great detail. What is it about pop culture that interests you so much — why is pop culture important?

JA: Because more than anything else it tells the truth about us at any given time, any chosen decade. Elvis, *Playboy, Cosmopolitan,* John Wayne, James Bond, *Carry On, MASH, Happy Days,* Rambo, Schwarzenegger, *The X-Files,* Jerry Springer, *Big Brother,* the stuff we choose, the charts, the ratings, the box office, the sales figures, they don't lie. The media, although part of the popular culture, the BBC, Fox News, the tabloids, academia, the pressure groups, the special interests, the axe-grinders, the advertisers, they all lie because they have an agenda, they're politically motivated, they're social engineers. But their lies also tell the truth about us.

As I say in my book on sex films, I'm a guy, I like to look at naked girls. There, I said it. But to watch TV or read the papers, with their censors, "regulators", "standards", and earnest, finger-wagging, furrow-browed pundits, you'd think that it was just me. I make this point, one way or another, in every book I've written, it's in there somewhere. I am basically a good, decent, kind, honest man, if I say so myself. I just happen to like violent movies, sex films, trashy pulp TV, dirty jokes, childish cartoons... but I'm not some solitary weirdo, living in a pure and pristine world of superior beings, these are commercial mass market entertainments enjoyed worldwide, so it's not just me. Other people lap up questionable or lowbrow things I don't — celebrity scandal sheets, tabloid TV, disaster porn, serial killer films, banal pop music, genteel murder mysteries, money-grabbing game shows... What we really read,

watch, look at, and listen to while we lie to ourselves and others is what we actually seek out, pay for. That's popular culture.

Until all of us, men and women, can be honest about what we want and like, we're doomed to live lives of misery and frustration... and we only get one life. Pop takes no prisoners, it lays us bare. Did you laugh at that joke, or didn't you? Why are you playing war games on your computer? Why are you lusting after that good-looking man or woman and not the fat ugly one? Why is afternoon television full of fictional murders? Suddenly all that political correctness, the phoney sexual politics, the posing and posturing, the complaining and tutting, the petitions and filling in forms, the indignant letters, the pious disapproval, it all looks pretty damn stupid.

We're back to guilty pleasures. I'm not saying lap up any old rubbish and ignore the arts. I'm not saying dismiss morality, spirituality, or conscience. I'm not saying we should all behave like Henry Miller. I'm just saying be honest about who you are and what you like. Stop all this raging hypocrisy. I'm a middle-aged man, but if I want to watch *Yogi Bear,* or a man in a Godzilla suit trampling cardboard buildings, or *Flying Disc Man from Mars,* or Maria Forsa having an orgasm, well, that's me sorted. I'm off to my wall of DVDs and the bores and dullards can watch mainstream TV. Sucks to be the rest of you!

Okay, I've finished!

You *did* ask!

EIN: Your book, *Irwin Allen Productions 1964-1970: A Critical History,* is an engrossing examination of four of television's most exciting and enduring science-fiction series: *Voyage to the Bottom of the Sea, Lost in Space, The Time Tunnel* and *Land of the Giants*. One element that many readers appreciated was your impressive episode by episode evaluations for each show (my copy of the book is very dog eared!) This must have been a labour of love! How long did it take you to research, watch and write this release, and what revelations did you discover as part of the process?

**JA:** I can't say I learned much, it was more about passing on what I already knew and wanted to say to likeminded people. I learned very early on in life, because I thankfully came from a time and was raised with a family that didn't spare your feelings, and there was a lot of laughter and joy at other people's expense, that nobody else I knew was remotely interested in all my useless trivia! So I wrote to get it out of my system, and sent it to magazines where people shared my interests. Even today, only a handful of my friends and acquaintances in "the real world" have even the vaguest idea of what I do, and I only tell them if I'm asked. That means that when I'm "off duty" I'm truly relaxing. Then I go back to my own little world. But I won't deny I enjoy those rare moments when someone says "oh my God, you're Jon Abbott!". But mostly they don't, and I can tell you for a stone cold fact that none of my family have read barely a word I've written! My daughter walked in the room once, took one look at the rubber monster stomping around the Seaview, and said "My God, Dad, you do watch some crap", then walked out again. I was laughing for days. Days. No, they couldn't care less.

I say I didn't learn anything from writing the Irwin Allen book, that sounds a bit arrogant, but I do know

most of the Allen shows back to front. *UNCLE* and *Batman* were a joy, because I got to rediscover the shows. I'd cherry-picked a few *Batman* off-air, and been seeing the *UNCLE* movies fairly regularly, but I'd just bought *UNCLE* on DVD, hadn't seen it for a while. The Cannell book was a voyage of discovery, the Elvis book was a breeze but I had to do a lot of reading, and the book on time travel movies and TV I've got lined up was absolutely fascinating to research. Firstly, I had to look up all the history, which is never dull. And then when I started I thought there were maybe two or three dozen movies? There's *hundreds*.

It's difficult to say how long any book takes, because I'm always working on several projects at once, and the commissioned work comes first. With the Irwin Allen book, I was always watching one series or another, sometimes watching an episode specifically to write about it, sometimes just for pleasure and noticing something. Eventually, of course, I got to the point where I had to start filling in the blanks. I take notes in longhand initially, then type it up while I can still interpret my scrawl, then rethink, revise, rewrite, re-read. At least half my work-time is spent re-reading and re-writing, and although that sounds like a slog, it's the part of the process I most enjoy. The blank page is a terror. It sounds silly, but if I freeze I just start by "talking" to the page, as if it's asked me a question. I answer very bluntly and simply, and then slowly the clever stuff appears.

**EIN:** Stephen J. Cannell created, wrote, story edited or produced some of the most recognisable TV series of the 1970s to 1990s including *The Rockford Files, Greatest American Hero, Baa Baa Black Sheep, Hunter* and

*Hardcastle and McCormick.* Your 2009 book, *Stephen J. Cannell Television Productions: A History of All Series and Pilots,* is a comprehensive coverage of Cannell's series. Many of Cannell's series had somewhat flawed or reluctant protagonists. You note that Cannell changed the face of the action-adventure genre. Please tell us about this.

**JA:** It's all in the book, but very bluntly, he put the humor into a rather absurd genre that took itself far too seriously. The chapter on *The Rockford Files* says it better than I can here ("His gun is deadly, mine's in the cookie jar!" is a great line!), and the sections on *Greatest American Hero, Riptide,* and *The A-Team* are among the best things I've ever written. All the other shows then followed his lead, *Magnum* and *Moonlighting* for example, but it was the movies that did for him, because franchises like *Lethal Weapon* and *Die Hard,* and one-offs like *Blind Fury* and *Cliffhanger,* basically did what Cannell was doing, but on the big screen, with huge budgets. Of course Cannell himself was influenced by his predecessors, the Republic serials and early buddy shows like *UNCLE* and *I Spy,* as well as contemporaries like Eastwood and Altman, but his personal legacy is enormous, massive. I started the project back in the very late '80s, when he was still working, because all the attention was going to Bochco and MTM, attention they deserved, but no-one seemed to be noticing Cannell except a handful of TV buffs. He was getting lumped in with his old muckers Glen Larson and Donald Bellisario and all that grey-haired Silverman/Hargrove crap, and that just wasn't right. I wanted the book to give him contemporary recognition for what he'd accomplished and was doing then, but it ended up a history. I'm glad he saw it and liked it though. His people asked McFarland for a contact address, and I okayed it, but a few months later he was gone. Damn shame.

**EIN:** You have a number of other books released in 2015, *Cool TV of the 1960s: Three Shows That Changed The World* and *Strange New World: Sex Films of the 1970s.* Please tell us about them.

**JA:** Can I just be real lazy and direct everyone to my Author's Page on Amazon? It's all there, exactly as I want to say it, and *Cool TV* is already out, with *Strange New World* due in July. It's late because when I got the proof, what looked fine on the computer screen didn't quite cut it on the page, so I've completely reformatted it, and that meant another couple of weeks re-doing the index! But it'll be worth it when it's ready. I'm super-pleased with both of them.

**EIN:** Do you recall a little known single season (1961) British thriller, *The Mask of the Clown?* I ask as someone who fondly remembers this program (apparently tapes still exist of all episodes) and who discovered that the legendary Brian Clemens was the script writer (Clemens aka Tony O'Grady is notable as the writer of episodes of classic programs including *The Avengers, Danger Man, The Professionals* and *Bugs*).

**JA:** Sorry, no. If it's out there, I'm surprised no-one's released it on DVD. Network do that sort of stuff.

**EIN:** Jon, I have to ask, as a child of the 60s which TV show trading cards did you collect?

**JA:** Literally anything with a TV connection. If it wasn't related to a TV show, I just wasn't interested. If it was, I wanted it. And that wasn't just cards, it was toys, comics, mugs, models, you name it. The most exciting time of the year was Christmas, because that was when the Annuals came out... and they were good-looking books in the '60s, thick and on good paper, with some thought and effort behind them, less so as the '70s wore on, and rip-offs today. Now it's basically one comic, in hardback. The *Tom and Jerry* annuals for 1971 and 1972 could almost be subtitled "The Best of Harvey Eisenberg", and Leo Baxendale used to illustrate his own characters for the Odhams books, he didn't farm 'em out to other artists. As a child, every year I asked Santa for the *TV Comic* annual! *I had to have it!*

I still collect cards now, got books of 'em. My memories are Hanna-Barbera sweet cigarette (!) cards, now called candy sticks but without the cards, and when I was about fourteen, me and my two school mates collecting *Star Trek* (*"What Are Little Girls Made Of?"* with the blue borders) and *Land of the Giants*. I had the full set of *Star Trek*, and a few years ago I obtained the one card I was missing from *Land of the Giants!* I also remember everyone collecting the monochrome Beatles and *UNCLE* cards with the fake autographs. How weird was that? Love cards. I'm a total trading cards nerd.

EIN: Patrick McGoohan's seminal series *The Prisoner*. As a teenager I was transfixed by this obtuse, complex show and one which, at the time, I struggled to understand. How did this series impact you?

JA: When it was first on, I was eleven years old, raised on Bond, *UNCLE,* and *The Avengers,* and took it all at face value, quite literally. It was repeated when I was about fourteen, and then I got it. I saw it again when I was in my early twenties and was greatly amused at the thought of grown adults puzzling over "the meaning" of what was obviously a satirical microcosm of British society, free but not free, free as long as you fit in and conform. The *Tally-Ho* was obviously the *Mail/Express,* the cheery loudspeaker you couldn't get away from was the BBC, Number Two was faceless officialdom, the bubbles were the police, the heavy mob. How could you not get it? It was the subject of the first full-length article I ever had published, in *Starburst* magazine. There was a fan club that was filmed for a Channel Four documentary dressed in all the gear, running around the London locations, acting out scenes from the episodes. I casually and I thought harmlessly referred to them in the piece as "a weird little fan club" and one of 'em wrote to the mag saying they *weren't* weird, and that the meaning of the show was still open to debate. My god, in the last episode of the show everything is labelled! So that was the beginning of my controversial writing career. Embrace your weirdness, that's what I say. Otherwise you just come across as *really* weird...

EIN: McGoohan's themes of individualism (retaining one's identity), conformity, state control, rebellion, etc are as relevant, arguably even more relevant today, as they were in the swinging 60s. Do you agree?

JA: Absolutely. Timeless, even today, with everyone so much more tolerant generally, but super-*in*tolerant of certain opposing views. In those days, non-conformity was all about the counter-culture, being wacky and offbeat, not wanting to join the rat race, and so on. Today, it's more about everybody thinking and feeling the same about "issues", no dissenting from the approved view, and facts, feelings and opinions be damned. You're assumed to be on message, and so is everyone else. "We" have decided what is "okay" and "not okay", and even more sinister, what is "true".

It's extraordinary the absolute nonsense people will just take on board without an iota of evidence or common sense. It used to be about empirical proof, now it's about what we choose to believe, then force the facts to fit. If you can't buy the scientists, bury them. As a free-thinking individual, all you need to do is just think, think for thirty seconds, can this be true? Can it? How can it?

When I was a kid, the two words you heard all the time in the playground were "prove it". Someone was quoted in the press just a few days ago, complaining without a hint of irony or shame, that no-one would take his opinions on board because the scientific community was demanding double-blind proof with placebo testing, but he felt it was "too important" to wait for the results! And the newspaper just printed this as a valid opinion! He hasn't got time to wait for the evidence! It's terrifying, beyond satire.

Having said that, *South Park's* done some wonderful stuff on "accepted wisdom" — the day after *The Day After Tomorrow,* and the smoker being beaten up outside the Museum of Tolerance and all that... But when university professors are telling their students "there's no such thing as a fact" you know we're beyond hope.

What did they say in *The Prisoner?* "Questions are a burden to others". I'd like to boot them out of a top floor window and prove gravity to them.

**EIN:** I found the 2009 remake of *The Prisoner* starring Jim Caviezel and Sir Ian McKellen interesting but ultimately disappointing. What are your feelings about it?

**JA:** It might sound odd, but I've never seen it. I used to reluctantly watch these reboots and revamps because I thought I ought to, but they're all so bloody awful and just such an obvious bad idea that I mean to, just to have an opinion, but often just don't get round to it. I used to say to my wife, I've got to watch this, people will ask me about it. Now I just think, you know what? Life's too short. I figure if it's a surprise success, like *Doctor Who* was, I'll hear about it. It's tough enough watching the 'return of's...' with the original cast, only older. I still haven't seen *The Avengers* with Fiennes and Thurman, *Wild Wild West, I Spy,* or *Get Smart,* just off the top of my head. I've only seen about twenty minutes of *Lost in Space,* introducing the characters, and a bit from the end. The only ones I liked were *My Favorite Martian* with Christopher Lloyd (but then I had no nostalgia for the original), and oddly, *The Green Hornet,* which I thought was both fun and respectful. There was a moment when I expected a blast of the original theme, but they didn't! But I know I'm in the minority with both. I'm also in the minority with the *Top Cat* movie. Yes, the story and the bad guy sucked, but there was a lot of fanboy stuff in there that I loved. It was a brave try. Such a shame they screwed it up. But they did.

I suppose the best way to do a 21st century version of *The Prisoner* would be to tackle things like political correctness, eco-twaddle that defies scientific fact, an "obesity epidemic" that completely misunderstands the words 'obesity' and 'epidemic', and the anti-smoking fascists, who have undone forty years of steady anti-smoking progress with their draconian bullying. There's no shortage of subjects. The reactionaries hate everybody, of course, always have, always will, but the liberals are weird. There's always a couple of groups it's okay to persecute with the full force of smug self-righteousness, and another couple of segments of society that are golden, immune to being criticised or questioned about anything.

**EIN:** Sadly, another of the icons of popular culture television, Patrick Macnee, passed away recently. He shared an interesting trait with the late Patrick McGoohan in that they both would not act using guns (McGoohan refusing that his *Danger Man* character, John Drake, use a gun and Macnee suggesting a classy umbrella instead of a gun for his John Steed character in *The Avengers*). How do you rate *The Avengers* and *The New Avengers* in the pop culture television hierarchy and what is your view of Patrick Macnee (the dapper and cool John Steed) as a pop culture icon?

**JA:** Very sad, but at least he had a good run and went peacefully. Guns in action films are like swearing in dialogue, if you can't use 'em it makes the writers work harder. *Taxi's* Louie de Palma, for example, was much wittier than Eddie Murphy in *Beverly Hills Cop* because he had to be. That said, swearwords are hilarious when used sparingly, and I love a good shoot out Chow Yun Fat style! Let's face it, *Danger Man* was a snore-fest, and *UNCLE* was never more exciting than when they pulled their guns out! Calling Doctor Freud...!

I think the Emma Peel era of *The Avengers* and *The Sweeney* are equally placed at number one for the Greatest British TV series of all time, and are likely to stay there! I would place John Steed, with Emma Peel, as the number one TV icons, most of the others are probably sit-com figures. *The New Avengers* was a very troubled series, as we know, and like most revivals was probably best not attempted. I realise it's difficult to leave these things alone given the profit potential and the lack of good ideas, but they rarely work out. The biggest problem *The New Avengers* had was that the 1960s was the epitome of creativity and style, and the 1970s was the exact opposite. I've always said I wouldn't have wanted to see a 1970s *UNCLE,* and I feel the same about *The Avengers. The New Avengers* proves me right. Both series closed just in time in my opinion.

**EIN:** Please tell us about some of your favourite TV shows from the 1960s?

**JA:** It's quicker to list the ones that disappointed me when I finally got to see them again either via VCR or cable and satellite. All of them were as good, or even better than I remembered, particularly as I was seeing many in color for the first time, with the exception of *My Favourite Martian* and *Green Acres,* both of which I was dismayed to discover were staggeringly unfunny through adult eyes. *The Beverly Hillbillies* and *I Dream of Jeannie* stood up wonderfully. *Voyage to the Bottom of the Sea* was much better than I remembered when they ran a few after a ten year gap in the early '80s. I didn't see the other Irwin Allen shows in colour until the late '80s, because my family didn't have colour TV in the early '70s, when they had last been on, and I thought the rough edges would show, but they were superb, looked great. Everyone used to say oh Jon, they won't be as good as you remember them, but in almost every case they've been as good, or better.

**EIN:** Jon, I know you are a big fan of *The Man From UNCLE*. What are your thoughts on the (long overdue) upcoming film version starring Henry Cavill as Napoleon Solo and Armie Hammer as Illya Kuryakin? The film trailers so far released suggest it will be a fun outing with liberal doses of action and humour. And unlike the classic television series which reflected a strong friendship between the two leads, the new film features a neat (and quite amusing) 21st century sensibility (read: tension) between the two leads. What do you think of this change in narrative and also Cavill and Hammer as the leads?

**JA:** I'm dreading *UNCLE*. I'd have liked to have seen the Tarantino one that was aborted, because if anyone had half a chance it's the *Kill Bill* guy, but nothing could live up to my hopes. The one they've made has been on the shelf for so long it looks like a dead duck. The best I hope for with these things is that they'll revive interest in the original. I hate it when they disrespect the original, or fail to understand it. First do no harm! But I'm genuinely just not interested. I cannot think of a *single instance* where they brought something back and improved on the original.

**EIN:** Considering the original TV series, was it Napoleon or Illya for you?

**JA:** Sharyn Hillyer, mate. No, seriously, the great thing about *UNCLE* was the teamwork, the interplay between Solo and Kuryakin. The first buddy films? I think so. Anyhow, whenever they separated them for too long, the show suffered slightly. But you needed to split them up occasionally so that you could enjoy them getting together again. Same with Steed and Emma, Doug and Tony, and Kirk and Spock. The friendship between the characters, the chemistry between the actors, is crucial. I love the look on Emma Peel's face when Steed turns up at the end of "The House That Jack Built". And Kirk's, when Spock turns up in "Wink of an Eye". Blink and you miss it.

**EIN:** The '60s was also a key time of comic books, particularly the DC and Marvel super heroes. What is your view on the near glut of superhero films released in recent years?

**JA:** Glut is the right word. It was way too soon to do *Spider-Man* again, and as flawed as *Fantastic Four* was, it was okay *when it stuck to the comics*. This latest one looks horrendous. It's all too much too soon. I've only just seen *Thor 2,* and still haven't got round to *Captain America 2* yet. It's like children drawing a picture in pencil and then creasing up the paper as they furiously rub an eraser over it all and start again. And then doing it worse. I thought the first two Toby McGuire *Spider-Man* were okay, and like everyone, thought *Iron Man* was wonderful. *The Avengers* was great when it got going, but a bit slow to start for the kids. The second *Hulk* was an improvement, great battle, but when will they work out that the kids want to see the Hulk, not Bruce Banner. And am I the only person who's noticed that the CGI on the recent *Spider-Man* films is *vastly* inferior to the 2001 movie? Shouldn't this stuff be getting better? I also hate the way the actors' egos mean that the heroes are constantly tearing off their masks. But the thing that really grinds my gears is all these silly white boys shouting racist every time someone dares complain about Nick Fury or Johnny Storm or whoever suddenly being reinvented as black. Imagine the outcry *from exactly the same people* if John Shaft or Foxy Brown was recast as white? Surely the racist act is to turn an established white character black just to tick a demographic box? What could be more patronising or condescending than that? And I loved the multi-cultural Asgard, that was hilarious. Apparently it's okay to be "racist" to the Scandinavians. But it's great to see the comics I read as a kid turned into contemporary entertainment. No-one had heard of Marvel Comics when I was reading them!

EIN: Of all the books you have written what is your favourite?

JA: This is so corny, and it's not even original, but it's so true. Your books are like your kids, you love them all for different reasons. The Irwin Allen book is special because it was the first, and is still selling, but the Cannell book just lays there and I thought it would sell better because the shows are more recent. I thought it was by chance perfectly timed to catch the nostalgia market, but no. And yet I'm as proud of that book as any, and it's some of the best stuff I've written. The Elvis Films was my first self-published, so that's warm and fuzzy, and as I said earlier I couldn't be more happy with Cool TV and Strange New World, they've turned out just as I'd hoped. I'm livin' the dream. I just hope it doesn't all go tits up somehow.

EIN: Are you working on, or do you have specific subjects for any other books?

JA: I have a list of about a dozen subjects I would like to tackle if I live to be one hundred and fifty. Next is the Irwin Allen/Cool TV treatment for Desilu, a quick dust-off and revise for a Time Travel Movies project that pre-dates the Irwin Allen book would you believe, and a third I want to keep under wraps in case somebody nips in

and does it first (there's already another time travel book been announced, not a swipe, just bad luck). I have no idea which of these will be ready first. Also, I'm thinking Cool TV 2...!? I just hope I live long enough to finish them!

EIN: Jon, before we roll the final credits is there anything else you would like to say to EIN readers?

JA: Only that I hope this has been interesting to other people, and not just a massive ego-stroke for me. I've enjoyed it, anyway...!

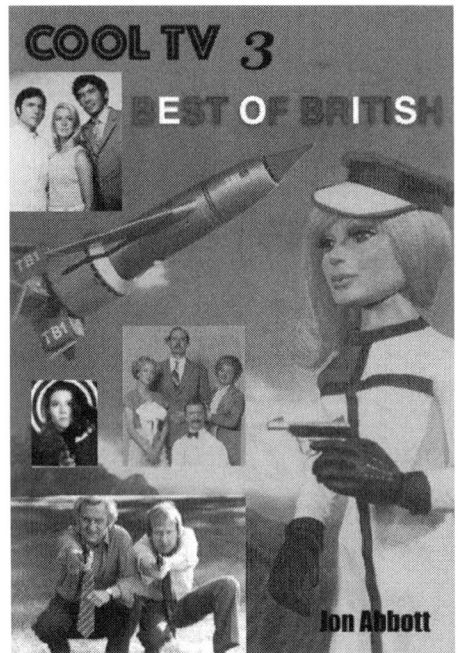

*If we all make it to 2020, this one's next...! Love, Jon...*

Printed in Great Britain
by Amazon